For Joanna Tinker,
my dearest friend

Contents

Preface
Apology, Summary, and Thanks

I have a message from God unto thee.

> —Ehud to Eglon, Judges 3

A is not yet B.

> —Ernst Bloch, his summary of his life's work

> For who can tell but the Millennium
> May take its rise from my poor cranium?
>> —Thomas Spence, *The Constitution of Spensonia*

In an essay on Spenser, Louis Adrian Montrose analyzes some subversive statements that an Essex laborer named John Feltwell made about Queen Elizabeth, then comments, "The rantings of a rural malcontent would perhaps be unworthy of such attention if they did not serve to make a point of larger significance about the relations of power in Elizabethan society." No doubt. But perhaps it's also true that modern theories of power in early modern society aren't worth much attention if they don't make a point of larger significance about ranting rural and urban and vagabond malcontents. Pretty often, those malcontents already have a theory of social power that we may have mistaken for mere ranting. After all, critical reflection wasn't invented last week by academic theorists. And sometimes, if we listen hard, they seem to be throwing their voices— ranting at us from a future that's better than theirs, better than ours, too.

In this book, I talk about some seventeenth-century malcontents, what upset them, what they said about it, and what they did about it. I argue that the radical praxis of working people played a crucial role in the English Revolution, the first capitalist and anti-capitalist revolution, and that it can help us better understand that struggle and the struggles of our own time.

Because it's a polemical book about a polemical era, I anticipate a polemical response, so I want to get a quick word in about what I'm trying and not trying to do. First, I've taken a preposterously pre-post-marxist approach. I know that an up-front declaration like this sounds ass-backwards: if a hidden agenda seems nasty, then an exposed one looks positively impudent, even though I formed it in the course of reading, thinking, and writing, not beforehand. Moreover, my particular agenda, humanist marxism, isn't exactly the soupe-du-jour in contemporary anglophone universities, where humanism is a foolishness unto Heideggereans, and marxism a stumbling block unto anticommunists. Nowadays, the donnish victory yelp of "post-marxism" proclaims even the most whimpering and patrician neo-marxism not only vulgar but anachronistic: since the master plot of human emancipation only started walking in 1789, and dropped dead in 1989, a new marxist study of the English Revolution sounds both premature and passé. In a voice sometimes subtle but always vulgar—so I vainly hope—this whole book responds to that argument. For the moment, I'll just say that these triumphalist elegies sound like whistling in the dark. When I look around me, I see hopeful red specters haunting Europe and Chiapas and Buffalo. And when I look back at seventeenth-century England, I see red baby ghosts crawling down Coleman Street through Putney Church to George Hill.

Second, I hope other literary critics will read this book, but I know it doesn't look much like traditional literary criticism, or structuralist discourse analysis, or postmodernist cultural studies. I do, in fact, talk a good deal about language, writing, and genre, but I focus not on Milton or Marvell, still the classic authors for a discussion of literature and the English Revolution, but on popular libels against King Charles and the Duke of Buckingham in 1628, soldiers' speeches in 1647, Digger prophecies in 1648–52, and Fifth Monarchist and republican pamphlets against Cromwell's Protectorate in 1653–58. I also hope historians will be interested, but I know this book won't feel much like what they're used to. The introduction contains too much theory and polemic, and the book as a whole is neither a tightly focused monograph nor a narrative of the revolutionary decades. Except in passing, I don't discuss the beginning of the Revolution in 1640–42, its regicidal crisis in 1649, or the Restoration of 1659–60. Nor do I discuss at any length such crucial topics as mainstream revolutionary Independency, Presbyterianism, Quakerism, plebeian neutralism, or royalism. In short, I haven't even tried to write a comprehensive and continuous historical narrative. That's not because I don't believe in empirical, historical truth. I do, and I've tried hard to get my facts straight. Nor do I share the current disdain for the grands récits of historians like Marx, Gardiner, Firth, Tawney, Hill, Manning, Stone, and Thompson. Their récits still sound pretty damned grand to me. So do those of their successors, such as Perry Anderson, Robert Brenner, Ann Hughes, Peter Lake, Peter Linebaugh, Jeanette Neeson, David Norbrook, and Ellen Meiksins Wood. I regularly dig into the common treasury they've established, and I'd be pleased to think I've left a mite or two of my own behind.

However, in this book, I've tried to do something else: examine the popular praxis organized in five radical projects. With their retro New Left overtones, those terms probably sound a little quaint, particularly alongside my Old Left subtitle, and some camouflage would have been prudent—maybe a crisp eurotitle like *Reading/Writing Revolution: A Cultural Poetics of the English Civil War.* But that wouldn't sit right. I'm concerned with more than culture, so I'm not inclined to talk about the Revolution under the heading of "poetics"—a pleasant form of labor more familiar to professors like me than to the soldiers, housekeepers, and farmers whom I write about. "Work" comes closer to the mark, and "praxis" hits home, for it suggests the power of workers to lay claim to and modify their own work through class struggle. For me, "praxis" means goal-oriented action—action both imposed and elected, action planned, accomplished, and reflected upon. It includes both verbal and non-verbal action, and I don't assume that the former always determines the latter. People don't write revolutions, but fight them, and just as not all writing is fighting, neither is all fighting writing. Gramscians in their offices sometimes forget what Gramsci in custody tended not to: that counter-hegemonic discursive struggle usually takes place in the shadow of coercion, armed struggle, suffering, and death. Of course, when all is said and done, Ehud's dagger is a pen as well as a pike. But of course, all never is, so it's a pike as well as a pen.

By *radical project*, I mean praxis organized in a collective effort to totalize society by changing it from an oppressive inhuman thing controlling people from without, to a human process that people control for themselves in a relatively democratic way. That's at best a down payment on an argument, at worst a musty exercise in romantic anticapitalism. Even I feel a little awkward writing this way. Not, however, because I feel like I'm intruding on the seventeenth century, but because I feel like it's intruding on me: amid the grim, grinding torpor of class war in the year 2000, and the whimsical, bored, or hostile reaction to utopian projectors and to hot and bothered rhetoric (like "class war in the year 2000"), the English 1640s and 1650s feel like a rich seedbed for ranting, loud-mouthed projects in human emancipation. That's what first drew me in twenty years ago, when I read Christopher Hill's ever-astounding *The World Turned Upside Down: Radical Ideas in the English Revolution*: projects, projects, everywhere—projects so remarkable that their defeats trump our victories.

In part one, I locate my work inside contemporary seventeenth-century studies. In chapter 1, "Cornet Joyce's Commission," I contrast "hierarchy" and "association" as two seventeenth-century ways of conceptualizing society and political praxis. Then I criticize two theoretical approaches to early modern England that developed independently, but within the general culture of contemporary anticommunism. In chapter 2, I consider the revisionist historians of seventeenth-century England. In chapter 3, I turn to the work of Michel Foucault and the new historicist literary critics influenced by him. Because both groups tend to identify with the perspective of sovereign power and resist the study of popular political practice, they find themselves compelled to resort to mere contingency to explain historical change.

In chapter 4, I present my own approach. I argue that such key marxist concepts as base and superstructure, class, the mode of production, and surplus labor help explain early modern England, and do not by any means jar with a nuanced analysis of politics, status, religion, ideology, culture, and the public sphere; indeed, they positively require it. I consider the twentieth century's two primary controversies over the social interpretation of the English Revolution: the debate over the rise of the gentry, and the debate over the transition from feudalism to capitalism. I turn to Robert Brenner's historical writing, Brian Manning's *The English People and the English Revolution*, and Jean-Paul Sartre's *Critique of Dialectical Reason* for a model of structural history from below that combines a study of the shape of class struggle with an analysis of the vernacular ideology and praxis of the English laboring classes: the poor, wage laborers, and small producers who envisioned an English Revolution quite distinct from that of Cromwell and his capitalist allies. Considering some of Marx's own utopian meditations on small production and historical transition, I argue that the failure of the English Revolution was the failure of land reform. I conclude by suggesting that literary critics of early modern English culture could escape some of their conceptual impasses by engaging more seriously the work of the British marxist historians, who have focused on the experience of the English laboring classes in the epoch of transition from feudalism to capitalism.

In part two, I take up a series of radical projects stretching from 1625 to 1660. Chapter 5 focuses on the 1620s, when large segments of the English ruling and laboring classes allied with each other against the absolutist project of the Caroline state. After suggesting that tyrannicidal theory and practice limit the extent to which we can view early modern England as a patronage system, I examine resistance to the would-be absolutism of early Stuart England, including parliamentary speeches, sermons, street riots, naval mutinies, and John Felton's assassination of the Duke of Buckingham, favorite to both James and Charles. I consider the assassination itself, Felton's trial and execution, and a large group of anonymous but widely circulated manuscript poems depicting him as the apocalyptic hand of God acting outside the sphere of corrupt civil law. By asserting the authors' right to assume a public voice counseling or criticizing the king, they help explain the movement of many early Stuart citizens from kingly subjects to godly and republican revolutionaries. I conclude with some recollections of the assassination by radical opponents of Charles and Cromwell.

Chapter 6 moves to 1647 and the Puritan New Model Army. When Parliament tried to disband its victorious army and establish a Presbyterian–monarchist settlement, the New Model soldiery elected a body of Agitators who created an armed public sphere capable of action as well as debate. Against Mark Kishlansky (who sees New Model soldiers forming a tradition-bound hierarchy) and C. B. Macpherson (who sees them as proto-capitalist possessive individualists), I see them as workers struggling to maintain control over their own labor by organizing themselves into a military soviet. In the Putney Debates of November, radical soldiers appropriated traditional social rhetorics, developed a new definition of liberty based in labor, and overcame their grandee officers. They then worked to transform the nation under *The Agreement of the People*, failing only when the grandees crushed their mutiny at Ware. Even more than Pride's Purge or the regicide, this was the turning point of the English Revolution: the first open and bloody struggle over whether it would be the bourgeois revolution of a new capitalist ruling class or a democratic revolution of small producers.

Chapter 7 considers Fifth Monarchist opposition to Cromwell after he dismissed Barebone's Parliament in 1653. I focus on the career of Anna Trapnel, a Baptist prophetess who based a complex oppositional praxis in the forms and the authority of the household's intimate sphere and the congregation's pre-political public sphere, providing a unifying focus for the small producers, housewives, and laborers who formed the scattered Fifth Monarchist collective under assault. I examine her spectacular debut at Whitehall, where her ecstatic prophecies allowed her to take over from silenced male Fifth Monarchist preachers, her journey to Cornwall, her imprisonment in Bridewell, and her final, marathon bouts of prophesying, from October 1657 to November 1659. I conclude with some reflections on anti-sectarian Restoration misogyny and on the role of radical religion in the history of English feminism.

Chapter 8 takes up former Agitator Edward Sexby. I begin by narrating the final decade of his life, when he moved from debating Cromwell at Putney to serving as his emissary to the Huguenots of the Fronde to plotting his assassination. Sexby's eclectic conspiracies reveal both an unusual organizational energy and intelligence, and the limitations of radical political activity cut off from the sort of popular basis that the Agitators enjoyed. I discuss *Killing Noe Murder*, Sexby's tyrannicidal pamphlet of 1657, which translated contemporary republican theory into practice, invoking radical theories of popular sovereignty to oppose Protectorate theories of *de facto* rule. I conclude by considering the legacy of this pamphlet, the nature of tyrannicide as political praxis, and the afterlife of Sexby's arguments in contemporary debates between advocates of natural law and of *de factoist* decisionism.

The final chapter, "The Diggers' *Hortus Inconclusus*," jumps backward to 1648–50 and outward to the rural English poor. I begin with the recent renaissance of local studies, which encourages us to turn from such totalizing categories as ideology, class, and revolution to the small, hard facts of local history, deference, festivity, and the experience of the body. I call this a false opposition, for the Diggers' praxis moved them from a particular sort of local experience—the wage labor and hunger of dispossessed small producers—to a totalizing theory of history, exploitation, and class struggle.

In their prophetic theory and their agrarian practice, the Diggers criticized the nostalgic paternalism of neo-feudalists and the instrumental utopia of capitalist improvers. They proposed an agrarian general strike that would destroy the English class structure and a utopian project that would inaugurate a millennium for small producers. The Diggers' communist georgic walks out of step with the aristocratic pastoral of the landholders, and associates with revolutionary social theory and practice in the common fields and forests of the contemporary world, where capitalist accumulation proceeds apace, while workers try to trip it up.

In this book, I try to resist what E. P. Thompson calls "the enormous condescension of posterity"—that perennial effort to ignore early modern poor and working people altogether, or to see them unreflectively acting out a role scripted for them by the ruling class or a totalitarian world-view or "episteme." Through what Sartre calls a *regressive–progressive analysis*, I attempt to establish "regressively" the pressures or determinations acting on individual and collective actors, and then, "progressively," their attempts to understand, appropriate, fuse, and transform those determinations, bending them toward a distinct future. The dialectical reason dissolved in their praxis, and produced by it in turn, is distinguishable from but not radically different from or inferior to our own attempts to understand it.

Because my book turns to the British marxist historians, to Sartre, and to Marx himself, I know that it rides athwart a good deal of historical and literary critical writing about early modern England. Lest anyone think I haven't noticed that fact, I've tried in the chapters of part one to reflect on my approach and the approaches of others. But these chapters are less a methodological *a priori* than a reflective afterword. For the most part, I wrote them after writing chapters 5 through 9, and you might read them that way, too. And I hope that the later chapters have a particular coherence and interest of their own as well as a place in a larger argument about class struggle in seventeenth-century England. To paraphrase Sartre on Valéry: Anna Trapnel is a petit bourgeois spinster, no doubt about it, but not every petit bourgeois spinster is Anna Trapnel.

For that matter, neither am I. After working up these arguments, my main feeling isn't smug satisfaction at having reconstructed the network of determinations that constrained early modern radicals, but envy at their creative intelligence and courage in understanding that network and struggling to transform it. I hope some of that envy peeks through from time to time.

I'm over my head in debts, but it feels good to count them up and hear again in my mind all these sweet smart voices. Alpha: the dedication was easy and tough. I talk below about Winstanley's god, who is immanent in bodies, in labor, in all matter and history. Because he can't localize this god, Winstanley calls him *Reason*. Now I usually call my wife *Joanna*, but she gives me the same problem, for she's everywhere in me and in these chapters. She inspired and corrected them, praised and scoffed at them, and cajoled them right out of me. All the while, her ferocious love and wit kept me laughing. So how can my thanks begin or end?

Twenty-five years ago, Jason Rosenblatt led me toward seventeenth-century studies and made me want to become a teacher. Seventeen years ago, when he was supervising my dissertation on seventeenth-century utopias, Harold Toliver quietly asked, "Where's Winstanley?" then kindly let me be. Here, Hal, finally—thanks for the extension. Twelve years ago, when I began writing this book, Ed White became my student, my dear friend, and my best reader and teacher. Our discussions through the years run through all these pages, and I owe him more than I can say.

Ed, Tony Bradley, Huck Gutman, and Julie Rubaud were wonderful comrades in Vermont—old times there are not forgotten. With his genius for friendship, Tony gave me constant support and encouragement. Huck gave me an early critique that stuck with me. Julie, now of the Diggers Mirth Collective Farm in Burlington's Intervale (which offers its produce for the delight and recreation of all those who dig, or own that work), wrote an undergraduate thesis that helped me think about debate at Putney. Christopher Hill opened this period up for me as he has for so many others. Sometimes, when I want to scare myself, I try to imagine what seventeenth-century studies would look like without him—it's not a pretty sight. I'm grateful to David Norbrook, whose work on Renaissance literature and politics has been a continuing inspiration, for his friendship and for a sustaining dialogue about literature and society in seventeenth-century England. Thanks to Stephen Greenblatt, not only for his brilliant writing, but also for several kindnesses without which I might not have had the salaried leisure to argue with it here. This book wouldn't exist at all without the ministrations of Mike Sprinker, who died in August 1999. I know I'll have to stand in line to call him an ace editor, a happy brawler, a good Red, and a blithe spirit.

In Buffalo, I've been lucky to work with a number of brilliant young scholars. Lew Daly zealously scrambled our teacher/student relationship, teaching me about seventeenth-century class struggle and the radical sociology of religion. Alan Gilbert helped me appreciate the widespread cultural importance of small production. Katharine Gillespie taught me about radical domesticity in England and America. Catharine Gray taught me about women's writing and counterpublic spheres in seventeenth-century England. Simon Joyce led me through crime, cultural studies, and the Irish pubs of North London. Julia Miller taught me about the Ladies' Land League and other Irish malcontents.

For helpful readings of various chapters, I'm grateful to Lew, Alan, Simon, and Julia, and to Sarah Barber, Anna Beer, Alastair Bellany, Alan Bewell, Tony Bradley, Dick Burt, Rebecca Bushnell, Norah Carlin, Ken Dauber, Art Efron, Margaret Ferguson, Stephen Greenblatt, Jean Howard, Mick Jardine, Rosemary Kegl, Chris Kendrick, Peter Linebaugh, David Norbrook, John Rogers, Jason Rosenblatt, Molly Rothenberg, Carola Scott-Luckens,

Alan Sinfield, Nigel Smith, Mike Sprinker, Ramya Sreenivasan, Keith Stavely, Ed White, and Sue Wiseman. Sarah lent me her study of Henry Marten before its publication and sent me transcripts from the Marten Papers. Anna kindly transcribed several manuscript poems for me. Carola sent me a copy of her superb dissertation on seventeenth-century women prophets. Nigel shared his encyclopedic knowledge of seventeenth-century England. Chris Fitter, Martin Jenkins, and Brian Manning read the manuscript for Verso and gave expert criticism. Thanks also to Jane Hindle at Verso and to my copy editor, Justin Dyer, who saw the manuscript through its transformation into a book.

Thanks also to Sharon Achinstein, BJ, Linda Bogdan, Barbara Bono, Patty Bradley, Andrew Bradstock, Bruno, Bernard Capp, Coco, Walter Isaac Cohen, Diggers 350 (with their short-lived but glorious camp atop George Hill), John Dings, Vic Doyno, Kevin Dunn, Stanley Fish, Barbara Foley, Clem Hawes, Frances Henderson, Ariel Hessayon, John Hirsch, the Holstun boys (Mike, Britt, and Clay), William Hunt, Dina Kuzminer, Pete Lund, Olivier Lutaud, Charles Molesworth, Bob Montgomery, Stephen Orgel, Valerie Pearl, Pogo, Tim Raylor, John Rowe (master teacher), Sara Rubinstein, Jim Slevin, Lawrence Stone, Dan Vitkus, Bill Warner, Ellen Meiksins Wood, David Wootton, Michael B. Young, Robert Zaller, Paul Zarembka, and to the staffs of Talking Leaves Bookstore, Lockwood Library at SUNY Buffalo, and the Bodleian Library at Oxford University.

I'm indebted to the University of Vermont, to the chairs of English and the Dean of Arts and Sciences at SUNY Buffalo, to the American Council of Learned Societies, and to the National Endowment for the Humanities (which gave me a fellowship for 1990–91) for release time, travel money, and research and publishing grants. But in the last instance, as the saying goes, I'm beholden to the American workers whose hard work, taxes, and tuition have made my easy work even easier. That sounds both pompous and abstract, alas, but the debt is real.

Earlier versions of my arguments here appeared as "Ranting at the New Historicism," *English Literary Renaissance* 19.2, 189–226, © 1989, *English Literary Renaissance*; "'God bless thee, little David!': John Felton and His Allies," *ELH* 59.3, 513–52, © 1992, The Johns Hopkins University Press; "Ehud's Dagger: Patronage, Tyrannicide, and *Killing No Murder*," *Cultural Critique* 25, 99–142, © 1992 *Cultural Critique*; "Introduction" and "Rational Hunger: Gerrard Winstanley's *Hortus Inconclusus*," in *Prose Studies* 14.3 (1991), 1–13, 158–204, rpt in James Holstun, ed., *Pamphlet Wars: Prose in the English Revolution*, 158–204, © 1992, Frank Cass & Co., Ltd; and as "Was Marx a Nineteenth-Century Winstanleyan? Communism, George Hill, and the *Mir*," *Prose Studies* 22.2 (1999), rpt in Andrew Bradstock, ed., *Winstanley and the Diggers 1649–1999*, © 2000, Frank Cass & Co., Ltd. Thanks to the Ashmolean Museum for permission to reproduce the print of John Felton on the cover.

Omega: see Alpha.

—Buffalo, New York, May 1, 2000

On texts, quotations, and frequently cited works

I modernize printing conventions and spelling most of the time and punctuation infrequently. I've tried to follow Old Style dating, except that I take the year to begin on January 1, not March 25. I usually refer to early modern books, pamphlets, newsbooks, and broadsides by author, short title, and year of publication; most were published in London. For more information, see Carolyn Nelson and Matthew Seccombe, *British Newspapers and Periodicals, 1641–1700*, New York 1987; Donald Goddard Wing, comp., *Short-Title Catalogue of Books Printed in England, Scotland, Ireland, Wales, and British America and of English Books Printed in Other Countries, 1641–1700* (3rd edn, vol. 1; 2nd edn, vols 2 and 3, New York 1982–94), and *ESTC on CD-ROM*, British Library Board, Reed Technology and Information Services 1998. I've abbreviated references to the following works:

B Thomas Birch, ed., *A Collection of the State Papers of John Thurloe*, 7 vols, 1742.

BD T. H. Aston and C. H. E. Philpin, eds, *The Brenner Debates: Agrarian Class Structure and Economic Development in Pre-Industrial Europe*, Cambridge 1985.

BMR Robert Brenner, *Merchants and Revolution: Commercial Change, Political Conflict, and London's Overseas Traders, 1550–1653*, Princeton 1993.

CCSP W. Dunn Macray, ed., *Calendar of the Clarendon State Papers Preserved in the Bodleian Library. Vol. III: 1655–1657*, Oxford 1876.

CFMM B. S. Capp, *The Fifth Monarchy Men*, London 1972.

CH Richard Cust and Ann Hughes, eds, *Conflict in Early Stuart England: Studies in Religion and Politics 1603–1642*, London 1989.

CM G. E. Aylmer, ed., *Parliament, the Civil War and the Conquest and Administration of Scotland: Sir William Clarke Manuscripts in Worcester College, Oxford (1640–64)*, 17 reels, Brighton 1979. Page references to original Ms. foliation.

CP C. H. Firth, ed., *The Clarke Papers: Selections from the Papers of William Clarke*, 4 vols, London 1891–1901, vols 1 and 2 rpt London 1992.

CSPD *Calendar of State Papers, Domestic Series, of the Reign of James I, 1603–25*, 11 vols, 1859, rpt Nendeln 1967; *Charles I, 1625–1649*, 23 vols, 1802–69, rpt Nendeln 1967; *1649–1660*, 13 vols, 1875–86, rpt Vaduz 1965. I refer by volume and page and assume the series will be apparent.

CSPV *Calendar of State Papers and Manuscripts, Relating to English Affairs, Existing in the Archives and Collections of Venice and in Other Libraries of Northern Italy*, 38 vols, London 1864–1940; rpt Nendeln, Liechtenstein, 1970.

D *A Declaration of the Engagements, Remonstrances, Representations,*

> *Proposals, Desires and Resolutions from His Excellency Sir Tho: Fairfax, and the generall Councel of the Army*, 1647.

DA   Simonds D'Ewes, *The Autobiography of Sir Simonds D'Ewes, Bart., During the Reigns of James I. and Charles I*, 2 vols, London 1845.

DNB   *Dictionary of National Biography*, L. Stephen and S. Lee, eds, 63 vols, London 1885–1900.

DRD   David Wootton, ed., *Divine Right and Democracy: An Anthology of Political Writing in Stuart England*, Harmondsworth 1986.

F   Frederick W. Fairholt, ed., *Poems and Songs Relating to George Villiers, Duke of Buckingham; and His Assassination by John Felton, August 23, 1628*, London 1850.

FCA   Charles H. Firth, *Cromwell's Army: A History of the English Soldier during the Civil Wars, the Commonwealth and the Protectorate*, 2nd edn, London 1912.

FD   Charles H. Firth and Godfrey Davies, *The Regimental History of Cromwell's Army*, 2 vols, Oxford 1940.

G   Ian Gentles, *The New Model Army in England, Ireland and Scotland, 1645–1653*, Oxford 1992.

GHCP   Samuel Rawson Gardiner, *History of the Commonwealth and Protectorate, 1649–1656*, 4 vols, London 1913–16.

GHCW   Samuel Rawson Gardiner, *History of the Great Civil War, 1642–1649*, 4 vols, London 1893.

GHE   Samuel Rawson Gardiner, *History of England from the Accession of James I. to the Outbreak of the Civil War, 1603–1642*, 10 vols, London 1883–84.

GZ   Richard Greaves and Robert Zaller, eds, *Biographical Dictionary of British Radicals in the Seventeenth Century*, 3 vols, Brighton 1982–84.

HS   Thomas Healy and Jonathan Sawday, eds, *Literature and the English Civil War*, Cambridge 1990.

LM   Don M. Wolfe, *Leveller Manifestoes of the Puritan Revolution*, 1944; rpt New York 1967.

M   John Milton, *Complete Prose Works of John Milton*, 8 vols, New Haven, CT, 1953–83.

MECW   Karl Marx and Frederick Engels, *Collected Works*, 47 vols, New York 1975–97.

NP   *The Nicholas Papers*, 4 vols (Camden n. s. 40, 50, 57; third series 31), London 1886–1920.

P   William S. Powell, *John Pory, 1572–1636*, Chapel Hill, NC, 1977.

P&L   A. S. P. Woodhouse, ed., *Puritanism and Liberty*, 3rd edn, London 1986.

PRO   State Papers in the Public Record Office, in *State Papers Domestic, Charles I, 1625–1648*, 206 reels; and *State Papers Domestic, Interregnum, 1649–1660*, 96 reels, Brighton 1981–86.

RHC   John Rushworth, *Historical Collections of Private Passages of State* [Part One, distinguished as "1"], London 1659. *Historical Collections, The Fourth and Last Part* [4], London 1701.

S   Edward Sexby, attrib. "William Allen," *Killing Noe Murder: Briefly Discours'd in Three Questions*, 1657.

SCDR   Jean-Paul Sartre, *Critique of Dialectical Reason, Vol. 1: Practical Ensembles*, London 1991.

SSM   Jean-Paul Sartre, *Search for a Method*, New York 1968.

T   [Anna Trapnel], 990-page printed folio with missing title page, Bodleian Library, shelfmark S.42.I.Th, after November 30, 1659.

TCS   Anna Trapnel, *The Cry of a Stone*, 1654.

TFC   Rodney Hilton, ed., *The Transition from Feudalism to Capitalism*, London 1976.

TLS   Anna Trapnel, *A Legacy for Saints*, 1654.

TM   Rawlinson Mss. A, Bodleian Library; manuscripts by John Thurloe and his correspondents.

TRP   Anna Trapnel, *Anna Trapnel's Report and Plea*, 1654.

TVK   Anna Trapnel, *A Lively Voice for the King of Saints and Nations*, 1658.

W   Gerrard Winstanley, *The Works of Gerrard Winstanley*, Ithaca, NY, 1941.

WCP   Austin Woolrych, *Commonwealth to Protectorate*, Oxford 1982.

WIR   Charles Webster, ed., *The Intellectual Revolution of the Seventeenth Century*, London 1974.

WSS   Austin Woolrych, *Soldiers and Statesmen: The General Council of the Army and Its Debates, 1647–1648*, Oxford 1987.

PART ONE

HIERARCHY AND ASSOCIATION

1

Cornet Joyce's Commission

We had the sky, up there, all speckled with stars, and we used to lay on our backs and look up at them, and discuss about whether they was made, or only just happened—Jim he allowed they was made, but I allowed they happened; I judged it would have took too long to *make* so many.

—Mark Twain, *Huckleberry Finn*[1]

In recent years, many critics and historians have gazed raptly at the spectacles of power in Renaissance England—the progresses, masques, and public theater that gave Tudor and Stuart courts idealized pictures of themselves, triumphing over the forces of disorder. I'll begin with a different sort of spectacle—one that showed Charles Stuart an orderly antimasque he wasn't expecting and didn't much like.

In June 1645, the New Model Army won the Battle of Naseby and gained the upper hand in its war with the king's forces. A year later, Charles gave himself up to the Scots, who sold him to Parliament for £200,000 in January 1647. Parliament held him at Holmby House, Northamptonshire, in the company of four gentlemen of the bed-chamber, several parliamentary commissioners, and a small garrison. A period of relative calm followed, but tensions mounted among four political entities ostensibly at peace with each other: the Anglican king, the largely Presbyterian Parliament (with its Scots and English allies), the Presbyterian and Independent "grandees" or Army leadership, and the Army's largely Independent and sectarian rank and file. The Army began to fear that Parliament might return Charles to the Scots, thus squander-ing the blood and sweat they had expended in the first civil war, and demanding more in a second.

In May, the New Model began to consider countermeasures, which coalesced around 28-year-old George Joyce, formerly a tailor to the Army's parliamentary nemesis, Denzil Holles, and now a cornet in the lifeguard of General Thomas Fairfax. In late May, Joyce assembled out of three regiments near Oxford a formidable troop of five hundred, perhaps as many as a thousand, and arranged to rendezvous with them at Holmby. This extraordinary body proceeded under an ambiguous authority, with

1. I'm with Jim.

no written warrant from Parliament, Fairfax, or Cromwell. When a parliamentary emissary asked who commanded them, "Answer was made him, all commanded, and yet were under command."[2] A beast with many heads *and* military discipline—the paralyzing horror of the early modern ruling class.

Joyce traveled to London, consulted with Cromwell, and set out for Holmby. Arriving on Wednesday, June 2, somewhat ahead of his troops, he met the king nearby at Lord Spencer's bowling green. The next morning, he wrote a letter, probably to Cromwell, requesting instructions, which suggests he had not yet decided to take Charles into custody. But later that day, he told the parliamentary commissioners he intended "to secure his Majesty's person, and to protect them, there being a secret design as they were informed, to convey or steal away the king, and to raise another army to suppress this under his excellency Sir Thomas Fairfax." That night, after Joyce promised not to harm him, dismiss his attendants, or force his conscience in matters of religion, Charles promised to ride away with him.[3] The next morning, Joyce's assembled troop agreed to these same terms. Except for a brief interlude in November and December 1647, when he escaped to Carisbrooke Castle, Charles remained in Army custody until January 1649, when he mounted the scaffold outside Whitehall.

Joyce's action transferred Charles from a Presbyterian body still committed to some version of the traditional constitution, to a radical Independent body working toward a somewhat hazy but potentially republican and regicidal future. But for the moment, I'm more interested in a brief exchange between Charles and Joyce, just before they rode away together. When Charles asked him to produce the commission authorizing his action, Joyce invoked the earlier parliamentary order that the Army secure the king's person, then the need to keep Charles from falling into hostile hands and reigniting the war, then the general authority of the soldiers of the Army as the only instrument of peace in the kingdom. Unsatisfied, Charles persisted. Finally, drawn up at the head of his troops, Joyce gave a satisfactory response, which he preserved in an account that slips between first and third person:

> The king . . . asked, whether I had nothing in writing from Sir Thomas Fairfax our general, to do what I did: the cornet desired the king he would not ask him such questions, for he did conceive he had sufficiently answered him before: then said the king, I pray Mr. Joyce deal ingenuously with me, and tell me what commission you have. The Cornet's answer was, here is my commission. Where, said the King? He answered, here: his Majesty again asked, where? He answered, behind me, and desired his Majesty that that might satisfy him: whereupon the king smiled; and said, it is as fair a commission, and as well written as he had

---

2. *CP* 1.23, 25. [George Joyce], *A True Impartiall Narration*, 1647, 3. I draw primarily on this tract, probably by Joyce himself. Rushworth reproduces it, with some silent revisions (*RHC* 4.513–17). See also *WSS* 106–14.

3. *CP* 1.118–19; Joyce, *True* 4; *CM* 41.55ʳ.

seen a commission written in his life. A company of handsome proper gentlemen as he had seen a great while.[4]

Charles proceeded to ride away with Joyce and his troop.

How should we conceptualize this exchange? I can think of three ways,
which I will christen "Clarendonian," "Nietzschean," and "dialectical."
Identifying with the revisionist historians of early modern England who
have revived the history of the "Great Rebellion" constructed by Edward
Hyde, Earl of Clarendon, we might see it as the encounter of monarchical
order and popular disorder: in a time of constitutional chaos, a renegade
cornet seizes the initiative from his commanders, the parliament commanding them, and the king ostensibly commanding them all.[5] But this
model doesn't work very well—it's too hard to align the players. Bold
though he was, Joyce presented his aim as securing "the king in another
place, from such persons as should cunningly or desperately take him
away contrary to order, which was endeavored very earnestly (as we are
informed) by some that are enemies to the peace of the kingdom."[6]
Joyce's deference and the orderliness of his troops contrast sharply with
Charles's impulse to promise, renege, and jockey for a better deal—a
royal disorderliness that would play no small part in bringing him to the
scaffold twenty months later.

Second, adopting the briskly demystifying perspective of Nietzschean
postmodernism, we might see this exchange as the encounter of legitimacy with power: the turmoil of civil war produces a grimly humorous
moment of *Realpolitik* when the absent warrant exposes the glimmering
sword, revealing the will to power beneath all *de jure* claims to abstract
right. But George Joyce sits uneasily in the Nietzschean role of marauding
and form-giving blond beast. His indecision the day before about what
course to take and his stammering reluctance to override all forms of
legitimacy suggest a political actor reflecting on authority while simultaneously creating and claiming it. Directly after this exchange, the king
returned to an older model of authority, saying that "I do acknowledge
none to be above me here but God," and Joyce didn't press the point.[7]
Under examination by Fairfax, Cromwell, Charles, and Parliament's commissioners a few days later, Joyce insisted that he had the consent of the
king and his commissioners for his action.[8] And in a July pamphlet, Joyce
justified his action by appealing to the very traditional grounds of "the law
of nature, nations, this kingdom, and our own commissioners derived
from the Parliament for its foundation."[9]

Third, we might—and I do—view this exchange as a dialectical encounter of experience and ideology. "Dialectical" is, to say the least, a loaded

4. Joyce, *True* 9.
5. See, for instance, C. H. Carlton's account of Joyce in *GZ*.
6. *True* 5.
7. *True* 9.
8. Fairfax, *Another Letter from His Excellency Sir Thomas Fairefax*, 1647, 3.
9. *Vindication of His Majestie and the Armie*, 1647, 4.

term. For the moment, I'll define dialectics after Sartre as the movement of totalizing praxis by which historical actors reflect on prevailing forms of authority and on their own practical activity, and then act in such a way as to fuse and transform both. Joyce's gesture condenses a dialectical movement between two models of politics, one established, one emergent. The first, which appears in Charles's demand for a commission, implies a descending or *hierarchical* vision of authority. For Charles, a cornet can act only by virtue of a commission from above. Charles demurs in the tones of a nervous hierarch who has just noticed a few weak links in the great chain of being and its mundane military auxiliary, the chain of command. The second, which we can see in Joyce's reluctant gesture toward his troops, implies a lateral or *associative* vision. Here, authority derives from the freely chosen activity of a collective: the military praxis of the first Civil War, the sore and sweaty experience of a hard ride from London and Oxford, and the danger of Presbyterian and royalist attack. Shared history, shared work, shared peril.[10] This collective quality appears even in the syntax of *A True Impartial Narration*, whose anonymous author shifts without warning from Joyce's "I," to the "we" of his troop, to the "we" of the whole Army.

Joyce's authority emerged dialectically under the prodding claims of an alternative, more conservative authority. Charles impetuously pushed Joyce into a new political identity, forcing him to say something that he didn't want to hear, and that Joyce didn't exactly want to say. It's one thing to base one's action on loyalty to the king and resistance to his evil advisors; it's quite another to invoke the collective praxis and power of a cavalry troop. True, Joyce retreated into a more deferential "loyalist" rhetoric in his *Vindication of His Majestie and the Army*, but he did not abandon this new form of authority, for he took the trouble to record his response for posterity, and many personal narratives and newsbook accounts echoed it with some consistency. Similar appeals to the authority of martial praxis would resonate through the political debates of the ensuing months, and, indeed, throughout the forties and fifties: in the Army's insistence throughout the summer that it was more than Parliament's "mere mercenary Army," in the Agitators' efforts to turn the same claim against their grandee leaders during the Putney Debates of the autumn, and in the claims of radicals like Winstanley and Trapnel that they had participated in the revolutionary struggle whose hard-won fruits were being expropriated by a new ruling class.

The English Revolution created an extraordinary ferment for new

---

10. Joyce wrote someone on June 4 announcing he had the king in custody (*CP* 1.118–19). Cromwell may have been Joyce's silent partner, but modern historians who see a grandee mastermind behind Joyce follow the lead of Hobbes (*Behemoth*, 2nd edn, Chicago 1990, 138) and Charles himself, who said he would suspect Fairfax and Cromwell's collusion unless they hanged Joyce (Gertrude Stevenson, ed., *Charles I in Captivity*, London 1927, 77). Fairfax, who tried to return the king to Holmby, called Joyce an "arch-Agitator" (*Short Memorials*, 1699, 112–17).

modes of radical associative praxis incorporating action and rationality, and opposing the hierarchical praxis of the ruling class.[11] By focusing on this opposition, rather than one between, say, order and disorder, or legitimacy and power, or a premodern and a modern episteme, or on the consensual bonds that undercut any apparent opposition, I associate myself with a marxist and (in part) a liberal tradition of writing history rather than with a revisionist or postmodernist one, and with radical seventeenth-century political actors and theorists like Cornet Joyce rather than royalists like King Charles. Now I don't think that a doughty declaration of solidarity resolves all interpretive problems in a flash, leaving us free to speak immediately with these seventeenth-century political actors and writers. Moreover, the conflict between hierarchy and association moved around in an interesting way, as we'll see when it reappears in the debates of the New Model Army at Putney, and when Leveller radicals declare associative solidarity with the deposed king. It's just that, so far as history concerns itself not simply with what historical actors did and said, but with their own understandings of what they did and said, some of those understandings will seem truer and, finally, ethically preferable to others.

I won't apologize for muddling together descriptive and normative terminology—not because I think everyone should follow suit, but because everyone already does so, with varying degrees of self-consciousness. In historical writing, the worst sort of normative principle fails to recognize itself as such, insists that it emerges magically from the order of things, and refuses to defend itself in the sort of debate with alternative principles that leads to historical knowledge and better models.[12] People frequently attack the sort of history I propose to practice as "whig history," though they often do so selectively, from the point of view of an alternative but unacknowledged whig history. Scratch a Tory, or even a postmodernist, and find a whig. If we deny the normative dimensions of descriptive history, then we defer or deform the process by which scholars judge rival truth claims and normative standards: presenting empirical evidence, marshalling arguments about theoretical presuppositions, and staging the

---

11. Early modern English speakers could intend by "society" a sort of activity as well as a thing (Raymond Williams, *Keywords*, rev. edn, New York 1983, 291–5). I hope my slight lexical awkwardness in referring to "association" (no article) and to "associative" processes will gesture elegiacally toward their fervent belief that their creative, collective activity could transform the world. For me, "association" includes theories of "lateral" collective sovereignty like Winstanley's as well as theories of ascending popular sovereignty like those John Sanderson discusses in *"But the people's creatures": The Philosophical Basis of the English Civil War*, Manchester 1989.

12. See the capitalist moral economy at work in Lawrence Stone's Introduction to the reissue of R. H. Tawney's *The Agrarian Problem in the Sixteenth Century*, 1912; rpt New York 1967. Using a demographically oriented history with "a more objective and more statistical manner," he rejects Tawney's moral condemnation of early capitalist landlordism. But he also commiserates with landlords who failed to get their "fair due" from fixed rents hollowed out by price inflation, and therefore attacked the "unnaturally favorable position" of copyholders by turning them into leaseholders and wage laborers (xi, xii, xv). Nature abhors an unextracted surplus.

debate between different historiographical fields. However gratifying it is to claim the high ground of brute facticity and pelt one's opponents with charges of *a priori* interpretation, that claim doesn't form an argument. It advances anticommunist solidarity, but not historical knowledge.

By refusing to acknowledge fundamental conflicts between more-or-less consciously formulated normative principles in seventeenth-century England, and by insisting that it knew only one culture and class, revisionists and postmodernists produce a relatively impoverished model of the period as either the conflict of order and disorder, or the power-driven struggle of all against all. Similarly, by refusing to address responsibly the rival claims of liberal and socialist historians, they produce a relatively impoverished hermeneutical method. Now I don't believe in the unmitigated evil of all forms of hierarchy, or the unmitigated good of all forms of association. Complicating counter-examples leap up from the New Model itself in its zealous murder and mutilation of unarmed royalist camp followers at Naseby, and its anti-"papist" praxis in burning alive the refugees huddling in St Peter's Church, Drogheda.[13] But finally, I prefer free association to hierarchy, for it tends to constitute and nurture the human essence, while enforced hierarchy tends to distort and mutilate it.[14] So far, these theses remain merely polemical claims. But for the moment, I'm content with Joyce's "Behind me." This two-word epiphany redefines him as an integral part of a pledged group on a level with a king, and gives us a compressed version of the creative practical consciousness of the working men and women who made the English Revolution. Marx's *The Eighteenth Brumaire* contains a somber aphorism about the relation between structure and agency: "Men make their own history, but they do not make it just as they please." George Joyce reminds us that we can reverse those clauses without contradiction.[15]

---

13. *GHCW* 2.252. *GHCP* 1.111–25.
14. I hope this last sentence will at least protect me from any charge of a *covert but insidious* essentialism. But I also hope that any professors inclined to sniff will offer up for inspection the radically antiessentialist idioms they deploy in their workplace against sexual blackmail or denial of tenure on ideological grounds or mundane corporate-academic thuggery. Everyday life sets important limits to theoretical antihumanism, for those who are antihumanists in their books and lectures tend to be humanists in their jobs and in their skins.
15. *MECW* 11.103. The Communards reminded Marx of the same thing (*MECW* 22.307–59).

2

Historical Revisionism
and the Perils of Chronism

But at least as suspicious as the immaturity (fanaticism) of the undeveloped utopian function is the widespread and ripe old platitude of
the way-of-the-world philistine, of the blinkered empiricist whose world
is far from being a stage, in short, the confederacy in which the fat
bourgeois and the shallow practicist have always not only rejected
outright the anticipatory, but despised it.

—Ernst Bloch, *The Principle of Hope*

As for "revisionism," this is either a truism or an absurdity. There is no
need to readapt a living philosophy to the course of the world; it
adapts itself by means of thousands of new efforts, thousands of
particular pursuits, for that philosophy will be one with the movement
of society.

—Jean-Paul Sartre, *Search for a Method*

> The Solemn League and Covenant
>   Now brings a smile, now brings a tear.
> But sacred Freedom, too, was theirs;
>   If thou'rt a slave, indulge thy sneer.

—Robert Burns

Introduction

During the last quarter century, a new group of historians has rejected
what it sees as an atrophied and mythical "whig" vision of early modern
England, whether a stately liberal progress or a socialist long march. The
liberal vision looks back in pride at Parliament's seizure of the initiative.
It traces its own tradition through S. R. Gardiner and C. H. Firth,
culminating in Lawrence Stone's *The Causes of the English Revolution*.[1] The
socialist vision looks back in sorrow at the defeat of the Levellers in 1649
and the Diggers in 1650, but finds reassuring precedents for proletarian
revolution in the bourgeois revolutions of 1642 and 1689. This vision
commences with Marx himself and moves through R. H. Tawney and the

---

1. London 1986.

Historians' Group of the Communist Party, culminating in Christopher Hill's *The World Turned Upside Down: Radical Ideas in the English Revolution.*[2] The new historians reject such potted historical schemes and begin to reconstruct the past in its own terms. Because they *look again* at documents previously seen askance, if at all, the old orthodoxy dubs them *revisionists*—like "politically incorrect," an ostensibly marxist swearword become an honorific. For who save the most hidebound mythologizing liberal, the most myopic relic of the Second International, could object to "looking again"? Who resists revision, other than purblind dogmatists?[3] To begin revising, they turn to primary documents and embark on modest but rigorous projects (local studies, biographies, parliamentary histories), since only patient empirical work can lead toward a new historical synthesis. They open themselves up to the possibility of a history based on precarious negotiations among individuals, on structural breakdowns in an administrative apparatus, on a welter of irreducible historical contingencies that make the past a more complexly textured thing. They abandon Manichean accounts of the "English Revolution" based in parliamentary and popular initiative, the quest for liberty, and class struggle, for a complex account of the "English Civil War." They see a totality of the bone, not the brain—one based in custom, consensus, and a hierarchical world-view, not in self-conscious ideologies and primal conflicts between forces of oppression and liberation.

Almost twenty years ago, Mary Fulbrook argued that any response to revisionism should critique its arguments about the insignificance of ideology, class, and long-term causes while preserving its empirical insights and extending them in a new program of research, and both efforts are well underway.[4] But originality and empirical richness bring no

2. Harmondsworth 1975.
3. For a thorough and thoughtful introduction to the historiography of the English Revolution, see R. C. Richardson, *The Debate on the English Revolution Revisited*, 3rd edn, London 1998. For discussions of revisionism, see 218–28, 236n.33, 237n.47; and Alastair MacLachlan, *The Rise and Fall of Revolutionary England*, New York 1996, 231–51. For some revisionist methodological statements, see Glenn Burgess, "On Revisionism," *The Historical Journal* 33.3, 1990; Paul Christianson, "The Causes of the English Revolution," *Journal of British Studies* 15.2, 1976; Barry Coward, "Was There an English Revolution in the Middle of the Seventeenth Century?" in Colin Jones, Malyn Newitt, and Stephen Roberts, eds, *Politics and People in Revolutionary England*, Oxford 1986, 9–40; and Conrad Russell, *Unrevolutionary England, 1603–1642*, London 1990, ix–xxx. For a classic collection of "post-revisionist" essays, see Richard Cust and Ann Hughes, eds, *Conflict in Early Stuart England* (*CH*), particularly the editors' introduction, and their later collection, *The English Civil War*, London 1997. Most "post-revisionist" critiques offer a liberal or "neo-whig" response focusing on oppositional ideologies. For marxist critiques incorporating a discussion of class struggle and the mode of production, see Perry Anderson, *English Questions*, London 1992, 284–93; Robert Brenner, *BMR*; Alex Callinicos, "Bourgeois Revolutions and Historical Materialism," *International Socialism* 43, 1989; Lewis C. Daly, "'Saith the Spirit, to This Shattered Earth': Mid-Seventeenth-Century Puritan Radicalism and the History of Religious Forms of Class Struggle," diss. SUNY Buffalo 1996; Christopher Hill, "Parliament and People," in *Collected Essays*, 3 vols, Amherst 1985–86, 3.21–64; and Ellen Meiksins Wood, *The Pristine Culture of Capitalism*, London 1991.
4. "The English Revolution and the Revisionist Revolt," *Social History* 7.3, 1982.

guarantees, as we can see when we examine the revisionist response to the two most important marxist studies of the English Revolution published in the last quarter century: Robert Brenner's *Merchants and Revolution* and Brian Manning's *The English People and the English Revolution*.[5] Each offers a detailed narrative based on a formidable program of primary research, and each has been ignored, dismissed on *a priori* grounds, or travestied by revisionist reviewers.[6] That's not too surprising, since revisionist history, like the other reified partial totalities of the capitalist academy, exists in large part to render such marxist narratives invisible, but it does make a theoretical and polemical retort essential. Moreover, the totalizing ambition of the historical revisionist project—considerably greater than its protestations of naive empiricism might indicate—deserves such a response. First, I will consider three errors revisionists see in liberal and marxist history: its tendencies to elevate methodological *a prioris* over empirical evidence, to see opposition instead of consensus, and to indulge in anachronism rather than reconstructing the past in its own terms. Then, I will turn to three revisionist attempts to provide a "positive" account of the origin and course of the English Revolution: the instability of a three-kingdom nation, the force of religion, and the contingent fact of King Charles's personality. I conclude by using Jürgen Habermas's analysis of various conservative reactions to the Enlightenment to locate English historical revisionism among other sorts of revisionism in other academic fields. My argument is that, in their effort to render collective social and ideological conflict invisible by attacking what they mistakenly see as a reductive liberal and marxist dualism, historical revisionists fall into a reductive capitalist monism.

Con: *A Prioris*, Opposition, and Whiggery

An *a priori* is like the smell of excrement, as Freud describes it: only that of others offends. But if *a prioris* follow us everywhere, they are not immutable, for they can help us discover new evidence that forces us to modify or replace them, as our own interpretive experience repeatedly

---

5. 2nd edn, London 1991.
6. On Manning, see John Miller, "Two Types of Historical Method," *Times Higher Education Supplement*, May 28 1976; and John Morrill, *The Nature of the English Revolution*, London 1993, 214–23. On Brenner, see Morrill, "Conflict Probable or Inevitable?" *New Left Review* 207, 1994; Simon Adams in *History Today* 45.3, 1995; and Conrad Russell in *The International History Review* 16.1, 1994, 129, who pleads a delicate inability to discuss the conclusion of Brenner's book because he "does not know for certain what 'feudalism' and 'capitalism' are"—a perennial stratagem, as Tawney eloquently pointed out in 1926: "After more than half a century of work on the subject [capitalism] by scholars of half a dozen different nationalities and of every variety of political opinion, to deny that the phenomenon exists; or to suggest that if it does exist, it is unique among human institutions in having, like Melchizedek, existed from eternity; or to imply that, if it has a history, propriety forbids that history to be disinterred, is to run wilfully in blinkers.... [An author] is unlikely, however, to make much of the history of Europe during the last three centuries if, in addition to eschewing the word, he ignores the fact" (*Religion and the Rise of Capitalism*, 1926; rpt New York 1962, xii).

confirms. A dialectical methodology can posit at most an *analytical* distinction between fact and theory, so that a new theory allows us to discover new facts, while new facts allow us to test prior theories, and the process of historical writing becomes the dialogue of discovery and testing. We will usually discover new facts more rapidly than we modify our theories, but in any reflective practice of historical writing—any practice that at least acknowledges it has an *a priori*—both processes will be in play. However, historical revisionism posits a *substantial* and *temporal* distinction between fact and interpretation, with histrionic modesty. Kevin Sharpe objects to Christopher Hill's reliance on "*a priori* assumptions"—not because they resist correction, but because they *are* assumptions. He introduces a collection of revisionist essays with the no-nonsense claim that "We have chosen to look at the history of early seventeenth-century parliaments from a new perspective—from the perspective of the early Stuart period itself."[7] Conrad Russell declares that revisionists "believe that the logically correct order of proceeding is to establish the correct events first, and to consider their explanation afterwards."[8] Praising the revisionist rigor of T. P. S. Woods, John Morrill says, "Old-fashioned Whigs may well lament the failure of revisionist historians to ask 'the big *why* questions,' but once enough historians have performed the kind of small service Mr. Woods has performed, the revisionists will be able to assemble a big answer to them." But revisionists have never been loath to pose big questions, even if they come up with small answers. Even the decision to move from "why?" to "how?" conceals a bold agenda: the revisionist effort to purge intention and ideology from historical explanation. Morrill himself has just characterized England in 1642 as a country "drifting unwillingly into civil war"—a plain style but a very big claim, each word of which (except, perhaps, "into") packs a wallop. "Drifting," for instance, replaces fluvial whig teleology with oceanic revisionist contingency. He concludes with a nostrum: "In scholarship, as in everything else, if we look after the pennies, the pounds will look after themselves."[9] But in scholarship, as in everything else, if we look after the pennies, we spend lots of time counting pennies, talking about pennies, fashioning a penny-based theory of society and history, and losing friends, but without discovering where the pennies came from (from the Bank of England? from someone else's labor? from heaven?), leaving ourselves with a shimmering coppery drift of unrelated facts that mound up into an all-purpose but paralyzingly *a priori* conclusion: "Things were very, very complex."

In his declaration of principles at the beginning of *The Rise of the New*

---

7. *Criticism and Compliment*, Cambridge 1987, ix; *Faction and Parliament*, Oxford 1978, 5.
8. *Unrevolutionary* x.
9. "Proceeding Moderately," *Times Literary Supplement*, October 24 1980, 1196. Barry Coward also finds a "drift of events" culminating in the English Revolution ("Was There" 26, 29, 31). Morrill alludes to Chesterfield's quotation from Secretary of the Treasury Lowndes, that "very covetous, sordid fellow."

Model Army, Mark Kishlansky also embraces this positivist method. He proposes to ignore "obviously biased informants," to make "sparing use" of retrospective accounts, and "to avoid the historiographical wars that have devastated study of this period."[10] But without some *a priori* principles of selection and judgment, how do we distinguish biased from unbiased sources? Shouldn't a true revisionism leave open the possibility that a Presbyterian heresiographer like Thomas Edwards, whom Kishlansky rejects, *a priori*, speaks in the value-free voice of moderate sweet reason? Even if he doesn't, isn't his very bias a historical *datum*? How can we hope to write a full history of any period when we begin by bracketing or effacing such crucial objects of historical inquiry as the retrospective accounts of Clarendon and Hutchinson? Such accounts form not in the private space of the distorting imagination, but in the turbulent subjective/objective stream of history itself, and they proceed to re-enter that stream, becoming *facts* in the continuing political history of the period. By attempting to bracket out historical sources tainted with retrospective *a prioris*, Kishlansky reveals an entire "chronistic" philosophy of history, which anachronistically bleaches out reflections and anticipations until each atomized moment, in sequent toil, disappears without remainder into the next. And by claiming to leave behind modern historiographical wars, Kishlansky attempts to set aside the entire collective enterprise of historical writing, which begins with dialogue, not *tabula rasa*. After ruling the *a prioris* of others out of order while perfuming their own, revisionists free their Comtean method to procreate undisturbed with their unacknowledged Burkean agenda and produce a hybridized historical positivism. The result is mulish, in more ways than one, and it severely damages, among other revisionist histories, Kishlansky's account of the New Model Army in 1647, as I will argue in chapter 6.[11]

Revisionists frequently diagnose an *a priori* propensity for seeing *opposition* where it doesn't exist. Both liberals and marxists, Conrad Russell says, work inside a Hegelian framework that sees progressive change arising from "a clash of opposites."[12] Typically, revisionists seek out some opponent's empirically elaborated *distinction* between two

10. Cambridge, MA, 1979, ix.
11. Revisionists' mistrust for retrospection implies their mistrust for print. Sharpe says that one must always check print against more authentic manuscript sources (*Personal Rule of Charles I*, New Haven, CT, 1992, xxii). Morrill faults Manning for using pamphlets and other print sources to understand the English Revolution, since the only "sources for a proper study of popular attitudes in the 1630s and 1640s" are "depositions, examinations, and other records of innumerable quarter sessions, assizes, King's Bench and Star Chamber" (*Nature* 230); the only audible proles are those in the dock. This point of method pursues a class agenda: the very institutions capable of asking questions, recording answers, and archiving manuscripts tended to be those of the ruling class, and many laboring-class readers could neither read nor write proper manuscript hand (Keith Thomas, "The Meaning of Literacy in Early Modern England," in Gerd Baumann, ed., *The Written Word*, Oxford 1986, 97–131). Kishlansky himself says fellow revisionist J. S. A. Adamson takes manuscript fetishism too far ("Saye No More," *Journal of British Studies* 30.4, 1991, 400).
12. *Unrevolutionary* ix.

seventeenth-century entities (Calvinist and Arminian, court and country, Parliament and Privy Council). After connecting the two in some fashion, they can then deny that this *distinction* forms an absolute *difference*, and smile in triumph. Such short work with binaries will be familiar to postmodernist literary critics, and within certain limits, one might call revisionism a rough-and-ready form of *deconstruction*. Johann Sommerville's *Politics and Ideology in England, 1603–1640*, a post-revisionist study of the conflicting political ideologies of early Stuart England, has proved a lightning rod for this approach.[13] Kevin Sharpe anxiously takes issue with Sommerville's "anxiety to find divisive and conflicting ideologies":

> For though his chapters rigidly distinguish absolutist theories from ideas of contract and law, much of his evidence suggests that they need to be discussed together—as tensions and ambivalences within a body of shared beliefs rather than as rival value systems. Both proponents of divine right and advocates of original popular sovereignty, he acknowledges, believed that the object of government was the common good.[14]

A proper rivalry between two value systems, then, would require one of them to reject the common good—an unlikely prospect in early modern England, outside of a particularly coarse morality play.

Revisionists like J. C. D. Clark frequently criticize an "oppositional" model of early Stuart parliaments:

> Parliamentary conflicts in 1604–29 do not reveal the existence of two "sides," two coherent groups of peers or commoners, whether Court or Country. . . . Many of the conflicts can be explained by individual reactions to the distortions of the system and of conventional expectations produced by the exceptional and widely resented dominance of Buckingham. . . . Equally, in the localities, the need for access to power at the centre prevented the emergence of a monolithic bloc in opposition to the royal administration. . . . We can answer with some certainty the question: do modern parties date from the Civil War or from the 1690s? The answer, I would suggest, is: they date from neither episode. In particular, if historians wish to treat Victorian parties as the paradigm, it is to the world after 1832 that we must look for their emergence.

Clark's argument personalizes conflict, thus eliminating anything that we might be inclined to call principled opposition: others do not so much *oppose* Buckingham on ideological grounds as *resent* him—no doubt because they envy him.[15] Clark's straw men seek conflicts among "coherent groups" and "monolithic blocs"—monads or nothing. But his closing

---

13. London 1986.
14. *Politics and Ideas in Early Stuart England*, London 1989, 286; see also Sharpe's "Religion, Rhetoric, and Revolution in Seventeenth-Century England," *The Huntington Library Quarterly* 57.3, 1994, 255; Russell on Sommerville in *Unrevolutionary* ix, and *The Causes of the English Civil War*, Oxford 1990, chapter 6; Kishlansky's critique of opposition in "The Emergence of Adversary Politics in the Long Parliament," *Journal of Modern History* 49, 1977; and Burgess's in "Revisionist History and Shakespeare's Political Context," *Shakespeare Yearbook* 6, 1995, 11.
15. *Revolution and Rebellion*, Cambridge 1986, 134, 139, 154–5.

tautology sits on a wobbly syllogism: all political opposition in Western democracies derives from organized, parliamentary political parties, so because early modern England lacked such parties, it lacked political opposition. Beginning with a false major premise (what *would* a Chartist, feminist, or Fenian make of it?) ostensibly taken on trust from unnamed whigs, he tacks on a minor premise that no one would deny, then deduces a perfectly valid, perfectly false conclusion that attempts to shut down any analysis of parliamentary and extra-parliamentary opposition. Adversary politics in post-Restoration parliaments suggests not so much a movement toward contention as the capitalist containment of subversion: by rendering a tamer sort of opposition "loyal" and functional, they rendered a fiercer sort "disloyal" and so more easily crushable. But we search Victorian Britain in vain for anything like the turbulent Parliament of 1626, which accused the Duke of Buckingham (and by implication, Charles) of being grossly corrupt, a papal fifth columnist, and perhaps even the poisoner of King James. Charles saved the duke from trial only by proroguing Parliament—an act that suggests he sensed opposition in Parliament, if not a parliamentary Opposition.

"Opposition," in fact, is a concept too important for understanding society more generally for us to make it contingent on the presence of a historically specific form like the parliamentary party. We should group it not with taxonomic concepts such as "fish" or "fowl," "monarchy" or "democracy," but with analytical concepts such as "culture," "gender," and "labor," which are intrinsic to any modern analysis of any conceivable society. Opposition in early Stuart England included the non-party-based but clearly oppositional politics of the parliaments; the committed Puritan opposition to Arminian and "papist" influences on civil and church government; the ethical and political rhetoric pitting "country" virtue against "courtly" corruption; pro-Palatinate popular culture, performance and publication of antityrannical drama; and the oppositional poetry of the neo-Spenserians, who hearkened back to an idealized Elizabethan era of Protestant political virtue. Much of this book will be an attempt to show how significant oppositional collectives emerge *from within* shared bodies of ideas: how the Protestant theology of the spirit could produce a severe split and a debate within the New Model Army; how the Puritan project of reformist solidarity known as Barebone's Parliament could become, within the space of twelve months, a conflict between Fifth Monarchist radicals and an Antichristian Protectorate; how the traditional and distinctly non-revolutionary solidarity of the common field could become the Diggers' model for the revolutionary transformation of England.

Revisionists have typically dealt with social (and socialist) histories of the Revolution by pretending that they don't exist—and the same applies to laboring people. In the Preface to *Parliamentary Selection*, Kishlansky presents a superficially modest defense: "But to study a hierarchical elite and to portray its values in its own terms does not constitute a statement of modern political preferences. . . . The historian's primary obligation remains to understand the past on its own terms."[16] But the first claim improperly collapses studying a group with portraying its values in its own terms. Moreover, if we allow the first "its own terms" to meld with the second, and so also collapse "a hierarchical elite" with "the past," then history from above wins game, set, and match. It is difficult to overestimate the importance of such moments inside revisionist prose, whereby questions about class, working people, and history from below are half-asked, quarter-answered, and blocked completely from further consideration.

So far as working people *act* in non-traditional ways, John Morrill tends to find them silent or unintelligible: "Thus in 1642 men desperately wished to avoid a conflict or, at least, to let it pass them by. The war began despite, yet also because of, the longing for peace. For while the moderates, as always, talked and agonized, the extremists seized the initiative."[17] We can hear the revisionist project at work in the confident generalization of "men desperately wished," in the rueful "as always," and in the paradox of "despite, yet also because of," which gracefully avoids the retort that would abolish it: that different groups of people with distinct interests and ideologies fervently longed for different sorts of peace. Most of all, we hear revisionism when those desperately pacific "men" of the first sentence reappear as the talkative agonizing "moderates" of the third, quietly annihilating the "extremists" by placing them outside the ken of reasonable political actors whose words and actions historians must examine carefully. Elsewhere, Morrill claims that nobody really referred to Charles as a tyrant during "the paper war" of 1641–42. But he can make this claim only by limiting himself to works printed "with the knowledge and consent of the two Houses (or at least of the Commons)," thereby eliminating works put out by "every crank and those with an eye solely to the market."[18] This bit of psychohistorical sorting eliminates such oblique but menacing speech acts as the republication in 1642 of John Ponet's *Shorte Treatise*, and the increasing outbursts of seditious speech, many of them by common people, during the Personal Rule.[19] And one may suspect that only suicidal bravado, not crankiness or greed, could have led to denunciations of the king as a tyrant in 1641–42, as Gerrard Winstanley later suggested: "You know that while the king was in the height of his oppressing power, the people only whispered in private chambers against him: but afterwards it was preached upon the house tops, that he was a tyrant and a traitor to England's peace; and he had his overturn."[20]

In arguing against a substantial early modern culture of opposition, revisionists have questioned the scope and the severity of censorship.

16. Cambridge 1986, xi.
17. *The Revolt of the Provinces*, London and New York 1976, 42.
18. *Nature* 285.
19. For seditious speeches, see John Cordy Jeaffreson, ed., *Middlesex County Records*, 4 vols, London 1886–92, *passim*.
20. *W* 502; Luke 12.3.

Sheila Lambert says works of "all complexions" were performed, preached, and printed in the 1630s, with relatively few formal prosecutions, so younger scholars should not be led astray by the "old myth of the struggle for the freedom of the press."[21] Glenn Burgess argues that early Stuart censorship aimed to prevent disorder, not to stifle critical opinion.[22] John Barnard and D. F. McKenzie challenge the classic whig hypothesis about an unleashing of the presses in the 1640s; given the brevity of most revolutionary-era pamphlets, the total volume of print may have remained constant.[23] But the very constituents of the oppositional early Stuart semi-public sphere point to the deeply felt reality of censorship: covert publication by scribes or overseas or with pseudonyms or false imprints, the circulation of potentially seditious manuscript newsletters, and the proliferation of an obliquely antityrannical Roman idiom on the stage, the page, and in political rhetoric.[24] Lambert's argument about the rarity of prosecution seems both beside the point (since censorship aims precisely to prevent oppositional writers from thinking, much less writing and publishing, dangerous thoughts) and contrary to the documented evidence, as Hill shows.[25] Burgess distinguishes between free speech in a structurally circumscribed public sphere and a destabilizing threat to the public order—a distinction that would have been anachronistically unintelligible to any member of the early modern ruling class. McKenzie forgets that censorship aims at persons as well as pages, the pace as well as the fact of publication. The entry of previously private persons into the public sphere after the *de facto* breakdown of censorship in the early forties, along with the explosive integration of practice and publicity through overnight publication, left all observers with the impression of a sea change: in 1641, depending on one's point of view, Babel loomed and gibbered, or the saints found their voices, like a mighty rushing of waters.

Kevin Sharpe observes that "We know of no voice that was silenced. Indeed, there were no real institutions or mechanisms of organized censorship."[26] Even if that sublime first sentence were true, its insouciant Newspeak would be chilling. And the second asks us to forget the Tower, the Master of Revels, Star Chamber, the Court of High Commission, the Stationer's Company, and Parliament. Referring to the "myth" of widespread censorship, Sharpe says it was never total and observes that "John Lilburne continued to publish despite the Star Chamber decree of 1637," thus boldly refuting an argument never made while deftly sidestepping the actual arguments that Charles severely punished some writers and distributors of unlicensed works in an unsuccessful effort to silence

---

21. "Richard Montagu, Arminianism and Censorship," *Past and Present* 124, 1989, 68.
22. *Absolute Monarchy and the Stuart Constitution*, New Haven, CT, 1996, 7.
23. Nigel Smith, *Literature and Revolution in England, 1640–1660*, New Haven, CT, 1994, 24; Smith's response is telling.
24. Annabel Patterson, "The Very Name of the Game," *HS* 21–37.
25. *A Nation of Change and Novelty*, London and New York 1990, 24–55, 195–217; and *Collected Essays* 1.32–71.
26. *Criticism* 37.

criticism.[27] And it seems worth remembering that the Caroline state arrested Lilburne in December 1637 for distributing books by Bastwick, convicted him, stripped him to the waist, tied him to the tail of a cart, whipped him every few paces of the two-mile trip from Fleet Prison to Westminster, and imprisoned him until November 1640, when the Long Parliament released him. True, while in prison, he wrote his first work, *The Christian Mans Triall*, about this very episode of censorship. But his ability skillfully to integrate this episode into an autobiographical oeuvre of Foxean persecution does not mean that it was not censorship.[28] Sharpe compares Charles's Personal Rule to "the emergency powers assumed by government in the name of common safety at a time of crisis," which "few question." Its efforts to identify English Puritan "collaborators" with the Scots resemble the modern "war against terrorism"; then as now, the state monitored the mails, "yet most of us do not live in fear of our mail being tampered with."[29] Britons who want a Bill of Rights and Americans who remember they already have one may not feel completely reassured.

The question of opposition brings us to the question of intellectual history, and the historical limits of the thinkable. In its first decade or so, the revisionist project tended to neglect intellectual history, but not out of any positive antipathy. The sheer, fractured complexity implicit in revisionist factions, local history, and contingencies may have threatened to spin off into the ether, but a very traditional model of the hierarchical Renaissance world-view always reeled it back in. Perry Anderson notes that revisionism, like modern conservatism more generally, has always taken pains to demote ideas so far as they might become divisive *ideologies*, but to promote them so far as they form unifying *world-views* that delegitimate any claim by an appeal to class or material interest.[30] For instance, Jonathan Clark rigorously subordinates "values" to "situations" and the unforeseeable play of contingent events, but he also makes orthodox Anglicanism the determining world-view of early modern England. His anti-idealist idealism strategically reduces the conceptual armory of his opponents to "mere" words (like "opposition" and "class") subject to "deletion," while elevating his own lexicon ("order," "hierarchy," "consensus," "orthodox religion") to the status of all-permeating, ideal forms, not even subject to debate. He even doubts whether the social base "has any existence outside contemporaries' perceptions." Approaching the deconstructive absolutism of Paul de Man himself, he argues that "revolution (like class, that other favourite) is a descriptive term, not a phenomenon. Studies of revolution as of class are studies of the use of words, not of things. . . . Such phenomena as 'class' are matters of *perception*."[31]

27. *Politics* 9; *Personal* 654, 651.
28. Pauline Gregg, *Free-Born John*, London 1961, 52–64, 75–84.
29. "The Personal Rule of Charles I," in Howard Tomlinson, ed., *Before the English Civil War*, London 1983, 53–78, 55; *Personal* 683.
30. *English Questions* 289.
31. *Revolution* 18, 32; "On Hitting the Buffers," *Past and Present* 117, 1987, 200; *Revolution*

Historians frequently mock literary critics for resorting to dated concepts like "the rise of the gentry" or "Parliament's seizing of the initiative," which bear dim traces of their origins in ancient undergraduate seminars. Literary critics might be forgiven a retaliatory snicker at the evergreen appeal to historians of E. M. W. Tillyard's *The Elizabethan World Picture*, if they were not busily tricking out that same world picture in postmodern dress, as I will argue in the next chapter.[32] Revisionism offers a traditional, top-down, church-and-king history of ideas, developed for the last decade or so by no one more than Kevin Sharpe. Particularly in his long essay, "A Commonwealth of Meanings," Sharpe finds pre-revolutionary England dominated by a number of hierarchalist commonplaces—the *concordia discors* of the Anglican *via media*, the monarch as head of the body, father of the family, or God of the cosmos.[33] We will see all of these commonplaces challenged or critically appropriated by radicals in part two. For the moment, I simply want to note that this approach embraces a hierarchical organicism of method as well as object: organic ruling-class ideas impress themselves on the body politic in an organic fashion. But if universally and gladly accepted, why did they require such frequent reiteration? Like all ideology, they must combine an instrumental or hierarchical dimension with a utopian or associative one. The body politic metaphor, for instance, could never have served the absolutist project if it had not balanced capital hierarchy with corporal association. Though conservative ideologists emphasized the first ideal, both continental and English radicals emphasized the second, turning the head into the good of the whole body, the monarchical head into a diseased and expendable body part. Machiavelli lauded Rome for removing the diseased "head" of the Tarquins and recovering its republican virtue.[34] In *Vindiciae, Contra Tyrannos*, Hubert Languet and Philippe du Plessis Mornay depict a body politic that glances apocalyptically toward the tottering idol of Belshazzar's dream in Daniel 7: the people may be the pedestal of the kingly Rhodian Colossus, but "he cannot remain standing without the people. Who would find it strange, then, if we conclude that the people is more powerful than the king?" And they appropriate for the people the kingly fiction identifying the mystical body of the king and the nation's immortal identity in

---

26n, 32. Compare de Man: "If we extend this notion beyond literature, it merely confirms that the bases for historical knowledge are not empirical facts but written texts, even if these texts masquerade in the guise of wars or revolutions"; *Blindness and Insight*, 2nd edn, Minneapolis 1983, 165. This masquerading text began to phosphoresce after de Man's Jew-hating wartime journalism came to light.

32. London 1943.

33. *Criticism; Politics*; Sharpe and Peter Lake, "Introduction" to Sharpe and Lake, eds, *Culture and Politics in Early Stuart England*, Stanford 1993, 1–20; Sharpe and Stephen N. Zwicker, "Politics of Discourse: Introduction," in Sharpe and Zwicker, eds, *The Politics of Discourse*, Berkeley and Los Angeles 1987, 1–20; Sharpe and Zwicker, "Introduction: Refiguring Revolutions," in Sharpe and Zwicker, eds, *Refiguring Revolutions*, Berkeley and Los Angeles 1998, 1–24; Sharpe, *Politics* 3–74.

34. *The Discourses*, Harmondsworth 1970, 157.

time, proclaiming the immortality of the people.[35] In *Of Reformation*, Milton pictures an English body politic suffering from a prelatical wen, then violates the decorum of organic fable by calling in from outside a "wise and learned philosopher," who recommends radical surgery.[36]

In this book, I'm attempting a materialist study of anti-hegemonic resistance, but one might also write a materialist study of hegemonic deference—clearly a much more widespread phenomenon in early modern England and all other cultures, including that of modernity—without abandoning a materialist for an idealist method. In his recent attempts to integrate revisionist political history and new historicist cultural history, Sharpe has drawn attention to the unifying force of hegemonic ideology: for instance, in Tudor England "the cooperation of the political nation and the obedience of the lower orders rested more on a culture of order than on physical coercion."[37] But even if we avert our eyes from the peasant risings and the groaning gallows of Tudor England, we will still see how extensively culture and ideology interweave with coercion, including the coercive denial of free access to the means of production.[38] In early modern England, as in most societies, hegemonic ideological domination and physical coercion need each other: just as constant physical coercion tends to be relatively inefficient at maintaining order and extracting surplus labor, so a hegemonic ideology of order, industry, and deference remains empty words if it cannot, from time to time, metamorphose into a jail, a gibbet, a cavalry troop, a husband's fist. Even in a capitalist state employing contractual means of domination, the state monopoly on public coercion comes in handy when a general strike threatens "the public safety," and the National Guard mobilizes to guard the nation from the people.

No doubt, the deference of an agrarian wage laborer to the capitalist landlord who hires him or that of a domestic laborer to her parish priest derives in part from a persuasive ideology of order, but it also derives from their prudent decision to continue reproducing their means of subsistence in the traditional fashion. The wage laborer may decide, quite reasonably, that he prefers servile poverty punctuated by patronizing harvest festivals to sulking destitution outside of the deferential community. The domestic laborer may decide that she prefers quiet and

---

35. George Garnett, ed. and trans., Cambridge 1994, 76, 90; Garnett attributes the work to both men.
36. *M* 1.583–4. This violated fable suggests *Paradise Lost*, where historical Satan confronts his allegorical progeny, Sin and Death, much to the dismay of Milton's neoclassical readers. For Milton, indecorously mixed media prophesy a traumatic transition: from unfallen innocence to fallen knowledge, from prelatical monarchy to regicidal republic. See R. Po-chia Hsia on the tension within the corporatist model of pre-Anabaptist Münster: "The consensus model argued or implies the rule of the body by its 'better parts,' whereas the corporatist model defended the equality of all the constituent members" (Hsia, ed., *The German People and the Reformation*, Ithaca, NY, 1988, 51–68, 66–7).
37. "The King's Writ," Sharpe and Lake, *Culture* 117–38; 117.
38. "Capital obtains this surplus labour without an equivalent, and in essence it always remains forced labour" (*MECW* 37.806).

obedience in church fellowship to a scold's bridle, censure and fines in a church court, and fractious isolation. Both may internalize their habits of obedience, for maintaining tacit resistance alongside active deference requires enervating psychic work on top of the physical work of subsistence and surplus production—the painful but seldom-studied casuistry of laboring-class everyday life. But in changed material circumstances, when a crisis in the political order or the mode of production makes possible new material choices, an old culture of deference can change quickly to tacit, or even vocal and active, resistance. During the English Revolution, new radical projects in non-hierarchical sociability emerged, revealing not only an enormous human creativity in the revolutionary era, and an explosion of experimental collectives, but the provisional and material (as opposed to "consensual and ideological") quality of deference before it and after it. Christopher Hill rightly sees the English Revolution as a touchstone for early modern England in general, for relatively brief moments of "hot" class struggle like 1642–60 help us to understand and interpret those long periods of order that they break up.[39]

Any attempt to replace the model of a consensually unified, early modern world-view with one containing meaningful differences, even self-conscious opposition, will soon draw a revisionist charge of *anachronism*: forcing modern categories onto a premodern society. Revisionists rigorously police contemporary historical writing for interloping modern phenomena, social models, and schemes of analysis. They may even quarantine a particular analytical term with complicating queries, demands for historical specification, insistences on lexical change. But when one notices that revisionists address these peremptory challenges only to their opponents and never to themselves, one may begin to suspect a strategic motive. This prerogative rigor regarding terminology and concepts aims not to keep the empirical discussion of historical change from starting off on the wrong foot, but to throttle it in its crib.

Among the contested terms is "revolution" itself. Revisionists prefer "English Civil War" to "English Revolution" to describe the events of mid-century on the grounds that premodern political thinkers could not even conceptualize a total and irreversible change. "Revolution" had the premodern sense of cyclical rotation, so we should follow Clarendon in seeing the ostensible "revolutionaries" of 1642–60 as "rebels": not

39. In *A Millennium of Family Change*, London 1992, Wally Seccombe reminds both left and right idealists that patriarchal deference has material foundations: "An unwillingness to face squarely the awkward fact that the self-interest of the oppressed is not unilaterally revolutionary leads to the substitution of an utterly idealist explanation for acquiescence or prudence" (33). See also Manning on the material dimensions of peasant deference (*English* 324–5), and that revisionist sage, Bertolt Brecht, on plebeian revolt in *Coriolanus*: "I don't think you realize how hard it is for the oppressed to become united. Their misery unites them—once they recognize who has caused it. 'Our sufferance is a gain to them.' But otherwise their misery is liable to cut them off from one another, for they are forced to snatch the wretched crumbs from each other's mouths. Think how reluctantly men decide to revolt!" (*Brecht on Theatre*, New York 1977, 252).

proto-Jacobin proponents of a genuinely new social order, but paleo-Elizabethan malcontents within an old one. But early modern apocalyptic thought certainly made it possible to think of irreversible change. Alger-non Sidney, that exemplary republican martyr, refused to be scared off by the epithet of "rebel," and offered a rational etymological counter-argument that subtly recalls the "good old cause": the word "rebellion" is "taken from the Latin 'rebellare' which signifies no more than to renew a war. . . . Rebellion being nothing but a renewed war . . . of itself is neither good nor evil, more than any other war, but is just or unjust according to the cause or manner of it."[40] Christopher Hill has shown that seventeenth-century speakers used "revolution" in something like its dominant modern sense.[41] And not just seventeenth- and twentieth-century conservatives, but seventeenth-century radicals could denounce a proposed revolution-ary settlement as mere rebellion which stopped short of its revolutionary intentions. We will hear such charges made by the Agitators in 1647, by the Diggers in 1649, and by Fifth Monarchists and republicans in 1653–58. One might almost define modern revolutions as those which introduce unresolved conflicts—for instance, those in France, Haiti, America (the Civil War), the Soviet Union, Ireland, China, and the host of postcolonial nations whose revolutions, built out of peasant and proletarian blood and sweat, produced new national regimes of capitalist exploitation. Modern revolutions may produce a fundamental social transformation, but they may also *stop short of* such transformations while introducing a new conflict and a new normative standard, even an *anachronistic* standard, whereby we measure the present against its past promises and future potential and find it wanting. A revolution is, like Ernst Bloch's *hope*, that which can be betrayed, but not completely.

Similarly, "radical" comes in for a sustained attack on the grounds that it properly belongs to the late eighteenth and early nineteenth century, or because it suggests a "root" difference over fundamentals foreign to the consensual politics of early modern England—a justified critique when directed against the foolish attempt to find this or that radical "ahead of his time."[42] But we can reject this foolishness in two significantly distinct ways. We can reduce a "radical" to the *a priori* unity of "his time" through some dubious enthymeme: "No less than Laud's sermons, Thomas Scott's pamphlets speak in the fundamentally religious idiom of his time, not in the secular idiom of political radicalism, so no less than Laud, Scott inhabits a traditional mental universe." Or we can explain the radical by expanding "his time" to a complex totality includ-ing significantly opposed ideologies, noting, for instance, the ideological chasm between a godly preacher in exile and an Arminian archbishop, the different visions of history and "his time" that they constructed, the

---

40. Jonathan Scott, *Algernon Sidney and the English Republic, 1623–1677*, Cambridge 1988, 56.
41. *Nation* 82–101.
42. J. C. Davis, "Radicalism in a Traditional Society," *History of Political Thought* 3.2, 1982. Christianson, "Causes" 41–3.

execution of the first by a Spanish agent, the second by a Puritan parliament.

Revisionists have almost always taken the former route, creating a perilously homogeneous early modern chronism. J. C. Davis laments the "muddled and anachronistic view of the radical, overlain with eighteenth and nineteenth century Whig, nonconformist and, alas, socialist views of what progress and therefore radicalism meant."[43] For Conal Condren, seventeenth-century political actors moved outside of traditionalism only at moments of "rhetorical mishap, eristic embarrassment, and argumentative isolation," so we can use "radical" only as an adjective in a seventeenth-century context.[44] For Sharpe, early modern England held only "one truth," so "there could no more be a contention over fundamental values in secular matters than in spiritual."[45] True, if "radicals" must kick free of conservatives in some absolute, ontological fashion, then of course no radicals lived in early Stuart England, or anywhere else. But if radicals are those who risk their ears, their livelihoods, their liberty, and their lives in principled conflicts with the ruling class (kings, priests, lawyers, landlords), then many radicals walked the fields and streets of early modern, early capitalist England. Indeed, compared to the university campuses of postmodern, late capitalist Britain and North America, they were thick on the ground.

How would this sort of lexical rigor look if turned against historical revisionism and used to judge its successes at understanding the past, "in its own terms," as the saying goes?[46] For instance, how might a whig respond to the following revisionist critique of long-term, liberal explanations for the English Revolution?

> Indeed, perhaps the most powerful version of the revisionist case was based on an analysis of the real, financial and material, causes of administrative and then political breakdown, causes which were in large part hidden from contemporaries and which their own categories of thought were unable to comprehend.[47]

A resentful whig in an eye-for-an-eye mood might say the authors have projected modern conceptions of Namierite atomism and the bureaucratic state apparatus onto a century that had no conception of—indeed, no terms for—such things. After all, the *OED* records no use of "financial" before 1769, no application of "administrative" or "administration" to government before 1661, and no use at all of "breakdown" before 1832, that *annus mirabilis* when Jonathan Clark's modernity spontaneously generated itself. Emboldened by these small triumphs, she might rise to interrupt in mid-sentence any revisionist referring to pre-revolutionary England using such terms as "royalist" (1643), "monarchist," "deference,"

---

43. "Radical Lives," *Political Science* 37, 1985, 167.
44. *The Language of Politics in Seventeenth-Century England*, New York 1994, 162.
45. *Politics* 11.
46. Burgess, "Revisionist" 9.
47. Sharpe and Lake, "Introduction" 2.

and "fanatic" (1647), "patriarchal" (1656), "consensual" (1754), "absolutist" (1830), "monarchism" (1838), "consensus" (1851), and "paternalism"
(1881—in Chicago!). "Anachronism" itself is a troubling late arrival: 1646
for a misdated fact, but 1818 (Coleridge's "anachronic") for an improperly
projected world-view. So an obsession with rooting out anachronism in
accounts of early modern England is itself anachronistic: the reflex of a
Romantic linear historicism that ignores the world-view of the period it
wishes to understand. Her fit passes and our whig sits down. A revisionist
protests that the seventeenth century certainly had the *concept* of administrative breakdowns, if not the word; even if it didn't, modern historians
should feel free to reconstruct them. And then we would be off and
running in an argument based on example, counter-example, and a
struggle for explanatory adequacy. I would finally side with the whig in
emphasizing long-term causes, but not to the exclusion of medium-term
"precipitants" and short-term "triggers." But my argument could never
be that the concept of an "administrative breakdown" is *anachronistic*, only
that it is *wrong* or *inadequate*.

For revisionists, anachronism usually derives from teleological historical
writing. But we can usefully distinguish at least three sorts of teleological
error. *Necessitarian teleology* argues that A inevitably became A' and could
not have become B or C. *Meliorist teleology* describes the movement from A
to A' as a progress. And *winner's teleology* argues that A' historians looking
into the past should forget about B and C—those dead ends of history
which lacked the good sense to join with A on its fortunate march to the
future.[48] We may accuse S. R. Gardiner with some justice of all three sorts,
though his capacious Victorian imagination and his own sectarian background brought him a considerable sympathy with the "losers" populating
his histories.[49] Some marxists, and Marx himself, insofar as he subscribed
to a rigorous modes-of-production narrative inherited from Adam Smith,
fall into all three sorts. Necessity comes with the "stagist" movement from
feudalism to capitalism to socialism to communism. Meliorism is trickier,
since marxism sees no smooth increase in human happiness, but it is at
least implied in the promise that class struggle and the development of
the productive forces will eliminate most human suffering. And winner's
teleology appears when some misty-eyed but stiff-lipped emissary of
Stalin or the Shining Path contemplates the "inevitable" (and therefore

48. On whig history and presentism, see Burgess, "Revisionism"; Herbert Butterfield, *The
    Whig Interpretation of History*, London 1963; Christianson, "Causes"; William H. Dray,
    "J. H. Hexter, Neo-Whiggism and Early Stuart Historiography," *History and Theory* 26.2,
    1987; and his "Presentism, Inevitability and the English Civil War," *Canadian Journal of
    History* 17, 1982; Russell, *Causes* 4–5; and Adrian Wilson and T. G. Ashplant, "Whig
    History and Present-Centered History," *Historical Journal* 21, 1988. Brendan Bradshaw
    discusses Butterfield's second thoughts in "Nationalism and Historical Scholarship in
    Modern Ireland," *Irish Historical Studies* 26.104, 1989.
49. Russell sees Gardiner and the liberal tradition sharing with marxists a Hegelian theory
    of change through conflict and a Darwinian theory of necessary and progressive change
    (*Unrevolutionary* ix; *The Origins of the English Civil War*, London 1973, 5–6).

hastenable) demise of tribal peoples, monks, aristocrats, peasants, kulaks, and small producers inhabiting the soon to be superseded modes of production.

But other liberals and marxists are not such easy game. Stone's *Causes of the English Revolution*—the favorite liberal quarry of revisionist whig hunters—reveals meliorism only. He concludes by celebrating the English Revolution's success at securing liberties eventually extended to all classes, but he does not dismiss superseded peoples and eras. Moreover, the revolutionary preconditions "made some redistribution of political power almost inevitable, and reform of the Church very probable, but whether these changes would come about by peaceful evolution, political upheaval, or force of arms was altogether uncertain, dependent on the wisdom, or lack of it, of the government, and the moderation, or lack of it, of the opposition."[50] Similarly, no teleological consensus unites all marxists. As I will argue in chapter 4, Marx himself worked up a powerful critique of the pseudo-Darwinian models of social evolution that he had embraced in some of his earlier writings. And "whig history," insofar as it implies a winner's teleology, has always seemed a strange epithet to apply to British history from below, which aims primarily at the depredations of capitalism, but secondarily at the indifference or active hostility of scientific socialism to the lived experience of ordinary working men and women. In his "Preface" to *The Making of the English Working Class*, E. P. Thompson criticizes the reformist socialism that ransacks the past for forerunners of the welfare state:

> It reads history in the light of subsequent preoccupations, and not as in fact it occurred. Only the successful (in the sense of those whose aspirations anticipated subsequent evolution) are remembered. The blind alleys, the lost causes, and the losers themselves are forgotten. I am seeking to rescue the poor stockinger, the Luddite cropper, the "obsolete" hand-loom weaver, the "utopian" artisan, and even the deluded follower of Joanna Southcott, from the enormous condescension of posterity.[51]

Christopher Hill echoes this passage in his Preface to *Liberty Against the Law*, and his entire oeuvre bears witness.[52] Indeed, it has always been a dumbfounding spectacle to see the author of *The World Turned Upside Down*, that magnificent and hopeful elegy to lost causes, presented as a condescending Left Whig.

And historical revisionists, ostensibly haters of everything whiggish, join unreconstructed liberals and orthodox dialectical materialists in embracing all three sorts of teleology. Winner's teleology appears in their briskly eugenic distaste for history focusing on "cranks, crackpots, screwballs and

---

50. *Causes* 146–7, 116.
51. New York 1966, 12–13; see Joanna Innes on Thompson's lifelong "assault upon teleology and determinism" in "Jonathan Clark, Social History, and England's 'Ancien Regime,'" *Past and Present* 115, 1987, 173.
52. London 1996, x.

fanatics, the nutters and kooks who appear in the wake of every genuine movement for social reform and who become the principal barrier to lasting change," in Kishlansky's words.[53] Sharpe worries that a "vast scholarly industry" has wasted "too many pages . . . on endeavors to find meaning in the writings of the civil war's madmen," on "minor sects and crackpots." We find almost no evidence of plebeian radicalism, but "we should not expect principled opposition from the illiterate and unsophisticated."[54] Meliorism appears in the condescension toward a past lacking their own capacity (inexplicable, or at least unexplained) to reflect on ideas, and in their tacit embrace of capitalist modernization theory (a whig theory of *economic* history). Anthony Fletcher traces the Revolution to "the imaginative poverty of the seventeenth century," which led to a material poverty, since it left the seventeenth century incapable of imagining the capitalist utopia of non-exploiting improvement: "This was a society in which people were made scapegoats for processes, which lacked the capacity to conceive of and weigh in the balance alternative political systems, which took a highly traditional view of the world as a place of 'limited good' where no one can prosper save at someone else's expense."[55] Walter and Wrightson trace early modern dearth and famine to "a marketing system as yet insufficiently developed to iron out regional inequalities of distribution"—an argument that Irish revisionists have found handy when working up a blame-free account of the Famine.[56] Like improving Tory landlords critical of Whig politics, revisionist critics of whig history gladly accept the economically whiggish retrospect offered by capital accumulation.

Necessitarianism poses a hard case at first, since revisionist "contingency" would seem to be the polar opposite of necessity. But the two merge as the absolute *other* to human freedom, for contingency is precisely the lived experience of serial necessity, which limits freely chosen praxis. Western humanists, anticommunists and communists alike, object to the economistic and "stagist" model of marxist history not because it eliminates the element of chance, but because it deprives human beings of agency, turning them into the mere vehicles of a history worked out in advance by the dialectic. When it fights the whig model of the English Revolution as a fundamental political and cultural change, revisionism offers a rival stagism describing a change from a unified premodernity to a unified modernity. Sometimes, revisionists see a thoroughly modern seventeenth century, as when Elton, Russell, and Burgess claim that early

---

53. Review of Christopher Hill, *The Experience of Defeat* (New York 1984), *Times Higher Education Supplement*, September 7 1984.
54. "Religion" 275, 284; *Politics* 306, 302–3, 303–4.
55. *The Outbreak of the English Civil War*, London 1981, 415.
56. "Dearth and the Social Order in Early Modern England," *Past and Present* 71, 1976, 31. See T. W. Moody on the Famine and John Wilson Foster's Protestant hymn to agrarian improvement—the churlishly spurned cure for Catholic Ireland's economic, spiritual, and even literary woes, in Seamus Deane, gen. ed., *The Field Day Anthology of Irish Writing*, 3 vols, Derry 1991, 3.576, 650.

Stuart England was already a limited monarchy, not an absolutism.[57] More often, they see it as thoroughly premodern, as when Davis emphasizes the orientation of all early modern political thinkers, including Gerrard Winstanley, to premodern *authority*, not modern *liberty*.[58] Both arguments demand a unbridgeable chasm between the traditional world and our capitalist world. The causes for this change are seldom clear—perhaps technological innovation, or demographic growth, or pure chance—but in any case, it helpfully enables us to dismiss as anachronistic any discussion of a fundamental social struggle in seventeenth-century England.

Even more necessitarian is the revisionist history in which nothing much happens at all—not in the seventeenth century, not before, and not after. Whether it reduces present to past or past to present, this history proposes neither abstract conceptual unity ("the history of class struggle in its various forms"), nor a mediated genetic continuity ("the growth of modern conceptions of constitutional liberty"), but a concrete and substantial unity. Alan Macfarlane sees the inhabitants of the ancient German forests as possessive individualists yearning toward capitalism even before they were English, while Jonathan Clark sees the deferential *ancien régime* of England persisting at least until 1832, the year of the first Reform Bill.[59] For Clark, even this late transition never really arrived, since modernity is nothing more than electrification plus the parish: "Seen less dogmatically, even the culture of the factory (that paradigmatically individualised world) can best be explained with the concepts of status, deference, paternalism, community and religious affiliation now so familiar to historians of the world before 1832."[60] Maurice Cowling revives the revisionist model of early modern politics when he writes the history of the Labour Party as a series of squabbles for power among a group of grasping individuals and factions.[61] In his revisionist study of the Agitators, Kishlansky coyly suggests that "a more cynical historian" than himself might see "some nest-feathering trade union issues at the back of appeals that would be popular with the soldiery."[62] Russell suggests that "every little historian born into

---

57. Sommerville discusses Elton and Russell's "no absolutism" argument in "English and European Political Ideas in the Early Seventeenth Century," *Journal of British Studies* 35.2, 1996, 170. See also Burgess, *Absolute* and "Revisionist."
58. "Religion and the Struggle for Freedom in the English Revolution," *Historical Journal* 35.3, 1992; see also Davis's "Radical Lives" and "Radicalism"; William Lamont, "The Religious Origins of the English Civil War," in Gordon J. Schochet, ed., *Religion, Resistance, and Civil War*, Washington 1990, 1–11; and J. G. A. Pocock, *Virtue, Commerce, and History*, Cambridge 1985, 54–71.
59. Ellen Meiksins Wood makes this argument about Macfarlane and Clark in *Pristine* 117–69. She criticizes Macfarlane's misreading of Tacitus (189–90n.23); compare Marx on J. Grimm's mistranslation of the same passage, which erases the ancient German commune by implying that "the Germans from the earliest times cultivated on individual farms like Westphalian squires" (*MECW* 42.558).
60. *Revolution* 40.
61. Anderson, *English* 286.
62. "What Must Be," Schochet, *Religion* 83–90, 89–90.

this world alive is either a little Calvinist or a little Arminian."[63] Sharpe says, "We are all, at heart, either royalists or Roundheads."[64] If we rightly spurn a reductive mode-of-production narrative with five stages and four changes, why should we clasp to our bosoms a two-stage, one-change narrative, much less its one-stage, no-change variant? In this bare-bones stagism, teleology collapses into archaeology, for *arche* and *telos* reveal only the history of the same—a traditional world-view continually reproducing itself.

Individually, these models of history without change contradict each other. Collectively, they contradict the absolute change model which they, contradictorily, also demand. But mere contradiction proves no obstacle, so long as everyone cooperates in fending off a dialectical alternative that would see the modern world arising from internal conflicts in a premodern world substantially distinct from it, with a crucial role in the working-out of those contradictions played by the collective praxis of working people.

Pro: Multiple Kingdoms, Religion, and Personalities

Ever since Russell's Introduction to *The Origins of the English Civil War*—something of a birth announcement for historical revisionism—revisionist$ have argued that "social change explanations of the English Civil War must be regarded as having broken down."[65] They mean the arguments associated with the mid-twentieth-century controversy over the gentry, which I will consider in chapter 4. But for the moment, I want to look briefly at the very concept of a "social change explanation" and its implied alternative. In most forms of historical discourse, as in everyday English speech, *society* is not a synonym for *economy*, but a name for something like the lived totality of human existence. Its opposites are not *culture* or *politics* (both of which, along with economy, comprise part of society), but perhaps *nature* and *the individual*. Even those are analytical not substantial opposites, since we can imagine *socialized nature* (worked matter) or *the socialized individual* (humans themselves) more easily than their unsocialized contraries. So what can it possibly mean when Glenn Burgess defines revisionism as "the rejection, not of social history, but of social determinism and reductionism, of holism"?[66] Certainly we all find that some models of social change reductively overestimate this or that factor, which we proceed to sully with a suffix: "economism," "culturalism," "idealism," "phonocentrism," "phallogocentrism," "technologism," and "essentialist humanism." But "*social* reductionism"? A *reductio ad totum*? This oxymoron

---

63. *Causes* x.
64. "Battles of Words and Swords," review of Mark Kishlansky, *Monarchy Transformed* (London 1996), *Sunday Times* (London), November 3 1996.
65. 1–31, 8.
66. "Revisionism" 616.

attempts to destroy the project of historical totalization by a strange sort of inversion and displacement that reduces it to economistic reduction.

Lawrence Stone's classic *The Causes of the English Revolution*, which revisionists frequently view as the quintessence of reductive liberal social change explanations, offers a complex, persuasive, and highly adaptable theory of causality to explain the breakdown of the monarchy in 1640 and outbreak of armed conflict in 1642. Drawing on the *Annales* division of history into long, medium, and short "times" or cycles, which overlap and combine in an intelligible but not easily predictable fashion, Stone traces long-term "preconditions" dating to 1529 (the instability of Tudor governance, economic growth, class change, the absence of foreign threats, intellectual change, and the rise of opposition), medium-term "precipitants" to 1626 (the political tensions generated by Buckingham and the Personal Rule), and short-term "triggers" to 1640 (the crises attendant on the Bishops' Wars and their aftermath, and the personality of Charles himself). Preconditions establish the possibility of a revolution, precipitants its probability, and triggers the revolution itself.

Stone's model offers itself up for marxist and even revisionist appropriation. Beginning with its title, Russell's *The Causes of the English Civil War* pays a sort of homage to Stone's book, which it does not mention. Russell turns Stone's eight "preconditions" into three structural "causes," largely eliminates Stone's medium-term "precipitants," and turns most of his "triggers" into seven "events and non-events." The personality of Charles catalyzes these causes, events, and non-events, producing the outbreak of hostilities.[67] Paul Christianson even attempts to press Stone's arguments into service as an argument against Stone himself, saying that "Long term movements form part of the background of causation, but they do not determine events unless viewed within a framework of inevitable progress"—a statement generally compatible with Stone's own analysis which nonetheless demands that we somehow attribute a teleological determinism to Stone by distinguishing a background causality from Stone's "preconditions" and "precipitants."[68] But Stone never denies an important role for contingencies, actions by individuals, and trivial causes. He insists only that they need to be seen in combination with long-term processes, actions of groups, and great causes, and grows exasperated, understandably, at revisionists who shear off one level of determination (preconditions), minimize another (precipitants), and elevate the third (triggers), while criticizing his book as reductive.[69]

Robert Brenner's *Merchants and Revolution* differs markedly from Stone's *Causes*, but its "social change" explanation for the Revolution has drawn similar revisionist critiques. Brenner says that, while the class interests and the political ideologies of the king and Parliament were markedly distinct,

67. 47, 117, 168.
68. "Causes" 47.
69. *Causes* 167.

and so exerted a pressure toward conflict of some sort, "It cannot, of course, be concluded that it was inherently impossible for the patrimonial monarchy and the parliamentary classes to reach agreement, or that conflict was inevitable."[70] Morrill responds that what Brenner calls his "social interpretation" of the crisis at mid-century might more accurately be called a "social-determinist" interpretation:

> Revisionism need not mean the lack of a social *interpretation*, so long as that means social *contexts* rather than social *causes*. Since Brenner is explicit that *Merchants and Revolution* does not argue for the inevitability of the Revolution, simply that a political collision between the monarchy and the landowning class was inherently likely, this fuzziness about what exactly he intends by a "social interpretation" is fairly debilitating.[71]

If Brenner had acted his appointed role of reductive and economistic vulgar marxist arguing for mechanical *causes* of the Revolution, he would have been *a priori* ignorable. But when he fails to do so, when he rejects the choice between *necessity* and *contingency* and operates in the properly historical realm of regularities, likelihoods, and structural pressures, he becomes unreadably fuzzy. Marxists are always mechanical and reductive determinists, except, of course, when they aren't, and then they aren't marxists.

So liberals like Stone and marxists like Brenner try to explain events by appealing to a larger social totality and a larger expanse of time—a social and historical *problematic* containing factors both economic and non-economic. Marxists may emphasize the former and liberals the latter. But for both, these factors derive in complex ways from other complex social totalities or formations, and one can trace them back, explain them, and the factors explaining them, and so on. This regress halts not when we reach an uncaused cause, a thing-in-itself, but when we feel we have adequately explained the phenomenon we wish to understand. Revisionists, on the other hand, employ a distinct and profoundly reductive method. They attempt to kick free of this endless regress and gain the safe ground of an *individuum*, a monad, a cause that is not an effect—in short, a *contingency*. But *contingent* is what Freud calls a "primal word" with antithetical senses. Transitively, *contingere* means *to touch, to affect, to cause*, and intransitively, *to befall, to happen*. When revisionists invoke contingency, they are typically trying to leave the transitive domain of cause and effect for the intransitive domain of happenstance, like an exhausted parent responding to a child's antinomian chorus of "Why? Why? Why?" with the thudding authoritarian coda of "Just because." In its early phases, revisionism rested secure with a primarily negative argument against the various "determinisms" that it encountered: events happened this or that way, but they *need not have*. In its later phases, revisionism has attempted to

---

70. *BMR* 665.
71. "Conflict" 114, 122, 113.

construct a more positive but still contingency-based explanation of the Civil War by tracing events to a small number of particular "primal contingencies" which need not be explained further. Concentrating on Russell's *The Causes of the English Civil War*, I would like to focus on three such contingencies: the structural difficulty of administering a three-kingdom nation; religion; and the personality of Charles I.

Russell rejects any attempt to explain the Civil War as "a purely English phenomenon," for "the main disruptive force in both England and Ireland was the problem of multiple kingdoms." James skillfully knitted together Catholic Ireland, Presbyterian Scotland, and Anglican England, but things began to unravel under Charles, in part because each of the three kingdoms had an imperial vision of religion and politics that it wished to enforce upon the others. Using the favorite metaphor of classical mechanics to describe the mounting crisis of 1639–42, Russell argues that "there was a constant billiard-ball effect of each of the kingdoms on the affairs of the others." But the cue ball was Scottish: the "'Scottish imperial' vision of British unity . . . involved forcing England into uniformity with the Scottish church." Philo-Scots (i.e., Puritan) soldiers in the English army of the Bishops' Wars become a "fifth column" who would "sap English will to fight." The "Scottish party" in England (i.e., the parliamentary opposition) issued the "Petition of the Twelve Peers," which placed its English sponsors "well the wrong side of treason" in its alliance with the Scots, creating a dynamic that determined the rest of the Civil War. Knowing that they had committed treason, and knowing that Charles knew it, the Twelve Peers "could not afford any settlement which gave them less than total success."[72] Meanwhile, in Ireland, Charles's lawyers sought revenues for an underfunded monarchy by finding forgotten land tenures or creating new ones, and "It was this growing insecurity of Catholic land tenure, rather than any direct measures of persecution, which increasingly created fears for Catholicism in Ireland."[73]

But claims for the rough equality of the three kingdoms under one sovereign sit uncomfortably with charges of treason. Moreover, it takes a palpable act of will to see seventeenth-century England, Wales, Ireland, and Scotland as hard and indivisible "individuals" roughly equal to each other, instead of complex societies in a structured hierarchy dominated by England. We collapse too much under the heading of an imperial drive if we equate a Covenanter attempting to maintain toleration for the Kirk with an Arminian insisting on British unity under the prayer book. Russell suggests English Puritans presented the Root and Branch Petition the day before Robert Baille's paper against Laud in order to "give English cover to that paper."[74] No doubt, if it had been presented the day after,

---

72. *Causes* 26, 27, 16, 65, 27, 31, 120; *The Fall of the British Monarchies 1637–1642*, Oxford 1991, 202; *Causes* 14; *Fall* 149–53. See also Sharpe, *Personal* 943, 945.
73. *Causes* 55–7.
74. Ibid. 180–81.

the evidence would have been even more damning, and equally immune to an alternative hypothesis of shared Scots and English Puritan interests. As Peter Lake says, the Scots never proposed to abolish episcopacy, and when tensions between Scots Calvinists and English Arminians faded after the settlement of May 1641, the "Scots party" in England continued to clash with English Arminians: "No doubt much remains to be learned about the London mob but it seems unlikely that many of the people who flocked from London to Westminster to petition Parliament were Scottish."[75] Nicholas Canny argues that England's attempted "anglicization" affected Ireland much more profoundly than Irish resistance did the English monarchy.[76] And how can we follow Russell in separating Irish anxiety over land tenures from English society and social conflict? If Charles's own unquestioned landholdings had been on a French scale, or if parliamentary supply had flowed freely from 1625 to 1640, what would have driven him to a high-stakes attempt to milk revenues out of Ireland through an extraordinary and destabilizing policy?

Martyn Bennett observes that the international dimensions of the conflict would not have been news to Gardiner or even Lucy Hutchinson.[77] So the choice we face is not "one kingdom or three?" but "what kind of three-kingdom history?" The revisionists' version derives from their growing sense that appeals to English contingency and faction cannot quite explain historical change. "Nation," then, becomes a large-scale, long-term explanatory horizon, and nations and national conflicts become primal contingencies. Since three-kingdoms theory exists primarily to hold off English social change explanations, we shouldn't be surprised that revisionist accounts of political developments in Ireland and Scotland tend to be relatively thin and anglocentric. But we gain nothing by *opposing* a three-kingdom explanation to a social change explanation, for kingdoms are never primal contingencies: what looks like a unified and imperial Scots *nation* from the English side of the border probably feels like a complex and divided Scots *society* on the other.

Religion, the second revisionist primal contingency, attempts to undercut a long-term social change explanation while offering up a short-term and relatively "contingent" explanation. On the one hand, the revisionists' hierarchical world picture rests in large part on a model of consensual religion that shuts down accounts based in theories of social change, collective interest, and principled ideological conflict. On the other, their penchant for psychohistory allows them to trace the political disturbances that did occur at mid-century to the religious sensibility of an individual like Charles, or the collective neurosis of a group like the godly. In *Revolution and Rebellion*, Jonathan Clark accuses new leftists ("the Class of

75. Review article on C. S. R. Russell, *The Huntington Library Quarterly* 57.2, 1994, 189, 191, 194; see also MacLachlan, *Rise* 244.
76. "The Attempted Anglicisation of Ireland in the Seventeenth Century," in J. F. Merritt, ed., *The Political World of Thomas Wentworth*, Cambridge 1996, 157–86, 157–8.
77. *The Civil Wars in Britain and Ireland*, Oxford 1997, xi–xii.

'68") of utterly ignoring "one auxiliary discipline which the revisionists were to find of immense importance in the understanding of early-modern England: theology.... The undervaluation of ... ecclesiastical phenomena is a reflection of modern assumptions that religion is a small, specialized and insulated area of national life."[78] Clark does not clearly define what he means by "theology," but it seems to be a cross between a timeless and hierarchical Anglican *via media* and the defensive contemporary practice of academic history, for he celebrates the collapse of "grand theories originating elsewhere in the academic world," and the renewed attention to those categories generated from within the historical profession itself and the periods it considers, including "hierarchy, allegiance and authority—concepts articulated within the practice of politics, law and religion." Further, he praises revisionism for its "renewed attention to religion *as religion* rather than as a sublimation of something else."[79]

But can one imagine any phrase more alien to William Laud, or William Prynne, or William Walwyn, or any other seventeenth-century person, than "religion *as religion*"? It suggests the turf-consciousness of a shrinking orthodoxy in a secular state or unpopular university department—indeed, precisely a "small, specialized and insulated area of national life"—not that totalizing and world-transforming immanent force of seventeenth-century English society. The generally meager revisionist account of early modern religion as religion recalls a lesson learned by at least some literary critics, with a painful sense of the years wasted in celebrating poem as poem or text as text: the reflexive noun intended to ring in an autonomous academic discipline more frequently sounds its death-knell, or a tinkling announcement of its retirement into ineffectual private life. Some marxists have run into a similar dead end with a tub-thumping insistence on "economy as economy," which simultaneously bloats and desiccates economy, making it the nominal essence of all society while destroying its interactive power to explain lived human experience. Speaking of twentieth-century English historians, Clark notes coyly that "It would not be possible without personal discourtesy to dwell on the extent to which a character-twisting hatred of orthodox religion was at the heart of the critique devised by some of the historians discussed."[80] Clark's forthright religious orthodoxy is bracing, but even here, he pulls his punches: where Anglicanism once saw itself as a full-scale theory of society and history, holding off sectarian threats to the divinely ordained social hierarchy, the collective rituals and ceremony of the Arminian church, and the immortal soul itself, it now wards off only threats to "character," that puny (and secular) mid-Victorian idol. Prelacy, like so many things, isn't what it used to be.

Other revisionist claims about seventeenth-century religion tend to be

78. 16, 106.
79. 23, 166, 108; see also 30, 91, 101, 108, 139.
80. 30n.

of a piece with Clark's, if not always so devoted to Anglo-Catholic sectarianism. Writing in 1990, Russell said that

> We have to explain, then, not only why some people might fight for religion, but also why, in the normal seventeenth-century structure of authority, it was normal to find religion and politics as closely intertwined as economics and politics are today.... It does not help that the word "religion" has slowly changed its meaning with the retreat of the State from religious enforcement, and that what takes place outside the South African Embassy may sometimes be nearer to seventeenth-century meanings of "religion" than what takes place inside St. Martin-in-the-Fields.[81]

This is reasonable and humane, but finally inadequate. For just as economy formed part of the twist back then for a tithe-hating tub preacher, so, too, did religion in 1990 for an anti-racist nun outside the embassy, and so it does still today for politically active believers.

John Morrill says that "The English civil war was not the first European revolution: it was the last of the Wars of Religion."[82] But the idea of some fundamental divide between sacred wars of religion and secular revolutions appears only inside a feebly credent or a feebly non-credent version of the history of ideas supplementing capitalist modernization theory, and it threatens to suck the life out of both sides of the divide. It implicitly denies the social and political vision of such "traditional" revolutionaries as the fourth-century Donatists and Circumcellions in Augustine's North Africa, the fourteenth-century peasants in Wat Tyler's England, and the sixteenth-century Anabaptists in Thomas Müntzer's Germany.[83] At the same time, it muffles the ideology of religious transcendence (whether superhuman or superindividual) in "modern" revolutionary movements such as the radical Dissenters and United Irishmen of London and Belfast during the 1790s, John Brown's abolitionists and Hung Hsiu-ch'üan's Taiping rebels during the 1850s and 1860s, Antonio Conselheiro's mille-narian communist cowboys in the Baía of the 1890s, and the liberation theologians of pan-Africa, from Turner to Delany to King to Malcolm to Tutu to Aristide to the religious basic communities of contemporary Brazil.[84] Ernst Bloch even finds "a constant, unwritten essence of Joachim of Fiore" in Bolshevik Russia:

> Several great peculiarities were thus able to spring up in Christo-romantic fashion on Bolshevist soil; the indisputable Bolshevik and equally indisputable

---

81. *Causes* 62, 63.
82. *Nature* 68.
83. Neal Wood, "African Peasant Terrorism and Augustine's Political Thought," in Frederick Krantz, ed., *History from Below*, Montréal 1985, 279–99; R. H. Hilton, *Bond Men Made Free*, London 1973.
84. On the United Irishmen, see Jim Smyth, *The Men of No Property*, New York 1992. On the Taiping Rebellion, see Eric R. Wolf, *Peasant Wars of the Twentieth Century*, New York 1973, 118–23. *Rebellion in the Backlands* [*Os Sertões*] (Chicago 1944), Euclides Da Cuña's tragic epic about Conselheiro and the Brazilian republic, casts oblique light on the capitalist English republic's destruction of the Diggers.

chiliast Alexander Blok gave an indication of this, thoroughly in the Joachite spirit. When in Blok's hymn, the "March of the Twelve," that is, of the twelve Red Army soldiers, a pale Christ precedes the revolution and leads it, this kind of presence of the Spirit is just as remote from the western Church-combines as it finds the eastern Church at least theologically open to it.[85]

The peasant rebellion—the most globally widespread and important form of social revolution in both the modern and the premodern world, and almost always fired by religious ideology—also muddies up Morrill and Russell's binary history.

Much of the revisionist attention to religion in the early Stuart era has turned to Laudian Arminianism, seeing Arminians sometimes as aggressive conservative radicals in their own right, more frequently as *via media* proponents of order and decency beset by Calvinist zealots.[86] Russell evenhandedly blames Charles as well as his Puritan opponents, emphasizing the innovative force of Arminianism and its role in increasing religious polarities and bringing on the war. And at times, he verges on a genuine, full-fledged attempt to account for the origins and the course of Puritan–Arminian collective struggle. But finally, he sees religion as a primal contingency—as (in Peter Lake's words) "a cloud of unknowing that continually disrupts the rational pursuit of otherwise attainable political ends," a "cause for conflict which was seemingly irreducible into other categories or forces," and a "deus ex machina."[87] For he cannot account for the rise of Arminianism other than by noting Charles's decision to favor it and his provocative marriage to a Catholic queen. Veering off into psychohistory, Russell observes that "Charges of popery and charges of Puritanism are both weapons in a struggle for power, and tell us a great deal more about those who used them than they do about those against whom they were used." Eliminating the cognitive dimensions of religious ideology, he reduces it to sheer instrumentality in a relatively unprincipled struggle driven by an almost Nietzschean will-to-power: what made religion a political issue was "the belief that it must be enforced."[88]

Russell turns from the wealth of evidence and argument about Puritanism to speculative accounts of its origin in an anxiously partial and premature rejection of orthodox religion. Russell's Puritans are imperfectly lapsed Catholics: their frantic antipopery suggests a fear they had "committed the sin of schism" and "a nagging unease in their own consciences." They are still idolaters: their desire "to destroy images and ceremony was

---

85. Ernst Bloch, 3 vols, *The Principle of Hope*, Cambridge, MA, 1986, 2.514–15.
86. On this controversy, largely inspired by the important work of Nicholas Tyacke, see Tyacke, "Puritanism, Arminianism and Counter-Revolution," Russell, *Origins* 119–43; and *Anti-Calvinism*, Oxford 1987. See also Andrew Foster's "Church Policies of the 1630s," *CH* 193–223, which includes a bibliography on the historians' controversy over Arminianism through the late eighties (217n.2), and for more recent work, Richardson, *Debate* 227–8.
87. Review essay on Russell, 185, 187; "Introduction" to Geoffrey F. Nuttall, *The Holy Spirit in Puritan Faith and Experience*, 1946; rpt Chicago 1992, ix–xxv, xv.
88. *Causes* 102–5, 198.

not because they were not attracted to them, but because they were." They are still orthodox communicants: their assurance of election served "the same psychological functions . . . as belief in the perpetual visibility of the church did for Catholics," just as their "attachment to predestination was in part because it gave some people back that certainty of which departure from Catholicism had deprived them."[89] These connections, reasonable enough in the abstract, suggest not so much a substantive identity as a structural moment within the praxis of sectarian self-understanding and self-transformation. And in any case, they did little to reassure English Arminians, who viewed with horror the social and political threats posed by the experimental predestinarian religion of English Puritans. No doubt, the individual Puritan saint's assurance of election did fulfill some of the same need for a sense of stability and corporate being as did the perpetual visibility and the ritualistic order of the Catholic church and of Laudian Anglicanism. But that assurance typically appeared inside and by means of fellowship in an *elected* Puritan congregation with a very particular religious structure of feeling: the associative solidarity of the Puritan pledged group contrasts powerfully with the individuated serial collective of the Arminian or Catholic parish, with its immutable disciplinary structures, its sacrament-centered religious practice, and its individuating promise or threat of a final judgment.

This revisionist propensity for psychohistory extends beyond Russell. Roger Lockyer says Buckingham's enemies, shamed by their inability to rise to his call for national greatness, found in him "the personification of their own neuroses."[90] Anthony Fletcher traces the English Civil War to sheer, cross-class cultural stupidity, when the Puritan fear of popery clashed with the monarchist fear of parity in an "abnegation of reason" and a "curious mixture of folly and idealism."[91] And in *Fear, Myth and History*, J. C. Davis says the Ranters existed only as "a projection of the fears and anxieties of a broader society. They were closer to the image of 'folk devils' projected in a 'moral panic' which reached its climax in the wake of the revolution of 1648–9."[92] In the twentieth century this neurotic displacement of the self became a whiggish exercise in narcissistic projection when the Historians' Group of the Communist Party (notably, Hill and A. L. Morton) flattered itself with a vision of the Ranters as a force of authentic, seventeenth-century proletarian subversion, fired by a pantheist and practical antinomian theology.[93] But for Davis, the Ranters formed a

---

89. Ibid. 85, 65, 73–4, 77, 79–80.
90. *Buckingham*, London 1981, 474.
91. *Outbreak* 409, 418.
92. Cambridge 1986, x.
93. Hill, *World*; Morton, *The World of the Ranters*, London 1970. For the ensuing controversy, see Davis's "Fear, Myth and Furore," *Past and Present* 129, 1990; Davis et al., "Debate: Fear, Myth and Furore," *Past and Present* 140, 1993; my "Ranting at the New Historicism," *English Literary Renaissance* 19.2, 1989; and Clement Hawes, *Mania and Literary Style*, Cambridge 1996. Davis's Ranter marxists are hard to find, but not the pantheistic antinomian Ranters he denies. See *A Justification of the Mad Crew in Their Waies and*

distinct group only if they were a sect with a uniform ideology: if they differed significantly among themselves (if they lacked absolute *identity*), and if they shared in the Protestant theology of the spirit (if they lack absolute *difference* from other groups), then the "Ranters" lack any collective identity at all. They fold back into a welcoming Protestant mainstream stretching from Ussher to Winstanley. The so-called Ranters "eschewed party and sought to moderate the passions of party, to emphasize the general substance of a Protestant, biblicist Christianity rather than the formalistic distinctions and divisions of denominationalism."[94]

"Protestant, biblicist Christianity" could do double duty for the non-party of early Stuart Arminians, and a truly ambitious revisionist treatment of religious consensus might well attempt to harmonize Laudian Arminians and Coppite Ranters. But for both, we need to consider discipline as well as doctrine, supplementing a study of the substantially if not utterly distinct ideologies and languages of early modern religious groups with a study of their forms of organization and practice. And we should avoid jumping prematurely to psychohistory by rejecting this or that ideology, whether Arminianism or antipopery or Ranting or Ranter phobia, as a deluded conspiracy theory. Even the most extreme prelates and sectarians acted in rational, self-interested ways through attacks on the conspiracies of their "fanatical" or "popish" opponents. "Conspiracy theories" are not individual psychopathological delusions that spread by contagion, but genuine forms of rough structural social analysis, anchored in competing group interests.[95]

When a Puritan artisan sees a Laudian rail of separation installed in his church and suspects a conspiracy of Antichrist, William Laud, and the Whore of Babylon, he does not simply stew in a paranoid delusion, but engages in a specifically religious form of totalizing thought. When an Arminian priest hears his murmurings as the conspiracy of Jack Straw, John Pym, and John of Leyden, he does not simply slip into a fear of folk devils, but engages in an alternative form of totalizing consciousness that rightly senses a threat to his entire way of life. In August 1641, the House published an order for taking away "all scandalous pictures out of churches"; a group of Essex commoners synthesized this nationwide religious directive with a local act of class struggle. The stained-glass

---

Principles (1650), which Davis himself reproduces (*Fear* 138–55) in an antinomian edition that shuffles its opening pages (in sequence, pages A2^v, A3^v, A2^r, A3^r).

94. "Fear" 102–3.

95. On dueling conspiracy theories in early Stuart England, see Richard Cust, *The Forced Loan and English Politics, 1626–1628*, Oxford 1987, 328–9; Ann Hughes, "Local History and the Origins of the Civil War," *CH* 224–53; Lake, "Anti-popery," ibid. 72–106; and Alexandra Walsham, "'The Fatall Vesper,'" *Past and Present* 144, 1994. In "The Value of Conspiracy Theory (forthcoming in *American Literary History*), Edward White diagnoses a tendency in American Studies (from Hofstadter's *The Paranoid Style in American Politics* to republican synthesis theory to recent idealist appropriations of public sphere theory) to reject conspiracy theory and thus abjure structural social analysis of any sort. He responds by analyzing conspiracy theory as part of plebeian self-creation and political action in colonial Pennsylvania.

windows in the chancel of Chelmsford Church depicting "the history of Christ from his conception to his ascension" also included "the escutcheons and arms of the nobility and gentry, who had contributed to the building and beautifying that fair structure":

> In obedience to the order the Church wardens took down the pictures of the blessed Virgin, and of Christ on the cross, and supplied the places with white glass. But the sectaries who understood the sense of that order better then the church-wardens, did rest very ill satisfied with this partial imperfect reformation: that therefore they might, according to the phrase of that times, make a thorough reformation, on the first of November in the evening, all the sectaries assemble together, and in a riotous manner with long poles and stones beat down and deface the whole window.

The monarchist author and the godly lower sort of Chelmsford came together and "understood" the implications of the House's order in a way that the House itself did not. The iconoclastic aesthetic/religious energy that the order unleashes produces a new intention, a new definition of "scandalous" with room for the scandal of church-sanctioned class domination, and a previously almost unimaginable act of religiously driven class struggle.[96]

For seventeenth-century Englishwomen and -men, including the radicals whom I consider in this book, "religion" is a name for social totality— for living in, thinking about, and transforming all of society, including both material structures and a "superstructure" of ideological forms, both objectively existing institutions and the subjective experience of inhabiting, creating, and transforming them. To avoid interpreting some religious phenomenon reductively, we should aspire not to its *autoduction* to itself (can that be any less reductive than its *heteroduction* to something else?), but to its systematic *eduction*—leading it out through the circuits of explanation, looping back through "religion" from time to time, with an enriched understanding. Atheists desiring to conduct a non-reductive study of religion will attempt to establish its existence *inside* social totality; theists will probably want to reverse the container and the contained; but neither will suggest that they constitute discrete spheres. In this book, I will examine not only the theology of the spirit informing the New Model Army, the Fifth Monarchists, and the Diggers, but the particular sorts of self-organization and group praxis it made possible: tyrannicide, egalitarian political debate, theatrical scenes of prophecy, communal digging as communal prayer. Religion sometimes acted as a limiting *mentalité* imposed in a top-down fashion on premodern political actors. But it also served those actors as *creative practical consciousness*.

For a full sense of the objective issues that led men and women into deadly struggle over religion, and of the subjective textures of devotional, communitarian, and ecstatic experience that defined seventeenth-century

---

96. [Bruno Ryves], *Mercurius Rusticus*, 1646, 22–3; see Hunt's discussion in *The Puritan Moment*, Cambridge, MA, 1983, 291–3.

religion, we need to turn from the revisionist account of religion to several alternative disciplines and subdisciplines: to social and intellectual and cultural historians, to post-revisionist historians interested in the socially resonant complexity of seventeenth-century religious thought and practice, to literary critics focusing on the languages of devotional self-fashioning, to feminist critics and historians examining the ways in which the Christian theology of the spirit made possible women's creative self-transformation, and, of course, to Christopher Hill's brilliant and voluminous studies of the ways in which early modern persons of different classes lived the complex textures of religious experience. We also need to turn directly to the discipline of "theology" that Clark invokes but leaves in the lurch. Contemporary seminaries, departments of religion, and departments of theology have little use for any absolute distinction between "religion" and "society"—neither in pastoral training, nor in historical and academic study, where the concepts of "the sociology of religion" and "liberation theology" provoke controversy but not an anathema. Biblical scholars such as George Mendenhall, Marvin Chaney, and Norman Gottwald have worked up a complex argument, thoroughly grounded in Ancient Near Eastern philology and archaeology, that the events recounted in Exodus, Joshua, and Judges began as a peasant and slave revolt led by *hapiru* outcasts (the word may be cognate with "Hebrew"). Later, the court of King David redacted accounts of this rebellion through a sort of monarchical whig historiography, producing the account we have today of an ethnic migration culminating in imperial conquest and nation formation. But the texts reveal strong evidence of a multiethnic Canaanite peasant rebellion permeating Israel's very theology:

> A model of the Israelite social system will incorporate the highly centralized and richly articulated religion of Yahweh. But it must do so sociologically by understanding the religion as a social phenomenon (institutionally and symbolically) and therefore related to all the other social phenomena within the system by the law of internal relations. This socioreligious inquiry must proceed without simplistic recourse to the tautological, philosophically idealist claim that because religion was central to the social system, it can be posited as the unmoved mover of the Israelite mutation.[97]

97. Norman K. Gottwald, "Sociological Method," in Gottwald, ed., *The Bible and Liberation*, Maryknoll, NY, 1983, 26–37, 35; see also the discussion (149–200) of Gottwald's epochal *The Tribes of Yahweh* (Maryknoll, NY, 1979); Marvin L. Chaney, "Ancient Palestinian Peasant Movements and the Formation of Premonarchic Israel," in David Noel Friedman and David Frank Graff, eds, *Palestine in Transition*, Sheffield 1983, 39–94; and George E. Mendenhall, "The Hebrew Conquest of Palestine," *Biblical Archaeologist* 25.3, 1962. In "'Saith the Spirit,'" beginning with these arguments and with other works of contemporary liberation theology, Lewis C. Daly has brilliantly reconstructed the theological contours of seventeenth-century class struggle, arguing that the Hebrew and Christian Scriptures offer an account of popular struggle for the land, which explains their perennial and world-wide appeal to peasant revolutionaries.

Like the appeal to multiple-kingdoms theory, the appeal to theology can never successfully separate past and present, idea system and social totality.

The practice of psychohistory frequently links the revisionist analysis of religion to the third revisionist primal contingency: the appeal to individuals. Once we reach an individual impulse or pathology that played an important political role, we can stop explaining, with the implicit assumption that "That's just the way a great lord or an enthusiastic prophet or a particular king *was*." In explaining the origins of the Civil War, Russell gives pride of place to Charles Stuart. Although he sees the war arising from seven short-term "events or non-events" clustering around the Bishops' Wars, which were in turn the product of three "long-term causes" (multiple kingdoms, religious divisions, an underfinanced monarchy leading to administrative breakdown), Charles handled them all so clumsily that one cannot imagine civil war without him. Russell speculates that a different succession could have prevented the war altogether, or transformed it. If Charles had died and his Calvinist sister Elizabeth had succeeded him, then the English would have united around active involvement in the continental wars of religion, and the Revolution might have happened "with most of the leading protagonists on opposite sides to those they in the event took," leaving "subsequent historians to write learned essays on the revolutionary potential of Arminianism."[98] Similarly, Morrill argues that "it was smallpox not inexorable historical laws that deprived England of James's elder son, who as Henry IX would probably have plunged England into the Protestant cause abroad and at home, quite possibly provoking a revolt by anti-puritan forces at home with a very different trajectory and outcome."[99]

Now we can always point to particular contingencies that did alter events, and to others that might have. Such counterfactual experiments open charming oblique prospects on a historian's fantasy life.[100] But like most dreams, these begin to bump into a reality principle. If we press unkindly on Russell's counterfactual scenario, it begins to buckle and crack. How has his Queen Elizabeth II become the English Gustavus Adolphus without his iron and copper mines, which generated revenues allowing him to pursue a sort of imperial Protestant absolutism, with no need of subsidies?[101] Why has a Puritan queen appointed these Arminian bishops? Can we really imagine them joining with the monopoly-holding

98. Russell, *Causes* 211; *Unrevolutionary* xxx; *Causes* 85–6, 212.
99. Morrill, *Nature* 51; "Conflict" 121. Contrast William Hunt's argument for the particular oppositional role *actually played* by the collective posthumous myth-making around the figure of godly Prince Henry, in "Spectral Origins of the English Revolution," in Geoff Eley and William Hunt, eds, *Reviving the English Revolution*, London 1988, 305–33.
100. Russell erases the Glorious Revolution in a Catholic triumph in "A Protestant Wind," in John M. Merriman, ed., *For Want of a Horse*, Lexington, MA, 1985, 103–8; J. S. A. Adamson the English Revolution in "England without Cromwell" and J. C. D. Clark the American in "British America," both in Niall Ferguson, ed., *Virtual History*, London 1997, 91–124, 125–74.
101. Perry Anderson, *Lineages of the Absolutist State*, London 1974, 172–91.

company merchants to oppose the very state power guaranteeing their status and their incomes? Where, exactly, will these right anti-monarchists come together to raise a rebellious army against the unified forces of the queen-in-parliament, the Calvinist nobility and gentry, their Covenanting allies, and the monarcho-Puritan English people? Sometimes, contrary-to-fact scenarios become contrary-to-sense.

A settlement like that of 1689, but with a more securely Protestant monarch, might have been possible; Levellers and republicans and Fifth Monarchists opposed to the Protectorate seem to have been contemplating such a thing during the 1650s, as I will show in chapter 8. But two further test cases suggest that we should always supplement any counterfactual thought experiment based in contingencies and personalities with long-term structural analysis and "social change" models. First, in 1624, after leaving off plans for the Spanish Match and joining the anti-Spanish Patriot coalition, Charles *did* become a Puritan prince something like his dead older brother Henry, and by advocating a more active English role in the wars of religion, he helped scare his father into a more strident anti-Puritanism.[102] But as king, Charles became a frustrated, would-be absolutist and antagonist of Puritan parliamentarians, and if they had acceded, Elizabeth or Henry might well have followed a similar course; whatever her earlier imperial Protestant ambitions, Prince Rupert's mother was no partisan of Parliament when fighting broke out. Second, the Revolution itself did produce a version of Russell's imagined godly Elizabeth II in the figure of Oliver I, whose career allows us to reconsider Russell's vision of placid Protestant consensus. Cromwell did, in fact, embark on a bloody policy of Protestant imperial conflict with the Irish, the Spanish, and the Dutch. But this did not by any means entail the disappearance of political opposition, as I will argue in chapters 6 through 9 below—an opposition that frequently appropriated the forms and the very texts of the earlier opposition to King Charles.

In the seventeenth century, as in the twentieth, large-scale regularities and small-scale contingencies *determined* each other in a reciprocal but not necessarily symmetrical fashion. The actions of individuals played a crucial role in this process. But "explanation via individuals" is not quite the same thing as "explanation via contingency." For a revisionist historian, Charles's sacramental Arminianism and absolutist personality are uncaused effects that anchor an entire high political narrative. But for a sociologist and historian of religion and ruling-class family life in early modern England, they might be effects—evidence within a large-scale analysis of the English church, or the very telos of a smaller-scale biographical study. Particular periods tend to produce particular sorts of contingencies—which is to say, contingencies tend to be transitive and historical,

102. Thomas Cogswell, *The Blessed Revolution*, Cambridge 1989.

not intransitive and primal.[103] And we should not presume that we are the first to notice them. Historical actors involved in life-and-death struggles face contingencies all the time, but without the academic anticommunist's freedom to sit back and celebrate the way they disrupt all purposive projects. If they fail to theorize them, and make them more governable inside a *project*, they themselves risk becoming passive atoms hurled about by the course of events. The revolutionaries who founded a regicidal republic were driven in large part by their fear that Arminian and absolutist Charles might promise and renege yet once more, or that the Stuart dynasty might "contingently" throw up yet another monarch like him or even worse—as, indeed, it did, in 1685.

Revisionism as New Conservatism

One may reasonably judge both the institutional power and the impending obsolescence of an academic school by measuring its ability to ignore contiguous fields and disciplines. And it would be difficult to overestimate the sheer insularity of revisionist British historians of seventeenth-century England—an *a priori* insularity which appears in their thoroughgoing prohibition of any comparative and sociological method that might challenge their argument that the English Civil War was by no means a social revolution. Aside from a tendentious reading of Macpherson, Hill, Manning, and Thompson, they maintain an almost pristine ignorance of marxist theory and history, including Marx and Engels themselves, western marxists, non-Europeans, cultural theorists, and sociologists. Despite a rich socialist historical literature focusing on premodern class struggle, revisionists still proceed as if speaking of such a thing were a sort of universally acknowledged category error. This ignorance extends to marxist and non-marxist studies of comparative revolution and social change that would extend beyond the realm of Britain. If Russell's *Causes of the English Civil War* revises Stone's *Causes of the English Revolution*, it also aims only at a specialist audience and shuns Stone's sociological and comparative interests; one simply cannot imagine turning a page in Russell's book and coming upon anything like Stone's passing consideration of the English Revolution inside a comparative framework including the Sioux Ghost-Dance Rebellion of 1890.[104] Revisionist insularity extends to similar work in adjacent periods of English history, as Clark has complained, and to genres straying beyond the monograph. Mark Kishlansky provides the exception that proves the rule in *A Monarchy Transformed: Britain 1603–1714*—a large-scale seventeenth-century narrative for non-specialists,

---

103. "One might try to find the unity of the disparate causes in a broader synthesis, to show that the incompetence of the eighteenth-century kings was effect as much as cause, etc., to rediscover circularities, and to show how chance is *integrated* in those 'feed-back' devices which are the events of History; and that it is instantly incorporated by the whole so that it appears to everyone as a manifestation of providence, etc." (*SCDR* 16).
104. Stone, *Causes* 6.

for beyond a brief introductory sketch, he presents "nothing on social, economic or women's history . . . little on local history and administration . . . no treatment of intellectual life—of literature, philosophy, science or the fine arts." Thus we return to the well-trampled turf of high political narrative.[105]

Moreover, revisionists produce a history not only substantively but formally anti-populist—almost calculated to bore the non-specialist reader. Struggling to demonstrate, with the utmost possible rigor, the self-enclosed *distance* of the past, revisionists frequently find it not simply wrong-headed but perhaps even immoral to try to learn from the past and connect it with the present. Lotte Mulligan and Judith Richards gently chide anyone turning to Gerrard Winstanley or Peter Chamberlen for help in understanding poverty today, and quote with approval Quentin Skinner's comment, "To demand from the history of thought a solution to our own immediate problems is . . . to commit not merely a methodological fallacy, but something like a moral error."[106] So we should not be surprised at the declining popular and international interest in British academic history.[107]

But revisionists need not feel lonely. Anyone familiar with Irish historical revisionism since the Civil Rights Movement of 1969 will note certain strong family resemblances. Irish revisionists find their "mythologizing" enemies among bourgeois and socialist republicans focused on 1798, the Famine, and 1916.[108] Since the Days of '68 and the bicentennial of 1989, French revisionists have denounced the republican heritage as a mythical continuation of Jacobin Terror.[109] Moving further afield, we can hear a sort of revisionism in Cambridge School political theory, which proposes a "linguistic turn" from bloated whiggish macrocategories such as right, justice, and liberty to the hard facts of local political languages, and in Clifford Geertz's celebrations of "local knowledge" in cultural anthropology against the totalizing and frequently marxist models of social anthropology. And literary critics may recognize some revisionist affinities with the postmodernist critique of the Enlightenment. While not exactly couched in terms of revisionism's pre-theoretical empiricism, postmodernism, too, rejects certain sorts of master narratives and turns to studies of microhistories, synchronic steady states, and various contingent jigglings.

---

105. ix.
106. "A 'Radical' Problem," *Journal of British Studies* 29, 1990, 146. For an unrepentant example, see Charles Avila's *Ownership*, Maryknoll, NY, 1983, which turns to patristic writings to understand the liberation struggles of poor Filipinos.
107. See David Cannadine, "Viewpoint," *Past and Present* 116, 1987; and Bradshaw on the "sheer competence" and "sheer dullness" of Irish revisionism ("Nationalism" 336, 337).
108. For Irish revisionist and antirevisionist writing, see Bradshaw's essay and the anthologies edited by Luke Gibbons (Deane, *Field Day* 3.561–680) and Ciaran Brady (*Interpreting Irish History*, Dublin 1994).
109. On French revisionism, see Callinicos, "Bourgeois"; George Comninel, *Rethinking the French Revolution*, London 1987; and E. J. Hobsbawm, *Echoes of the Marseillaise*, New Brunswick, NJ, 1990. Among English revisionists, only Clark mentions the French parallel (*Revolution* 5).

Revisionism is enjoying an international, cross-disciplinary success, and it would be brash to posit its imminent demise.[110]

But when do discrete attacks on revolutionary metanarratives begin to sound like part of an equally ideological counter-revolutionary meta-narrative? If one may pose such a question to such an anti-dialectical interpretive practice, when does a quantitative change become qualitative? The sheer proliferation of such contingency-based models requires a large-scale structural explanation that puts into doubt revisionists' professed self-understandings as innocent, empirical correctors of mythical whiggery. I would suggest that revisionisms have arisen in various academic disciplines relatively ignorant of each other as part of a coordinated capitalist attack on liberal democratic theory, academic marxism, history from below, liberation pedagogy, and "political correctness" in the university. That attack, in turn, has prepared the way for a full-scale capitalist assault on British and American public education itself, in the context of the winding-down of the postwar economic boom.

Moving to the context of intellectual history, we can understand the revisionist project in relation to three currents of anti-Enlightenment thought, as distinguished by Jürgen Habermas. He defines the *Old Conservatives* (Leo Strauss, Hans Jonas, Robert Spaemann) as those who "do not allow themselves to be contaminated by cultural modernism. They observe the decline of substantive reason, the differentiation of science, morality and art, the modern world view and its merely procedural rationality, with sadness and recommend a withdrawal to a position *anterior* to modernity." Second, *Neoconservatives* (the early Wittgenstein, the middle Carl Schmitt, the late Gottfried Benn, and Daniel Bell—I would add Michael Oakeshott) accept the economic advances of capitalism, but reject the destabilizing potential of cultural modernity, proposing that "politics must be kept as far aloof as possible from the demands of moral-practical justification." And third, postmodernist *Young Conservatives* (Bataille, Derrida, Foucault) abandon the rationalist and universalizing heritage of the Enlightenment for a decentered Nietzschean aesthetics of existence. Habermas insists that the Enlightenment contains within itself certain standards for self-critique and correction—including constitutional democracy, the welfare state, and the rational consideration of political means and ends in a public sphere. He argues for the continuing importance of what he calls "the project of modernity formulated in the eighteenth century by the philosophers of the Enlightenment." For Habermas, those conservatives who attempt an extrinsic and total critique of the Enlightenment lose the normative standards they need to perform that critique, and revert to reactionary pre-Enlightenment standards of order and being, or to

110. For a comparative discussion of various historical revisionisms, see Anderson, *English* 281–93.

ostensibly post-Enlightenment standards of difference and free play which begin strangely to resemble their pre-Enlightenment corollaries.[111]

In this chapter, I have considered the historical revisionist project as a complex totalization of these conservatisms. Neoconservativism dominates through its celebration of capitalist modernity—its whig theory of economic history combined with an attack on the Enlightenment heritage of liberalism and marxism as destabilizing political whiggery. But revisionism also incorporates substantial moments of Old Conservatism (by retreating to the consensual world picture of a sacrosanct premodernity) and of Young Conservatism (by venturing forth to the fatalist contingency of a *langue*-like postmodernity). Habermas's terms can help explain some of the squabbles within revisionist historiography—for instance, between the capitalist mainstream of revisionist Neoconservatism, and the more nostalgic Old Conservative royalism of J. C. D. Clark, J. S. A. Adamson, and sometimes Kevin Sharpe. But these revisionists unite with each other, and with the Young Conservative postmodernists whom I will consider in chapter 3, in their unmitigated opposition not to the critical spirit of the Enlightenment as a whole, but to its specifically marxist extension, which I will consider in chapter 4.[112]

111. "Modernity versus Postmodernity," *New German Critique* 22, 1981, 13–14, 9; see also his long treatment of the topic in *The Philosophical Discourse of Modernity*, Cambridge, MA, 1990.
112. Thanks to Ed White for help with this paragraph. Although the marxist philosophy of praxis gives Habermas a crucial critique of the Enlightenment's instrumental reason, it "does not afford the means for thinking dead labor as mediated and *paralyzed intersubjectivity*" (*Philosophical* 60–74, 65; see also 75–82). But from Marx on commodity fetishism to Sartre on the practico-inert, a crucial current of marxism has done just that. See Alex Callinicos, *Against Postmodernism*, New York 1990, 113–20.

3

Foucault, the New Historicism, and the Base Curiosity of the Plebs

The watchwords of the battle, written in characters which have remained legible throughout human history, read: "Rome vs. Israel, Israel vs. Rome." No battle has ever been more momentous than this one. Rome viewed Israel as a monstrosity; the Romans regarded the Jews as *convicted* of hatred against the whole of mankind—and rightly so if one is justified in associating the welfare of the human species with absolute supremacy of aristocratic values. But how did the Jews, on their part, feel about Rome? A thousand indications point to the answer. It is enough to read once more the Revelations of St. John, the most rabid outburst of vindictiveness in all recorded history.

—Friedrich Nietzsche, *The Genealogy of Morals* (1887)

But before I conclude, give me leave (friends) to tell you one thing, and to me it seems strange, that this very day some Independent ministers said, that they are fools who busy themselves in meddling with two such obscure books as the prophecy of Daniel, and the Revelation. Lord have mercy upon us! not meddle with the Revelation, when we are commanded to search into it, and understand it. But will you know the reason? There is so much of Babylon laid open in it, so much of Babylon discovered there in the civil powers of the world, and in the worldly church, the parish churches and the national churches, and so much against the Whitehall court of Triers, and the rest of [the] order of archbishops, and bishops, and deans, and all the great jurisdictions, and against all the parish priests and tithe-mongers, that it's no wonder they do not care to have men looking into the Revelation.

—Christopher Feake, sermon to Allhallows the Great Congregation, a spy's report in *The Thurloe Papers* (1656)

English professors have brought much offence in the world; but there is a discovering distinguishing time a-coming.

—Anna Trapnel, Bodleian Library, *S.1.42.Th* (1658)

Damiens's Remonstrance

After 1980, while revisionism rose to prominence in historical studies, the new historicism rapidly became a powerful force in North American literary studies. New historicists established themselves in departments of literature, in the catalogues of university presses, in new journals like *Representations*, and in older ones like *ELH* and *English Literary Renaissance*. They developed their arguments through cross-disciplinary dialogues with anthropologists and cultural historians, through debates and exchanges with feminists and British cultural materialists, and through critiques of other interpretive modes. In the words of Louis Adrian Montrose, the new historicism requires "a wholesale rejection of some prevalent alternative conceptions of literature: as an autonomous aesthetic order that transcends the shifting pressure and particularity of material needs and interests; as a collection of inert discursive reflections of 'real events'; as a superstructural manifestation of an economic base." To the first argument, Montrose proposes "the historicity of texts"—their involvement in political struggles and with nonliterary writing and practices. To the second and third, he proposes "the textuality of history"—its constitution by languages and sign systems, and the linguistic mediation of all our contact with it.[1]

I find much to admire in these new historicist theses, which are frequently implicit in my arguments above with historical revisionism. The new historicist propensity for textual gaps and conflicts, for unresolved ideological fractures, would seem to ally it with the marxist opponents of historical revisionism, and it would be wrong to conflate the church-and-king mob of revisionism with the transgressive subversives of the new historicism. Such European influences as Raymond Williams, Foucault, and Derrida have declared their critical affinities with historical materialism, and new historicists have, from time to time, found themselves the objects of vulgar red-baiting.[2] But finally, I think new historicism also

---

1. "Renaissance Literary Studies and the Subject of History," *English Literary Renaissance* 16.1, 1986, 8. The new historicism has not lacked for chroniclers, so I won't offer a summary overview. A good place to start is Montrose's "New Historicisms," in Stephen Greenblatt and Giles Gunn, eds, *Redrawing the Boundaries*, New York 1992, 392–418. See also Walter Cohen, "Political Criticism of Shakespeare," in Jean E. Howard and Marion F. O'Connor, eds, *Shakespeare Reproduced*, New York 1987, 18–46; Jean Howard, "The New Historicism in Renaissance Studies," *English Literary Renaissance* 16.1, 1986; Fredric Jameson, *Postmodernism, or, the Cultural Logic of Late Capitalism*, Durham, NC, 1991, 181–217; David Norbrook, "Life and Death of Renaissance Man," *Raritan* 8.4, 1989; H. Aram Veeser, ed., *The New Historicism*, New York 1989; Don E. Wayne, "The New Historicism," in Malcolm Kelsall et al., eds, *Encyclopedia of Literature and Criticism*, London 1990, 791–805; and Wayne, "Power, Politics, and the Shakespearean Text," Howard and O'Connor, *Shakespeare* 47–67.

2. For Foucault, see *Remarks on Marx*, New York 1991; for Derrida, his *Specters of Marx*, New York 1994; and the responses in Michael Sprinker, ed., *Ghostly Demarcations*, London 1999. On the connections between the New Left and the new historicism, see Catherine Gallagher, "Marxism and the New Historicism," Veeser, *New Historicism* 37–48. The paradoxical combination of new-historicist-as-fellow-traveler and new historicist anticommunism becomes more intelligible when we recall that early modern Anglicans could

effaces political struggle, downplays the creative practical consciousness of working people, and works to shut down history from below. I want to introduce this argument by returning to a new historicist touchstone: the opening pages of Michel Foucault's *Discipline and Punish*, which recount the public execution in 1757 of Robert François Damiens, an unemployed domestic servant from Artois who had attempted to assassinate Louis XV. After extracting Damiens's confession, the king's men tore him with pincers, burnt him with sulfur, poured boiling oil and molten lead, resin, and wax into his wounds, listened to his cries and confessions, tied him to horses, severed his sinews, drew him, quartered him, and burned him to ashes.[3] Foucault thinks the gathered crowds saw the execution as a sort of carnival; in the words of Nietzsche's *Genealogy of Morals*, one of the most important influences on his book, "Punishment, too, has its festive features."[4] The *ancien régime* punishes an attack on the king with "an almost theatrical reproduction of the crime in the execution of the guilty man," publicly turning him into "the symmetrical inverted figure of the king." Foucault contrasts this festive feudal Carnival of torture with the endless Enlightenment Lent of discipline. The latter transforms the penal subject through a program of incarceration, surveillance, and corrective training, as in Léon Faucher's distinctly non-theatrical rules "for the House of young Prisoners in Paris" of 1838, and Jeremy Bentham's panopticon. In the rest of his book, Foucault focuses on the "disciplinary archipelago" of prisons, schools, hospitals, and military barracks—a world no less cruel than the sovereign theater of punishment, but distinctly inferior as public spectacle.[5]

In a late essay, Foucault characterized his life's work as a history of *subjectification*, or "the different modes by which, in our culture, human beings are made subjects."[6] Damiens's death gives us his most striking example, and new historicist critics examining the penal and aesthetic spectacles of early modern England have found it irresistible. Scott Wilson imagines the populace at such spectacles: "They exult in the horror, they *enjoy* it. Now this enjoyment may be a measure of their oppression, but that is partly the point: the gaze of the oppressed enjoys oppression, enjoys the evil that is done in the name of the law."[7] Richard Wilson begins his study of discipline in Shakespearean comedy with an account of James's "theatrical" staging of Ralegh's near-execution in 1603.[8] Jonathan Goldberg juxtaposes the allegorical torture of Bonfont in *Faerie*

---

denounce Cromwell and the Independents as communists. Anticommunism always works as an intra- as well as interclass practice.
3. New York 1977, 3–6.
4. *The Birth of Tragedy and the Genealogy of Morals*, Garden City, NY, 1956, 198; see also 211–13.
5. *Discipline* 45, 29, 6–7. Neither Faucher (Malthusian economist and supporter of Louis Bonaparte) nor Bentham (inveterate opponent of natural law) seems particularly promising as an ambassador for the Enlightenment.
6. Hubert Dreyfus and Paul Rabinow, *Michel Foucault*, 2nd edn, Chicago 1983, 208.
7. *Cultural Materialism*, Oxford 1995, 148.
8. "The Quality of Mercy," *The Seventeenth Century* 5.1, 1990.

Queene 5, the actual torture of the Duke d'Ancre, and *Discipline and Punish*.[9] Thomas Cartelli explains the sovereign violence of Marlowe's Tamburlaine by looking at the skulls of rebellious nobles decorating London Bridge, and the publicly amputated hands of two seditious Elizabethan pamphleteers.[10] Leonard Tennenhouse compares Shakespearean theater and Damiens's scaffold as sites of public ritual and surveillance.[11] Stephen Greenblatt combines a meditation on aesthetic wonder and horror with a seventeenth-century English adventurer's tale of torturing a Chinese goldsmith to death.[12] Michael C. Schoenfeldt finds George Herbert's God practicing Foucauldian torture.[13] Thomas Healy frames Marvell's "Upon Appleton House" with a story of a mock Eucharist in which soldiers crucified a woman and forced her to eat her own flesh and drink her own blood.[14] I conclude my *A Rational Millennium* with a chilly little triptych of torture: Comenius's seventeenth-century proposal for a utopian program of disciplinary "didachography" that will print out identical enlightened students, Kafka's rationalized torture in *The Penal Colony*, and (implicitly) Foucault's disciplinary archipelago.[15] Gleefully splattering idealist theories of dispassionate beauty, Foucault and his followers aspire to the inquisitorial sublime. Indeed, in his *Philosophical Enquiry into Our Ideas of the Sublime and Beautiful*, Edmund Burke used Damiens's execution as a horrific benchmark against which to measure more subtly graded forms of aesthetic danger and pain.[16]

But something's missing. Foucault sublimely strips Damiens's story down to pure spectacle, without mentioning why he attacked the king in the first place, or how his allies responded. Though many critics have emulated the unblinking *sang froid* of Foucault's avant-gardiste gaze, not one has managed to cast a sympathetic glance toward the pre- and post-spectacular Damiens—Damiens on his feet, Damiens remembered. But Dale K. Van Kley has shown that his attack was not so much a madman's assault on the king's two bodies, as an act of solidarity with the parlement of Paris against Bourbon and Ultramontane absolutism. Even under torture, Damiens told his guards that he attempted to kill Louis "because his majesty had not listened to the remonstrances of his parlement." His attack was "an exceptionally strong, nonverbal sort of remonstrance on behalf of the parlement of Paris." Inside the parlement and outside, Damiens's execution and the persecution of his family contributed to the

9. *James I and the Politics of Literature*, Baltimore 1983, 2–3, 243n.4, 149–50, 271n.36.

10. *Marlowe, Shakespeare, and the Economy of Theatrical Experience*, Philadelphia 1991, 91–2.

11. *Power on Display*, New York 1986. See also Gillian Murray Kendall, ed., *Shakespearean Power and Punishment*, Madison 1998.

12. *Learning to Curse*, New York and London 1990, 11–15. In "Perils of Historicism," *New York Review of Books* 28.6, 1991, Ann Barton shows that Greenblatt makes this spectacle more theatrical by omitting its context in the commercial competition of English and Chinese imperialists in Java.

13. *Prayer and Power*, Chicago 1991, 121–2.

14. "'Dark all without it knits,'" *HS* 170–88, 180.

15. New York 1987, 308–13.

16. London 1958, 39–40.

"desacralization of the monarchy" and played an important part in the pre-history of the Revolution.[17] In *The Rights of Man*, Tom Paine asks, "Who does not remember the execution of Damiens, torn to pieces by horses? The effect of these cruel spectacles, exhibited to the populace, is to destroy tenderness or excite revenge; and by the base and false idea of governing men by terror instead of reason, they become precedents." Paine *explains* the passion of the French Revolutionary crowds by calling it an imitative response to the horrific violence of absolutism. No doubt, Foucault's neo-Bourbon box seat offers a sublime view of the scaffold, but a groundling view restores questions of reason and justice.[18]

Like Foucault, many new historicist critics tend to overestimate the role of top-down, oppressive subjectification, underestimating or denying altogether the role of rationally guided oppositional practice. To develop this thesis, I will consider two key aspects of Foucault's historical method: his practice of Nietzschean genealogy (with new historicist applications by Nancy Armstrong and Leonard Tennenhouse), and his focus on power (with applications by Stephen Greenblatt). I will then turn to the foundation of new historicist social theory in a model that juxtaposes social "system" with individual "subject." This model criticizes marxist totalization, but offers in its place a static, non-contradictory social totality. And it has difficulty explaining social conflict and historical change. I conclude by looking at the work of "post-revisionist" historians and critics, who have developed a formidable critique of both historical revisionism and new historicism. After discussing my affinities with this work, I suggest that, like those they criticize, post-revisionists have tended to bracket and ignore questions of economy and class.

Genealogy and Power

New historicism is literary Foucauldianism. Such a bald claim risks contradictory but equally damning charges of redundant self-evidence and reductionist distortion. On the one hand, the new historicism's debt to Foucault has not exactly gone unremarked. On the other, its polymorphous diversity should save it from the indignity of a family name. Montrose contrasts the protean plurality of "new historicisms" with the totalizing impulse of the doubly patronymic "Hegelian Marxism."[19] Similarly, Stephen Greenblatt argues that American critical affiliations like new historicism are "not linked to systematic thought. They are like our political parties, confusing to Europeans because they are important but

17. *The Damiens Affair and the Unraveling of the Ancien Régime, 1750–1770*, Princeton 1984, 43, 270.
18. *Political Writings*, Cambridge 1989, 70. For postmodernists contemplating the inconceivable complexities of the global system (a.k.a. "capitalism") as for Burke's contemporaries contemplating the unspeakable horrors of the Jacobin crowd, *the sublime* forms the giddy but authoritarian *ne plus ultra* of antitotalizing microthought: no more thinking, here be monsters.
19. "New Historicisms" 410.

ideologically evasive and inconsistent."[20] As an improvising *bricoleur* rather than a doctrinaire adept, the new historicist adapts a wide array of local knowledges to local interpretations.

But calling the new historicists "Foucauldian" is no more reductive than calling psychoanalysts "Freudian," historical materialists "marxist," and Republicans and Democrats "capitalist." It's not that new historicists never differ significantly from Foucault and from each other. It's just that Foucault became for them what he himself says Marx became for marxists, Freud for psychoanalysts: an "initiator of a discursive practice" who authorized his followers to analyze the disciplinary production of subjectivities, pose a certain body of questions about power and knowledge, and engage in certain disputes within certain limits.[21] More than any other postwar European writer, Foucault enabled left and liberal intellectuals to work up a non-marxist theory of cultural politics. And like Derrida before him, he found a welcoming home in the rich alluvium of American academic anticommunism, for his theory is not incidentally but constitutively opposed to history from below—the history of working men and women making their own lives.

In his 1971 manifesto, "Nietzsche, Genealogy, History," Foucault contrasts Nietzsche's "genealogy" or "effective [*wirkliche*] history" with "traditional history."[22] Where the latter describes the gradual, continuous unfolding of an idea present at the origin, genealogy insists on the contingency and unpredictability of all beginnings, on fragmentation and dispersal as the form of history, on the will to power as its content. More generally, genealogy gives us superior access to the irreducible philological materiality of the past. Where a traditional historical formalism asserts the universality and ideal status of some few treasured documents, genealogy displays a stern archival rigor:

> Genealogy is gray, meticulous, and patiently documentary. It operates on a field of entangled and confused parchments, on documents that have been scratched over and recopied many times.... Genealogy ... requires patience and a knowledge of details and it depends on a vast accumulation of source material.... In short, genealogy demands relentless erudition.

The dust-encrusted genealogist emerges from the archive brandishing a palimpsest saturated with dark marginal knowledge, and heretofore guiltily misfiled by anxious librarians of the Enlightenment. With all Monsieur Jourdain's delight at discovering he can speak *prose*, genealogists discover they can conduct systematic primary *research* and make empirical discoveries. But with all his selfish sense of *nouveau riche* proprietorship, they reject traditional history—no less dusty, no less erudite—because it tries to get "as near as possible, placing itself at the foot of its mountain peaks, at the risk of adopting the famous perspective of frogs," and because it

20. *Learning* 3.
21. *Language, Counter-Memory, Practice*, Ithaca, NY, 1977, 131.
22. *Language* 139–64.

fancies it can get at "what actually occurred in the past" and attain "objectivity, the accuracy of facts, and the permanence of the past."[23]

Second, with "its affirmation of knowledge as perspective," genealogy displays a superior consciousness of its own mode of existence in the political present. Where traditional historians "erase the elements in their work which reveal their grounding in a particular time and place . . . Nietzsche's version of historical sense is explicit in its perspective and acknowledges its system of injustice." Genealogy doesn't just retrieve knowledge, but creates it. It promises not "the slow exposure of the meaning hidden in an origin," but "the violent or surreptitious appropriation of a system of rules, which in itself has no essential meaning, in order to impose a direction, to bend it to a new will, to force its participation in a different game, and to subject it to secondary rules." But at the same time, it condemns traditional history for *its* attempts at violent appropriation—for "placing present needs at the origin," for attempting to "convince us of an obscure purpose that seeks its realization at the moment it arises."[24] There *is* a distinction between a forthright will to power in the present and one that dissimulates itself as a nostalgic philosophy of origins, but it may blur when we recall Foucault's own nostalgia for the wandering fools of medieval Europe, the bloody Bourbon theater of sovereign punishment, the *ars erotica* of ancient Rome and the eternal lubricious Orient.[25]

The introduction of *Discipline and Punish* brings these empiricist and "presentist" impulses together:

> I want to write the history of this prison, with all its political investments of the body that it gathers together in its closed-off architecture. Why? Simply because I am interested in the past? No, if one means by that writing a history of the past in the terms of the present. Yes, if one means writing the history of the present.[26]

If Foucault wishes to contrast a history that merely objectifies the past to one that reflects self-consciously on the historical quality of its own analytical categories, that seems unobjectionable enough, even salutary. But what distinguishes this approach from the array of competing historicisms? And hasn't dialectical history in particular always tried to conceptualize the simultaneous continuity and discontinuity of past and present, and the emergence of its own analytical consciousness and categories?

---

23. 139–40, 157, 158.
24. 156–7, 151–2, 148.
25. In *The History of Sexuality, Volume I*, Foucault longs to find the pleasure-seeking *ars erotica* of "China, Japan, India, Rome, the Arabo-Moslem societies" buried beneath the truth-seeking *scientia sexualis* of Western confession and psychoanalysis (New York 1978, 57, 70–71). Thus Foucault slights both the oppressive *scientia* regulating fertility and women's sexuality in more than half the world, and the big, bouncing *ars* of Western pleasure seeking.
26. 31.

Foucault distinguishes genealogy from traditional history on grounds that might also be seen to connect them.

I don't mean utterly to collapse Foucault's historical practice with that of all other historians. Nancy Fraser has usefully defined Foucauldian genealogy against several alternatives. Where structuralism and semiology analyze systems of signs, genealogy articulates practices. Where hermeneutics searches for deep meanings, genealogy reads layers of interlocking and contested interpretations. Where ideology critique evaluates systems of belief in terms of some normative truth, genealogy describes the production of truth effects. Where the history of ideas traces the development of unities, genealogy charts discontinuities and multiplicities.[27] But I do want to focus on another antagonist—the *deep* antagonist, to employ a non-genealogical adjective: where history from below begins with working men and women making their own lives and the lives of those who don't work, genealogy begins with the idea systems that ostensibly control these workers from above. Indeed, Foucault views any "traditional" historian practicing history from below as a rancorous leveller:

> His apparent serenity follows from his concerted avoidance of the exceptional and his reduction of all things to the lowest common denominator. Nothing is allowed to stand above him; and underlying his desire for total knowledge is his search for the secrets that belittle everything: "base curiosity." What is this source of history? It comes from the plebs. To whom is it addressed? To the plebs. And its discourse strongly resembles the demagogue's refrain: "No one is greater than you and anyone who presumes to get the better of you—you who are good—is evil." The historian, who functions as his double, can be heard to echo: "No past is greater than your present, and through my meticulous erudition, I will rid you of your infatuations and transform the grandeur of history into pettiness, evil, and misfortune." The historian's ancestry goes back to Socrates. This demagogy, of course, must be masked. It must hide its singular malice under the cloak of universals. . . . We can begin to understand the spontaneous historical bent of the nineteenth century: the anemia of its forces and those mixtures that effaced all its individual traits produced the same results as the mortifications of asceticism; its inability to create, its absence of artistic works, and its need to rely on past achievements forced it to adopt the base curiosity of the plebs.[28]

At first, this historian's quest for "total knowledge" and a social project to incorporate it in suggests the genealogist's quest for "relentless erudition" and effort to seize the past and twist it to a present purpose. Reading his blue books in the depths of the British Museum, then trying to put his knowledge to work in the International Working Men's Association, Karl Marx looks like some sort of genealogist as well as a "traditional historian." But the two part company—not primarily because of method, but because of class affiliation. Foucault's neo-Latinism of "plebs" condenses the liberal

27. *Unruly Practices*, Minneapolis 1989, 19–20.
28. *Language* 157–9; translation slightly modified.

citoyen and the marxist proletarian, denies the specifically modern quality of both, and ridicules both from an old–new perspective of aristocratic *health*. He tries to disqualify a plebeian history from below, plebeian historical audiences, a plebeian project of emancipation, and even an entire century, doomed to impotent sterility on the grounds of its base curiosity. Like Nietzsche, Foucault tries to found a new history somewhere beyond the rancorous binary of good and evil. And like Nietzsche, he winds up inhabiting a version of that binary: the vitalist opposition of fertility, health, and life, to barrenness, sickness, and death. Surveying the scabby mob from a wintry Zarathustran height, the genealogist looks red-blooded (not "anemic" or "ascetic"), maybe even blue-blooded (who hates the plebs, if not the patriciate?), but never, never sweaty. Genealogy is not only itself; it is also *not*-history-from-below, *not* the history of the self-constitution and praxis of groups, *not* the history of workers living their own lives.[29]

The Imaginary Puritan, by Nancy Armstrong and Leonard Tennenhouse, is the most ambitious attempt to address the English Revolution from the perspective of Foucauldian genealogy.[30] Like Foucault, Armstrong and Tennenhouse criticize whig or "traditional history" as "a just-so story that gives the operative categories of industrial cultures a location well in the past, thus allowing the present order of things to emerge as so many facts of human nature." They, too, reject the idea that we can know history itself apart from its present-day representations: "One must give up the whole pretense of knowing the past (which only conceals the effects of writing about it)." So they, too, like all genealogists, must raise one foot out of the self-satisfied present whose veiled interests traditional historians used to serve, the other out of the solid and knowable past about which they once made truth claims. But the anticipated pratfall never arrives, for they deftly set their feet back down again. First, their Foucault begins to merge with their present-centered whig storytellers: "In providing us with such an account, his point is never to make one see the past as it really was. His concern is wholly for the present." Second, the very sentence that abjures historical truth claims conjures them up again: "One must give up the whole pretense of knowing the past (which only conceals the effects of writing about it); one must show precisely when and how the most basic categories of modern culture developed and how they related to one another." But surely one should at least pretend to know the past when claiming *precision* in describing how the basic categories of the modern developed.[31]

For Armstrong and Tennenhouse, there is "no question" that the family

---

29. Habermas discusses the disturbing regressions of the postmodern quest for a new ethics in *Philosophical Discourse*. On Nietzsche's abhorrence of democracy, see Alain Boyer, "Hierarchy and Truth," in Luc Ferry and Alain Renaut, eds, *Why We Are Not Nietzscheans*, Chicago 1997, 1–20; and Norbrook, "Life."
30. Berkeley and Los Angeles 1992.
31. 3–4.

provides the extra-discursive "common ground" for interpreting discursive events, saving us from an atomized model of society as a mere "ensemble of discursive effects with which to account for the most basic categories of modern culture."[32] There may in fact be very *few* questions, since arguments about the family and gender rouse the interest of bourgeois intellectuals while arguments about political forms and class struggle provoke a snub or a yawn. But the appeal to a ground remains constant. Moreover, though they hesitate to make large-scale historical claims in their own names about the world outside the *domos*, they freely invoke such claims by others. Their Foucault, for instance, does not merely *argue* but "show[s]," "demonstrates," and "explains" historical theses. In *Discipline and Punish*, he "offers the reader a snarl of contingencies—theories, procedures, architectural drawings—that worked together to produce an entirely new understanding of crime." And British revisionist historians do not simply oppose but "debunk" and "refute" their liberal and marxist predecessors, "test" assumptions, and "discover" them to be lacking. They approach the archive like genealogists and "try to read material from the past with an artificially induced naiveté, as if they were not modern readers," remaining "conscientious" and "careful," in their "close investigations."[33] But close to *what*? What does one test an assumption against, if not some empirical datum, whether modestly posited, or boldly asserted? If one creates the documents one analyzes, how can one be conscientious and careful about doing so?

In their chapter on the English Revolution, Armstrong and Tennenhouse criticize an earlier generation of literary critics who followed liberal historians like Gardiner, who looked for evidence of the emergence of "institutional changes brought about by those who opposed the autocratic power of the Crown," and marxist historians like Christopher Hill, who read to find "signs indicating the emergence of a new class ethos around the ideal of individual freedom."[34] But they engage Gardiner only with a brief passage from the summary conclusion of *The History of the Great Civil War* and (seriously out of context) a passage from his introduction to *Constitutional Documents*, relying for the rest on R. C. Richardson's account of Gardiner in *The Debate on the English Revolution Revisited*. And they dispose of Hill by charging that he implants "categories of class" fully "two centuries before they actually organized popular thought." We might expect this charge to cut and run at the sight of Robert Kett's camp-men, or a sumptuary code banning proles in velvet, or at Jonson's *Masque of Queens*, Middleton's *Women Beware Women*, and Winstanley's *New Law of Righteousness*—which helped organize the class consciousness of, respectively, would-be absolutists, urban merchants, and the rural poor. But the argument holds firm, for in their chapter on the English Revolution, they

32. 4, 3, 69.
33. 8, 3, 54–6.
34. 47–68, 50–51.

preserve their history-of-the-present purity by neglecting to discuss the words or actions of any seventeenth-century political actors.[35] Foucauldian genealogists make bold truth claims while dismissing their opponents for doing the same thing. They practice a presentist history while dismissing their opponents as naively presentist whigs. And with an air of hermeneutical sophistication, they dismiss the practitioners of plebeian "traditional" history because they are so, well, *plebeian* and *traditional.* This gesture should command awe, if not emulation.

From genealogy to *power*: Foucault's master concept for discussing the disciplinary formation of subjectivity. In the first volume of *The History of Sexuality*, he defined power as neither a grouping of oppressive institutions, nor a mode of oppressive governance, nor a property owned by one group and coveted by another, but the "multiplicity of force relations" in a society. It forms both the "internal conditions" and "the immediate effects" of all social life. It cannot be located, for it forms "the moving substrate of force relations. . . . Power is everywhere; not because it embraces everything, but because it comes from everywhere." It doesn't *repress* primal energies, or human nature, or the proletariat; it *produces* new spaces, knowledges, and subjectivities.[36]

Foucault's concept has drawn fire from many quarters for failing to examine adequately the question of resistance.[37] Foucault might protest that he set out precisely to *critique* a Sartrean and marxist model of totalizing revolutionary praxis. In a 1971 interview with two Maoists, he observed, "I think that to imagine another system is to extend our participation in the present system. This is perhaps what happened in the history of the Soviet Union."[38] But Foucault's critique of a Hegelian or marxist totalizing history leads him to a totalization of his own on the level of power—a power that tends to be, *de facto* if not *de jure*, an instrument of state domination. In *Discipline and Punish*, he considers only two concrete cases of resistance: a Fourierist critique of liberal penal reform, and the urban crowds that gathered tumultuously around the scaffold, making heroes of those who assaulted the king's body. He concludes the book by focusing on the radical potential growing up inside the interstices of the disciplinary archipelago: "In this central and centralized humanity, the effect and instrument of complex power relations, bodies and forces subjected by multiple mechanisms of 'incarceration,'

35. 225, 54, 62.
36. 92, 94, 93; see also *Power/Knowledge*, New York 1980, 142.
37. See Nancy Fraser, *Unruly Practices* 17–34; Perry Anderson, *In the Tracks of Historical Materialism*, London 1983, 50–51; Callinicos, *Against* 80–88; Peter Dews, *Logics of Disintegration*, London 1987, 144–99; Habermas, *Philosophical* 266–93; Martin Jay, *Marxism and Totality*, Berkeley and Los Angeles 1984, 528; Carolyn Porter, "Are We Being Historical Yet?" *South Atlantic Quarterly* 87.4, 1988, 764–5; Edward Said, *The World, the Text, and the Critic*, Cambridge, MA, 1983, 244–5; and Charles Taylor, "Foucault on Freedom and Truth," in David Couzens Hoy, ed., *Foucault: A Critical Reader*, Oxford and New York 1986, 69–102, 90–93.
38. *Language* 230. Compare Jean-François Lyotard, *The Postmodern Condition*, Minneapolis 1984, 66.

objects for discourses that are in themselves elements for this strategy, we must hear the distant roar of battle." But this roar remains inarticulate, and we search Foucault's writings in vain for an analysis of resistant group praxis.[39]

Thus Foucault's *power* comes to resemble a mildly politicized version of Hegel's *Geist* or Derrida's *differance*: an analytical term derived from actual social relations and reified as the agency governing those relations—a form of reductiveness frequently attributed to marxists, but lampooned nowhere better than in *The German Ideology*:

> First of all, an abstraction is made from a fact; then it is declared that the fact is based upon the abstraction. A very cheap method to produce the semblance of being profound and speculative in the German manner.
>
> For example:
>
> *Fact*: The cat eats the mouse.
>
> *Reflection*: Cat—nature, mouse—nature, consumption of mouse by cat = consumption of nature by nature = self-consumption of nature.
>
> *Philosophic presentation of the fact*: Devouring of the mouse by the cat is based upon the self-consumption of nature.[40]

As revisionists denounce what they see as a reductive marxist class dualism, then replace it with a paternalist monism, so Foucault criticizes *class struggle* as reductive totalization, then replaces it with a *power/resistance* dyad that promptly collapses into a *power/power* monad.

This isn't to say that either Foucault or the new historicism presents us with an unrelieved vista of oppressive domination. But their ostensible anti-essentialism prevents them from systematically discussing any normative collective alternative to coercion. Foucault tended to move from ostensibly value-neutral descriptions of power, to politically engaged work without an explicit normativity, to arguments with an implicit but distinctly liberal and emancipatory ring.[41] As an example of the first approach, we might look to *Discipline and Punish*, where Foucault brackets the substantial claims of liberal theory and looks only at its forms, conducting a brilliant analysis of the will to power and knowledge inhering even in "humane" penal discipline. But by his own standards, any provisional bracketing should end in a discussion of what is to be done, and anyone alternately dazzled and bludgeoned by the mantra of "everything is political" may be forgiven for asking Foucauldians what they support for the polis they inhabit: a return to the jolly sovereign theater of torture? The liberal ideal of penal correction that attempted to replace it? Its socialist critique, which discusses penal means and ends according to current conditions and normative ideals of human nature? Or an end to law itself in a carnival of Dionysian criminality?

---

39. 287–9, 67–9, 308; thus the last words of Foucault's book ("le grondement de la bataille") pay homage to the dubious roar of Georges Bataille.
40. *MECW* 5.481.
41. Nancy Fraser, *Unruly Practices* 27.

Foucault opted for the last in a debate with Noam Chomsky on Dutch television in 1971, the same year he published "Nietzsche, Genealogy, History." At first, he seems to offer a radically distinct view of "the plebs," whose revolutionary violence he celebrates as almost an end in itself:

> Rather than thinking of the social struggle in terms of "justice," one has to emphasize justice in terms of the social struggle. . . . One makes war to win, not because it is just. . . . When the proletariat takes power, it may be quite possible that the proletariat will exert towards the classes over which it has just triumphed, a violent, dictatorial and even bloody power. I can't see what objection one could make to this.

Chomsky tries to show him:

> No Leninist or whatever you like would dare to say, "We, the proletariat, have a right to take power, and then throw everyone else into crematoria." If that were the consequence of the proletariat taking power, of course it would not be appropriate. . . . I think that one can and *must* give an argument, if you can't give an argument you should extract yourself from the struggle. Give an argument that the social revolution that you're trying to achieve *is* in the ends of justice, *is* in the ends of realizing fundamental human needs, not merely in the ends of putting some other group in power, because they want it.[42]

Chomsky shows commendable restraint, but there's no good reason to deny Foucault's *Lebensphilosophie* of irrational but life-affirming collective violence the good old-fashioned name of "fascism," even though it's not so much Himmler's beerhall fascism as the salon fascism of Yeats and Marinetti, or the lecture-hall left fascism stretching from Georges Bataille to contemporary postmodernist young conservatives, who celebrate the masses as a sublimely irrational force of violent resistance lying beyond the bourgeois torpor of reason, ethics, and judicial forms.[43]

In 1977, Foucault tried to mediate these two views. The plebs are "the permanent, ever silent target for apparatuses of power"—not a mere illusion, not a class outside of all power, but an effect of structure:

> The plebs is no doubt not a real sociological entity. But there is indeed always something in the social body, in classes, groups and individuals themselves which in some sense escapes relations of power, something which is by no means a more or less docile or reactive primal matter, but rather a centrifugal movement, an inverse energy, a discharge. There is certainly no such thing as "the" plebs; rather, there is, as it were, a certain plebeian quality or aspect (*"de la" plèbe*). There is plebs in bodies, in souls, in individuals, in the proletariat, in

---

42. "Human Nature: Justice versus Power," in Fons Elders, ed., *Reflexive Water*, London and Ontario 1974, 133–97, 180, 182, 184, 186.
43. Richard Wolin, "Left Fascism," *Constellations* 2.3, 1996. See also Foucault's discussions with French Maoists (*Language* 218–33, *Power/Knowledge* 1–36). Jean Baudrillard celebrates "the mass" as a revolutionary body, "dumb like beasts," in *In the Shadow of the Silent Majorities* (New York 1983, 28)—a serious contender for the nadir of postmodernist thought. See the critique by Callinicos, *Against* 86–7, and, for a powerful critique of modern antipopulism, John Carey's *The Intellectuals and the Masses*, New York 1993.

the bourgeoisie, but everywhere in a diversity of forms and extensions, of energies and irreducibilities.[44]

Foucault's indefinite pronouns and overlapping metaphors suggest his frustrated desire to discuss resistance without speaking of struggles between dominant and subordinate groups. But despite the vaguely positive tones, we have not really moved very far from the impotent, rancorous plebs of "Nietzsche, Genealogy, History," or the gleefully blood-spattered plebs of the Chomsky debate. So far as they are "curious" and exhibit critical rationality, the plebs become ascetic, anemic, and base. So far as they act, they become a mute but murderous proletariat. So far as they resign themselves to the condition of a non- or pre-rational energy or discharge, they exist only as a concept or quality—a *"de la" plèbe* permanently cut off from rational self-understanding and praxis. This is history from below, after a fashion, but it is also history without a head.

Foucault's plebs set out looking lustily Roman, but wind up looking vaguely Heideggerean—shuffling along in the peasants' shoes painted by Van Gogh, which Heidegger saw as the earthy emblems of chthonic Being.[45] The plebs I will examine below, on the other hand, wear the peasant clogs or *Bundschuhs* adopted as an emblem by the Alsatian peasants' union, when they marched against their high-booted, sixteenth-century princes, prompting an aristocratic Great Fear that shuddered through and beyond the English Revolution.[46] And they talk as they walk. Foucault advises political theorists to stop thinking of power as sovereign prohibition and start thinking of it as productive positivity—as "power without the king." But plebeian political theorists have never had the luxury of doing anything else, for they know in their brains as well as their bones that *power* is always the power to produce, or to extract what others produce.[47] As Gerrard Winstanley knew, the *kingly power* (a *"du" roi*?) of landlords easily survives the *power of the king*.[48]

Foucault's concept of power has opened one door for new historicists while shutting another. In *Shakespearean Negotiations*, Stephen Greenblatt reveals himself to be, like Foucault, a brilliant interpreter, and the chapters in the body of his book subtly situate Shakespeare's plays among Renaissance discourses of colonialism, sexuality, and exorcism.[49] But his theoretical introduction, which ponders the methodological implications of "social energy," is more troubling. Scholars who study social energy in Renaissance culture should abandon traditional history, with its search for an "originary moment." They should take up a power-centered genealogy, and study cultural production through "a subtle, elusive set of exchanges, a network of trades and trade-offs, a jostling of competing representations,

44. *Power/Knowledge* 137–8.
45. *Poetry, Language, Thought*, New York 1971, 32–7.
46. *MECW* 10.431.
47. *History* 91.
48. *W* 353, 381, 388–9, 436, 466.
49. Berkeley and Los Angeles 1988.

a negotiation between joint-stock companies." While "the circulation of social energy by and through the stage was not part of a single coherent, totalizing system," it did leave individuals "the products" of a system of dynamic circulation and exchange. Social energy underlies and connects all apparently diverse aesthetic and non-aesthetic phenomena, for "everything produced by the society," so far as it can *circulate*, joins those more properly aesthetic or experiential forms of social energy such as "Power, charisma, sexual excitement, collective dreams, wonder, desire, anxiety, religious awe, free-floating intensities of experience." Greenblatt's abjuration of totality begins to feel a little *pro forma.*[50]

Greenblatt traces his concept of circulation to Derrida and to "the circulatory rhythms of American politics." But along with "negotiation," it becomes his master metaphor for Renaissance culture.[51] In classic new historicist fashion, both terms condense an anti-formalist and an anti-communist polemic. As dynamic terms, they take us away from any simple idea of the work of art as a thing in itself, changing the hermetically literary world into a circulatory economy and leaving behind a certain idealist aesthetics. But we do not leave capitalist social theory as such, which turns obsessively to economy, presenting *value* as precisely a product of circulation and exchange. For when capitalist ideologists reduce cultural activity to economy and economy to circulation, they reduce men and women to the status of *homo oeconomicus*, metaphysically driven by a Smithian imperative to truck and barter. When they stop short at a strictly symbolic economy of circulation and exchange, they remain caught within those circulatory Hegelian modes of expression with which Marx regrettably "coquetted" in the first chapter of *Capital*, missing his fundamental claim in the succeeding chapters that labor, not exchange, produces value, that the ruling class expropriates value before circulating it, and that workers hoping to end that expropriation must respond not with further circulation, but with revolutionary struggle.[52] When they turn the structuralist master metaphor into a global conceit and present all of human culture, including economy, as a language-like circulatory phenomenon, they ignore the warnings of Saussure himself.[53]

Similarly, *negotiation* attempts to cancel both idealist and from-below theories of society. On the one hand, it rejects the idea of an absolute aesthetic origin or expression, for it suggests something pre-existent that one negotiates *with* and *for*. But on the other, it presupposes a class-specific encounter among parties who already possess some of this something and seek more of it. A Roman *negotiator* was neither patrician nor

50. 7, 12, 6, 19.
51. *Learning* 154.
52. *MECW* 35.19. On the premarxist limitations of new historicist "economy," see Richard Halpern, *The Poetics of Primitive Accumulation*, Ithaca, NY, 1991, 13–15; Norbrook, "Life" 105; and Jameson, *Postmodernism* 193.
53. *Course in General Linguistics*, New York 1966, 73, 80. See Sebastiano Timpanaro, *On Materialism*, London 1975, 135–58; and Anderson, *Tracks* 43.

plebeian, but a businessman, especially a banker. Negotiation was *nec otium*, but also *nec labor*—perhaps something like the anxious, mid-level busy-ness of modern academics and other members of the professional–managerial class. And the object of negotiation was always something more than a cultural effect of the negotiation itself. Even relatively immaterial objects of negotiation such as status, recognition, and favor at court reveal a material dimension (office, monopoly, property, title), which always implies the power to exploit and coerce. Any attempt to employ negotiation as a master concept for social analysis can avoid manifest bad faith only by excluding certain important sorts of class experience: no matter how hard we try to claim otherwise, a Puritan capitalist's relation to his English wage laborers and his Barbadian slaves will look rather more like coercion than negotiation.[54] Even those who reject the labor theory of value will probably concede that not everyone in early modern England could live by circulation and negotiation alone, and that nobody, absolutely nobody, enjoyed more than two or three degrees of separation from an arthritic laborer in a field.

Structure and Subject

Critics of the new historicism sometimes complain that it presents us with the spectacle of free human subjectivity ground down by sheer instrumental domination. Greenblatt suggests the inadequacies of this critique when he presents new historicism as a critical reconciliation of marxism and poststructuralism: while marxists like Fredric Jameson define capitalism as a regime of oppressive individuation, and poststructuralists like Lyotard define it as a regime of oppressive totalization, new historicists see it as a dizzying oscillation between the two:

> For capitalism has characteristically generated neither regimes in which all discourses seem coordinated, nor regimes in which they seem radically isolated or discontinuous, but regimes in which the drive towards differentiation and the drive towards monological organization operate simultaneously, or at least oscillate so rapidly as to create the impression of simultaneity.[55]

But social theory like Greenblatt's doesn't simply describe this movement. It also re-enacts it—oscillating so rapidly between a prematurely totalized "system" and "subject" that it blurs out those mediating collective categories, including classes, that comprise and create them. As a result, it attains only what Marx calls the "contemplative" materialism of Feuerbach and the Left Hegelians, which criticizes society yet cannot describe the productive relations that shape it: "The highest point attained by *contemplative*

---

54. In "Negotiation and New Historicism," *PMLA* 105, 1990, 480–81, Theodore Leinwand does briefly suggest that even the relations between slaveholders and slaves should be understood as negotiation, but he returns briskly to Elizabethan drama.
55. *Learning* 151; I think Greenblatt distorts Jameson and exaggerates his own distance from Lyotard.

materialism, that is, materialism which does not comprehend sensuous-ness as practical activity, is the contemplation of single individuals in 'civil society.'"[56]

Capitalist social theory in general moves away from a theory of historical *change* founded in the conflicting praxis of determinate/determinant *groups* in a developing social *totality*, to what Lukács calls the contempla-tion of static *oscillation* between a determined *subject* and a total *system*:

> The contemplative stance adopted toward a process mechanically conforming to fixed laws and enacted independently of man's consciousness and impervious to human intervention, i.e. a perfectly closed system, must likewise transform the basic categories of man's immediate attitude to the world: it reduces space and time to a common denominator and degrades time to the dimension of space.

Such a contemplative materialism oscillates between the "antinomies of bourgeois thought"—

> between subject and object, freedom and necessity, individual and society, form and content, etc. . . . It is important to realise at this point that although bourgeois thought only landed in these antinomies after the very greatest mental exertions, it yet accepted their existential basis as self-evident, as a simply unquestionable reality. Which is to say: bourgeois thought entered into an unmediated relationship with reality as it was given.[57]

Bourgeois contemplative materialism can't see beyond the early capitalist oscillations of early modern culture, as we saw with historical revisionism, which oscillates between atomized factions, contingencies, and personali-ties, and a consensual, unified, and hierarchical world-view, with an accompanying attack on any attempt to construct a "social change expla-nation" that would focus on mediating categories. This oscillation also appears in Montrose's characterization of the Foucauldian process of "subjectification" which, "on the one hand, shapes individuals as loci of consciousness and initiators of action; and, on the other hand, positions, motivates, and constrains them within networks of power beyond their comprehension or control"—two hands that look remarkably similar.[58]

This oscillation allows for distinct analytical emphases. Foucault first celebrated the resistant subjectivity of the mad, then focused on epistemes and the ruthlessly systematic disciplinary archipelago, then turned to a subject-centered aesthetics of existence grounded in classical antiquity and susceptible, perhaps, to a postmodern revival. In his late essay "What is Enlightenment?" he returned to the totalizing object of so much of his earlier criticism—not to reject or accept the Enlightenment out of hand, or to conduct a dialectical critique of it, but to reconstruct the critical

---

56. *MECW* 5.8.
57. *History and Class Consciousness*, Cambridge, MA, 1971, 89, 156.
58. "The Elizabethan Subject and the Spenserian Text," in Patricia Parker and David Quint, eds, *Literary Theory/Renaissance Texts*, Baltimore 1986, 303–40, 306.

"attitude" or "philosophical ethos" at its heart. But for Foucault, this contemplative ethos never focuses on the grand collective projects and groups of the critical and revolutionary Enlightenment: Babeuf and Owen, the United Irishmen and the Black Jacobins, the Sons of Liberty and the Floating Republic, Wollstonecraft's feminism and Fourier's, Thomas Spence's agrarian communism and the origins of English trade unionism. Rather, it turns to Constantin Guy, the "painter of modern life" celebrated by Baudelaire, and to Baudelaire himself and "the asceticism of the dandy who makes of his body, his behavior, his feelings and passions, his very existence, a work of art."

"Couldn't everyone's life become a work of art?" Foucault asks hopefully.[59] Yes, no doubt, but as Alex Callinicos observes, "To invite a hospital porter in Birmingham, a car-worker in São Paulo, a social security clerk in Chicago, or a street child in Bombay to make a work of art of their lives would be an insult—unless linked to precisely the kind of strategy for global social change which . . . poststructuralism rejects."[60] Truly, poststructuralism's critique of modernity (for instance, Foucault on liberal penality) towers over its normative vision, with its pathetic bourgeois appeals to *Homo ludens*, the pleasures of capitalist spectacle, and an aesthetics of existence redolent of the second *cappuccino* before the seminar. The latter deserves not just sober refutation, but peals of laughter. Three crudely Brechtian questions—unanswerable because unposable inside Foucault's genealogy: who built the arcades through which the dandy strolls? Who produced the commodities on display in its windows? Why in 1870 might they choose to turn the arcades into a barricade defending the Commune? Or, to return to the seventeenth century and the model of an Elizabethan world picture or early modern episteme: who hewed wood and drew water for Renaissance Man? Who washed his shirts and cooked his dinner? Why in 1641 might they join their fellow workers in a crowd desecrating a prelatical temple or surrounding and petitioning Parliament? Foucault's (and Greenblatt's) focus on artistic self-fashioning is appealing, but shouldn't we look beyond café cosmopolitanism to the actually existing collective artworks and popular drama of the modern and premodern world—to the commune and the crowd, the barricades and the shattered idol, the libelous ballad and the subscribed petition? Or to those more mundane artworks—a field, a meal, a child, an apocalyptic fuck, a deftly avoided fistfight? Art, and creative practical consciousness, are always all around. Culture is ordinary.[61]

Greenblatt has oscillated from an earlier emphasis on oppressive and relatively systemic totalization to an emphasis on relatively individual "wonder" and negotiation. In 1980, at the end of *Renaissance Self-Fashioning*, he reflected on a significant ambiguity in the title of his book: does it

59. *The Foucault Reader*, New York 1984, 32–50, 40–42, 350.
60. *Against* 90–91.
61. Raymond Williams, *Resources of Hope*, London 1989, 3–18; Bloch, *Principle, passim.*

refer to Renaissance people fashioning themselves, or to the Renaissance fashioning selves?

> In all my texts and documents, there were, so far as I could tell, no moments of pure, unfettered subjectivity; indeed, the human subject itself began to seem remarkably unfree, the ideological product of the relations of power in a particular society. Whenever I focused upon a moment of apparently autonomous self-fashioning, I found not an epiphany of identity freely chosen but a cultural artifact. If there remained traces of free choice, the choice was among possibilities whose range was strictly delineated by the social and ideological system then in force.[62]

Within this system, choice becomes no more than a minor, programmed oscillation, and by no means a free praxis capable of creating new alternatives. The later Greenblatt, like the later Foucault, shifted from system to subject, paying renewed attention to the individual subject's capacity for ecstatic "wonder," even when assaulted by the determining social forces of "resonance."[63] In three recent essays, he argues that a renewed attention to aesthetic wonder will provide us with a conduit to three premodern experiences of the sacred regrettably demystified by an instrumental rationalism associated with Protestantism. This contemplative aesthetics will allow us to experience the sacred intensities of transubstantiation, witchcraft, and bodily mutilation, without necessarily reviving the mass, witch-burning, and torture.[64] But though Greenblatt oscillates between the poles of system and subject, he does not leave the binary bedrock of capitalist social theory for a study of the diverse collective subjectivities of distinct and even antagonistic practical ensembles—for instance, the collective Protestant solidarities that led Anne Askew to choose the stake in 1545 rather than affirm the miracle of the mass. Indeed, when marxism encourages individuals to fuse their wondrous contemplation of present-day contradictions into a collective project aimed at resolving them toward a utopian future, it becomes tainted with a "moral imperative" grounded in "the primal organic unity that it posits as either paradisal origin or utopian, eschatological end."[65]

In this idealist history of ideas, a static idea system determines the subject from above or behind; that subject can at best assume a contemplative relationship to that system—never a comprehensive or transformative one. This model appeals not only to revisionist intellectual historians like Kevin Sharpe, but also to new historicists, who offer "a Renaissance as synchronically isolated and politically uniform as anything

62. Chicago 1980, 256.
63. *Learning* 161–83; *Marvelous Possessions*, Chicago 1991.
64. "Remnants of the Sacred in Early Modern England," in Margreta de Grazia, Maureen Quilligan, and Peter Stallybrass, eds, *Subject and Object in Renaissance Culture*, Cambridge 1996, 337–45; "Shakespeare Bewitched," in Jeffrey N. Cox and Larry J. Reynolds, eds, *New Historical Literary Study*, Princeton 1993, 108–35; "Mutilation and Meaning," in David Hillman and Carla Mazzio, eds, *The Body in Parts*, New York and London 1997, 221–42.
65. *Learning* 151, 149.

we find in E. M. W. Tillyard's *Elizabethan World Picture*."[66] In a late essay, Foucault sounds remarkably like Tillyard or Sharpe when he finds an early modern consensus about the top-down technics of state rule embodied in the metaphor of the ship of state—though in fact, like the body politic metaphor, it became a site of interpretive struggle between absolutists and republicans.[67] Revisionists join new historicists in constructing a world picture that renders opposition a metaphysical impossibility. Lotte Mulligan and Judith Richards say that radical change would have been "theoretically as well as practically unachievable" in early modern England, since any genuine radical would have been trying to move outside "the semantic field" and the "conceptual structures within which the society operated."[68] Walter Benn Michaels says that Theodore Dreiser could have formed a critique of American capitalism only by somehow standing outside society itself.[69] Speaking, it would seem, of all history, Jonathan Goldberg says that "to imagine the overthrow of the present state of things and to make a revolution would seem to involve the destruction of the very limits in which thoughts and actions occur, and there would seem to be no way to express this—and perhaps therefore no way for revolution to occur."[70]

The new historicism has always fallen obediently into ranks behind Jean-François Lyotard's postmodernist battle cry: "Let us wage a war on totality; let us be witnesses to the unpresentable; let us activate the differences and save the honor of the name."[71] Critiques of totalizing thought join a long tradition tying Hegelian and marxist methodological "totalization" to *totality* and then to *totalitarianism*. Foucault, for instance, sees marxism and Freudianism as "totalitarian theories" useful for research only if one curtails, divides, or overthrows their theoretical unity.[72] As Jameson says, such attacks join up with a long counterrevolutionary tradition which warns that any totalizing revolutionary politics leads inevitably to the Terror and *Nineteen Eighty-Four* (I would add "Münster"), and that we might well want to view such attacks as "a systematic repudiation of notions and ideals of praxis as such, or of the collective project."[73] But precisely because this repudiation is *systematic*, we should also see it as a praxis in its own right—a totalizing project no less

66. Lee Patterson, *Negotiating the Past*, Madison 1987, 63.
67. *The Foucault Effect*, London 1991, 93–4. For republican meditations on political mutiny, see George Buchanan, *The Powers of the Crown in Scotland*, Austin 1949, 96; Languet and Mornay, *Vindiciae* 75, 164–5, 168; and William Prynne and John Goodwin, quoted in Michael Walzer, *The Revolution of the Saints*, 1965; rpt New York 1972, 177–83.
68. "A 'Radical' Problem," 122–3.
69. *The Gold Standard and the Logic of Naturalism*, Berkeley and Los Angeles 1987, 18–19.
70. *James I* 264n.4.
71. *Postmodern* 82.
72. *Power/Knowledge* 80–81. John Morrill calls Robert Brenner's *Merchants and Revolution* a collection of "splintered insights . . . a splendid book when it is not arguing a positivist explanation of the English Revolution"—that is, an explanation of any sort ("Conflict" 113, 119).
73. *Postmodernism* 333, 401.

collective than the revolutionary projects it attempts to fragment and destroy. Alienated existence in a capitalist series is no less collective and intersubjective than revolutionary praxis in a fused group, and counter-revolutionary projects are still projects. The attempts by Count Ernst of Mansfield, Prince Metternich, and Richard Nixon to restore docile peas-ant seriality in Germany, France, and Vietnam were no less collective and goal-oriented than the Anabaptist, Jacobin, and communist peasant revolts they attempted to crush.

Similarly, Jameson shows that the most fervidly anti-totalizing interpre-tations always employ totalizing hermeneutics of their own—that the Nietzschean anti-hermeneutics of Deleuze, Guattari, Foucault, Derrida, Baudrillard, Lyotard, Kristeva, and Althusser always conceals a self-denying master code.[74] Althusser's structural marxism has particularly influenced cultural studies and the new historicism by rejecting the humanist critique of alienation and insisting on conjunctures of relatively independent histories—but not without a dissimulated deep structure.[75] In the mean-time, the repressed totalizing *project* returns as totalitarian *system*. Foucault says that "We experienced Sartre's generation as one courageous and generous, with a passion for life, for politics, for existence. . . . But we have discovered something else, another passion: a passion for the con-cept that I will call 'system' . . . an ensemble of relations that maintains and transforms itself independently of the things it relates."[76] Inside a poststructuralist tradition, this passion for system typically follows in the wake of Saussure's structural linguistics, with its founding division between a systemic *langue* in the synchronic present, and the contingent world of individual speech acts or *paroles* and of diachronic linguistic change. For instance, Montrose argues that the new historicist project "reorients the

74. *The Political Unconscious*, Ithaca, NY, 1981, 21–3.
75. Althusser's anti-Hegelian "history without a subject" attempts to move outside hermeneu-tics, but he falls back into an astonishing neo-Hegelianism in his enormously influential essay, "Ideology and Ideological State Apparatuses." He argues that all particular ideol-ogies are the product of an "ideology in general" that exists outside history, where it no doubt communes happily with other such immortal virtuous pagans as the Hegelian Absolute Idea and the Freudian and Lacanian unconscious, its immediate model. He also argues that "the category of the subject" produces *Ideology in general* and historically determinate *ideologies*. Just as capitalism transfers human agency from workers to the commodity fetishes they create, so Althusserian "science" transfers human agency from history to "categories." But in his Afterword, Althusser executes a baffling about-face by turning "ideology in general" from an agency into a mere analytical category, and by arguing that particular ideologies come not from the subject or ideology in general, but from class struggle. Thus he abandons his psychoanalytical determinism and returns to fundamentalist historical materialism, seemingly without being aware that he is doing so (*Lenin and Philosophy and Other Essays*, New York 1971, 127–86, 159–62, 170–71, 184–5). On the complex heritage of Althusser's writing, see Ted Benton, *The Rise and Fall of Structural Marxism*, New York 1984, and Perry Anderson's *Arguments Within English Marxism*, London 1980. Althusserianism had a more productive history in Europe and Britain, where it actively engaged a lively humanist marxist tradition, than in the United States, where it rather quickly assimilated itself to regnant anticommunist ideologies (poststructuralism, psychoanalysis).
76. *Dits et Écrits, 1954–1988*, 4 vols, Paris 1994, 1.514.

axis of intertextuality, substituting for the diachronic text of an autonomous literary history the synchronic text of a cultural system."[77] But he
simply substitutes one term of a deceptively comprehensive binary for
another, and fails to explain why "diachrony" entails bad totality, while a
synchronic text or social system does not.

In the French context of postmodernist theory, "totalization" probably
conjures up the specter of Sartre, whose massive *Critique of Dialectical
Reason* examines the relationship between totalizing projects and the
totalizing reason that tries to understand them. I will discuss Sartrean
totalization in the next chapter, but for the moment, I would simply
emphasize that it is not so much a realized *entity* as a malleable *intention*
embodied in the concrete praxis of a project. Sounding like Bloch, Sartre
stresses its negative relation to the present, its positive relation to the
future: "In relation to the given, *praxis* is negativity; but what is always
involved is the negation of a negation. In relation to the object aimed at,
praxis is a positivity, but this positivity opens onto the 'non-existent,' to
what *has not yet* been."[78] As Jameson says, totalization is

> that process whereby, actively impelled by the project, an agent negates the
> specific object or item and reincorporates it into the larger project-in-course.
> Philosophically, and barring some genuine mutation of the species, it is hard to
> see how human activity under the third, or postmodern, stage of capitalism
> could elude or evade this very general formula.[79]

Sartre describes dialectical criticism as a "regressive/progressive method"
that must "regressively" establish the various conditions of historical
possibility in a particular epoch and the determinations acting upon a
particular person—conditions and determinations that can never be
absolutely known *a priori*—before it "progressively" reconstructs the
attempted synthesis of a project. He faults Albert Guérin's marxist account
of the French Revolution by saying he "*totalizes too quickly.*" He leaps over
the essential regressive moment by "replacing real, perfectly defined
groups (*la Gironde*) by insufficiently determined collectivities (*the bourgeoisie* of importers and exporters)" and produces "that form of idealism—
called 'economism'—which Marx so often denounced."[80]

In the 1980s, Renaissance new historicists frequently fell into a "progressive" premature totalization by moving too quickly from some cultural
artifact to an absolutist world-view, ignoring crucial determinations by
economy, the laboring classes, radical religion, and by culture itself.[81]
More recently, they have turned from Foucault toward an *Annales*-style
cultural history of ideas and everyday life. But at the same time, they have
tended to fall into a "regressive" premature totalization—a synchronic

77. "Professing the Renaissance," Veeser, *New Historicism* 15–36, 17.
78. *SSM* 92.
79. *Postmodernism* 333.
80. *SSM* 45, 43.
81. I consider this omission in "Ranting," and "Ehud's Dagger," *Cultural Critique* 22, 1992.

culturalism that establishes multiple determinations and negotiations, but forbids the "progressive" and temporalizing synthetic movement of the project. By ignoring the subjective idea of a future guiding the individual project, and the intelligible movement of history itself, the new historicism, like revisionism, leaves us with the ever-ready claim that things were very, very complex. By trying to pre-empt any determinate statement at work inside a project of theoretical totalization, this *a priori* pluralism can itself begin to sound rather totalitarian.

As an interpretive method arguing for the essentially political and contested nature of all writing, literature included, we might have expected the new historicism to develop an intense interest in the English Revolution. But it has barely registered the revolutionary years, focusing instead on the exploration narratives, public and private drama, court culture, and the manuscript and print literature of pre-revolutionary England. Like the formalist critics they condemn, new historicists have tended to focus on the years 1580–1625 and to ignore the English Revolution, partly because they tend to view "politics" as something done *to* human subjects, or done in order *to create* them. The committed (but not uncontested) efforts of many early Stuart political and literary ideologists to construct a closed absolutist cultural economy lend themselves to such a treatment, and the new historicist passion for system has produced models of early modern culture as an analogical episteme, a patronage system, a series of theatrical spectacles, a cultural marketplace, a system for courtly self-fashioning or the circulation of social energy, a patriarchal mechanism for stamping out gender identity, a theological unity informed by Calvinist doctrine and discipline, an emergent ideology of imperial nation formation. But it has proved harder to describe a similar economy that would contain the revolutionary era: the turbulent twenties and simmering thirties, the popular tumults of 1640–42, the two civil wars, the rise of the New Model Army, the regicide and its aftermath, the formation of a royalist counter-culture in exile, the Leveller Rising of 1649, the innovative traditionalism of the Clubmen, the entry of women into a revolutionary public sphere, the burgeoning of political theory (patriarchalist, Hobbist, casuist, democratic, communist, republican), and sects (Independents, Separatists, Baptists, Ranters, Quakers, Muggletonians, and millenarians of various stripes)—all articulated in an explosion of presses, pamphlets, and newsbooks. The English Revolution calls for something more than a thick description or a philosophically rigorous debunking of the liberal humanist subject; it encourages us to view politics as something done *by* human subjects in groups—a complex array of elective practices by which people can at times remake themselves and their own history.

Change, Containment, and Subversion

New historicists seem to be uninterested in or incapable of addressing one of the most traditional meanings of "history": why social conflicts arise, and how and why society changes. The reason may be the new historicist debt to the tradition of Saussurean structural linguistics, whose inadequacies in providing an account of linguistic change—never mind social change in general—are notorious. As Sartre pointed out thirty years ago, Saussurean structuralism works better at explaining "steady-state" objects like a system of myth than at explaining entire human societies, which always have a history—even those "cold" societies that Lévi-Strauss saw as relatively static. Lévi-Strauss can only explain historical change as the product of some contingency: external events, war, or famine may alter the social system, but people themselves never modify the system— they are, "on the contrary, made by it."[82]

Like the revisionists' monographic imagination, the new historicists' focus on authors or epistemes usually allows them to ignore or nuance this problem. They can even deploy an arsenal of vaguely materialist concepts ("the middle class," "possessive individualism," "imperialism," "the market economy," "production," "circulation," "bourgeois subjectivity," "force relations," "print capitalism," "economy of X," "cultural capital"), so long as they never discuss where they came from, or what might lie outside of them. If revisionist historians of early modern England find capitalism always just around the next corner, and thus unmentionable, postmodern critics typically find it always just past the last one, and thus inexplicable. The new historicist anecdote at the beginning of a book or essay strategically shifts attention away from the question of diachronic historical *change* and toward the question of synchronic structural *homology*—the parallel functioning of the nonliterary anecdote, the literary work, and the social system.[83] Here, they follow Foucault, who jump-starts his books with striking emblematic diptychs: the ship of fools vs the asylum, Pomme's analogical cure of a hysteric vs Bayle's clinical observation of meningitis, Damiens's scaffold vs Faucher's itinerary.[84] Foucault's sheer artistic brilliance stuns and dazzles while drowning out those embarrassing questions about causes and transitions which will be properly posable only if "a theory of scientific change and epistemological causality was to be constructed." While we await such an unlikely development, we should maintain a pious silence and contemplate these epiphanic moments when "the mode of being of things . . . was profoundly altered."[85]

---

82. Sartre, "Replies to Structuralism," *Telos* 9, 1971, 111–12. See also the critiques of Saussure by Timpanaro, *Materialism* 147–50; and V. N. Vološinov, *Marxism and the Philosophy of Language*, Cambridge, MA, 1973, 56–60, 116–17.
83. Jameson, *Postmodernism* 192–3.
84. *Madness and Civilization*, New York 1973, 3–37; *The Birth of the Clinic*, New York 1975, ix–x; *Discipline* 3–7.
85. *The Order of Things*, New York 1970, xxiii, xxii.

But when we abandon a periodization based in class struggle and the mode of production for a modernizing journey from the world we have lost to the world we have now, or with a hop, skip, and jump through the epistemes, or with a postmarxist shuffle from the industrial era of production to the post-industrial era of information, or with a meta-master-narrative lamenting our fall from an authentic primitive era of mythic micronarratives into an Enlightenment era of delusively emancipatory metanarratives, we may very well lose the totalizing or explanatory quality of historical materialism. But by no means do we avoid a total claim to mastery.[86] Foucault's emblems and new historicist anecdotes amalgamate *contingency* (their out-of-nowhere quality) with a certain *necessity* (their striking poetic immediacy), implying an oscillatory theory of history characteristic of the structuralist and poststructuralist tradition, and capitalist history more generally. As Perry Anderson says, poststructuralism's vision of history began as a "total and initial determinism" and ended in "the restatement of an absolute final contingency, in mimicry of the duality of *langue* and *parole* itself."[87] Rejecting both Christian and Greek (and marxist) conceptions of history, Foucault finds that proper or "effective" history demands acceptance of "only one kingdom, without providence or final cause, where there is only 'the iron hand of necessity shaking the dice-box of chance.'"[88] Rejecting historical materialist teleology, Ernesto Laclau and Chantal Mouffe find the postmarxist social sciences transformed by a new "logic of contingency."[89] Rejecting "social change interpretations" of the English Revolution, with their focus on individual and collective agency inside a contradictory and mutable structure, Mark Kishlansky finds that properly revisionist history must discover how "contingent circumstance in a traditional environment dictated the course of events."[90] Structure/Agency thickens into System/Subject, which stiffens into Necessity/Contingency, or *Tyche Tyrannos*: the dead hand and dead end of postmodernist, postmarxist, and revisionist social theory.[91]

When their critics press them to address squarely the question of historical change, and "contingency" proves a shaky ally, postmodernists try to hobble "history" with question-begging adjectives, so that it becomes "autonomous," "seamless," "transparent," "positivist," "linear," "progressive," "whig," "chiliastic," or "eschatological" history—a God- or

---

86. On Foucault's model of power/knowledge as a total theory, see Callinicos, *Against* 85; and Dews, *Logics* 188.
87. *Tracks* 50–51.
88. *Language* 155, quoting Nietzsche's *The Dawn*.
89. *Hegemony and Socialist Strategy*, London 1985, 3.
90. "What Must Be" 83.
91. Since capitalist historians usually ignore workers, their turn to "contingency" is no great surprise. Marxists ignoring the agency of the state or the ruling class might be forced to a similar expedient. But contingency itself, as the metaphysical conflation of freedom and necessity, suggests the spectral return of the wage laborer, "who is compelled to sell himself of his own free-will" (*MECW* 35.753)—increasingly, in a labor market emphasizing "contingent" or "just in time" labor.

Enlightenment- or Marx-sick vision of the Big Story. For instance, when Lyotard's avant-garde, waging its war on totality, turns from a synchronic to a diachronic axis, its enemy changes from structural totality to "metan-arratives."[92] Laclau and Mouffe find in marxist history the "eschatological" belief that "an absolutely united working class will become transparent at the moment of proletarian chiliasm."[93] Don E. Wayne says that new historicists eschew "the eschatological or teleological connotations of the term 'history.'"[94] In his introduction to *The New Historicism*, H. Aram Veeser spurns those "defenders of linear chronology and progressive history, whether marxists or Whig optimists." In the same volume, Green-blatt finds "chiliastic expectations" in Jameson's "eschatological" marxist history, while Montrose groups the "Marxian master narrative" with "the great code of Christian figural and eschatological history."[95] In 1971, Jameson responded to these arguments with his usual eschatological prescience by noting that they do not so much assimilate marxism to religion as religion to marxism, revealing it to be a complex, totalizing hermeneutic with worldly aims.[96] With these anticlerical pejoratives—including that anticommunist chestnut, always presented as a fresh and cheeky aperçu, that pronounces marxism an unselfconscious religious fanaticism—new historicists reveal their difficulty in leaving the court and stage for a concrete discussion of religion and the religious impetus behind social change in early modern England. Radical religion formed the primary medium of totalizing and transformative thought for early modern radicals, including those whom I consider in this book. Their chiliasm gave them not a realized model of the New Jerusalem, but a crucial tool for thinking about and working against the oppressions of their day. For them, *apokalypsis* forms neither a *totalized state of being* nor a *transparency of the signifier* but a *totalizing project*—a praxis of uncovering, critical thought, struggle, defeat, and sometimes even victory.

A traditional, Smithian model of historical change as the magical self-generation of modernity frequently haunts a number of ostensibly anti-teleological models. For instance, in *Hegemony and Socialist Strategy*, a work of unrivalled authority for postmarxist cultural studies, Laclau and Mouffe retool a synchronic structural analysis as a diachronic historical analysis, overcoming vulgar marxist schemes of linear history by turning the French Revolution into its own cause: "The democratic principle of liberty and

92. *Postmodern* xxiv. Lyotard blames marxist and liberal metanarratives for Auschwitz, and says that "In Nazism there were plenty of lefts" ("Defining the Postmodern," in Lisa Appignanesi, ed., *Postmodernism, ICA Documents 4 and 5*, London 1986, 6–7, 6; and quoted in Philippe Lacoue-Labarthe, "On the Sublime," ibid. 7–9, 9). Since Nazis killed hundreds of thousands of communists and tens of millions of others in the name of anticommunism, this exquisite aphorism recalls revisionist efforts to blame the Holocaust on European Jewry.
93. *Hegemony* 84.
94. "New Historicism" 794.
95. Veeser, "Introduction," *New Historicism* i–xvi, xv; Greenblatt, "Towards a Poetics of Culture," ibid. 1–14, 5; Montrose, "Professing" 20.
96. *Marxism and Form*, Princeton 1971, 116–18.

equality first had to impose itself as the new matrix of the social imaginary; or, in our terminology, to constitute a fundamental nodal point in the construction of the political." The French Revolution "was the first to found itself on no other legitimacy than the people."[97] Laclau and Mouffe sneak into the "pre-democratic" world a germinal version of the "democratic" intentionality whose very emergence they purport to explain, while their franglais reflexive verbs do heroic work in reinstalling a neo-Hegelian Spirit of the Age as the identical subject/object of history.

In moments of particular stress, anticommunist history and criticism may even turn to marxist schemes of historical change. In *Discipline and Punish*, after telling us that "where power is concerned," one must abandon "the metaphor of property," Foucault reintroduces not just the metaphor but the thing itself when he describes the birth of modern power:

> Furthermore, as it was acquired in part by the bourgeoisie, now free of the feudal burdens that once weighed upon it, landed property became absolute property: all the tolerated "rights" that the peasantry had acquired or preserved . . . were now rejected. . . . With the new forms of capital accumulation, new relations of production and the new legal status of property, all the popular practices that belonged, either in a silent, everyday, tolerated form, or in a violent form, to the illegality of rights were reduced by force to an illegality of property. . . . Or, to put it another way, the economy of illegalities was restructured with the development of capitalist society. The illegality of property was separated from the illegality of rights. This distinction represents a class opposition.

Foucault even reinvents Marx's analysis of primitive accumulation as a twofold process: "If the economic take-off of the West began with the techniques that made possible the accumulation of capital, it might perhaps be said that the methods for administering the accumulation of men made possible a political take-off in relation to the traditional, ritual, costly, violent forms of power."[98] Friedrich Martin Foucault, the genealogist of power and Being, briefly morphs into Karl E. P. Foucault, the historian of capitalism and struggles over property and popular rights.[99]

The new historicist system/subject model does not altogether ignore opposition. Rather, it changes opposition from the diachronic project of an oppositional collective to a synchronic function of the system itself. In Stephen Greenblatt's phrase, it effects *the containment of subversion*—the process by which one sort of practice incorporates and turns to its uses a contrary one. Greenblatt developed this concept in his studies of Tudor

97. 154–5.
98. 28, 85–7, 220–21.
99. Ferry and Renaut note Foucault's recourse to incompatible "Nietzscheo-Heideggerean" and marxist registers of explanation (*French Philosophy of the Sixties*, Amherst, MA, 1990, 71–81). See also Teresa L. Ebert on Judith Butler: "for all Butler's discursive displacements, the concealed, sutured-over *base* of her own theory is still the *economic base*" (*Ludic Feminism and After*, Ann Arbor, MI, 1999, 219).

and Stuart culture.[100] And we can find analogs in the writings of Mandeville (private vices, public benefits), Adam Smith (the invisible hand), Hegel (the cunning of reason), and many others. Indeed, marxists have found a contained subversion model crucial for understanding the systemic genius of capitalism, which makes functional the mobile and unemployed population and the impulse to compete and accumulate—"subversive" forces that terrified earlier ruling classes. In "On the Jewish Question," Marx himself shows how formal democracy's potential subversiveness can wind up being contained by and reinforcing the structural inequalities of capitalist civil society.[101] Marcuse updates Marx with his theory of "repressive desublimation."[102] Speaking of Gramsci's conception of hegemony, a model of domination through strategic toleration, Raymond Williams observes, "It can be persuasively argued that all or nearly all initiatives and contributions, even when they take on manifestly alternative or oppositional forms, are in practice tied to the hegemonic: that the dominant culture, so to say, at once produces and limits its own forms of counter culture."[103] Sartre traces the way in which reified collectives work to transform subversive, self-affirming *praxis* into contained, system-affirming *exis*.[104] And historical materialists should welcome Greenblatt's dissection of the "fatuous and presumptuous" argument of left avant-gardist formalism that "certain rhetorical features in much-loved literary works constitute authentic acts of political liberation."[105]

But all too frequently, the theory of contained subversion becomes a global theory of society or a metaphysic implying that only the discovery of moments of preordained failure can count as sophisticated criticism—an impulse born, perhaps, of the fear of being caught out in a moment of uncauterized new left idealism. The concept of contained subversion has proved particularly attractive to new historicists encountering what looks like opposition to Tudor/Stuart absolutism. Janet Halley finds that, when Elizabethan Familists practiced radical equivocation by assigning private meanings to prescribed words and practices so as to conform outwardly to Anglican church discipline, they had already "spoken their own prohibition; the heretics' subversive sign has been subverted by a textuality of the state."[106] For Richard Wilson, *Julius Caesar* siphons off "the subversiveness of popular festivity in the representation of a deflected and contained rebellion," thus anticipating "the counterrevolution of the Cromwellian

100. See his discussions of Marlowe's characters (*Renaissance* 209), of "contained subversion" in Thomas Harriot's exploration narrative and Shakespeare's *Henriad*, and of "salutary anxiety" in *The Tempest* (*Shakespearean* 21–65, 138). See also *Learning* 92–3.
101. *MECW* 3.146–74.
102. "Repressive Tolerance," in Herbert Marcuse, Robert P. Wolff, and Barrington Moore, Jr, *A Critique of Pure Tolerance*, Boston 1965, 56–83.
103. *Marxism and Literature*, Oxford 1977, 114.
104. *SCDR* 255.
105. *Learning* 166.
106. "Heresy, Orthodoxy, and the Politics of Religious Discourse," *Representations* 15, 1986, 320.

Commonwealth" and "the coercive strategy of those subtle London masters who 'stir up servants in an act of rage' . . . the better to control them." Not only does aristocratic cunning contain plebeian subversion, but Shakespeare's Elizabethan play prophetically contains the entire English Revolution.[107] The revisionist historian Glenn Burgess criticizes the contained subversion model for exaggerating the absolutist severity of early modern England, which he sees rather as a softer-edged consensual totality. But the thing if not the name reappears when he argues that "patterns of conflict found in late-Tudor and early-Stuart England reinforced stability and order rather than undermining them."[108] When Richard Burt and Jonathan Goldberg encounter early Stuart republicanism in political theory, historical writing, literature, and drama, they argue that it is, at best, a form of absolutism in a self-deceptive guise—analogous to modern "humanism" in its impulse to dissimulate its rancorous will to power.[109] Jonathan Dollimore warns that, when we piece together the shards of history from below, we may well find only "the self-division intrinsic to (and which thereby perpetuates) subordination." We can ever find in "a repressed subculture that most utopian of fantasies: an alternative to the dominant, which is simultaneously subversive of it and self-authenticating."[110]

But this is a fantasy dreamed by a straw man. "Self-authenticating" opposition hardly covers the whole field, and may not cover any of it—it would be hard to find this romantic concept at work in the writings of any early modern radical group, or even any Romantic one.[111] Any claim that subversion lurks inside society or language or being as such must remain problematic for a marxist tradition—as we can see in Marx and Gramsci's own committed work in communist political organizing, and in Williams's continuation of the passage I quote above: "it would be wrong to overlook the importance of works and ideas which, while clearly affected by hegemonic limits and pressures, are at least in part significant breaks beyond them."[112] And Sartre distinguishes between that *locally* contained subversion that we know as a *trap*, whereby a military force uses its opponents' freedom of movement to lure them to their own destruction, and the more common phenomenon of simple *failure*:

> For every *praxis*, to some degree, takes account of its areas of ignorance, reckons on *probabilities* (in the strict sense of the term), makes wagers, and takes risks.

107. " 'Is This a Holiday?' " *ELH* 54, 1987, 41.
108. "Revisionist" 11.
109. Burt, " 'A Dangerous Rome,' " in Marie-Rose Logan and Peter L. Rudnytsky, eds, *Contending Kingdoms*, Detroit 1991, 109–27, 111, 122; Goldberg, *James I* 72–6, 96–7, 190.
110. "Introduction" to Dollimore and Alan Sinfield, eds, *Political Shakespeare*, Ithaca, NY, 1985, 2–17, 14–15.
111. More recently, both Dollimore (*Sexual Dissidence*, Oxford 1991) and Alan Sinfield (*Faultlines*, Berkeley and Los Angeles 1992) have preferred "dissidence" to mechanically contained "subversion." See particularly Sinfield's fine critique of the "entrapment" (or "contained subversion") model of culture (38–42).
112. *Marxism and Literature* 114.

The freedom of an action which ends in failure is simply freedom which fails, since the fundamental relation of the organism to its environment is univocal. Matter does not make a constitutive return to praxis in order to transform it into a controlling fatality.[113]

"Praxis" for Sartre, like "hope" for Bloch, is that which *can be* disappointed—not that which *can't be* (like the telos of linear history), not that which *must be* (like "contained subversion").

In its more extreme form, the contained subversion model joins in the larger anticommunist effort to depict collective conflicts as functional aspects of the social whole, deluded projections of the pathological individual, or both. Capitalist ideologists must transform what looks like a dream of a distinct future into an oblique, neurotic reinforcement of the present. Jameson sees something like contained subversion implicit in the system/subject model favored by capitalist ideologists in general, whether the "harder" analysts of totalitarian domination (Weber, Foucault), or the "softer" celebrators of an all-penetrating society of consumption (Baudrillard, Daniel Bell): "the model of the 'total system' would seem slowly and inexorably to eliminate any possibility of the *negative* as such, and to reintegrate the place of an oppositional or even merely 'critical' practice and resistance back into the system as the latter's mere inversion."[114] Similarly, Adorno observes that bourgeois cultural politics since Hegel has tried "to unmask anyone who seeks to change things as both the genuine child and the perverse product of the whole which he opposes, and has insisted that the truth is always on the side of the whole, be it against him or present in him."[115] We can see variants in the New Critical fondness for the *concordia discors* as an aesthetic ideal, the revisionist model of functional factional striving, and Foucault's vision of the penal discipline that produces and circulates delinquents.[116] The specifically new historicist version of this argument typically assails "utopian" (read, "marxist") thinking, but springs from a stifled utopia of its own: the end of the postwar economic boom and the counterculture in the early 1970s, when liberal-left Western academics began to project their experience onto all the world and all of history.[117] From a position of transcendental synchronic critique, postmodernist cynicism jettisons transcendental historical idealism prematurely, without adequately thinking *through* it. Having mislaid the rational kernel, it contemplates the radical idealist husk with archly bemused or melancholy or horrified disgust. Any "eschatological"

---

113. *SCDR* 237.
114. *Political* 91.
115. *Prisms*, London 1967, 106–7.
116. *Discipline* 257–92.
117. For Terry Eagleton, "almost every central feature of postmodern theory can be deduced, read off as it were, from the assumption of a major political defeat" ("Where Do Postmodernists Come From?" in Ellen Meiksins Wood and John Bellamy Foster, eds, *In Defense of History*, New York 1997, 17–25, 23). David Suchoff links new historicist contained subversion to Cold War ideology in "New Historicism and Containment," *Arizona Quarterly* 48.1, 1992.

oppositional practice that failed to deliver the New Jerusalem on schedule must have been controlled all along from a secret office in Babylon.

And indeed, if we see all opposition as that of subversives struggling to attain an Archimedean vantage point outside language and culture from which to criticize the dominant order, then, of course, they will be recontained; the autonomous subversive subject will be revealed as a self-mystified product of the dominant social system itself. But when we replace this melancholy whiggery with an analysis of praxis, the subversive becomes a mere revolutionary—a less dashing figure, perhaps, but also one less prone to facile deconstruction. Actual revolutionaries, from early modern Europe to the present, tend to set out not from some will-to-subvert, but from a normative principle—often a very traditional one claiming to be the betrayed and abandoned essence of society as a whole. Just as modern radicals claim to be champions of democracy and friends to the people, so early modern radicals claim to be restorers of Apostolic purity in religion (Protestant radicals in general), the protectors of king and commonwealth from evil counselors (John Felton and his friends), defenders of England's ancient liberties against Norman usurpers (Levellers), God's allies against Antichrist and the Beast (Fifth Monarchists), defenders of the Good Old Cause (republicans), restorers of Edenic common preservation (Diggers). In fact, I think we could draw a significant general contrast between the fundamentally *immanent dialectical critique* practiced by early modern radicals, who typically reject ruling-class *hypocrisy*, and the fundamentally *extrinsic hierarchical denunciation* practiced by their opponents, who typically attack radical *monstrosity*. If contained subversion is an important "synchronic" principle whereby the ruling class "thinks" its own resistance and attempts to make it functional, using the delusive dream of a radically distinct future to reinforce the present, then equally important is the dialectical and "diachronic" principle of subverted containment, whereby an oppositional collective "thinks" the ruling class, discovers its self-divisions, appropriates its functional structures and ideologies, and integrates them in an oppositional project, using the contradictions of the hierarchical present to realize the dream of an associative future.

Post-revisionism and Its Prospects

The constitutive revisionist dilemma: after we have shown the pure "chronistic" self-identity of a premodern epoch, utterly alien to our own, why study history at all, except for the guild-proud pleasures of a pointless master contemplating his pointless apprentices? The parallel postmodernist dilemma: after we dispose of natural law, human nature, liberty, utopia, and *the future*, how can we provide a ground for social critique? Even if we can, why bother? As Habermas asks Foucault, "if it is just a matter of mobilizing counter-power, of strategic battles and wily confrontations, why should we muster any resistance at all against this all-pervasive power circulating in the bloodstream of the body of modern society, instead of just adapting ourselves to it?"[118] The illusionless postmodern ideologist who attacks those sentimental and anachronistic historians seeking exemplary early modern revolutionaries begins to resemble the premodern ideologists of hierarchy attacking those revolutionaries as the many-headed hydra. Gazing at the poems, pageants, and plays of early modern England, new historicists take on the melancholy of Max Weber contemplating the modern world's post-religious iron cage of bureaucratic domination, even when (especially when) they add a Nietzschean exordium to turn this melancholy science into a gay one, full of canny negotiation and rapt wonder.[119] And there is little to choose between inhabiting one's "natural" (and therefore immutable) link in the premodern great chain of being, and hugging one's "socially constructed" (and therefore immutable) node in the postmodern network of subjectification. Second nature might as well be first nature if there is no possibility of a third.

But there is always a third. Despite revisionists' frequent proclamations of victory in the historiographical wars, they have received sustained criticism. Similarly, amid a colliding host of annunciatory prolegomena, furious critiques, and elegiac summings-up, the very name "new historicism" has acquired a fine patina, and a census of literary critics might turn up no more self-identified "New Historicists" than "New Critics." If the name fits at all, it would appear that former new historicists are moving beyond courtly literature toward a model of early modern England that does not pronounce the English Revolution an *a priori* impossibility. "Cambridge Studies in Renaissance Literature and Culture," a recent book series edited by Stephen Orgel, promises something like a new new historicism, which would move well beyond the anecdote, opening itself up to British scholarship and to allied methodologies, including marxism. Stephen Greenblatt and Catharine Gallagher have just written a study of the new historicism, which should be a turning point of sorts.[120]

Nonetheless, I think that a critique of these two intellectual movements is by no means beside the point, for neither was all that new in 1980, and neither is all that old in 2000. With a familiar manifesto rhetoric, each began by exaggerating the previous strength of its predecessors, its own newness, and the heroic magnitude of its triumph over them. In the whiggish tones of a smug amphibian, Foucault observes that "Marxism exists in nineteenth-century thought like a fish in water: that is, it is unable to breathe anywhere else."[121] Poor Sartre, the "last Hegelian" and "last marxist," whose *Critique* was "the magnificent and pathetic attempt by a nineteenth-century man to think the twentieth century," lies flopping like a beached trout.[122] Jonathan Clark concludes his revisionist manifesto

118. *Philosophical* 283–4.
119. *The Protestant Ethic and the Spirit of Capitalism*, New York 1958, 181.
120. *Practicing the New Historicism*, Chicago 2000.
121. *Order* 262.
122. *Dits* 1.541.

by noting the ages of the British marxist historians, those "voices from the past—a surprisingly remote past." With a sly wink, he observes, "To a large extent, the debate is one between generations; it will be resolved in the way all such debates have to be settled."[123] Here we see whig history in full flush ("My generation will survive yours!"), and the coarse but immensely gratifying archetype of all irony ("You're dead, and I'm not!"). But Clark's comment is no more profound as a reflection on the complexities of intellectual history than it is generous as the observation of a youngish but—alas, like all of us—aging scholar. Every man or woman that is born of a woman hath but a short time to live, and afterlives are tricky to calculate. The same is true for all authors, even Jonathan Clark, and of the books they write, and it is not clear that the time, times, and half-a-time of the new millennium will find Clark's *Revolution and Rebellion* (1986) less remote than Christopher Hill's *The World Turned Upside Down* (1972), or Lawrence Stone's *The Causes of the English Revolution* (1972), or E. P. Thompson's *The Making of the English Working Class* (1963), or Herbert Aptheker's *American Negro Slave Revolts* (1943).[124] If Brixton or Belfast or Oakland explodes next year, my money will be on the old boys.

But in any case, we should remember that the product of capitalist intellectual labor demands that effect of newness that is a secondary quality of all commodities. Anyone who has internalized revisionism's false memory of its radical break with an alleged whig–marxist hegemony from 1945 to 1975 will encounter with surprise the actual records of that past, for earlier attacks by liberals on marxist "reductionism" anticipate uncannily later revisionist attacks on liberal reductionism.[125] We might best see revisionism as a passing mutation within anticommunist historiography, whereby a conservative avant-garde first retools its anticommunist arguments for a bit of internal purging and policing by conflating anticommunist liberals with marxists, then grudgingly readmits the former to the fold. The marxist *Other* remains constant, however. Habermas's argument about the Enlightenment and its conservative critics, which I presented in the conclusion of the previous chapter, highlights the longer-term contours of intellectual postmodernity, revealing ostensibly avant-garde intellectual movements as conceptual moments in a larger history rather than discrete stages. This awareness may in turn encourage skepticism toward last week's claims for a seismic shift in the global terrain of intellectual inquiry. Such shifts seldom take us far from an attack on marxist reduction and Cartesian dualism, a celebration of local texture over logical structure, and a top-down history of ruling-class ideas, all of which we could trace back to John Crowe Ransom, if not to Coleridge. The postcolonial cultural

---

123. *Revolution* 70.
124. New York 1993.
125. See, for instance, J. H. Hexter's famous quarrel with Christopher Hill, before he became a ferocious liberal opponent of revisionism. For Hexter, Hill, and the ensuing controversy, see *The Times Literary Supplement*, October 24, November 7, November 14, and December 12 1975.

theory passionately embraced by North American academics in the last decade has efficiently replaced the third term of the multiculturalist trinity, "gender, race, and class," with "nation," but it does not move noticeably beyond the well-furnished culs-de-sac of Young Conservative received wisdom. For instance, Homi K. Bhabha transforms "Marx's reserve army of migrant labour" into "Nietzsche's mobile army of metaphors, metonyms, and anthropomorphisms," warning us with authentic Nietzschean hauteur that we must not "too hastily associate with the spontaneous and primordial *presence* of the people in the liberatory discourses of populist ressentiment." No doubt, the absent yet somehow also resentful plebs are anxiously waiting for us to make up our minds.[126]

Habermas's scheme should encourage us to maintain not only a critical skepticism toward the "new," but also a conservative openness to the unexhausted utopian truth content of the "old" that the avant gardes claim to have superseded. A response to the system/subject model ruling both revisionist political history and new historicist literary history has been underway for some time now through a study of oppositional culture in early modern England. Indeed, one could argue that this study has always been underway. A theoretically adventurous criticism determined to demonstrate its seismic break with all existent criticism might be inclined to characterize the period of 1935–77 as the benighted epoch of high formalism, when the New Critics' fixation on lyric poetry and the independence of literature *qua* literature from its historical and political context should have made revolutionary-era pamphlets quite invisible. Yet during this period appeared excellent editions of the Army Debates; of the writings of Oliver Cromwell, the Levellers, the Diggers, and Harrington; and the first volumes of that prodigious corporate achievement, the Yale *Complete Prose Works of John Milton.* This period also saw the work of a number of brilliant writers on Puritanism and the revolutionary era who were by no means given to glib denunciations of historicism and celebrations of irony and paradox: William Haller, Perry Miller, A. S. P. Woodhouse, Don M. Wolfe, Geoffrey Nuttall, Joseph Frank, Pauline Gregg, Christopher Hill, A. L. Morton, David Petegorsky, H. N. Brailsford, Olivier Lutaud, J. G. A. Pocock, Brian Manning, Sacvan Bercovitch, and many others. Typically, these writers practice a mix of social and intellectual history some distance from the poststructuralist emphasis of the newer literary historicisms, and most are humanists, even *Christian* humanists.[127] But it never occurred to any of them to polarize literary and

126. "DissemiNation," in Bhabha, ed., *Nation and Narration*, New York 1989, 291–320, 315, 317. For a critique of anticommunist postcolonial criticism, see Aijaz Ahmad's *In Theory*, London 1992; and "Postcolonial Theory and the 'Post-' Condition," *Socialist Register 1997*, London 1997.

127. "Humanism" seems to be one of those "essentialisms" that may be safely defined in essentializing terms, then jettisoned. For some response, see Kate Soper, *Humanism and Anti-Humanism*, La Salle, IL, 1986; Ferry and Renaut, *French Philosophy*; and Michael Landmann's "Talking with Ernst Bloch," *Telos* 25, 1975. Bloch acknowledges Marx's critique of Feuerbach's humanism, in which "the genus *man* is absolutized, a dull dew

non-literary writing, and their diverse disciplinary associations make recent pronouncements about the epochal, imminent merger of literary and historical studies seem a little stale. Their concrete study of language in culture and of the English Revolution has not yet been thoroughly assimilated by revisionists or postmodernists studying seventeenth-century England.

Despite some exaggerated visions of an absolutist episteme ruling early modern literature, critics of Renaissance English drama have seldom been able to follow revisionist historians in claiming that no one could imagine, much less advocate, tyrannicide before 1649.[128] If we wish to consider the ability of early Stuart citizens to assemble in groups and think critically and collectively about authority, tyranny, and resistance, then Parliament's failure to debate *Vindiciae, Contra Tyrannos* tells us less than London's obsession with antityrannical revenge tragedies and Roman plays—cultural productions that looped back around into political practice, as we will see in chapter 5, when I consider the Senecan idioms praising John Felton for assassinating the Duke of Buckingham. Cultural materialist critics, whatever their overstatements about the extent to which the public stage *actually* deconsecrated Renaissance sovereignty—perhaps never all that consecrated in the first place—have shown the futility of pretending that Renaissance drama was an absolutist state apparatus and ignoring those fifth-act heaps of noble bodies. The classic work here is Dollimore's *Radical Tragedy*: though it overestimates the oppressive unity of Christian providentialism and underestimates the power of capitalist surplus extraction in maintaining ruling-class hegemony, it remains a brilliant and trailblazing study.[129] Most encouraging of all, there are signs of increasing critical interest in the pamphlet wars of the Revolution, and in restoring the middle of the century to early modern literary history. In recent years, publishers have reissued classic collections of primary documents, and published several new ones.[130] Miltonists have spread their

---

of love pours out with repetitious 'man' and 'humanity' and blurs all opposites and distinctions in false toleration." This *man* "can go chase himself," but the "historical efficacy of humanism has not, it seems to me, been given its full due, for humanism is dealt with as a criminal offense by every Stalinistic state absolutism. At the end of the Stalin era, it was enough to say the words 'humanist socialism' to be in danger of prison. Can then a concept be so invalid, if it was considered so dangerous by the repressive, degenerate nonfulfillment of socialism?" (171). True enough, but a little disingenuous, given Bloch's late break with Stalinism.

128. Neither Morrill (*Nature* 285–306), nor Burgess (*Absolute*), nor Russell, who argues that the "doctrine of resistance was literally unmentionable" (*Fall* 460), seriously considers drama as a medium of early Stuart resistance theory.

129. See Dollimore's Introduction to *Radical Tragedy*, 2nd edn, New York 1989, xi–lxviii; Franco Moretti, "'A Huge Eclipse,'" in Stephen Greenblatt, ed., *The Power of Forms in the English Renaissance*, Norman, OK, 1982, 7–40; Rebecca W. Bushnell, *Tragedies of Tyrants*, Ithaca, NY, 1990; Albert H. Tricomi, *Anticourt Drama in England, 1603–1642*, Charlottesville, VA, 1989; and Susan Wiseman, *Drama and Politics in the English Civil War*, Cambridge 1998.

130. *DRD*; Howard Erskine-Hill and Graham Storey, eds, *Revolutionary Prose of the English Civil War*, Cambridge 1983; William Walwyn, *The Writings of William Walwyn*, Athens, GA, 1989; Joad Raymond, ed., *Making the News*, New York 1993; Nigel Smith, ed., *A Collection*

nets wider, rediscovering an interest in Milton's contemporaries as something more than background or context.[131] Several literary critical books, collections of essays, and special issues of journals have focused largely or exclusively on revolutionary-era writers, and others are in the works.[132] The renewed critical attention to early modern women writers has brought long-overdue attention to the women writers of the revolutionary era.[133] Several book-length studies of revolutionary-era writing from a generally literary-critical perspective have appeared in recent years.[134]

On the level of theory and method, the revisionist and new historicist challenge has been taken up by a diverse group of post-revisionists. Historians such as Sarah Barber, Alastair Bellany, Richard Cust, Ann Hughes, Peter Lake, and Johann Sommerville have shown the existence of an anti-absolutist, Puritan, and even republican culture in early Stuart England. Literary critics such as Sharon Achinstein, Joad Raymond, and Nigel Smith have reconstructed the oppositional rhetorics and genres of seventeenth-century republicanism and radical sectarianism. No book better embodies this longstanding post-revisionist focus on oppositional culture than David Norbrook's *Poetry and Politics in the English Renaissance*[135]—a study that rivals Greenblatt's *Renaissance Self-Fashioning* in its ambition, its achievement, and its effort to bring recent work in cultural theory into play in the interpretation of English Renaissance culture. Both

---

of Ranter Writings from the 17th Century, London 1983. In 1971, the Cornmarket Press (London) produced a massive facsimile reprint of revolutionary newsbooks in a series entitled "The English Revolution."

131. Sharon Achinstein, *Milton and the Revolutionary Reader*, Princeton 1994; David Armitage, Armand Himy, and Quentin Skinner, eds, *Milton and Republicanism*, Cambridge 1995; Thomas N. Corns, *Uncloistered Virtue*, Oxford 1992; Laura Lunger Knoppers, *Historicizing Milton*, Athens, GA, 1994; David Loewenstein and James Grantham Turner, eds, *Politics, Poetics, and Hermeneutics in Milton's Prose*, Cambridge 1990; Annabel Patterson, *Reading Between the Lines*, Madison 1993; John Rogers, *The Matter of Revolution*, Ithaca, NY, 1996; Elizabeth Skerpan, *The Rhetoric of Politics in the English Revolution*, Columbia, MO, 1992.

132. Sharon Achinstein, ed., "Special Issue: Gender, Literature and the English Revolution," *Women's Studies* 24, 1994; Francis Barker et al., *1642: Literature and Power in the Seventeenth Century*, Colchester 1981; Thomas N. Corns, ed., *The Literature of Polemical Strategy from Milton to Junius*, London 1987; Corns and David Loewenstein, eds, *The Emergence of Quaker Writing*, London 1995; *HS*; James Holstun, ed., *Pamphlet Wars*, London 1992; Joad Raymond, ed., *News, Newspapers and Society in Early Modern Britain*, London 1999; Claude J. Summers and Ted-Larry Pebworth, eds, *The English Civil Wars in the Literary Imagination*, Columbia, MO, 1999.

133. See below, chapter 7 n.20.

134. Lois Potter, *Secret Rites and Secret Writing*, Cambridge 1989; Joad Raymond, *The Invention of the Newspaper*, Oxford 1996; my *Rational Millennium*. In a series of essays, his editions of the Ranters, George Fox (*The Journal*, Harmondsworth 1998), and Marvell (forthcoming from Longman), his study of sectarian writing and language theory (*Perfection Proclaimed*, Oxford 1989), and his survey of the literary and polemical genres of mid-seventeenth-century England (*Literature and Revolution*), Nigel Smith has done more than any other literary critic to bring the English Revolution into seventeenth-century literary studies. For a review of recent historical and literary critical studies of seventeenth-century political discourse, see Paul Hammond, "Review Article: The Language of the Hive: Political Discourse in Seventeenth-Century England," *The Seventeenth Century* 9.1, 1994.

135. London 1984; 2nd edn, Oxford forthcoming.

begin with Thomas More, and both consider Spenser and Sidney at length. But their differences are also significant. Where Greenblatt writes six chapters on individual writers, Norbrook reveals the influence of S. R. Gardiner and British narrative historical writing by surveying English literary and political history from More to the young Milton. Where Greenblatt's reigning opposition is that between system and subject, Norbrook's is that between courtly culture and radical humanism—that is to say, between two different articulations of system and subject within a developing social totality. After considering More's republicanism, Norbrook considers the apocalyptic Protestantism and poetry of social reform by Tudor commonwealthsmen like Bale and Crowley, the radical Protestant poetics of Spenser and Sidney, the neo-Spenserian opponents of Ben Jonson in early Stuart England, and the millenarian poetry of the young Milton. More recently, his *Writing the English Republic* has developed and deepened this project with a virtuoso reconstruction and analysis of the seventeenth-century republican literary imagination.[136] I have not done justice to these post-revisionists in this chapter. The heft and authority of their work have already altered the shape of seventeenth-century studies. By showing the collective ideological conflicts defining the literary, religious, and political culture of early Stuart England, they have ably challenged one foundational assumption of capitalist social theory: the opposition of system and subject, which leads to the premature totalization of dominant culture as the entirety of culture, of a particular sort of ruling-class subjectivity as "the subject" itself, and of particular works as cultural synecdoches.

But in demonstrating that ideas matter and even conflict, these post-revisionists have left another capitalist foundational assumption almost untouched. If we define *culture* as the realm of ideology in its broadest sense, *economy* as the reproduction of real material existence, and *society* as the lived totality incorporating both, then a practice of "cultural studies" that never defines *not-culture*, a practice of ideology critique that never pauses to talk about *not-ideology*, risks falling into a culturalist reductionism that must either avoid historical explanation altogether, or fall back on a theory of contingency. It is too soon to tell which way this ideologically "liberal" post-revisionist current will turn—whether it will remain focused on the dialogue to the right with revisionist history, or commence a serious dialogue to the left. But like its revisionist and postmodernist antagonists, it tends to assume that a formulaic rejection of economism adequately settles accounts with the marxist tradition. For instance, Steven Pincus's *Protestantism and Patriotism: Ideologies and the Making of English Foreign Policy, 1650–1668*, a sophisticated post-revisionist history, is marred by a mechanistic, *a priori* separation of politics and religion from economic interest—frequently through a critique of Brenner's *Merchants and*

136. Cambridge 1999.

Revolution.[137] In a recent essay pointing toward a reconciliation of revisionists and post-revisionists, the brilliant post-revisionist historian Peter Lake exults in the "luxurious and rather rare indeterminacy and multivocality of the post-revisionist moment." He proclaims the relative independence of politics while ignoring society, claims that post-revisionists discovered the idea of multiple, non-necessitarian metanarratives, and groups marxism and Christopher Hill with capitalist modernization theorists singing hymns to the "benefits of modernity, the controllability of the historical process, the benign capacity of the state to intervene and shape the economic and social development of the nation"—a staggering distortion of Hill's work.[138] Here, by implying that a theory of history as class struggle necessarily implies a whig theory of history as progress, Lake reprises a crucial revisionist argument; but as Perry Anderson says, Butterfield himself was aware that these theories are "quite separable."[139] Three recent collections of revisionist and post-revisionist essays have no room for marxist work save as an extramural object of critique.[140] There are even signs that new historicist literary criticism may join in this emergent consensus by shifting from a "hard" to a "soft" model of the early modern/capitalist total system. As invocations of panoptic Jacobean absolutism begin to sound histrionic and silly, and as neo-new historicists turn from "subjectification" to a model of circulation, negotiation, criticism, factional politics, and fundamental consensus, they move closer not only to an *Annales*-style history of steady-state *mentalités*, but also to the revisionist model of a hierarchical but flexible early Stuart state.

But the history of the revisionist project suggests the perils awaiting any such accommodation. Twenty years ago, dissociating political and religious ideas from their social context, revisionism proceeded in short order to deny their importance and the importance of principled conflict. So a mere reiteration of the importance of ideas and ideologies, however subtle and carefully elaborated, will likely prove no more than a holding action. Robert Brenner suggests a likely supplement:

> One of the best ways to restore principled conflict over the constitution and religion to its proper place at the center of the interpretation of seventeenth-century politics is to reassociate constitutional and religious ideas with the sociopolitical and economic contexts from which they arose—the experiences

---

137. Cambridge 1996, 13n, 40, 97.
138. "Retrospective" to Merritt, *Political World* 252–83, 283, 257.
139. *English* 285.
140. Sharpe and Lake, *Culture*; Cust and Hughes, *CH* and *The English Civil War*. One might plead the dearth of marxist professional historians and literary critics of the period, but as Christopher Hill notes, "Those of us who had tenure before the cold war heated up were lucky to retain our positions: there was no promotion and no recruitment of Marxists into the profession in the fifties" (quoted in Harvey Kaye, *The Education of Desire*, New York 1992, ix). Bold British exorcisms of Hill's "school" (Tyacke, "Puritanism" 119) are almost as ludicrous as bellicose American jeremiads against marxist economism triumphant.

they were designed to comprehend, the interests they were shaped to further, and the structures they in effect defended or tended to transform.[141]

Given the realities of institutional power, the terms of the debate are understandable: a post-revisionist historian analyzing early Stuart parliaments will hear more revisionist demands that she consider the consensualist *mentalité* of the time than marxist demands that she articulate high political arguments with material production and class struggle, so she will probably spend most of her time on a pre-emptive or conciliatory response to the first critique. But the intellectual rationale for this rightward address is not so apparent, for post-revisionism has more to learn from historical materialist theories of society than from anticommunist theories of culture. And in time, deprived of its living and breathing connection to economy, culture makes a poor substitute for society—indeed, a poor substitute for itself.

141. *BMR* 648.

4

Class Struggle and the English Revolution

"Society" is not a valid object of discourse. There is no single underlying principle fixing—and hence constituting—the whole field of differences.

—Ernesto Laclau and Chantal Mouffe, *Hegemony and Socialist Strategy*

And you know, there is no such thing as society. There are individual men and women, and there are families.

—Margaret Thatcher

Commotions for these reasons want not a stout captain as a plebeian wittily answered the Duke of Norfolk (sent against the commons in Suffolk and asking that who was their captain) that Poverty was their captain with his cousin Necessity.

—John Milton, *Commonplace Book*

The Usual Suspects

Why is marxism so boring? With a sigh of relief, Stephen Greenblatt abandons its "mechanics of culture" for the supple cultural poetics of the new historicism:

> And I would say that one long-term commitment of any cultural poetics or new historicism—which is always, to some extent, an anti-historicism—would be to *intensify* and not to lose that sense of surprise. One of the problems with Marxist aesthetics was that it tended so easily to round up the usual suspects, and tended so much to collapse what looked remarkable into the predictable, the familiar, the same. But in fact one's experience of life is *precisely* of things that you can't possibly have predicted. *Afterwards* they may look inevitable or you may project back.[1]

Now marxist aestheticians who aren't quite dead yet may struggle feebly against Greenblatt's premature elegy.[2] They may doubt that everyone's life is so full of delicious surprise. If they happen to be feeling particularly

1. "'Intensifying the Surprise as well as the School': Stephen Greenblatt Interviewed by Noel King," *Textual Practice* 8.1, 1992, 125–6.
2. Marxism's relations with Foucault and the new historicism are controversial. See Porter, "Are We"; Suchoff, "New Historicism"; Gallagher, "Marxism"; my "Ranting"; and Richard Halpern, who finds more common ground than I do (*Poetics* 1–15).

beleaguered and petulant, they may also want to spread some of the tedium around, pointing to the mechanical predictability of, say, a pedestrian new historicist anecdote. And if they're acquainted with Kant's sublime and its teeming progeny, they may not be completely flabbergasted by Greenblatt's own quest for such predictably unpredictable aesthetic limit experiences as "wonder," "intensity," "the remarkable," and "the marvelous." Still, one probably knows what he means. If the first two commandments for scholars are "Never lie" and "Never ignore exploitation and suffering," then the third is "Never bore," and marxists are as guilty as anyone of breaking it.

But is Greenblatt tired of the marxist argument or of its tiring subject matter? When we drone on and on about exploitation, class, and all the usual suspects, should he hear the tedious product of a bad method, or a sensitive response to a sad history? Discussing the regrettably static and mechanistic base/superstructure metaphor, Terry Eagleton suggests an answer:

> History ... indeed displays a remarkable self-identity from start to finish, presents a strikingly monotonous, compulsively repetitive narrative all the way through. What all historical epochs have in common is that we can say with absolute certitude what the vast majority of men and women who populate them have spent their time doing. They have spent their time engaged in fruitless, miserable toil for the benefit of others. Arrest history at any point whatsoever, and this is what we will find. . . . Those who celebrate history as change, difference, plurality, unique conjuncture, and who hone their theoretical instruments accordingly to capture something of this precious specificity, simply blind themselves politically and intellectually to this most scandalous of all transhistorical truths.[3]

Like Greenblatt's new historicism, marxism must remain, to some extent, an antihistoricism: by doggedly returning us from the kaleidoscopic plurality of culture to the monochrome of exploitation, and by struggling to comprehend the true, heroic particularity of any worker's hard-won foray into the world-transforming realm of revolutionary freedom, it attempts to keep culture from degenerating into a series of unpredictable but thin and tedious moments of surprise.

Eagleton is working with Marx's discussion of freedom and necessity— that existential dyad underlying all modes of production, even the communism Marx yearns for:

> In fact, the realm of freedom actually begins only where labour which is determined by necessity and mundane considerations ceases; thus in the very nature of things it lies beyond the sphere of actual material production. Just as the savage must wrestle with Nature to satisfy his wants, to maintain and reproduce life, so must civilised man, and he must do so in all social formations

---

3. "Base and Superstructure in Raymond Williams," in Eagleton, ed., *Raymond Williams*, Boston 1989, 167.

and under all possible modes of production. With his development this realm of physical necessity expands as a result of his wants; but, at the same time, the forces of production which satisfy these wants also increase. Freedom in this field can only consist in socialised man, the associated producers, rationally regulating their interchange with Nature, bringing it under their common control, instead of being ruled by it as by the blind forces of Nature; and achieving this with the least expenditure of energy and under conditions most favourable to, and worthy of, their human nature. But it nonetheless still remains a realm of necessity. Beyond it begins that development of human energy which is an end in itself, the true realm of freedom, which, however, can blossom forth only with this realm of necessity as its basis. The shortening of the working-day is its basic prerequisite.[4]

Marx's mundane conclusion jars with the eschatological marxist utopia of anticommunist caricature, though it, too, might seem positively extra-terrestrial to a seventeenth-century copyhold tenant seeing his meager earnings melt away in taxes, fines, and tithes, or a twentieth-century worker coming home to her second shift of unpaid domestic labor, or driving from his full-time to his part-time job. In their more idealist writings of the 1840s, Marx and Engels had predicted that necessity would more or less disappear in an artisan's utopia of freely chosen praxis. Here, after decades of political organizing and studying political economy, Marx has lost his youthful optimism, but he continues to hope for "the modest Magna Charta of a legally limited working day."[5] A fully human history will begin only in a future realm of freedom no longer subject to mechanical determination by natural necessity and the arti-ficial necessities produced by regimes of class exploitation. Far from an inhuman economism that would chain all human "superstructural" activ-ity to a determining base, marxism is an anti-economistic humanism prophesying that human freedom, which class society has largely purged from the base, alienated to the superstructures, and deformed in the process, might reconquer large segments of the base itself. The ferocious fear of marxism as economic reductionism lashes out at marxist bearers of bad news about the prehistoric past and present, displaces onto them its own unspeakable suspicion that economic exploitation really *is* essen-tial and eternal, then tries to drown out their good news that the realm of necessity can be rolled back, uncovering a larger realm of human freedom, a utopian weekend that makes constant, creeping inroads on the work week.

Class struggle is the road from one realm of necessity to another, and from the realm of necessity to the realm of freedom. In this book, I will argue that the English Revolution was a class struggle. By that, I don't mean the quasi-natural collision of a declining gentry, or the aristocracy, or the feudal countryside with a rising gentry, or the bourgeoisie, or a

4. *MECW* 37.807.
5. Ibid. 3.229–58, 5.47, 35.307.

proto-capitalist London. Rather, I mean the struggle among various groups that were endeavoring to maintain or transform the relations of production. The two-part prologue to this struggle assured that England would not become an absolutist tax/office state like France. First, the English aristocracy and increasing numbers of the gentry and even yeomen renters waged a class war of primitive accumulation by attacking feudal tenures claimed by the church, the state, and peasant commoners and copyholders, transforming the land into their own absolute property. Second, the Tudor monarchy unwittingly accelerated this capitalist transformation. When he broke from Rome, Henry VIII gained an enormous body of church lands, comprising perhaps a quarter of the realm, and thus an unprecedented opportunity to found an absolutist state independent of parliamentary subsidies. But to finance his futile wars against the French, he sold off most of these lands, weakening himself and strengthening the English gentry and new nobility: "One of the drabbest and most inconsequential foreign wars in English history thus had momentous if still hidden consequences on the domestic balance of forces in English society."[6]

Henry made it likely that any English absolutism would be fretful and largely symbolic, compromised by its lack of a standing army and its material dependence on English landholders. To use James Harrington's materialist terminology and, in part, his analysis of the Tudor revolution, Henry introduced a destabilizing "imbalance" between the agrarian "foundations" of the state and its political "superstructures." The monarchy negotiated this imbalance through careful statecraft during most of the sixteenth century and teetered on the verge of open political conflict in the 1620s. It regained some temporary equilibrium through funding stopgaps and strategic royal alliances during Charles's "Personal Rule" of the 1630s. But he initiated a new phase in the struggle by attempting to turn England into an absolutist class-state through forced loans and various forms of extra-parliamentary taxation, which fell primarily on the English laboring and parliamentary classes.[7] This bold, absolutist project

---

6. Anderson, *Lineages* 124–5.

7. I'll refer to English smallholders, small producers, wage laborers, and poor as the "laboring classes" because "the working class" refers to a later class formation. "The middling sort" came into common usage during the urban class struggles of the 1640s (Keith Wrightson, "Estates, Degrees, and Sorts," in Penelope J. Corfield, ed., *Language, History, and Class*, London 1991, 30–52, 50–51). In *The English People and the English Revolution*, Brian Manning uses the term to highlight the role of that class of small producers beneath the wealthy gentry and above wage laborers and servants. But it can work to hide the widening seventeenth-century rift between those middling persons becoming capitalists and those becoming wage laborers, as Norah Carlin has shown. She proposes "the exploited classes" as an alternative ("Marxism and the English Civil War," *International Socialism* 10, 1980–81, 112; see also Manning, "God, Hill and Marx," review of Christopher Hill, *The English Bible and the Seventeenth-Century Revolution* [London 1993], *International Socialism*, ser. 2, Summer 1993, 83–4). But I also wish to include those small producers, agrarian and urban, who had some immediate access to the means of production—a group analytically distinct from wage laborers, if also partially overlapping with them, and sharing their struggles with the English ruling class. Similarly, I will refer

was by no means a moribund feudalism: "It is only within the insular context of Whiggish English historiography that Charles's policy can be labelled reactionary and anachronistic rather than progressive. Seen from the continent of Europe, the objectives and methods of Charles, Laud and Strafford were precisely those in which the future lay."[8] But it was a precarious project, with a weak material foundation. The resulting proliferation of absolutist cultural production was neither the symbolic expression of an absolutist state and society (the old historicist and revisionist model), nor the discursive construction of absolutism (the new historicist model), but a structural symptom of and supplement to a state unable to transform society according to its absolutist desires.[9]

From 1640 to 1641, the parliamentary classes struggled with the king, producing the Grand Remonstrance in November 1641. Immediately thereafter, the English laboring classes entered active political life, as crowds of London and provincial petitioners rallied to Parliament. As Brian Manning has shown in *The English People and the English Revolution*, the ruling classes in Parliament then split between a party of order siding with the king, and a popular party siding with the mobilized laboring classes. After the latter won the first Civil War in 1646, two factions within it began struggling to define the meaning of the Revolution. A capitalist faction struggled to prevent the resurgence of absolutism, establish capitalist state forms, and stifle a popular faction, which struggled in turn to create a genuine social revolution enfranchising a political nation of male small producers. This struggle began with tensions inside the New Model Army and continued through the regicide, the Leveller mutiny at Burford, and the various movements of laboring-class sectarian opposition in the late forties and the fifties: the Levellers, Diggers, Ranters, Fifth Monarchists, and Quakers. Because capitalist revolutionaries failed to transform English society, a large section of the nation remained neutral after the death of Cromwell in 1658, and absolutist forces were able to restore their rule, though not without some significant concessions to capitalist

---

to would-be absolutists, lords, and gentry exploiting precapitalist political/economic rights, and to emerging and expanding capitalists, as the "ruling classes"—those sometimes antagonistic groups able to extract the surplus labor of others by one means or another.

8. Stone, *Causes* 132.

9. New historicists frequently base their reading of literature as political/symbolic *work* on Lévi-Strauss's argument about Caduveo face painting in *Tristes Tropiques* (New York 1975, 178–97), as interpreted and generalized by Jameson in *The Political Unconscious* (77–80). Lévi-Strauss notes that Caduveo visual artists repeatedly create symmetrical designs around an oblique axis, dreaming about the egalitarian kinship moieties painfully denied them by their harshly hierarchical society. But while myth may provide a formal resolution for a logical contradiction, this resolution is "an impossible achievement if, as it happens, the contradiction is real" (*Structural Anthropology*, New York 1963, 229). The Caduveo repeated these dreams precisely because they never gained such moieties. Similarly, in their proclamations, political treatises and sermons, court masques, patronage poetry, and Arminian church rituals, early Stuart absolutists kept dreaming about an independence of parliamentary supply precisely *because* they never gained it. Meanwhile, the English parliamentary and laboring classes dreamed other dreams.

parliamentary interests, which were reaffirmed and extended in the settlement of 1688–89.

I will begin by arguing for the crucial importance of several marxist concepts and models for understanding early modern history, including base and superstructure, mode of production, class (as distinct from status), and class consciousness. Then, I will discuss marxist theories of primitive accumulation, bourgeois revolution, and the English Revolution.[10] I'm particularly concerned with the way in which the seventeenth-century laboring classes subjected the first capitalist revolution, in both its economic and political aspects, to a thoroughgoing theoretical and practical critique from its very inception. Crucial though their arguments are, neither Blake nor Fourier, neither Marx nor Morris, neither Weber nor Foucault nor Habermas was the first to criticize the instrumental rationality and will to power of revolutionary capitalism. The Agitators, the Levellers, the Diggers, Anna Trapnel, and Edward Sexby, among many others, got there first.

Base, Superstructure, and Hierarchies of Determination

In the Preface to *A Contribution to the Critique of Political Economy*, Marx moves in a breath from his most notorious model of society to his most famous chiasmic aphorism:

> In the social production of their existence, men inevitably enter into definite relations, which are independent of their will, namely relations of production appropriate to a given stage in the development of their material forces of production. The totality of these relations of production constitutes the economic structure of society, the real foundation, on which arises a legal and political superstructure and to which correspond definite forms of social consciousness. The mode of production of material life conditions the general process of social, political, and intellectual life. It is not the consciousness of men that determines their existence, but their social existence that determines their consciousness.[11]

A series of near-parallelisms bedevils the passage: what are the relations among *relations of production, structure of society, real foundation of society,* and

---

10. For accounts of marxist interpretation of the English Revolution, see Richardson, *Debate* 124–40, 148–9, 184–202; Norah Carlin's *The First English Revolution* (London 1983), and her "Marxism." Christopher Hill, one of the most brilliant and prolific historians of the twentieth century, has accumulated a body of marxist work impossible to summarize in a footnote. See Donald Pennington and Keith Thomas, eds, *Puritans and Revolutionaries*, Oxford 1978; Eley and Hunt, *Reviving*; Harvey Kaye, *The British Marxist Historians*, Cambridge 1984, 99–130; Richardson, *Debate* 124–40, 185–7; and MacLachlan's *Rise*. Brian Manning's *The English People and the English Revolution* (1976) remains the premier narrative and analytical marxist account of the Civil War and the Revolution, through the regicide. He has recently extended it with *1649: The Crisis of the English Revolution*, London 1992; and *Aristocrats, Plebeians and Revolution in England 1640–1660*, London 1996. Brenner's formidable *Merchants and Revolution* (1993) is the most important large-scale marxist account of the Revolution published after Manning's.
11. *MECW* 29.263.

social existence? Among *arising, conditioning,* and *determining*? Among *social consciousness, social, political,* and *intellectual life,* and *consciousness* plain and simple? Why should relations be "appropriate to" forces? Why does Marx create a mere "negation of the negation" by turning consciousness into a pure reflection of material existence, with no independence or semi-autonomy? And most of all, why this deterministic model of "real foundation" or base and the (unreal?) superstructures? This metaphor's reductively spatial and static quality has proved all too attractive both to mechanistic dialectical materialists and to mechanistic anticommunists eager to score quick points against them.

The Gordian perplexities of the Preface derive less from the gnarly nature of things than from Prussian censorship: Marx was frantic to publish a major work in German, but Prussia mandated a jail term for anyone stirring up class hatred, hence his remarkable failure even to mention "class," much less "class struggle," in the Preface.[12] But this leaves us with the base/superstructure metaphor, which "has always been more trouble than it's worth," as Ellen Meiksins Wood says.[13] I, too, would prefer to drop it altogether for a model of "society," "social formation," or "complex social totality" with a "hierarchy of determinations," generally preserving the first place in the hierarchy for the reproduction of material human existence. But Marx deserves two defenses. First, the mainstream of critical marxism has returned repeatedly to the question of economic determination, complicating it in various ways. Marx began worrying this metaphor five sentences after its birth, when he revised it into the relation between "the economic conditions of production," whose transformation shapes class conflict, and the "the legal, political, religious, artistic or philosophic—in short, ideological forms in which men become conscious of this conflict and fight it out."[14] An ideological superstructure where people become conscious of class conflict and then fight it out is something more than mechanically determined appearance; an economic base where they tend not to do so is something less than autonomous essence. As Gramsci asks, quoting from memory, " 'Man acquires consciousness of social relations in the field of ideology': is not this an assertion of the necessity and the validity of 'appearances'?"[15]

Following Raymond Williams, I will argue that we can hold on to the proposition that "base determines superstructure" only if we transform each term, restoring the *practices* for which they stand. "Base" changes from a "fixed economic or technological abstraction" into "the specific activities of men in real social and economic relationships." "Determination" changes from a mechanical and predetermined process into "the setting of limits and the exertion of pressures." A "superstructure" changes

12. Arthur M. Prinz, "Background and Ulterior Motive of Marx's 'Preface' of 1859," *Journal of the History of Ideas* 30, 1969.
13. *Democracy Against Capitalism,* Cambridge 1995, 49.
14. *MECW* 29.263.
15. *Selections from the Prison Notebooks of Antonio Gramsci,* New York 1971, 138; see also 375–7.

from a merely reflected content into a "range of cultural practices." Historical materialism offers a theory of society as a complexly structured totality and process in which the "base" of material production regularly shapes the non-economic superstructures more than they shape it.[16] I have said "shapes" rather than "determines," which still suggests mechanical causality, despite Williams's struggles to rescue the word.[17] And I have said "regularly" not "always" or "necessarily" because marxism is more at home in the empirical realm of history than in the ideal realm of absolute logic, where anticommunists prefer to meet it and hold it to the reductive choice of "rigorous necessity or indeterminate contingency?"

This concrete hierarchy implies complexity, not reductive simplicity. Following Sartre, I will argue that "the concrete" is not the hard, indivisible nugget of fact beloved of both revisionist and postmodernist positivists, but "the hierarchical totalization of determinations and of hierarchized relations."[18] Sartre alludes to a methodological discussion in *The Grundrisse*. Marx begins with an ostensibly "real and concrete" concept like "population," which nonetheless gives only a "chaotic conception of the whole" until it is traced to its various structural and historical determinations (classes, wage labor, capital, exchange, division of labor, prices, etc.), and "From there it would be necessary to make a return journey until one finally arrived once more at population, which this time would be not a chaotic conception of a whole, but a rich totality of many determinations and relations."[19] Through this regressive/progressive double movement, or *totalization*, Marx "will be able to show the action of superstructures on substructural facts." In Sartre's example of Flaubert (later expanded in his massive unfinished biography, *The Family Idiot*), these "regressively" reconstructed determinations include "*Madame Bovary*, Flaubert's 'femininity,' his childhood in a hospital building, existing contradictions in the contemporary petite bourgeoisie, the evolution of the family, or property, etc."[20] This regressive analysis produces no more than a "hierarchy of heterogeneous significations" if we do not develop it by introducing a "progressive" moment of analysis, which aims to recover

> the totalizing movement of enrichment which engenders each moment in terms of the prior moment, the impulse which starts from lived obscurities in order to arrive at the final objectification—in short, the *project* by which Flaubert, in order to escape from the petite bourgeoisie, will launch himself across the various fields of possibles toward the alienated objectification of himself and will constitute himself inevitably and indissolubly as the author of *Madame Bovary*

16. Williams, *Problems in Materialism and Culture*, London 1980, 34, 31–2. For some important discussions of base and superstructure, see Williams's whole essay (31–49); Eagleton, "Base"; Ellen Meiksins Wood's discussion of Thompson (*Democracy* 49–75); and Norman Geras, "Seven Types of Obloquy," in Leo Panitch, ed., *The Socialist Register 1990*, London 1990, 1–34, 9.
17. *Problems* 31–2; *Keywords* 98–102; *Marxism* 83–9.
18. *SSM* 49.
19. *MECW* 28.37–45, 37.
20. *SSM* 92; see also 85–166 and 51–2n.

and as that petit bourgeois which he refused to be. This project has *a meaning*, it is not simply the negativity of flight; by it a man aims at the production of himself in the world as a certain objective totality.

My own project in part two of this book is precisely an exercise in Sartrean regressive/progressive analysis of several seventeenth-century projects. Regressively, I try to establish the objective determinations (material, religious, political, gendered, autobiographical, discursive) acting upon John Felton, the Agitators, Anna Trapnel, Edward Sexby, and the Diggers. Progressively, I try to show the subjective and synthetic contours of their particular projects, which all comprise "the subjective surpassing of objectivity toward objectivity," as they combine in a seventeenth-century program of resistance by small producers to an absolutist or emergent capitalist state.[21] The product is not simply the bare thesis that the English Revolution was a class struggle, but also the argument that this class struggle took a particular shape partly because of the complexly determined and determining projects of working people.

Second, Marx's statement was not a dissertation but an aphorism: a local and strategic attempt to hack out some breathing room for historical materialism inside a choking thicket of Hegelian idealism. And the need for such ground-clearing aphorisms has not disappeared, even inside ostensibly materialist contexts. For if marxists have nothing in particular to like about the base/superstructure metaphor, they still have something to fear from its critique: the disappearance of economy and the very concept of determination. For instance, many readers assimilate Williams's essay on base and superstructure to a comfortably idealist rejection of the economic, or an argument for the "relative autonomy" of the superstructures, which leads to new reifications: the base becomes as a mere thing which can be safely ignored, while the relatively autonomous superstructures become too complex to analyze systematically, and determination becomes overdetermination verging on indeterminacy. Contemporary practitioners of cultural studies seldom take the time to specify what is *other than* culture, so by definition (by the definition of "definition"), they never define culture itself. They post clear warning signs on the road to reductive economism, but leave unmarked the equally reductive road to culturalism. In the early modern, military sense of the term, they practice economic *reduction* in its crudest form by besieging economy and reducing it to an unspeakable nullity. In her summary "Post-Script" to the highly influential anthology *Cultural Studies*, Angela McRobbie replaces "society" with "culture," calls Fredric Jameson and David Harvey economistic reductionists, declares that class is not everything then implies that it is not anything, forbids the concept of a hierarchy of determinations, and defines politics for postmarxist academics as the

21. *SSM* 44–5, 97, 146–7. On Sartre's concept of totalization, see Jay, *Marxism* 331–60; and Thomas R. Flynn, *Sartre, Foucault, and Historical Reason. Volume I: Toward an Existentialist Theory of History*, Chicago 1997, 106–13.

"ample opportunity to become involved in educational and cultural policy-making"—the glimmering, can-do utopia of bright, young postmarxist managers.[22]

The very phrase "cultural materialism" should worry materialists as much as traditional idealists, for it provides another way to ignore the reproduction of real material existence. If all culture is material, then culture is "base" and everything is base; if everything is base, then nothing is base, and the concept of determination disappears.[23] Williams delivers a critique of Lukács's "totalization" that might better be directed toward the "cultural materialism" that he himself named:

> If we come to say that society is composed of a large number of social practices which form a concrete social whole, and if we give to each practice a certain specific recognition, adding only that they interact, relate and combine in very complicated ways, we are at one level much more obviously talking about reality, but we are at another level withdrawing from the claim that there is any process of determination. And this I, for one, would be very unwilling to do. Indeed, the key question to ask about any notion of totality in cultural theory is this: whether the notion of totality includes the notion of intention.[24]

If we bump into a modest but formidable historical assertion ("The economic base has *regularly and complexly shaped* culture"), then discreetly step away and bravely enter the lists with a bold but puny logical assertion ("The economic base *necessarily and mechanically determines* culture"), we have left the domain of historical argument, defined by empirically complex but intelligible regularities, pressures, and limits, for the cozy partial totality of anticommunist philosophy and idealist cultural theory. There are victories to be won here, but they are roughly on a level with a triumphant demonstration that, after all, gravity does not always and mechanically determine ballet. The base/superstructure model will remain useful so long as the preferable concept of human practices in a totalized hierarchy of determinations meets with an anticommunist appropriation that erases the hierarchy and brackets or naturalizes economy, class struggle, and individual and collective intentionality.

Three arguments may help to explain the extraordinarily regular priority of economy. Marx and Engels make the first one in *The German Ideology*, when they sneer at Feuerbach's antimaterialist idealism:

> So much is this activity, this unceasing sensuous labour and creation, this production, the foundation of the whole sensuous world as it now exists that, were it interrupted only for a year, Feuerbach would not only find an enormous

22. "Post-Marxism and Cultural Studies," in Lawrence Grossberg, Cary Nelson, and Paula A. Treichler, eds, *Cultural Studies*, New York 1991, 719–30, 721.
23. Williams's interviewers make a related argument in a discussion of *Marxism and Literature*, and Williams concedes the point: *Politics and Letters*, London 1979, 351–3; see also Eagleton, "Base" 169.
24. *Problems* 36.

change in the natural world, but would very soon find that the whole world of men and his own perceptive faculty, nay his own existence, were missing.[25]

No society in a condition of material scarcity that fails to organize its own material reproduction can survive very long, and this organization can never be merely spontaneous or automatic. That such a crude truism still carries a significant charge of critical meaning does no credit to contemporary academic discourse. Second, as I argued in the previous chapter, historical explanations that systematically scant or ignore economy, thus removing the potential for *conflict* and *contradiction* implicit in the base/ superstructure model, tend to falter when they shift from synchronic description to diachronic explanation. And third, the ordinary language of early modern England implies a hierarchy of base and superstructure, as we can see in the "basic" terrors called up to end all discussions of "superstructural" political reform. It's worth taking seriously the hysterical ruling-class fear that any social reform will set loose a marauding group of peasant communists (John Ball, Wat Tyler, John of Leyden) struggling for a community of property and of women. For instance, in response to the attack on episcopacy by the Root and Branch Petition, Sir John Strangeways warned that "if we made a parity in the Church we must at last come to a parity in the Commonwealth"; it is difficult to imagine anyone warning that communism might lead to congregational church government.[26] This *reductio ad Münsterum* condenses the fears that economic communism will destroy the reigning forms of surplus extraction, and that sexual communism will destroy the reigning forms for transmitting ruling-class property and reproducing labor power.

Paradoxically, one of the strongest reasons for preserving a base/ superstructure model—at least as a strategic moment in a larger marxist theory of society—is that it preserves the cultural or ideological superstructures as a domain of potential agency and free praxis. All social theory incorporates a theory of "necessity" or determinations. Because capitalist social theory tends to deny or minimize the importance of the base, it tends to locate these necessities in the realm of the superstructures, thus crowding out or utterly denying the human capacity for relatively free collective praxis, and creating a sort of culturalist or ideological determinism. As I have argued, both revisionism and the new historicism tend to deny the realm of the superstructures as a domain for creative revolutionary praxis, or reduce it to some stunted form: the (surprisingly Hegelian)

---

25. *MECW* 5.40. Marxist feminists might direct a supplementary sneer toward Marx and Engels as well as Feuerbach regarding any interruption of the physical reproduction of labor power.

26. *The Journal of Sir Simonds D'Ewes*, New Haven, CT, 1923, 215. Compare the 1965 address of Congressman Jamie Whitten to the Delta Council: "Voting rights is merely a front for a massive takeover by militant agitators. Once seized, this power will be used to control industry, agriculture, and even labor"; quoted in Clyde Woods, *Development Arrested: Race, Power, and the Blues in the Mississippi Delta*, London 1998, 166. For a compendium of early modern ruling-class terrors, see Christopher Hill's "The Many-Headed Monster," in *Change and Continuity in Seventeenth-Century England*, Cambridge, MA, 1975, 181–204.

freedom only to recognize and submit to necessity, the strictly contemplative and subject-centered aesthetic agency of the individual-as-artist, the
spectacular cultural reproduction of ruling-class ideology, the ersatz free
agency of the cultural system as a whole known as "contingency," the
cultural theorist's inexplicable freedom to describe the metaphysical
impossibility of free human activity.

By contrast, Marxist social theory dialectically relates freedom and necessity, collectivity and individuality. It emphasizes the elements of necessity and
compulsion defining the economic realm, including the differentiated
and class-specific but also universal human interaction with nature (earth,
air, water, fire, wool, wood, seeds, wombs, stomachs), and the second-level
necessities imposed by oppressive relations of material production. But at
the same time, because it acknowledges these necessities, marxism finds
an extraordinary importance in the superstructures as "the legal, political,
religious, artistic or philosophic—in short, ideological forms" in which
people become conscious of this class conflict and "fight it out." They
form a crucial realm combining necessity and freedom in a complex way
that we cannot know ahead of time. Not despite but precisely because of
the determining power of the economic base, superstructural religion
becomes the most important ideological form of the English Revolution—
a practical domain in which radical Protestants could recognize, exercise,
and extend a measure of relative freedom, and turn it onto the realm of
social or political necessity. In every chapter below, I consider the sociology of radical religion, but I do not propose to "reduce" religion to
economy. Rather, I aim to understand the way in which religious actors
confronted an oppressive state and economy and tried to transform them
into something like the kingdom of freedom, or of God.

Status and Class

When I refer to *class* in the rest of this book, I mean the shared
relationship of a group of people to a particular mode of production—
to a specific historical organization of the forces of production, to its
own laboring activity, and to other classes. This is a relationship both
imposed and self-created, both structural and conceptual, a relationship
that people live, feel, ignore, and think about, sometimes critically. For
most people throughout history, it is a also a relation of *exploitation*: the
ruling class's systemic extraction of surplus labor from the laboring class,
over and above the necessary labor that it performs in order to keep living
from day to day. And *class struggle* consists of this very exploitation and
resistance to it. It need not take the form of a pitched battle between
political parties with unified class consciousness. Indeed, ruling classes
can struggle through the mere threat of physical coercion, or through
ideological projects, or through local organizational stratagems, so long
as they function to limit or prevent the emergence of laboring-class
struggle; and laboring-class struggle can consist in the breaking of tools,

theft (disexpropriation), and pre-political ideological projects through which workers define themselves as something other than surplus producers.[27]

In the chapter on "Labour Rent" in the third volume of *Capital*, Marx provides an important formulation:

> The specific economic form, in which unpaid surplus-labour is pumped out [*ausgepumpt*] of direct producers, determines the relationship of rulers and ruled, as it grows directly out of production itself and, in turn, reacts upon it as a determining element. Upon this, however, is founded the entire formation of the economic community which grows up out of the production relations themselves, thereby simultaneously its specific political form. It is always the direct relationship of the owners of the conditions of production to the direct producers—a relation always naturally corresponding to a definite stage in the development of the methods of labour and thereby its social productivity— which reveals the innermost secret, the hidden basis of the entire social structure, and with it the political form of the relation of sovereignty and dependence, in short, the corresponding specific form of the state. This does not prevent the same economic basis—the same from the standpoint of its main conditions—due to innumerable different empirical circumstances, natural environment, racial relations, external historical influences, etc., from showing infinite variations and gradations in appearance, which can be ascertained only by analysis of the empirically given circumstances.[28]

Marx suggests the explanatory primacy of class. But this does not mean it is an unmoved mover, a "primal contingency" of the sort I have described at work in revisionist history, for other "factors," other "circumstances" and "influences," which seem not to have been mechanically generated by abstract productive relations, also affect at least the "appearance" of the productive relations. Moreover, the state form, "the relation of rulers and ruled," which is largely *determined by* production, also determines production in turn, "reacts upon it as a determining element," which

27. I am much indebted here to G. E. M. de Ste Croix's superb discussion in *The Class Struggle in the Ancient Greek World*, Ithaca, NY 1981, 31–111.

28. *MECW* 37.777–8. This passage in the third volume of *Capital* is a touchstone for political marxists: see Maurice Dobb, *TFC* 58n., 166; de Ste Croix, *Class Struggle* 51–2; Brenner, "The Origins of Capitalist Development," *New Left Review* 104, 1977, 64; and Ellen Meiksins Wood, *Democracy* 53–9. See also the entries on "mode of production" by Susan Himmelweit in Tom Bottomore, ed., *A Dictionary of Marxist Thought*, 2nd edn, Oxford 1991; and by Bob Jessop in John Eatwell, Murray Milgate, and Peter Newman, eds, *Marxian Economics*, New York 1990. Marx verges on technologism when he asserts that the relations of production always *naturally* correspond to the productive forces, if that's what he means by his "definite stage"—an argument that should trouble those marxists who see the motor of history as the *contradiction* between productive forces and relations as well as those who focus on the relations. On forces and relations, see Laurence Harris in Bottomore, *Dictionary*; G. A. Cohen, *Karl Marx's Theory of History*, Princeton 1978, 134–80; Cohen, "Forces and Relations of Production," and Robert Brenner, "The Social Basis of Economic Development," both in John Roemer, ed., *Analytical Marxism*, Cambridge 1986, 11–22, 23–53; Ellen Meiksins Wood, *Democracy* 129–40, and "Explaining Everything or Nothing?" *New Left Review* 184, 1990; Comninel, *Rethinking* 166–70; and Callinicos's criticisms of Brenner, Wood, and Comninel in "Bourgeois" 161–4, and "The Limits of 'Political Marxism,'" *New Left Review* 184, 1990.

suggests that the primacy of production is only logical and quantitative, not temporal and absolute. In the rest of this chapter, Marx considers both the binary structural relation between surplus producers and surplus appropriators, and the plural relations among various forms of land rent, including labor rent, produce rent, and money rent, present in a pure state or in mixtures, within the feudal mode of production. He also considers the way in which the dynamic of feudal land rents generated the classic tripartite system of capitalist agriculture: the proletarian agrarian wage laborer receiving wages and generating surplus value for the capitalist tenant farmer, who transfers some of that surplus to the capitalist landlord as rent.[29] This structure, which is of enormous importance for understanding the early modern English birth of capitalism, has the rhythmic complexity of the musical triplet, for it sets a historically specific "three" against the abstractly familiar and even universal "two" of surplus producers and appropriators. "Class" and "the mode of production" thus counterbalance a strong impulse toward binary analysis with a historical impulse toward more complex, empirical elaboration.

But contemporary history and literary criticism are more likely to present class as a historically determinate idea—perhaps relevant to the modernity which first thought it, but not without strain, or not at all, to premodernity, which lacked the conceptual apparatus to think about classes, and perhaps the social reality of classes as well. As the argument goes, any attempt to discuss class and class struggle before 1832, or 1789, or 1689 falls into a fatal anachronism, for it projects backward dichotomous modern categories. A properly historicist approach will turn instead to that society's own modes of self-understanding—specifically, its complex and multivalent categories of estate, degree, order, status, and sort.[30] Writing of early modern England, Anthony Fletcher and John Stevenson argue that "a class society in our period had not yet arrived," and that "English society in this period cannot readily be interpreted in class terms."[31] Derek Hirst says "localized horizons" situating labor in the household made it difficult for workers to identify with workers elsewhere, so "class" is a problematic term.[32] As we have seen, Armstrong and Tennenhouse accuse Christopher Hill of anachronistic recourse to "categories of class."[33] In his study of early modern sodomy, Gregory W. Bredbeck says, "I recognize an implicit difficulty in speaking of 'class' in precapitalist societies."[34] David Kastan rejects as "silly" the idea that there

29. *MECW* 37.783–8.
30. In my discussions of class and status below, I am indebted to R. H. Hilton, *The English Peasantry in the Later Middle Ages*, Oxford 1975, 3–19; Neal Wood, *The Politics of Locke's Philosophy*, Berkeley and Los Angeles 1983, 7–23; Manning, *1649* 49–78; and de Ste Croix, *Class Struggle* 81–98.
31. "Introduction" to Fletcher and Stevenson, eds, *Order and Disorder in Early Modern England*, Cambridge 1985, 1–40, 4, 19; the readiness is all.
32. *Authority and Conflict*, Cambridge, MA, 1986, 12.
33. *Imaginary Puritan* 62.
34. *Sodomy and Interpretation*, Ithaca, NY, 1991, 27n.

was no such thing as an unconscious before Freud, but not the class and Marx corollary, since class truly comes into existence "only when people discover themselves as a class"—in the nineteenth century. David Underdown finds that "Class is a concept that can be applied to seventeenth-century English society only with the greatest possible caution. . . . It is not so easy to detect the element of consciousness necessary to transform a status or occupational group into a class. Most people still thought of themselves in 'vertical,' local terms: as members of communities."[35]

Keith Wrightson suggests some similar distinctions when he charts a movement from a medieval *three* to an early modern *many* to a modern *two*—a movement that points to a fundamental change in the social world. Late medieval writers tended to speak of three functional "estates" or "orders," as in John Wycliff's distinction among "prestis, lordis, labourers" and William Caxton's among "clerkes," "knyghtes," and "labourers." Early modern writers multiplied these categories in schemes of "degree." For instance, Wrightson notes that, in the *Voyce of the Last Trumpet*, Robert Crowley distinguished "beggars, servants, yeoman, priests, scholars, learned men, physicians, lawyers, merchants, gentlemen, magistrates, and women!" Modern writers, on the other hand, move toward a binary formulation. Writing in 1825, William Cobbett spoke "not in terms of 'estates' or 'orders,' differentiated by social functions, but in terms of 'classes' distinguished and evaluated primarily on economic criteria."[36]

Of course, schemes of estate, hierarchy, and degree do not refer exclusively to the mode of production, but to rich and resonant social differences in a distinctively premodern social totality, in which questions of economy are complexly interwoven with questions of religion, literacy, warfare, family structure, and culture. But these early modern schemes of social structure would collapse and become meaningless if they were not at least *partly* and even, I would argue, *primarily* class relations. We should not overlook the economic interdependence of "lordis" and "prestis," and the dependence of both on laborers. Indeed, Caxton presents an ought-laden and ethical but also rigorously economic theory of the estates in the very passage that Wrightson quotes:

> The labourers ought to pourveye for the clerkes and knyghtes suche thinges as were nedeful for them to lyve by in the world honestly; and the knyghtes ought to defende the clerkis and the labourers, that there were no wronge don to them; and the clerkis ought to enseigne and teche these ii maner of peple and to adresse them in their werkis in such wise that none doo thinge by whiche he sholde displese God ne lese his grace.[37]

---

35. Kastan, *Shakespeare After Theory*, New York 1999, 242n.2; Underdown, *Revel, Riot, and Rebellion*, Oxford 1985, 168; "Community and Class," in Barbara C. Malament, ed., *After the Reformation*, Manchester 1980, 147–65, 156. See Neal Wood's similar examples in *Politics* 12–13.
36. "Estates" 30–32. Marx and Engels see a similar simplification (*MECW* 6.482–5).
37. Wrightson, "Estates" 30.

The laborers' "pourveyance" speaks for itself. The fighting of the lords suggests a status attribute implying an entire ethic of gentle self-fashioning and political conflict, but also a specifically feudal form of economic activity, becoming antiquated in Caxton's day: sheer military force enables lords to reproduce themselves economically by extracting surplus from "their" peasants and preventing their lordly rivals from claiming that surplus.[38] And the priestly professional–managerial class works to reproduce this very form of coercive surplus extraction, arguing for its divine necessity in this world, its withering away in the next. Partisans of the "no-class-yet" argument forget that anticlerical passage in *The German Ideology*, where Marx and Engels trace class society to the moment when mental labor split off from manual labor, and priests appeared as the "first form of ideologists."[39] All this is not to say that, when we rip away the veil of medieval "estates" or early modern "degree," "status," and "sort," we will discover the naked face of economic exploitation; we may discover simply another veil. But even if it's veils all the way down, they will become rather flimsy and difficult to grasp if we insist on reducing them to a strictly ideological weft and ignore their material woof.

We can no more separate the late medieval "knyghtes" and "clerkis" and "women" strictly from economy than we can strictly limit the modern "middle class" and "working class" and "women" to it; if we continue using "status" as a way to discuss human relations that were not immediately economic, we must remember that this is just another way of discussing relations that were *mediately* economic. Premodern systems of status are always, among other things, ways of thinking about, reproducing, and even transforming class relations, and, as such, deserve scrupulous study from a marxist perspective. And something resembling the ostensibly modern binary class division between surplus producers and appropriators appears inside the apparently pluralist premodern schemes of status. Wrightson notes that the very impulse to classify in detail seems to be a ruling-class self-obsession, with gentry ideologists providing a finely detailed analysis of their own class fractions, but displaying much less interest in the variegations of the "orders" beneath them, who tend to merge into a single group.[40] Crowley's classification, for instance, groups perhaps eighty percent of the population in "servants." William Harrison's very influential scheme in *The Description of England* (1577) provides another binary division when it distinguishes the three sorts comprising the ruling class (gentlemen, citizens and burgesses of towns, and yeomen), from that "fourth sort of people" who have "neither voice nor authority in the commonwealth, but are to be ruled and not to rule other," those who are "day labourers, poor husbandmen, and some retailers, . . . copy holders, and all artificers, as tailors, shoemakers, carpenters, brickmakers,

---

38. Robert Brenner, "Dobb on the Transition from Feudalism to Capitalism," *Cambridge Journal of Economics* 2, 1978, 128.
39. *MECW* 5.45.
40. "Estates" 41.

masons, etc."[41] The ruling classes themselves move even more strongly toward binary schemes at moments of class discord, redirecting their taxonomic energies toward the dike holding back the many-headed beast, the monstrous hydra, the rank-scented and mutable multitude.

A similar binary formulation regularly emerges from a peasant or laboring-class perspective. John Feltwell—that ranting rural malcontent with whom I began this book—testified that "The Queen is but a woman and ruled by noblemen, and the noblemen and gentlemen are all one, and the gentlemen and farmers will hold together so that the poor can get nothing"—a ranting conspiracy theory that gets closer to the structural tendencies of late sixteenth-century English agrarian capitalism and patriarchy than do many modern schemes.[42] All the groups I consider in part two produce similar binary classifications: oppositions between the godly and the popish (chapter 5), the freeborn people-in-arms and the oligarchic Parliament (chapter 6), the Good Old Cause and the tyrannical and Antichristian Protectorate (chapters 7 and 8). In chapter 9, we will see that Gerrard Winstanley was a perpetual fount of metaphoric social binaries: Saxon and Norman, Jacob and Esau, lamb and dragon, common preservation and self-preservation, common field and enclosure, power of love and kingly power, and many more. Such classifications reveal to Carlo Ginzburg the "totally dichotomous view of the class structure, typical of a peasant society."[43] But perhaps this view is not only typical of peasants, but also, in important ways, *true*, and based in a particular form of situated practical and theoretical consciousness. While none of these binaries is simply a distinction between surplus producers and surplus appropriators, none of them fails to be significantly determined by that distinction.

Countless scholars in the human sciences have warned us to be wary of reductive dichotomies. From deconstructionists problematizing the binaries of Western metaphysics, to Foucauldians criticizing the idea of power as domination, to historical revisionists criticizing whiggish models of political opposition, to postmarxists attacking populist models of binary conflict in the name of pluralist radical democracy, to theorists from various fields replacing confrontational "capitalist imperialism" with the pluralist, holist, and quasi-natural "globalization," social theorists spend so much time attacking binary oppositions that any claim for their explanatory power must seem willfully contrary, like a Wildean–Leninist aphorism. Even Fredric Jameson backs off from binaries by invoking Derrida (who deconstructs their fundamentally ethical core) and Nietzsche (who reveals their dissimulated will-to-power).[44] But here, Sartre is the better historical materialist: instead of rejecting binary ethical thinking as dichotomous false consciousness, he anchors it in relations of production. Even the most rancid ethical binary—say, the ruling-class fear and loathing of the

41. Ibid. 34.
42. F. G. Emmison, *Elizabethan Life*, Chelmsford 1970, 57.
43. *The Cheese and the Worms*, Harmondsworth 1982, 16.
44. *Political*, 113–15; see also *Postmodernism* 62. But see Jameson's discussion in *Marxism* 233.

base plebs—derives from "interiorised scarcity" when the relations of production "are established and pursued in a climate of fear and mutual mistrust." The unproductive surplus-appropriating groups, "which are perpetually in danger of liquidation because they are the absolute Other living off the labour of Others, interiorise this ambivalent alterity and comport themselves like gods, as if they were Other than human, or as if they alone were humans in the midst of a different, sub-human species."[45] The concept of surplus appropriation *explains* that perennial crop of ethical binaries that keeps mysteriously springing up, ripe for deconstruction or complication or denial.[46] And the most important theorists of this binary—those who not only describe its structure but imagine its abolition—have not been deconstructive philosophers, or marxist historians, or even leaders of the vanguard party. They have been those tribal peoples, peasants, slaves, serfs, maroons, small producers, proletarians, feminists, and masterless men and women engaged in class struggle, fighting to maintain or fuse in their very persons the identities of surplus producer and surplus appropriator.

These no-class-yet arguments are clearer about the mutual exclusivity of "status" and "class" than about the meaning of the two terms, creating strategic confusions.[47] Sometimes they ask "status" to replace class. If we take a hereditary status category such as gentry birth and define it as the closest thing to a class category the period gives us, then look at the English Revolution and find wealthy and poor gentry on both sides of the conflict, we can conclude that class is simply irrelevant for an understanding of the Revolution—that the Revolution was at most a shift of power within the gentry, and perhaps no more than an administrative breakdown that left status/class relations undisturbed.[48] For instance, Conrad Russell descends momentarily to history from below when he refers to the portentously unnamed sons of "a Colchester baker, a London merchant, a Westminster tallow-chandler, and a Reading draper," only to reveal that they became the Arminian bishops Harsnett, Andrewes, Neile, and Laud.[49] The Puritan radical Robert Greville, Lord Brooke, noted with disgust the bishops' derivation "*Ex fæce plebis.*"[50] But Russell has confused birth status with class, and he might as well claim that class had no bearing on the Homestead Strike because Andrew Carnegie was born to a weaver's wife. Stuart absolutism, like the Bourbon absolutism that filled its bureaucratic state offices with a corps of fecal *philosophes*, like Puritanism and capitalism, offered careers open to talent. Precisely because of their plebeian origins, these Arminian bishops maintained strong class loyalty

---

45. *SCDR* 149–50, translation slightly modified.
46. "Binaries will lose their historical existence not through reading protocols but by abolishing class" (Ebert, *Ludic* 131).
47. Neal Wood, *Politics* 12–13.
48. Manning criticizes attempts to treat the gentry as a class in *1649* 68–9.
49. *Causes* 3.
50. *A Discourse Opening the Nature of that Episcopacie*, 2nd edn, 1642, 3.

to the absolutist class/state that underwrote their wealth through the extra-economic extraction of surplus labor.

More commonly, anticommunist social theorists ask "status" to stand in for everything that is not class, everything that differentiates and individualizes persons by cultural and political and familial and other criteria not immediately economic, turning "the status system" into a rough synonym for "ideology," or for a total social idea system or discourse that interpellates docile early modern subjects. Following this definition, what would it mean for us to say that status, not class, defines premodern society? At the very least, we should be able to explain how premodern societies managed to organize their material reproduction and extract surplus labor. Either premodern material reproduction organized itself and surplus labor extracted itself spontaneously or with no great fuss, or status organized material reproduction in some way outside of class relations, or some mechanism other than status or class organized material reproduction. The first alternative seems improbable or impossible on the face of things. The second implodes, for fickle marxists unwedded to particular terms might well prove disturbingly eager to swap their model of a complex, ideologically overdetermined class system for a complex, economically overdetermined status system that organizes material production. The third is abstractly possible, but difficult to imagine concretely outside of science fiction.

Conversely, what would it mean to claim that modern society is *not* a status society—to say that it organizes social relations with no significant recourse to categories of social organization that are not *immediately* economic? Theorists of modern ideology, from orthodox marxists to orthodox anti-marxists, have agreed in little except the thesis that modern ideologies are at least partly independent of the economic base, and postmarxists like Laclau and Mouffe studying modern society have so diminished class relations and elevated ideology and identity that the non-class struggles waged by the new social movements begin to resemble uncannily the non-class conflicts among premodern status groups. Even if we reject such arguments, how can we even begin to talk about twentieth-century capitalism without mentioning nationality, race, politics, gender, age, religion, rural or urban, healthy or sick, and cultural affiliations of various sorts? For instance, if we stick to economy and eschew status, how can we even begin to understand Proust?[51] Proponents of the no-class-yet vision of the early modern world may grudgingly issue a conditional exit visa to interloping marxist historians: "So long as you avoid premodern society, you may apply your definition of class to modern society." But such offers are always made in bad faith, and marxists know they will find unsympathetic immigration officials on the other side of the border, for the space between class-not-yet and class-no-more shrinks to a nullity. Not

---

51. See Michael Sprinker's historical materialist study, *History and Ideology in Proust*, Cambridge 1994.

even the sooty bastions of ostensibly class-determinist nineteenth-century modernity are safe, as we can see when postmarxists like Gareth Stedman Jones try to detach the Chartists from a class politics.[52]

The work of periodization, then, comes down to a choice between a history-of-ideas approach differentiating periods by their ruling idea systems and driven by a quasi-natural dynamic of contingency, modernization, demographic change, or technological innovation; and a historical materialist approach differentiating historical epochs by their respective "mode of production" (which emphasizes economy but also preserves a structurally vital role for non-economic factors), and driven by a dynamic of class struggle. The division between premodern status and modern class is, like most forms of binary periodization, both too reductive and too divisive. On the one hand, it minimizes the sheer diversity in premodern schemes of status, which assume the form of a "classical" social hierarchy only through the plagiarism of early modern writers, or the interpretive decisions of modern historians.[53] On the other, it tends to hide the fact that all historical epochs reveal both economic and non-economic forms of social differentiation—along with indigenous attempts to understand their interrelation. This mixture is apparent even when denied, as when Keith Wrightson discusses the status-based early modern locality:

> It was not a society dominated by class affiliation; for however strong the awareness of status within a specific local context, broader class consciousness was inhibited for those below the level of the gentry by their lack of alternative conceptions of the social order, their envelopment in relationships of communality and deference, by the localism which gave those ties force and meaning and by a lack of institutions which might organize and express a horizontal group consciousness of a broader kind.

But just before this passage, Wrightson says, "The most vital of social relationships were established and maintained within a specific local context and it was in this context that the hegemonic activity of the national ruling class, their domination of the social consciousness of their inferiors, was most successful."[54] The near-sighted localism of "status society" does not descend from above but emerges from ruling-class efforts to fragment the unity of the laboring classes. Localism suggests not

---

52. Ellen Meiksins Wood, *The Retreat from Class*, London 1986, 102–15; *Democracy* 72–3.
53. Wrightson, "Estates" 44. In a bolder prototype for Wrightson's argument, Peter Laslett called pre-industrial England a "one-class society" on the grounds that a class is "a number of people banded together in the exercise of collective power, political and economic," so that only the ruling class of premodern England was part of society proper (*The World We Have Lost*, 2nd edn, New York 1971, 23–4). This bit of moebius logic would seem to allow for a two-class society only in a society with two ruling classes. Laslett mistakes the hegemony of a ruling class over a working class for the sheer passivity or even the nonexistence of the latter—a common enough mistake, though seldom theorized so proudly. See Christopher Hill's devastating review of Laslett's book (*Change* 205–18).
54. *English Society 1580–1680*, New Brunswick, NJ, 1982, 64–5.

that class struggle is irrelevant, but that it is being waged successfully by the ruling classes—a do-or-die necessity for a ruling class threatened by the crisis of peasant resistance in late medieval Europe.[55] And of course, such functional localism is by no means limited to the premodern world, as we can see when we recall Marx on the merely "local interconnection" among the atomized peasants of Louis Bonaparte's France, or the atomized practico-inert of Sartre's serial bus queues, or the racism, sexism, nationalism, and consumerism that attempt to divide and localize capitalist workers.[56] At the same time, the capacity to recognize, analyze, and work against this ruling-class localism is by no means the prerogative of the modern world, as we will see below in the attempts by radicals to move beyond the locality through networks of organization, publication, and physical movement. The most important oppositional entities of the revolutionary era—radical religion, the Puritan New Model Army, and the English revolutionary public sphere—were precisely attempts to overcome the localist hegemony of the parish.

Indeed, the postmodern (but also marxist) critique of whig or progressive or genetic history might be usefully turned against the idea of a gradually developing, slowly accreting class consciousness that only properly emerges with, say, the People's Charter. Class consciousness—reactive or progressive, ruling class or laboring class, successful or unsuccessful, inhabits and defines all modes of production. As I will argue in chapter 6, England was never closer to a small-producers' revolution than in November 1647, when Levellers and Agitators tried to bring the New Model Army together at a single rendezvous to subscribe *The Agreement of the People*. But this is not to limit class consciousness to early modernity. In 1381, forty or sixty or a hundred and ten thousand English peasants gathered at Blackheath. Their army of ten thousand took possession of London and drove Richard II to seek refuge in the Tower. Their leader Wat Tyler pressed beyond a call for a repeal of the poll tax to a demand for radical transformation in the relations of production through an end to servile and forced labor. Richard responded by organizing himself and his remaining forces to disperse the peasants and slay their leaders. The peasants responded in turn by resisting efforts to re-enserf them—a resistance with unimagined but world-historical consequences.[57] How can we begin to explain such events without a concept of class consciousness?

The explanatory power of status becomes clearest when we distinguish it analytically, not historically, from class. When we cease to argue that concepts of class are irrelevant to the outbreak of the English Revolution, on the grounds that the novel "status" groupings of parliamentarians and royalists contained all classes, we can begin to notice the particular social function of religion as a cross-class "status" ideology: when Charles I

55. *BD* 283.
56. *MECW* 11.187–8; *SCDR* 256–70.
57. R. B. Dobson, *The Peasants' Revolt of 1381*, London 1970.

attempted to turn the enormously powerful religious ideologies of the English church to an innovative class project by using them to strengthen a hierarchical, absolutist state, the opposing, cross-class ideology of anti-popery helped English Puritans resist him. Similarly, the cross-class ideology of army solidarity can help us understand both the success of the Agitators' revolutionary project of laboring-class unity in the face of ruling-class oppression (first that of Parliament, then that of the grandees), and then the failure of that project, when General Fairfax re-established hierarchical army solidarity. A history focused on gentry "status" and one focusing on class are by no means incompatible, if we see gentry status as the ideological vestige of an earlier class formation.[58] It is no accident that the two assassins whom I consider below, John Felton and Edward Sexby, were members of the declining gentry. The status sense of a gentleman, cut free or evicted from the productive relations that underwrote it and forced to soldier for wages, metamorphosed into oppositional ideology: into Felton's vision of a godly parliamentary monarchy opposing the duke's recusant absolutism, or into Sexby's vision of a smallholders' republic opposing Cromwell's apostate junta. In Williams's terms, this *residual* class identity survived as a status site from which to negate the *dominant* class structure of the present, and to imagine an *emergent* future distinct from both past and present.[59]

Class Consciousness and the Public Sphere

The revisionist distinction between premodern status society and modern class society suggests the classic marxist distinction between the "class-in-itself," a group of people "bound by similar production relations when it is not (yet) conscious of itself," and the "class-for-itself," a group of people bound by similar production relations and "conscious of itself as a class in opposition to other classes, and acting accordingly."[60] This distinction is useful for holding off the no-class-yet argument that sees class as too exclusively a matter of consciousness, and opens up into an important debate in marxist theory over the relation between structure and agency.[61] But if indeed the history of all hitherto existing society is the history of class struggle, and if class struggle always requires class consciousness, then all history and so all relations of production contain at least a sedimented trace of class consciousness. Marx and Engels's depiction of French peasants as rural idiots is lazy shorthand, at best. The devotion of Western European peasants to smallholding and the traditions of village

58. Karl Kautsky, *The Materialist Conception of History*, New Haven, CT, 1927, 263; Neal Wood, *Politics* 12–13.
59. *Marxism* 121–7.
60. G. A. Cohen, *Karl* 76.
61. Regarding E. P. Thompson's ostensible voluntarism and subjectivism, see Ellen Meiksins Wood's argument (*Democracy* 78–84) with G. A. Cohen (*Karl* 74–7) and Anderson (*Arguments* 40).

communality derives not from rustic instinct but from a cultural memory of late medieval struggles to escape serfdom.[62]

True enough, despite claims of bourgeois ideology critics, class can never be merely be *thought* or *spoken*. But neither can it be merely a structural location, much less a thing like water or fire. Water may flow and fire may burn without fluid or fiery intention, but class simply cannot exist in the present without being thought, spoken, and intended. The forces of production themselves always incorporate a certain knowledge or technology, including a conceptual and linguistic component, or they cease to be forces of production at all. And the relations of production must be continually thought and voiced. A slave who knows how to cooperate with other slaves to move a bale of cotton displays class consciousness; so does the lady of a manor when she calculates the competitive practice of her fellow landowners to determine how much rent she can rack out of her tenants without driving them away. Of course, people speaking of "class consciousness" typically mean not this sort of instrumental knowledge functioning within a mode of production, but the revolutionary solidarity of a class struggling to transform itself and the mode of production it helps to constitute, or to preserve itself against the transformative efforts of some other class. But a revolutionary situation can transform the former sort of consciousness into the latter.

This transformation appears in the radicalization of two seventeenth-century discursive forms, the petition and the remonstrance. The petition originated in a hierarchical and medieval world, and implied in its very structure a *local* appeal from low to high: "Petitioning implies a belief in a natural order of society protecting the interests of rich and poor alike, which the authorities can be expected to enforce once the misdeeds of individuals are brought to their notice."[63] But during the Revolution, petitions grew larger in scope and ambition, becoming a crucial component of the revolutionary English public sphere, and a medium more of lateral *association* than of hierarchical *appeal*. It is difficult to imagine the radical praxis of London small producers in the 1640s without them. The 15,000 citizens who subscribed the Root and Branch Petition of December 1640, and the troop of 1200–1500 who delivered it to the House, helped put a new edge on the petitionary "please."[64] Similarly, the Commons typically directed its remonstrances to the Lords or the king, with no radical designs on the social order. But when it published the Grand Remonstrance of November 1641, a critical review of Charles's entire reign, before he had a chance to respond to it, Sir Edward Dering sensed a violation of generic decorum: "When I first heard of a Remonstrance, I did not dream that we would remonstrate downward, tell stories to the

62. *MECW* 6.488, 4.309; *BD* 43–5.
63. Underdown, *Revel* 118.
64. Manning, *English* 53–7, 104–7. On petitions, see also Fletcher, *Outbreak* 191–227; Annabel Patterson, *Reading* 57–79; and David Zaret, "Petitions and the 'Invention' of Public Opinion in the English Revolution," *American Journal of Sociology* 101.6, 1996.

people, and talk of the king as of a third person. The use and end of such Remonstrance I understand not: at least, I hope, I do not." By proposing an extraordinary alliance between the parliamentary classes and the non-political classes, the House turned an in-itself and localist discursive form into a for-itself act of class consciousness—one that helped generate in turn the reactive class consciousness of the royalist party.[65] We will see similar transformations in each chapter below—for instance, in chapter 9, the Diggers' efforts to turn the traditional solidarities of the common field and the guildhall into models for the revolutionary transformation of all England, and even the world. This sort of bipedal praxis, with one foot in the residual past and another stepping tentatively into the emergent future, is a much more common phenomenon in early modern radicalism—indeed, in radicalism more generally—than the *ab nihilo* radical straw man that revisionists and postmodernists love to hate.

The movement from an instrumental, in-itself class consciousness to a revolutionary for-itself class consciousness has some affinities with the process that Jürgen Habermas describes in *The Structural Transformation of the Public Sphere*. Pre-capitalist or absolutist publicness was by no means a separate sphere of debate, but "something like a status attribute." It "pretended to make something invisible visible through the public presence of the person of the lord," representing through formal rituals of hierarchical display some ostensibly pre-existent "aura" intimately tied to the physical being of the monarch or noble, and embodied in insignia, dress, demeanor, rhetoric, and the joust. The bourgeois public sphere, on the other hand, grew out of the need of early capitalist traders for market information, so that the traffic in commodities interacted with the traffic in news, and "the news itself became a commodity." From this capitalist context grew the institutions of public reason and debate, and the link never completely broke: to be an *homme*, to be a *citoyen*, was also, in practice, to be a *bourgeois*, with a public identity authorized by an income and an education, and Habermas accepts in large measure Marx's withering critique of the bourgeois marketplace of ideas.[66] Nonetheless, he resists seeing the movement to the new bourgeois regime of publicity as a mere illusion of liberation, for, by its very nature, the bourgeois public sphere could not help opening up to a larger and larger public. Though it deluded itself about its egalitarian quality, it retained a genuinely anti-authoritarian potential that distinguished it from the premodern alignment of status and blood, and it asserted a fundamental right to the public exercise of reason: "The public sphere of civil society stood or fell with the principle of universal access. A public sphere from which specific groups would be *eo ipso* excluded was less than merely incomplete; it was not a public sphere at all." The primary structural transformation Habermas sees in the degraded realm of contemporary mass culture was not so

65. Manning, *English* 106.
66. Cambridge, MA, 1989, 7, 21, 122–4.

much an exclusion as an incorporative, degrading expansion, which transformed the open formation of public opinion into the managed neo-feudal practice of public relations, mass communications, and the manufacture of consent.[67] Habermas's arguments have begun to shape post-revisionist studies of seventeenth-century England.[68] I would like to consider two strengths in Habermas's argument, then two weaknesses. First, Habermas draws attention to communicative media and institutions as historical phenomena in their own right, not mere vehicles for a history independent of them. His definitions of premodern and modern publicity can help us appreciate how rapidly seventeenth-century England moved from premodern status display to modern forms of public debate. We might locate the shift generically in the movement from the early Stuart court masque, with its defining moment of *unveiling* the actual nobles who frequently appeared on stage as actors, to the pamphlet or newsbook of the revolutionary era, with its defining activities of *analysis, polemic,* and *defense,* leading, frequently enough, to the discovery of a previously unsuspected knowledge, even *apokalypsis*—an unveiling of quite a different sort. I particularly focus on the seventeenth-century public sphere in chapter 6, where I examine the Agitators and the Putney Debates, but I consider it in every other chapter as well, even those (like chapters 5 and 8) that focus on the secretive and conspiratorial activity produced by throttled publicness.

Second, in examining the genesis of the public sphere, Habermas draws attention to the specifically *pre-political* forms of sociability that create habits of publicness, preparing the way for the full-scale, even oppositional, political public sphere. His primary examples are the networks of trading news, the "intimate sphere" of bourgeois family life (with its "audience-oriented privacy"), and the literary and political culture of Restoration coffeehouses and Bourbon salons. In this book, I will examine a number of other institutions of pre-political publicness: the covert discursive culture of newsletters, gossip, and manuscript poetry (chapter 5), the New Model Council of the Army (chapter 6), the "intimate sphere" of Puritan domestic life (chapter 7), and the public culture of voluntary religion (every chapter). Given Habermas's tendency to view the public sphere as a secular phenomenon, on the grounds that "the Church" was an institution that "lost the character of representative publicity," we can usefully supplement his rather scanty account of seventeenth-century England with A. S. P. Woodhouse's account of the Puritan dialectic of

---

67. 37, 85, 195.
68. Achinstein, *Milton* 9, 58; Dagmar Freist's *Governed by Opinion*, London 1997, 13–17; Donald L. Guss, "Enlightenment as Process," *PMLA* 106.5, 1991; David Norbrook's "Life" and "*Areopagitica*, Censorship, and the Early Modern Public Sphere," in Richard Burt, ed., *The Administration of Aesthetics*, Minneapolis 1994, 3–33; Raymond, *News*; and David Zaret, "Religion, Science, and Printing in the Public Spheres in Seventeenth-Century England," and Lloyd Kramer's response, "Habermas, History, and Critical Theory," both in Craig Calhoun, ed., *Habermas and the Public Sphere*, Cambridge, MA, 1992, 212–35, 236–58.

separation and analogy.[69] Radical Puritans could request toleration for a segregated "order of grace," which ostensibly posed no threat to the "order of nature," including state power. But that order of grace soon began to assert itself, revealing the prophetic good sense in King James's anxiously Erastian warning, "No bishop, no king." In 1647, an anonymous partisan of the New Model argued that, if God insists on freedom of conscience for individuals in matters of religion, then even more must he allow it in the less important realm of civil government.[70] In Woodhouse's striking phrase, "the lessons of the conventicle will not be forgotten in the forum."[71]

I would also like to suggest two criticisms of Habermas's model. First, the bourgeois public sphere never floated free of the "private sphere" of class society: its preconditions and the very substance of its discussions tended to be class-specific. Habermas is fitfully aware of this, but the same is not true for all of his interpreters: David Zaret, for instance, criticizes Habermas as a base-and-superstructure economic determinist and cheerily denies any significant conflict between capitalism and a critical public sphere, in the seventeenth century or the twentieth.[72] Donald Guss sees Milton's *Areopagitica*—the touchstone for seventeenth-century public sphere theory—as a class-neutral celebration of plurality, difference, openness. And David Norbrook observes of *Areopagitica*, rightly enough, that "it is reductive to see the assault on monopolies of discourse simply as a rationale for laissez-faire capitalism."[73] For one thing, actual capitalist societies are seldom averse to censorship or industrial and media monopoly. What I would add is that we can still see *Areopagitica* as part of the specifically bourgeois public sphere of the revolutionary Independents in 1644, and Milton as a bourgeois revolutionary, so long as we remember the tempered awe and horror of *The Communist Manifesto*, which opens with an encomiastic philippic to the world-transforming revolutionary bourgeoisie, and of *The Eighteenth Brumaire*: "But unheroic as bourgeois society is, it nevertheless took heroism, sacrifice, terror, civil war, and battles of peoples to bring it into being."[74]

Milton's project in revolutionary bourgeois publicness becomes clearest in his tract's peroration, where he tries to tie himself to the affections of his parliamentary audience by conjuring up the spirit of Robert Greville, Lord Brooke, who had died the year before in the siege of Lichfield

---

69. *Structural* 266n.62. *P&L* [58–60]; see also John Saltmarsh's words (ibid. 184), and Zaret ("Religion" 223) and Guss ("Enlightenment" 1163) on religion and the seventeenth-century English public sphere.
70. *The Army Harmelesse* 22.
71. *P&L* [58–60]. In *Areopagitica*, Milton links the freedom of the conventicle and the freedom of unlicensed publication (*M* 2.541).
72. "Religion" 215–16, 231; "Petitions" 1543. Kramer notes that Zaret attacks Habermas's alleged economic determinism only to embrace a print technology determinism—a common technique for demarxing Habermas ("Habermas" 248, 257n.1).
73. "*Areopagitica*" 11.
74. *MECW* 6.482–96, 11.104.

Cathedral. As a parliamentary radical, a defender of John Lilburne, an opponent of the privileges of the East India Company, a founder of the Committee for a General Rising, and the author of a plea for freedom of conscience in *A Discourse Opening the Nature of that Episcopacie, which Is Exercised in England* (1641), Brooke embodied Milton's opening praise of the freely publishing "master spirit."[75] As a leading Puritan colonizing aristocrat, he was also up to his neck in the sweat and blood of English indentured servants, Irish deportees, and West African slaves. Just as a mercantile thread runs through the imagery and the substance of Milton's pamphlet, so a discursive, "public sphere" thread runs through Brooke's aristocratic capitalism: during the superficially quiescent 1630s, innovative commercial networks integrated aristocrats like Brooke, capitalist new merchants, and Puritan ministers in such projects as the Massachusetts Bay Company, the Additional Sea Adventure to Ireland, the Bermuda Company, and the Providence Island Company. These networks established habits of cooperation and communication, created a form of "private sphere" publicness, and helped create the Puritan revolutionary coalition of 1642.[76] Milton's project of a (limited) libertarian flight from the political specification of the sayable comes together handily with the new merchant's flight from the political specification of the shippable, and both require us to see a mixed bourgeois program of emancipation and domination.

This argument brings me to my second critique of Habermas. In seventeenth-century England, as in so many times and places, we need to speak of public spheres rather than a public sphere, and resist the classically ideological implication that the ruling classes existed (or, at least, thought and talked) before the laboring classes. Habermas admits the class limitations of the bourgeois public sphere, then criticizes them from the point of view of Marx's *Eighteenth Brumaire*. But he also claims that the "plebeian public sphere" associated with the French Revolution, the Chartists, and the February Revolt on the Continent was no real public sphere at all, but an instrument for public pressure that degraded the public sphere into "an arena of competing interests fought out in the coarser forms of violent conflict," ultimately producing the contemporary "refeudalization" of the public sphere wrought by capitalist modernity, which Habermas discusses at great and despairing length.[77] In thus combining a fierce critique of modern reification with a relative lack of interest in proletarian cultural institutions, Habermas followed in the steps of his teacher, Adorno.

From very early on, his model drew skeptical queries about the primacy of the bourgeois public sphere, and the extent to which it escaped

---

75. *M* 2.560–61. On Brooke, see Levack's entry in *GZ* and Ann Hughes, *Politics, Society and Civil War in Warwickshire, 1620–1660*, Cambridge 1986, 121–6.
76. On Brooke and these networks, see *BMR* 48, 156, 182, 243, 273, 276, 404, and particularly 394–5.
77. *Structural* 122–29, 168, xviii, 131–2, 195, 141–250.

specifically bourgeois interests. For instance, Oskar Negt and Alexander Kluge find a proletarian public sphere in a wide variety of sites, from the labor movement to the cracks and crevices of a degraded capitalist mass culture.[78] With characteristic intellectual generosity, Habermas acknowledges these critiques:

> A different picture emerges if *from the very beginning* one admits the coexistence of competing public spheres and takes account of the dynamics of these processes of communication that are excluded from the dominant public sphere. . . . The exclusion of the culturally and politically mobilized lower strata entails a pluralization of the public sphere in the very process of its emergence.[79]

Such modifications are important if we wish to avoid jumping from the new historicism's reductively absolutist England to a public sphere theory's reductively bourgeois variant.

Specifically, we need to look beyond the classical republicanism of the university-educated aristocrats and gentry, which has thus far drawn most attention from public sphere theorists, to a larger group of writers and actors who also believed in fundamental popular sovereignty, and tried to create new forms of popular government, new institutions of democratic discourse, and a social revolution that would prevent the emergence of a new oligarchy. In chapter 5, I argue for a sort of cross-class Caroline oppositional publicness that stretches from plebeian street riots to learned, humanist poetry. Similarly, in the tumultuous days of 1640–42, we see not a uniformly "bourgeois" public sphere, but pamphlets and petitions issuing from small producers and even wage laborers and women, who create in their very bodily presence behind their petitions an *empowered* public sphere that Parliament took very seriously. In chapter 6, I argue that the "grandee" or agrarian capitalist leaders of the New Model Army organized a public sphere *in reaction to* the soldiery's plebeian public sphere. In chapters 7 and 8, I argue that sectarians and popular republicans came together in a radical public sphere opposed to the Protectorate. And in chapter 9, I consider the Diggers' attempts to creative an innovative rural publicness through publication and networks of inter-commune communication.

Original Theft and the Transition

Marxists define and debate "bourgeois revolution" as furiously as non-marxists denounce and dismiss it.[80] The concept lies at the center of the

---

78. *The Public Sphere and Experience*, Minneapolis 1993; they append an anthology of excerpts on the public sphere of the British labor movement, beginning with Chartism (187–200).
79. "Further Reflections," Calhoun, *Habermas* 421–61, 425, 426.
80. Perry Anderson finds the concept strangely undeveloped even in the writing of Marx and Engels. Examining a wide array of bourgeois revolutions, he finds them all to have been variously "overdetermined": from above by conflicts with feudalism or absolutism, from below by conflicts with peasants or proletarians, from within by divisions within the bourgeoisie, and from without by foreign conflicts, frequently with other bourgeois states

twentieth century's two most important historical controversies about the
social origins of the English Revolution: from the 1940s to the 1960s, the
debate over the gentry, with its aftermath in the rise of historical revisionism; and in the same period, the debate over the transition from feudalism
to capitalism, with its aftermath in the Brenner Debate. R. H. Tawney's
"The Rise of the Gentry, 1558–1640" (1941) prompted the first debate,
which occurred mostly among non-marxist historians and focused on the
origins of the English Revolution.[81] Tawney saw a conflict building in
sixteenth-century England between a feudal aristocracy allied with the
monarchy, and improving gentry landlords allied with the industrialists
and traders of the towns. While the aristocracy declined, the gentry rose,
producing a political imbalance that culminated in the English Civil War.
After World War II, Lawrence Stone built on Tawney's arguments but
stressed the role of overexpenditure in the aristocracy's decline. H. R.
Trevor-Roper attacked Stone's argument, then Tawney's, offering an
alternative social interpretation in which not a rising gentry but a declining and resentful "mere gentry" cut off from court office forced the
English Revolution. J. H. Hexter questioned the idea of a social explanation of any sort, though he did emphasize the increasing military power
of the greater gentry, and the resulting increase of political power in the
House of Commons. Defense, attack, and counterattack followed.

Though anticommunist historians still enjoy exhuming and pummeling
the "traditional social interpretation," it has collapsed for a lack of
evidence, and its partisans have trimmed their sails. As Brenner says, they
found it impossible to distinguish clearly between a declining regressive-
feudal agrarian aristocracy, and a rising progressive-capitalist agrarian
gentry, or to show why the latter group only should have been capable of
agrarian innovation and improvement. Like the young Marx, they relied
on Adam Smith's "techno-functionalist" account of historical change,
which finds the motors of history in the self-developing market, division
of labor, and forces of production. With the concept of a proto-bourgeois
gentry, they smuggled into the feudal mode of production a germinal
version of the capitalist mode whose appearance is to be explained:
"Because this first model ultimately assumes the transition to capitalism in
order to explain it . . . it ends up depriving the associated account of
revolution of much meaning or point."[82] Indeed, Marx anticipated this
critique in *The Grundrisse*, where he criticizes the Smithian vision of

---

(*English* 105–18). This taxonomy is very helpful, particularly if we add "small producers"
to those below. See also Robert Brenner, "Bourgeois Revolution and the Transition to
Capitalism," in A. L. Beier, David Cannadine, and James M. Rosenheim, eds, *The First
Modern Society*, Cambridge 1989, 271–304; Callinicos, "Bourgeois"; and Ellen Meiksins
Wood, *Pristine* 1–19.

81. Tawney, *History and Society*, London 1978, 85–128. On this debate, see Richardson (*Debate*
113–25), Brenner (*BMR* 638–44), and Stone's Introduction to *Social Change and the
Revolution in England, 1540–1640* (New York 1965), a collection of primary materials and
recent historical writing relevant to the debate.

82. "Bourgeois" 273; see also 295–6 and *BMR* 640.

economic history and, implicitly, his younger self: "Production, as distinct from distribution, etc., is to be presented as governed by eternal natural laws independent of history, and then *bourgeois* relations are quietly substituted as irrefutable natural laws of society *in abstracto*. This is the more or less conscious purpose of the whole procedure."[83]

The debates among mostly marxist economists, sociologists, and historians over the transition between feudalism and capitalism are almost as old as the debates over the gentry, but they are still unfamiliar to most non-marxist historians and literary critics. Maurice Dobb sparked the first phase of the debate with his *Studies in the Development of Capitalism*, a ground-breaking attempt to synthesize previous scholarship in a study of the *historical* course of capitalist development through class struggle, which became a founding text for the British marxist historians.[84] Paul Sweezy responded, prompting further responses by Dobb, Kohachiro Takahashi, Rodney Hilton, Christopher Hill, Georges Lefebvre, Giuliano Procacci, Eric Hobsbawm, and John Merrington.[85] In 1976, Robert Brenner sparked the second phase with his essay "Agrarian Class Structure and Economic Development in Pre-Industrial Europe," which prompted responses by M. M. Postan and John Hatcher, Emmanuel Le Roy Ladurie, Guy Bois, Rodney Hilton, and J. P. Cooper, among others, and, in turn, a long response by Brenner.[86] Though Brenner subjected Dobb's arguments to a sympathetic critique, he carries on his "political marxism" by tracing the transition to class struggle and the conflicting relations of production— not to the autonomous development of forces or to their conflict with the relations.[87] Later developments in political marxism include Ellen Meiksins Wood's *Pristine Culture of Capitalism*, Brenner's *Merchants and Revolution*, and Wood's *Democracy Against Capitalism* and *The Origin of Capitalism*.[88] The transition debates provide a remarkably useful model for understanding the relation between the transition from feudalism to capitalism and the English Revolution. Though seldom mentioned by revisionist historians and utterly unknown to postmodernist literary critics, they bear directly on the methodological problems I have discussed in the previous two chapters, and their focus on a "class struggle" or "political marxist" model of interpretation helps explain the importance of the laboring

83. *MECW* 28.25.
84. 1947; rev. edn, New York 1984. On Dobb, see Kaye, *British* 23–69; and Brenner, "Dobb."
85. Collected in *TFC*.
86. Collected in *BD*. For links between the two phases, see Brenner's "Origins" and "Dobb"; Manning's "The English Revolution and the Transition from Feudalism to Capitalism," *International Socialism* ser. 2, Summer 1994; and the comments by Hilton (*BD* 1), who introduced both collections. Given the specter of reductive socialist orthodoxy, it's amusing to contrast the medium for the transition debates (the wide-ranging, international, comparatist, and blood-flecked brawl among an international group of academic and non-academic writers) with that for historical revisionism (the clubbishly polite anthology of essays by mostly British academic historians writing about Britain).
87. The term "political marxism" derives from Bois's claim that Brenner practices a "political and voluntarist marxism" (*BD* 227).
88. The last book (New York 1999) gives an excellent overview of the entire debate.

classes in the English Revolution—though not without problems, as I will argue.

The very terms by which we know the two debates suggest their distinct trajectories. Whereas the first begins with essential "status" identities like "gentry" and "aristocracy," then traces their "rise" and "fall," the second begins with the totalizing structural concept of the mode of production, then examines structured struggle between groups comprising it—groups formed and transformed by the struggle itself. Specifically, it begins with Marx's concept of primitive accumulation.[89] In its classic, agrarian English form, this entailed a transition from a mode of production in which the ruling classes extracted surplus labor from peasants by non-economic, political means, to one in which they extracted it by economic means alone. Where feudal lords had lived off legally sanctioned produce rents and feudal services, capitalist landlords lived off rents paid them by tenant farmers, who lived off the value produced by agrarian wage laborers, who lived off their wages.

The term "primitive accumulation" suffers partly from a bad translation of Marx's *ursprüngliche Akkumulation*, partly from his ill-considered decision to retain and mock the mystifying terminology of classical political economy rather than strive for descriptive accuracy. Marx rejected earlier ideas of accumulation that suggested an automatic or conflict-free process. He mocks notions of accumulation through bourgeois abstinence with a sarcastic fable about the "frugal élite" and the "lazy rascals," noting that bourgeois elites have always been more interested in their workers' abstinence than in their own.[90] He ridicules Edward Gibbon Wakefield's idea of a primitive accumulation based in society's consensual decision to separate into groups of workers and capitalists: "the mass of mankind expropriated itself in honour of the 'accumulation of capital.'" And he attacks the "obviously and nonsensically circular" argument that spontaneously accumulating capital could have called into existence the very exploited workers whose labor created it.[91]

A better term for this process might be *original division* or *expropriation* or *theft*. All the individual "moments" of the capitalist mode of production—means of subsistence, instruments of labor, raw materials, and living labor—exist ahead of time, inside the feudal mode of production. Primitive accumulation recasts them in their specifically capitalist form by a *political* act of *separation*:

> In actual history it is notorious that conquest, enslavement, robbery, murder, briefly, force, play the great part. . . . The process, therefore, that clears the way

---

89. See Marx on the transition in *The Grundrisse* and in the first volume of *Capital* (*MECW* 28.421–32, 35.704–61).
90. *MECW* 35.587–94, 704. Contrast Weber's "Protestant ethic," through which the self-imposed "worldly asceticism" of bourgeois Protestants unintentionally accumulates capital, with Marx's "'spirit' of Protestantism," through which Henry VIII expropriated the Catholic church and its hereditary sub-tenants (ibid. 35.711–12).
91. Ibid. 35.754, 28.432.

for the capitalist system, can be none other than the process which takes away
from the labourer the possession of his means of production; a process that
transforms, on the one hand, the social means of subsistence and of production
into capital, on the other, the immediate producers into wage labourers. The
so-called primitive accumulation, therefore, is nothing else than the historical
process of divorcing the producer from the means of production.

This divorce leaves laborers doubly free: "free from the old client or
bondage relationships and any obligatory services, and free also from all
goods and chattels, from every objective and material form of being, *free
from all property.*"[92]

As primitive accumulation separates the immediate producers from the
means of production, so it separates the exploiting class from the means
of coercion. Or to be more accurate, it differentiates the ruling class's
power to extract surplus from its power to coerce. The feudal landlord
loses the juridico-political privilege and power that previously allowed him
to extract surplus by squeezing it from his tenants or plundering it from
his fellow lords, and becomes a capitalist landlord who can extract surplus
by economic means only. Meanwhile, the central state claims a monopoly
on juridico-political power, including the power to exercise legal coercion
and violence. It usually exercises this power from a distance in an
ostensibly class-neutral fashion. But it also works hand-in-hand with capitalists to protect the property relations that regularly extract surplus labor
through the invisibly coercive medium of the wage form.[93]

In some uses of the term, "primitive accumulation" proper occurred
only once, in pre-capitalist England, and the agrarian capitalist "takeoff"
in England certainly poses special problems of explanation. But Marx also
uses the term to describe the continuing, global process that divorces
immediate producers from the means of production and transforms
agrarian use rights into absolute property rights. He refers to colonial
New England's war against the Indians, Liverpool's slave trade, and the
Highland clearances as primitive accumulation, presumably because they
separated Algonquians, West Africans, and Scots clansmen from the
means of production. And he refers to New World smallholders as a sort
of truculent new peasantry who must be divorced from their new colonial
farms by new state policies of "systematic colonization."[94] Since Marx
never sets a firm terminus for primitive accumulation, it is difficult to see
why we should absolutely distinguish dispossessed peasants in early modern England and in modern Chiapas. Original theft is always also this
morning's.

The political marxist interpretation of the transition argues that we
must turn from an exogenous to an endogenous model of social change:

92. Ibid. 35.705–6, 28.431. See also Brenner on the ongoing role of political force in all
   class relations, all forms of surplus extraction (*BD* 11).
93. This second act of separation is implicit in Marx's *MECW* 35.705, 723–31. See also Ellen
   Meiksins Wood, *Democracy* 19–48.
94. *MECW* 35.741, 747, 755–9.

the mode of production is not a closed and relatively stable functional system which can only be disturbed by some quasi-natural outside force, but a dynamic and contradictory whole shaped by class struggle. Dobb criticized as non-marxist the exogenous account based in the growth of some external "factor" such as "population or productivity or markets or division of labor or the stock of capital." For instance, all by themselves, feudal traders will have no revolutionary significance, for their very existence depends on their cooperation with the feudal mode of production. Nor should we expect that productive forces and technology lead the way in development, for productive relations form "the shell within which technical growth itself proceeds."[95] Paul Sweezy responded with a vigorous exogenous critique: the feudal mode of production contained a certain dynamism, but we must seek the true motor of historical change outside it, in the rapid expansion of trade, which revealed the inefficiencies of the feudal manor, defined wealth as an end in itself, developed new tastes in the feudal ruling class, accelerated the rise of the towns, and encouraged serfs to flee the land. Trade, then, helped to generate a new system of production for exchange, not consumption.[96]

Dobb insisted that a properly marxist account of class structure must begin not with consumption or exchange, but with relations of production: the particular way in which the ruling classes pump surplus labor out of the laboring classes.[97] The feudal mode of production, then, reveals the ongoing conflict between a peasantry with direct, unmediated, non-market-based access to the means of production (primarily the land), and a lordly ruling class which gains access to peasant surplus only by "extra-economic compulsion"—feudally mandated rents, fines, services, and tithes. Feudalism declines because of an endogenous political struggle between peasants striving to limit rents and lords striving to increase them: "The disintegration of Feudalism (and hence its final and declining stage) came *not* as the result of the assault upon it of an incipient 'Capitalism' in the guise of 'merchant capital' wedded to 'money economy,' as has been commonly supposed, but as a result of the revolt of the petty producers against feudal exploitation."[98] "External" forces like demographics, trade, and technological innovation certainly played a role in the transition, but they were subordinate to those feudal class relations that assured the daily reproduction of material existence.

As Kohachiro Takahashi comments, in an essay friendly to Dobb, "If we say that historical development takes place according to external forces, the question remains, however, how those external forces arose, and where they came from."[99] If we cannot say, or if we suggest that they somehow generated themselves, then they come to serve the mystified

95. *Studies* 12, 17, 23.
96. *TFC* 33–56.
97. Ibid. 57–67, 98–101, 165–9; *MECW* 37.777–8.
98. *TFC* 100.
99. Ibid. 79.

explanatory function of the revisionist "primal contingencies" I discussed in chapter 2: after we smuggle a historical phenomenon specific to capitalism (like "proto-capitalist market towns") into the precapitalist era, capitalism can surreptitiously give birth to itself. But since trade, markets, and towns were always aspects of feudal production as such, we cannot assume that they would by themselves compel a transition to capitalism.[100] Since feudal peasants could subsist materially by virtue of their claim to the land, they felt no need to specialize, innovate, and produce surpluses for the market, and certainly none to become wage laborers by dispossessing themselves of the land. Since feudal lords could reproduce themselves materially by virtue of their ownership of the means of political and military coercion, they felt no need to market surpluses. With no market competition, they tended to focus not on the improvement that would be crucial to agrarian capitalism, but on the military power that would enable them to forestall the non-market "competition" of peasants eager to reduce surplus extraction, or of fellow lords eager to encroach on their territory and their surpluses.

Only inside the capitalist mode of production did something like an impulse to improve and increase relative surplus value predominate, for commodities, labor power, means of subsistence, and means of production all circulated in a market, which enforced market-oriented behavior. Because the tenant farmer has no direct access to the means of production, he relies completely on the market for his material reproduction. He *must* improve the lands he rents, minimize wages, and aggressively market surpluses. If he does not, he will lose his lease to an underbidding competitor. Similarly, because they have no direct access to the means of production and subsistence, direct producers *must* sell their labor to earn wages. Capitalism, then, is the first mode of production with a built-in impetus to improvement, competition, and market-oriented activity. Only inside capitalist relations of production did markets, trade, cities, convertible husbandry, and soil-enhancing fodder crops contribute to the momentum of continuous improvement and innovation; persistence in an appeal to exogenous explanations in the face of this explanatory failure begins to look like an ideologically motivated effort to evacuate history of class agency.[101] Brenner's argument led Bois to charge him with pursuing "a voluntarist vision of history in which the class struggle is divorced from all objective contingencies."[102] But the only voluntarism Brenner sees is the relatively impure sort that appears under objective economic compulsion, when a primal threat to material reproduction prompts class struggle; this is notably distinct from the relatively pure and metaphysical voluntarism that sees unfettered *Homo oeconomicus* automatically realizing his will-to-accumulate. So far as Brenner suggests a theory

100. Ibid. 133, 116, 170–95.
101. Brenner, "Dobb" 12; "Origins" 41.
102. *BD* 115.

of economic human nature, he sticks with the more general (and empirically, almost tautologically, verifiable) model of individual humans and collectives driven by the need to reproduce themselves materially, not by a will-to-production, much less a will-to-capitalist-improvement. Economic activity serving material reproduction in a capitalist economy (say, producing a single, inedible crop for market) might be positively suicidal elsewhere.

Political marxists deny themselves any recourse to the reassuringly autonomous genetic processes that provide the motor of change in various related versions of "bourgeois revolution" theory: the rise of the gentry, the market, trade and merchant capital, the towns, the forces of production. Rather, they pursue a historical materialist method combining structural analysis of the pressures or struggles likely to originate within a particular mode of production, with a historical analysis of particular social and political struggles, and the transitive contingencies they respond to and produce. Such an approach resists the binary blackmail threatened by revisionists and postmodernists, for the results are neither inevitable nor purely contingent. Class struggles tend to produce outcomes which are neither clearly intended prior to the struggle, nor utterly unrelated to the interests embodied in the struggle. For Dobb and Brenner, the key moment of transition lies in the widespread fourteenth-century crisis of the European peasantry. The key structurally conditioned pressure was the impulse of peasants to minimize lordly surplus extraction, and the impulse of feudal lords to maximize it. Through "political accumulation," the lords attempted to improve the military means of coercion, which could lead them to interfere with the reproduction of the immediate producers, and encourage non-productive competition with other lords. The result was soil exhaustion and the demographic collapse of fourteenth-century Europe, aggravated by the particular historical contingency of the plague. To maintain their accustomed levels of extracted surplus, feudal lords throughout Europe began squeezing their reduced peasantry so hard that peasants responded with armed struggle.[103]

Both Dobb and Brenner insist that all modes of production contain certain "laws," or at least regular tendencies and impulses, based in the ruling form of surplus extraction. Feudalism tends toward economic stagnation and crises of underproduction because its relations of production discourage technological innovations and encourage the division of peasant holdings through inheritance into smaller and smaller parcels, while capitalism tends toward sustained growth and crises of overproduction because its relations of production mandate a constant, competitive

103. Brenner, "Dobb" 125–6. On political accumulation, see his *BD* 236–42; "Social" 31–2; and "Feudalism," Eatwell et al., *Marxian Economics* 170–85, 174–6. On the European crisis of 1378–83, born of the plague, population collapse, rising living standards for the poor, and renewed ruling-class efforts at expropriation, see Michel Mollat, *The Poor in the Middle Ages*, New Haven, CT, 1986, 193–233.

attempt to extract more relative surplus value through improvement, technological innovation, and the engrossment of smallholdings. But when we turn to the question of *transition*, before the particular, determining logic of the new mode of production solidifies, then a historically specific and "political" explanation becomes more important.

For instance, Brenner argues that the fourteenth-century general crisis of European feudalism led to radically different results. In most of Europe east of the Elbe, the lords managed to defeat and re-enserf the peasantry. In much of Western Europe, particularly France, the peasantry gained substantial political independence of the lords and something like an agrarian freehold. Consequently, the seigniorial lords fostered a centralization of state power, producing an absolutist tax/office state as the instrument for extra-economic surplus extraction. This state operated at the expense of the peasants at first, but eventually the lords as well—an outcome that undermined economic development, eventually sinking the French economy deep into the general economic crisis of the seventeenth century.[104] English lords, like their French cousins, failed to maintain extra-economic, political controls over their peasant tenants, thus losing a traditional mode of surplus extraction. But they retained their broad demesnes and sufficient feudal powers to keep their peasant leaseholders from gaining full property rights.[105] Given the lords' difficulty in extracting surplus directly from the peasants, they began extracting it mediately, through their hold on the land. Peasants with copyhold tenure could own property semi-permanently, paying fixed heriots or fines only at the moment of inheritance or sale. The lords did all they could to turn copyhold into leasehold, which would allow them to set contract terms upon the expiration of leases—the sort of absolute property right that would be a prerequisite for engrossment, improvement, and the rise of agrarian capitalism:

> The unintended consequences of the actions of English peasants and lords aiming to maintain themselves as peasants and lords in feudal ways was thus to introduce a new system of now-capitalist property relations in which the direct producers were free from the lords' extra-economic domination but also separated from their full means of reproduction (subsistence). In the upshot, tenants without direct access to their means of reproduction, had no choice but to produce competitively for exchange and thus, so far as possible, to specialize, accumulate and innovate.[106]

This argument about unintended consequences may recall the revisionist and postmodernist appeal to contingency and critique of teleological history. True, political marxist contingency tends to be impure and transitive; feudalism imposed a pressure toward a finite number of "contingent" resolutions. But the resemblance remains, and no marxist need

104. *BD* 288, 290.
105. Ibid. 293.
106. Brenner, "Feudalism" 184.

flee it in terror, since dialectics is, among other things, precisely the historical logic of unintended effects.

Paradoxically, the late fourteenth-century moment of the English peasants' greatest victory against feudalism began the transition to the capitalist mode of production that would expropriate their descendants and turn them into proletarians. By the early seventeenth century, England had become an agrarian capitalist economy, based in the classic tripartite structure of capitalist landlord, capitalist tenant farmer, and proletarian agrarian wage laborer. In 1600 Thomas Wilson saw a countryside transformed not by a rising class surpassing a declining class, but by the internal transformation of the English ruling class:

> The gentlemen, which were wont to addict themselves to the wars, are now for the most part grown to become good husbands and know as well to improve their lands to the uttermost as the farmer or countryman, so that they take their farms into their hands as the leases expire, and either till themselves or else let them out to those who will give most.

As a result, most English yeomen have decayed into dependent servants, though some have profited enough from their leases that they have become gentlemen.[107] F. M. L. Thompson estimates that landlords extracted about two-thirds of the income from land by the end of the seventeenth century.[108] G. E. Mingay estimates that this figure rose to eighty to eighty-five percent by 1790.[109]

I will not attempt a full summary of Brenner's account of the transition, but I would like to emphasize several points that bear on the revisionist and postmodernist critique of social change explanations of the English Revolution, and to my discussion below of the role that small producers played in it. Dobb and Brenner suggest that we reject exogenous and economistic accounts of the transition relying on quasi-natural, automatic processes that exist quite apart from human agency, because they don't adequately account for the development of capitalism in late medieval England, and its failure to develop earlier or elsewhere. At first glance, this critique of *a priori* "forces first" economism resembles the revisionist and postmodernist critique of all marxism as economism. In the first phase of the debate, Paul Sweezy argued for something like an inevitable dissolution of feudalism based on its essential "laws and tendencies," including the rise of trade, towns, demand for luxury items, and so on.[110] In the second phase, Guy Bois criticized Brenner's "political marxism" as a "voluntarist vision of history" that divorces the class struggle from

107. Joan Thirsk and J. P. Cooper, eds, *Seventeenth-Century Economic Documents*, Oxford 1972, 752.
108. "The Social Distribution of Landed Property in England Since the Sixteenth Century," *Economic History Review*, 2nd series, 19, 1966, 513.
109. *English Landed Society in the Eighteenth Century*, London 1963, 23–5.
110. *TFC* 40.

such laws of development as may be peculiar to a specific mode of production. Could one, for instance, imagine trying to account for the nature of the development of capitalism in the nineteenth and twentieth centuries solely by reference to social factors, without bringing into the picture the law of capitalist accumulation and its mainspring, that is to say the mechanism of surplus value?[111]

This "law," "mainspring," and "mechanism" suggest precisely the sort of marxist orthodoxy frequently attacked (if seldom located) by historical revisionists, among other anticommunists.

But John Morrill strangely echoes Bois in his anticommunist attack on Brenner's *Merchants and Revolution*: "Brenner has written an unfashionable book in that the great majority of historians have turned their backs on *social-determinist* interpretations (what Brenner less accurately calls *social interpretation*) of the crisis in mid seventeenth-century England."[112] At first, Bois and Morrill seem to mean something quite different when attacking Brenner's "social" determinism: where Bois sees Brenner elevating the superstructural "social factors" of political self-organization over the economic base, Morrill sees him disguising as a "new social interpretation" yet another reductive marxist attempt to favor the economic base over the "superstructures" of politics, religion, and pure contingency. In sum, Brenner/Bois = Morrill/Brenner. But finally, Bois and Morrill mean something very similar by "social" determination: the specifically historical study of a complex social formation combining economic and non-economic (mainly, political) factors. Both present Brenner's "social" whole as a reductive part. In sum, Brenner/Bois = Brenner/Morrill. Like Sartre's totalizing progressive/regressive method, like Eagleton and Williams's materialist hierarchy of determinations, political marxism is neither a *cultural* materialism grounded in the superstructures, nor an *economistic* materialism grounded in the base, but a *historical* materialism grounded in class struggle.[113] As we saw in chapter 2, we find the stagist teleology of the Smithian tradition not only among "forces first" and dialectical materialist marxists, but among historical revisionists working from a "modernization" or "commercialization" narrative. And so far as they have any theory of historical change at all, we find it among postmodernist literary critics of the Renaissance, who employ something like Sweezy's exogenous explanation: their focus on the courts, streets, and stages of London suggests his dynamic urbanism; their fixation on print media and other forms of discursive agency suggests his technologism; and their view of society as a language-like phenomenon defined not by production and struggle but by circulation and negotiation suggests his "circulationism," as Dobb christens his focus on markets and exchange.[114]

111. *BD* 115.
112. "Conflict" 114.
113. Kaye, *British* 21–2. See Ellen Meiksins Wood on the omnipresence of the political and social despite the "primacy of production" (*Democracy* 24).
114. *TFC* 71.

But all this discussion of the transition from feudalism to capitalism still leaves us some distance from a political marxist account of bourgeois revolution in general, the English Revolution in particular. We may classify Dobb and Brenner as political marxists who emphasize both the mode of production and class struggle in explaining historical change. But where Dobb viewed the English Revolution as a "crucial historical moment" when capitalists overthrew a feudal ruling class, Brenner tended in his writings of the seventies and eighties to limit the English "bourgeois revolution" to economy alone, stretching it out into an agrarian long revolution of at least two centuries. He found precedent in Marx's economically focused model of primitive accumulation, which "appeared to undermine the historical and theoretical foundation of the theory of bourgeois revolution."[115] Rather than describing one class supplanting another, Brenner concentrates on the *internal* transformation of the agrarian ruling class, whereby feudal aristocrats became capitalist landlords seeking competitive leases, while wealthier peasants became capitalist tenant farmers and poorer peasants became proletarian agrarian wage laborers. But this argument leaves unanswered Dobb's earlier question to Paul Sweezy: if the English state was already capitalist by 1642, then what was the English Revolution about?[116] By implying that it need not have happened, Brenner came strangely close to the revisionists.

In *Merchants and Revolution* (1993), Brenner addressed this problem by offering a full-scale reinterpretation of the English Revolution through 1653.[117] Brenner sharply distinguishes the absolutist company merchants and merchant adventurers whose ability to profit rested on royal monopoly and charter, and the capitalist interloping or "new" merchants excluded from the companies and compelled to adopt capitalist techniques, including such competitive innovations as the organization of the slave trade and of production itself in North America and the Caribbean. The Civil War became inevitable only in 1640 or so when these capitalist new merchants came together with a majority of the agrarian capitalist ruling class in Parliament and the radical city movement, and when the absolutist monarchy came together with the company merchants and the conservative city movement.[118] The new merchants contributed their organizational expertise to the petitioning campaigns of

---

115. *TFC* 31–2. *BD* 308; "Bourgeois" 295.
116. *TFC* 62.
117. For some reaction to Brenner's book, see Christopher Hill, "Trading Places," *The Guardian* (May 4 1993); Alex Callinicos, *Theories and Narratives*, Durham, NC, 1995, 131–6; and the forum in *New Left Review* 207 (September/October 1994), with reviews by John Morrill, Ian Gentles, and Alex Callinicos. In "Maurice Thomson's War," *London Review of Books* 15, 1993, Perry Anderson drives home the importance of Brenner's book, but questions his accounts of religion, the small producers of London, territorial divisions in the war, and the thoroughly capitalist quality of the English ruling class. Brian Manning also points to residual feudal aspects of English landholding and to Brenner's neglect of the manufacturing districts ("English").
118. *BMR* 316, 354, 359–71, 454. In this account of party formation, Brenner acknowledges (364, 454, 666) his debt to Manning's *The English People and the English Revolution*.

1640–42, their funds and ships to the First Civil War. They also supported the New Model in its 1647 conflict with London's "political Presbyterians" and their company merchant allies.

Thus Brenner delivers two blows to the Smithian "bourgeois revolution" model, which pits the dynamic capitalist city of manufacturers and merchants against the feudal agrarianism that would "fetter" it. Where his earlier writings reconstructed the capitalist dynamism of early modern English agriculture, *Merchants and Revolution* finds absolutist English merchants in competition with properly capitalist ones. Paradoxically, Brenner simultaneously offers something like a classic "bourgeois revolution" conflict between an absolutist class-state comprising the monarchy itself, its clients, its state clergy, and its company merchants, all reliant on the centralized political extraction of surplus; and a capitalist-led group comprising much of the landed ruling class in Parliament, the colonial interloping merchants, the Puritan clergy associated with them, along with their radical allies among the English laboring classes. Brenner even finds capitalist industrialization, but in an unusual site: "The most spectacular and revolutionary commercial-industrial development of the Interregnum was the introduction of sugar planting in the West Indies. . . . The sugar plantation was a factory set in a field."[119] In some ways, this argument feels more traditionally marxist than Christopher Hill's later interpretation of the Revolution as Puritan and parliamentarian in its intention, bourgeois only in its outcome.

Small Producers and the English Revolution

In other ways, Brenner diverges from the British marxist historians, with their focus on men and women making their own history. Despite his inclination to see class struggle as the real engine of history, *Merchants and Revolution* displays no great interest in the English laboring classes. This is partly a matter of the project Brenner chooses: he does not *fail* to write Christopher Hill's richly textured cultural history from below, but undertakes a distinct and complementary history emphasizing structural analysis of the transition. But the problem goes beyond this, for as he teases out the logic of economic change in England after 1381, when English peasants ended their enserfment, Brenner tends to overlook the English laboring classes. The exception that proves the rule is that small segment of laboring-class traders who transformed themselves into capitalist new merchants. In Brenner's account, these traders tend to absorb the quite distinct class projects of radical small producers. Right through to 1649, he says a "radical alliance" including political independents, new merchants,

---

119. *BMR* 161. Compare C. L. R. James on the "huge sugar-factories" of San Domingo, whose slaves were "closer to a modern proletariat than any group of workers in existence at the time," and his argument for the crucial role of the French maritime bourgeoisie, enriched by these slaves, in the origins of the French Revolution (*The Black Jacobins*, New York 1963, 85–6, 58; see also 392).

domestic traders, and artisans maintained "a roughly consistent identity—
a set of continuing if often mutually antagonistic, core components." This
is fair enough for the early forties, and Brenner speaks with insight about
the splits between moderates and Levellers, and the Commonwealth's
failure in 1653 through its inability to choose between "the radicalism of
artisans and small tradesmen" and "the traditionalism of the old landed-
class rulers."[120] But he slips too quickly past the conflicts that preceded
and followed. After the summer of 1647, when laboring-class New Model
soldiers broke with their grandee officers, this conflict never disappeared.
It went dormant during the Second Civil War and the brief radical
experiment of Barebone's Parliament. But it broke out violently in the
Army mutinies at Ware in 1647 and Burford in 1649, and the sustained
resistance to the Protectorate by ex-Levellers, republicans, Fifth Monarchists, and Quakers. A marxist account of the Revolution should be able
to account for the fact that the new merchant Maurice Thomson and the
Fifth Monarchist-to-be Anna Trapnel, who walked in fellowship in William
Greenhill's radical Independent congregation during the mid-forties, had
taken different paths by 1654, when Thomson sat on Cromwell's High
Court of Justice, furthering his career as a slave-trading merchant, while
Trapnel lay in a trance outside Whitehall, prophesying furiously against
the Protectorate on behalf of sectarian small producers.

To return to Perry Anderson's categories for discussing bourgeois
revolution: Brenner examines the English bourgeois revolution's overdetermination from above (conflict with the absolutist state and its
clients), from within (the split within the English capitalist ruling class),
and from without (its Western plantations and commercial conflicts with
the Low Countries), but tends to slight its overdetermination from below:
bourgeois reactions to and struggles with the initiatives of the English
laboring classes.[121] Paradoxically, Brenner's narrative of historical change
comes to resemble that history based on "ruling-class choice and imposition" alone that he astutely criticizes in Wallerstein.[122] Throughout the
revolutionary era—from the petitioning days of 1640–42 to the rise of the
New Model to the Fifth Monarchist move toward social and cultural
revolution to the Quaker scare of the late fifties—the laboring class
determined ruling-class choices by making choices of its own.

In bracketing the laboring classes, and specifically the experience of
small production grounding their political praxis, Brenner also sidesteps
the question of transitional economic forms—an important unresolved
aspect of the Dobb/Sweezy debate. Dobb saw two centuries of deteriorat-
ing feudalism between the lords' loss of the clear power to extract a
surplus by coercion, and the laboring class's divorce from the means of
production. Here, we see "petty production of the worker-owner, artisan

---

120. *BMR* 537, 635.
121. *English* 105–18.
122. "Origins" 59.

or peasant type, which was not yet capitalist," though the majority of English small tenants were still tied to the remnants of *de facto* feudal compulsion.[123] Sweezy saw the transitional period as, not a *mixture* of feudal and capitalist modes of production, but a form in which "the predominant elements were *neither* feudal *nor* capitalist"—namely, a period of "pre-capitalist commodity production" in which the laboring classes still owned the means of production, but produced for exchange among themselves or on the market. Because Sweezy's argument threatens to leave us with two co-existent modes of production, Dobb insists we should continue to speak of a feudal England, however decayed, until the bourgeois revolution of 1642.[124]

Brenner has responded to Sweezy and Dobb's quarrel by emphasizing the sharpness of the break, though without the sort of detailed social or local analysis that would allow him to rule out transitional forms. But some of his most sympathetic marxist readers have denied that capitalism ruled English agrarian production by the beginning of the seventeenth century. Hill notes that the English state abolished most feudal tenures only during the Revolution, thus weakening peasants' non-market claims to the means of production.[125] Manning says that most English people lost access to the means of production only after the Revolution.[126] Anderson emphasizes the "ideologically" feudal quality of landholding and social relations, which continued to exercise a determining pressure on the mode of production itself.[127] Callinicos argues that Brenner's model fails to take into account such class struggles as the eighteenth-century conflicts over common right visible in E. P. Thompson's portrait of a society no longer feudal but not yet utterly capitalist, and the transitional mode of production forming the very foundation of new merchant wealth: the unwaged, indentured and enslaved labor of the New World plantations.[128]

The idea of transitional or co-existent modes of production need not debilitate marxist history. Rodney Hilton, for instance, characterizes the period after the 1380s, after the near-disappearance of servile villeinage, as a time of diminishing rents, high real wages, rising peasant prosperity, and "relatively untrammeled petty commodity production."[129] Before they were turned into proletarians, a substantial segment of the English laboring classes lived as subsistence farmers or small commodity producers, as urban or rural artisans who owned their own means of production, as women practicing domestic industry for subsistence or small exchange, as farmers or artisans or even wage laborers with some measure of

123. *Studies* 19–20.
124. *TFC* 19–20, 49–50, 42–63.
125. "Trading."
126. "English" 84.
127. "Maurice" 16.
128. *Theories* 35, 134, 232n.106.
129. *BD* 133–4.

common right that kept them from absolute dependence on the market, as masterless men and women seeking occasional work and a place to squat. No doubt, they were part of a transitional economic formation, with some of them rising into the class of capitalists while most fell into the class of free wage laborers those capitalists would exploit. But they were more than what they had been or what they and their descendants would become. They also lived out their lives through the relative independence they remembered, experienced, and hoped to extend. Thus, while I think Ellen Meiksins Wood and Harvey Kaye are right to group Brenner with the British marxist historians, I also think his work requires the complement of theirs—not just for adding cultural and ideological richness to his economic account, but for their attention to an entire class experience that tends to get lost in his account of the transition and the new merchants' revolution: that of English small producers after the decline of serfdom.

Much of the work of the "British" marxist historians, in fact, has focused on the particular political and cultural forms through which the laboring classes resisted proletarianization. While British capitalists continued struggling to expropriate the means of production from the immediate producers, the immediate producers of Britain and the entire Atlantic economy continued to find customary and innovative grounds to resist them. The entire corpus of Christopher Hill's work, particularly since *The World Turned Upside Down* (1972) and continuing to *Liberty Against the Law* (1996), has considered popular resistance to residual feudal or emergent capitalist expropriation—whether immediate resistance by Diggers, Fifth Monarchists, and the countless English poor resisting submission to the discipline of wage labor, or mediate ideological forms of resistance that we can see in sectarian religion, mechanic preaching, and literature. Hill writes history from below even when considering ruling-class figures. His Milton, for instance, is not only a bourgeois Puritan intellectual shaped by residual aristocratic humanism and emergent possessive individualism, but also a radical shaped by an oppositional "third culture" of antinomian sectarianism, based largely in the class experience of the laboring classes.[130]

I think the way ahead for marxists studying the English Revolution lies in a structural analysis from below that would synthesize the culturalist approaches of Hill and A. L. Morton with the economic and structural approaches of Anderson, Brenner, and Wood.[131] Brian Manning's *The English People and the English Revolution* (1976) is the closest approach thus far to such an analysis. Anticommunist historians and literary critics still scant or ignore Manning's book, despite (or perhaps because of) its skill in integrating a structural analysis of the class conflict leading up to the outbreak of hostilities with an analysis of the ideologies and forms in

130. *Milton and the English Revolution*, New York 1977.
131. Thanks to Ed White for the phrase.

which the English people became conscious of that conflict and fought it out. It puts the English laboring classes at the very center of the Revolution as innovative political actors and theorists in their own right. Manning concentrates on the "middling sort of people"—working people not reduced utterly to poverty or wage labor.[132] Manning's approach contrasts strongly with the usual somnambulistic turn to ruling-class initiative. For instance, Mark Kishlansky commences his revisionist account of the New Model Army in 1644 with the Self-Denying Ordinance and a parliamentary debate over the military failures of the Earl of Manchester.[133] Though frequently critical of Kishlansky, Ian Gentles follows suit.[134] But Manning begins with a London petition of July 7 1643 that encouraged Parliament to bypass Essex's defensive military tactics and institute a ten-thousand-man Puritan army. This petition led to the establishment of a parliamentary "Committee for the General Rising" under Henry Marten. When Parliament formed the New Model in the following year, it was trying not only to replace the stalled war effort conducted by the aristocratic parliamentary "right," but also to co-opt and contain the popular, extra-parliamentary "left."[135]

Manning's structural account of the Civil War's outbreak avoids the beloved (because easy to refute) model of straightforward self-expression by a rising revolutionary class. Instead, he examines the dialectical interaction of Parliament with the crowds of Londoners and provincial petitioners—previously "private" persons forming themselves into a revolutionary force under the pressure of economic distress, the threat of armed royalist reaction, and an ideology of Puritan antipopery. Fearing that the king would use force against them, Pym and his parliamentary associates appealed to the populace and condoned their petitioning campaign, which prompted a reactionary royalist party of order. Like the New Model, then, the royalist party has a plebeian origin: "The intervention of the people in the politics of the Long Parliament drove a wedge into the ruling class and divided it, and assured the triumph of the popular party. King, Lords and bishops were defeated: this was achieved not by the Commons, but by the mob."[136] The people's action had at least two significant effects. First, they created a precedent for a fundamental and ongoing alteration in the shape of English political life, based on the entry of private persons into various public realms (publishing, preaching, arguing law, governing, military leadership). Second, they created a new normative ideal of the people's safety as the highest law, and a model of the state as not the creator but the creature of the people—particularly those who had freely offered their blood and their labor for its preservation.

132. *English* 230–41.
133. *Rise* 28–33.
134. *G* 4–10.
135. *English* 312–13, 316–18.
136. Ibid. 210, 180.

Manning doesn't assume a clear class *demarcation*, for the parliamentarians were certainly a mixed group comprising nobles, Puritan clergy, gentry, capitalist new merchants, and the laboring classes, and set against a royalist group comprising king, Anglican clergy, gentry, company merchants, and the laboring classes. And in this as in all wars, the largest volume of the blood spilled on both sides was laboring-class blood. But he does describe a class *dynamic* explaining the complexity of motivations on both sides. Many became royalists not out of their liking for absolutism, but out of their fear of levelling democracy, while rebels took arms for significantly mixed reasons:

> Inevitably a wealthy parliamentarian squire and a poor parliamentarian peasant or craftsman would not see the conflict in the same terms: the former took up arms against other squires for political or religious reasons; the latter took up arms against royalist squires because they were squires as well as for political or religious reasons.[137]

Even putting aside Manning's substantial evidence for laboring-class hostility toward the ruling classes, the later schisms within the parliamentarian party become almost unintelligible if we fail to hypothesize significantly divided class motives. Manning's anticommunist readers sometimes complain that he doesn't provide an adequately Manichean vision of class conflict, but his account would probably have satisfied Mao Tse-Tung, whose "On Contradiction" (1937) argues that "Qualitatively different contradictions can only be resolved by qualitatively different methods"—the contradiction between the colonies and imperialism by national revolutionary war, the contradiction between proletariat and bourgeoisie by communist revolution. The Kuomintang and the Communist Party united in democratic revolution under Sun Yat-sen, split in class struggle from 1927 to 1936, reunited after 1935 against Japanese imperialism, and, of course, split once again after Mao wrote.[138] Similarly, the English parliamentary ruling class and the radical laboring class united against "popish" Arminianism in 1641, moved into substantial antagonism after 1647, reunited against Charles in the Second Civil War and in Barebone's Parliament, and split again with the formation of the Protectorate.

In the usual mode of British academic history, Manning seldom mentions marxist concepts or reflects explicitly on the interpretive principles he employs. When he does, the results can be unsatisfactory, as when he defines class by ideology and subjectivity ("ethos" and "feelings"), by tautology ("Whether or not a conflict is a class conflict depends on the extent to which it involves class issues"), and by fiat ("A revolutionary struggle is a class struggle").[139] But his practice is much better. His account shows how conflicts grow up *within* received and traditional forms without,

---

137. Ibid. 265.
138. *Four Essays on Philosophy*, Peking 1968, 23–78, 38, 47.
139. *Aristocrats* 71.

at first, any explicit revolutionary intention. He considers how cyclical economic crises (the depression of the twenties and thirties) were aggravated by political causes (the absolutist squeeze tactics of the Personal Rule), then conceptualized by the core ideology of antipopery, which welded together the class fractions comprising the parliamentarian/ popular party. Barry Reay observes that Manning provides "what could be described as the dialectics of the revolt within the Revolution"—one which supplements and complements Christopher Hill's more ideologically oriented work on the culture of radical sectarianism.[140]

Despite sharp idiomatic differences, Manning's account of the days of 1640–42 strongly resembles Sartre's classic account of the storming of the Bastille in 1789, which shows how an isolated and fragmented *serial collective* with its principle of unity outside itself changed into a revolutionary *fused group* with an internal principle of unity.[141] For Sartre, the unity of the fused group is always its own product, but also, frequently enough, the unintended consequence of action by another group or groups. The citizens of Paris, serially isolated by cold, hunger, and economic crisis, saw the electors of Paris beginning to move out of pure seriality by continuing to sit after royal decrees had dismissed them. Menaced by troops sent to surround Paris and restore order, they formed a revolutionary crowd. Similarly, during the Personal Rule, despite the sufferings imposed by Ship Money and other royal attempts to squeeze revenue from the English populace, almost all of Manning's Londoners and provincials remained serially isolated monarchists. Even if they engaged in spasmodic acts of resistance, and pre-political acts of experimental sociability, they continued to find their unity in the king or the local guild or the English church. But with the example of parliamentary opposition, particularly its trial and execution of Strafford, and with the fear of popish massacres in England suggested by the Irish rebellion, their seriality faded and they began fusing into a public, political existence.[142]

Both Sartre and Manning describe the formation of revolutionary groups and ideologies through praxis: not the revisionist model of a sheer disconnect of intentional action and effect, with historical actors stumbling in the dark from one act to another; not the ostensibly "liberal" or "marxist" model of fixed revolutionary intention mechanically generating revolutionary action; not even Christopher Hill's model of a revolution with parliamentary and Puritan origins, and unintended class

---

140. "The World Turned Upside Down: A Retrospect," Eley and Hunt, *Reviving* 53–71, 61. Reay compares Manning's analysis of the Revolution's beginning to his own analysis of its conclusion, when a Quaker scare cemented the ruling-class consensus underlying the Restoration (*The Quakers and the English Revolution*, London 1985, 81–100). Manning's complementary account in *Aristocrats* emphasizes hatred of oligarchical rule and the excise among various classes (119–36).
141. *SCDR* 351–63; see also his discussion in *SSM* 117–24.
142. Manning, *English* 57–69.

revolutionary effects.[143] Rather, both focus on the dialectical *process* of revolutionary will formation, in which intentional actions produce more or less unintended consequences, which become in turn the means for reflective clarification of those intentions and for forming new ones. As Sartre puts it, "The consequences of our acts always end up by escaping us, since every concerted enterprise, as soon as it is realized, enters into relation with the entire universe, and since this infinite multiplicity of relations goes beyond our intention." But the very fact that humans *do* things without intending to indicates a difference between human and inhuman action: "It is men who *do* and not avalanches." This very frustrated *doing* becomes integrated in the reflective praxis of later projects, and Sartre denounces as "marxist formalism" and even "Terror" that whiggish impulse to dematerialize the purposes historical actors posit for themselves and reduce the dialectical movement of history to an unwitting pursuit of a predetermined goal.[144]

Marx and Engels were certainly not immune to this sort of terror in all of their writing, which frequently embraces a Smithian modernization model, particularly with regard to the countryside, as in Engels's reference to the "silent vegetation" of pre-industrial peasants, Marx's reference to French peasants as a "sack of potatoes" whose devotion to their smallholdings he blames for the successes of Louis Napoleon, and their joint reference to capitalism rescuing peasants from "the idiocy of rural life."[145] But this is not by any means the whole story. In their later years, Marx and Engels returned to anthropological studies and read avidly accounts of "primitive communism" surviving among the Iroquois, the Irish, South Asians, North Africans, and Slavs.[146] After the emancipation of the Russian serfs in 1861 and the rise of Russian Narodism, Engels and especially Marx grew fascinated with the possibility of a direct transition from the *mir*, or Russian peasant commune, to advanced communism.[147] When

---

143. For the later Hill, the English bourgeoisie was bourgeois only by virtue of its "objective position" in the mode of production, and did not truly become a class "for itself" until late in the Revolution, or even later: like all bourgeois revolutions, the English Revolution was bourgeois primarily in its outcome, not its originating intention, for "bourgeois revolution . . . does *not* mean a revolution made by or consciously willed by the bourgeoisie" (*Collected* 3.112, 95; see also 94–124 and *Change* 278–82). This argument cedes too much to revisionists criticizing the traditional social interpretation, while maintaining a Smithian *apriorism* in which the final cause of capitalism reaches back into history to snap the fetters preventing it from giving birth to itself. See also Hill, "The Theory of Revolutions," in David Horowitz, ed., *Isaac Deutscher*, London 1971, 115–31, 127–8.

144. *SSM* 47–9.

145. *MECW* 4.309, 11.187, 6.488.

146. See Lawrence Krader, ed., *The Ethnological Notebooks of Karl Marx*, Assen 1974; and *The Asiatic Mode of Production*, Assen 1975.

147. See Teodor Shanin, ed., *Late Marx and the Russian Road*, New York 1983, a superb collection of nineteenth-century documents and twentieth-century reflections on them. For further discussion and some connections to seventeenth-century England, see my "Was Marx a Nineteenth-Century Winstanleyan? Communism, George Hill, and the *Mir*," *Prose Studies* 22.2, 1999, rpt in Andrew Bradstock, ed., *Winstanley and the Diggers 1649–1999*, London 2000.

N. K. Mikhailovsky described the first volume of *Capital* as (in Marx's words) "a historico-philosophical theory of general development, imposed by fate on all peoples, whatever the historical circumstances in which they are placed," Marx insisted on the "quite disparate results" of similar phenomena occurring in "different historical milieux." For example, the expropriated free peasants of ancient Rome became, not the capitalist wage laborers of early modern Europe, but slaves.[148] In correspondence with the exiled Narodnik Vera Zasulich, he suggested that the *mir* might become "the fulcrum for social regeneration in Russia." What threatened it was not History, not the dialectic, but the political project of the capitalist state, the landed proprietors, and the wealthier peasants, who wished "to turn the poor peasants—that is to say the majority—into simple wage-earners."[149]

Marx's late discussion of the *mir* suggests the political marxist theory of history as class struggle in particular historical contexts, not the unfolding of an immutable and irreversible process. In a temporally paradoxical phrase, Sartre says it "clearly shows that, for Marx, the history of the noncapitalist and pre-capitalist societies of the past *is not over and done with*"—that is to say, they aren't finished, and they aren't finished changing.[150] As this discussion redeems marxism from its characterization as an unequivocally unilinear and mechanistic teleology, so it redeems small production in seventeenth-century England from its whiggish characterization as a doomed transitional form. Marx's theory of the *mir*'s utopian potential bears most immediately on the Digger commune. But it is also relevant to the democratic utopia of small producers implicit in the radical praxis of other groups I will examine in part two, and still others that I do not (Quakers, Levellers, Clubmen, New England Separatists). The English Revolution was a bourgeois revolution overdetermined from below, but it was also a small-producers' revolution overdetermined (in this case, *crushed*) from above. For the failure of the English Revolution was primarily the failure of land reform. Among many others, Kevin Sharpe has offered a culturalist explanation for the Restoration: unlike other, more successful revolutions, the English Revolution failed to draw the people to it through a richly imagined revolutionary iconography.[151] But he ignores the material dimensions of republican failures and successes: the revolutions of France and Mexico flourished less because of their successful cultural revolutions—significant though those were—than because they gave peasants a material stake in the republic. The contrast with "Commonwealth" England (Winstanley, among others, noted the unfulfilled promise of the term) couldn't be stronger.[152]

148. *MECW* 24.196–201, 617n.227.
149. Ibid. 24.370–71, 360n.
150. *SCDR* 140; see also 142.
151. "'An Image Doting Rabble,'" Sharpe and Zwicker, *Refiguring* 25–56.
152. On the failure of agrarian reform, see Joan Thirsk, "Agrarian Problems and the English

The anonymous Leveller manifesto, *The Mournfull Cries of Many Thousand Poore Tradesmen* (1648), presents a brief but trenchant analysis of the nation's economic connectedness: taxes, custom, and excise force country people to raise the price of food, while keeping them from buying goods manufactured in the towns. The author asks,

> Is not all the controversy whose slaves the poor shall be? Whether they shall be the King's vassals, or the Presbyterians' or the Independent faction's? . . . You have in your hands the king's, queen's and prince's revenues, and papist lands, and bishops, and deans, and chapters lands, and sequestered lands, at least to the value of eighteen hundred thousand pounds by the year, which is at least five hundred thousand pounds a year more than will pay the navy, and all the army, and the forces which need to be kept up in England and Ireland.[153]

Eleven years later, after the state transferred these lands to private ownership, the Hartlibian Moses Wall tried to draw Milton's attention to another lost opportunity:

> You complain of the nonprogressency of the nation, and of its retrograde motion of late, in liberty and spiritual truths. It is much to be bewailed; but yet let us pity human frailty when those who had made deep protestations of their zeal for our liberty both spiritual and civil, and made the fairest offers to be asserters thereof, and whom we thereupon trusted; when those being instated in power, shall betray this good thing committed to them, and lead us back to Egypt. . . . Besides whilst people are not free but straitened in accommodations for life, their spirits will be dejected and servile. . . . Also another thing I cannot but mention, which is that the Norman Conquest and tyranny is continued upon the nation without any thought of removing it; I mean the tenure of lands by copyhold, and holding for life under a lord (or rather tyrant) of a manor; whereby people care not to improve their land by cost upon it, not knowing how soon themselves or theirs may be outed it, nor what the house is in which they live for the same reason; and they are far more enslaved to the lord of the manor, than the rest of nation is to a king or supreme magistrate![154]

A concerted effort to convert copyhold to freehold and enclosed commons and captured lands to public use could have secured the English Revolution by quickly expanding the property-holding political nation, raising up the peasantry as allies to rural and urban small producers, lifting the burden of free quarter and the excise, and providing a material ground for the creative sectarian experiments in self-governance unleashed by the Civil War. But the ruling classes were unpersuaded. For instance, a few months after Wall's letter, Milton's *Proposalls of Certain Expedients* proposed not the end of copyhold and the relief of the poor, but the classic utopia of capitalist improvement: the "just division of waste commons whereby the nation would become much more industrious,

---

Revolution," in R. C. Richardson, ed., *Town and Countryside in the English Revolution*, Manchester 1992, 169–97.

153. *LM* 276, 277.

154. *M* 7.511.

rich, and populous."[155] In February 1660, in the *The Readie and Easie Way*, he envisioned the county community as "a little commonwealth" ruled by "the nobility and chief gentry," who would make and apply laws "without appeal," creating a county oligarchy to complement the national oligarchy of his perpetual Grand Council.[156] Milton concludes his jagged and valiant pamphlet with Jeremiah's desperate appeal to the "earth, earth, earth!"— but spares not a thought for the land, land, land.[157]

No one better theorized this revolution that never came to be, the lost utopia of the English Revolution, than Gerrard Winstanley, who therefore gets the last word in this book. But he was by no means alone. Though largely urban, the Fifth Monarchy Men proposed to abolish copyhold and customary tenures in favor of freehold. The manifestos for Thomas Venner's Fifth Monarchist risings also propose turning all conquered estates into a common treasury so as to eliminate tithes, taxes, excise, and customs.[158] Mary Cary warned Barebone's Parliament to maintain control of the lands it had liberated, which would defray taxes, excise, and customs, "those great burdens of the people."[159] The Levellers also attended to agrarian problems and grew increasingly interested in reforming "base tenures" like copyhold, hoping that such an effort would underwrite the liberty of urban as well as rural small producers. Richard Overton concludes *An Appeale, From the Degenerate Representative Body* (1647) by demanding that the state restore the enclosed commons to the free use of the poor.[160] In 1650–51, John Lilburne and John Wildman helped to defend the rights of smallholding fenmen in the Isle of Axholme.[161] In 1652, while exiled to the Low Countries, Lilburne read Peter Chamberlen's *The Poore Mans Advocate*, Plutarch's *Lives*, and Machiavelli's *Prince* and *Discourses*. Inspired by the *Lex Agraria* of the Gracchi, he wrote the Levellers of Hertfordshire advocating a program of social welfare for the indigent, and a moderate settlement of lands on all soldiers. H. N. Brailsford says that the Levellers "would have peopled the English countryside with an enfranchised peasantry, so securely planted on the soil that it would have dared to stand erect." He attributes the Levellers' defeat to their failure to maintain an adequate focus on rural needs, but this was a quantitative and strategic, not an absolute and predetermined failure: "They did enough for the tenants' cause to provoke Cromwell and the gentry to crush them, but not enough to mobilise the villages as their resolute allies."[162]

---

155. Ibid. 7.338.
156. Ibid. 7.383, 458–9.
157. Ibid. 7.383, 388; these passages remain in April's revised edition (ibid. 7.458–9, 462).
158. *CFMM* 147. William Medley, scribe, *A Standard Set Up*, 1657, 20; [Thomas Venner,] *A Door of Hope*, 1660, 10.
159. [Attrib. M. R.—i.e., "Mary Rand"], *Twelve Humble Proposals*, 1653, 13.
160. *LM* 194–5.
161. Keith Lindley, *Fenland Riots and the English Revolution*, London 1982, 188–222.
162. *The Levellers and the English Revolution*, Stanford 1961, 611–14, 441, 450. See also his analysis of the near-Digger Buckinghamshire pamphlets (444–6) and his eloquent

The Clubmen, perhaps the largest popular movement of the era, and frequently neutralist, if not royalist, present a more challenging case. Non-marxist historians have returned to them again and again in an effort to deny the popular basis of the Revolution.[163] But this argument works only if we agree to see the parliamentarians and the grandees' New Model as unremittingly radical. They offered the Clubmen little more than plunder and enforced free quarter in the short term, perhaps a new landlord in the long term, and no clear social revolutionary program.[164] But John Morrill has pointed out the Clubmen's Levellerish calls for local autonomy and liberty from arbitrary power. The Somerset Association, for instance, argued that "it is possible that a parliament may err (and that foully) as well as a general council"—an argument suggesting the Diggers' more revolutionary plebeian critique.[165] Their traditions of village democracy, their experimental clubs of "associates," and their published declarations and petitions suggest that, as Brian Manning says, they "belong with the history of popular movements and of popular intervention in politics during the English Revolution."[166] If we could refrain from collapsing active neutralism into passive traditionalism, a full-scale examination of the Clubmen next to the Diggers would make an important contribution to our understanding of the revolutionary era.

Robert Brenner observes,

> As almost all sections of the alliance of forces that made the revolution of 1648 were aware, any formal democratic settlement would have restored the conservative gentry to power. This was simply because, with the important exception of London (and of course the army), relatively few areas in the nation had experienced significant radicalization during the Civil War years.[167]

But this sounds a little too inevitable. A counterfactual analogy: after the American Civil War, the emancipated Southern slaves were less accustomed to self-governance than the English laboring classes in 1649, and they constituted a much smaller part of the population. Yet with the assistance of the occupying Union Army, they quickly began moving into positions of power and forming institutions of mutual aid. Ten more years of occupation, with a program of land reform benefiting poor whites as well as blacks, might have rooted out the plantocracy and created a self-sustaining, biracial agrarian populism. This populist South might then have elected representatives capable of joining Northern radicals in resisting the depredations of Northern capitalist magnates. Similarly, in

---

account of a visit to the last English open field at Laxton, which he compares to the village community in the Pathan borderland of India, and the *mir* near Vladimir, in which "there was to the last a lively sense of community and fellowship, which sprang from the collective ownership of the fields" (420–22).

163. On the Clubmen, see Morrill, *Revolt* 98–111, 196–200, and Underdown, *Revel* 156–9.
164. Hill, *Change* 204.
165. *Revolt* 101.
166. *Aristocrats* 84; see also 137–41 and *English* 30–31 and 431n.86.
167. *BMR* 539.

1649, the Commonwealth could have begun a genuine program of land reform aimed at restoring enclosed commons and liberated absolutist lands to the poor, transforming copyhold into freehold, ending all tithes, converting some captured lands to state property, and easing or eliminating taxation. If an ascetic army of officers more interested in nurturing popular justice than in gorging on land had enforced such a program for ten years, it is difficult to imagine the transformed English people acquiescing in the Restoration settlement.

But to return to factual assertion: in the wake of the Depression of 1873, the Northern and Southern ruling class came together to arrange the election of Rutherford B. Hayes, the withdrawal of occupying Union troops, and the end of Reconstruction in a racialized reign of terror that has not yet ended.[168] Similarly, the New Model grandees and their allies embarked on a land rush that left the laboring classes outside the freeholding political nation, fragmented the revolutionary cause, and ultimately ushered in the Restoration. In both cases, the laboring classes failed to unify their rural and urban fragments, cement a bond with the Army, and institute a genuine social revolution grounded in small-producer democracy. These failures were real and tragic, but not necessary or inevitable. Indeed, the descendants of seventeenth-century English and nineteenth-century American workers, who continued to struggle against proletarianization and in some measure succeeded, saw and see no such inevitability. As E. P. Thompson has observed,

> Our only criterion of judgement should not be whether or not a man's actions are justified in the light of subsequent evolution. After all, we are not at the end of social evolution ourselves. In some of the lost causes of the people of the Industrial Revolution we may discover insights into social evils which we have yet to cure. . . . Causes which were lost in England might, in Asia or Africa, yet be won.[169]

They might even be won in Manchester or the Mississippi Delta.[170]

Early Modern Studies and the British Marxist Historians

No marxist contemplating the course of twentieth-century intellectual history can hold on to the notion of a unilinear and progressive history. It's easier to spot a number of promising roads not taken. In a 1986 essay, Raymond Williams considered the brief efflorescence of Soviet cultural theory that he christened "the road from Vitebsk," referring to a town in which P. N. Medvedev, V. N. Vološinov, and M. M. Bakhtin engaged in an innovative program of workers' education and developed a cultural theory that shunned both the orthodox pressure toward economism and the

---

168. Howard Zinn, *A People's History of the United States*, New York 1990, 194–205; C. Vann Woodward, *Reunion and Reaction*, Boston 1966.
169. *Making* 13.
170. Clyde Woods, *Development*.

Russian Formalist rejection of all literary responsiveness to collective human purposes and struggles. But Medvedev and Vološinov disappeared into the Gulag, and bourgeois Western cultural theory took the road toward Geneva, Vienna, and Paris instead, with disastrous results for any socialist who wishes to see culture as the product of creative practical consciousness in a context of material scarcity.[171] We could certainly point to other such roads. The utopian populism of Ernst Bloch's *Principle of Hope* lies some distance from both Adorno's melancholy reification theory and Benjamin's messianic technologism—both of them gravitating toward high culture and metaphysics, both of them much more easily assimilated to regnant postmodernist and anticommunist modes of idealist literary theory; like utopia itself, Bloch's time seems to be forever *not yet*.[172] Sartre's *Critique of Dialectical Reason* first appeared, unpropitiously, in 1960, just as structuralism poured over France, and it finally arrived in English translation in 1976, just as that wave reached the English-speaking world. But now, forty years later, after the exhaustion of the postmodernist project in a morass of contingency and power, as post-postmodernists begin working their way toward an analysis of collective agency, it may be time for Sartre's *Critique* to rise again from the depths. Though certainly not without its own problems, its unsurpassed phenomenology of practical ensembles, its anticipation of recent efforts to resist the structural marxist evacuation of reflective human agency, its ferocious attack on reductive and aprioristic marxism, and its fundamentalist marxist insistence on the priority of class, labor, and human need could play an important role in contemporary struggles to escape the aporias of postmodernist thought.[173]

Just as Sartre remains the excoriated but un- or underread and unassimilated Other for the postmodernists whom I examine in chapter 3, so do the British marxist historians for the revisionists whom I examine in chapter 2—and for their post-revisionist successors. This group, not always British, includes the original members of the Historians' Group of the Communist Party (Maurice Dobb, Christopher Hill, Rodney Hilton, Eric Hobsbawm, Victor Kiernan, A. L. Morton, George Rudé, John Saville, Dorothy Thompson, E. P. Thompson, and Dona Torr), along with a number of students, allies, and sometimes critics (Perry Anderson, Robert

---

171. *The Politics of Modernism*, London 1989, 171; see also 151–62.
172. Jamie Owen Daniel and Tom Moylan, eds, *Not Yet: Reconsidering Ernst Bloch*, London 1997. See also Ernst Bloch, *Literary Essays*, Stanford 1998—an edition that presents Bloch as an aesthetician, an Expressionist, a "public intellectual," anything but a Red.
173. The second volume appeared in French in 1985, and in English as *Critique of Dialectical Reason, Vol. II (unfinished): The Intelligibility of History*, London 1991. On Sartre, see Thomas R. Flynn's *Sartre and Marxist Existentialism*, Chicago 1984; *Sartre, Foucault* (and its forthcoming companion volume); Mark Poster's *Existential Marxism in Postwar France*, Princeton 1975; and Fredric Jameson's edited special issue of *Yale French Studies* 68 (1985) entitled "Sartre after Sartre." For a brilliant, sympathetic critique of Sartre that draws on the then-unpublished manuscript for the second volume of the *Critique*, see Anderson's *Arguments* 50–53. The whole chapter, "Agency" (16–58), which focuses on the interrelations of E. P. Thompson and Louis Althusser, is of the greatest interest for considering the mode of production in marxist social theory.

Brenner, Terry Eagleton, Peter Linebaugh, Brian Manning, Marcus Rediker, Raymond Williams, and Ellen Meiksins Wood).[174] They, too, grew up in part through experimental efforts in workers' and adult education, and they, too, fell into a conflict with the Communist Party, and most left in 1956. We might summarize the group's collective achievement under four headings. They formulated a "class struggle" model of social change distinct from the idealist history of ideas and orthodox economism. They focused on history from below—on working people themselves, but also on history as a whole reconceptualized from their perspective. They reconstructed a compelling account of popular and radical intellectual traditions. And with their attention to lived human praxis, with all its byways and dead-ends, they constructed a *historical* materialist alternative to both liberal whig history and dialectical materialist stagism, displaying a profound interest in embodied marxist utopia: those women and men who were *not yet* proletarian in their labor or their intellectual traditions.[175]

For the last twenty years or so, while the mainstream of Renaissance literary studies has produced historical/biographical studies and editions, the interpretive avant-garde has engaged a continental tradition of anticommunist and antihumanist theory, producing the Renaissance new historicism, among other interpretive modes. I argued in the previous chapter that this avant-garde has reached an interpretive impasse. I think that one way out might be a serious engagement with the work of the British marxist historians. Thus far, the dialogue has been slight. Its development would ask literary critics to cast off their endemic anticommunism, and that will take a heave and a grunt, particularly in the US, where Miltonists and Romanticists unable to ignore Christopher Hill and E. P. Thompson frequently manage to slough off the historical materialist dimensions of their arguments—a common enough American strategy with dubious foreign imports.[176] It would ask them to move beyond the philosophical critique of essentialism and the discursive analysis of subject formation, to the historical analysis of the transition from feudalism to capitalism, the class struggles that accompanied it, and the early modern practical ensembles conducting and created by those struggles. It would also ask them to continue expanding their definition of "literature" (or at least, of "writing worth sustained and careful analysis") to include those works in which laboring-class women and men made their own lives and

---

174. See Kaye's sympathetic studies of the group (*British* and *Education*) and Alastair MacLachlan's critique (*Rise*).

175. I am indebted to Harvey Kaye (*Education* 100–101) and to Lew Daly for this summation.

176. Compare the de-marxing of structuralism, "critical theory" (including Habermas), "cultural studies," and "postcolonial theory"—no great surprise, given the bone-deep practical anticommunism of the US, which has murdered more people in its name than any nation except Nazi Germany. Even to name American anticommunism is to risk a retaliatory but self-denying instance of it. If all this sounds like a strident digression, that's exactly my point: like Graham Greene's insouciant Pyle, Americans remain, for the most part, hysterically oblivious to the blood they have shed in Korea, Indochina, Latin America, and elsewhere. Oops, a megadeath!

conceptualized their own practical activity. And given the agrarian origins of English capitalism, it would ask them to supplement their court- and London-focused interpretive practice with renewed attention to the countryside.

Such a dialogue would require a disciplinary leap no greater than that required by the theory revolution of the seventies and eighties, which brought literary critics into dialogue with anthropologists, semioticians, philosophers, and psychoanalysts. Second, it would offer a considerable historical overlap: the traditions counting as "theory" in recent years have typically focused on modernity and postmodernity, making for a sometimes productive but usually strained bridging effort, and the formulaic depiction of early modern British women and men as premature postmodernists has begun to cloy. But from Maurice Dobb's *Studies in the Development of Capitalism* to T. H. Aston and C. H. E. Philpin's collection *The Brenner Debates*, from Rodney Hilton's studies of the Peasant Rising of 1381 to J. M. Neeson's study of commoning in late eighteenth- and early nineteenth-century England,[177] the British marxist historians have made the early modern transition from feudalism to capitalism the very center of their work. Third, the recent "culturalist" interest in postcolonial theory and the Atlantic world could benefit considerably from recent marxist studies of the role of waged, indentured, enslaved, and free labor in shaping the black, white, and red Atlantic of the seventeenth century, from England to Africa to the Caribbean to North America—themselves an implicit or explicit critique of the insular habits of the British marxist historians.[178] And fourth, literary critics' abiding commitment to questions of gender, particularly if developed through a further dialogue with materialist feminist theory and history, could add a great deal to marxist discussions of the transition, since gender and the reproduction of labor power are glaring omissions from the British marxist account of the transition.

But what texts am I talking about? Didn't the laboring classes tend to be illiterate? And didn't somebody once say "the ideas of the ruling class are in every epoch the ruling ideas"? During the past twenty years, early modern literary studies has been transformed by the consideration of gender, including the discovery or rediscovery of an entire canon of texts by and about women, lesbians, and gay men (texts once all but invisible), and by a systematic effort to ask new questions about gender (questions once all but unposable). A similar turn to class could highlight the social practice and imaginative ideal of small-producing men and women, a group which is neither feudal nor capitalist nor mechanically and inevitably transitional between the two, and which extends from Piers Plowman to More's Utopians to Milton's Adam and Eve to Mary Collier to John

---

177. Neeson, *Commoners*, Cambridge 1993.
178. Theodore W. Allen, *The Invention of the White Race*, 2 vols, London 1994 and 1997; *BMR*; Paul Gilroy, *The Black Atlantic*, Cambridge, MA, 1993; C. L. R. James, *Black Jacobins*; Peter Linebaugh and Marcus Rediker, *The Many-Headed Hydra*, London 2000.

Clare's commoners, and from English to Gaels to Algonquians to Ibo. A systematic effort by early modern literary critics and intellectual historians to consider particular works, writers, and genres inside a framework focused on class struggle and the transition from feudalism to capitalism could not only enrich the account of the transition developed by the British marxist historians, but develop and transform it. I would be jumping the gun to predict just what shape that transformation might take, but I hope it comes, and I hope this book contributes to it.

PART TWO

RADICAL PROJECTS

5

The Deference of John Felton

We are a game at cards; the Council deal,
The lawyers shuffle, and the clergy cut,
The king wins from the losing commonweal
The duke keeps stakes; the courtiers work, and put
The stock far from the city; thus all jump
Still cross; for why? Prerogative is trump.

—anonymous ms poem, 1620s

But there will never be any lack of servile courtiers, who do not keep to any honorable position, but reach such a stage of insolence that they say that God, angered at the people, sends tyrants, whom he sets up as executioners, who punish those who deserve to be punished. I own that this is true, but it is equally true that God has called poor and almost unknown men from the ranks of the common people to execute vengeance on an arrogant and worthless tyrant.

—George Buchanan, *De Iure Regni apud Scotos*

This death expresses at the same time the impossible revolt of his people, hence his *actual* relation with the colonizers, the radical totality of his hate and refusal, and finally the inward project of this man—his choice of a brief, dazzling freedom, of a freedom to die.

—Jean-Paul Sartre, *Search for a Method* [1]

Introduction

On the morning of Saturday, August 23 1628, George Villiers, Duke of Buckingham, awoke at his lodgings in Portsmouth, where he was organizing an expedition to relieve the besieged Huguenots of La Rochelle. After breakfast, while making his way through a crush of soldiers and clients so he could visit King Charles at nearby Southwick Park, he paused to speak with one of his colonels. At that moment, a lieutenant named John Felton stabbed him in the left breast with a ten-penny knife. He died almost instantly. Felton was captured, interrogated, tried, and condemned. On

---

1. Sartre refers to the death of an African worker who stole an airplane in England, flew south, and crashed.

November 28, he was hanged at Tyburn, and his body was suspended near Portsmouth, where it rotted in the open air.

That's a good, drop-dead chapter opening, but it's a little deceptive so far as its bloody anecdotal form promises an argument for the essentially personal or theatrical quality of political life. A revisionist historian taking up this episode might want to focus on Felton's personal motivation and argue that he acted because of patronage denied, not political conviction. A new historicist might extend this argument into a more dramatic and metaphysical realm, arguing that the spectacle of Felton's body shows us that the most theatrical acts of opposition wind up serving the interests of sovereign authority. For fear of vulgar, romantic populism, both would probably concentrate on the career of Buckingham, that exemplary client, patron, and Renaissance self-fashioner, who seems almost to have been conjured up by Marlowe's Gaveston, Chapman's Bussy, and Jonson's Sejanus.[2] But in this chapter, I will argue that Felton's intimate and theatrical encounter with Buckingham arose from and opened up into a larger collective and ideological conflict. I will focus on Felton as well as Buckingham. Political actors like Felton, who associate themselves with nascent political opposition, help make the Revolution a comprehensible event rather than a contingency. Like Damiens's attack on Louis XV, Felton's on Buckingham was a rationally motivated act, and it moved England a step forward on the path leading—not necessarily, but intelligibly—to revolution.

This old-fashioned argument about opposition invites a charge of teleology, anachronism, and infidelity to sources, so I want to emphasize my reliance not on what people "must have" been thinking, but on what they actually wrote—in diaries, newsletters, confessions, prophecies, and, above all, manuscript poetry about the duke and Felton. Many of these poems have been readily available for 150 years in Frederick Fairholt's *Poems and Songs Relating to George Villiers, Duke of Buckingham; and His Assassination by John Felton, August 23, 1628*, while others reside in those manuscript archives that revisionists so frequently criticize others for slighting. But Roger Lockyer's biography of Buckingham and Kevin Sharpe's *Criticism and Compliment*, two notable revisionist accounts of the period, make little use of them. True, in a later essay, Sharpe and Peter Lake do mention "the vulgar invectives and libels against the Duke of Buckingham that circulated amongst the people," which "replicated, albeit in a rather demotic form, the charges of his peers."[3] But this argument itself replicates a rather patrician model of cultural transmission, whereby aristocratic discourse seeps into the deme and circulates turbidly among mutable many. And it does no justice to the sophisticated poetry produced and circulated among the various anti-Buckingham

2. On Buckingham, see Henry Wotton's *A Short View of the Life and Death of George Villiers*, 1642, rpt *Reliquiae Wottonianae*, 1685, 161–83; and Lockyer, *Buckingham.* See also J. H. Elliott and L. W. B. Brockliss, eds, *The World of the Favourite*, New Haven, CT, 1999.
3. "Introduction" 11.

classes. The oppositional sentiments appearing in this poetry could not readily appear in public. As John Eliot discovered to his distress, a direct attack on Buckingham in a pamphlet or in Parliament was a booking slip for a room in the Tower. But an anonymous manuscript poem attacking the duke or even the king could circulate freely and become an active medium for culturing a new form of oppositional political consciousness.[4]

The subculture defined by and defining this opposition will never come into focus if we insist that Caroline England must have been a deferential unity if it was not riven by sharply defined and antagonistic political parties. Felton and his friends emerge neither from a monolithic absolutist cultural system, nor from a self-consciously regicidal republicanism, but from an oppositional *structure of feeling*—Raymond Williams's term for a body of lived beliefs and collective values that stops short of a formal ideology, extending "over a range from formal assent with private dissent to the more nuanced interaction between selected and interpreted beliefs and acted and justified experiences." Structures of feeling are frequently more accessible to specifically *cultural* analysis than to any other approach.[5] If we focus on the textures of Caroline culture, we will see a political opposition thinking its way slowly toward revolution and regicide, but doing so *inside* a monarchist and loyalist frame of reference: an engraving of 1628 depicts Felton holding his hat deferentially in one hand, his dagger in the other.[6] The assassination and the poems reflecting

---

4. In *Fleeting Things*, Cambridge, MA, 1990, 49–66, Gerald Hammond wrote the first significant study of the poems for more than a century, comparing them to those commemorating the execution of Strafford. On the early modern culture of libel, see above all the works of Alastair Bellany, including "The Poisoning of Legitimacy? Court Scandal, News Culture and Politics in England, 1603–1660," diss., Princeton University 1995; "'Raylinge Rymes and Vaunting Verse': Libellous Politics in Early Stuart England, 1603–1628" (Sharpe and Lake, *Culture* 285–310); and his two forthcoming books, *The Politics of Court Scandal in Early Modern England* (Cambridge) and *Death of a Favourite* (Manchester). The latter will include our preliminary catalogue of the Buckingham/Felton poetry. See also Adam Fox's "Ballads, Libels and Popular Ridicule in Jacobean England," *Past and Present* 145, 1994; and Thomas Cogswell's "Underground Verse and the Transformation of Early Stuart Political Culture," in Susan D. Amussen and Mark Kishlansky, eds, *Political Culture and Cultural Politics in Early Modern England*, Manchester 1995, 277–300. On newsletters, see Richard Cust's "News and Politics in Early Seventeenth-Century England," *Past and Present* 112, 1986; Ann Baynes Coiro's "Milton and Class Identity," *Journal of Medieval and Renaissance Studies* 22.2, 1992; Andrew Mousely, "Self, State, and Seventeenth-Century News," *The Seventeenth Century* 6, 1991; and Sharpe's *The Personal Rule*, which questions the importance of newsletters in culturing an oppositional public sphere (683–90). William S. Powell's study of John Pory (*P*), includes a microfiche edition of Pory's newsletters.

5. *Marxism* 132–4.

6. "The Lively Portraiture of Iohn Felton who most Miserably kil'd the right Honorable George Villiers Duke of Buckingham August the 23 1628," in the Sutherland Collection at the Ashmolean Museum (see jacket illustration). This may be the portrait of the "assassinate" commissioned by Abraham Darcie to adorn a group of his poems commending Buckingham, licensed by Secretary Conway, then denied by Laud, who feared a veiled satire (*CSPD* 3.xv, 281, 346). Darcie or "Abraham De Ville Adrecie" was a poet (see *Honors True Arbor*, 1625) and translator of Camden, Casaubon, Du Moulin, and Sleidan.

upon it reveal a gestating ideology of revolutionary resistance that would culminate in the Revolution, the regicide, and resistance to Cromwell.[7]

In "Good Clients Gone Bad," I argue that tyrannicides like Felton dramatically mark out the limits of the early modern patronage system. In "Buck, King of Game," I consider opposition to Buckingham as the project of a class coalition directed against the project of the absolutist Caroline class-state. In "God bless thee, little David!" I consider the assassination itself and Felton's subsequent interrogation and execution. In "Felton at Colonus," I examine a number of anonymous poems reflecting on these events, and in "Noble Felton Resolutions," some later recollections.

Good Clients Gone Bad: Patronage and Tyrannicide

The study of literary and political patronage has become a boom industry.[8] Whereas liberal and socialist historians have focused on clashing ideologies and classes leading to the English Revolution, revisionists have focused on the personal rivalries contained within a distinctively premodern patronage system. Even Derek Hirst, who has written an important critique of revisionism, describes patronage as a universal and relatively humane "social lubricant."[9] Meanwhile, new historicist literary critics have called patronage not only the socioeconomic context in which poets and dramatists write, but the very subject matter and goal of their writing. They have produced numerous critical studies focusing on patronage, on writers particularly associated with it, on genres such as the court

7. Compare the career of the preacher Thomas Scott. In 1623, he fled from Stuart and Anglican censorship to Utrecht. He republished his radical English works and wrote many new ones until assassinated in 1626 by a former Spanish agent. His forthright attacks on popery, Spain, and Gondomar, the Spanish ambassador, and his support of the House of Commons and anti-episcopal Christianity, form a canon unlike that of any other contemporary English author. John Felton's indirect assault on Charles's absolutism through Buckingham resembles Scott's on James's pro-Spanish policy through Gondomar. Felton's foreordained execution and Scott's Continental exile put both temporarily beyond the pressures of censorship and the patronage system, making them precursors to the relatively uncensored sectarians and radical presses of the revolutionary era. In effect, they become the oppositional unconscious of their time, and prophets of more material and collective opposition in the forties and fifties. On Scott, see Markku Peltonen, *Classical Humanism and Republicanism in English Political Thought 1570–1640*, Cambridge 1995, 229–70; and Peter Lake, "Constitutional Consensus and Puritan Opposition in the 1620s," *The Historical Journal* 25.4, 1982.

8. For three important collections, see Cedric C. Brown, ed., *Patronage, Politics, and Literary Traditions in England, 1558–1658*, Detroit 1993; Guy Fitch Lytle and Stephen Orgel, eds, *Patronage in the Renaissance*, Princeton 1981; and Sharpe and Zwicker, *Politics*. See also Richard Helgerson, *Self-Crowned Laureates*, Berkeley and Los Angeles 1983; Arthur F. Marotti, *John Donne, Coterie Poet*, Madison 1986; Stephen Orgel, *The Illusion of Power*, Berkeley and Los Angeles 1975; and Don E. Wayne, *Penshurst*, Madison 1984. New historicist arguments about the importance of patronage frequently resemble those of traditional historicists. John Buxton argues for a closed and relatively conflict-free economy of patronage, sadly lost in the modern world, in *Sir Philip Sidney and the English Renaissance*, London 1954. I am indebted for this point to M. D. Jardine's fine essay "New Historicism for Old: New Conservatism for Old?" in Brown, *Patronage* 291–309.

9. "The Place of Principle," *Past and Present* 92, 1981; *Authority* 31.

masque central to it, and on other genres, showing for instance that Elizabethan poets write their sonnet sequences to gain political as well as erotic favor. Arthur F. Marotti argues that "almost all English Renaissance literature is a literature of patronage."[10] Invoking Marotti, Jonathan Goldberg drops the "almost," and he calls Ben Jonson a "representative voice—perhaps the representative voice—of Jacobean culture, creating its language and being created by it, the voice that most fully reproduces his society."[11] Even Stanley Fish, a frequent critic of the new historicism, shares Goldberg's appreciation of Jonson's ability to establish something like autonomy within a closed symbolic and economic order.[12] Indeed, he sees modern academic criticism inhabiting a patronage world: it can be oppositional "only in an internal sense as younger critics look for arguments and methods by which they can be distinguished from the older practitioners they hope to replace."[13]

In these arguments "patronage" frequently becomes "the patronage system"—something considerably more total and mechanistic than a structure of feeling. Werner L. Gundersheimer begins his "Patronage in the Renaissance" in a reserved tone, calling patronage only "one of the dominant social processes of pre-industrial Europe," and noting that humanists like More and iconoclastic Protestant radicals frequently opposed it. But by the end of his essay, these opponents to patronage have become the foolish utopian Gonzalo of *The Tempest*, and patronage has changed from part to whole: "The political and social orderings in European societies in the Renaissance are mirrored in their structures of patronage."[14] Sharpe and Zwicker find patronage to be only one among many determinants of literary production in the Renaissance, but also, somehow, "the cynosure of all political and social relationships. To see literary relations as part of the system of clientage is to chart the history of literary production." Their metaphor calls up the totalitarian astrology of the Stuart masques themselves: just as the masque circles around and focuses on the polar monarch viewing it, so all early modern culture revolves around patronage, and so, too, should all study of the period.[15] Indeed, in a long essay on early Stuart culture, Sharpe comments, "We have studied the world picture of early modern England as one might study a court masque."[16]

Now one might object that all such attempts to reconstruct *world pictures* produce masque-like accounts that contain conflict and silently exclude enormous domains of human experience. If *patron/client* stands tall as a model for considering the *king/poet* relation, it staggers when we move to

10. "John Donne and the Rewards of Patronage," Lytle and Orgel, *Patronage* 207–34.
11. *James I* xiv, 230.
12. "Authors-Readers," *Representations* 7, 1984.
13. "Driving from the Letter," in Mary Nyquist and Margaret W. Ferguson, eds, *Re-membering Milton*, New York 1987, 234–54, 250.
14. Lytle and Orgel, *Patronage* 3–23, 3, 23.
15. Sharpe and Zwicker, *Politics* 15, 13.
16. Sharpe, *Politics* 63.

master/apprentice and *landlord/tenant*, and stumbles when we turn to *bishop/ Baptist* and *sister/sister*. And if patrons create clients by granting them the right to extract surplus labor from a third party, then no society can ever be simply a patronage system. Like the potlatch relation to which anthro-pologically informed critics frequently compare it, the patronage system contains a crucial economic dimension: its conspicuous display of unpro-ductive and excessive expenditure reinforces the symbolic power of the absolutist class-state, and so also the legitimacy of its non-market-based extraction of surplus—a process quite distinct from potlatch. But in the normal course of things, such arguments will never come up, and "the patronage system" will serve as an ersatz *mode of production*, allowing critics to continue working undisturbed inside a chiasmic closed loop: the literature of patronage/the patronage of literature. Arguments for society as a patronage system are powerful precisely because they render inaud-ible certain sorts of evidence, opposing arguments, and methodological questions.

This impulse toward systematization also appears in Sharpe's *Criticism and Compliment: The Politics of Literature in the England of Charles I*, winner of the Royal Historical Society's Whitfield Prize for 1987, and perhaps the first revisionist attempt to supplement a high political narrative with an explicit account of culture. For Sharpe, "patronage describes not a condition of servility, but all social and political relationships, relation-ships of *mutual* dependency," and he argues for the importance and moral seriousness of such Caroline court poets as Davenant, Carew, Townshend, and Shirley.[17] They "were not mere acolytes of kings; they provided counsel as well as celebration, criticism as well as compliment" and each engaged "the fundamental ethical and political questions of his day."[18] Though previously seen as the mere mushrooms of a decaying court, these clients were its most astute critics: "It is no contradiction in terms to suggest that opposition to 'the court,' or at least to a prevailing faction or policy, was articulated by a courtier, or that criticisms of 'the court' could be made by a courtier to a courtier."[19]

Sharpe's argument about criticism at the center complements the revisionist argument about authority at the periphery, where ruling ideas penetrate and compromise the ostensible radical. One can get no closer to actual opposition than the patronage system's self-correcting mecha-nisms for containment: "the commonweal was one ethical community" and "one political community from the highest ... to the lowest," a community which "shared a common discourse" and "common values."[20] Even Milton becomes a covert courtier who inhabited "that common world of Renaissance humanism which is all too often fragmented by those who erect too rigid boundaries of 'court' and 'country,' or

17. 291.
18. 223, 178.
19. 93.
20. 16, 266, 53.

'Anglican' and 'puritan.' "[21] All those historians who have stressed divisions within this common culture—Perez Zagorin, Margot Heinemann, Martin Butler, David Norbrook, Lawrence Stone, and, of course, Christopher Hill—are importers of "a priori assumptions." Everyone in this (rather significantly mixed) group suffers from "that most dangerous of historical ailments, anachronism; from, that is, the translation into early Stuart England of the ideas and politics of a later age."[22]

In chapter 2, I called this a strangely prerogative argument, since all historians approach texts with assumptions open to rational examination and debate. Furthermore, Sharpe's *a priori* devotion to a one-culture hypothesis rivals Zagorin's to a division between country and city. And his own critical practice shows that there is more than one way to be anachronistic. We may indeed slip into genetic anachronism by searching a period so minutely for anticipations that we miss what's most important to that period itself. But we may also slip into an abstractive anachronism by focusing so closely on certain phenomena like patronage that we fail to place them in the field of contemporary phenomena that give them shape and being. As Mary Fulbrook observes, "Metatheoretically, such exaggerated stress on patron–client relationships is at least as philosophically degrading as any other form of downplaying the autonomy of human action—such as seeing men merely as agents of historical forces—and therefore should be rejected by revisionists on their own arguments."[23] When Sharpe turns patronage into a system governing all of culture—when he can find no alternative or oppositional practices for patronage to ally with, oppose, repress, work on—he detaches it from its context and purges it of its true political materiality.

As a result, Sharpe creates a curious hybrid version of the history of ideas that we might refer to as empiricist platonism—a hybrid defined by a doctrinaire hostility to the theory of others and an inability to focus on the dialectical formation of contradictory ideas and discourse in practice. Terms such as "virtue," "truth," "nature," "love," "reason," and "passion" float into Sharpe's ken as if there were no need to consider struggles over them. Davenant saw virtue and truth as "the absolute standards which prescribe and ought to determine how men behave in society and in politics"; but we never consider how a classical republican might define "virtue." Courtly poets saw love as "the cynosure of human relationships" and "the cynosure of relationships that constituted medieval and early modern government"; but Sharpe never acknowledges that Anne Bradstreet, Milton, and the Ranters might not have viewed love as did the starry-eyed encomiasts of Caroline patriarchy.[24] Carew's country house poems "transcend their particular circumstances" as "representations of an idealized nature which was central to Carew's ethics and social values";

21. 273.
22. ix, 52.
23. "English" 262.
24. *Criticism* 61, 62, 168.

but Sharpe never considers the copyholder's view of Saxham manor.[25] Sharpe finds a lexical touchstone in *commonwealth*, and he uses it to assert the commonalty of early modern English thought and practice.[26] But this highly contested word made Thomas Elyot anxious: "There may appear like diversity to be in English between a public weal and a common weal, as should be in Latin, between *Res publica* and *res plebeia*."[27] Even Sharpe's favorite monarch deserts him here: while detained at Holmby House, Charles frequently talked with James Harrington, then one of his Gentlemen of the Bedchamber, and "loved his company," but "he would not endure to hear of a commonwealth."[28] Because Sharpe takes the protestations of courtier poets at face value and shuns any "anachronistic" scheme of historical explanation, he can discuss political change only in their highly abstract and ethical vocabulary, adopting the incredulous response of Charles and his courtiers to the appearance of revolutionary opposition. Quoting Davenant's argument for the necessity of "oppressing the people" (and this in a chapter entitled "The Politics of Love"), Sharpe employs free indirect discourse to meld his voice with that of the court: Charles "confronted men dominated by appetite and passion, who threatened to subvert all reason," men who appeared "weak in mind" and "beasts, creatures of sense but not of reason." As an explanation of the Revolution, this leaves something to be desired. For instance, what prompted these passionate but weak-minded beasts to act collectively?[29]

In an essay on *Macbeth*, David Norbrook suggests a modest way out of the dilemmas created by a one-culture or system/subject model. He remarks that new historicists tend to see political options

> polarized between total submission to power, authority, and the state on the one hand and radical subversion on the other.... Such a focus fails to do justice to the many Renaissance thinkers who had a conception of political order which involved neither hereditary monarchy nor total anarchy, and a conception of linguistic order which permitted rational communication without reinforcing feudal social relationships.[30]

Norbrook focuses on the Scots humanist George Buchanan, but his argument applies more generally to the theory and practice of tyrannicide. Though tyrannicide aims to destabilize and transform divine right absolutism and courtly culture, we cannot reduce it to an irrational force of pure metaphysical negation or "subversion," for it grows from deep roots in the history of Western republicanism. Tyrannicidal theorists carefully engaged the political languages of dominant culture, and their

---

25. 128.
26. See "A Commonwealth of Meanings," *Politics* 3–71.
27. Williams, *Keywords* 71.
28. John Aubrey, *Aubrey's Brief Lives*, Harmondsworth 1982, 208.
29. *Criticism* 300–301. For a similar new historicist argument about the centrality of patronage, see Robert C. Evans's *Ben Jonson and the Poetics of Patronage*, Lewisburg, PA, London, and Toronto 1989, and my critique in "Ehud's Dagger" 111–12.
30. "*Macbeth* and the Politics of Historiography," Sharpe and Zwicker, *Politics* 78–116, 79.

opponents found their arguments despicable but perfectly intelligible. I will discuss early modern resistance theory in more detail below, when I consider the career of Edward Sexby, but given the tendency of some historians and critics to argue the centrality of the patronage system with Johnsonian stone-kicking empiricist hubris, it might be useful here simply to chart a brief premodern anti-tyrannical genealogy: Aristotle and Cicero in the classical world; Aquinas and John of Salisbury in medieval Europe; Machiavelli and the sixteenth-century classical republicans in the Italian states; Buchanan, Knox, and the other "monarchomachs" of Reformation Scotland; Marian resistance theorists such as John Ponet and Christopher Goodman; Huguenots such as Hubert Languet and Philippe du Plessis Mornay, and their antagonistic heirs in the Catholic League; Spanish Jesuits such as Mariana and Suárez; and English republicans such as John Milton, Marchamont Nedham, John Wildman, James Harrington, John Streater, and Algernon Sidney.

Indeed, tyrannicidal practice erupts inside what we might take to be a court-dominated subculture. True, an early modern patronage system worked reasonably well within certain material circumstances and limits. For instance, after the near-destruction of Huguenot power, a patronage system founded in substantial royal landholdings and a bureaucracy of farmed-out offices defined Bourbon absolutism. But in England, where skimpy royal landholdings could not maintain an absolutist state, the patronage system began breaking down, particularly when early Stuart monarchs began asking it to provide not a supplement to but a substitute for the political and economic relation of the king in Parliament. Increasingly, awarding patronage to one client meant withholding it from another, and the slighted client didn't always linger and try again. When Robert Carr, Earl of Somerset, Buckingham's predecessor as favorite to James, decided he wished to marry Frances Howard, James agreed to annul her marriage to the Earl of Essex. Thereafter, Essex pursued a military career, sided with parliamentarian opposition to the king, became the patron of an oppositional circle, and, when the Revolution broke out in 1642, commanded the parliamentary army.[31] As we will see, John Felton's career follows a parallel trajectory. When Buckingham rebuffed his pleas for back pay, he changed from an anonymous and impoverished soldier-client outside the political nation, to a tyrannicide, and the toast of the oppositional Caroline public sphere. In describing a consensual ideology informing a one-class patronage system, revisionists and new historicists argue that the political is the personal—that seemingly collective and ideological struggles are actually personal or factional clashes within a more or less unified social order. We might do better to turn this

31. One libeler praised Essex's efforts on behalf of the Palatinate, while another called him "the kind whelp / Of Good Eliza's lion" who helped the "royal offspring" (Princess Elizabeth) starved by Buckingham's attention to "panders, minions, pimps, and whores" (*F* 60, 69).

around and argue that, in the turbulent history of early Stuart England, the personal rapidly becomes political.

Buck, King of Game

Clearly, we must not attempt to align Buckingham with a party of papist courtiers set off against a party of Puritan parliamentarians, for he patronized parliamentary Calvinists as well as Anglican bishops, and advocated war with Catholic Spain and France as well as Charles's marriage to Spanish and French princesses. In 1623, when he failed to negotiate the Spanish Match and returned home, England welcomed him with antipopish enthusiasm. In 1624, he headed a national coalition of parliamentary "Patriots" and extra-parliamentary antipapists agitating for a godly war with Spain.[32] But we should also acknowledge that, four years later, he had become "without doubt the most unpopular man in England," in the words of his most recent and sympathetic biographer.[33]

His monopoly of patronage and court office made him notorious. True, the "corruption" of gifts, bribes, and the sale of offices and monopolies so permeated the Jacobean patronage system that we might rightly see it exercising an instrumental, administrative function.[34] And the very concept of corruption is somewhat foreign to the decayed feudalism and would-be absolutism of early Stuart England, a mode of production that had not fully separated the spheres of state and economy. But the sheer magnitude of Buckingham's corruption prompted others to begin differentiating those spheres. The channels of patronage, greatly broadened at the time of James's accession, had narrowed by 1613, largely because Buckingham received rewards and offices equal to those received by Elizabeth's entire peerage during her 45-year reign, prompting those members of the ruling class excluded from patronage to oppose what they came to see as a destructive courtly corruption.[35] Sir Simonds D'Ewes remarked that Buckingham was "generally conceived to be the main cause of the sale of that multitude of English, Scotch, and Irish hereditary honors, of the aversion of hearts between the king and his subjects, and of all the other mischiefs in church and commonwealth."[36] When the Commons impeached Buckingham in May 1626, it accused him of purchasing political offices in which he had an immediate interest, becoming Great Admiral of England, General Governor of

32. Cogswell, *Blessed passim.*
33. Lockyer, *Buckingham* 463.
34. Linda Levy Peck, "Corruption at the Court of James I," Malament, *After* 75–93.
35. J. H. Hexter, "The English Aristocracy, Its Crises and the English Revolution, 1558–1660," *Journal of British Studies* 8, 1968, 57–8. Sharpe discusses aristocratic resistance to Buckingham in "The Earl of Arundel, His Circle and the Opposition to the Duke of Buckingham, 1618–1628," Sharpe, *Faction* 209–44.
36. *DA* 1.380.

the seas and ships, Lord Warden of the Cinque Ports, and Constable of the Castle of Dover.[37]

He was therefore able to engage in those absolutist forms of political surplus extraction that had been the privilege of the king, the company merchants, and the Anglican clergy. His 1626 bill of impeachment noted that he had monopolized trade-related state revenues, extorted money from the East India merchants, and claimed warrant as Great Admiral to seize a French ship and its cargo, leaving English merchants exposed to French retaliation. He gathered so many privileges that he was able to deny the company merchants their traditional monopolies, driving them into a temporary alliance with the capitalist new merchants in the Parliament of 1626.[38] Charles aggravated this resented imbalance with the Forced Loan of 1626–27, and his prerogative assault on those who refused to pay, including the Five Knights.[39] If we expand our definition of class struggle beyond the conflict of industrial bourgeoisie and proletariat, then we can begin to see emerging an alliance of the parliamentary classes with the small-producing extra-parliamentary laboring classes, united by an ideology of antipopery and resistance to corruption, and by their common interest in resisting the absolutist class-state embodied in the person of the all but impervious Buckingham.[40]

Buckingham also gained a reputation as a papal fifth columnist by sponsoring a series of disastrous English forays into the Thirty Years War: Mansfield's expedition to the Palatinate, the assault on Cadiz, Louis XIII's assault on the Huguenots of La Rochelle with the help (it was suspected) of English ships provided by Buckingham (all 1625), and the disastrous 1627 attempt to relieve La Rochelle, which culminated in England's humiliating defeat at the Isle of Rhé, and some French mockery:

> The upshot of a French libel now sung at Paris is, that though the Duke of Buckingham be not able to take the Citadel of Rhé, yet is he able to take the Tower of London, which may be construed in many ways. The French king's saying to the Savoy ambassador, as he came that way, was, "Alack," said he, "if I had known my brother of England had longed so much for the Isle of Rhé, I would have sold it him for half the money it hath cost him."[41]

Perhaps one third of the 50,000 men whom the king and Buckingham pressed into service between 1624 and 1628 died in battle, of wounds, or

---

37. S. R. Gardiner, *The Constitutional Documents of the Puritan Revolution, 1625–1660*, 3rd edn, Oxford 1906, 7–13; *Documents Illustrating the Impeachment of the Duke of Buckingham in 1626*, Westminster 1889.

38. *BMR* 225.

39. Cust, *Forced*.

40. One libeler would depict Felton as a sort of neo-Spenserian Sir Guyon, whose Protestant "zeal" disenchanted an absolutist England, where "One proud man did mate / The nobles, gentles, commons of our state" (*F* 69–70). Such antipopery, which locates Buckingham and his recusant mother within a long series of "popish plots" against England, became the religious and political ideology unifying the English people in opposition to the court. See Lake ("Anti-popery") and Manning (*English* 12–13).

41. *P* 121.

of disease.[42] Of 7833 soldiers who accompanied Buckingham to Rhé, only 2989 returned—John Felton among them.[43]

Topping off these charges, many believed that Buckingham had hurried King James to his grave. Dr Ramsay, a royal physician, reported that, after an illness, his physicians found James "reasonably well recovered, and in their judgments past all danger, till, in their absence, George Duke of Buckingham ministered to him a potion, and gave him plasters, after which he soon fell into a great burning and distemper, which increased more and more until his decease."[44] Dr Craig, another royal physician, was prosecuted for accusing Buckingham and his mother of poisoning James.[45] And by May 1626, from the safety of the Continent, George Eglisham, the Marquis of Hamilton's lifelong friend and protégé, and physician to James, published a Latin tract against the duke, *Prodromus Vindictae in Ducem Buckinghamiae*, and an English translation titled *The Forerunner of Revenge*, listing "Franckfort" as the place of publication. Eglisham begged Parliament to bring Buckingham to trial, charging that he had poisoned the Marquis of Hamilton, who died three weeks before James, because Hamilton resisted marrying his son to Buckingham's niece, and that he and his mother administered a fatal potion and plaster to the ailing but recovering king in the absence of his physicians. Eglisham uttered menacing words against the new king:

> It is justice that maketh kings, justice that maintaineth kings, and injustice that bringeth both kingdoms and kings to destruction to fall in misery, to die like asses in ditches or more beastly deaths, with eternal infamy after death, as all histories from time to time do clearly testify.... [O]ur late monarch of happy memory King James ... hath often publicly protested, even in the presence of his apparent heir, that if his own son should commit murder or any such execrable act of injustice, he would not spare him, but would have him die for it, and would have him more severely punished than any other.[46]

Published, copied, and recopied, the pamphlet became notorious and circulated widely.[47] Attorney General Robert Heath examined Alexander Bushey, who bought or borrowed a copy, copied out five others, and sold them "to relieve his wants."[48] Zuane Pesaro, Venetian Ambassador, reported that "The king is incensed against the author of the book and the Parliament against the accused."[49]

42. Michael B. Young, "Buckingham, War, and Parliament," *Parliamentary History* 4, 1985, 62, 64. On Rhé, see *GHE* 6.167–200.
43. *CSPD* 2.454.
44. *DA* 1.263.
45. *GHE* 5.313–16; *Bishop Burnet's History of His Own Time*, 6 vols, Oxford 1823, 1.29; and *CSPV* 19.416.
46. 4, 9. On Eglisham, see *DNB* and *CSPD* 1.337.
47. The Folger Shakespeare Library owns two manuscript copies (V.a.470, X.d.236), the Bodleian at least one (Ms. Wood D.18, 88–97), and Bellany lists others ("Poisoning" 539n.54).
48. *CSPD* 2.17.
49. *CSPV* 19.416.

At times, the controversy verges on trivial melodrama, but in attempting to quash it, Roger Lockyer moves into an act of sympathetic mind reading that is, if anything, even sillier:

> It may well be that the remedies which Buckingham administered did more harm than good, but he acted with the best intentions. It was not Machiavellian cunning that prompted him, but simply a desire to ease the sufferings of his "dear dad and gossip." . . . The Duke felt bereft by the King's death and could not hide his grief. . . . On this occasion, as on a number of others, Buckingham's physical collapse shows the strains upon him had become intolerable.[50]

Of course, these strains could also have arisen from remorse, dissimulation, or fear of discovery. Hugh Ross Williamson's chatty account of Buckingham provides an altogether preferable analysis. He finds the medical evidence consistent with poison and notes Buckingham's estrangement from the king after his return from Spain in 1623, his resentment at the king's favor toward Gondomar, and Charles's deep affection for him: "from every point of view, it seems to me that Buckingham had reason to desire James's death, though this is a very different thing from asserting that he poisoned him."[51]

The poetic libels frequently refer to the poisoning of Hamilton and James.[52] John Russell may refer to both in *The Spy* when he asks, "Is there not / Unslaughtered or unpoisoned left one Scot?"[53] An ally of Buckingham thought the rumors serious enough to warrant drawing up a manuscript counter-narrative of James's last days which says that James requested the potion and plaster, adds that they speedily cured the ague of several people in the king's immediate circle, and lists the names and addresses of those persons and other friendly witnesses.[54] The final resolution in the House's 1626 bill of impeachment against Buckingham stopped just short of a murder charge when it charged him with "an act of transcendent presumption and of dangerous consequence" in medicating the king.[55] In 1628, the parliamentary radical Thomas Scott reported in his journal that "all the realm" suspected Buckingham of poisoning the king.[56] Precedents lay ready to hand in the rumors that Dr Lopez

---

50. *Buckingham* 234.
51. *George Villiers*, London 1940, 171–4.
52. *F* 20, 10, 11, 20, 50, and 51.
53. A1ᵛ. This remarkable, long pamphlet poem of 1628 refers to events only though mid-1627, but its title page emphasizes its emulous publication in "Strasburgh" on the very day of Felton's lunge; see *CSPD* 3.266 for a manuscript copy. A. W. Pollard and G. R. Redgrave identify the author ("I. R.") as John Russell in *A Short-Title Catalogue of Books Printed in England, Scotland and Ireland*, 2 vols, rev. edn, New York 1976–94. Russell was BA (1628) and MA (1632), Magdalene College, Cambridge, and priest at Chingford, Essex, from 1634 to 1687 (J. Venn and J. A. Venn, comps, *Alumni Cantabrigienses*, 10 vols, Cambridge 1922–27, 1.3.500).
54. *A relation concerning the plaister and potion given to K. James*, Ms. V.a.402 68ʳ–70ᵛ, in Folger Shakespeare Library; thanks to Tom Cogswell for guiding me to this work.
55. Gardiner, *Constitutional* 20–22.
56. Mary Frear Keeler, Maija Jansson Cole, and William B. Bidwell, eds, *Proceedings in Parliament 1628*, 6 vols, New Haven, CT, 1983, 6.132–3.

attempted to poison Queen Elizabeth, that Somerset poisoned Prince Henry, that Somerset and Frances Carr poisoned Sir Thomas Overbury. Indeed, some rumors held that Buckingham himself, in his earlier, godly incarnation, had been poisoned because of his imagined opposition to the Spanish Match.[57]

Such poison scares exhibit a certain strategic rationality, for they enable commoners to turn claims of royal prerogative and the *arcana imperii* against themselves, and channel debauchery or an ethical lapse into a political crisis. Conrad Russell sees Charles as a ruler "to whom there was no alternative," since opposition in early Stuart England required either a rival claimant to the throne (who didn't exist) or a rival army (which didn't exist until 1640).[58] But he forgets that deference to one prince could function as opposition to another. Precisely because King James himself had linked regicide with monstrous patricide, Charles's opponents could set his father's words against his favorite's actions.[59] We might compare the recurrent efforts by Puritans to set a once or future godly prince against a contemporary tyrant or scourge: Queen Elizabeth and Prince Henry against Kings James and Charles, martial Prince Charles and his Calvinist sister Elizabeth against pacific King James, Citizen Charles Stuart against Oliver Tyrannus, King Jesus against all merely human princes. Like most forms of early modern radicalism—like Protestantism and humanism more generally—the formally conservative rhetoric of early modern tyrannicide employs a utopian past for radical purposes, advocating restoration, not innovation. Languet and Mornay's Huguenot theory of resistance appealed to medieval theories of natural law against the new theories of absolutism formulated by Bodin. Moderate Anglicans and Puritans attacked Caroline Arminianism not as a rusty fetter on rising capitalism, but as a dangerous innovation. And as we will see, the June 1628 parliamentary remonstrance accused Buckingham of "some secret working to introduce into this kingdom *innovation* and change of holy *Religion*."[60]

The opposition to Buckingham employed a deferential rhetoric focusing on evil counselors misleading the king, but everyone concerned recognized the oblique attack on Charles. Lucy Hutchinson commented, "The whole people were sadly grieved at these misgovernments, and, loath to impute them to the king, cast all the odium upon the Duke of Buckingham, whom at length a discontented person stabbed, believing he did God and his country good service by it."[61] During Buckingham's impeachment, someone gave a paper to the king saying that "the great

---

57. *Diary of Walter Yonge, Esq.*, London 1848, 74.
58. *Unrevolutionary* xiii–xvi.
59. *DRD* 99–100.
60. *RHC* 1.628–30. On the subversive innovation of Caroline absolutism, see "A Satyre on the D. of B." (*F* 49–50).
61. *Memoirs of the Life of Colonel Hutchinson, with a Fragment of Autobiography*, London and Vermont 1995, 69. In 1628, when Felton was held in the Tower, her father, Sir Allen Apsley, was Lieutenant.

opposition against the duke, was stirred and maintained by such as seek the destruction of this free monarchy, because they find it not ripe to attempt against the king himself, they endeavor it through the sides of the duke."[62] Responding through his Lord Keeper to an earlier House attack on Buckingham, Charles said, "and therefore His Majesty cannot believe that the aim is at the Duke of Buckingham, but findeth that these proceedings do directly wound the honor and judgment of himself and of his father."[63] In June 1628, the king prophesied to Buckingham, "George, there are some that wish that both these and thou might perish. But care not for them. We will both perish together, if thou doest."[64] Summing up the House's 1626 Bill of Impeachment, John Eliot, Buckingham's former ally and client, invoked the "sacred name" of the king and protested he had no desire "to reflect the least ill odor on his majesty or his most blessed father of happy memory." Yet he also linked the duke and Sejanus, and Charles responded, reasonably enough, "He must intend me for Tiberius!"[65] In 1628, Pierre Matthieu's life of Sejanus appeared in two separate translations with the same title, *The Powerfull Favorite, Or, the Life of Aelius Sejanus*, ostensibly published in Paris; one offered a mirror for magistrates by including a fine engraving of Charles facing the title page.

Private persons did not hesitate to set themselves in public opposition to Buckingham. In November 1625, Christopher Hogg accused Buckingham of poisoning the king and was interrogated and whipped.[66] John Rous worried that "Our King's proceedings have caused men's minds to be incensed, to rove and project . . . looking towards the Lady Elizabeth," which "is fearful to be thought of."[67] In November 1626, the Privy Council told the Lord Chief Justice that Thomas Brediman had prophesied that a military mutiny would "kill the Duke of Buckingham and perhaps the king too," replacing them with a free state, or with the King of Bohemia and his wife, Princess Elizabeth.[68] In July 1628, the Privy Council directed the Cornish justices of assize to prosecute two seamen who had reported the king slain by the duke.[69] In *The Spy*, John Russell puts the opposition of the 1620s into a larger moderate Protestant context. He hearkens back fondly to Elizabeth, Drake, Ralegh, and the defeat of the Armada; celebrates Essex, Warwick, and Horace Vere; criticizes James for his pacifism; and denounces Gondomar, English Arminians, and particularly Buckingham, whom he accuses of poisoning James, plotting against

---

62. Sir Richard Baker, *A Chronicle of the Kings of England*, London 1660, 481.
63. Gardiner, *Constitutional* 5.
64. Henry Ellis, ed., *Original Letters Illustrative of English History*, 3 vols, London 1825, 3.253.
65. John Forster, *Sir John Eliot*, 2 vols, London 1864, 1.545, 549, 552; see also *DA* 2.186; Bellany, "Poisoning" 526. Hill discusses the role of allusive language in the culturing of early modern political opposition (*Nation* 37).
66. *CSPD* 1.160, 164, 187, 230, 260, 261, 286.
67. *The Diary of John Rous*, London 1856, 19.
68. *Hist. Ms. Comm.* 15th Report, Appendix part II, 290–91; *CSPD* 1.471–2, 2.41, 73, 331.
69. Forster, *Eliot* 2.338.

Charles, and popish treachery at Rhé.[70] Spenserian poets such as William Browne, Henry Reynolds, and Michael Drayton attacked Buckingham by attacking the corruptions of court poetry. Even Ben Jonson, in his masque entitled *The Gypsies Metamorphosed*, may have glanced critically at Buckingham by casting him and his family as rapacious gypsies.[71] In any case, someone turned an inoffensive song from that masque into a libelous prayer that entreats God to save "My sovereign from a Ganymede / Whose whorish breath hath power to lead / His Majesty which way it list," denouncing Buckingham as "that slime . . . / That keeps my sovereign's eyes from viewing / The things that will be our undoing."[72]

Opposition to Buckingham merged with hatred of ganymedes in the 1620s, for early modern charges of sodomy merged readily with charges of popery, poisoning, sumptuary excess, and corruption in general.[73] When Buckingham left James to go to Spain with Charles, one writer commented that "Buckingham, his spouse, is gone, / And left the widowed king alone." An anonymous poem described Jove and Ganymede at war with all the other gods, including Vulcan, Mars, Venus, Juno, Diana, and Proserpina, who all

> threaten without mercy
> To have him burned
> That so hath turned
> Love's pleasure arsy versy.[74]

A 1626 poem attacked Buckingham for disrupting the proper relationship between the wifely Parliament and the husbandly king—James, Charles, or both. After boasting that the Parliament has been true to the king while offering Buckingham its ass to kiss, the poet accuses him of practicing

> An art sprung from a blacker seed,
> Then that which he poured in that [reed?]
> Whom we call Guido Fawkes
> Who if he fired had his vessel

70. E1ᵛ–E3ʳ.
71. Dale B. J. Randall, *Jonson's Gypsies Unmasked*, Durham, NC, 1975; Norbrook, *Poetry* 224–6, 245–7; Martin Butler is skeptical in "'We are one mans all,'" Brown, *Patronage* 247–67.
72. Allan H. Gilbert attributes the revision to William Drummond in "Jonson and Drummond or Gil on the King's Senses," *Modern Language Notes* 62, 1947. In "Ben Jonson and an Unknown Poet on the King's Senses," *Modern Language Notes* 74.5, 1959, C. F. Main suggests some anonymous Jacobean satirist. For other versions, see *CSPD* 3.240 (*PRO* 16/111/51) and Norman K. Farmer, "Poems from a Seventeenth-Century Manuscript with the Hand of Robert Herrick," Supplement to *Texas Quarterly* 16.4, 1973, 137–41. Farmer suggests that Herrick, Buckingham's chaplain at Rhé, copied this and several other libels into his commonplace book. Ann Baynes Coiro persuasively challenges Herrick's authorship ("Milton" 271n.).
73. See Bellany, "Poisoning" 456, 458–80; and Alan Bray, *Homosexuality in Renaissance England*, London 1982; and "Homosexuality and the Signs of Male Friendship in Elizabethan England," in Jonathan Goldberg, ed., *Queering the Renaissance*, Durham, NC, 1994, 40–61.
74. Farmer, "Poems" 144–5, 130–31.

> Of sulfur standing on bare trestle
>   In his sepulchral walks:
> Could not have so dispersed our state,
> Nor opened Spain so wide a gate
>   As hath his graceless grace.[75]

The writer suggests not simply that the king has a ganymede, but that he is one—i.e., that he is the passive partner in gay sex: as the grains of Guy Fawkes's gunpowder nearly blew up Parliament, so Buckingham's seed will blow him up. His corrupting influence leaves the body politic wide-reamed and prone to Spanish penetration. In 1627, Dominick Roche, a Limerick alderman, said the King of Spain broke off the Spanish Match when he found that Charles as well as James committed "unnatural crimes" with Buckingham.[76] In 1628, someone printed Sir Francis Hubert's long poem *Edward II*, prompting him to bring out two authorized versions in 1629.[77] On February 18 1628, John Harris, preacher at St Margaret's Church in Westminster, preached before the Commons (and later printed) a fast-day sermon entitled *The Destruction of Sodome*, which portentously denounced England as well as Sodom, corrosive wealth and contempt for the poor as well as sodomy. With monarchomachic overtones, he called on negligent magistrates to censor the wicked and cleanse the streets of corruption.[78]

In 1627, Star Chamber prosecuted three fiddlers from Sussex for singing a brilliant, arsy-versy ballad:

> Then let us sing all of this noble duke's praise,
>   Come love me where as I lay
> And pray for the length of his life and his days,
>   The clean contrary way.
>   O the clean contrary way.
>
> And when that death shall close up his eyes,
>   Come love me where as I lay,
> God take him up into the skies. . . .[79]

And so forth. Heath denounced libels as "the epidemical diseases of those days," and the judges sentenced the fiddlers to be festively whipped and

75. Bodleian Ms. English Poetry 50 14^{r-v}; thanks to Alastair Bellany for a transcript.
76. Robert Pentland Mahaffy, ed., *Calendar of State Papers Relating to Ireland, of the Reign of Charles I. 1625–1632*, 3 vols, London 1900, 1.489. Charles and Buckingham seem to have been passionate friends, not lovers, but the early modern border between those two identities was even more porous than it is now. In "On His Majesty's Receiving the News of the Duke of Buckingham's Death," Edmund Waller compared Charles's grief to Achilles' for Patroclus and Apollo's for Hyacinthus and Cyparissus—analogies that might have been too daring outside an elegy (Herschel Baker, ed., *The Later Renaissance in England*, Boston 1975, 247).
77. *Poems*, Hong Kong 1961, xxxix–xli.
78. 44. Ben Jonson heard his friend Zouch Townley, later author of a poem on Felton, preach at St Margaret's (*CSPD* 3.360).
79. *F* 11–13.

carried on horseback "the clean contrary way"—facing their horses' tails.[80] But libelers kept it up after Buckingham's death, singing, "What fiddlers sung, now all may freely say, / The Duke is gone the clean contrary way."[81] John Russell archly echoed the refrain in *The Spy*.[82] And John Eliot— probably the parliamentarian's son—later alluded to the failure of Charles's agents in punishing the fiddlers, saying that "If they went the people's tongues to stay, / Doubtless they went the clean contrary way," then attached "a new ballad for the fiddlers": a wittily obscene satire against Buckingham and Charles's Catholic queen.[83]

An ingenious chronogram on Buckingham's name appeared in 1628, allegedly before his death:

> georgIVs DVX bVCkInghaMIae = *MDCXXVIII*
> Læto iam sæclo tandem sol pertulit annum;
> Noni non videat, quæsumus, alme, diem.
> Thy numerous name with this year doth agree
> But twenty-nine, Heaven grant thou never see![84]

"Upon the D. of B." creates a venereal conceit by parsing Buckingham's name:

> Our Charlemagne takes much delight
> In this great beast so fair in sight,
> With his whole heart affects the same,
> And loves too well *Buck—King* of *Game*.

This buck "doth so bark and pill the trees" that "The foresters say, while he's alive / The tender thickets ne'er can thrive." After the hunters slay the buck, the nation rejoices and "few are sad." The speaker concludes with dangerous sententiousness:

> A *buck*'s a beast; a *king* is but a man,
> A *game*'s a pleasure shorter than a span;
> A beast shall perish; but a man shall die,
> As pleasures fade. This be thy destiny.

The poem is finally awkward, ineloquent, and uncontrolled, but interesting for that very reason. The duke and the king are inseparable—indeed, the duke contains the king inside his own name. The duke shall die, but the king is "but a man," and a man shall die, too. Even if the writer hasn't set out to menace the king, his violent hatred of Buckingham spills over into the threat of regicide.[85]

---

80. British Library, Lansdowne Ms. 620 ff. 50ʳ–51ʳ. See *CSPD* 2.185, 233, 240, 242, 246.
81. Bellany, "Poisoning" 134–5.
82. E2ʳ.
83. *Poems*, 1658, 81–92.
84. D'Ewes attributes it to William Harreise (*DA* 1.389–90), Fairholt to John Marston (*F*xvi). The day after the assassination, Osborne sent Wentworth a version of the same chronogram and another for IaCobVs stVarDVs Magnae brItannIae reX—also totaling 1628 (J. P. Cooper, ed., *Wentworth Papers, 1597–1628*, London 1973, 303).
85. *F*5–6. James Priest or Preest's libel of April 1629 echoes the poem (*CSPD* 3.533–4, 4.39).

We can hear a similar voice in the writer of the anonymous manuscript headnote to a copy of "The Duke Returned Again," a satire by a veteran of Rhé which attacks Buckingham as the son of a recusant, a military bungler, and the murderer of James. The writer says the poet wrote "a bitter verse, which savors more of an envious and detracting wit, and violent passion, than of a sound and settled judgment." Then, alternating pro- and anti-Buckingham perspectives, he comments,

> Which title how deservedly he hath gained, God knows; but if we look into his speech made in the Council Chamber, April 4th 1628, we shall find him (if his tongue and heart agree) the king's favorite, the country's loyal and well-devoted subject. But to hear him of the former opinion welcome him home, who shall speak for all the rest, with viperous (though I hope undeserved) bitterness, as followeth.

He questions the poem's perspective, then questions his questioning, then preserves, reproduces, and (presumably) circulates the poem itself, revealing what we might call the *forensic* voice of these authors.[86]

He also notes that some have called Buckingham the "Achan of our English Israel." Achan the Judahite and his family became favorite figures for Buckingham and his recusant family on the make: in Joshua 7, after Achan keeps some "accursed" Babylonish spoils of battle, all Israel stones him and his family to death, then burns them to ashes. The anti-Buckingham "Satire on the D. of B." prays that "the host not rest / Till Achan die."[87] Another poem directs a prayer-petition to Queen Elizabeth as a Marian intercessor for "her now most wretched and most contemptible the commons of England." In a voice that modulates from queenly delicacy to Joshua's ferocity, she advises England to cleanse itself:

> There is an execrable thing lies hid,
> Such a sin as modesty doth forbid
> My sex to name: till that be brought to light
> And Achan punished, look to be put to flight.[88]

After the assassination, we will hear Elizabeth's neo-Spenserean voice from heaven echoed by Buckingham's neo-Senecan voice from hell.

June 1628 was particularly turbulent. Eleanor Davies predicted Buckingham would die in August, and according to one report, he received a copy of her prophecy.[89] Parliament examined Pierce Butler, an Irish

---

86. *F* 19–24.
87. Ibid. 50.
88. Farmer, "Poems" 147–9, 168–9; in 1642, someone printed another version as *The Humble Petition of the Wretched and Most Contemptible, the Poore Commons of England*. Radical Protestants frequently invoked Achan as the archetypal cursed figure preventing a thorough national reformation. See A. Ar.'s *The Practise of Princes*, 1630, 9; and *The Troublers Troubled, or Achan Condemned and Executed*, a sermon that Samuel Fairecloth preached before the House of Commons in April 1641, the month before Strafford's execution. Milton planned a tragedy on the subject in the early forties (*John Milton, Poems Reproduced in Facsimile*, Menston 1972, 36).
89. Esther S. Cope, *Handmaid of the Holy Spirit*, Ann Arbor, MI, 1992, 51–2.

diviner, after he testified that Buckingham had gained the king's affections through witchcraft.[90] On the 5th, the whole nation celebrated with bonfires and bells at the false report of Buckingham's commitment to the Tower.[91] On the 7th, Charles assented to *The Petition of Right*, one of the landmarks of English constitutional history.[92] Conrad Russell emphasizes that *The Petition* marked an ideological turning point: where previous parliaments had defended this or that liberty, the 1628 Parliament in this document "first saw these liberties as collectively threatened by a threat to the ideal which held them all together, the ideal of the rule of law."[93] On June 14, a Scot named Wilson caused an incident that John Rous recorded in his diary:

> That the duke, being at bowls with the king and other noblemen, his hat was on, which a Scottish man seeing, took it off, and threw it on the ground. He then offered to spurn him; but said the king, "George let him alone; he is drunk." "No," said the Scottish man, "neither drunk nor mad, but a subject, as I thought he had been, of whom if you knew but what I know, you would not so esteem him as you do."[94]

Wilson's insistence on hat honor does not altogether hide his presumption. His "deference" would find one echo in August, when Felton claimed he had saved the king from the duke, and two more in the early forties. First, the petition accompanying the Grand Remonstrance asserted the petitioners' "loyal affections, obedience and service," while warning Charles against those "malignant parties" who had corrupted the Privy Council. Second, the Houses voted "that an army shall be forthwith raised for the safety of the King's person"—the outbreak of the Revolution.[95]

That same day, two months before Buckingham died in part for Charles, his astrologer, Dr John Lambe, died in part for him, in a striking episode of what Alexandra Walsham has called the "street wars of religion" in the 1620s.[96] A pamphlet of 1628 claims that, after Lambe's arraignment at the assizes of Worcester on charges of witchcraft, "the high sheriff, the foreman of the jury, and divers others of the justices, gentlemen there present, and of the same jury, to the number of forty died all within one fortnight."[97] In 1624, a jury found him guilty of raping eleven-year-old Joan Seagar and sentenced him to hang, but Secretary Conway ordered him released. Lambe became a confidant of Buckingham and his mother,

---

90. *CSPD* 1.321; *CSPV* 19.416.

91. Isaac Disraeli, *Curiosities of Literature*, 3 vols, London 1824, 3.440.

92. *DRD* 68–71.

93. *Parliaments and English Politics, 1621–1629*, Oxford 1979, 343; Russell's powerful revisionist account of the Parliament of 1628 emphasizes the disruptive agitation of the Commons (323–89); Sommerville stresses the ideological conflict over royal prerogative (*Politics* 163–73).

94. 17. See also Keeler et al., *Proceedings* 6.100, 117; *CSPD* 23.282; *DA* 2.198.

95. Gardiner, *Constitutional* 205, 203, 261.

96. " 'The Fatall Vesper' " 59. Walsham analyzes a 1623 episode of providentialist antipopery with striking substantial and formal parallels to the furor surrounding Felton's deed.

97. *A Briefe Description of the Notorious Life of John Lambe*, Amsterdam 1628, 12.

perhaps by advising them about the duke's troubled brother, John Villiers, Viscount Purbeck, rumored to be the victim of sorcery.[98] On Friday the 13th, when Lambe left the Fortune Playhouse, a group of apprentices battered him through the London streets. When he died the next morning, the Privy Council threatened to revoke the city's charter and levied a substantial fine on the city companies.[99] But despite a vigorous attempt to find the guilty parties, the Privy Council arrested nobody, and the libelers' rough music continued the apprentices' lambasting:

> The devil in hell will roast him there
> Whom th'apprentices basted here
> In hell they wonder when he rams
> Among the goats to see a lamb.[100]

Martin Parker's broadside ballad celebrating the attack appeared with a woodcut previously used for editions of Marlowe's *Doctor Faustus*. The king sent Parker to Newgate, along with his bookseller Henry Gosson and his printer Elizabeth Allde.[101] Mead reported a libel posted in Coleman Street:

> Who rules the Kingdom? The King. Who rules the King? The Duke. Who rules the Duke? The Devil. . . . Let the duke look to it; for they intend shortly to use him worse than they did his doctor; and if things be not shortly reformed, they will work reformation themselves. . . . They say his Majesty (and he had reason) was much displeased.[102]

Evidently, the need to destroy (or "reform") the corruptly counseled person could survive the destruction of the corrupt counselor—a message with threatening overtones for the king as well as the duke. We can detect a similar muted threat in a couplet that was probably the most popular English poem of 1628: "Let Charles and George do what they can, / The duke shall die like Doctor Lambe."[103]

On June 16, four days after the king accepted *The Petition of Right*, the House presented its Remonstrance, which lamented the deaths of English soldiers and sailors, the censorship of Puritans, the toleration of recusants like Buckingham's mother, and the favor shown to Neile, Laud, and other proponents of Arminianism, that "cunning way to bring in

---

98. Leba M. Goldstein, "The Life and Death of John Lambe," *Guildhall Studies in London History* 4.1, 1979. See also Bellany, "Poisoning" 554–87.

99. *F* xv.

100. "An Epitaph" in Yale University Beinecke Library, Ms. Fb 140, 1.

101. Hyder E. Rollins, ed., *A Pepysian Garland*, Cambridge, MA, 1922, 278–82. Goldstein, "Life" 28–9.

102. Ellis, *Original Letters* 3.252. The Aldermen reportedly imprisoned and perhaps hanged one Thomas Foster, who said he had taken down one of the placards to read it, then put it back up. See Valerie Pearl, *London and the Outbreak of the Puritan Revolution*, London 1961, 77; Goldstein, "Life" 30.

103. *F* xv. In 1660, an anonymous republican directed it toward Charles II and George Monck (*Valley of Achor* B1ᵛ). This brilliant poem deserves generic christening (the villiersknell?) and contemporary emulation.

Popery." It accused Buckingham of plotting England's popish ruin by gathering an excess of military power to himself, weakening coastal defenses, and conspiring with European Catholics. Someone reported to the Commons that he had had responded, "Tush, it makes no matter what the Commons or Parliament doth, for without my leave and authority, they shall not be able to touch a hair of a dog." He denied the story, but it had already begun to spread.[104] One satire stripped him down to the language of pure tyrannical invective. He addresses the House as "you giddy-headed multitude," and brazenly repeats the charges against him— that he poisoned James and Hamilton, lost Rhé, gained James's affection by magic, sold political offices, and used Lambe's philters to seduce women. He neither confirms nor denies, but pleads executive privilege:

> I'll give you better counsel, as a friend,
> Cobblers with their latchets ought not to transcend,
> Meddle with common matters, common wrongs,
> To the House of Commons common things belong.

Standing "extra sphaeram," he declares he will not be inserted into their judicial proceedings: "My power shall be unbounded in each thing, / If once I use these words, *I and the king*." He declares that Parliament will never prove he had a hand in poisoning James, and spurns London's threat: "Though Lambe be dead, I'll stand, and you shall see / I'll smile at them that can but bark at me."[105] The effect is that of a Renaissance Machiavel's mid-play soliloquy.

On June 19, an anonymous parliamentary diarist recorded a libel posted at the Exchange and elsewhere threatening "that if the King did not take the Duke's head by midsummer, they would take it."[106] On the 26th, a newsletter reported that the king had responded to the Remonstrance by proroguing the Parliament until October; it followed with some seditious speeches, many of them echoing the Remonstrance, attributed to a Scot named Robert Melvin.[107] In July, a number of alleged robbers, fleeing a hue and cry in County Carmarthen, created a diversion by spreading a story that Buckingham had murdered the king. This prompted a panic in Loughor, which spread to Swansea and beyond, leading to a lengthy investigation by Heath,[108] who proposed examining and jailing those who spread libels.[109] In July 1628, some inhabitants of Wellinborough reportedly called the king's troops "the Duke of Buckingham's rogues" and threatened to cut their throats.[110] In August, Buckingham stalked out of a Globe revival of Shakespeare's *Henry VIII*, right after the scene depicting

104. Keeler et al., *Proceedings* 4.311–17, 6.346n.12; *RHC* 1.619–27, 627.
105. *F* 28–31.
106. Keeler et al., *Proceedings* 6.118.
107. *P* 125–6. On Melvin, sometimes "Melvyn" or "Melville," see *P* 126–7; *RHC* 1.627; Bellany, "Poisoning" 550–51, and *CSPD* 3.103, 149, 172, 173, 180, 213, 363, and 364.
108. *CSPD* 3.210, 221, 236, 272, 273.
109. Ibid. 3.218.
110. Ibid. 3.227; *PRO* 16/110/56.

the execution of an earlier Duke of Buckingham—though some observed he should have stayed to see the fall of Cardinal Wolsey, "who was a more lively type of himself, having governed this kingdom eighteen years, as he hath done fourteen."[111]

These libelers and street rowdies handle the *arcana imperii* with a rough familiarity bordering on contempt. Like parliamentarians speaking publicly against Buckingham, they insist on the right to enter into public life and debate Buckingham's (later Felton's) merits and demerits, acknowledge traditional principles of order, lament fallings-off from them, and glance prophetically toward alternative principles that might take their place. In the relatively anonymous space of the streets and the circulated manuscript, they engage in something like a repressed republican *conversazione civile*. This conversation reveals neither an unquestioning absolutist loyalty nor a millenarian regicidal ardor, but it can help us understand how some early Stuart citizens moved from the first position to the second.[112]

"God bless thee, little David!"

John Felton was born around 1595 to a family of impoverished Suffolk gentry related to the Earl and Countess of Arundel.[113] His mother Eleanor was the daughter of William Wright, the mayor of Durham.[114] His father Thomas was an avid official hunter of recusants. After a critical report by Henry Spiller, a Catholic clerk working under him, he lost his office and, imprisoned for a debt to Spiller, died in Fleet Prison. Though dogged with accusations of corruption, Spiller gained influence through friends at court, rising "from the Exchequer and Pipe Offices to become a Justice of the Peace for Middlesex, a knight, a member of many government commissions, a prominent courtier and a close adviser to the king."[115] Eleanor Felton received a generous state pension, but her son Edmond

---

111. Robert Gell's report in *DA* 2.210.
112. Most historians hesitate to speak of English republicanism before 1642, or even 1649, but republicanism is a discursive as well as a state form. On republican writing and practice, see David Norbrook (*Writing*) and Peltonen (*Classical*). Bellany sees attacks by Felton's friends as "a symptom of incipient republicanism" ("Poisoning" 640). Felton found justification for his action in some books which called it lawful "to kill an enemy to the republic" (*RHC* 1.638).
113. Thomas Birch, *The Court and Times of Charles the First*, 2 vols, London 1848, 1.450. Timothy Raylor gives the best account of the Felton family in "Providence and Technology in the English Civil War: Edmond Felton and His Engine," *Renaissance Studies* 7.4, 1993, 400. See also the *DNB* entry by Sidney Lee and the accounts by Rous (*Diary* 25–34), D'Ewes (*DA* 1.376–90), and Carleton (*F* xvii–xxi). Bellany challenges Carleton's authorship ("Poisoning" 590n.), but for convenience I will continue to call him the author. On Buckingham, Felton, and the assassination, see the letters collected by Ellis (*Original Letters*), Powell (*P*), and Birch (*Court*); and James Howell, *Epistolae Ho-Elianae*, 9th edn, London 1726; Edward Hyde, *The History of the Rebellion and Civil Wars in England*, 1888; rpt Oxford 1958; Isaac Disraeli, *Curiosities* 3.427–67; Forster, *Eliot* 2.349–75; and *GHE* 6.344–76.
114. *CSPD* 3.349.
115. Raylor, "Providence" 400.

commenced a crusade against Spiller, whom he suspected of poisoning his father.[116] If John concurred, then the assassination may have been partly a displaced act of revenge against an upstart popish favorite suspected of poisoning a beloved paternal figure.

In any case, his father's ruin put an end to Felton's hopes for living as a gentleman, forcing him into the army as a professional soldier. According to Yonge, he came back from military service in the United Provinces a "great Puritan" who abhorred the cursing and drinking of "debauched people."[117] He served under Sir Edward Cecil and a Captain Leigh in the 1625 attack on Cadiz, Buckingham's miserable attempt to repeat Ralegh's glorious expedition of 1596, and a debacle significant enough to feature as the third charge in the Grand Remonstrance of 1641.[118] He was among those veterans of the expedition deposited in Munster in December, and in November 1626, received £12 12s. for service under Leigh in Ireland.[119] After Leigh died, Felton applied twice for command of his company in the Rhé expedition, with the recommendations of Sir William Uvedale and Sir William Becher.[120] In Hyde's account, Felton told Buckingham that if he did not have a captain's place he could not live, and the duke responded he would have to hang then—a grievous insult to a decayed gentleman.[121] Felton probably owed his bad luck with Buckingham to Sir Henry Hungate, with whom he had quarreled during the Cadiz expedition. According to D'Ewes, Felton "discovered" Hungate's "secret lust" and "received from him a most base revenge, being wounded by him in his bed very dangerously," whereupon Hungate worked to deprive Felton of his due promotion.[122] Still, he served in the 1627 expedition to Rhé.[123]

Many accounts of Felton, from the seventeenth century to the present, try to explain his assassination of Buckingham on personal grounds, whether psychological or monetary. On August 28, his own brother, Edmond—himself no blithe spirit—spoke of John's "melancholy disposition . . . sad and heavy and of few words."[124] Elizabeth Josselyn, the wife of a stationer, who lodged with Felton in the Fleet Lane home of Thomas and Ann Foot, called him a melancholic given to few words and much

116. *CSPD* for James 9.222, 10.162; for Charles 1.141, 551; 4.310–11.
117. Bellany, "Poisoning" 619.
118. Captain Leigh was probably Edward, but may have been Sir Anthony. See John Glanville, *The Voyage to Cadiz in 1625*, Camden n.s. 32, Westminster 1883, 122; and *CSPD* 1.78, 101. On Cadiz, see *GHE* 6.1–23.
119. Mahaffy, *Calendar* 1.172. Victor Treadwell, *Buckingham and Ireland, 1616–1628*, Dublin 1998, 294–5.
120. *CSPD* 2.238.
121. 1.43; see also 1.53.
122. 2.382–3. Was Hungate trying to fuck him? On Hungate, see the *DNB* on Felton and *P* 129.
123. *DA* 1.382.
124. *PRO* 16/114/31; *CSPD* 3.274. Raylor suggests that the Felton boys' melancholy was congenital or a pose suggesting thwarted genius or gentry virtue ("Providence" 400).

reading.[125] She accused him of borrowing and failing to return a copy of *The History of the Queen of Scots*—perhaps the *Histoire de Marie Royne d'Ecosse* ("Edinburgh" 1572), a Huguenot translation of Buchanan's very popular antityrannicidal *Detection of the Doings of Mary Queen of Scots*.[126] Foote reported that Felton kept company with one Billingsley, probably the Henry Billingsley in trouble with the duke and imprisoned because of his "insufferable carriage" and attempts to break the regal monopoly over the foreign post.[127] An anti-libel called him a "frenzied miscreant" with "private spleeny heartburns."[128] Hyde said that Felton's "melancholic nature" was aggravated by "frequently hearing some popular preachers in the city."[129] Henry Wotton, Thomas May, David Hume, Frederick Fairholt, and John Forster all offered a similar diagnosis.[130] In *The Three Musketeers*, Alexandre Dumas added a dollop of erotomania: his Felton kills Buckingham at the seductive instigation of the villainous Milady.[131] Even modern accounts present the bookish poor as moping melancholics. Mildred Ann Gibb calls Felton "a man of morbid religious passion, given to much reading and brooding, who had gradually come to see in himself a divinely selected instrument of vengeance."[132] Lockyer calls him "a melancholy man, much given to reading, and of few words. He was the prototype of the puritan 'fanatics' who were to appear in extraordinary numbers when the great rebellion broke out in the 1640s"—strong testimony to the perennial appeal of Clarendonian history and of humor physiology.[133]

The second strategy for personalizing Felton's action presents him as a disappointed client. This argument fits snugly into the revisionist and new historicist account of early modern political conflict as the motiveless jostling of individuals and factions within a consensual patronage system rather than the ideological conflict of groups. Sidney Lee sees Felton as a disgruntled office seeker.[134] Drawing on a second-hand report that contradicts several first-hand ones, Conrad Russell suggests he went to Portsmouth to clamor for back pay and stabbed Buckingham only when

125. Felton's widowed sister, Elizabeth Done, may have been the Widow Donn who in 1638 shared the smallish parish of St Bennet Gracechurch with the Thomas Foot who became an alderman, lord mayor, a leading political Independent, and a regicide (T. C. Dale, *The Inhabitants of London in 1638*, 2 vols, London 1931, 1.40; Pearl, *London* 315–16).

126. *CSPD* 3.343; thanks to Tim Raylor for the suggestion. See James Emerson Phillips, *Images of a Queen*, Berkeley and Los Angeles 1964, 61–2, 252–3n.

127. *CSPD* 3.332; 1.220, 221, 231, 405, 466, 572, 2.6, 106, 436, 590, 591, 3.177.

128. Bellany, "Poisoning" 632.

129. 1.53.

130. Wotton, *Short* 22–3. Thomas May, *The History of the Parliament of England*, 1647; rpt London 1812, 6; David Hume, *The History of England*, 6 vols, Boston 1854, 5.47; *F* xxvi; Forster, *Eliot* 2.374.

131. New York 1940. In *John Felton*, London 1870, Edward Stirling rewrote Dumas for the London popular theater: his righteous Felton kills haughty Buckingham for dishonoring his daughter.

132. *Buckingham*, London 1935, 317.

133. *Buckingham* 459.

134. *DNB*.

refused.[135] Now by all accounts, Buckingham did owe Felton £80, but most witnesses credited Felton's claim that his desire for the public good was his foremost motive. Dudley Carleton, who was present at the assassination and helped preserve Felton for trial, said that he invoked his unpaid arrears, his Protestantism, and the House's Remonstrance against Buckingham.[136] Wotton thought it unlikely that Felton would "so deface his act, as to make the duke no more than an oblique sacrifice, to the fumes of his private revenge" against Hungate. Only "the prince of darkness itself" could discover Felton's true motive, but he noted that Felton blamed Eglisham's pamphlet and the House's Remonstrance.[137] Even if we admit that tyrannicides like Felton act partly out of a sense of injured merit (and there's no good reason to deny this), why should we insist on seeing ideology and individual experience as mutually exclusive (as if ideology were something mechanically imposed upon individuals), or as names for the same thing (as if ideology were a public rationale for personal pique)? Rather, Felton complexly fused his personal and public motives: as a gentleman forced into military service, then subject to labor without pay and the humiliation of a public rebuff, he generalized the injury to his status and his stomach as an injury to the nation, and undertook a project that he thought would heal both at once.

Felton hired a Holborn scrivener, George Willoughby, to draw up a petition for his back pay. In July, visiting Willoughby's shop, Felton found him making copies of the House's June Remonstrance, whose printing had been banned. He took one copy to a nearby tavern and read it through, then took it away with him, promising (and failing) to return it.[138] Struck with the thought of assassinating Buckingham, Felton fasted and prayed for two months to make sure that his plan was not "a temptation of the Devil . . . and when his resolutions were still the same to accomplish it, he then took the incitation to proceed from God himself, redoubled his courage, and heartily prayed for divine assistance to finish it."[139] Perhaps he imitated the deliberative delay of the Jacobean dramatic revenger, or heeded Languet and Mornay's warning about mistaking a dangerous tyrannicidal notion for divine inspiration.[140] Under examination, Felton claimed to have heard "a sermon at St. Faith's Church under

135. *Parliaments* 392. Russell draws on Osborne's letter of August 24 to Wentworth, but omits the lesson he drew from Buckingham's death: "A just reward for killing a poor mariner the day before with his own hands, for a little sauciness, as it is said, in asking his pay as the lieutenant did" (Cooper, *Wentworth* 303).
136. Ellis, *Original Letters* 3.258.
137. *Short* 22–3.
138. Forster, *Eliot* 2.336–7. On August 28, Lord Chief Justice Richardson and Heneage Finch examined Willoughby, who received a copy of the "Charles and George" epigram from a baker's boy by way of a pantler, and passed it on to a counselor at law by way of the counselor's son—a cross-class circulation that suggests the ubiquity of duke-hatred (*CSPD* 3.274, 360). Heath traced one Buckingham libel back through fifteen people to a "Mr. Hebe" (*CSPD* 3.195, *PRO* 16/109/34).
139. *DA* 1.383.
140. *Vindiciae* 62, 171–2.

Paul's, where the preacher spake in justification of every man in a good cause to be judge and executioner of sin, which he interpreted to be him."[141]

On Monday, August 18, he resolved to kill Buckingham. Setting himself his suicidal task, Felton methodically left the patronage system for the realm of freedom. The next day, he borrowed money from his mother and bought a dagger from a cutler near Tower Hill. Because he had injured his left hand in battle, he fastened the dagger in his right pocket so he could reach it easily.[142] Thinking he would be killed in the act, he sewed into in his hat a defiant self-vindication consisting of a sentence said to be copied from Geffray Fenton's *Golden Epistles*, adding a sentence of his own:

> That man is cowardly and base and deserveth not the name of a gentleman that is not willing to sacrifice his life for the honor of his God his king and his country. Let no man commend me for doing of it, but rather discommend themselves as to the cause of it, for if God had not taken away our hearts for our sins he would not have gone so long unpunished.[143]

Before commencing the seventy-mile trip to Portsmouth, he asked a church "by the conduit in Fleet-Street" to say prayers for him on Sunday, August 24, "as a man disordered and discontented in mind."[144]

Meanwhile, Buckingham gamely prepared in Portsmouth for another foray into the Continental wars of religion: an expedition to liberate the besieged Huguenots of La Rochelle.[145] He consulted with Charles,

---

141. William Sanderson, *A Compleat History of the Life and Raigne of King Charles*, 1658, 123. In a sermon before the king, Bishop Matthew Wren accused Puritans of sharing with Felton the belief that one may justly slay anyone opposed to one's party (Forster, *Eliot* 2.367n.). Felton's examiners asked him "if the Puritans had no hand therein" (*RHC* 1.638). In his hyperventilated *Folly and Madnesse Made Manifest* (1659), William Fiennes, Lord Saye and Sele, compared Quaker enthusiasts to Felton, who claimed "impulses of the spirit" to kill Buckingham (7).

142. Birch, *Court* 1.401.

143. *F* xxi. Fenton, translator of Guicciardini's republican *Storia d'Italia*, shared secretarial duties to Lord Grey in Ireland with Edmund Spenser. I haven't found this sentence in *Golden Epistles*, his humanist epistolary conduct manual of 1575, but several chapters might have caught Felton's eye. "The Original of Tyranny and Idolatry, together with the Punishments of Tyrants and Idolaters" emphasizes Nimrod's political tyranny as well as his moral disobedience. "There Are no Greater Riches than Honour, nor Poverty more Intolerable than Infamy," stresses Hebrew and Classical exempla of heroic individual action. And in "A rebuke to ambition under the speech of a savage man uttered in the Senate of Rome," a captive German says God allows evil men "to assemble and heap great things, to the end that when they are in their most security and delight, he might shew his power to their general confusion." After he denounces Rome, he offers himself up to death at its hands (195–200).

144. Forster, *Eliot* 2.350. The location suggests the Felton family's church, St Dunstan's in the West, where John Donne still held the living and sometimes preached; see John Stow, *The Survey of London*, London 1987, 349. News of the assassination reached St Dunstan's on Sunday, just after the sermon, during the psalm. Some stood up rejoicing, while others swooned in grief, and among the latter—or so they claimed—Felton's mother Eleanor and his sister Elizabeth Done (*CSPD* 3.277).

145. La Rochelle fell on October 18, between Buckingham's death and Felton's (Lockyer, *Buckingham* 459–60).

received intelligence reports, negotiated with Huguenots, and tried to control his fractious troops, chronically unpaid and mutinous because of his general improvidence. He and the king had frequently resorted to martial law, including exemplary hangings, which Parliament viewed as a dangerous prerogative encroachment on common law. *The Petition of Right* condemned the "commissions for proceeding by martial law . . . lest by color of them any of your Majesty's subjects be destroyed or put to death contrary to the laws and franchises of the land."[146] But the conflict continued. On June 2, Secretary Coke warned Buckingham that mariners had mutinied aboard the *Nonsuch*, and warned him and the king against a second assault on La Rochelle.[147] On Friday, August 22, Buckingham faced down a naval mutiny in Portsmouth. When a sailor who had affronted him earlier in the month was led to the gibbet, a group of his comrades attempted to rescue him. Buckingham and some loyal troops drove them back on shipboard, killed two, then proceeded to hang him.[148]

Alternately riding and walking, Felton arrived in Portsmouth on Saturday morning, August 23. On his way into town, he iconoclastically sharpened his knife on a stone cross in the highway, "believing it more proper in justice to advantage his design than for the idolatrous intent it was first erected."[149] He joined the throng at Buckingham's lodgings in 10 High Street. Between 9 and 10 that morning, Buckingham set out for the king's lodgings at nearby Southwick Park, the seat of the Norton family. Amid the press of English and Huguenot soldiers and sailors, Felton lunged at Buckingham, stabbed him in the chest, and called out, as the Earl of Cleveland recalled, "God have mercy upon thy soul!"[150] Accounts of Buckingham's last words vary. D'Ewes attributes to him that posthumous present perfect that one might have thought an expository convention of Renaissance drama: "God's wounds! The villain hath killed me!" Chastising this blasphemy, D'Ewes says that Felton "had greater care of Buckingham's soul than Buckingham himself had."[151] A poetic libel gave an alternate account of Buckingham's blasphemy: "He cried out (s'blood) and out came blood indeed."[152] Buckingham's wife, pregnant at the time, came out from her chamber on the second floor, saw her dying husband, and swooned.[153]

Somehow, Felton eluded detection in the crowd. When some searchers

146. *DRD* 170–71. See Lindsay Boynton, "Martial Law and the Petition of Right," *English Historical Review* 49.311, 1964.
147. *CSPD* 3.146.
148. A letter to Rous says Buckingham would have spared the condemned sailor (*Diary* 27; *GHE* 6.348). Conway suggests he killed one sailor with his own hand (*CSPD* 3.268; *PRO* 16/114/7), but Richard Hutton doubts this (*The Diary of Sir Richard Hutton, 1614–1639*, W. R. Prest, ed., Selden Society Supplementary Series 9, London 1991, 73–4).
149. William Sanderson, *Compleat History* 123.
150. *F* xvii–xviii; Forster, *Eliot* 2.355; Captain Harvy in Keeler et al., *Proceedings* 6.214–15.
151. *DA* 1.381–2, 384.
152. V. L. Pearl, and M. L. Pearl, "Richard Corbett's 'Against the Opposing of the Duke in Parliament, 1628,'" *Review of English Studies* n.s. 42.165, 1991, 34n.
153. *F* xx.

remembered that Buckingham had been speaking heatedly with some Huguenots, they cried out "A Frenchman! A Frenchman!" Felton mistook this cry for his own name, and "most audaciously and resolutely drawing forth his sword, came out and went amongst them, saying boldly, 'I am the man, here I am.'"[154] Hyde described him "with open arms very calmly and cheerfully exposing himself to the fury and swords of the most enraged, as being very willing to fall a sacrifice to their sudden anger, rather than to be kept for that deliberate justice which he knew must be exercised upon him."[155] But Carleton, Thomas Morton, and others saved him and took him to the house of the Governor of Portsmouth.[156] Carleton, Sir John Mennes ("Captain Mince"), Viscount Dorchester, Secretary Coke, and Secretary of State Edward Nicholas commenced the interrogation:

> Captain Mince tore off his spurs, and asking how he durst attempt such an act, making him believe the duke was not dead, he answered boldly that he knew he was dispatched, for 'twas not he, but the hand of Heaven that gave the stroke, and though his whole body had been covered over with armor of proof, he could not have avoided it.[157]

Felton changes himself from a mere private person into the hand of God.[158]

Before and after the deed, Felton insisted on his ideological motivation. When he set out for Portsmouth, he left behind a letter containing four dangerous republican aphorisms:

> 1. That there is no alliance nearer to any, than the alliance to his country. 2. The safety of the people is the chiefest law. 3. No law more sacred than the welfare of the commonwealth. 4. God himself hath enacted this law, that whatsoever is for the profit, or benefit of the commonwealth should be accounted lawful.

Felton claimed to have copied them from Fenton's *Golden Epistles*.[159] The officer who took Felton into custody after the assassination found him to

154. Ellis, *Original Letters* 3.257–8; *DA* 1.384; Forster, *Eliot* 2.356; *PRO* 16/114/7, 20.
155. *History* 1.85.
156. *DA* 1.384.
157. Howell, *Epistolae* 203. Mennes, with James Smith, compiled two poetic miscellanies, *Musarum Deliciae* (1658) and *Wit Restor'd* (1658). The latter contains a number of poems on Buckingham and Felton. A James Smith wrote the pro-Felton poem, "On Felton's Arraignement" (*F* 71–2). See Timothy Raylor's *Cavaliers, Clubs, and Literary Culture*, Newark 1994; and his reprint edition of the miscellanies (Delmar, NY, 1985). On Nicholas, see *F* xxii.
158. On the interrogation, see also Carleton's account (*CSPD* 3.271; *PRO* 16/114/20). Many libelers referred to Felton's inspired "hand" and "arm," perhaps trying to detach the assassination from a private person and give it an independent force as an act of God or violated nature. In 1660, Algernon Sidney signed the book for visitors at Copenhagen University, "*Manus haec inimica tyrannis* [This hand is an enemy to tyrants]" (*DRD* 21). Too late, Webster's Bosola resolves, "The weakest arm is strong enough that strikes / With the sword of justice" (*The Duchess of Malfi*, London and New York 1993, 5.2.337–8).
159. *CSPD* 3.326–7. See also Birch, *Court* 1.401; and Isaac Disraeli, *Curiosities* 3.460–61. I haven't found these aphorisms in Fenton's book; a manuscript miscellany in the

be "a very bold resolute young man, and doth not repent his act, as persuading himself that he hath done good service to the king, state, and country."[160] In mid-September, Edward Dering found him in jail, owning his action "with the bosom of a quiet settled constancy" and "professing he would do it were it to do again."[161] At his arraignment on November 27, his indictment was read and "he confessed the fact, but added that he did it not maliciously, but out of an intent for the good of his country."[162]

His fellow soldiers and sailors christened him "Honest Jack," and asked the king to spare him.[163] Alvise Contarini wrote that "all, save the king and the favorites," so rejoiced at Buckingham's death that "it has been very difficult in many parts of the kingdom to prevent bonfires and other rejoicings."[164] Gathering crowds turned Felton's journey to the Tower of London into a triumph: "multitudes of people . . . with a general voice cried, 'Lord comfort thee,' 'The Lord be merciful unto thee,' or such like words." As he passed through Kingston upon Thames, an old woman cried out in typological solidarity, "Now God bless thee, little David!" and he entreated the crowds to pray for him. An anagrammatist turned Felton's name into "No Flie not." Suggesting parliamentary guilt by association, his guards conveyed him to the Tower cell occupied by John Eliot after his inflammatory summing-up of the House's 1626 bill impeaching the duke.[165] But through September and October, crowds flocked to the Tower to see Felton, departing "in tears and prayers that he may remain firm."[166] The state investigated a number of persons accused of drinking healths to him.[167] At Felton's going from the bar after his condemnation, one lawyer grumbled, "How easy it is to rescue and save him, if men had any courage!"[168]

This support for Felton extended well beyond the lower classes. Francis Nethersole, agent for Elizabeth of Bohemia, complained that "the base multitude in this town drink healths to Felton," but he also observed "infinitely more cheerful than sad faces of better people." Though he

---

Bodleian also records them (Malone 23, 133). The second aphorism translates Cicero's "salus populi suprema lex esto," from *De Legibus* 3.3.8 (*De Re Publica, De Legibus*, London and Cambridge, MA, 1966). Combined with the figure of an axe sending Charles's head flying, it would form the battle standard for Major William Rainsborough, Army radical and future Ranter. See Ian Gentles, "The Iconography of Revolution," in Gentles, John Morrill, and Blair Worden, eds, *Soldiers, Writers and Statesmen of the English Revolution*, Cambridge 1998, 91–113, 108. The signature "Johan: Felton" in a copy of *M. Tulli Ciceronis Epistolarum Selectarum, Libri Tres* (1626) does not much resemble Felton's autograph (Lockyer, *Buckingham* between 364 and 365); thanks to Sara Rubinstein and the University of Michigan library for a photocopy of the former.

160. Rous, *Diary* 28.
161. Forster, *Eliot* 2.359n.
162. Birch, *Court* 1.444–5.
163. *F* xxviii; Ellis, *Original Letters* 3.260–61, 265.
164. *CSPV* 21.283.
165. Ellis, *Original Letters* 3.260, 261, 265.
166. *CSPV* 21.337; see also *RHC* 1.638.
167. *CSPD* 3.268, 277, 325.
168. Birch, *Court* 1.438.

condemned them, he also hoped for a reconciliation of king and people, "the stone of offense now being removed by the hand of God."[169] In September, Giovani Soranzo, Venetian ambassador to the Netherlands, told the Doge and Senate that Elizabeth feared the report might prove false, while Zorzi Zorzi, ambassador to France, reported Richelieu reveling at the news.[170] Lord Henry Percy sent the news to his brother-in-law, James, Earl of Carlisle, in Venice, saying that "the desirer and plotter of your ruin and destruction is possessed with a death not unfit for him, because correspondent to his life, which was granted by all men to be dishonorable and odious."[171] Sir John Oglander observed that, although Buckingham was the greatest of royal subjects in Europe, his sudden and strange death showed that "all must look for the like that maintain their greatness merely on the favor of the Prince, without the merits of their own or the approbation of the commonwealth." He added some meteorological corroboration: before Buckingham's death it rained almost every day, "But after his death, ensued for all the harvest and till Allhallowtide such fair weather as all the country people wished he had been killed a month sooner. It was noted that after Felton's death and his hanging in chains we had not one fair day a long time after."[172] In his journal, Thomas Scott concurred, and added a commentary on Psalms 116, a psalm of thanksgiving to God for deliverance from death.[173] In September, Sir Robert Savage said that he would have killed Buckingham if Felton had not, and was sent to the Tower.[174] A manuscript miscellany contains a remarkable learned discourse on the assassination in the form of a letter to a friend. Combining poetry and prose, Latin and English, classical and scriptural sources (Buckingham as Catiline, Felton as Phineas), the author denounces favorites in general, and Buckingham in particular, as that "upstart mushroom favorite" and "poisonous kind of creature," which "every good man will hate," who is to be "no more esteemed than a mad dog or bull slain by any or many of the multitude." He defends Felton's decision to slay the "monster" without giving him time for repentance, models his own impassioned writing on Felton's heroic deed, and begs the king to honor Felton as a hero of the nation, or to ignore any repentance extorted by torture.[175]

Even Ben Jonson came under suspicion. Heath examined him on October 26 on charges that he had written the verse libel "To His

169. *CSPD* 3.268, *PRO* 16/114/7.
170. *CSPV* 21.282, 305.
171. *CSPD* 23.291–2.
172. *A Royalist's Notebook*, London 1936, 40, 42.
173. Keeler et al., *Proceedings* 6.236.
174. *CSPD* 3.326. On Savage, see also *P* 111.
175. Bodleian Library, Malone Ms. 23, 165–90; 184, 169, 173. This miscellany includes several poems about Buckingham, Felton, and Strafford. It quotes Numbers 25 on Phineas and compares Felton (174–6). Given that Phineas skewered a Hebrew man and a Midianite woman *in flagrante*, the allusion may carry a sexual charge against the duke.

Confined Friend Mr. Felton," and because he had given a dagger to the actual author, Zouch Townley, who escaped safely to the Hague.[176] Alexander Gill the Younger, formerly an usher and Milton's tutor at St Paul's School, celebrated the occasion with an episode of drunken raillery in the cellar of Trinity College, Oxford, saying "that our king was fitter to stand in a Cheapside shop, with an apron afore him and say 'What lack ye?' than to govern a kingdom. . . . That the duke was gone down to Hell to meet King James there. . . . He was sorry that Felton had deprived him of the honor of doing that brave act." His seized papers called James and Charles "the old fool and the young one," said it was a common thing in London to drink Felton's health, and contained a version of the libelous revision of Jonson's "The Five Senses." Star Chamber tried and censured him, threatened a fine and his ears, then dismissed him with temporary loss of liberty and office.[177] Laud called Buckingham's death "the saddest accident that ever befell me, and should be to all good Christians," and "the saddest news that ever I heard in my life," and thought Gill's words devoid of "all humanity."[178]

Charles was disconsolate.[179] Alvise Contarini, the Venetian ambassador, wrote that he originally intended to spend £10,000 on a state funeral, but changed his mind "because of the expense and the risk of a popular tumult."[180] In another account, he wanted to help pay off some of the duke's debts, and feared "some foul treason of his like to be discovered."[181] Fearing a popular attack that would desecrate the corpse, Charles buried the duke surreptitiously in Westminster Abbey on September 10 or 11, but he added an armed guard, "carrying their pikes and muskets upon their shoulders as in a march, not trailing them at their heels, as is usual at a mourning. As soon as the coffin was entered the church, they came all away without giving any volley of shot at all. And this was the obscure catastrophe of that great man."[182] Sir Richard Weston, Chancellor of the Exchequer, warned that any attempt to build a great tomb for the duke while James still lacked one would bring a great popular outcry. Charles did not complete the duke's grand tomb in Westminster Abbey until 1634.[183]

The stories of Felton in prison range from portraits (typically by clergy)

---

176. *CSPD* 3.ix–x. A copy of Russell's *The Spy* contains Jonson's signature (Norbrook, *Writing* 54n.63).
177. Ellis, *Original Letters* 3.276–7. *CSPD* 3.viii–xi, 319; 4.xv–xix, 362, 393. William Chillingworth may have informed on Gill (*CSPD* 3.326; John Aubrey, *Brief* 159).
178. *CSPD* 3.269, 319. Charles Carlton, *Archbishop William Laud*, London 1987, 73; William Laud, *The Works of the Most Reverend Father in God, William Laud, D.D.*, 7 vols, 1847, rpt New York 1975, 7.15–18; H. R. Trevor-Roper, *Archbishop Laud, 1573–1645*, London 1962, 456. Laud received the news while at Croydon, investing the Arminian ultra Richard Montagu (*RHC* 1.635).
179. *CSPD* 3.268.
180. *CSPV* 21.337.
181. Birch, *Court* 400.
182. Ellis, *Original Letters* 3.399.
183. *GHE* 6.356–7.

of a recovering melancholic, horror-stricken at his action, to accounts (typically by lawyers and other laity) of a pious and somewhat chastened but basically unrepentant tyrannicide. Mead reported hearing that "Two grave and learned divines were sent to him by order from His Majesty, to try if, by working upon his conscience, they could get out of him who were his complices and confederates." One divine reported to Mead that Felton wished to receive communion and to wear ashes, sackcloth, and a halter as tokens of humiliation. When one of these divines, Dr Brian Duppa, told Felton that his sudden murder might have slain Buckingham's soul as well as his body, he allegedly "fell into a bitter weeping, and professed this deed of his to be a fearful, and a crying sin."[184] But another informant told Mead of quite a different Felton. At Heath's suggestion, and with the support of Laud and Lord Dorset, Charles suggested that Felton be racked and encouraged to name his "complices." When Dorset told Felton to "prepare yourself for the rack," he replied,

> I do not believe, my lord, that it is the king's pleasure, for he is a just and gracious prince, and will not have his subjects to be tortured against the law. I do again affirm upon my salvation that my purpose was known to no man living, and more than I have said before I cannot. But if it be his majesty's pleasure, I am ready to suffer whatsoever his majesty will have inflicted upon me. Yet this I must tell you by the way, that if I be put upon the rack, I will accuse you, my Lord of Dorset, and none but yourself.[185]

Like the assassination itself, Felton's retort deflects anti-tyrannical resistance from the king toward one of his mediaries. His judges ruled unanimously that "Felton by the law ought not to be tortured by the rack, as no such punishment is known to or allowed by our law." Blackstone later applauded them for ending official judicial torture in England.[186] This was a little premature, since judicial torture on the king's prerogative persisted until 1640 at least, while more covert torture survived well into the twentieth century, as suffragists and Irish political prisoners have testified, but we should note the formal illegality of judicial torture in Britain and the popular prejudice against it.[187]

The King's Bench Bar arraigned and convicted Felton on November 27. A London minister told Mead that Felton "wept most bitterly *for that sin*, as he called it—*that great sin*," and that the ministers who stayed with him struggled to save him from despair. One lawyer told Mead's informant that Felton said "he was sorry he had taken so faithful a servant from

---

184. *CSPD* 3.326–7; *PRO* 16/116/101.
185. Birch, *Court* 1.401–2. Felton threatened Laud, not Dorset, in some accounts (Bulstrode Whitelocke, *Memorials of English Affairs*, 1682, 11; *RHC* 1.638).
186. *Commentaries on the Laws of England*, 4 vols, Philadelphia 1825, 4.328; *GHE* 6.359n.
187. Erasing Felton's sardonic gallows humor and the judges' principled resistance, Rosalind Miles says they refused to torture Felton because he was "clearly quite deranged" (*Ben Jonson*, London 1986, 235). According to a French summary, Kazimierz Baran's essay ("Tortury w Angielskim Procesie Karnym," *Czasopismo Prawno-Historyczne* 31.2, 1979) considers Felton's case at length.

so gracious a lord." But another swore that he said "he was sorry if he had taken away so faithful a servant to his majesty as Mr. Attorney had related." A "gentleman of Lincoln's Inn" told Mead that, when the king's attorney emphasized Buckingham's quality and denounced Felton for having slain "so dear and near a subject of the king's, so great a counselor of the state, the general of his majesty's forces, admiral of the seas, etc.," Felton responded, "I am sorry both that I have shed the blood of a man, who is the image of God, and taken away the life of so near a subject of the king, as Mr. Attorney hath related."[188] As Felton's dagger reveals Buckingham's corporal humanity and removes him from his titles, so his confession reveals the duke's spiritual equality with all descendants of Adam and Eve, and his political equality with all subjects of the king. After passing sentence, the judges suggested Felton's popery or atheism by noting that he had not taken communion for two years. He responded that he had acted only for the good of his country, and added, "Here is the hand . . . that did the deed, and I wish it may be cut off and then my body disposed at the king's pleasure." The judges denied the request.[189] Even this reversion to an earlier mode of analogical corporal punishment begins to look like a claim for individual agency—perhaps with a recollection of Scaevola's loss of his hand in the defense of Rome, which Felton's poetic allies recalled.[190]

Another version of Felton's confession shows him working within and against the rhetoric of criminal repentance:

> I confess I did sin in killing the duke; and I am sorry that I killed a most wicked and impenitent man so suddenly, but I doubt not but that great good shall result to the church and commonwealth by it; and I assure myself that God hath pardoned this and all my other sins in and through the merits and blood of Jesus Christ my savior.

The insincere confession under duress, one of the most sublime products of the human imagination, deserves the greatest analytical reverence. By admitting his sin, Felton mitigates it, for his penitence elevates him above his "wicked and impenitent" victim. His sin may in fact lie not in the act itself, but only in its suddenness. Further, he suggests that, in moral terms, the murder was rather ordinary, and so reasonably grouped with "all my other sins," which God had already pardoned. Finally, he stresses the fact that the good to both church and state offset the evil of his deed—as if he had not sinned at all, but taken on a Christ-like propitiatory martyrdom. Felton resists the judicial pressure to become an iconic penitent and dramatizes the power of a private person to consider, compare, weigh

---

188. Birch, *Court* 1.444–6. See *CSPD* 3.398 and *PRO* 116/121/78 for Heath's speech moving Felton's execution.
189. *P* 133.
190. *F* 45, 68–9.

cause against cause, sin against sin, and take on a public and deliberative role.[191]

That same afternoon, Felton's relatives, the Earl and Countess of Arundel and their son Lord Matravers, brought him money to give away at his execution and a winding sheet. On the 28th, Felton thanked God— not the king—for giving him so long to repent, prayed that the king's heart would be "knit together" with that of the Parliament, prayed for the King and Queen of Bohemia, praised Buckingham's widow, asked her and all the duke's servants to forgive him, and forgave his hangman. After he was hanged and cut down, he showed some signs of life. When the woman hired to wrap him in a winding sheet refused to give him aqua vitae to revive him, the gathered crowd cursed her.[192] *The Prayer and Confession of Mr. Felton*, a short pamphlet of 1628 printed (presumably) with official sanction, echoes many of these details, but adds that Felton blamed his own sin and the seduction of the devil. I see no need either to deny the authenticity of this account, or to assume it tells the whole story about Felton's state of mind. Felton remains a monarchical subject, and we remain some distance from the Puritan regicides, with their ideologically elaborated self-vindications at the Restoration.[193] The king originally intended to bury Felton in the usual spot for "common malefactors," but at the insistence of Buckingham's widow, he had Felton's body dressed in the clothing he had been wearing at the time he stabbed the duke, sent by coach to a spot two miles outside Portsmouth, and hung up by chains in the open air.[194]

Felton at Colonus

Several cavaliers (Carew, Carey, Davenant, Shirley, Waller) wrote sympathetic elegies for Buckingham, but most poets approved of Felton's action.[195] Even those works that tried to maintain some critical distance from Felton continued that forensic voice of public disputation we saw in the satires of the living duke. If a pro-Buckingham copyist, and not the pro-Felton author, produced the ambivalent title of "In Commendacion of Felton's

191. *DA* 1.385–6. On confession as resistance, see Patricia Marbry Harrison, "Religious Rhetoric as Resistance in Early Modern Goodnight Ballads," in Sally McKee, ed., *Crossing Boundaries*, Turnhout, Belgium, 1999, 107–25.
192. Birch, *Court* 1.450. Peter Linebaugh discusses popular struggles for the bodies of the hanged, who could sometimes be revived and escape further punishment, in "The Tyburn Riot Against the Surgeons," in Douglas Hay, Peter Linebaugh, and E. P. Thompson, eds, *Albion's Fatal Tree*, New York 1975, 65–118.
193. J. A. Sharpe, "'Last Dying Speeches,'" *Past and Present* 107, 1985.
194. *P* 136, 139.
195. Bellany ("Poisoning" 628–40) and Gerald Hammond (*Fleeting*) discuss the "anti-libels" supporting Buckingham. See also Gervase Warmstrey, *Virescit Vulnere Virtus: England's Wound and Cure*, 1628; rpt ed. Henry Huth, *Fugitive Tracts Written in Verse which Illustrate the Condition of Religious and Political Feeling in England and the State of Society There During Two Centuries*, London 1875, vol. 2; and Robert Spence's *Illustrissimi Fortissimique Domini, D. Georgii Villerii Buckinghamiae Ducis* (Edinburgh? 1629?), a long Latin poem, which contains some execrations against Felton.

Fowle Murther of the Duke," then some contradiction still remains, for the copyist has at least taken care to preserve the poem's jubilant sentiments.[196] We see a similar title and effect in a poem somewhat more favorable to Buckingham, "A Charitable Censure on the Death of the D. of B.," which directs charity and censure toward both Felton and the duke. It opens by responding to the Buckingham-in-hell motif that appears in so many of these poems: "What! shall I say now George is dead / That he's in hell? Charity forbid." The poet focuses less on Buckingham than on his own struggle to speak no ill of the dead: "If to the kingdom he did harm, / Yet thy tongue still thou ought'st to charm." He finally settles on Buckingham's role in breaking off negotiations for the Spanish Match as an honorable memory.[197]

In "On the Murder of the Duke of Buckingham," Owen Feltham records the pro-Felton voices, condemns them, merges with them, and attempts to disengage himself from them once again:

> Canst thou be gone so quickly, can a knife,
> Let out so many titles and a life? . . .
> Let the rude genius of the giddy train,
> Brag in a jury, that it hath stabbed Spain,
> Austria, and the skipping French; yea all
> Those home-bred papists that would sell our fall.
> The eclipse of two wise princes' judgments sure
> Thou was't, whereby our land was still kept poor.

The poet moves from caesural wit directed toward the over-titled duke, to aristocratic contempt for the mob, to railing antipopery that unites him with that very mob and its rude genius, perhaps Felton. Later in the poem, he moves into genuine elegiac language, praising the "flowing nobleness" of Buckingham. If he should "speak the vulgar," he would praise Felton as a second Brutus, but one who should receive only "Such bays as heathenish ignorance can give." He concludes with a complex condemnation of Felton that merges "the vulgar" with "the people":

> But then the Christian, checking that, shall say,
> Though he did good, he did it the wrong way;
> And oft they fall into the worst of ills,
> That act the people's wish without their wills.

With effort, one can perhaps distinguish ethically between those who merely wish for something and those who act on the wish, but the distinction does not clearly work to the advantage of the mere wishers. In any case, the poem ends inconclusively, as the poet struggles to preserve conventional codes of ethical behavior and social deference while acknowledging a political and even providential necessity that overrides them. This capacity for conflict bordering on contradiction ("wish"

196. *F* 67–9.
197. Ibid. 50–51.

without "will") points to a mode of tyrannicidal dialectical thinking such as we can see, most famously, in Marvell's "Horatian Ode."[198]

Another poem is memorable not only for its bold workmanship (it gamely rhymes "Felton" and "smelt on"), but for the way it collapses tyrannicidal agencies: "Felton, awake, and cheer thyself from sorrow, / Thy hand must strike the duke, and that tomorrow." The speaker—whether the poet, England, Felton himself, or even God—tells Felton that "thou only art set on / By him, whose justice doth attend thy doom," and it concludes with a casuistically strained combination of condemnation and forgiveness:

> Pray heavens grant pardon, and thyself assure,
> The country's service striveth to procure
> The day ne'er ending with prayers joined with thine,
> To obtain forgiveness for the bloody crime.

The need to slay Buckingham presses so closely that the poet issues a sort of Protestant indulgence: like Felton forgiving his hangman, he imaginatively forgives a bloody crime before its commission.[199] Several fictionalized gallows speeches dramatize Felton's impenitent penitence, quite like Felton's own in jail. "Felton's Farewell" externalizes his divided psychological state, in which "Sorrow and joy at once possess my breast"—his private grief at having to leave his friends (not at having killed the duke), his public joy at having rescued his country. "To Charles," also in Felton's voice, presents the oxymoronically "bold pious petition / Of free bound Felton," who tells Charles, with a humble presumption reminiscent of Wilson the Scot, that "I your servant . . . have set you free."[200]

"Upon the Duke's Death" supplements the prorogued Parliament through an explicitly forensic poetry that submits both Felton and Buckingham to trial.[201] The poet begins by entertaining two "short arguments": that regardless of Buckingham's offenses, he ought to have been tried by law, not cut down by a private person; and that regardless of Felton's virtue, he ought to be condemned, since he acted outside the law. First, the poet notes that Charles corrupted the regular course of law when he dissolved the 1626 Parliament to protect the duke:

> When law was offered, it was then neglected;
> For when the Commons did, with just intent,
> Pursue his faults in open parliament,
> The highest court of justice, so supreme,
> That it hath censured monarchs of the realm;
> There might his grace have had a legal trial,

---

198. Ibid. 54–5. Gerald Hammond's excellent reading first compared Marvell (*Fleeting* 62–3); *Andrew Marvell*, Frank Kermode and Keith Walker, eds, Oxford 1990, 82–4.

199. "1628: Feltons dream Aug. 22nd being the night before the murder," Bodleian Library, Tanner Ms. 465, 102ʳ.

200. *F* 76, 72–4.

201. Ibid. 52–4.

> Had he not it opposed with strong denial.
> But he then scorned and proudly set at naught
> The House, and those that him in question brought.
> Therefore when the law or justice takes no place
> Some desperate course must serve in such a case.

The poet may be echoing the debates in the Parliament of 1628 over kingly prerogative, such as the extra-legal powers Charles claimed to justify imprisoning the Five Knights who resisted the Forced Loan. While the Commons grounded prerogative power in common law, the king appealed to his divine right—an argument that could potentially abrogate any human law whatsoever. Such arguments conjure up the balancing divine prerogative embodied in the inspired hand of a tyrannicide. The "desperate course" returns to the natural law of political self-defense, which the poet figures by a movement out of juridical into body politic imagery: "A rotten member, that can have no cure, / Must be cut off to save the body sure."

In response to the second argument, the speaker begins with temperate piety: "What shall we say? was it God's will or no, / That one sinner should kill another so? / I dare not judge." But he proceeds immediately to judgment:

> yet it appears sometime
> God makes one sinner 'venge another's crime;
> That when as justice can no holdfast take,
> Each other's ruin they themselves should make.

As in the denouements of countless revenge tragedies, which also take place in a state of nature emerging from the corruption of civil society, God employs an extra-legal agent, then removes him from the purged state to prevent a further cycle of vengeance.

Yet the poet goes further, elevating Felton by linking him with God, and threatening Charles by linking him with Buckingham. Even before the passage quoted above, the poet says that "By Felton's hand God wrought his [Buckingham's] overthrow." And in the last eight lines, Felton changes from God's instrument to God's hand to God himself:

> But howsoe'er it is, the case is plain,
> God's hand was in't, and the duke strived in vain:
> For what the Parliament did fail to do
> God did both purpose and perform it too.
> He would no threat'nings or affronts receive,
> Nor no deep policies could him deceive;
> But when his sin was ripe it then must down:
> God's sickle spares not either king or crown.

Felton did not usurp parliamentarian authority; God took that delegated political power back into himself—as the legislative language of "purpose" and "perform" underlines—and transferred it temporarily to Felton.

When Charles thwarts regular parliamentary power, God may empower extraordinary agents, and even merge with them, as the ambiguous subject (God or Felton?) of the last four lines shows. In moving from the narrative past tense of "was" to the sententious present tense of "must down" and "spares not," the poet may simply reflect the characteristically awkward/ eloquent fluidity of seventeenth-century tenses. But this unsparing apocalyptic sickle also glances toward a particular king, and perhaps toward the "crown" of kingship itself.

Though many of these poems reveal learned humanist hands at work, and sit happily in manuscript commonplace books and poetic miscellanies alongside poems by Donne, Jonson, and the cavalier poets, they tend to employ an oppositional and antipapist aesthetic, as Buckingham's partisans saw. The anonymous author of "To Felton's Freindes" constructs an extended critique of the radical religious casuistry at work in the pro-Felton poems. Felton is "Confirmed on earth, and that he may be crowned / God must the author of this deed be found."[202] Carew says that Felton was driven by "blinded zeal," while Davenant says that "the precise / Do relish murder as a sacrifice," and fears that oppositional poets will "drink town breath, t'infuse some qualm / That may convert the story to a psalm."[203] One brilliant epigram confirms these fears:

> The pale horse of the Revelation
> Hath unhorsed the horseman of our nation,
> And given him such a kick on his side
> (At Portsmouth) that he sware, and died.

In Felton's kick, apocalyptic defeats courtly horsemanship. The author juxtaposes colloquial diction and millenarian imagery partly for humorous effect, but he also prefigures the way in which radical sectaries would infuse everyday social and political life with chiliastic energies during the next three decades.[204] In one poem, Buckingham becomes a closet papist villain in the employ of the Antichrist, secretly plotting "the ruin of heaven's favorite, / Reformed religion." Another attacks the "blockheads made bishops," while another makes Felton a Christ-like figure working the "redemption" of his nation.[205] "On Felton's Arraignment" offers an almost apocalyptic elegy: until Felton's deed, "all thy fellow saints have waited long, / And wearied time with expectation." In "To His Confined Friend Mr. Felton," Zouch Townley exclaims, "All we by him did suffer, thou for all," turning Buckingham into a guilty Adam and Felton into a self-sacrificial Christ or Second Adam.[206] In D'Ewes's account, Charles

202. J. A. Taylor, "Two Unpublished Poems on the Duke of Buckingham," *Review of English Studies* n.s. 40, 1989, 238.
203. Gerald Hammond, *Fleeting* 52–3, 55.
204. *F* 63. Bellany analyzes Rubens's equestrian portrait of Buckingham (1627) as the determined horseman of the English nation ("Poisoning" 490–91).
205. *F* 42, 49, 69; see also 71.
206. Ibid. 75.

himself joined in this providential interpretation when he asked, "Who can prevent a stroke from heaven?"[207]

The poems in Fairholt's collection so frequently associate Felton with the tyrannicides of Hebrew and classical antiquity that we may reasonably call them "republican." Even before Buckingham died, Richard Corbett defended him in a poem linking his opponents with the monarchomach George Buchanan.[208] The author of "Felton Commended" evoked the "magic thralldom" of the state under Buckingham, saying that he created "Iliads of grief" by casting away great sums of money. But the cult of courtly conspicuous consumption (he mentions Gerard Honthorst's portrait of Buckingham as Mercury) has been disenchanted and destroyed: "Naught but illusion were we, 'til this guile / Was by thy hand cut off, stout Maccabee."[209] In "To Charles," Felton proclaims his tyrannicidal affiliations, maintaining nominal piety and obedience as a civil subject while asserting his status as a divinely sanctioned tyrannicide:

> I know what Phineas did; and Heber's wife,
> And Ehud, Israel's judges, with Eglon's life:
> And I did hear, and see, and know, too well,
> What evil was done our English Israel,
> And I had warrant sealed, and sent from heaven,
> My work to do, and so the blow is given.

The poet even goes so far as to deify Felton when he has him ask, "And must I die? yet shall I live again: / To dust I must; but I shall rise to reign."[210] The author of "Upon the Duke" shows Buckingham in the *Mirrour for Magistrates* tradition, posthumously realizing his own identity as a tyrant, Felton's as a tyrannicide:

> but, oh the gall:
> My murtherer's lamented; hark! they call
> Him, noble Roman, second Curtius;
> Undaunted Scaevola, that dared thus.[211]

Similarly, the author of "Felton's Tombstone" says that Felton's "valor great did prove a Roman spirit."[212] He may be alluding to a statement by the living duke, as he prepared his 1628 assault on La Rochelle: "Some of his friends had advised him, how generally he was hated in England, and how needful it would be for his greater safety to wear some coat of mail

---

207. *DA* 1.386.
208. *F* 32; Pearl and Pearl, "Richard Corbett's" 32–9.
209. *F* 69–70.
210. Ibid. 72–4. Thomas Scott the parliamentarian interwove a commentary on Judges 3 (on Othniel and Ehud) with a discussion of Felton's assassination (Keeler et al., *Proceedings* 6.243).
211. *F* 45.
212. Ibid. 77

or some other secret defensive armor: which the duke, slighting, said, 'It needs not; there are no Roman spirits left.' "[213]

These poems repeatedly evoke the language and forms of Renaissance tragedy—not the monarchical tragedy of transition, which warns against untuning the string of degree, but the sort of tragedy that Sidney praises, which "maketh kings fear to be tyrants."[214] In particular, they bring home to England the conventions of revenge tragedies set in the Mediterranean world, as we can see in their frequent recourse to the Hades of Thomas Kyd and the English Senecans, and their casuistical struggle to defend revenge inside a conservative Christian ethical framework. In Caroline England as in Renaissance drama, thwarted justice usually produces anti-tyrannical tragedy, which submits kingly perverters of civil law to a retributive divine or natural law. The poet appropriates the techniques of tyrannical rule and turns them against the ruler: just as the king's priest, judge, or torturer forces the prisoner to confess his sin, so the poet forces Buckingham to admit his abuses of power. The posthumous soliloquies by Buckingham provide him with the confessional voice of a dying Machiavel proclaiming his tardy repentance. In the "Prosopopeia on the Duke," attributed to one "Jo. Heape," Buckingham confesses his conspiracy with Rome and Spain, and hints at his identity as a treacherous ganymede and poisoner: "I that my country did betray, / Undid that king that let me sway / His scepter as I pleased."[215]

Buckingham reviews his career in "Upon the Duke," a long dramatic soliloquy complete with introduction, "Protasis," and "Catastrophe." He begins with his entry "on this world's theater" as a "monarch's minion" with "naked chin," and recalls his Epicurean pleasure in banquets and masques, and contempt for "mediocrity" and notion of an afterlife. His tragic hubris led him to pry into the "ark of state affairs" and the "royal cabinet of secrets," until "the affectation of a higher state / (That sin that first of all the heavens did hate) / Took up my utmost thoughts." The rest of the poem compares him to Hebrew, Greek, and Continental tyrants. In another classic motif from revenge tragedy, he laments his sudden execution, with no time to repent, and begs his friends to "howl my tragic fall," which may also be their own: "Justice hath begun; / Some friends, I fear, must bleed ere she hath done." As he begins to reveal the names of these friends, dawn and the lark arrive and chase him away.[216] Other poems extract confessions from Buckingham by inserting him into tragic dialogues with Charon and with Dr Lambe. In another, Buckingham improbably confesses the justice of his punishment and prophesies the anagrammatical revenge that will be visited on him:

---

213. *DA* 1.381.

214. *Selected Prose and Poetry*, 2nd edn, Madison 1983, 129. See also Bushnell, *Tragedies*.

215. *F* 51–2. *A Full, True and Particular Account* (1700?), based on "Monsieur d'Ablancour, *le Vie le Grand Duc de Buckingham*," recounts an unsuccessful attempt by the ghost of Buckingham's father to convince his son to moderate his conflict with the people.

216. *F* 36–46; on Buckingham's sudden-death damnation, see also 54, 57, and 59.

O famous Felton! Thy valor yet I love! . . .
I know each letter of my name shall be
A theme for their inventions, to let flee
Abroad to all the world, even my black deeds.[217]

Another poem comically shows Buckingham indulging a compulsion to repeat: he writes his mother that he has become "heir apparent to th'infernal state," and tells her that their kindred may find places in hell, while Pluto, currently unattached, may even choose her for his wife.[218]

The last and most powerful poem in Fairholt's collection, "Felton's Epitaph," also employs tragic conventions, but of a different sort. Focusing on Felton's death and the grisly display of his decaying body, it becomes, in effect, a brief *Antigone*.[219] Felton becomes a tyrannicidal saint who combines Antigone's heroic individual opposition to tyranny with Polyneices' sacred festering body:

Here uninterred suspends (though not to save
Surviving friends, th'expenses of a grave)
Felton's dead earth; which to the world shall be:
His own sad monument. His elegy
As large as fame; but whether bad or good
I say not: by himself 'twas writ in blood:
For which his body is entombed in air,
Arched o'er with heaven, set with a thousand fair
And glorious diamond stars. A sepulcher
That time can never ruinate, and where

217. Ibid. 56–63, 59.
218. "The copy of a letter," Bodleian Library, Tanner Ms. 465, 103ᵛ.
219. *F* 78. I have modernized the version in David Norbrook and H. R. Woudhuysen, eds, *The Penguin Book of Renaissance Verse, 1509–1659*, London 1992, which is based on British Library, Sloane Ms. 826, 197ʳ, adding the Latin motto sometimes attached to other versions. Seventeenth-century readers and copyists made it extraordinarily popular. Margaret Crum's *First-Line Index of English Poetry, 1500–1800* (Oxford 1968) lists thirteen versions in the Bodleian. Yale's Beinecke Library owns two (see first-line index), and the Folger Shakespeare Library six more (Mss. V.a.97, V.a.125, V.a.319, V.a.322, V.b.43, W.a.135). The Leicestershire County Record Office holds a copy (Herrick Ms. DG 9/2796, 10–11). The British Library attributes one copy to "H: Ch:," whom its catalog identifies as Henry Cholmley (BL Ms. Add. 15226, 28ʳ⁻ᵛ)—an identification that jars with the anti-Felton poem immediately following attributed to the same author (J. A. Taylor, "Two" 236n.), though printed copies in *Wits Recreations* (1658) and *Wit Restored* (1658) repeat the identification. For additional printed copies, see *The Wars, and Causes of Them, Betwixt England and France* (1697) and *A New Collection of Poems Relating to State Affairs* (1705; see Pearl and Pearl, "Richard Corbett's" 236). Bellany has found an anti-Felton parody of this poem, and another poem which, because of verbal echoes, would seem to be either a source for or (more likely) an homage to "Felton's Epitaph." It calls his hanging body "a spectacle of dread, / A pendant sword o'er proud ambition's head" ("Poisoning" 654–8; British Library Add. Ms. 15226, 28ʳ⁻ᵛ; Bodleian English Poetry Mss. e.14, 76ᵛ). Ashmole Ms. 38, a poetic miscellany in the Bodleian Library, identifies the author as "D: Donn"—as [Dr] John Donne—an identification we should not reject out of hand, given that the miscellany also contains six poems unquestionably by Donne, one of them his elegy to the Marquis of Hamilton, which focuses so indiscreetly on the grotesqueries of Hamilton's corpse (which Eglisham, among others, took for signs of poison) that it suggests opposition to Buckingham as his poisoner.

Th'impartial worm (which is not bribed to spare
Princes corrupt in marble) cannot share
His flesh; which if the charitable skies
Embalm with tears; doing those obsequies
Belong to men shall last, til pitying fowl
Contend to bear his body to his soul.

CŒLO TEGITUR QUI NON HABET URNAM
[THE HEAVENS COVER THE GRAVELESS]

The poet begins formally, with closed, end-stopped couplets that ring familiar elegiac changes. He confronts directly the difficult occasion of his writing: if elegy aims to produce memorial language that will take the place of an absent body, then Charles, like Creon, tries to stifle elegy by refusing burial. He explicitly acknowledges and implicitly denies this attempt through his memorable claim that Felton's body has become its own monument. Felton's death, like that of Elizabeth Dury in Donne's "The First Anniversary," suggests the death of the earth: by remaining above ground, Felton's body, his "dead earth," becomes a monument "to the world" as well as to itself. He edges dangerously forward by calling Felton "As large as fame," but immediately demurs, saying, "but whether bad or good / I say not."[220] He seems to be moving from pity to fear, preparing to detach himself from errant and presumptuous Felton.

But only for a moment. The line concludes not by lamenting Felton's act, but by praising his heroic, self-sacrificing individualism. The constrained and anonymous elegist declares emulous solidarity with Felton's tyrannicidal writing, which employed the revenger's ink of choice: "by himself 'twas writ in blood."[221] The poem moves away from its neat couplets. Its enjambed lines, with their near-rhyme or repeating rhyme endings, take on the prophetic cadences of a Miltonic verse paragraph. Once again, the author identifies Felton with the world, but this time to suggest their common eternity, not their common death. The entire cosmos arches around Felton's suspended body. A conventional meditation on death (which levels all men) becomes a vehicle for hierarchical inversion: Felton has freed himself from the conqueror worm, who (like Felton) spurns bribes while eating away "Princes corrupt in marble"— whether dead princes in tombs, or living ones in palaces. The poem concludes with Felton's apotheosis, as the pitying fowl effect the sympathetic removal of his body which tyrannical authority attempted to

---

220. Compare Wotton's comment on Felton's lingering after his action to be recognized, "as if, in effect, there were little difference between being remembered by a virtuous fame, or an illustrious infamy" (*Short* 25).
221. On revengers writing in blood, see also *F* 68; Hieronimo's fatal play and penknife in *The Spanish Tragedy*, London and New York 1994, 4.4.202; and Thomas Fuller on Felton in Herschel Baker, *Later Renaissance* 754.

prevent.[222] As their wings bear his body upward to his soul, the poet's initial reluctance to pronounce upon his fate seems to have disappeared. Felton began the poem as a combination of Antigone and Polyneices; he concludes it as the prophetic and anti-tyrannical Oedipus, ascending from the grove at Colonus.[223]

Noble Felton Resolutions

Why do people circulate dangerously self-incriminating libels? Perhaps not despite the risks they entail, but because of them: a private person who composes, passes on, or receives a libel simultaneously binds himself to others and others to himself through their mutual implication in a prosecutable offense—a threatening solidarity directly opposite to the appetitive competition of writing and circulating patronage poetry. Libelers leave the hierarchical but atomized serial collective intended by the absolutist project, and even the spontaneous fused group of the anti-popish mutiny or street riot, for the more formally structured associative unity of the pledged group. Members of this group, Sartre says, exercise "terror" over themselves and each other through the pledge—an over-statement, but one that helps explain the "contentious" fowl of "Felton's Epitaph," that strange note of antagonism that we can hear in many of the verse libels, and even Felton's farewell note.[224] Inside this emergent republican structure of feeling, a friendly/threatening rivalry or emulation pulls individual libelers into the future defined by a totalizing oppositional project in which they avert their eyes from the king, and keep their eyes on each other.

Of course, Felton's action did not have the effect that he and his partisans prophesied, but it did push the nation toward civil war. No new favorite emerged, but Charles did not exactly enter into a cordial relationship with Parliament and the commonwealth at large. He

---

222. These birds may represent Felton's friends: in an account of December 1628, his body and its gibbet mysteriously disappeared (*P* 143), but *A Relation of a Short Survey* (1634) reported them still there (*Camden Miscellany* 16, 1936, 39).

223. The poem's motto reinforces its tyrannicidal genealogy. Norbrook and Woudhuysen trace it to Lucan's *Pharsalia* 7.819, which condemns Julius Caesar for refusing proper burial to defeated republicans (*Penguin* 770). Norbrook points out the lightly veiled menace in the implied analogy between Charles and Julius Caesar (*Writing* 55). That ascetic republican humanist Raphael Hythloday invokes the phrase in Book 1 of More's *Utopia*, New York 1992, 5. So does Kyd in *The Spanish Tragedy*. Shortly before he lays waste the royal houses of Spain and Portugal to avenge his son Horatio, whose murdered corpse remains above ground for most of the play, Hieronimo delivers his great "Vindicta mihi" speech:

> If destiny deny thee life, Hieronimo,
> Yet shalt thou be assured of a tomb;
> If neither, yet let this thy comfort be,
> Heaven covereth him that hath no burial. (3.13.16–19)

With its prologue and epilogue in a Senecan underworld, Kyd's ever-popular play was one of the greatest literary influences on Felton's friends.

224. *SCDR* 417–44.

dismissed the 1629 Parliament and did not call another until 1640, relying instead on his increasingly ineffective personal rule by ministers and privy council, and the influence of his wife. In practical terms, Buckingham's death changed little, since Charles struggled to imitate his policies and avoid any suspicion that he had simply been the duke's tool. But his enemies did begin to see the king more clearly as the actual cause of their grievances.[225] And neither Buckingham's abuses nor Felton's response to them disappeared from the memories of English radicals. Whatever the short-term and contingent reasons for the Revolution, the parliamentarians and plebeians who made it had long-term memories.

A paper left in his window warned Viscount Conway to "look to himself, for there is another Felton and another knife ready for his throat as well as there was for the duke, and bade him to tell his great friend the lord treasurer (i.e. Weston) as much."[226] In March 1629, the Middlesex Sessions sentenced John Olliver to hard labor for threatening to "Felton" an enemy.[227] In May, John Donne delivered to Archbishop Laud a libel found in St Paul's Yard, which cast him in a ducal role: "Laud, look to thy self: be assured thy life is sought. As thou art the fountain of all wickedness, repent thee of thy monstrous sins, before thou be taken out of the world, etc. And assure thy self, neither God nor the world can endure such a vile counselor to live."[228] In 1632, Matthieu's life of Sejanus reappeared as part of *Unhappy Prosperity*, with a second edition in 1639. Both included Matthieu's address to the French king describing the work as a "mirror that flattereth not . . . which at the same instant it sheweth the stain, taketh it away," emphasizing "that a prince ought to be very careful to conserve his authority entire." Its translator, Sir Thomas Hawkins, also translated Manzini's *Politicall Observations upon the Fall of Sejanus*, with two issues in 1634, and reissues in 1638 (as part of *Remarkable Considerations*) and 1639 (as part of the second edition of *Unhappy Prosperity*). In 1634, someone revived *Doctor Lamb and the Witches*, a play since lost.[229] In 1638, Francis Lord Cottington forwarded to Secretary Windebank a letter by "D. D." lamenting the fact that, since the dismissal of the "last unfortunate Parliament the kingdom has languished by means of ravenous projectors," and adding that, wherever he meets three people in any part of England, "two of them exclaim bitterly against the government, as ready to entertain the Turk or any other as the present, if there were any offer; nay some with bitter oaths professing mischief with Felton, from whose rage God bless his Majesty, who cannot

225. L. J. Reeve, *Charles I and the Road to Personal Rule*, Cambridge 1989, 37.
226. Treadwell, *Buckingham* 295.
227. Jeaffreson, *Middlesex* 3.108.
228. R. C. Bald, *John Donne*, New York 1970, 506.
229. Alfred Harbage and Samuel Schoenbaum, *Annals of English Drama 975–1700*, London 1964, 132.

choose but know these things."[230] The street literature associated with the anti-prelatical march on Lambeth Palace in May 1640 threatened "that Charles and Marie do what they will, we will kill the archbishop of Canterbury like Dr. Lambe."[231] In October 1641, a London sermon publicly praised Felton.[232]

In 1642, three pamphleteers recalled James's alleged poisoning. Another edition appeared of *The Forerunner of Revenge*, while *King James His Judgement of a King and a Tyrant* began a list of anti-tyrannical queries with, "When our good King James his death was by one of his physicians tendered to the king, and Parliament, to be examined, why the Parliament was eft soon dissolved?" And *Strange Apparitions* showed James, Hamilton, Buckingham, and Eglisham coming together in hell: after Eglisham's denunciation, the duke admits poisoning the king and the marquis and having Eglisham assassinated in Holland.[233] In 1643, someone reprinted Dudley Digges's introduction to the parliamentary bill of impeachment against Buckingham, which calls an excessive trust in court favorites "the original of all the public grievances, and combustions of this kingdom."[234] In 1644, the speaker of *Hell's Hurlie-Burlie* described his recent visit to hell, where he saw the pope's contest with Satan for supremacy. While there, he gave Satan two 1628-style poetic satires: one shows Buckingham challenging Satan's powers and threatening to rule him as he did James and Charles, while the other places him in an infernal procession with Dr Lambe and the Seven Deadly Sins. He misses Buckingham, however, for Satan has sent him topside to lead the assault on the godly English army.[235] In *The Court and Character of King James*, Sir Anthony Weldon presents Buckingham as James's poisoner and a "monster" justly taken off by Felton.[236] Arthur Wilson's *The History of Great Britain* suggests the duke and his mother poisoned Hamilton and James; it includes an engraving of the latter poisoning.[237] In 1648, a shorter version of Eglisham's pamphlet appeared as *A Declaration to the Kingdome of England Concerning the Poysoning of King James*. It eliminates Eglisham's introductory epistles to King Charles and to Parliament, but retains the account of Buckingham's poisoning of James, adds a subtitle (*Together with King James His Protestation Concerning Our Sovereign Lord the King that Now Is*), and commences with James's threat against his own son should he turn murderer—an anecdote which had acquired a new menace in the move toward the regicide.

In 1645, speaking in St Dunstan's, the Felton family church, Joan

---

230. *CSPD* 13.89–90.
231. Keith Lindley, *Popular Politics and Religion in Civil War London*, London 1997, 34.
232. *GHE* 10.30.
233. Eglisham survived until at least 1630 (*CSPD* 4.168), but a royal agent might have murdered him after that.
234. D. D., *A Speech Delivered in Parliament*.
235. The first satire adapts an earlier libel (*F* 34–6).
236. 1651, 160–63, 199–201.
237. 1653, 285–90.

Sherwody allegedly called the king "a stuttering fool," asking "Is there never a Felton yet living? If I were a man, as I am a woman, I would help to pull him to pieces."[238] In 1646, with her customary disdain for finite verbs, Lady Eleanor Davies saw the Lord Admiral's assassination prefigured in the wounding of the seven-headed sea beast in Revelation 13:

> Where shews here, besides the healing of that foul sore the Kings-evil, Porchmouth's blow, but a butcher's knife given, how cured. Also what an insatiable mouth by him opened; daily fed with such gifts, offices, and titles of honor not a few; wanting no kindred to be supplied. This aspiring man Buckingham, from the beast deriving his name, so much bound to the dragon his patron, rather than to Saint George. This supporter of the Spanish faction, colored, or cloaked under Arminianism: that beyond expectation after ten years, his father's unlucky favorite who continued his too, from 1625 March, until 1628 August, two and forty months, or three years and half before his pay received, not behind with it then. Being as not unknown forewarned of that very month, Caesar, as he foretold of the Ides of March.[239]

Davies collapses into an eternal prophetic present the Anglo-Hebraic conflict of Saint George and the Dragon, the quality of Felton's blow as a symbolic revenge for pay arrears, Buckingham's association with Spain, and her own 1628 prophecy of the duke's death. If we allow her the modest (by her usual standards) fudge factor of counting both the first and the last month, the time between James's death on March 23 1625 and Buckingham's on August 23 1628 does indeed suggest the "time and times and half a time" of biblical apocalyptic (1 year + 2 years + 1/2 a year = 42 months).

In November 1647, a newsbook warned General Fairfax, recently relocated to Putney, that "there are Feltons in the Army, very near his bosom."[240] In December, the Leveller printer John Harris warned that, if Cromwell continued "to advance lawless ambition and strengthen irregular attempts . . . he may chance in the midst of his golden hopes meet with Buckingham's fate."[241] In February 1648, John Lilburne reportedly told John Wildman the words of an unnamed "Gentleman" (probably Henry Marten), who suspected Cromwell of colluding with the king to maintain a tyranny:

> This Gentleman, said he, takes upon him a noble Felton resolution, that (rather than a kingdom should be enslaved to the lust of one man) he would dispatch him (namely Cromwell) wherever he met him, though in the presence of the General Sir Thomas Fairfax himself, and for that end, provided, and charged a pistol, and took a dagger in his pocket, that if the one did not, the other should dispatch him.

238. Jeaffreson, *Middlesex* 3.93, 120.
239. *The Revelation Interpreted* 3–4.
240. *Mercurius Melancholicus* 10/30–11/6/47.
241. "Sirrahniho," *The Grand Designe* B2^v.

Marten, so the story goes, broached his plan to a fellow member of the House, who shut him up in a room in Whitehall and warned Cromwell; and Wildman said that "he knew three other men (at the same time) had taken up the same resolution of killing Cromwell, and there was not one of them that knew the intentions of another."[242] That same month, *A Declaration of the Commons* again charged Buckingham with poisoning King James.[243]

In October, John Harris deconsecrated the captive king by mocking the healing virtue of his spittle, then asking when exactly he became the Lord's anointed—"after the poisoning of his brother Harry, or his father?"[244] In December, an anonymous author, probably Thomas Scott the regicide, included the fiasco at the Isle of Rhé and the suspicious deaths of King James and the Marquis of Hamilton in his indictments of Charles.[245] In January 1649, Charles's prosecutor John Cooke repeated the charges against Buckingham and added that Charles "dissolved that Parliament [of 1626], that so he might protect the duke from the justice thereof, and would never suffer any legal inquiry to be made for his father's death."[246] In 1628, while a student at Christ's College, Cambridge (one of whose fellows was Joseph Mead, theorist of the millennium and avid reader and circulator of newsletter accounts about the assassination), Milton called Junius Brutus "that second founder of Rome and great avenger of the lusts of kings." In *Eikonoklastes* (1649), he accused Charles of breaking off Parliament to protect Buckingham from prosecution on charges of poisoning James, "besides other heinous crimes." In *The First Defence* (1651), he reiterated the charge, added that Charles "did not only absolve the slayer of the king and of his father from all blame in the highest council of state, but also dissolved Parliament to keep the whole affair from any parliamentary investigation," and questioned "the purity and continence of one who is known to have joined the Duke of Buckingham in every act of infamy."[247]

During the Protectorate, Cromwell's former allies began to see him as a tyrant, then conspired with Charles II and other royalists on the Continent to establish a Leveller republic or a constitutional monarchy. Opposition coalesced around John Wildman and Edward Sexby, whom we will meet again. After Sexby's capture and death in the Tower, his servant Samuel Dyer testified that Wildman had asked Sexby, "Shall such a tyrant live? (meaning the Lord Protector): No, if there be (or might be)

---

242. [Walter Frost,] *A Declaration of Some Proceedings* 15.
243. Thomas Burton, *Diary of Thomas Burton, Esq.*, 1828; rpt New York 1974, 2.382n. Bellany, "Poisoning" 690–95.
244. *Mercurius Militaris* 10/10–10/17/48.
245. *A New Paire of Spectacles*, 1649, 2–3.
246. *M* 3.351–2.
247. Ibid. 1.267, 4.372, 4.408–9; see also 4.451. On Milton and Mead, see Hill, *Milton* 33–5.

two Feltons to be found."[248] In a crowning irony, Cromwell had become the object of a conspiracy between regicidal republicans and the sons and namesakes of Charles Stuart and George Villiers.

248. *B* 6.830. Later recollections include *The Fate of Favourites; Exemplified in the Fall of Villiers, Duke of Buckingham (Prime Minister to their Majesties King James and King Charles I)*, London n.p., 1734, a synthetic, pro-Felton account of Buckingham's career, trial, and assassination whose anachronistic subtitle and anonymous publisher suggest a warning to Walpole. It was reissued in 1735 as *The Life and Deserved Fall, of George Villiers, Duke of Buckingham, (Prime Minister to King James and King Charles I. . . . To Which Is Added, an Essay on the Rights of British Subjects in Electing Members of Parliament)*, and with the original title in 1740. In 1769, an anonymous advertisement for an assassin of Lord Bute recalled Felton's precedent. See John Brewer, "The Misfortunes of Lord Bute," *Historical Journal* 16.1, 1973, 6.

6

New Model Soviets:
The Agitators and Martial Praxis

The conditions of Social Democratic action are radically different. This action grows historically out of the elementary class struggle. It thus moves in the dialectical contradiction that here the proletarian army is first recruited in the struggle itself, and too, only in the struggle does it become aware of the objectives of the struggle. Here, organization, enlightenment, and struggle are not separate mechanically, and also temporally, different moments, as is the case with a Blanquist movement. Here, they are only different sides of the same process.

—Rosa Luxemburg, *Organizational Questions of Russian Social Democracy*

For the Army are acted by their own *principles*; they are an army *understand* themselves.

—John Saltmarsh, *A Letter from the Army*

Agitate! Agitate! Agitate!

—Frederick Douglass

Organize! Educate! Agitate!

—Eugene V. Debs

Armed Prophets

I'll begin with two famous prologues:

> This is true liberty when free born men
> Having to advise the public may speak free,
> Which he who can, and will, deserves high praise,
> Who neither can nor will, may hold his peace;
> What can be juster in a state than this?

That the meeting was for public businesses; those that had anything to say concerning the public business, they might have liberty to speak.

In the first, the epigraph to *Areopagitica* (1644), John Milton translates a passage from Euripides' *Suppliants*, turning *touleutheron* into "free born"—already a popular catchphrase.[1] By beginning with a learned translation,

1. *M* 2.485; Hill, *Change* 219–38.

he immediately enters into Renaissance humanism's philological conversation with the past. The body of *Areopagitica* conjures up the very center of republican civic consciousness by adding the *conversazione civile*, the public discussion of political ends and means.[2] But what if we disingenuously answer Milton's rhetorical question? It's good for the freeborn man to speak freely and win the toleration or praise of an autonomous public or state authority, but it's better to get a rational response in kind, perhaps even a modification of that authority itself. *That's* what can be juster. Milton's epigraph hints that early modern writers may jump out of an absolutist regime of licensing and censorship, only to fall into a capitalist regime of repressive toleration, in which the state authority finds it can safely *tolerate* an oppositional but impotent public opinion. If it cannot translate public debate into political forms, the most eloquent defense of free speech risks enclosure and management, perhaps inside the efficiently policed sphere of bourgeois authorship. In *The Prince*, Machiavelli reminds unarmed prophets or political innovators of Savonarola's fiery execution—an end not unlike the one Milton barely escaped in 1660.[3] But he had already faced the quieter impotence of the unarmed prophet in the public sphere. While his unlicensed *Areopagitica* drew no punishment or repression from Parliament, neither did it affect in any material way Parliament's view of prior licensing, which continued in one form or another through the forties and fifties—and, indeed, to this day.[4]

In the second passage, Oliver Cromwell calls to order the Putney Debates, the most famous debates in English history.[5] He calls for a discussion of the *res publica*, the "public business," but in the course of the

---

2. Eugenio Garin, *Italian Humanism*, New York 1965, 50–56, 151–69.
3. New York 1977, 18.
4. Michael Lieb and John T. Shawcross, eds, *Achievements of the Left Hand*, Amherst, MA, 1974, 305.
5. *CP* 1.226. In the library of Worcester College, Oxford, H. A. Pottinger discovered a fair copy of the original shorthand transcript of the debates among the official papers of William Clarke, Secretary to the General Council of the Army in 1647–49; the microfilm edition (*CM*) includes an introduction by G. E. Aylmer. C. H. Firth edited a four-volume selection of the debates and related documents as *The Clarke Papers* (*CP*; 1891–1901); the reissue of the first two volumes (London 1992) contains a preface by Austin Woolrych. The New Model Army and its debates have interested literary historians of the period almost not at all, but social and political historians to the point of obsession. In *Cromwell's Army* (*FCA*), Firth says, "A civil war is not only the conflict of opposing principles, but the shock of material forces" (v); later histories have added greatly to our understanding of the political narrative, but they have not replaced Firth's social, intellectual, and material history of the Army. A. S. P. Woodhouse's classic *Puritanism and Liberty* (*P&L*) includes a text of the debates, an excellent introduction, and a generous selection of supplementary documents. The third edition (London 1986) includes Ivan Roots' introduction and a bibliography of recent criticism. Because Woodhouse emends and interpolates too freely for me, I quote Firth's edition, modernizing his spelling but retaining his punctuation. I will discuss below the influential accounts of the debates by C. B. Macpherson and Mark Kishlansky. Austin Woolrych presents a full narrative of the debates and the events leading up to them in *Soldiers and Statesmen* (*WSS*). Ian Gentles presents a larger-scale narrative history in *The New Model Army* (*G*). On the Levellers, see Brailsford, *Levellers*, and David Wootton, "Leveller Democracy and the Puritan Revolution," in J. H. Burns and Mark Goldie, eds, *The Cambridge History of Political Thought, 1450–1700*, Cambridge 1991, 412–42.

debates, Cromwell frequently sounds like he would gladly assume the position of Milton's statesman, who listens to advisors, awards praise, then makes his own decisions. But circumstances have altered. Political authority, military power, and the capacity for debate have come to rest in the same persons: the soldiers as well as the general officers of the New Model Army. The Army became "at once a sort of fourth estate in the realm, and a body not less representative than the (not very representative) Parliament at Westminster."[6] As the most powerful military force in the nation, with a claim rivaling Parliament's own to represent the English people, and a relatively egalitarian forum for debate in the General Council of the Army, the New Model of 1647 brings us closer to an empowered public sphere than does any other body of the revolutionary era.

Here I'm invoking Habermas's great *Structural Transformation of the Public Sphere*, which focuses on the origins of the bourgeois public sphere in eighteenth-century Europe. Like so many others writing in his shadow, I'm suggesting that he got his dates wrong. He might well respond that the General Council fell short of the bourgeois public sphere in important ways. For instance, as its radical members learned to their regret, General Fairfax could convene and dismiss it at will. But the eighteenth-century bourgeois public sphere had weaknesses of its own. In Habermas's account, it emerged only by virtue of its structural separation from the state and from the "private sphere" of civil society. This separation made the public sphere a realm of relative freedom formally open to all adult men. But civil society systematically deformed it through implicitly class-based criteria for admission (free time, education, bourgeois acquaintances), and by using it to drain off dissent from the private sphere, leaving it a relatively untouched realm of necessity. Arguably, the bourgeoisie solidifies its rule through a new demarcation of state, family, public sphere, and private sphere.

In such situations, the laboring class tends to emancipate itself not by gradually subverting the bourgeois public sphere from within, but by organizing itself, generating its own public sphere, and winning over important segments of the army—that vital component of the state which provides the ultimate coercion underwriting bourgeois hegemony. The public sphere of the New Model Army, like the proletarian public spheres of England, France, and the United States, sprang up not *after* the bourgeois public sphere, but alongside it, even before it, out of the fundamental social existence of the soldiers: the "private sphere" of their military labor. Any successful revolutionary struggle requires counter-coercive force as well as counter-hegemonic rhetoric, and as a formidable and relatively democratic army, the New Model moved beyond advising the state to transforming it. Radical liberals like Habermas chronically underestimate the role of force in history. So do some marxists, as Perry Anderson notes when he contrasts Gramsci's

6. *P&L* [20].

overemphasis on ideological "wars of position" with Trotsky's insistence on the military "wars of maneuver" that emerge at moments of revolutionary crisis, such as the October Revolution.[7] Here, we might compare (and contrast) the Bolsheviks' success at winning over important parts of the Czar's army, which became Trotsky's Red Army, with the Levellers' attempts to win over the New Model Army in 1647, culminating in the Putney Debates. The New Model soviet offered not only an important predecessor to the Enlightenment public sphere, but an anticipatory critique of its inherent weaknesses.

On January 27 1645, after a series of military defeats and sustained popular criticism, the House of Commons passed the ordinance instituting the New Model Army under the command of Sir Thomas Fairfax. The New Model won its decisive battle at Naseby in June, conducted a series of successful sieges, and turned the tide of the war. In June 1646, the royalists lost Oxford. Charles handed himself over to the Scots, who sold him to Parliament in February 1647 for £200,000. With active hostilities at an end, Parliament faced a new potential rival in its own army. When it tried to disband the New Model and send some of its regiments, under faithful Presbyterian officers, to subdue Catholic Ireland, soldiers and officers alike began to resist, issuing petitions articulating their reasons for doing so. In April, eight cavalry regiments elected "Agitators," or representative spokesmen, to further this resistance. In early June, after Cornet Joyce took the King into custody, thirteen regiments rendezvoused near Newmarket Field, covenanted together, and formed a General Council of the Army distinct from the Council of Officers.

What sort of thing was the New Model Army during this contentious year of peace? Liberal historians have seen it as the first of the great revolutionary citizen armies of the modern world, a body animated by Leveller and radical Puritan ideology. And they have tended to see at Putney a genuine, principled debate among the relatively egalitarian and authoritarian currents set loose by the Revolution. Several recent accounts of the Army and the debates have defined themselves against this view. Mark Kishlansky has minimized the role of radical democratic ideology in the Army, emphasizing instead the Army's traditional belief in a consensual hierarchy uniting officers and men. In *The Political Theory of Possessive Individualism*, C. B. Macpherson offers a similar argument, though he finds not a traditionalist but a proto-bourgeois consensus. And those few postmodernist philosophers, historians, and literary critics who have considered the New Model have tended to view it as a state apparatus of top-down discipline. Like Kishlansky and Macpherson, they tend to minimize its internal debates and the democratic praxis of its soldiers.[8]

7. "The Antinomies of Antonio Gramsci," *New Left Review* 100, 1976–77, 75–8.
8. Foucault, *Dits* 1.124–30; Francis Barker, "In the Wars of Truth," *HS* 91–109; my *Rational Millennium* 88–91.

But the New Model in 1647 presented something qualitatively new in English history: a victorious Army generating its discipline and sense of collective identity *out of itself*, changing from the voiceless instrument of others to an active force seeking to new-model the entire nation. In this chapter, I will argue that we can best understand the Putney Debates not with a top-down model of consensualist or liberal or disciplinary ideology, but with a bottom-up model of martial praxis. In "Something New," I argue that Army radicalism emerged neither magically *ab nihilo*, nor irrationally through reaction to pure contingency, but dialectically from the Army's material conditions and its reflection on its experience in the war and with its own officers. In "No Courtesy!" I characterize the Putney Debates not as a traditional search for consensus, but as a conflict between the grandees' hierarchical vision of collective life, and the associative vision of the radicals. In "Possessive Individualism and the Expense of Blood," I examine the relation between these visions and the seventeenth-century debate over politics and property. And in "Contingency and Martial Law at Corkbush Field," I examine the end of the Putney Debates, and their strange continuation in the grandees' repression of an Army mutiny.

Something New: The Emergence of the Agitators

In *The Rise of the New Model Army*, Mark Kishlansky argues that Army radicalism emerged slowly, painfully, and reactively during the course of 1647, producing a change both monumental and regrettable:

> As the events of the summer had shown, parliamentary politics had been replaced by force. Votes superseded debate; confrontation replaced conciliation; action had overcome reason; radical politics had emerged. New participants, unimagined when the struggle began, now crowded the political scene. . . . At the juncture of Civil War and Revolution they now stood, and if the impulse of the future was to turn the world upside down, the wisdom of the past had been to make it whole.[9]

Where traditional politics of parliament sought holistic reconciliation through reason and wisdom, these pushy new men sought confrontation through impulsive force and violence. Surprisingly, Kishlansky finds the agent of transition not in some radical rakehell, but in arch-Presbyterian Denzil Holles, who tried to master the Army through an innovative but ultimately self-destructive party politics in the House of Commons. In the summer of 1647, Kishlansky says, the Army embodied the conservative wisdom of the past, for it tried to resist Holles, eliminate the rule of party, and restore this lost wholeness. But after it was infected by Holles's party politics and duped by crafty Levellers, the New Model, too, begin acting in a "radical" fashion. Kishlansky's argument preserves a

9. 271–2.

ruling-class origin for history in the initiative of Holles, and denies the possibility of plebeian critical consciousness and reflective praxis: since the New Model did not mechanically follow a radical script, it must have wandered into radicalism by responding in an impulsive, *ad hoc* manner to contingent events in Westminster and elsewhere.[10] In a later essay, Kishlansky declared victory: "we now agree" that New Model radicalism dates from 1647, not from its creation, that it derived *ad hoc* from contingent circumstances, not from ideological struggle, and that it owed little to the Levellers and radical religion.[11]

It's no great surprise to find no Manichean conflict between coherent and highly disciplined political parties in 1647, but the turbulent history of the period hardly suggests consensus. Kishlansky's claim that the Army became politicized only in the summer of 1647 holds true only if we define a *political* body narrowly as one internally divided and engaged in formal debate. But if we see as "political" a violent struggle with the army of a reigning monarch over the future contours of a state, then the New Model was political from its very inception. Moreover, if we draw too sharp a line between groups we define as hierarchical, consensual, and non-political, and those we define as radical, oppositional, and political, we risk overlooking those material sites that enable a group of the first sort to become a group of the second. The internally politicized New Model of 1647 had a generative prehistory in the relatively egalitarian praxis of three pre-political sites. First, the cavalry troop, which paved the way for the egalitarian discursive culture of the Army's public sphere. Troopers usually owned their own arms and horses, and when they were paid, they received three times as much as infantry. Firth says a cavalry trooper was a "capitalist, in a small way"; I would say "a military small producer."[12] Woolrych explains the emergence of the Agitators from the horse regiments by pointing to their greater mobility and so ease of communication among scattered regiments, to their greater literacy and politicization. The cavalry troop was the ideal unit for representative organization, since it "numbered a hundred men, few enough to know each other well but numerous enough to need spokesmen or delegates if action needed to be concerted or agreements negotiated."[13] Second, Fairfax's Council of War fostered the habits of dialogue and debate that spread through the ranks in 1647. In 1645–46, these

---

10. If Kishlansky sees the soldiery as pre-ideologically reactive, J. S. A. Adamson has trouble seeing them at all. His New Model simply followed the lead of an elite group in the House of Lords led by William Fiennes, Lord Saye and Sele. In "Politics and the Nobility in Civil-War England," Adamson turns Saye into the guiding genius of *The Heads of the Proposals* and Kishlansky into an "unreconstructed whig" (*Historical Journal* 34.1, 1991, 255). See also "The Baronial Context of the English Civil War," *Transactions of the Royal Historical Society* 5.40, 1990; and "The English Nobility and the Projected Settlement of 1647," *Historical Journal* 30.3, 1987. I'm persuaded on most counts by Kishlansky's responses in "Saye What?" *The Historical Journal* 33.4, 1990; and "Saye No More."
11. "What Must Be" 84.
12. *FCA* 40.
13. *WSS* 61–2.

councils, which included the general staff and all regimental commanders, met before major battles and debated strategy and tactics. When
open hostilities ceased, the Council diminished in military importance,
but "As soon as the army began to intervene in State affairs it became
the organ through which the general opinion of the army found
expression."[14] Third, and most important, the gathered congregations.
In *Cromwell's Army*, Firth emphasized the role of radical religion in incu-
bating revolutionary ideology, and most historians have followed suit.[15]
Brian Manning points to evidence of radical Puritanism even in Essex's
army.[16] Murray Tolmie has argued that the separate churches of London
fostered a sense of oppositional solidarity among New Model soldiers.
Indeed, New Model regiments also tended to be congregations—an
extraordinary development, which superimposed a relatively democratic
form upon a military hierarchy.[17] Ian Gentles says that radical religion in
the New Model produced high morale, an impulse to transform civil
society, and a willingness to employ ruthless methods against armed and
unarmed opponents.[18]

Revisionists have not been convinced. Though willing enough to invoke
religion as a bulwark against economic and ideological explanations of
the Revolution, they tend to back off from analyzing radical religion as a
political ideology and a material practice. John Morrill discusses the
turmoil in the Army in 1647 with little attention to religion, though he
himself has argued that the English Revolution should be rechristened
"the English Wars of Religion."[19] Kishlansky discounts the role of sectarian
radicalism in the New Model, noting that only nine preachers officially
attended to the Army. But he admits that this very lack fostered lay
preaching, which disturbed religious conservatives even more.[20] On April
26 1645, both Houses forbade preaching by anyone not ordained in a
reformed church, directing this order specifically to the attention of
Fairfax and the Army.[21] But this could have been no great comfort to
"Tom Tell-Troth," a Presbyterian satirist who attacked pamphlets by Dell,
Saltmarsh, and Goodwin, the "seducing chaplains of the Army"—all of
them ordained ministers.[22] *The Third Part of Gangraena*, by Thomas
Edwards, brims with nightmares about the Army spreading religious
infection throughout the nation.[23] Another Presbyterian feared that, after
the New Model occupied London, ordained preachers would be "daily

14. *FCA* 57, 59. Compare the egalitarian strategy sessions of the Chinese Red Army (the
    "Ironsides"!), Agnes Smedley, *The Great Road*, New York 1956, 240.
15. *FCA* 313–48.
16. *English* 344–5.
17. *The Triumph of the Saints*, Cambridge 1977, 144–73.
18. *G* 87–119.
19. *Nature* 307–31, 33–4.
20. *Rise* 70–73.
21. *Die Sabbathi 26. April, 1645.*
22. *Works of Darkness Brought to Light*, 1647, 11.
23. 1646, 21–3, 30–31, 41–7, 95–6, 107, 110–11, 172–4, 179–80.

affronted in the discharge of their ministry by every rude soldier, and mechanic, standing up in the time of preaching, prayer, as they have done in other places." In the classic mode of reactionary polemics, he fears these mechanic preachers will seek places for themselves while pretending to attack the system of places: "Will not all the frogs and rabble of sectaries from all parts of the kingdom come up hither, and London become the sink of all errors and confusion? And shall they not all by the power of the Army have free quarter, and be maintained of the rich men's estates for preaching to them?"[24] In *The Character of a Moderate Intelligencer*, "J. C." (perhaps John Cleveland) attacks sumptuary and vocational disorder: "I do abhor a woman should wear breeches, / A priest that fights, a man at arms that preaches."[25]

Responses by Army partisans suggest that these attacks were more than Presbyterian hysteria. *Vox Militaris* argues that the very want of preachers in the Army led soldiers to "the mutual edification one of another."[26] In January 1646, speaking for preaching soldiers, W. G. says "I confess (if this be to be accounted an insolency) it is such a kind of insolency as scarce any Army in the world was ever complained of before." He simply denies that any preaching soldier claims to be "by special appointment . . . set apart to that office"—a claim that rebuts the charge of their resentful desire to gain paid ecclesiastical office for themselves by implying the superfluity of that very office.[27] In June 1647, J. P. defended the right of all to preach, including women, and denied any fundamental distinction between preaching and prophesying, between exhorting a few met by chance and hundreds met by plan: "The more the merrier, if it be lawful." He attacked the established clergy and infuriated his imagined Presbyterian colloquists by referring to their "wages" and invoking the opinions of "Martin Mar-Priest" (Richard Overton).[28] The officer-Agitator Edmond Chillenden defends mechanic and Army preaching from the Westminster Assembly by combining St Paul's words on women preachers, Christ's spiritist retort to Nicodemus, and John's vision of Christ as the sharp-tongued apocalyptic Son of Man:

> The word of God came not from you, neither came it to you only, but as well to the rest of the saints, besides you, feeling the wind bloweth where it listeth, hold not back, neither hinder the blowings or breathings of it lest God come and fight against you with the sword of his mouth, and slay you before him, because you will not let him reign over you nor his people.[29]

The venerable "liberal" point about the role of radical religion in the Army still holds.

24. *Some Queries Propounded to the Common-Councell*, 1647, 10.
25. 1647, 12.
26. 1647, 9.
27. *A Just Apologie for an Abused Armie*, 1647, 17.
28. *Certaine Scruples from the Army*, 1647, 9, 13, 16, 23.
29. *Preaching without Ordination*, "To the Nationall Synod or Assembly"; 1 Cor 14.36; John 3.8; Rev. 1.16.

When one considers the entire array of writings and discursive practices surrounding the New Model at war—newsbooks from various sides, manuals of discipline, sermons, radical civilian speech and writing about the Army—we clearly see that it had become a pre-political public sphere, poised to become a political public sphere in peacetime.[30] Richard Baxter abhorred the "seductions" of this public sphere, with the conservative Puritan's classic ambivalence toward print. On the one hand, he uses the written word to hammer at popery, beginning his *Reliquiae* by remembering that God took the trouble to "instruct and change" his father "by the bare reading of the Scripture in private, without either preaching or godly company, or any other books but the Bible."[31] On the other hand, he fears that print will lead soldiers toward the solitary vice of unguided heretical reading:

> A great part of the mischief they did among the soldiers was by pamphlets, which they abundantly dispersed; such as R. Overton's, *Martin Mar-Priest*, and more of his; and some of J. Lilburne's, who was one of them; and divers against the King, and against the ministry, and for liberty of conscience, etc. And soldiers being usually dispersed in their quarters, they had such books to read when they had none to contradict them.

Such men refuse proper containment inside military orders: "I heard the plotting heads very hot upon that which intimated their intention to subvert both church and state. . . . Many honest men of weak judgments and little acquaintance with such matters" are sucked into this new public sphere, "seduced into a disputing vein," where they make it "too much of their religion to talk for this opinion and for that. Sometimes for state-democracy, and sometimes for church-democracy." Orthodox soldiers easily became "ready instruments for the seducers," who were "men that had been in London, hatched up among the old Separatists." Baxter fought a losing battle in disputing sectaries during his two years attached to the Army, for in "all places where we went, the sectarian soldiers much infected the countries, by their pamphlets and converse, and the people admiring the conquering army, were ready to receive whatsoever they commended to them."[32] In April 1647, one newsletter writer said "Some of the soldiers do not stick to call the Parliament-men tyrants; Lilburne's books are quoted by them as statute law." Another called the whole Army "one Lilburne throughout, and more likely to give than to receive laws."[33] We shouldn't reject such overheated claims outright. Conservative terrors in the present may be a relatively good index of the future changes threatened by opening up the public sphere to workers.

Revisionists have tried to dissociate the Army from Leveller ideology as

---

30. On newsbooks and the Army, see Raymond, *Invention* 196–200.
31. *Reliquiae Baxterianae*, 1696, 2.
32. 2, 53, 56; rpt *P&L* 387–9.
33. *P&L* [23]; see also *GHCW* 3.236–7.

well as from radical religion. Barry Coward argues Army agitation could not have been radical because it arose from economic demands.[34] John Morrill separates the Levellers' "jam" issues from the Army's "bread and butter" issues of indemnity and back pay.[35] Mark Kishlansky says we must see Army radicalism as either the mechanical and total "penetration" of the Army ranks by a pre-formed and coherent Leveller ideology, or as a "reactive" and "contingent" process which "developed circumstantially."[36] But if the soldiers were not the passive tools of the Levellers, neither were they the passive victims of circumstances or their own needs. When wage laborers enter into politics, discussions of wages become political. The accounts of the Army in 1647 reveal the gradual appearance of collective consciousness among the soldiery under the pressure of primal, existential fear. In a pamphlet of May 3, the soldiers plead with and threaten Parliament: "Is it not better to die like men than to be enslaved and hanged like dogs? Which must and will be yours and our portion, if not now looked into, even before our disbanding."[37] A letter of late May, perhaps by Ireton, shows soldiers responding in unanticipated ways to the "contingency" of parliamentary threats:

> I doubt [suspect] the disobliging of so faithful an Army will be repented of; provocation and exasperation makes men think of that they never intended. They are possessed, as far as I can discern with this opinion, that if they be thus scornfully dealt withal for their faithful services while the sword is in their hands, what shall their usage be when they are dissolved?[38]

The soldiers' road to Putney resembles John Felton's to Portsmouth. Suffering the soldier's perennial malady of unpaid arrears, Felton read a parliamentary remonstrance against the duke and changed from a lieutenant chafing inside the patronage system to a tyrannicide stabbing into it. Also suffering from unpaid arrears, fired by the solidarity born of its victories in 1645–46, and fearing prosecution, piecemeal disbandment, and transport to Ireland, the New Model encountered radical religion and Leveller ideology and changed from parliamentary instrument to revolutionary agent.

On or before March 18, a petition later known as *The Humble Petition of the Officers and Souldiers of the Army* began circulating among the soldiery. It demanded indemnity from prosecution for wartime actions, payment of arrears, relief for wounded ex-soldiers and the widows and children of the slain, and assurance that no one would force volunteers outside the kingdom.[39] The Council of Officers debated it on March 21. On March 24 appeared *A Warning for all the Counties*, an impassioned anonymous

34. "Was There" 26.
35. *Nature* 307–31.
36. "What Must Be" 84.
37. *The Apologie of the Common Souldiers* 7.
38. *CP* 1.101–2.
39. *D* 1–2.

pamphlet. It declared solidarity with the Army, radicalized an aristocratic idiom by condemning "the many-headed monster of Presbytery," and attacked the Solemn League and Covenant as a tyrannical contract imposed from above. Far from seeing the Army as Parliament's instrument, it claimed the Army's "equal interest" with Parliament in the affairs of the nation, and "as the one hath the word to vote, so hath the other the sword to act." Previewing the Putney Debates, it combined republican, English, and scriptural idioms of resistance: "Is there never a Roman spirit left, that dare interpose, and protest for his country, against these destructive counsels, and votes for Norman bondage? . . . Rouse up your spirits, and secure your selves, and your birthrights."[40] The House tried and failed to identify author, printer, and publisher.[41]

On March 26 appeared *An Apollogie of the Souldiers to All Their Commission Officers in Sir Thomas Fairfax His Armie*. It anticipates the substance and the rhetoric of the Agitator tracts that would appear through the spring and summer, invoking the "law of nature" and "the liberty of the subject" to argue against arbitrary disbandment of the New Model. The imprisonment of Levellers such as Overton and Lilburne has given the Army a taste of what it might expect after disbandment, and "it had been better for us never to [have] been born, or at least to have been an army, than that those honest people, who have shewn themselves with us, and for us in these our sad calamities . . . should suffer either imprisonment of body, or any other tyrannical ungodly persecutions." It pronounces Fairfax simply one in a series of their generals, warns that Parliament would try to separate officers from soldiers by promising estates to the former, and signs off with "Your servants so far as we may." If we accept this unsigned pamphlet as a genuine product of the soldiers—and I see no good reason to hesitate—then the first published Army manifesto also reveals the beginnings of Army/Leveller solidarity, and of radical/grandee conflict.

Fairfax tried to squelch *The Humble Petition*, but it had moved beyond his control. On March 30, Parliament published *A Declaration of the Lords and Commons Assembled in Parliament*, which came to be known as the *Declaration of Dislike*. Adding grievous insult to the threat of capital injury, it called those supporting the petition "enemies to the state, and disturbers of the public peace"—a phrase that echoed through the polemics of the coming months in a fashion rivaled only by Edmund Burke's offhand reference to the "swinish multitude" a century and a half later. A letter of April 3 from the General's headquarters at Saffron Walden asks, "have the soldiers only, who have been instruments to recover the lost liberties of the nation, fought themselves into slavery? Sure there is right of petitioning for us, as well as there was a *Petition of Right* for the Parliament."[42] Parliament disrupted its own chain of command by ordering certain

40. 10, 6, 14, 10, 16.
41. *WSS* 35.
42. *RHC* 4.446.

regiments to Ireland without notifying Fairfax.[43] The regiments began to elect representative "agents," "adjutators," or "agitators" to meet and confer with their general officers. The agitators first appear in a letter by a Suffolk Presbyterian, who refers to a meeting of Ireton's regiment in Ipswich on April 15, when soldiers discussed their resistance to disbandment or being sent to Ireland, and "As for the petition, they now speak it openly that they will send it up with two out of every troop."[44]

Kishlansky suggests that "We do not know how they were selected, and I am extremely dubious that it was by ballot, or what their charge was."[45] Morrill suggests they were not "elected" by the soldiers but "coopted by the officers."[46] But this scenario would require us to see Agitator Sexby as Fairfax's creature, and to ignore the newsbook that clearly describes their election on May 13 and their meeting two days later at Bury, with each foot representative backed by a four pence contribution from each soldier in his regiment.[47] *The Solemne Engagement of the Army* of June 5, probably by Ireton, says the soldiers chose their Agitators through a two-step, democratic process:

> [T]he soldiers of this Army ... were enforced to an unusual, but in that case necessary, way of correspondence and agreement amongst themselves, to choose out of the several troops and companies several men, and those out of their whole number to choose two or more for each regiment, to act in the name and behalf of the whole soldiery of the respective regiments, troops, and companies, in the prosecution of their rights and desires in the said petition.

Ireton goes on to describe *future* elections, saying that the Council of the Army would consist of general officers "who have concurred with the Army in the premises, with two commission-officers and two soldiers to be chosen for each regiment who have concurred and shall concur with us in the premises and in this agreement." Ireton's vague "us" and passive voice suggest that he wanted to root out regimental democracy as much Morrill and Kishlansky want to deny it ever existed in the first place.[48] But he had no luck. The threat of disbandment and even execution as enemies to the state had transformed the serial collective of New Model soldiers into a fused group, which in turn transformed itself into an internally structured pledged group.[49]

The Agitators addressed a letter to Fairfax on April 25. On April 28, they sent another, entitled *The Apologie*, with signatures by two representatives from each of eight New Model cavalry regiments, including Edward Sexby, William Allen, Thomas Shepherd, Nicholas Lockyer, and

---

43. *WSS* 50–51.
44. *GHCW* 3.236–7; *WSS* 44. When tracing the origins of the Agitators, Kishlansky (*Rise* 204) and Gentles (*G* 175) overlook this letter.
45. "What Must Be" 88.
46. *Nature* 249.
47. *The Perfect Weekly Account* 5/12–5/19/47.
48. *P&L* 401, 402. On elections, see also *G* 175.
49. *SCDR* 417–44.

twelve others.[50] They also sent copies, dated April 30, to Cromwell and to Skippon, then sitting as MPs, who turned them over to the Commons on the same day.[51] *The Apologie* refers in memorable but less than conciliatory terms to a "plot" concocted by "some who have lately tasted of sovereignty; and being lifted beyond their ordinary sphere of servants, seek to become masters, and degenerate into tyrants."[52] On April 30, the House called Sexby, Allen, and Shepherd, and examined them individually about *The Apologie*, but they refused to interpret or defend its specifics because the several regiments had produced it jointly. When asked the meaning of its veiled but menacing reference to "tyrants," one of them replied, "That the letter being a joint act of those several regiments, they could not give a punctual answer, they being only agents; but if they might have the queries in writing, they should send or carry them to the several regiments, and return their own answer together with and comprised in the rest."[53] The Agitators gum up the works of one sovereign assembly by invoking their own duties as representatives of another; power and safety lie in a claim not to be utterly oneself. Presbyterian MPs found this retort extraordinarily impudent—Holles later remarked that Parliament should have hanged one of the three as an example, "as Mr. Cromwell afterwards did their fellows."[54] He had encountered (and in fact, had helped to generate) a radical new mode of political authority. With the emergence of the Agitators, the troops, companies, and regiments were organized not only by a hierarchical authority descending from Parliament to generals to officers to common soldiers, but by an associative authority spreading outward from elections conducted by individual soldiers.

On May 3 the Agitators printed *The Apologie of the Common Souldiers*, which included *The Apologie* and *A Second Apologie*, signed more prudently only by "your soldiers."[55] This remarkably radical piece calls for "an end to all tyranny and oppressions so that justice and equity, according to the law of the land, should be done to the people and that the meanest subject should fully enjoy his right, liberty and properties in all things." That last phrase suggests economic and political arguments to come. With no more than a telltale whiff of "Lilburnian principles," Kishlansky

50. *G* 175; *WSS* 57.
51. Cromwell's copy as printed by Prynne in *The Hypocrites Unmasking* (1647) closely resembles Fairfax's, but its printed date of March 30 is, I assume, a misprint for "April." Prynne's title of "A Letter of the Agitators to Leiutenant Generall Cromwell" may record the first use of "agitator." If it's a back-formation, we must look to *A Letter of the Agitators to Leuitenant Generall Cromwell* of May 29 (*D* 16). "Agitator" appears interchangeably with "adjutator." "Agitation" meant "stirring, disturbing" by 1567, and "doing the work of another" by 1634 (*OED*, "agitate" II.5). See *GHCW* 3.243–4n.
52. *D* 8.
53. *RHC* 4.474. Another account (*CP* 1.430–31) derives from Bodleian Library Tanner Ms. 88, 84.
54. *Memoirs*, 1699, 90.
55. Around May 6, they reprinted the first as a broadside entitled *For Our Faithfull and Ever Honored Commanders*.

supposes that some London civilians wrote *A Second Apologie*, along with *An Apollogie of the Souldiers* of March 26. Though he spurns *a priori* historical interpretation, it would seem that his thesis about the separation of the Levellers and the Army has become a principle for sorting and disqualifying evidence as well as a conclusion derived from it.[56] I have found no Army statements either owning or disowning *An Apollogie of the Souldiers*, so I'm content to follow the title's attribution. The recent experience of Sexby, Allen, and Shepherd in the House adequately explains the anonymity of *A Second Apologie*. And by reprinting it along with *The Apologie* in the *Book of Declarations*, Fairfax suggested that he, at least, did not find Army grievances utterly incompatible with Lilburnian principles.[57]

Kishlansky claims that the Army had refused all along "to meddle in matters of state," and that, by the beginning of the summer of 1647, the "soldiers were still unaware that their grievances were symptoms of a national malady rather than a local discomfort. . . . Only slowly would the army and the Levellers find common cause."[58] But *An Apollogie of the Souldiers* suggests that some in the Army made common cause with the Levellers by late winter, and Thomason's manuscript copy of *An Unanimous Answer of the Souldiers to the Comissioners' Propositions* (June 2) links together the Army's traditional grievances with a demand that Parliament relieve "the four Commoners of England who have lately petitioned the Parliament." Kishlansky also contradicts charges by the City, by the House, and by Kishlansky himself, who notes the Army's June 15 petition for the impeachment of the Eleven Members—a fairly dramatic bit of state-meddling.[59] On July 6 and again on July 16, a group of Agitators petitioned Fairfax to intervene for the imprisoned Lilburne, Overton, Musgrave, and others, with whom they declared their "fellow feeling."[60]

Kishlansky argues that the "appearance of the Agitators was innovative, not radical," and compares the elected soldier representatives of the Spanish Army in Flanders.[61] But whatever the precedents, the English ruling class could not believe its eyes in the summer of 1647; as Woolrych says, "there had been nothing really like the Agitators, either in the range of their objectives or in the sophistication of their organization."[62] Fairfax

---

56. *Rise* ix–xiii, 205, 332n.99.
57. *D* "5" [i.e., 7]–11. *Heads of Some Demands*, an anonymous, unpublished piece from Saffron Walden inserted between two pieces dated May 3, denounced Parliament in similar tones, concluding with a Levellerish declaration of popular sovereignty, parliamentary subordination, and the political "birthright" conferred by Magna Charta (*CM* 18r–v).
58. "The Army and the Levellers," *The Historical Journal* 22.4, 1979, 811, 805.
59. "Army" 810.
60. *CM* 41.164v, 103v–104r; *CP* 1.171. In "Journey to Putney" (Schochet, *Religion* 63–82), Barbara Taft agrees with Brailsford (*Levellers*) that, with Lilburne and Overton in jail, Walwyn helped establish Army/Leveller ties in 1647. Sexby also looks like a good bet.
61. *Rise* 205–6.
62. *WSS* 61.

claimed that "the power of the Army I once had, was usurped by the Agitators." He attempted to suppress them near the headquarters, but "this was only as the cutting off a hydra's head; for they began again . . . in more remote corners of the Army. . . . The Army was almost wholly infected with this humor of Agitation."[63] Hyde later recalled that the House's temper "raised another spirit in the Army," leading to mechanic preaching.[64] With a shudder, William Waller remembered that a spirit was haunting Westminster:

> The House received advertisement, that the Army began to be haunted with apparitions, certain spirits, and dominations, conjured up out of the body of the soldiery, under the title of Agitators; things never known before, in any army in the world, and now set up, in confutation of Ecclesiastes, to shew, that there might be a novelty under the sun.

He called their grievances "the particulars, wherein the Army, as a parliament, required satisfaction of the Parliament."[65] Prynne saw them "acting more like a Parliament and supreme dictators than soldiers."[66] Holles had trouble pinning them down. He compared them to the aristocratic supreme council of the Irish rebels, but admitted that they were commoners "chosen out of every regiment." They wished to "set up a new form of government in the Army," but they were also "instrumental to their masters," the mere creatures of "Cromwell and his fellows," who, "standing behind the curtain, laughed in their sleeves, and pleased themselves to see the game which they had packed, play so well." They were a "mercenary army," none of them worth a thousand pounds a year, and most of them mere tradesmen, "a notable dunghill, if one would rake into it, to find out their several pedigrees."[67]

Prynne called them class levellers, like John of Leyden and the German Anabaptists—a frequent motif.[68] In July, "Tom Tell-Troth" charged that the Army aimed to take the place of its betters:

> The grand design and main intent
> Is to new mold the Parliament.
> The Army then and country-clown
> Will turn the kingdom upside down.[69]

One newsbook called the reformed New Model a monstrous birth, with its feet "where the head should grow, / And Head (where feet should be)

63. *Short* 103, 107, 116.
64. *History* 3.32.
65. *Vindication of the Character and Conduct of Sir William Waller, Knight*, London 1793, 112–13, 123.
66. Kishlansky quotes Waller and Prynne (*Rise* 206, 332–3n.) but doesn't explain their error in thinking the Agitators a novelty.
67. *Memoirs* 86–8, 149; see Brailsford, *Levellers* 176–7.
68. *The Totall and Finall Demands*, 1647; see also the anonymous *Sine Qua Non*, 1647.
69. *Works* 8.

below."[70] Attributing to the Agitators the terminology that Harrington would employ in *Oceana*, one pamphleteer says they claim the people are the "foundation" of political "superstructures" such as kings, princes, and potentates, so that "the tail shall dictate to the head, the breeches to the brainpan."[71] Another says that the Agitator "may lineally derive his pedigree from the ancient grand Agitator Judas. . . . he differs in nothing from a Jew, but in his poverty." Just as the sun shining on the slime of the Nile breeds up monsters, so "the good whores of the kingdom and a troop fornicating together" breed up Agitators:

> This politic bubo is the clap, the gonorrhea of martial authority, which the champion lady got when she overstrained herself at Newmarket. . . . Solomon says there is no new thing under the sun, and the philosopher says *non datur multiplicatio specierum*: I wonder what they could for shame say, were they alive now, and saw but an Agitator.[72]

Another pamphlet, which Thomason collected during the Putney Debates, verges on taxonomic terror as it struggles to classify the Agitator, that "late spurious monster of John Lilburne's generation, compounded of those sects unto one body, an Anabaptist, a Jesuit, a Separatist, and a Seeker." The Agitator hates all civil and church order and ordinances, and is both heretic and Jesuit, atheist and zealot, tyrant and tyrannicide, condemner of and seeker after deans and chapter lands, both a communist who desires to abolish rents and tithes and a seeker after those very rents. He is

> a common enemy to all, a true friend to none, a wandering meteor, a raging wave of the sea, a new upstart mushroom, all head and no body, white in the morning, black worm eaten, and rank poison before night, and hates a Scot and Presbyterian more than either pope or devil. He was begotten of Lilburne (with Overton's help) in Newgate, nursed up by Cromwell at first by the Army, tutored by Mr. Peters, counseled by Mr. Walwyn and Musgrave, patronized by Mr. Marten, (who sometimes sits in council with them though a member) and is like to die nowhere but at Tyburn, and that speedily, if he repent not, and reform his erroneous judgment, and his seditious treasonable practices against king, Parliament, and martial discipline itself.

The author can characterize the Agitator only in reactionary and atavistic terms: a spurious claimant to a hereditary throne, a disease threatening the body politic, a criminal brought up short by a menacing allusion to Tyburn—the uproarious and ever-ready punchline for early modern

---

70. *Mercurius Melancholicus*, 11/6–11/11/47.
71. *Hampton-Court Conspiracy*, 1647, 5.
72. *An Agitator Anotomiz'd*, 1648, A1ʳ, A2ʳ, A2ᵛ, A3ʳ. I've guessed "whores" for a missing word.

ruling-class satirists.[73] These hysterical attacks focus on mythological or sexual generation in order to screen out a quieter but still terrifying innovation: the Agitators' democratic election by the soldiery.

During the spring and summer of 1647, the Agitators led and the general officers followed, as a newsletter observes: "The officers now own [ally themselves with] the soldiers and all that's done and do begin to bestir themselves."[74] They established their headquarters at Bury St Edmunds in Suffolk, some distance from Army headquarters, maintained themselves through subscriptions from the soldiers, and heard the regimental petitions of May.[75] An encrypted letter from (evidently) one Agitator to others, which describes the House's May 25 vote to disband the New Model and destroy its power, suggests the passionate and energetic activity of the Agitators:

> Gentlemen,
>
> My best respects. I rid hard and came to London by 4 this afternoon. The House hath ordered and voted the Army to be disbanded, regiment by regiment. The General's regiment of foot on Tuesday next to lay down their arms in Chelmsford Church, and they do intend to send you down once more Commissioners to do it of Lords and Commons; they will not pay more than two months' pay, and after we be disbanded to state our accompts and to be paid by the excise in course. This is their good vote, and their good visible security. Pray, gentlemen, ride night and day; we will act here night and day for you. You must by all means frame a petition in the name of all the soldiers, to be presented to the General by you the Agitators, to have him in honor, justice, and honesty, to stand by you, and to tell Skippon to depart the Army and all other Officers that are not right. Be sure now be active, and send some 30 or 40 horse to fetch away Jackson, Gooday, and all that are naught, and be sure to possess his soldiers, he will sell them and abuse them; for so he hath done, he engaged to sell them for eight weeks' pay. Gent. I have it from (59) and (89) that you must do this, and that you shall expel [them] out of the Army; and if you do disappoint them in the disbanding of this regiment namely (68) you will break the neck of all their designs. . . . Now, my lads, if we work like men we shall do well, and that in the hands of (52); and let all the (44) be very instant that the (55) may be called to a (43) and that with speed; delay it not, by all

73. *The Character of An Agitator,* 1647, 3, 7. *Mercurius Melancholicus* tells the Agitators that "Tyburn groans for you" (11/6–11/13/47; see also 11/13–11/20/47). *A Lenten Litany* (1647) prays God

> That it may please thee to assist
> Our Agitators, and their list,
> And hemp them with a gentle Twist,
> *Quaesumus te, Domine.*

The Second Part to the same Tune, collected by Thomason on November 13, two days after Charles's escape from custody, links Joyce, Ireton, and Cromwell to Cataline and Ravillac, and rhymes "Crumwell" and "loves a Bum-well."

74. *CP* 1.112.
75. *G* 162.

means and be sure to stir up the counties to petition, and for their rights to make their appeal to (55) to assist them. You shall hear all I can by the next. So till then I rest.

Yours till death,

102.[76]

The writer proposes mutiny against Presbyterian officers who had allied themselves with Parliament, and even against General Skippon. And by advocating a nationwide organization of the counties, he inverts Parliament's effort to atomize the Army through disbandment. Through conspiracy, coded communication, hard riding, and the publication of defiantly public manifestos, the Agitators hoped to revolutionize the Army and the nation.

On May 4, an anonymous unpublished piece advised the soldiery to protect against the abduction of the king, assure the trustworthiness of the general officers, and appoint a Council of the Army. With a striking self-consciousness about the revolutionary function of print, the author advocates something like a Jacobin correspondence society—a "party of able pen men at Oxford and the Army," with presses "to satisfy and undeceive the people." It would "hold correspondence with the soldiers and well affected friends in the several counties of the kingdom, for prevention of uproars, interposition of parties, for disarming the disaffected, and securing the persons of projecting parties, namely Presbyterians." On May 18, another letter to the Agitators spoke of the necessity for a printing press, which would help counteract Parliament's attempts to disband the Army.[77] These efforts succeeded: after Fairfax helped set him up with Henry Hills in Oxford, John Harris printed for the Army, but also for the Agitators.[78]

On May 20, Skippon, Cromwell, Ireton, and Fleetwood tried to assure Parliament they would maintain control of the Army by formally considering regimental petitions.[79] But as Kishlansky has observed, these regimental petitions of May 13–15, which Firth largely passed over when extracting *The Clarke Papers*, did little more than further the self-organization of the Army.[80] They responded to the parliamentary commissioners' queries about discontents in the Army, but their common substance and even phrasing suggest that they also opened a further channel for

---

76. *CP* 1.100–101.

77. Ibid. 1.22–4, 85–6. Firth nominates Edward Sexby as author of the first letter, comparing his May 17 letter to the Agitators: "If there be not a press got into the Army we shall be at a loss" (ibid. 1.82–3, transcription of *CM* slightly modified).

78. See "Harris, John" in H. R. Plomer, *A Dictionary of Booksellers and Printers Who Were at Work in England, Scotland and Ireland from 1641–1667*, London 1907; and Falconer Madan, *Oxford Books*, 3 vols, Oxford 1912, 2.452. On the Army's press, see Holles (Gregg, *Free-Born John* 174) and Richard Baxter, *Reliquiae* 61.

79. *CP* 1.94–9.

80. *Rise* 210. The unnumbered pages of *CM* 90 contain most of the originals, with a fair copy in *CM* 41 105ᵛ–30ʳ. Morrill tabulates the petitions' arguments in *Nature* 331. *Divers Papers from the Army* (1647) published the protests of Rich's regiment, along with a summary under ten heads of the various regimental responses.

"correspondency and actings" amongst the regiments. Though some regiments—particularly those far from the larger muster at Saffron Walden—proclaimed loyalty to Parliament, most spoke with one voice against arbitrary disbandment, prohibition of petitioning, non-payment of arrears, lack of indemnity, labeling of loyal officers as delinquents, attacks on the Army by the likes of Thomas Edwards in *Gangraena*, and, above all, against the *Declaration of Dislike*, "the very thoughts of which we utterly abominate," as Rich's regiment said.[81] Kishlansky claims that "Lilburnian rhetoric and Lilburne's cause, so much in the air in the capital, were also absent from the Army's petitions."[82] But the petitions of Fairfax and Hewson's regiments have, as Woolrych notes, a Leveller flavor, for both protest against preserving laws in an "unknown tongue" and the long imprisonment without trial of "the free men of England."[83]

On May 19, fourteen Agitators (including Sexby, Allen, and Shepherd) warned the regiments against the "dividing and so the destroying designs" of the Parliament, emphasizing the need for solidarity—a topic that would come up again at Putney.[84] But the Commons passed its motion for disbandment on May 25, and the Lords concurred. In late May, the Agitators wrote the troopers in General Poyntz's Northern Association, advising them of recent Army conflicts with Parliament and encouraging their solidarity.[85] On June 25, the Agitators sent them another letter, later printed as *The Copy of a Letter Printed at New-Castle, July the 6, 1647*, encouraging them to elect Agitators who would establish correspondence. They found a willing audience. On July 8, Poyntz's own troops arrested him, led him bootless through the streets of York, and held him in Pontefract Castle. On July 13, Thomason collected *A Declaration and Representation from the Forces of the Northerne Associations*, in which sixteen Northern Agitators declared their desire to associate with the New Model.[86] These events marked a significant victory, since Poyntz would almost certainly have joined Parliament and an invading Scots army against the New Model.[87] A coded letter of May 28 seems to refer to the projected seizure of the magazine at Oxford, a vital task assigned to George Joyce, who accomplished it around June 1.[88] A fictional dialogue acquired by Thomason on May 27 shows a soldier asking a minister, "But I pray you resolve me in this; may not we soldiers go and fetch his majesty from Holmby, and carry him to his place in Parliament?"[89]

In May, ninety-seven officers sent a petition to Fairfax protesting their

---

81. *CP* 1.98, *CM* 41.113ᵛ.
82. *Rise* 212.
83. *CM* 41.116ʳ⁻ᵛ, 119ᵛ–120ʳ; *WSS* 81.
84. *CP* 1.87–8.
85. Ibid. 1.89–92.
86. *CM* 21.180ʳ; *CP* 1.167–9; *G* 172–3.
87. *WSS* 148.
88. *CP* 1.105, 114n.
89. T. C., *The Red-Ribbond News from the Army*, 1647, 7.

loyalty to him but also to "those by whose authority they were raised."[90]
On May 29, a letter of intelligence reported that the soldiers had begun
to purge, and even beat, their Presbyterian officers, and to petition Fairfax
for a general rendezvous, "and if he scruple it, it will be done however."[91]
A petition to Fairfax of May 29, subscribed by thirty-one Agitators, entreats
him to a general rendezvous.[92] In his bold stroke of June 4, Cornet Joyce
took King Charles into Army custody, as we saw in chapter 1. Fairfax and
his generals tried to contain this radical momentum within an officer-
dominated collective. On June 5, the Army met near Newmarket, hooted
their "ill-affected" (Presbyterian) officers off the field, and subscribed *The
Solemne Engagement of the Army*, one of the most important documents of
the revolutionary era. It was "essentially a military covenant, whereby the
whole Army entered into a mutual pledge not to allow itself to be
disbanded or divided until it received satisfaction on certain stated
matters."[93] It formed a new corporate body which came to be known as
the General Council of the Army, consisting of the general officers and
four elected representatives (two officers, two soldiers) "to be chosen for
each regiment," which General Fairfax would convene at will.[94] The
General Council became the first, formalized site for the military public
sphere, but not the last. *The Solemne Engagement* concludes prophetically:

> Neither would we, if we might and could, advance or set up any one particular
> party or interest in the kingdom, though imagined never so much our own, but
> should much rather study to provide, as far as may be within our sphere or
> power, for such an establishment of common and equal right, freedom, and
> safety to the whole as all might equally partake of, that do not, by denying the
> same to others, or otherwise, render themselves incapable thereof.[95]

We might read this as a straightforward premodern attack on party, and a
pledge of obedience to the powers that be. But the vow to institute
"common and equal right" that "all might equally partake of" does not
seem calculated to reassure Presbyterian oligarchs, while the threat to
disenfranchise those who resist foreshadows the Army's occupation of
London and Parliament in August, and even Pride's Purge. On June 14
appeared *A Declaration or Representation from Sir Thomas Fairfax and the Army
Under His Command*—probably written by Ireton, but, as Brailsford suggests, its radical spirit implies Agitator pressure. In its most famous phrase,
it declared the New Model was "not a mere mercenary army, hired to
serve any arbitrary power of a state, but called forth and conjured by the
several declarations of Parliament to the defense of our own and the
people's just rights and liberties."[96] "Called forth" has some overtones of

---

90. *CM* 21ʳ⁻ᵛ.
91. *CP* 1.111–13. Another report concurs (*RHC* 4.498).
92. *Two Letters of His Excellency Sir Thomas Fairefax*, 1647, 10–11.
93. *WSS* 117.
94. *G* 173; *P&L* 401–3, 401, 402, [22].
95. *P&L* 403.
96. *D* 36–46, 39; *P&L* 404; see Brailsford, *Levellers* 216–23.

Protestant vocation, but in seventeenth-century English, "conjure" con-
notes political conspiracy and witchcraft—an extraordinary calling forth
that, unlike mercenary hire, could not be canceled at will, and that left
the Army free to move beyond the letter of parliamentary declarations to
their spirit and sense in order to defend the safety of the people.

The imprisoned Levellers viewed the *Solemne Engagement* with suspicion.
Overton warned that Fairfax would turn the Agitators into a body "only
for advice and consultation, not for control and conclusion."[97] Lilburne
argued that Cromwell had stolen power from the Agitators "and solely
placed it in a thing called a Council of War, or rather a Cabinet Junto of
seven or eight proud self-ended fellows."[98] But they underestimated the
extent of the grandees' compromise, which we can see in a metaphor
Ireton uses to justify resistance to Parliament: "the soldiery may lawfully
hold the hands of the general who will turn his cannon against his army
on purpose to destroy them."[99] Pauline Gregg notes that Henry Parker
used this favorite argument of resistance theorists in his *Observations*, and
Lilburne in his pamphlets and letters to Cromwell.[100] As an anonymous
conservative warned, it contained subversive implications for the grandees
as well as the king: "Consider that if you let loose the bands of government, and you that are officers by your own example . . . teach the soldiers
to disobey the Parliament, that lesson will serve to teach them likewise
how to resist their own officers."[101] Indeed, Wildman and Rainsborough
turned this image against the grandees at Putney.[102] In April 1649, a
rebellious Leveller would quote the passage back at Cromwell.[103]

While the names of the elected Agitators did tend to disappear from
the manifestos issued by Fairfax in the name of the Council of War, they
continued vigorously outside the Council. On June 16, twenty Agitators
published *A True Declaration of the Present Proceedings of the Army*, which
justified their decisions not to disband and to cashier pro-Parliament
officers. On June 21, in *A Copie of a Letter Sent from the Agitators of His
Excellency Sir Thomas Fairfax's Armie, to all the Honest Sea-men of England*, the
Agitators tried to recruit the considerably more conservative navy to their
cause.[104] In July appeared *The Humble Petition of the Wel-Affected Young Men,
and Apprentises*, in solidarity with the Army; it contained a comradely reply
by the Agitators, including Sexby ("Ed. Sepbe"). On July 15, Thomason
acquired *A Vindication of the Army*, a broadsheet intended to be "set up, in
parish churches, and public places throughout this kingdom." It recites

97. *LM* 188.
98. *Ionahs Cry out of the Whales Belly*, 1647, 9.
99. *D* 40.
100. *Free-Born John* 219; [Henry Parker,] *Observations upon some of his Majesties late Answers and
Expresses*, 2nd edn, 1642, 16.
101. *The Lawfulness of the Late Passages of the Army*, 1647, 16.
102. *CP* 1.272–3.
103. A. L. Morton, *Freedom in Arms*, New York 1974, 231, 234.
104. *LM* 142–53. See also the address to the Masters of the Society of Trinity House in
Journals of the House of Lords for 1647 (284).

the Army's grievances and concludes with a scriptural exhortation to liberation and solidarity: "ye may be free if ye will, be free now and ever, now or never, this is the seventh year, the year of jubilee."

The Agitators seem to have been in contact with Lilburne, probably through Sexby. In a July 6 letter to King Charles, the royalist Sir Lewis Dyve, imprisoned in the Tower with Lilburne, accused them of planning to dissolve the House of Commons, and paid them inadvertent tribute: "These men . . . are of such a temper, as they will not be thought to act anything for their own particular ends, but only as in reference to the common good, and the offers of honors and rewards they abominate, yet they will feed as greedily upon fair hopes, if handsomely set before them, as any people that ever I met with." He also refers to a plan to send fifty emissaries, one to each county, to encourage popular solidarity with this plan.[105] *Two Letters Written out of Lancashire and Buckinghamshire*, a pamphlet of July 12, prints one letter describing sectaries flocking to hear two representatives of the Army who had arrived with books, letters, and news, and another describing New Model dragoons who came to Newport and "post up and down the country their agents, with letters and instructions."[106] On July 12, the Agitators sent an eloquent republican missive to the forces in Wales. It attempted to shame them into ignoring their contractual pasts by imagining the reproaches of their progeny if they should let slip an unprecedented revolutionary opportunity.[107] Before July 15, a published letter encouraged soldiers to maintain their solidarity and establish committees to keep up correspondence with the Agitators.[108] On July 15, an anonymous pamphlet printed by the Army's printers repeatedly invoked the doctrine of *salus populi*, citing Calvin and Peter Martyr to argue that lesser magistrates may pressure and even punish superior powers.[109] The first major debate of the General Council occurred on July 16 at Reading.[110]

Meanwhile, London was in an uproar. The Army had impeached Holles and the other Eleven Members in June, and they left the Commons on June 25; that same day, a parliamentarian tract compared Fairfax's army to those of Jack Cade and the Münster Anabaptists.[111] Probably in early July, John Wildman wrote Fairfax encouraging him to relieve the city.[112] On July 26, a Presbyterian mob forced both Houses to pass resolutions sympathetic to City Presbyterians. On August 4, the Army began its bloodless occupation of London and restored to the two Houses those

---

105. "The Tower of London Letter-Book of Sir Lewis Dyve, 1646–1647," *The Publications of the Bedfordshire Historical Record Society* 38, 1957, 65.
106. 1647, 3–4, 6. On July 13, Thomason collected *A Copie of that Letter*, which claims to reproduce the Agitators' letter to Lancashire. See also *Some Queries* 10.
107. *CP* 1.158–61.
108. *A Declaration from the Agitators*, 1647, 22.
109. *The Grand Informer*, Oxford 1647, 7.
110. *CP* 1.176–214.
111. *IX Queries Upon the Printed Charge*, 1647.
112. *CM* 90, no pagination.

sympathetic members whom the mobs had purged. Holles fled to
France.[113] While the Agitators called for the expulsion of MPs who sat
during the mob occupation of Parliament, many of the Army's Presbyterian opponents, including Generals Massey and Poyntz, departed for
the Continent.[114]

As the transfer of the king to Parliament's control and the departure of
the Scots widened the rift between Parliament and the Army, so the
taming of a recalcitrant Presbyterian opposition in Parliament widened
the rift between grandees and Agitators. On August 10, Dyve wrote the
king that "The General and Cromwell and all the grandees both of the
Army and the two Houses are as eagerly bent to destroy the Agitators as
to suppress their greatest adversaries, the Presbyterian faction."[115] We
might best see the Putney Debates as an attempt to adjudicate the claims
of two public "parties" with conflicting interpretations of the *Solemne
Engagement of the Army*. The grandees' party saw it ratifying a hierarchical
Army. Their position appears most clearly in *The Heads of the Proposals*,
which Ireton (probably) drafted in mid-July. It proposed to extend the
franchise, regularize elections and meetings of Parliament, and partially
abolish episcopacy, but it maintained the traditional polity of England
based in king, Lords, and Commons, and sought reforms in a traditional
fashion, through repealable laws of Parliament.[116] Ireton and Cromwell
discussed *The Heads* with the king and with fellow members of Parliament,
frequently presenting their own opinions as the opinions of the Army—
or so radicals charged. Fairfax gathered his manifestos and reissued them
in early October as *A Declaration of the Engagements*, a grandee-friendly
chronicle of the Army's summer, with no Agitator-signed documents
between *The Humble Petition* of May 19 and *The Humble Proposals of the
Adjutators* of September 13. Its frontispiece depicts seated officers with
hats, standing soldiers without, and Fairfax presiding over all as the most
distant but also the largest figure.

The radicals, on the other hand, saw *The Solemne Engagement* changing
the Army from a hierarchical to an associative collective. In *Putney Projects*,
John Wildman lambasted *The Heads* and argued for the Army's power to
govern itself democratically.[117] The author of *A Plea for the Late Agents of
the Army* saw *The Solemne Engagement* dissolving the New Model and re-
creating it as a democratic body ruled by the General Council, a body
"wholly new, and in a way diverse or different from all martial courts or

---

113. In George Wither's *Carmen Expostulatorium* of August, the Army's entry into London
   disrupts the very deliberative progress of the poem; its reportorial looseness and
   openness to future events contrasts strongly with the tragic and sacramental impulse of
   His Maiesties Complaint, an anonymous poem of June 24, which deifies Charles, now in
   Army custody, by adapting to his situation Christ's plaint on the cross in Herbert's "The
   Sacrifice."
114. *The Humble Address of the Agitators of the Army to His Excellency Sir Thomas Fairfax*, 1647, 7.
115. "Tower" 77.
116. *D* 112–20; excerpts in *P&L* 422–6.
117. Excerpted in *P&L* 426–9.

councils of war, that ever the sun beheld in a mercenary army, and as different from the council by which this army was formerly governed." Its proceedings were "not to be constituted by the Gen.'s will, *or according to the degrees of offices of men in the Army,* but in a parliamentary way by soldiers' free election." The author underlines the sheer novelty of the egalitarian military collective, noting that the soldiers at Newmarket engaged in verbal and physical attacks on their Presbyterian officers, and "this in the face of the Gen.," which would have been capital offenses under traditional martial law. It concludes by asking readers to compare the *Book of Declarations* with the current actions of Cromwell and Ireton, now "transcendently kingified and lordified."[118]

In early November, Dyve described radicals as intensely suspicious: just as the danger of an alliance between Presbyterians and the king had forced them to take the initiative by seizing the king, so the danger in November of an alliance between the grandees and the king encouraged them to push for a new, non-monarchical settlement.[119] To complete the analogy, the fear of an invading Scots army loomed once more. In early September, John Lilburne's letter entitled "Advice to the Private Soldiers" counseled them to select new Agitators to limit the corruptions introduced by long-standing in office.[120] In late September, Dyve wrote the king that "new agents" had replaced the old Agitators in six regiments and were holding meetings "in town with divers other well-affected brethren of the city."[121] Actually, only five regiments elected new Agitators, though Sexby, representing the General's, may well have remained radical enough to win re-election, thus representing a sixth. Woolrych suggests he retained his old status in part perhaps to serve as a link between the new agents and the General Council.[122] The new agents did not actually claim to replace the old ones, but their meetings with the Levellers suggest a new level of political radicalism.

These meetings produced the manifesto entitled *The Case of the Armie Stated,* subscribed by eleven New Agents, and, on October 18, two of them presented it to Fairfax.[123] It claimed that *The Solemne Engagement* had dissolved the Army's hierarchical structure and its dependence on Parliament, reconstituting it as an egalitarian collective ruled by the General Council, in which General Fairfax's vote would count no more than that of the meanest soldier Agitator. Subscribed by eleven new Agitators, it

118. *Plea* A1ᵛ, A2ʳ. The Folger Shakespeare Library owns a copy of *A Plea* with penned additions (italicized above) that read more like authorial revisions than commentary; these appeared in print in Lilburne's reprint of *The Plea* (titled *A Defence for the Honest Nonsubstantive Soldiers of the Army*) in *The Peoples Prerogative* (1648, 42–4; *LM* 243–7). If Lilburne wrote *A Plea,* he had significantly changed his mind about the radical potential of the General Council. On December 22, he defended *A Plea* in an argument with Ireton, who called it "full of falsehoods and mistakes" (Lilburne, *Peoples* 56).
119. "Tower" 96.
120. *WSS* 213, 192.
121. "Tower" 90.
122. *WSS* 203–4.
123. Ibid. 207. For the text, see *LM* 196–222; excerpts in *P&L* 429–36.

proposed a manhood franchise (except for delinquents) with no special place for king and lords, criticized the General Council for its subservience to Parliament, and proposed a radical social program that would have repealed statutes against conventicles, returned enclosed common land to the poor, and ended tithes, monopolies, and imprisonment for debt. Most important, it called for an unalterable "law paramount" that would prevent parliamentary backsliding.[124] On October 23, Fairfax's *Papers from the Armie* tried to discredit the New Agents, and he sent *The Case* to a committee for discussion. This committee sent a letter to the New Agents detailing its responses. On October 27, Robert Everard, a New Agent for Cromwell's regiment, brought the response of the New Agents and their Leveller associates: *The Agreement of the People*.[125] This work offered a shorter version of *The Case* in a new, more assertive form: it was no longer a proposal for reasoned consideration but a petition calling for popular subscription, and already supported by sixteen regiments.[126] The grandees invited its authors and sponsors to the meeting of the General Council scheduled for October 28.[127]

The Putney Debates continued in one form or another until November 9, but those we know best occurred on October 28, October 29, and November 1. William Clarke, assistant to John Rushworth (secretary to General Fairfax and the Council of War), recorded them in shorthand—transferring a skill developed in the sermon-copying congregation to the new political public sphere. Two principal grandees attended. Lieutenant General Cromwell, who presided over the debates, would become Lord Protector in 1653 and die in office in 1658. His son-in-law, Commissary General Henry Ireton, the primary grandee theorist and speaker, died in 1651 during the New Model's Irish campaigns. Lord Saye was at Putney at the "Council of War" on Sunday, October 31, and possibly at the debates themselves the next day, but he did not speak.[128] No other members of Cromwell's "cabinet council," as Dyve calls them—St John, Vane, and Lambert—attended.[129] General Fairfax would certainly have led the grandees against the Agitators, whom he abhorred, and his considerable prestige on all sides might have muffled the debate. But he was ailing and did not rejoin the Council until early November, after the recorded debates.

The radicals formed a larger and more varied group. John Lilburne

124. *LM* 215–16, 212. On this matter of a formal constitution, see Taft, "Journey" 71, and "For the Noble and Highly Honoured the Freeborn People of England" an epistle of November 5, signed by ten Agitators, in *A Declaration from the Severall Respective Regiments in the Army to All Free-born Commons of England.* The twelve-point program for social reform in *The Case* circulated as *Propositions from the Adjutators of Five Regiaments of Horse presented to his Excellency on Munday, Octob. 18, 1647.*
125. *LM* 223–34; excerpted *P&L* 443–5.
126. *WSS* 214–15; *G* 199.
127. See Cromwell's account of these preliminaries (*CP* 1.229–30).
128. *Mercurius Elencticus*, 11/5–11/12/47.
129. "Tower" 77, 84.

would no doubt have assumed leadership, and his irrepressible eloquence might well have turned the debate into yet another state drama of virtue speaking the truth to power. But the Lords continued to hold him in the Tower, with (so he charged) the collusion of the grandees. The highest ranking debater was Colonel Thomas Rainsborough. Dyve pronounced him a blood enemy and rival to Cromwell, and revealed that he met with Lilburne in the Tower for two hours on the night of October 31, between the second and third days of the debates.[130] A year after the debates, a royalist raiding party killed him in Doncaster, depriving the radical cause of one of its most eloquent spokesmen. His brother William also spoke; the Army dismissed him after the Leveller Rising of 1649, and he later became a Ranter. The radicals included several Agitators. Though still a private in Fairfax's regiment of horse, Edward Sexby was the most vocal. William Allen, a Baptist, and Agitator for Cromwell's regiment, later became a republican opponent of Cromwell.[131] Edmund Rolfe was Agitator for Colonel Hammond's regiment of foot, Richard Deane for Robert Lilburne's regiment of horse, and Nicholas Lockyer for Colonel Rich's.[132]

Two civilian Levellers from London attended. Maximilian Petty worked actively in Leveller circles and would later co-author *The Second Agreement of the People* and become a member of James Harrington's Rota Club. John Wildman attended, in tacit acknowledgment of his role in drafting *The Case of the Armie*. As "John Lawmind," he wrote and published *Putney Projects*, a scathing critique of the grandees' performance in the debates. But for allegorical aptness, Wildman's patronym rivaled his anagram: he became the political associate of Sexby, the second Duke of Buckingham, James Harrington, Algernon Sidney, and Shaftesbury; conspired against the lives or reigns of six sitting rulers of England (Charles I, Cromwell, Charles II, James II, and William and Mary); and died in bed. Benjamin Disraeli called him "the soul of English politics in the most eventful period of this kingdom."[133]

Several other radicals spoke during the three days of recorded debates. Hugh Peter, former New Englander, judge of Ann Hutchinson, Army chaplain, regicide, and deliverer of a benediction on the king's execution, died on a Restoration scaffold in 1660. Sir Hardress Waller, regicide, died a political prisoner on the Isle of Jersey in 1666. William Goffe, regicide, fled to Connecticut, where, as "Walter Goldsmith," he died in 1679, or shortly thereafter. John Hewson, shoemaker and regicide, died in exile in Holland in 1662. Robert Tichborne, regicide, became Lord Mayor of

130. Ibid. 89, 95–6. Hugh Ross Williamson discusses Rainsborough in *Four Stuart Portraits*, London 1949. The Rainsboroughs had New England and "new merchant" connections; one of their sisters became John Winthrop's fourth wife, while another married his fourth son. On the antipathy of Cromwell and Rainsborough, see *CP* 1.245n.

131. Paul H. Hardacre, "William Allen," *Baptist Quarterly* 19, 1962.

132. We should distinguish this Lockyer from the Independent minister of the same name, and from the Leveller martyr Robert, executed in 1649.

133. *Sybil*, London 1926, 15; thanks to John Dings for this reference. On Wildman, see Maurice Ashley, *John Wildman*, London 1947.

London in 1656; he was imprisoned from the Restoration until his death in 1682. Robert Everard was an Agitator for Cromwell's regiment, a General Baptist, a Leveller, and later a convert to Catholicism. Henry Lilburne, John's youngest brother, became Lieutenant Governor of Tynemouth Castle, declared for the king, and died during the assault led by Sir Arthur Haselrig. Francis White had been summarily dismissed from the General Council in September for claiming that all power derived from the sword—a sword wielded by the grandees only when the soldiers felt their commands to be just—but he returned for the second day of the debates. He participated reluctantly in the Leveller mutiny at Burford in 1649, and drowned in 1657 while on the Commonwealth's business. Others included Captain George Bishop (later a conspirator with Sexby and Wildman against Cromwell, defender of religious toleration, and a leader of the Bristol Quakers), John Jubbes (Army radical, opponent of Cromwell, emigrant to Jamaica), Edmund Chillenden (button-seller, Fifth Monarchist, and keeper of a Restoration coffee house), Lewis Audley, John Merriman, John Clarke, Nicholas Cowling, and John Carter. Many more persons present at the debates evidently did not speak. Thus began the Putney Debates.[134]

"No Courtesy!": Consensus vs Conflict at Putney

Contemporary scholars of politics and culture frequently turn to the concept of consensus. Sometimes, working from a history of ideas methodology, they assume that a single idea system or episteme must unite all earlier epochs, so that any apparent conflict must be a trick of the light. Sometimes, they suggest that something in language itself works against any fundamental social conflict. In a linguistically Burkean argument against the Weathermen and campus dissidents, J. G. A. Pocock says that speech itself provides "a context too rich and complex to be unmade all at once by any great cultural revolution, or made to yield to any one set of revolutionary demands."[135] As we saw in chapter 3, postmodernist cultural critics frequently imply that all resistance to a dominant cultural consensus fails inevitably (or never really began) because the order of discourse always already contains it. Insofar as Bakhtin and his liberal appropriators reify "dialogism" in the novel and in literature as a positive, pluralist good in itself, they fall into a similar "consensual" idealism.[136] Even Habermas, so far as he takes the conventions of ordinary language as a standard for adjudicating social conflicts, falls into what Perry Anderson calls an "angelism" of language which attempts to invert the French "diabolism" of language and supply "the salve of consensus to society."[137] And revisionist historians frequently

---

134. I draw on *GZ* for most of the information in this paragraph.
135. *Politics, Language and Time*, 2nd edn, Chicago 1989, 273–91, xi.
136. Ken Hirschkop, "Is Dialogism for Real?" *Social Text* 30, 1992, 103.
137. *Tracks* 64.

depict early modern England as a consensual and hierarchical polity free of the party politics and ideological conflicts characterizing modernity. For Glenn Burgess, early Stuart Englishmen shared a "consensual 'world view,'" so their indubitable conflicts over power, wealth, and strategies created only "a tension within a single intellectual system," not fundamental disagreement over first principles.[138] J. C. Davis briefly demurs, observing that "The contrast between conflict and consensus is overdone and unrealistic," but he resolves this contrast (this conflict?) on the side of consensus, both for the seventeenth century and for the present: "the consensus emerging amongst historians in recent years is that religious unity remained a virtually universal priority amongst the godly in the 1640s and 1650s."[139] And in "Consensus Politics and the Structure of Debate at Putney," Mark Kishlansky argues that the Putney Debates were not really debates. They reveal a premodern collective searching for consensus, not modern political parties striving for victory: "Seventeenth-century debates were designed to achieve unity and unanimity. . . . The necessity of maintaining the army's unity had been demonstrated time and again. . . . Unity was an unshakable standard against which all action had been measured. . . . [T]he maintenance of unity was the fundamental principle to which all attempted to adhere. . . ."[140]

And indeed, this is Cromwell and Ireton's rhetoric, if not their own practice: they repeatedly express shock at the idea that anyone would arrive with precommitments, "resolutions," beliefs tied to interests. Cromwell, who calls the meeting to order, also calls for "order" in the presentation of opinions, and adds, "I shall offer nothing to you but that I think my heart and conscience tends to the uniting of us, and to the begetting a right understanding among us, and therefore this is that I would insist upon." He regrets the "general loose debate" and asks, "Let us be united in our doing."[141] With the intuitive sensitivity of a New Journalist, Kishlansky calls the grandees' attempt to defer debate of the *Agreement* "not a tactic, but a point of principle" based in deeply held beliefs.[142] At the same time, he blames the radicals for the debates' "failure"—a peculiar and very interested way to characterize them, as we will see. They disintegrate amid "the churning undercurrent of practices destined to destroy the army's unity," including Wildman's "provocative interruptions," "flaring tempers, Wildman's rudeness, Rainsborough's sarcasm," and the desire of some "to resolve contested issues by votes rather than

---

138. *The Politics of the Ancient Constitution*, University Park, PA, 1993, 167–8.
139. "Religion" 508, 529.
140. *Journal of British Studies* 20, 1981, 52, 56–7. Compare Achinstein's Habermasean argument that "Unity was first" at Putney (*Milton* 108). I think interest was first—or, rather, an interested clash between distinct models of unity.
141. *CP* 1.229, 238, 287, 288–9.
142. "Consensus" 61.

concurrence."[143] Slighting the contentious eloquence of both Ireton and Sexby, he calls Thomas Rainsborough the only debater who did not work to minimize dispute, with the likely reason being a "personal grievance"— his desire, frustrated by Cromwell, to retain his Army command after becoming a Vice Admiral.[144]

Of course, in the abstract, all debaters struggle for consensus, but the appeal to modernity for a contrast seems to me suspect. A marxist listening to contemporary political debate between Democrats and Republicans in the US Senate might hear no debate at all, but a family quarrel between the center-right and hard right wings of the Business Party, with a preordained capitalist consensus. And Kishlansky's argument begins to sound unwittingly *a priori.* In *The Rise of the New Model Army,* he sees the Army as a whole bearing the conciliatory and holistic wisdom of the past, while Denzil Holles unwittingly bore the contentious and fractious impulse of the future. In his analysis of the Putney Debates, Cromwell and Ireton take the first role, Rainsborough and the Levellers the second. And his basic historical paradigm suggests the nostalgic metaphysical plot par excellence: the fall from unity, identity, and wholeness of being into multiplicity and alienation.

Of course, revisionists have no monopoly on this paradigm, which goes back to Plotinus, if not further. But if we refuse to *locate* a particular form of nostalgia in the experience and struggles of a particular group, then we risk an unselfconscious identification with that group. Kishlansky, for instance, allows his narrating voice to merge with the grandees to create a free-floating Voice of the Age: "If unity could be maintained, if each man could check his own self-interest, if none came precommitted, a free debate could achieve consensus."[145] But Putney reveals something less preordained, something more genuinely contentious. Kishlansky's revisionist model of consensus does in fact play an important role in the debates—not as the determining horizon of discourse, but as the particular strategic rhetoric of the grandees. Again and again, they attempt to derail the debates by invoking a consensual, pre-political unity presided over by the ancient constitution, precedent, and property. Again and again, they fail, for the radicals press forward by invoking natural law and insisting on a rational discussion of political interests, ends, and means— a discussion capped with a vote. In the process, the radicals demystify the rhetoric of consensus, revealing it for one party rhetoric among others.

Cromwell and Ireton tend to focus on the preconditions and procedures for orderly debate rather than its substance. They spend much of the first day pondering the justice of changing engagements from *The*

---

143. Ibid. 69, 67, 66, 67. For Kishlansky, Agitators and Levellers are always churning up otherwise cheerful soldiers; cf. the "churning undercurrent of Agitator hostility toward the houses" that had compromised the Army's debates in July, and the repeated "meddling" of civilian Levellers ("The Army" 817, 811, 815, 824).
144. "Consensus" 55.
145. Ibid. 62.

Solemn League and Covenant (which subordinated the Army to Parliament) to *The Agreement of the People*. Cromwell warns, "before we take this [*The Agreement*] into consideration, it is fit for us to consider how far we are obliged, and how far we are free." Ireton desires "only to put things into an orderly way."[146] Though far and away the most long-winded speaker, Ireton grows alarmed at the prospect of one radical speech (by Petty) building on another (by Rainsborough): "I think we shall not be so apt to come to a right understanding in this business, if one man, and another man, and another man do speak their several thoughts and conceptions to the same purpose."[147] He sees an emerging oppositional consensus as anarchy itself. But the radicals are keenly aware that discursive forms have strategic uses: when Colonel Robert Tichborne proposes that the House follow the form of sending laws to the king for his consent, Wildman interrupts, "No courtesy!"[148] The grandees may have been attempting to delay substantive discussion in the hopes that Fairfax would recover and bring his extra-rational authority to bear on the debates. But the radicals worry that a few days' delay might undo them—whether through the return of Fairfax, or the invasion of a Scots army in aid of the king and a Presbyterian settlement. Captain Lewis Audley, for instance, fidgets furiously throughout the debates: "Mr. Wildman says, if we tarry long, if we stay but three days before you satisfy one another, the King will come and say who will be hanged first."[149]

The very concept of "unity" became intensely problematic during the debates: "To Cromwell's insistence on unity, the Agitators had for some time been asking 'unity for what?'"[150] Looking back on Cromwell's unity rhetoric in the summer of 1647, William Walwyn submitted it to the final eschatological division: "To unite, or divide, is not the thing; but whether in good, or evil, is the main of all; and by which, my adversaries and I shall one day be judged, though now they have taken the chair, and most uncharitably judge me of evil in every thing wherein I move, or but open my mouth."[151] The conflict is not between grandee unity and radical individualism, but between two models of unity: the grandees' hierarchical unity based in consensus and military deference, and the radicals' associative unity based in debate and a democratic vote. In fact, radicals had already mounted an attack on certain sorts of "division." On May 19, in *A Letter sent from the Agitators to the Severall Regiments*, the agitators reported the "dividing and so the destroying designs" of Parliament in trying to separate officers and soldiers.[152] They repeat the charge a month later in

146. *CP* 1.240, 232.
147. Ibid. 1.313.
148. Ibid. 1.405.
149. *CP* 1.265; see also 252, 288, 331, 339–40.
150. Christopher Hill, *God's Englishman*, New York 1970, 94.
151. *Writings* 392. The strong echo of this passage in *The English Souldiers Standard* (Morton, *Freedom* 240) strengthens Brailsford's claim (*Levellers* 498) for Walwyn's authorship of that work.
152. *CP* 1.87.

their letter to the "honest seamen of England."[153] *The Case of the Armie* advocated the Army's radical solidarity with itself and with the people, complaining that "the Army is divided into quarters so far distant that one part is in no capability to give timely assistance to another, if any design should be to disband any part by violence suddenly." Furthermore, it called for a utopian unity that would press for "all their and our own rights and freedoms as soldiers and commoners. Let us never divide each from other till those just demands be answered really and effectually."[154]

The first full speech of the debates, by Edward Sexby, confronts directly the dangers of an abstract search for consensus:

> We have been by providence put upon strange things, such as the ancientest here doth scarce remember. The Army acting to these ends, providence hath been with us, and yet we have found little of our endeavors; and really I think all here both great and small (both officers and soldiers), we may say we have leaned on, and gone to Egypt for help. The kingdom's cause requires expedition, and truly our miseries with our fellow soldiers' cry out for present help. I think, at this time, this is your business, and I think it is in all your hearts to relieve the one and satisfy the other. You resolved if any thing should be propounded to you, you would join and go along with us.
>
> The cause of our misery [is] upon two things. We sought to satisfy all men, and it was well; but in going to do it we have dissatisfied all men. We have labored to please a king, and I think, except we go about to cut all our throats, we shall not please him; and we have gone to support an house which will prove rotten studs, I mean the Parliament which consists of a company of rotten members. . . .
>
> I shall speak to the Lieutenant General and Commissary General concerning one thing. Your credits and reputation hath been much blasted upon these two considerations. The one is for seeking to settle this kingdom in such a way wherein we thought to have satisfied all men, and we have dissatisfied them—I mean in relation to the king—The other is in reference to a parliamentary authority (which most here would lose their lives for), to see those powers to which we will subject our selves loyally called. . . . These things I have represented as my thoughts. I desire your pardon.[155]

Sexby begins by tendering his desires and ends by begging for pardon, but the whole speech reveals a talent for throwing down the gauntlet. The Agitators had not been *summoned* by the grandees but *sent* by their regiments, bearing their resolutions. In characterizing Parliament as a house supported by rotten members, Sexby condenses and appropriates architectural and body politic imagery and establishes radical alliances. Richard Overton had recently called the Presbyterian members of Parliament "corrupt and putrefied members."[156] And in September, shortly before the grandees removed him from the Council, Major Francis White

153. *LM* 145.
154. Ibid. 201, 211.
155. *CP* 1.227–8.
156. *LM* 167.

told them "that they were repairing an old house and that when they were laying the top stone, it would fall about their ears."[157] Sexby's speech underlines the discrete and even antagonistic *interests* emerging into a debate in the public sphere. The possibility of satisfying all, even as a rhetorical ideal, is forever lost. In this face-to-face address of a cavalry trooper to his generals, we see that the world of deferential consensus, if it ever truly existed, was much blasted. Invoking the biblical archetype for holy separation, Sexby insists that the only possibility of a consensus lies not in the rotten Egypt of the past, but in the Canaan of the future.

Rainsborough briefly acknowledged the importance of formal unity, then subordinated it to matters of substance:

> Truly I think we are utterly undone if we divide, but I hope that honest things have carried us on thus long, and will keep us together, and I hope that we shall not divide. Another thing is difficulties. Oh, unhappy men are we that ever began this war; if ever we looked upon difficulties, I do not know truly that ever we should have looked an enemy in the face.

On the second day of debate, he moved "That the Army might be called to a rendezvous, and things settled."[158] Ireton responded by distinguishing regular divisions (for instance, generals dividing and distributing their soldiers to various camps) from divisions that destroy an army (for instance, Parliament's earlier attempt to send some New Model forces to Ireland, and the attempts of some—the New Agents?—to sow dissent in the ranks). The latter sort of division destroys an army's traditional discipline and leaves it "no more an army than a rotten carcass is a man."[159] Rainsborough responded, "If this gentleman had declared to us at first that this was the sense of the Army in dividing, and it was meant that men should not divide in opinions—to me that is a mystery." An unnamed Agitator diverted Ireton's charge: "Whereas you say the Agents did it, the soldiers did put the Agents upon these meetings. It was the dissatisfactions that were in the Army which provoked, which occasioned those meetings, which you suppose tends so much to dividing."[160] After a reading of *The Agreement*, Cromwell revealed the true nature of his fear:

> Truly this paper does contain in it very great alterations of the very government of the kingdom, alterations from that government that it hath been under, I believe I may almost say since it was a nation. . . . How do we know if, whilst we are disputing these things, another company of men shall not gather together and put out a paper as plausible perhaps as this?

He begins to fear a Swiss confusion, with one "canton," even one county, against another.[161] As so frequently in the seventeenth century, a

---

157. *The Copy of a Letter Sent to His Excellency Sir Thomas Fairfax*, 1647, 1.
158. *CP* 1.246, 346.
159. Ibid. 1.348.
160. Ibid. 1.349.
161. Ibid. 1.236–7.

suggestion of constitutional change prompts a conservative terror focused on the hydra-headed offspring of Babel and the republic.[162]

Some radicals attending the first day's debate seem to have spent that night composing an account of it for the soldiery who could not attend. The next day, October 29, Thomason acquired *A Cal to All the Soldiers of the Armie, by the Free People of England*.[163] It analyzed the stratagems of "crafty politicians and subtle Machiavellians," particularly Cromwell and Ireton's good cop/bad cop routine. Examining their rhetoric of divisiveness and unity, it remarked that they "talked of nothing but faction, dividing principles, anarchy, of hanging punishing, yea, and impudently maintained that your regiments were abused." It called the hysterical charges of anarchy "an old threadbare trick of the profane Court," and warned, "beware that ye be not frighted by the word *anarchy*, unto a love of *monarchy*, which is but the gilded name of *tyranny*; for anarchy had never been so much as once mentioned amongst you, had it not been for that wicked end."[164] It faulted Cromwell and Ireton for delivering accommodating speeches to the Commons "in the name of the whole Army," attacked Charles as a "man of blood," and invoked the most radical interpretation of *The Solemne Engagement*, reminding its readers that "WITH A WORD, YE CAN CREATE NEW OFFICERS; necessity hath no law, and against it there is no plea, the safety of the people is above all law."[165]

The grandees tried two strategies to derail the rational momentum of the debates. First, they declared their self-abnegating willingness to withdraw rather than create divisions. Ireton said that it did not matter to him whether England has a king, lords, or property—so long as he saw God's hand at work, he would submit to whatever came. Rainsborough responded, "For my part I differ in that. I do very much care whether a king or no king, lords or no lords, property or no property." He then added, "But as to this present business," and returned to the matter at hand in the debate.[166] Cromwell twice offered to withdraw himself from the Army rather than remain opposed to any consensus in favor of *The Agreement*, but Audley rejected this as a strategy of delay aimed at subverting the process of debate and resolution: "I see you have a long dispute that you do intend to dispute here till the tenth of March. . . . You have brought us into a fair pass, and the kingdom into a fair pass, for if your reasons are not satisfied, and we do not fetch all our waters from your wells, you threaten to withdraw yourselves."[167] Rejecting Cromwell's

---

162. Richard Jackson calls the Agitators "Babel's bricklayers" in *Quæries Proposd for the Agitators*, 1647, 1.

163. Perhaps because of its frenzied, overnight composition and publication, the pamphlet consists of two parts, numbered separately; Woodhouse excerpts it (*P&L* 439–43).

164. *Cal* 1.4, 5, 6. These words preview Rainsborough's words on October 29 (*CP* 1.308), but Wildman may also have been the author (*WSS* 227–8).

165. *Cal* 1.7, 2.5, 2.7 [i.e. 8].

166. *CP* 1.296, 304.

167. Ibid. 1.251, 328–9, 331.

histrionic selflessness, Rainsborough returned the debates to the rational adjudication of collective interests:

> This Gentleman says if he cannot go he will sit still. He thinks he hath a full liberty, we think we have not. There is a great deal of difference between us two. If a man hath all he doth desire; but I think I have nothing at all of what I fought for, I do not think the argument holds that I must desist as well as he.

He responded to Cromwell's hesitancy to take a vote by saying, "If it be put to the question we shall all know one another's mind. If it be determined and the resolutions known, we shall take such a course as to put it in execution."[168]

Second, the grandees attempted to disqualify their opponents by accusing them of individual willfulness. When Edward Sexby expressed his *resolution* not to give up his birthright, the word rankled, since it implied private will. Ireton responded, "I am sorry we are come to this point, that from reasoning one to another we should come to express our resolutions," and accused Sexby of making "a public disturbance upon a private prejudice."[169] But in the public sphere of a formal debate, such charges draw counter-charges: those who champion the public interest against the schemes of merely private men find themselves subject to the same charge, and so forced to debate the nature of the public interest. "Public" then comes out of the unexamined lifeworld and into the forum of rational debate. Sexby's first speech had already accused Cromwell and Ireton of "blasting" their own reputations by representing as the opinion of the entire Army their personal opinion that Parliament should make further addresses to the king.[170] Wildman seconded him in *Putney Projects*.[171] Cromwell and Ireton become merely private men who have misrepresented the public consensus of the General Council and the Army as a whole.

In the course of the debates, Sexby made only four recorded speeches, but each was a striking rhetorical performance, and he exercised an unusual influence on the course of the debates by goading Cromwell into four highly willful denunciations of his willfulness.[172] After the second, Rainsborough defended Sexby with a brief critique of deference: "I wonder how that should be thought willfulness in one man that is reason in another."[173] Sexby defended himself even more eloquently:

> I am sorry that my zeal to what I apprehend is good should be so ill resented. I am not sorry to see that which I apprehend is truth, but I am sorry the Lord hath darkened some so much as not to see it, and that is in short [this:]. Do you think it were a sad and miserable condition, that we have fought all this

168. Ibid. 1.334–5.
169. Ibid. 1.323–4.
170. Ibid. 1.228.
171. 1647, 43.
172. *CP* 1.227–8, 229; 322–3, 328; 329–30, 333; 377–8, 378.
173. Ibid. 1.329.

time for nothing? . . . Concerning my making rents and divisions in this way—as a particular, if I were but so, I could lie down and be trodden there. [But] truly I am sent by a regiment. If I should not speak, guilt shall lie upon me, and I think I were a covenant breaker. I do not know how we have [been] answered in our arguments, and I conceive we shall not accomplish them [our engagements?] to the kingdom when we deny them to ourselves. I shall be loath to make a rent and division, but, for my own part, unless I see this put to a question, I despair of an issue.[174]

Kishlansky sees Sexby's confession as a sincere one.[175] I'm more struck by his skill in placing himself among the Lord's sheep, Cromwell among his goats. He sarcastically appropriates Cromwell and Ireton's self-abnegating rhetoric of the day before. And his response recalls his March 30 defense before the House of Commons: as a representative of a regiment, he is himself and not himself; if he were to form a consensus with Cromwell, he fears he would betray the pledged group of his regiment. By reintegrating himself into a collective—the regiment he represents—Sexby brilliantly (and divisively) resists Cromwell's attempt to individuate him as self-willed, and with the collective authority produced by this previous vote electing him, he presses for a vote on *The Agreement*.

It's always hard to align certain political languages neatly with certain political positions, because people struggle *for* authoritative language, not just *with* it, and because speakers frequently find themselves occupying the rhetorical positions of their former opponents. At Putney, the grandees came surprisingly close to the patriarchalist position of James VI/I and Robert Filmer. Cromwell argues that the Army must "conform to the parliament that first gave them their being," and the soldiery to the orders of their general. In response to Rainsborough's assurance that there could be no forcible leveling of estates, since the commandments prohibit such a thing, Ireton ventures tentatively onto patriarchalist ground, trying to shore up the besieged authority of the hierarchical state with the (presumably) unassailable authority of the patriarchal family:

> Now then, as I say, I would misrepresent nothing; the answer which had anything of matter in it, the great and main answer upon which that which hath been said against this rests, that seemed to be: that it will not make the breach of property: that there is a law, "Thou shalt not steal." The same law says, "Honor thy father and mother"; and that law doth likewise extend to all that are our governors in that place where we are in. So that, by that there is a forbidding of breaking a civil law when we may live quietly under it, and a divine law.[176]

174. Ibid. 1.330.
175. "Consensus" 64–5.
176. *CP* 1.369–70, 310. See also Thomas Jordan's *Rules to Know a Royall King, from a Disloyall Subject* (1647) and the anonymous *The Case of the Army Soberly Discussed* (1647), which argues that many in the army are "servants and prentices not yet free, and children unmarried, whose parents are yet living, who but in obedience to the Parliament, and for the public service, would never have suffered them to go from them to be soldiers, and do not allow of any of their dealings" (4).

Rainsborough responds with nominal piety toward the metaphor:

> I would fain know what we have fought for, and this is the old law of England and that which enslaves the people of England that they should be bound by laws in which they have no voice at all. The great dispute is who is a right father and a right mother. I am bound to know who is my father and mother, and I take it in the same sense you do, I would have a distinction, a character whereby God commands me to honor, and for my part I look upon the people of England so, that wherein they have not voices in the choosing of their fathers and mothers, they are not bound to that commandment.[177]

By inserting "right" and "choice" into the hierarchical metaphor, Rainsborough strains it to the breaking point—as do radical political theorists who advise the body to remove a rotten head and attach a new one.

Religion forms the most contested political language at Putney. Don M. Wolfe sees a struggle between grandee piety and Leveller–Agitator secularism.[178] Kishlansky argues that religion helped to ensure that there was no real struggle at all, since "Unity, after all, had a divine model."[179] But Putney shows us rather a struggle between two economies of religion and politics. When the grandees invoke religion as an anti-rational brake on the egalitarian public sphere of debate and action, the radicals collapse religion and politics, charging the military and political action of the New Model with a religious fervor; when the grandees separate the spheres of nature and grace, the radicals reconnect them. This radical strategy appeared a month before the debates in A Discovery of the New Creation, a sermon that the Particular Baptist Thomas Collier preached to the Army at Putney, taking for his text 2 Peter 3.13: "Nevertheless we look for new heavens, and a new earth, wherein dwelleth righteousness." Collier's sermon moves with the accretive logic of sectarian écriture, but it also methodically defuses two forms of conservative theocratic rhetoric: Augustine's deferred millennialism and Paul's defense of de facto rule. In a wrenching reversal, Collier attacked those who distance God by projecting him beyond the heavens, calling them possessed by "low and carnal thoughts." He held off anti-political millennialism by arguing that Christ would come not in the body, but in the spirit of his active, striving saints. He then reduced the Solemn League and Covenant, the Presbyterians' revolutionary high-water mark of 1643, to the Mosaic Old Law:

> Here is the vanity of such persons that seek to uphold forms, fleshly actings, and fleshly compactings, the old ministry fetched out of human abilities, the wisdom of the flesh limiting the spirit to those human qualifications where he appears least, all these, both persons and things must bow down to the slaughter.

And he produced one of the most astonishing early modern readings of Romans 13, the favorite text of de factoist conservatives:

---

177. CP 1.310–11.
178. Milton in the Puritan Revolution, 1941; rpt New York 1963, 160.
179. "Consensus" 57.

This is the great work that God hath to effect in the latter days of the gospel, to reduce magisterial power to its primitive institution, that you may see Rom. 13.1: "There is no power but is ordained of God, and it is ordained for the punishment of them that do evil, but for the praise of them that do well." Although this end hath been a long time loosed, yet now God will reduce it to this institution.

Collier changes St Paul from an apologist for the powers that be to a revolutionary comrade of the powers that are becoming. He continues with a detailed list of "national grievances" and "temporal oppressions," including tyrannical laws, law French, prerogative power, tithes, and free quarter. He begs the Army to do something "for the kingdom that may engage their hearts unto you," underlining the inadequacy of prior engagements. He, too, warns that God will pour contempt on them "if once you turn aside from the public to your own private interests."[180]

To return to the debates proper: Cromwell had been and continued to be the object of fierce anti-sectarian polemic, but at Putney, he came to occupy the conservative position of his Presbyterian enemies, while the radicals assumed the sectarian role for themselves. At Putney, God the distant hierarch debates God the immanent associate. Theocratic bombast reached its high point in the debates in Lieutenant Colonel William Goffe's rhapsodic speech of October 28, famous for mentioning "God" or "the Lord" thirty times.[181] Goffe recalls God's special providences to his Army, laments the Army's current falling off from him, and prays for a reformation. This led to a resolution for a prayer meeting on the next day, and to the grandees' attempt to sidetrack the rational discursive momentum of the debates. Ireton worried aloud that many in the assembly, including himself, had forgotten God so much that they rushed into judgment and action, where "the main thing is for everyone to wait upon God."[182] Anticipating the next day's prayer meeting at the Quartermaster General's residence, Cromwell tried to bring God onto the side of grandee consensus through a devious pronoun shift, but he also revealed a certain wariness about religious rhetoric:

I hope we know God better than to make appearances of religious meetings as covers for designs for insinuation amongst you. . . . I pray God judge between you and us when we do meet, whether we come with engaged spirits to uphold

180. Collier, *A Discovery of the New Creation*, 1647, 15, 8, 28–9, 33–4, 36–8, 39–40; excerpted in *P&L* 390–96. Thomason collected his copy on October 28, which suggests some coordination with *The Agreement* and the debates. John Saltmarsh's letter of the same day to the Council of War exhorted them to "think it no shame to pass over into more righteous engagements" (rpt *Englands Friend Raised from the Grave*, 1649, 5). In the Whitehall Debates over how much liberty of conscience to grant in the revised *Agreement of the People*, Collier argued that the Hebraic judicial law had "no reference to us under the gospel," so the magistrate must derive his power either from God (in which case "let him shew it") or from "the agreement of the people"—or perhaps "*The Agreement of the People*" (*CP* 2.125).
181. *CP* 1.253–5.
182. Ibid. 1.256–7.

our own resolutions and opinions, or whether we shall lay down ourselves to be ruled [by him] and that which he shall communicate.[183]

But this program of pious delay failed, for Wildman spoke of a "desire to return a little to the business in hand," and the debates moved into a long and important discussion of pre-engagements.[184]

Moreover, the radicals spent an introspective night, and the next day, after the prayer meeting, they discovered a scriptural idiom which was not quite what the grandees had in mind; religion did not chill forward spirits, but fired them with millenarian ardor. It isn't clear when William Clarke began recording the speeches of the second day, October 29. But against Cromwell's wishes, it seems that what started out as a prayer meeting turned into a discussion of political liberties and the franchise.[185] This unpunctuated shift of speech genres suggested the very breakdown of spheres that the grandees dreaded, and encouraged new speakers to step forth. Captain John Clark began with a nonpartisan proposal that the Council submit the candle of reason to the spirit of God, not the other way around.[186] Then Goffe shared his meditations of the evening, which focused on the Book of Revelation, speaking of "the conjunction that is between Antichrist, or that mystery of iniquity in the world carried on by men that call themselves [the] church, that certainly it is with the conjunction of men in places of power or authority in the world, with kings and great men." He defines the "mystery of iniquity" (2 Thess. 2.7) as that recurrent tendency for Rome's enemies to romanize in turn, once they gain power. He proposes that they inquire whether or not they had endeavored to set up that power and that party (pretty clearly royalists) "which God hath engaged us to destroy." And he followed this exhortation with a claim that "What we do according to the will of God will not tend to division"—subtly but significantly distinct from a claim that division tends against the will of God. He concludes by calling for unity in the campaign against "the enemies of God."[187] The habits of introspective Puritan spirituality allow the individual saint to back the most radical proposal with the most impersonal authority imaginable.

The appeal to divine authority had become part of the debate, not an escape from it. Indeed, religion gives political novices like Robert Everard a dangerous foot in the door:

For my part I am but a poor man, and unacquainted with the affairs of the kingdom, yet this message God hath sent me to you, that there is great expectation of sudden destruction, and I would be loath to fill up that with

183. Ibid. 1.258, 279.
184. Ibid. 1.259.
185. The second day's debate took place at the Quartermaster General's residence, the site of the prayer meeting, not in Putney Church (*WSS* 230–31). The record proper begins only after some briefly noted "discourses of Commissary Cowling, Major [Francis] White, and others" (*CP* 1.280)—an inauspicious start for the grandees.
186. *CP* 1.280–81.
187. Ibid. 1.282–5.

words. We desire your joint consent to seek out some speedy way for the relief of the kingdom.[188]

Because the grandees' prayer meeting had become a convocation of plebeian prophets, Cromwell tentatively attempted to adjourn it, but he failed, and the debate then moved into its discussion of the franchise and the nature of political right, which we will consider in the next section.[189] Monday, November 1, the third day of debates, began with even more immediate connections of divine revelations to constitutional specifics. Captain Francis Allen revealed that God, who seems to have been running a skeptical eye over Ireton's *Heads of the Proposals*, told him to take away the "negative voice" or veto power of the king and the Lords, while Captain John Carter reveals "that he found not any inclination in his heart as formerly to pray for the king." When Cromwell tries to deny the authenticity of this testimony, Goffe defends the importance of considering revelation, noting that God speaks in different ways in different times, but at the present through the collective:

> God does not now speak by one particular man, but in every one of our hearts; and certainly if it were a dangerous thing to refuse a message that came from one man to many, it is a more dangerous thing to refuse what comes from God, being spoke by many to us. . . . it seems to me evident and clear, that this hath been a voice from heaven to us, that we have sinned against the Lord in tampering with his enemies.[190]

Goffe collapses popular debate and the divine will—a strategy opposite to Cromwell's exhortation to pious delay. We might compare *A Just Apologie for an Abused Armie*, in which "W. G." (perhaps Goffe) says that God took Fairfax away early in the Battle of Naseby to show his forces that they won by God alone—a radical and egalitarian bit of providence.[191] Similarly, in *A Glimpse of Sion's Glory*, Jeremiah Burroughs says, "The voice, of Jesus Christ reigning in his Church, comes first from the multitude, the common people."[192] While Fairfax is away, God and the New Model soldiery can unite in holy war or holy debate.

We have no records of Edward Sexby's fellowship in any gathered congregations, but he reveals a mastery of scriptural idioms in a brief jeremiad: "The Lord hath put you into a state . . . that you know not where you are. You are in a wilderness condition. . . . I think that we have gone about to heal Babylon, but she would not be healed. . . . We are going about to set up the power of kings, some part of it, which God will destroy."[193] Cromwell lamely questions Sexby's sincerity, quibbles with his

188. Ibid. 1.285–6; it's also possible this was William Everard, later the first leader of the Diggers.
189. Ibid. 1.286.
190. Ibid. 1.367–8, 374.
191. 1647, 6; *G* 469n.89.
192. *P&L* 234.
193. *CP* 1.377.

use of Scripture, and retreats to a pious delaying tactic: "I cannot but renew that caution that we should take heed what we speak in the name of the Lord. . . . I am one of those whose heart God hath drawn out to wait for some extraordinary dispensations, according to those promises that he hath held forth of things to be accomplished in the later times."[194] In a very long, Goffe-like speech, Ireton proclaims his self-abnegating readiness to submit to God even if he sees it "good to destroy, not only King and Lords, but all distinctions of degrees—nay if it go further, to destroy all property . . . if I see the hand of God in it I hope I shall with quietness acquiesce, and submit to it, and not resist it"—a cheap and general declaration of piety intended to hold off discussion of *The Agreement*. But later he admits the "human constitution" of property.[195]

Most important, within the very norms implied by the public sphere of the General Council, the radicals won. Their attempt to collapse rational debate and a providential war against Antichrist and his allies leads Cromwell himself to articulate a rational principle by which the voice of God might be determined. He recalls Paul's attempt to control the prophetic energies of the early Christian churches by limiting the authority of those who claimed immediate revelation: "That which he speaks was, that at such a meeting as this we should wait upon God, and the voice of God speaking in any of us. I confess it is an high duty, but when anything is spoken I think the rule is, let the rest judge!"[196] But in a nation of prophets or an assembly like that at Putney, where the prophets hold a voting majority, this delay was only temporary. The General Council would attain "consensus" by a vote, not by an appeal to some principle prior to interests. And a discussion of interests requires us to consider labor and warfare as well as rhetoric—sweat and blood as well as words.

Possessive Individualism and the Expense of Blood

In *The Political Theory of Possessive Individualism*, C. B. Macpherson argues against seeing the alienated capitalist model of the human personality as some modern falling-off from an earlier phase of hearty pre-capitalist democracy, since seventeenth-century British possessive individualists created that model, along with capitalism and liberal democracy. They saw the individual as "essentially the proprietor of his own person or capacities, owing nothing to society for them. The individual was seen neither as a moral whole, nor as part of a larger social whole, but as an owner of himself." Society consisted of no more than the market relations among a group of such proprietors, and "What makes a man human is his freedom from other men. Man's essence is freedom. Freedom is proprietorship of

194. Ibid. 1.378–9.
195. *CP* 1.296, 310–11.
196. 1 Cor. 14.29. *CP* 1.375.

one's own person and capacities." The limitations to this market-based model of society and consciousness appeared only in the nineteenth century, when "an industrial working class developed some class consciousness and became politically articulate. Men no longer saw themselves fundamentally equal in an inevitable subjection to the determination of the market."[197]

Macpherson's book controversially links together three political philosophers and one group whom others have struggled to distinguish. He nudges the received model of Hobbes to the left, saying that his retooled absolutism rests on an essentially bourgeois theory of radical individualism. He leaves Harrington more or less where Tawney left him: as a prophet of the rising or "bourgeois" gentry, with his classical republican identity shorn off. He grounds Locke solidly in a philosophy of human nature based on absolute property. And most controversially, he moves "the Levellers" (his name for civilian and Army radicals) to the right: because they assert the interests of a modestly propertied petite bourgeoisie against the landed aristocracy and the poor, they prefigure radical liberals, not radical democrats. At Putney, he says, they proposed merely to double the franchise, excluding "servants" (including all wage earners) and "beggars" (including all receivers of alms). Like Kishlansky, Macpherson emphasizes the radicals' ties with the grandees, but where Kishlansky sees them sharing an essentially backward-looking metaphysics of religious hierarchalism, Macpherson sees them sharing an essentially forward-looking ideology of bourgeois individualism. The Levellers failed because they thought "in terms of proprietorship, and a proprietorship not so very different in kind from their opponents."[198] Though he avoids any significant discussion of Marx, he works from a classically Marxist suspicion of bourgeois democracy, seeing its egalitarian pretensions as a screen for class inequalities in civil society. We might compare "On the Jewish Question," where Marx defines bourgeois liberty as a right "based not on the association of man with man, but on the separation of man from man. It is the *right* of this separation, the right of the *restricted* individual, withdrawn into himself."[199]

Macpherson's rigorous demystification of liberal humanist individualism has attracted postmodernist cultural critics, as they seek out individualist, subject-centered, transcendental fictions and reveal their social construction. But most historians have been more skeptical. Norah Carlin points out that "servants" forms a ductile category—that many young men working as apprentices or domestic servants had high hopes of leaving their servant status behind and setting up an independent household.[200] Keith Thomas says Macpherson overemphasizes the role of the franchise in the larger Leveller program of political emancipation. Both Thomas

197. Oxford 1962, 3, 142, 271.
198. 158, 151.
199. *MECW* 3.162–3.
200. *First* 23.

and A. L. Morton say he overlooks the narrow seventeenth-century definition of "servants" and "beggars," and so underestimates the significance
of the Levellers' proposal to expand the franchise to non-servants.[201] Iain
Hampsher-Monk finds Macpherson leaning too far toward the "liberal"
world, overlooking the conservative, communitarian, and distinctly pre-
capitalist meaning for the radicals of such key terms in these debates as
"equity" and "propriety."[202] Thomas, Morton, and Anthony Arblaster find
Macpherson misconstruing the very object of his study, which is, after all,
a *debate*.[203] In struggling to establish a Leveller consensus that would
underlie the entire debate, Macpherson discounts the variety of radical
opinion and bases too much of his argument on a single statement by a
distinctly peripheral figure, the Leveller Maximilian Petty, who proposed
to disenfranchise servants and apprentices dependent on the will of their
masters.[204] Macpherson himself lists at least a dozen passages when the
radicals seem to demand universal male suffrage, but "the only consistent
construction of the debate as a whole suggests that the Levellers (and
their opponents) assumed that servants and alms-takers, as well as crimi-
nals and delinquents, had lost their birthright."[205]

But philosophers with a historical bent, particularly marxist ones,
should beware of constructing debates too consistently. Macpherson falls
into a form of economic reduction that one may criticize from within the
marxist philosophy of history. Arblaster notes that, by conflating figures
like Hobbes and the Levellers, Macpherson employs a schematic model
that reduces history to a stagist transition from one non-contradictory
mode of production to another, with each essentially unified by the
consensual ideology of its ruling class. If the Levellers are not feudal serfs,
then they must be bourgeois—specifically, a party of petty bourgeois
liberals masquerading as radical democratic plebeians. But particularly at
moments of intense revolutionary conflict like 1647, we need not limit
ourselves to a two-class model of society.[206] Certainly, Marx himself felt no
such compulsion in *The Eighteenth Brumaire of Louis Napoleon*: if the struggle
of bourgeoisie and proletariat finally determined the non-revolution of
1848, this struggle becomes intelligible only inside a complex historical
narrative charting the interactions and struggles among the aristocracy of
finance, the industrial bourgeoisie, the landed bourgeoisie, the small
bourgeoisie, the army, the Parisian proletariat and lumpenproletariat, the
clergy, the peasantry, and the intellectuals.[207]

201. "The Levellers and the Franchise," in G. E. Aylmer, ed., *The Interregnum*, London 1972,
    57–78; Morton, *World* 197–219.
202. "The Political Theory of the Levellers," *Political Studies* 24.4, 1976.
203. Arblaster, "Revolution, the Levellers and C. B. Macpherson," Barker et al., *1642* 220–37.
204. *CP* 1.342. In "Maximilian Petty and the Putney Debate on the Franchise" (*Past and
    Present* 88, 1980), Christopher Thompson argues that Petty's other speeches point in a
    more radical direction (*CP* 1.294, 300, 312–13, 335–6, 336, 351–2).
205. *Political* 125, 122.
206. "Revolution" 232–3.
207. *MECW* 11.99–197.

At times Macpherson himself sounds more like a disillusioned liberal than a marxist: in his book, as in so much leftish social and cultural theory, the "aha!" that accompanies a demystifying discovery of "mere" workplace concerns with hours and wages reveals the distance between salaried academics, with a distant memory or no experience at all of time clocks, and their wage-earning objects of study. But the superficially "possessive individualist" struggle for higher wages and a shorter workday lies at the very center of Marx's historical analysis of class struggle in *Capital*. Marx does not utterly reject the possessive individualist model of the human essence, but emancipates and collectivizes it. Communism would replace alienated "proprietorship" with the free association of direct producers—the freedom to labor in a calling, to associate, to help determine the direction of group praxis, including productive labor. Moreover, possessive individualism never rules the field: *Homo oeconomicus* must associate with others in order to remain living *Homo* of any sort, and the most degraded ideological defense of atomized necessity in the private sphere of civil society seeks out a supplementary utopian theory of collective freedom in some other sphere, whether the state, the church, the aesthetic or political public sphere, the intimate sphere of the family, or even insubordinate practices of association within the private sphere itself.

For instance, the hierarchical necessity of the New Model chain of command exists alongside a utopian domain of free, associative collectivity in the congregation and prayer meeting, the General Council, and even inside the regiments themselves insofar as they chose to cashier royalist officers and elect representative Agitators. Moreover, if the New Model had consisted of pure possessive individualists, we would expect to see soldiers' demands for back pay predominate over their collective demands. But the question of arrears did not loom large in the tumults of 1647.[208] In demanding pensions for their wounded comrades and their survivors, in denouncing the ethical assault on their collective honor in *The Declaration of Dislike*, and in resisting their piecemeal disbandment or transfer to Ireland, the soldiers of the New Model did not embrace possessive individualism but spurned it.

Macpherson argues that radicals turned to possessive individualism because it gave them a valid justification for bourgeois theories of obligation.[209] Thus he inverts Marx's aphorism: "It is not the consciousness of men that determines their existence, but their social existence that determines their consciousness."[210] New Model soldiers were, among other things, workers, and if they were not exactly proletarians, their movement through a particular sort of labor to a new sort of consciousness suggests Marx's analysis of the dialectical emergence of proletarian class

208. *G* 48, 52.
209. *Political* 82. Macpherson glances at but then ignores the Diggers and the communitarian aspects of Leveller ideology itself (ibid. 272–3, 154–7).
210. *MECW* 29.263.

consciousness. In the classic account of *The Communist Manifesto,* one revolutionary class project emerges as the unintended consequence of another. Capitalists call together expropriated small producers or their descendants as proletarians working under a regime of industrial discipline. Through the wage contract, they extract the surplus value they create and simultaneously destroy the pre-capitalist or feudal mode of production. But in producing the proletariat, they unintentionally allow it to gain consciousness of itself. As the proletariat discovers its epochal productive powers, it begins to reflect critically on the oppressive relations of production that called it into existence, then organizes itself for the class struggle that will transform or destroy those relations.[211] Similarly, the English parliamentary ruling classes, including the grandees, call soldiers together under a regime of military discipline. They direct them in battle and prevent the king's efforts to turn England into an absolutist state, independent of parliamentary supply. But in producing the New Model Army, they unintentionally allow it to gain consciousness of itself. As the New Model discovers its epochal powers of nation formation, it begins to reflect critically on the oppressive political relations that called it into existence, then organizes itself for the struggle that will transform or destroy those relations.

This is not to equate Putney in October 1647 with the English Midlands in 1848 or St Petersburg in 1917. For one thing, warfare demands a very special sort of labor, with a temporal, ethical, and existential status distinct from that of productive labor. New Model soldiers were by no means communists, and a year and a half after the Putney Debates, they would help to repress the Diggers. Moreover, whether enlisted or impressed, soldiers typically joined the Army under circumstances quite distinct from the capitalist work contract, that ulcerous amalgam of legal freedom and economic necessity. But their radicalism contains at least two important "proletarian" aspects: first, they organized themselves politically in their workplace, the regimental muster. Second, their labor—their collective martial praxis—grounded their claims to political authority. The public sphere of the Army did not resemble the bourgeois public sphere analyzed by Habermas so much as it did the soviets of the 1920s: "there had been nothing like this spontaneous outbreak of democracy in any English or continental army before this year of 1647, nor was there anything like it thereafter till the Workers' and Soldiers' Councils met in 1917 in Russia."[212] The General Council of the Army was not a united bourgeois or proto-bourgeois public sphere, with the Putney Debates as a rational discussion among "as if" equals. Rather, it was an unsuccessful grandee/

---

211. Ibid. 6.492–3; see also 35.750.
212. Brailsford, *Levellers* 181, 410–12. See also Hill (*World* 63) and Woolrych, who says George Joyce acted at Holmby "as *primus inter pares* in what can well be likened to a military soviet" (*WSS* 109–10). Callinicos discusses democracy in the soviets (*The Revenge of History*, University Park, PA, 1991, 17–18, 97–8, 110–19). See also Leon Trotsky, *1905,* New York 1971.

capitalist attempt to contain and manage the public sphere of laboring-class radicals and their civilian allies. For the rest of this section, I will concentrate on the conflict between the grandees' model of political life as a hierarchical property (a model with no affinity at all with the institutions of egalitarian publicness), and the radicals' model of an associative praxis. This conflict appears in two conflicting accounts of the meaning of the war, two notions of the franchise, two models of the law, and ultimately two ideas of the human essence.

Ireton clearly articulates the grandee model: "All the main thing that I speak for is because I would have an eye to property." For Ireton, all discussions return sooner or later to real property: no person has a right to determine laws in the kingdom "that hath not a permanent fixed interest in this kingdom." Such an interest lies in "the persons in whom all land lies, and those in corporations in whom all trading lies." No man should have the franchise who can lift up and carry his "interest" about with him—"He that is here today, and gone tomorrow, I do not see that he hath such a permanent interest." Those without freehold property may claim a place to stand and the right to breathe and travel the highways unimpeded, but they have no more political right than do foreigners. In a phrase that would be immediately intelligible to Edmund Burke, Ireton sees political life as a sort of common law inheritance which, like freehold property itself, stretches back "beyond memory."[213] Pocock explains Ireton's logic:

> For Ireton the land must be freehold, or at least assimilable to the legal concept of freehold tenure; it must be capable of being conceived of as an inheritance at common law, which was itself an inheritance of customs from time immemorial, since there was no other way of anchoring the individual, from birth and at the moments of majority and inheritance, within a structure of law and property he could be obliged and committed to defend.[214]

For the grandees, the connection of property and politics is something more than an analogy, since property formed a precondition for political right, ensured that this right would be an entailed inheritance, and formed the very object of most political discourse. The grandees cannot imagine what politics might consist of other than the adjudication of rival claims to property, which makes them worry about what landless plebeians would get up to once enfranchised. If a state gives the vote to "any man that hath a breath and being," it will "destroy property. . . . show me what you will stop at; wherein you will fence any man in a property by this rule."[215]

The first day's debates focus on the grounds for engagements—not a topic that immediately suggests property right. But it leads Ireton to the landholder's primal fear: if we admit the possibility of revoking prior

213. *CP* 1.306, 302, 308, 300.
214. *The Machiavellian Moment*, Princeton 1975, 376.
215. *CP* 1.314.

engagements, then the only ground for such a revocation can be natural right, which conjures up the specter of communism. One must abide by covenants freely entered into:

> Take away that[, and] I do not know what ground there is of anything you can call any man's right. I would very fain know what you gentlemen, or any other, do account the right you have to anything in England, anything of estate, land, or goods, that you have, what ground, what right you have to it.[216]

In chapter 4, I called this fearful argument the *reductio ad Münsterum*, whereby emancipation in one sphere immediately threatens to infect others more vital. Here, if anywhere, we see the "organic" quality of early modern society, or the early modern domino theory of anarchic emancipation, or the conservative perspective on Woodhouse's dialectic of separation and analogy.

But Ireton's redbaiting homily for landlords falls flat at Putney. While it might have done him yeoman's service at the gentry hearthsides of Attenborough, Oxford, or the Middle Temple, it fails to move an assembly of (mostly) impoverished radicals, who simply do not have that much to lose. Moreover, religion provided Thomas Rainsborough with an easy retort: "That there's a property, the law of God says it; else why God made that law, 'Thou shalt not steal?'"[217] More important, the radicals had an alternative model of law that could conceive of the human personality apart from the transmission of property through time—namely, a populist and present-centered theory of natural law supplemented by a critical and historically centered theory of positive law or the "law of nations."[218] The radicals shied away from explicitly endorsing radical natural law, perhaps under the pressure of Ireton's attempt to link it to communism. Still some of their most quoted and most eloquent statements argue that right flows from (male) human nature, not from bloodline, status, or property ownership. Thomas Rainsborough said, "I think that the poorest he that is in England hath a life to live as the greatest he."[219] His brother William

216. Ibid. 1.263. Compare Pocock, who says Ireton is "not so much defending a particular form of property as seizing the high ground in debate"—an interesting metaphor but a dubious argument, since it separates property forms from the authority of legal systems underwriting and underwritten by them (*Virtue* 57).

217. *CP* 1.309.

218. On Levellers, Agitators, and natural law theory, see *P&L* [87–95]; Richard A. Gleissner, "The Levellers and Natural Law," *Journal of British Studies* 20.1, 1980; Gregg, *Free-Born John* 217–18; Ellen Meiksins Wood and Neal Wood, *A Trumpet of Sedition*, New York 1997, 84–6; and Richard Tuck, *Natural Rights Theories*, Cambridge 1979. In *The Declaration* of June 14, Ireton yoked natural law to its staid chaperon by referring to "the law of nature and nations" (*D* 40). Wildman echoed him in *The Case of the Army* and the Putney Debates (*LM* 205; *CP* 1.260). Natural law was by no means intrinsically radical, for just as there was an associative body politic, so there was a hierarchical law of nature: Richard Jackson's tenth query for the Agitators asks how army commanders can ensure that the common soldiers "shall not rebel against the law of nature in abominating all ability of brain and spirit, exceeding their own proportion" (*Quæres* 3).

219. *CP* 1.301; he may have been remembering Lilburne's *Charters of London*: "the poorest that lives hath as true a right to give a vote, as well as the richest and greatest" (Brailsford, *Levellers* 117).

added, "the chief end of this government is to preserve persons as well as estates, and if any law shall take hold of my person it is more dear than my estate."[220] When Rich worries about leveling in England, where "five to one ... have no permanent interest," Thomas Rainsborough warns that, in a plutocracy, "the one part shall make hewers of wood and drawers of water of the other five, and so the greatest part of the nation be enslaved."[221]

Turning from natural law, Wildman proposes a critical vision of positive law or the "law of nations" as the spoils of conquest: "Our very laws were made by our conquerors; and whereas it's spoken much of chronicles, I conceive there is no credit to be given to any of them; and the reason is because those that were our lords, and made us their vassals, would suffer nothing else to be chronicled." Wildman's conventional anti-Normanism acquires new force when pronounced inside a victorious army with the power to undo the Conquest.[222] On the other hand, Thomas Rainsborough attacks Ireton's idea of common law as a placid accretion of property and right:

> I hear it said, "It's a huge alteration, it's a bringing in of new laws," and that this kingdom hath been under this government ever since it was a kingdom. If writings be true there hath been many scufflings between the honest men of England and those that have tyrannized over them; and if it be read, there is none of those just and equitable laws that the people of England are born to but that they are entrenchments altogether.[223]

In the abstract, Wildman's view of the law as the instrument of the conquering and ruling classes conflicts with Rainsborough's view of the law as a record of popular resistances, and both jar with a concept of natural law. But all three came together in a vision of law as class struggle and mutable praxis rather than property and patrimony, and they comprise essential components of any critical history of the law.[224]

An implicit controversy between these two visions of politics and law emerges around the very word "propriety" or "property." For the grandees, it refers to the real property that grounds political right; for the

---

220. *CP* 1.320.
221. Ibid. 1.315, 320; Rainsborough alludes to Josh. 9.21, 23, 27.
222. Ibid. 1.318. Richard Baxter shuddered at the rhetorical questions of Army radicals: "They said, what were the lords of England but William the Conqueror's colonels? or the barons but his majors? or the knights but his captains?" (*Reliquiae* 51).
223. *CP* 1.246; Firth glosses, "All the good laws we now enjoy were innovations once, and entrenchments on the rights of the king or the lords."
224. In "The Norman Conquest and the Common Law," *The Historical Journal* 24.4, 1981, R. B. Seaberg argues that the Levellers' distinction between the common law's tyrannical procedures and its frequently libertarian substance explains how "they could both criticize English law as a creature of Norman force and call on it for support and defense" (794).

radicals, it refers to natural right.[225] After Ireton asks how this expansion of the franchise will make it possible to "fence any man in a property," Rainsborough responds, "I desire to know how this comes to be a property in some men, and not in others." Rainsborough's "this" presumably refers to political right, not property right, but at least a trace of ambiguity persists. Colonel Rich then chimes in with his warning against leveling, and Rainsborough reiterates his argument:

> I should not have spoken again[.] I think it is a fine gilded pill, but there is much danger and it may seem to some, that there is some kind of remedy[.] I think that we are better as we are, that the poor shall choose many[.] Still the people are in the same case, are overvoted still, and therefore truly sir I should desire to go close to the business, and the thing that I am unsatisfied in is how it comes about there is such a propriety in some freeborn Englishmen, and not others.[226]

Again, Rainsborough uses the term ambiguously, and Cowling introduces another political language with a similar ambiguity: "Whether the younger son have not as much right to the inheritance as the eldest?" By "eldest son," Cowling presumably means those with a forty-shilling freehold enfranchised by *The Heads of the Proposals*, and by "younger son" all freeborn Englishmen. But others adopted this metaphor to argue against primogeniture, and even for communism.[227] Cowling almost seems to be trying to aggravate Ireton's fears.[228]

225. On the early modern lexical shift from "property" as indicating one of several rights or uses different persons might have in the same object (say, a tract of land) to the more absolute modern definition, see Hampsher-Monk, "Political"; G. E. Aylmer, "The Meaning and Definition of 'Property' in Seventeenth-Century England," *Past and Present* 86, 1980; and Margaret Sampson, " 'Property' in Seventeenth-Century English Political Thought," Schochet, *Religion* 259–75.

226. In my version of this crucial speech, I simply modernize spelling, create the first two bracketed periods from apparent commas (Clarke himself frequently fails to distinguish them), and add the third (*CM* 65.42ᵛ). Firth's version (*CP* 1.315–16) is considerably freer, and Woodhouse's freer still, for he separates "the poor" from "the people" by changing punctuation, adding a conditional phrase, and twice turning an indicative *are* into a subjunctive *be*: "But there is much danger, and it may seem to some that there is some kind of remedy [possible]. I think that we are better as we are [if it can be really proved] that the poor shall choose many [and] still the people [be] in the same case, [be] over-voted still" (*P&L* 64). Macpherson uses Woodhouse's text to argue that Rainsborough "would prefer the present property qualification rather than risk that 'the poor' should out-vote 'the people.' . . . The text is not entirely clear, but it is difficult to see what other construction can be put on it" (*Political* 128). In my reading, which follows Rainsborough's populist thorough bass through this day of the debates, "the poor" and "the people" are the same, and "as we are" refers to *The Agreement*'s call for manhood suffrage, not the current franchise.

227. Joan Thirsk, "Younger Sons in the Seventeenth Century," in *The Rural Economy of England*, London 1984, 335–58.

228. Cowling's metaphorical fervor rends the veil and lets a little Digger light shine in, but his next speech suggests a historical vision closer to Harrington's: the medieval Commons used the traditional forty-shilling freehold to avoid being overbalanced by the Lords with all their vassals, but "Now the case is not so: all slaves have bought their freedoms" (*CP* 1.316). The argument recalls Bacon's in *History of King Henry VII* (*Works*, 14 vols, Boston 1861, 11.11–389), which Cowling read by 1650 (*A Survey of Tyrannie*

Sexby's even more contentious speeches reveal that "birthright," like "property," has one foot in each side of the conflict. After Ireton tries to ground political right in real property, Sexby delivers his most famous speech:

> I see that though it [the liberty of the people] were our end, there is a degeneration from it. We have engaged in this kingdom and ventured our lives, and it was all for this: to recover our birthrights and privileges as Englishmen, and by the arguments urged there is none. There are many thousands of us soldiers that have ventured our lives; we have had little propriety in the kingdom as to our estates, yet we have had a birthright. But it seems now except a man hath a fixed estate in this kingdom, he hath no right in this kingdom. I wonder we were so much deceived. If we had not a right to the kingdom, we were mere mercenary soldiers. There are many in my condition, that have as good a condition, it may be little estate they have at present, and yet they have as much a right as those two who are their lawgivers, as any in this place. I shall tell you in a word my resolution. I am resolved to give my birthright to none.[229]

"Birthright," one of the most resonant metaphors in the debates and indeed in all the Leveller writings of the summer, combines a conservative vehicle and a radical tenor. Ultimately, it derives from Genesis 25, where Esau trades his birthright to his younger brother Jacob for a mess of pottage. On the one hand, it's akin to "natural right," the right men have by virtue of simply being born, and the story had a clear and immediate application at a time when Parliament was offering the pottage of disbandment pay to soldiers willing to give up their hard-won stake in the Revolution. But its origin in the domain of patriarchal primogeniture inoculates it against anticommunist calumny. Sexby saw his birthright as simultaneously a lost "privilege" to be recovered through warfare, a quality inhering in one's personality like natural right, and something one could alienate to others through a social compact—though he "resolves" not to do so.[230]

But natural right is more than a rhetoric: just as the grandees' limited franchise derives from a vision of common law anchored in real property (which is to say, ownership of the means of production and so the power to appropriate the labor of others), so the radicals' vision of an expanded franchise derives from a vision of natural law anchored in their own labor. If the grandees see natural law as a roguish and willful impulse, the

---

28–9), and which Harrington would use to describe the destruction of feudal England's "modern prudence" (*The Political Works of James Harrington*, Cambridge 1977, 45, 157–8, 197n.3).

229. *CP* 1.322–3.

230. Perhaps Sexby echoed Overton's *A Defiance*: "I'll not sell my birthright for a mess of pottage, for justice is my natural right" (Morton, *World* 217). On "freeborn" and "birthright," see Lilburne's *Englands Birth-Right Justified*, 1645; Thomas, "Levellers"; and Hill, *Change* 219–38.

radicals anchor it in the collective labor of the New Model soldiery.[231] Where the grandees see Parliament as fathers who have given the Army birth and being, or as owners who have hired them as laborers, the radicals see themselves as owner-producers who have elected for them-selves a particularly hazardous sort of labor. They advance this case by drawing together the egalitarian idioms of labor and expense, on the one hand, of blood and life, on the other. A March pamphlet insisted that "the people are not so stupid, but do expect a more exact accompt and simple satisfaction, then they have had, for their profuse expense of wealth and blood."[232] A broadside poem of July asked,

> Is this the upshot then? We that have spent
> Our best of fortunes for a parliament?
> We that have sweat in blood, marched o'er the land,
> And where our feet did tread, our swords command? . . .
> Who gave your Senate being? the laws their breath?
> Was't not our blood? our hazarding of death?
> And will you counsel murther? fit to slay
> Even those by whom you sit, or whom, you stay?[233]

A Declaration or Representation referred to "the purchasing of such rights and liberties as they have enjoyed through the price of their blood, and we, both by that and the later blood of our dear friends and fellow soldiers, with the hazard of our own, do now lay claim to."[234] In May, Rich's regiment invoked "the price of our blood" and "the scarlet dye of our valiant fellow-soldiers' blood," while Lambert's complained that "after so great expense of blood, treasure, and time, we look for execution of justice but behold tyranny and oppression."[235] In a letter to the cavalry of the Northern Army, the Agitators of horse said the freedoms of the nation had been "purchased" by "many of our dearest bloods."[236] The Case of the Armie referred to the liberties "purchased by blood," to the wars which caused "the expense of so much blood," and "the price of blood" with which "the people have bought their rights and freedoms."[237] The Agree-ment of the People recalled "the examples of our ancestors, whose blood was often spent in vain for the recovery of their freedoms."[238] Francis White complained about the House's concern for the king, and lack of any

---

231. This is why I think Gleissner shouldn't try to remove the discussion of natural law at Putney "from the limitations of time and place" and resituate it "in the mainstream of realist philosophy" (76)—a mainstream that would drown Agitator "Buffe-Coate" (CP 1.235) without a second thought.
232. A Warning for all the Counties, 4–5.
233. I. H. [John Harris?], The Souldiers Sad Complaint.
234. P&L 404–5.
235. CM 41.113ʳ, 124ʳ.
236. CP 1.91.
237. LM 204, 213, 214.
238. Ibid. 226, 228.

desire "to gratify the exhausted commons for the expense of so much treasure and blood."[239]

The phrase became a plebeian blazon for the Good Old Cause. In 1649, *The English Souldiers Standard* asserted that the people's "just rights and liberties . . . purchased with so vast expense of blood," authorized them to hold their generals' hands when they reversed their cannons.[240] Winstanley claimed "universal liberty and freedom" as the people's "birthright," which "we have bought with our money, in taxes, free-quarter, and blood shed," and observed that the Hebrews earned Canaan "by the purchase of their blood and labor," contrasting the capitalist English settlement he feared.[241] In September 1654, the Baptist and Fifth Monarchist *Declaration of Several of the Churches of Christ* accused Cromwell of giving "advantage to Charles Stuart or some others, to invade us, our lives, our relations, afresh, by open wars, inundation of blood and mischief, so as seems to make void and uneffectual many years' wars, with vast treasure, expense, and blood."[242] The next month, in their *Humble Petition*, the Three Colonels warned Cromwell that "the price of our blood is brought to the utmost crisis of danger."[243] In his *Declaration of the Free and Well-Affected People of England* (1655), John Wildman referred to "the expense of so much precious Christian blood, for the settling the rights and liberties due unto us as men and Christians."[244] In *A Copy of a Letter from an Officer of the Army in Ireland*, "R. G." hoped that a free parliament in 1656 would compensate the people of England for their "expense of blood and treasure."[245] And in *Killing Noe Murder* (1657), Edward Sexby told his fellow soldiers that, under Cromwell, they had "purchased nothing but our slavery with the price of our blood."[246]

The metaphor may seem tame and tedious to us, but it seems to have had an abiding power for the New Model. It probably originated with Paul's words about Christ in his warning to the Ephesian elders (*presbuterous*) in Acts 20.28: "Take heed therefore unto yourselves, and to all the flock, over the which the Holy Ghost hath made you overseers, to feed the church of God, which he hath purchased with his own blood." Significantly, it refers not to the guilty shedding of another's blood, but to the willing expense of one's own. Where the recurrent references to Charles as "that man of blood" point toward regicidal state violence, "the expense of blood" points toward labor and even class struggle: the collective existential investment in replacing one political system with

239. *The Copy* 5.
240. Morton, *Freedom* 234.
241. *W* 256, 524.
242. 15.
243. Thomas Saunders, John Okey, and Matthew Alured, *The Humble Petition of Several Colonels of the Army*, 1654.
244. Whitelocke, *Memorials* 606.
245. 23.
246. *S* 14.

another.[247] By yoking "expense" and "blood," the radicals formed an implicit critique of possessive individualism. Unlike wage laborers in general, combat soldiers can never lose sight of the intimate and inseparable connection between their labor and their human essence. They cannot view their labor as a substance alienated for a time in exchange for wages, and then taken back again, since it is so hazardous that it threatens the very existence of the laborer; alienated blood is alienated for good.[248] Nor can he easily think of his relation to his fellow soldiers, upon whom he depends for his very life, as a mere relation among proprietors. After all, Parliament's very attempt to restore them through disbandment to the state of disconnected possessive individuals sparked their outraged protests and drove them into vocal radicalism. Just before the debates began, the New Agitators addressed their regiments, saying, "Gentlemen, we doubt not but the hazarding of our lives together for our country's freedom, have so endeared us each to other, and so imprinted the principles of common freedom in our hearts, that it's impossible to divide us from each other, whilst we insist upon the same principles."[249] Thomas Rainsborough's ferocious challenge to the grandees underlined the utopian power of this associative impulse: "I am loath to leave the army with whom I will live and die, insomuch that rather then I will lose this regiment of mine the Parliament shall exclude me the house, [or] imprison me."[250]

The image of the New Model as possessive individualists typically emerges from their enemies. Nathaniel Ward, the "Simple Cobbler of Agawam," compared their defeating the king then turning on Parliament to hired sailors driving off pirates then seizing the ship from its owners.[251] But the New Model soldiers themselves spurned any attempt by their leaders (Parliament first, later the grandees) to view them as mere wage

247. The author of *A Cal*, possibly Wildman, called the king "a man of blood; over head and ears in the blood of your dearest friends and fellow commoners" (2.5), but the idea of blood guilt appealed to conservatives like Christopher Love as much as to radicals. See Patricia Crawford, "'Charles Stuart, That Man of Blood,'" *Journal of British Studies*, 1977, 51; Hill, *English* 324–31. For the distinction between an individual and a collective/ structural ethics of political struggle, see Sarah Barber's *Regicide and Republicanism*, Edinburgh 1998.

248. Maternal praxis trumps martial praxis as a form of dispossessive individualist labor. As countless works by and for early modern women reveal, pregnancy and childbirth entailed a starkly predictable expense of blood, frequently fatal (Antonia Fraser, *The Weaker Vessel*, New York 1984, 59–80). But more or less mandatory married sexuality made it hard for women to view maternal praxis as an elective activity like that of the citizen soldier. I haven't seen any early modern discussions of childbearing as a sort of productive labor, though the idea of Protestant motherhood as vocation comes close. The threat of military conscription and compulsory pregnancy in the US continues to cast the shadow of unfree labor over these two primal sorts of praxis.

249. *Two Letters from the Agents of the Five Regiments of Horse*, 1647, 4.

250. *CP* 1.245.

251. *Resona Recessus*, 1647, 6. See also Samuel Butler's character of "A Soldier" as one who "pawns his life to get his living," who "exposes life and blood to sale, and is willing to consign his body over to death or slavery for any man, that will advance most upon it" (*Characters and Passages from Notebooks*, Cambridge 1908, 313).

laborers. Indeed, no word aroused more New Model loathing than "mercenary." Ireton's June 14 *Representation* declared the New Model "not a mere mercenary army, hired to serve any arbitrary power of a state, but called forth and conjured by the several declarations of Parliament to the defense of our own and the people's just rights and liberties."[252] *The Case of the Armie* recalled the passage twice.[253] In a fictional dialogue, a minister counsels a soldier to be prudent in demanding his arrears: "If that be the only, or the main groundwork of the soldiers' intentions, then both in all the good that they have well done: and in whatsoever they shall do, they are but merely mercenary, which (I confess) is but a base term, if deserved by military men."[254] As we have just seen, Ireton heard his own word thrown back at him in the Putney Debates, when Edward Sexby responded to him, "I wonder we were so much deceived. If we had not a right to the kingdom, we *were* mere mercenary soldiers."[255] We can also hear this argument in *The Mercenary Soldier* and *The Zealous Soldier*, two companion broadsides of April 1646. The Falstaffian Mercenary Soldier, a martial possessive individualist, leases out his services to the highest bidder and defines himself by getting and spending wages: "No money yet, why then let's pawn our swords, / And drink an health to their confusion." The Puritan Zealous Soldier engages in goal-directed activity, and claims a stake in defining it: "I fight not, for to venge my self, nor yet, / For coin, but God's true worship up to set." Long before we hear Whigs attacking the corruptions threatened by mercenary standing armies, we hear a citizen army furiously protesting attempts retroactively to turn its freely elected martial praxis into the mercenary warfare of possessive individualists.

The radicals found their final, formidable rhetorical redoubt in the authority of their labor. After Ireton pressed once again the freehold franchise as "the most fundamental part of your constitution," Thomas Rainsborough made an unusual move into sarcasm, and began to formulate a class-based critique of the war:

> Sir I see, that it is impossible to have liberty but all property must be taken away. If it be laid down for a rule, and if you will say it, it must be so. But I would fain know what all the soldiers have fought for all this while? He hath fought to enslave himself, to give power to men of riches, men of estates, to make him a perpetual slave. We do find in all presses that go forth none must be pressed that are freehold men. When these gentlemen fall out among themselves they shall press the poor shrubs to come and kill [one another for] them.[256]

252. *P&L* 404.
253. *LM* 205, 207.
254. T. C., *Red Ribbond* 7.
255. *CP* 1.323, Austin Woolrych's emphasis (*WSS* 239n.). See also Lilburne's broadside *All Worthy Officers and Souldiers*, written in the wake of the Army–Leveller mutiny in April 1649.
256. *CP* 1.325–6. Firth glosses "shrubs" with Jotham's parable of the trees and brambles in Judges 9.7–15.

By voicing the unvoiced motives behind the taking-up of arms, Rainsborough began the modern historians' debate over the causes of the English Revolution. Either the revolutionary troops were unthinking instruments in the struggle of one group of gentlemen for the land of another, or they intended to gain liberty for themselves in the form of a manhood franchise. Rainsborough only suggests this second possibility. Rather than invoking some earlier declaration of principle, he presents his position tentatively, as a rhetorical question, feeling his way toward a positive claim by ventriloquizing Ireton. In response, Ireton delivers an equally speculative reading of the unvoiced motives of 1642, and a fantasy of the capitalist future. The soldiers of the kingdom fought because of the danger "that one man's will must be a law," because they preferred to be ruled by "the common consent of those that were fixed men and settled men," and because they wanted the opportunity to acquire such a fixed interest: "Every man that was born in it that hath a freedom is a denizen, he was capable of trading to get money and to get estates by, and therefore this man I think had a great deal of reason to build up such a foundation of interest to himself."[257]

Sexby's response was simultaneously metaphoric, pronominally vague, and ferocious:

> Do you [not] think it were a sad and miserable condition that we have fought all this time for nothing? All here both great and small do think that we fought for something. I confess many of us fought for those ends which we since saw was not that which caused us to go through difficulties and straits to venture all in the ship with you. It had been good in you to have advertised us of it, and I believe you would have fewer under your command to have commanded. But if this be the business, that an estate doth make men capable to choose those that shall represent them—it is no matter which way they get it, they are capable—I think there are many that have not estates that in honesty have as much right in the freedom [of] their choice as any that have great estates.[258]

Here, in the fragile public sphere of the General Council, a private trooper accuses his generals of lying or speaking with important silent reservations. He also reminds them of their dependence on the men they commanded in battle, and in the conclusion of this speech, which we considered above, promotes himself to colonel by insisting that he speaks with the voice of an entire regiment, "not as a particular."

Ireton responded by asking whether those who declared for Parliament from the beginning of the war and those who engaged at Newmarket did so with the idea "that they should have as great interest in Parliament men as freeholders had," or with the idea of supporting "the liberty of parliaments," for "Unless somebody did make you believe before now that you should have an equal interest in the kingdom, unless somebody do make that to be believed, there is no reason to blame men for leading so

257. *CP* 1.326–7.
258. Ibid. 1.329–30.

far as they have done; and if any man was far enough from such an apprehension that man hath not been deceived." Rainsborough and even the civilian Wildman replied that the war was not over—that its earlier phases had to be completed by an additional phase of democratic and perhaps tyrannicidal struggle. Wildman says that God provides no concrete guidance about civil matters, only that we should try to be "like unto God," which is to say, practice justice and mercy, be meek and peaceable. But he moves instantly to a statement with threatening import: if we kill common soldiers in battle without a second thought, why may we not kill their commander, "the great actor of this, and who was the great contriver of all"?[259]

It's no easier to determine retrospectively the nature of an unvoiced intention or a silent covenant than it is to determine God's will on some concrete political point, but in both cases, the General Council was up to the challenge. Woolrych argues that the Council voted to enfranchise all but servants and beggars at the end of the second day of debating, and that Clarke might have suppressed this fact from his record on instructions from the grandees.[260] Kishlansky says that the "failure" of the Putney Debates "revealed not only the erosion of consensus politics, but the emergence of attitudes toward political decision making which were as revolutionary as the policies that had generated them."[261] But the Putney Debates failed only from the grandee perspective that Kishlansky silently adopts. For the radicals, whose drive to a vote began on the first day, they were a resounding success. So far as the radical public sphere failed at Putney, it failed not in its efforts to push its agenda through the General Council, but in its later effort to democratize the civil society of army discipline which had helped bring it into being.

Contingency and Martial Law at Corkbush Field

The *Clarke Papers* contain only a skeletal summary of the debates of November 3–9.[262] To reconstruct them, we must rely on pamphlets, newsletters, newspapers, and retrospective accounts. Even after mustering only three negatives (Cromwell, Ireton, and Rich?) against the franchise clause of *The Agreement*, the grandees refused to say die. In the November 8 meeting, Cromwell attacked "the danger of their principles who had sought to divide the Army. That the first particular of that which they called the *Agreement of the People* did tend very much to anarchy"—an argument which itself tended very much to anarchy, since it reopened a matter already decided by due process. After some objections by Captain William Bray, Cromwell moved the question, "Whether that the officers and Agitators be sent to their quarters, yea, or no?" The Council resolved

259. Ibid. 1.333, 335, 384.
260. *WSS* 243–4, 256–7n.
261. "Consensus" 69.
262. *CP* 1.410–18.

that "in regard the General shortly intends a rendezvous of the Army, and forasmuch as many distempers are reported to be in the several regiments whereby much dissatisfaction is given both to the Parliament and kingdom through some misrepresentations," the officers and Agitators should be returned to their regiments "until the said rendezvous be over, and until his Excellency shall see cause to call them together again according to the *Engagement.*"[263]

Why did the radicals, whose agenda had dominated the Council for more than ten days, agree to end their own power? Woolrych and Gentles suggest they sensed the disintegration of their own support in the ranks and of Army unity in general, but they admit the weakness of their evidence. Woolrych relies on two pamphlets. The first, *A New Declaration from the Eight Regiments in the Army* (November 22), was "to some extent a piece of headquarters propaganda," and it bore no signatures.[264] And the second appeared in circumstances that encourage a certain skepticism. Henry Denne's *The Levellers Design Discovered* appeared on May 24 1649, a few days after his death sentence for joining in the disastrous Army–Leveller mutiny at Burford. He gained a pardon only when he publicly repented, blamed Levellers for dividing the Army from its divinely appointed leaders, and claimed that Fairfax dismissed the Council a year and a half earlier, in response to petitions from most of his regiments asking him to restore the Army's customary discipline.[265] But with the possible exception of *The Humble Remonstrance and Desires*, a petition of November 3 attributed to Colonel Hewson's regiment of foot, but unsubscribed and printed by the Army's official printer, none of these petitions survives, nor does any other reference to them. Gentles also refers to *Sea-Green & Blue*, an anonymous Leveller response to Denne, which seems to confirm that the Agitators had grown alienated from their regiments.[266] But it denies that most of the regiments recalled their Agitators, insists that those which did had been misled, and invokes Wildman's *Putney Projects*.[267]

I think the radicals were taking a calculated risk. Two nearly identical pamphlets emphasize that, while they may have had the numbers, Fairfax held the trump card in his ability to dissolve the Council at will.[268] The radicals made necessity a virtue and asked him to end the debates in the General Council and send them home to their regiments. At the same time, they hoped to reconstitute the New Model soviet in a new, more powerful form by returning to the regiments, relaying information, debating, gathering almost the whole of the Army at a single rendezvous, and

263. Ibid. 1.411–13.
264. *WSS* 263n.
265. 4–5.
266. *G* 503n.
267. 10–11.
268. *A Copy of a Letter Sent by the Agents of Severall Regiments of His Excellencies Army*, dated November 11; and *A Letter Sent from Severall Agitators of the Army*, printed by John Harris, acquired by Thomason on November 12, and excerpted in *P&L* 452–4.

subscribing *The Agreement of the People.* Thus the Agitators hoped to extend the radical unity produced by the summer's general rendezvous at Newmarket.

But the grandees also had a strategy. On November 8 or 9, they dissolved the Council, then reneged on their promise for a unified rendezvous, revealing a "strange unconstancy" by calling for three dispersed rendezvous.[269] Kishlansky argues that the dissolution aimed "to restore the army's unity by returning officers and Agitators to their regiments in preparation for a rendezvous."[270] But this unity was of a rather special sort, for it was founded on a strategic division. Woolrych denies that the Council anticipated a single rendezvous and questions the radicals' account of grandee deception: he says that no other source referred to a single rendezvous, that Fairfax "would certainly" have informed Parliament of any decision for a single rendezvous, and that he "certainly" announced to the General Council on November 8 a plan for a "rendezvous of the army, general in the sense of including all its units within marching distance but not in that of assembling them all at the same place on the same day."[271] But *The Solemne Engagement of the Army* makes it plain that a "general rendezvous" was a single rendezvous like that at Newmarket, not "the several and respective rendezvous" prescribed by Parliament to fragment, discipline, and dismantle the victorious New Model.[272] The *Resolves and Humble Advice of the Councel of War* to Fairfax of May 29 called for a general rendezvous of the regiments at Newmarket, and objected to the "dishonor" implied by disbanding them piecemeal.[273] Both *A Copy of a Letter Sent by the Agents* and *A Letter Sent from Several Agitators of the Army* claim that "our friends obtained *a* general rendezvous" in the November 8 meeting of the Council. The accounts by Clarke and Rushworth concur.[274] So does *A Letter from His Excellency Sir Thomas Fairfax, to Mr. Speaker,* which seems to have been written on the 8th, though collected by Thomason on the 11th.[275] So does its draft in the Clarke Manuscripts.[276] *A Perfect Diurnall* published Fairfax's address to the House on the 9th and referred to his plan for "*a* rendezvous."[277]

Henry Walker's pro-grandee newsbook, *Perfect Occurrences,* said that a report came "from the army" on November 10 (presumably, "from the General," since the Council had been disbanded) that there would be a rendezvous headquartered at Ware, "whether they shall be rendezvoused together, or several rendezvous (as most probable) is not yet resolved."[278]

269. *A Copy* 2, 3.
270. "Consensus" 68.
271. *WSS* 260–61.
272. *D* "25" [i.e., 27].
273. *Two Speeches.*
274. *CM* 65.88ʳ; *CP* 1.412; *RHC* 4.866.
275. Title page, A2ʳ.
276. *CM* 65.89ʳ.
277. 11/8–11/15/47, emphasis mine.
278. 11/5–11/12/47.

By the next day at the latest, Fairfax had resolved on the latter option. Only Rushworth, in his retrospective account, indicates a plan for more than one rendezvous, strategically appending the phrase to "their respective rendezvous" to the text of the agreement preserved in *The Clarke Papers*.[279] Both Woolrych and Gentles say that the convalescing Fairfax might have had some difficulty addressing each regiment individually at a single muster during autumnal daylight hours—true enough, but why should two or three days' worth of addresses at one site have taxed him more than traveling among three separate rendezvous?[280] No historical method should sophisticate itself so far as to rule out the possibility of *a lie*; in the meeting on the 8th, Fairfax may simply have lied or spoken with a silent reservation. Furthermore, the sketchy quality of the General Council's records for these days is itself of some interest. If Woolrych rightly supposes that the grandees instructed Clarke not to record the overwhelming vote in favor of the *Agreement*'s expansion of the franchise on October 29, perhaps they also told Clarke not to record their promise of a single rendezvous, which led the General Council to assent to an adjournment of its meetings.[281] Such a narrative fits both the evidence and the missing evidence. But if need be, another explanation allows us to stop deferentially short of this charge, and it's consistent with the narrative of the radical pamphlets, and with Fairfax's reluctance to recognize the legitimacy of the General Council. When they found themselves about to resume the identities of general officers, the grandees found it rather easy to overlook, override, or change their minds about decisions made in the relatively egalitarian public sphere of the Army. Thomas Fairfax, first among equals in the General Council of the Army, is not quite the same person as General Fairfax. When the latter breaks free from the democratic discursive constraints on the former, prerogative will out. From the radicals' perspective, the fragmented "general" muster betrayed the deliberative process of the General Council; from the grandees', it marked decisively the movement from the associative and deliberative realm of the Army's public sphere to the hierarchical and instrumental realm of Army discipline. The grandees might even have had another excuse, though one likely to confirm the worst free-born suspicions of francophone perfidy: given the ambiguous number of "*the* rendezvous" in English, they might have been able to tell themselves that they intended something quite different from what the radicals heard.

In any case, November 9 kicked off a dramatic struggle.[282] On the one

---

279. *RHC* 4.868; *CP* 1.415; *P&L* 455.
280. *WSS* 266–7; *G* 219. Woolrych tries to discredit the radicals' account in *A Copy* of Fairfax's duplicity by saying it mistakenly claims Ireton flounced out of the General Council on November 6, not November 5 (*WSS* 260, 261n.45). But I don't see why this error should lead us to discount all of *A Copy*'s arguments. Moreover, like Firth, I think *A Copy* gets the date right (*CP* 1.440–41).
281. *WSS* 243–4.
282. Ibid. 276–99.

hand, radicals fostered mutiny by encouraging all the regiments to attend the first rendezvous at Corkbush Field near Ware. Their unifying text was a new edition of *The Agreement* which, when properly folded and inserted into soldiers' hats, revealed the discursive associative blazon of "England's Freedom and Soldiers' Rights,"—a pledge not to a leader, but to each other.[283] On November 11 appeared *A Copy of a Letter Sent by the Agents of Severall Regiments of His Excellencies Army*, subscribed by fifteen Agitators, with no representative from Rich's regiment, but with Sexby explicitly joining the new Agitators for the first time. Thomason noted that it was "scattered up and down the streets by the Agitators." It demanded a general rendezvous, comparing the grandees' strategy of divided rendezvous with Parliament's attempts earlier in the year to break the Army's strength through dispersed musters, disbandments, and shipments to Ireland.[284] The next day, John Harris published *A Letter Sent from Several Agitators of the Army*, with many of the same signatories as for *A Copy*, and some new ones. Taverns in and around London hosted meetings of Levellers, New Agents, and friendly MPs such as Henry Marten.[285] The Agitators even attempted to enlist the House, presenting it with a copy of *The Agreement* and a new petition, delivered by Lord Grey of Groby. On November 9, the House rejected it as "destructive to the being of Parliaments."[286]

But the grandees had also been busy. They won a number of concessions from Parliament. On November 13, a troop in Whalley's regiment issued a declaration in support of Fairfax and against the new Agitators. More important, the grandees turned to their advantage a (probably) unanticipated development: on November 11, the King escaped from Army custody in Hampton Court and fled to Carisbrooke Castle on the Isle of Wight. Explanations vary for the king's escape at this critical moment: perhaps a mere coincidence, perhaps his fear of an Agitator plot to assassinate him, perhaps strategic negligence by Cromwell intended to distract the Army.[287] But the upshot was to unite the New Model in relation to an exterior threat, as in June 1646, when it had defeated the royalists at Oxford, Charles commenced negotiations to hand himself over to the Scots, and the Agitators had not yet emerged from the ranks.

Fairfax appeared at each rendezvous with copies of *A Remonstrance from His Excellency Sir Thomas Fairfax, and His Councell of Warre, Concerning the Late Discontent and Distraction in the Army*, his response to *The Agreement*. It offers the nation regularized parliamentary elections but not manhood suffrage, back pay and physical safety but not democratic self-governance to the Army. Marshalling a squad of hierarchalist commonplaces, he

283. Ibid. 281.
284. 4.
285. *G* 220–21.
286. *Two Petitions*, 1647; *WSS* 276.
287. *WSS* 278–9, 268–76; Gregg, *Free-Born John* 203–5.

furiously attacks the New Agitators: they assumed the name of agents without any authority and "labored to make parties and factions in the Army." They acted "as a divided party from the said Council and Army, and associating themselves with, or rather (as we have just cause to believe) giving themselves up to be acted or guided by divers private persons that are not of the Army." And they threatened "the dissolution of all that order, combination, and government, which is the essence of an army."[288] It concludes with a blank spot to be filled in with the name of the regiment, and spaces for soldiers to subscribe, declaring their satisfaction in Fairfax and their willingness to be "subject to his excellency, his Council of War, and (every one of us) to our superior officers in this regiment and the Army, according to the discipline of war." Morrill hopefully suggests that the grandees "ordered a series of separate rendezvous to sound out rank-and-file opinion (a repeat of the Saffron Walden procedures)."[289] But in *A Letter from His Excellency Sir Thomas Fairfax, to Mr. Speaker*, he says the rendezvous aimed only to restore the "ancient discipline" of the Army (title page). He offered his soldiers not an opportunity to air grievances, but a martial law version of Hobson's Choice: the ancient discipline of the Army or death.

On November 15, when Fairfax met with seven regiments at Corkbush Field for the first rendezvous, Rainsborough presented him with a copy of *The Agreement* in the form of a petition, but Fairfax used his *Remonstrance* to enlist solid support. Colonel Thomas Harrison's regiment, which Fairfax had not ordered to the rendezvous, also arrived. After brief resistance, they removed the copies of *The Agreement* tucked in their hats, and swore allegiance to the general. Then Robert Lilburne's regiment of foot arrived, and they proved more truculent. Ordered to march north in October, they had been resisting the general's orders for more than a month. George Gregson, major to Colonel Pride, attempted to restore them to military discipline. They stoned him.[290] At this moment, with a charismatic and beloved rival leader in Thomas Rainsborough, a body of sympathetic troops drawn up, a published manifesto/constitution in *The Agreement* to provide an ideological rallying point, and the first blow struck, the Agitators brought seventeenth-century England closer to a genuinely popular democratic revolution than ever before or after.

But it didn't come close enough. Cromwell charged into the ranks with a drawn sword and demanded the regiment's submission. Fairfax conducted a court martial, found eight or nine soldiers guilty, and sentenced them to death. He pardoned all but three, whom he ordered to draw lots.

288. Firth notes the strong echoes of Ireton's attack on "divisions" during the second day of the debates (*CP* 1.348n).
289. *Nature* 326.
290. Kishlansky disputes the claim that there was a mutiny of any sort in "What Happened at Ware?" *The Historical Journal* 25.4, 1982. Morrill agrees (*Nature* 386). But Gentles asks, reasonably enough, "If breaking the head of a higher officer in the presence of one's commander-in-chief does not constitute mutiny, what does?" (*G* 505n.202; see also 219–26 and *WSS* 283–5).

The two winners then shot the loser, Richard Arnold. Woolrych characterizes this act as "remarkably (though characteristically) lenient." By the
monstrous standards of martial law, which would have allowed Fairfax to
execute everyone in both mutinous regiments, this is true enough.[291] But
as the author of *A Plea for the Late Agents of the Army* points out, the nation
was at peace, and the radical transformation of the Army at Newmarket
had put an end to the prerogative imposition of martial law.[292]

And Fairfax's calculating execution of Arnold appears horrid enough.
He formed a hierarchical spectacle that symbolically reversed the emergence of the Agitators from the ranks through a process that rationally
adjusted choice and interest. To begin with, he reverted to an earlier, pre-
Engagement deliberative body, calling not some version of the egalitarian
Council of the Army, but a Council of War comprised of appointed
officers. This body in turn reverted to the pre-revolutionary form of
exemplary punishment, seeing to it that "divers mutineers for example
sake were drawn forth, three of them were tried and condemned to
death."[293] As the regicides would find while awaiting the names of those
excepted from the Act of Oblivion, prerogative power resides in the ability
to set examples and make exceptions. By having the condemned men
draw lots to distinguish the shooters from the shot, Fairfax integrated
pure contingency and even a quasi-Calvinist moment of "election" into
the process. Unlike the Arminian God of Goffe and Collier, who merges
with a collective democratic struggle, the Calvinist God of Corkbush Field
arbitrarily individuates for salvation and damnation.[294] Fairfax's stratagem
has proven equally effective with historians like Firth, who obligingly
refers to hapless Private Arnold as a "ringleader."[295] Where the regiments'
election of Agitators associated them in a new egalitarian collectivity, a
pledged group with its internal principle of unity, Fairfax's spectacle of
chance, fear, and blood skillfully reordered them into a traditional
hierarchy with no unity outside the will of Fairfax. Each individual in this
serial collective—and the three "ringleaders" in particular—sees himself
as absolute Other to each of his comrades, and each one of them as his.
The soldiers prudently weighed their long-term interest in political self-
determination against their medium-term interest in speedy payment of

291. *WSS* 285.
292. 3–4. Compare *The Petition of Women* of May 1649, which invoked *The Petition of Right*
against the application of martial law in peacetime—specifically, the execution of the
Leveller rebel Robert Lockyer (*P&L* 368).
293. *A Full Relation of the Proceedings at the Rendezvous of the Brigade of the Army that Was Held in
Corkbush Field*, 1647, 5.
294. In April 1649, Fairfax ordered three officers charged with treason to draw lots: "in two
of them was written 'Life given by God,' and the other a blank.'" When they hesitated,
he had a child distribute them (*FCA* 288; see also *Mercurius Militaris* 4/17–4/24/49). If
Fairfax was monstrous toward the prisoners, he was diabolical toward the child.
On early modern lotteries, see Keith Thomas, *Religion and the Decline of Magic*,
Harmondsworth 1971, 139–46.
295. *FCA* 361.

arrears and their short-term interest in not being shot, and decided to follow orders.

After a visit by John Saltmarsh and two chastising letters he wrote to Fairfax and Cromwell (*Englands Friend*), the grandees and radicals achieved a reconciliation of sorts, but by no means did the Army democratize itself.[296] In December, Parliament substantially met the material demands of the Army. For all practical purposes, the General Council dissolved on January 4 1648, and Fairfax replaced it with various councils of officers alone. Early in 1648, the grandees disbanded thousands of New Model soldiers, singling out Harrison's mutinous regiment for particular cuts.[297] The Council of Officers discussed and approved *The Second Agreement of the People*, then submitted it to Parliament for its consideration only, and Interregnum England never saw the franchise extended to the freeborn.

The Agitators' associative spirit of 1647 reappeared in 1649, which saw efforts to revive the General Council, attacks on tithes and the excise, and open mutiny. But because they were uncoordinated, these attacks never had a serious chance of success.[298] A directive of February 1649 severely limited the rights of the Army to petition.[299] In March, five troopers protested and were punished. In April, an Army–Leveller mutiny demanded that the grandees re-establish the General Council and restore freedom to petition. Trooper Robert Lockyer led a mutiny of Captain Savage's troop, Whalley's regiment. A firing squad shot him on April 27. Though the mutiny seems to have been over pay alone, his funeral developed into a massive Leveller rally. The Army command cashiered William Thompson, a corporal of Whalley's regiment, in September 1647, but he continued to linger in the vicinity of the Army. In December, he published *Englands Freedom, Soldiers' Rights*, which insisted that the *Solemne Engagement* had new-modeled the Army and put an end to any traditional form of martial law, making it "absolute murder" to shoot Richard Arnold at Ware.[300] In May 1649, he gathered two or three hundred men in Banbury and issued a manifesto: "Through an inavoidable necessity, no other means left under heaven, we are enforced to betake ourselves to the law of nature, to defend and preserve ourselves and native rights." They proclaimed themselves

> gathered and associated together upon the bare accompt of Englishmen, to redeem ourselves and the land of our nativity, from slavery and oppression, to avenge the blood of war shed in the time of peace, to have justice for the

296. Saltmarsh's prophecies appeared as *Wonderfull Predictions* on December 29, then (recast in ballad form and oddly royalized) as *Strange and Wonderful Predictions* (Hyder E. Rollins, ed., *Cavalier and Puritan*, New York 1923, 195–200).

297. *G* 233.

298. On the turbulent spring of 1649, see Manning, *1649* 173–216.

299. *CP* 2.191–2.

300. *LM* 248–58, 255.

blood of M. Arnold shot to death at Ware, and for the blood of M. Robert
Lockyer, and divers others who of late by martial law were murthered at London.

They invoked the precedents of Dutch resistance, the principles of
Newmarket and Triploe Heath, and the right of soldiers to hold the
hands of generals turning their cannon against their own armies.[301]
Colonel Reynolds and three troops attacked and scattered them on May
10. Two regiments mutinied in Salisbury, but Cromwell overwhelmed
them at Burford Church on May 14, and proceeded to execute Corporal
Church, Corporal Perkins, and Cornet James Thompson, William's
brother. On May 16, William Thompson fought to the death in Welling-
borough, Northamptonshire.[302] Meanwhile, Edward Sexby, whom we
might have expected to find in the thick of the Leveller Risings, was
working loyally for Cromwell opening mail packets in Dover and Portland.[303] But as we will see, his later career would show that Cromwell had
failed to bring the associative democratic energies of the Army under the
strict control of martial law.

Were the Agitators radical liberals of the rising bourgeoisie, or radical
democrats of the poorer and middling sort? Recent arguments about the
Levellers also illuminate their military allies. Morton sees the Levellers
"thinking in terms of a largely pre-capitalist society of small producers."[304]
Thomas highlights their "faith in human equality and natural right,
modified by traditional patriarchal assumptions about the place of women,
apprentices and household servants, and further tempered by a specifically Leveller desire to eliminate clientage and dependence on great
persons."[305] Wootton concludes that the Levellers proposed to enfranchise
"those who were entitled to wear their hats at home"; radical though the
Levellers' proposal for an extended franchise was, they were finally
committed to the idea of a "householder franchise" that would "level" the
political differences between aristocrats and such independent small
producers, but exclude women, children, and household servants.[306] We
may plausibly compare these civilian small producers to the soldiers of
the New Model. Despite their relatively egalitarian collective martial praxis
in the New Model, the Agitators did not explicitly propose a radical
transformation of English civil society. After the transfer of royalist and
church lands to private hands, and provision for the back pay of the
Army, civil society was to remain, for all practical purposes, untouched.

But should we define this class of small producers as the progenitors
of nineteenth-century industrial capitalism, and write them off as

301. *Englands Standard Advanced*, 1647, 2, 3.
302. *GZ*. In 1659–60, Agitators reappeared in the Army, but this came to nothing (Hill,
     World 346–7).
303. *CSPD* 1.135, 140.
304. *World* 216; he is quoting A. L. Merson.
305. "Levellers" 70.
306. Wootton, "Leveller" 432. See also Manning, *English* 387–424.

"proto-bourgeois"? Surely this smacks of historiographical whiggery, and in any case, it would ignore the fact (demonstrated in eloquent detail by E. P. Thompson in *The Making of the English Working Class*) that most of these small producers were not early capitalists, but the ancestors of or the very same persons as early proletarians. Jeff D. Bass wryly suggests that Ireton and Rich need not have feared communist leveling: if the expanded franchise had led the poor to make a successful grab for property, then they, too, would soon have had a permanent and fixed interest in the kingdom.[307] But this is more than a joke if we see the Leveller/Agitator project as, not a land grab, but an effort to preserve small property and the democracy it underwrites against capitalist engrossment. As Norah Carlin points out, we should not overlook the genuine radicalism in the Leveller and Agitator defense of the rights of small property in an era when the "middling sort of people" were splitting between capitalists and proletarians. Many, including most marxists, have forgotten "the appeal of small property (especially in land, as in twentieth-century revolutions) to those who have not got it." She also points to the protests of seventeenth-century English artisans: in struggling to regulate their own productive activity, they were neither proto-capitalists nor proto-wage slaves, but the creators and defenders of a corporate guild ethos and an ideal of fraternity that should receive as much attention as the ideal of liberty.[308] In this chapter, I have argued that we should see a similar collectivist guild ethos, not a possessive individualism, animating the soldiery of the New Model, the true artisans of the English commonwealth.

In their fear of being duped by the cunning of capitalist reason, leftist historians and critics frequently adopt an overly rigorous scheme of class relations, overlooking the utopian surplus value in the enormously various "bourgeois" tradition, the parts of which do not go without remainder into the whole. For instance, consider the bourgeois radicalism of Tom Paine, a Quaker-born latter-day product and prophet of this class of small producers, who felt constrained in part 2 of *The Rights of Man* to defend himself from having proposed a "leveling system" in part 1.[309] But he also concludes part 2 with a proposal to decrease taxes on consumption, increase land taxes, add an income tax, and institute a comprehensive social welfare program with public financing of maternity benefits, education, housing, work programs, and old age pensions.[310] Recent editions of Paine's works by Hook and Kuklick have excised many of these proposals, the latter without benefit of clear ellipses—an omission that restores Paine handily to the Cambridge History of Political Thought by

---

307. "'Levellers': The Economic Reduction of Political Equality in the Putney Debates, 1647," *The Quarterly Journal of Speech* 77.4, 1991, 439.

308. "Marxism" 120; "Liberty and Fraternities in the English Revolution," *International Review of Social History* 39, 1994.

309. *"Common Sense," "The Rights of Man," and other Essential Writings of Thomas Paine*, Introd. by Sidney Hook, New York 1969, 235.

310. Marilyn Butler, ed., *Burke, Paine, Godwin, and the Revolution Controversy*, Cambridge 1984, 107–21.

removing him from the Atlantic History of Class Struggle.[311] If we reduce Paine to "the bourgeoisie," we perpetrate a subtler version of this excision. Similarly, if we reduce the civilian and Army radicals at Putney to possessive individualists, we overlook the democratic and collectivist currents inside seventeenth-century radicalism, which never quite died.

311. Paine, Hook, ed., 279; Paine, Kuklick, ed., 194–203. Too late to refer to it in the body of this chapter, I read Samuel Dennis Glover's excellent essay "The Putney Debates: Popular Versus Élitist Republicanism," *Past and Present* 164, 1999, 47–80, which reveals a radical plebeian dimension in English classical republicanism, and a republican

7

The Public Spiritedness of Anna Trapnel

Let your women keep silence in the churches: for it is not permitted unto them to speak; but they are commanded to be under obedience, as also saith the law. And if they will learn any thing, let them ask their husbands at home: for it is a shame for women to speak in the church. What? came the word of God out from you? or came it unto you only?

—St. Paul, 1 Cor. 14.34–6

Shut up he explained.

—Ring Lardner, "The Young Immigrants"

The secret voice of thunder hath a louder report, than men's great cannons.

—Anna Trapnel, *Report and Plea*

Handmaids Discovered and Revealed

Revisionists like Conrad Russell frequently reject a binary model for describing social conflict.[1] They might want to consider the advantages of a trinary model. New groups typically emerge into political life not subversively or *ab nihilo*, but through a clash within or between other groups. In 1641–42, a conflict between the monarchical and parliamentary wings of the English ruling class made an opening for the London crowds. In 1647, the Agitators emerged through a clash between Parliament and its generals. In 1789, the Parisian masses entered into active political life after a clash between the Bourbons and the Estates General, and the ensuing clash between royalist and republican whites in San Domingo made an opening for blacks and mulattos, slave and free. In the history of feminism as well, radical innovation arises not from the expressive autonomy of the radical, but from a conflict within the dominant order. Or better, the radical works up her autonomy by working upon this conflict. That series of largely male homosocial clashes known as the English Reformation (Catholic vs Reformer; Anglican vs Presbyterian; Presbyterian vs Independent; Independent vs Baptist; All vs Quaker) created a series of openings for women sectarians to enter into active

---

1. *Unrevolutionary* ix–x.

political life. I'll begin with two male-authored works that emerged from
the conflict between proponents of episcopal and Puritan church government. From quite distinct perspectives, both see the emergence of sectarian women as something quite new under the sun.

Traditional misogynous writings of early modern England, such as
Joseph Swetnam's infamous *Arraignment of Lewd, Idle, Froward, and Uncon-
stant Women* (1615), tended to draw on an ancient stock of recognizable,
proverbial misogynous lore: the traditional *plus ça change* humor of false
etymology (woe-to-man), genealogy (Eve's daughters and the crooked
rib), and bodily satire (woman's ungovernable tongue and insatiable
"tail").[2] But in the early 1640s, the popular attacks on episcopal government produced a new sort of misogyny. Almost by definition, women
religious radicals belonged to that novel "gangrene" of mechanic or "tub"
preachers, since they moved into preaching not from the universities
through state or gentry appointment, but from a non-religious sphere of
labor, perhaps even the household itself, through the special inspiration
of the holy spirit.[3] Consequently, antisectarian misogynists of the Revolution locate women preachers and prophetesses not in the eternal present
of male whimsy, anxiety, raillery, and hatred, but in particular times and
places.

The title page of *A Discoverie of Six Women Preachers* (1641) names four
particular places and six particular women who have made *news* "pleasant
to be read, but horrid to be judged of." The anonymous author tries to
control and contain these women, but he systematically undercuts himself.
First, he traces their spiritual claims to a monstrously oral plebeian desire
for base material food and drink. One Anne Hempstall calls together a
group of her "bibbing gossips," whose "thoughts were bent more upon
the strong water bottle, than upon the uses or doctrines which their holy
sister intended to expound unto them," and she herself regularly swigs
aqua vitae. But strong waters fortify the weaker vessel: she mounts a stool
and commences a remarkably sober, two-hour sermon. First, she recounts
her dream of Anna, the 84-year-old prophetess of Luke 2.36, then decides
that she should imitate her; strangely, the author lets this vow stand,
making no effort to break up the prophetic sorority. She then moves into
a Pauline exordium on hair length as an aid to gender differentiation,
taking her text from just before Paul's classically misogynous claim that
"the head of the woman is the man."[4] But Hempstall appropriates Paul's
authority by revoicing him and speaking authoritatively about the head of
her head. The author mocks the length of her sermon, combining the

2. R. Howard Bloch discusses misogynous writing as conventional "citation" in "Medieval
   Misogyny," *Representations* 20, 1987.
3. Katharine Gillespie notes the literal domestic publicity implied by "tub preaching" in her
   "Table Talk: Seventeenth-Century English and American Women Writers and the Rhetoric
   of Radical Domesticity," diss., SUNY Buffalo 1996, 39–40.
4. 1 Cor. 11.3.

traditional fear of female tongues with the newer fear of Puritan lungs. But he leaves its content untouched and uncriticized.

Despite the author's claim of an inattentive audience, Hempstall moves her holy sisters to emulation. Mary Bilbrowe, a bricklayer's wife, "desired them to be all with her the next morning, and after sermon, they should have a good fat pig to breakfast, besides a cup of sack or claret to wash it down." She invites them all to sit (on piles of bricks), and mounts a pulpit (made of bricks) to commence her sermon, but is drawn away to an assignation either commercial or sexual. Pigs, booze, bricks, and sex: the grossly material world debunks female pretensions to the spirit. All this should produce a hearty Erastian laugh, but the author slips when he worries that such women might "take their ministers' office from them." These women are not base aliens but dangerous competitors, occupying the same material plain with clerics—a common priestly fear.[5]

The author concludes with a sneer at these congregations or "female academies," adding that "where their university is I cannot tell," but "Bedlam or Bridewell would be two convenient places for them"—the uproarious female-gendered equivalent to the hempen punchline favored for male sectaries.[6] But as receptacles for political prisoners, Bedlam and Bridewell were still potentially public sites distinct from the grim semiprivate village *Gemeinschaft* of bridling, battering, and spousal rape typically offered to wayward and froward women in earlier misogynous literature.[7] Lady Eleanor Davies, confined to Bedlam as mad in 1637, would turn it into a symbolically charged site of state persecution in her later prophecies. As we will see, Anna Trapnel would do the same with Bridewell. The pamphlet concludes not with Swetnam's smugness, but with genuine fear: "At this time I have described but six of them, ere long I fear I shall relate more, I pray God I have no cause, and so for this time I conclude." Here we see the classic, market-oriented open-endedness of the pamphlet press, but also an anxious prophecy that the next two decades would amply confirm.[8]

5. *Discoverie* 3–4. *A Strange Wonder* (1642) warns that "there is no whore to a Holy whore, which when she turns up the white of her eye, and the black of her tail when she falls of her back, according as the spirit moves her" (4). *Lucifers Lacky* (1641 or 1642) warned against the antiepiscopal London crowds attempting "to rob Levi of his due" and concluded with a crude woodcut of a tub preacher and a preaching woman captioned, "When Women preach, and cobblers pray, / Then fiends in Hell, make holiday." *A Spirit Moving in the Women-Preachers* (1646) combines economic and sexual anxiety about an irregular sort of tithing: sectarian women will transfer their husbands' estates to their seducers, "furnishing their pretended holy brother of the separation, or schism, with whatsoever he pleases" (3). *Tub-preachers overturn'd* (1647) alludes to sectaries who have "crept into widows' houses, and have bewitched or deceived silly women" (5).

6. When a Baptist preacher heard Sarah Latchett preach against him in his own church, he proposed Bridewell as a proper place for "such an idle housewife" (Phyllis Mack, "The Prophet and Her Audience," Eley and Hunt, *Reviving* 139–52, 139).

7. David Underdown, "The Taming of the Scold," Fletcher and Stevenson, *Order* 116–36.

8. We have no independent confirmation of these prophetesses, but that's not to say that they were merely discursive constructs. As Achinstein says, reports of terrifying radical women may indicate homosocial conflict between monarchist and republican patriarchs,

The actual material sites of female self-education were the separating congregations of Independents and Baptists, and the female conventicles and discussion groups associated with them. We can see a record of one such group—a congregation of Dublin Independents—in John Rogers's *Ohel or Beth-Shemesh* (1653), particularly his chapter entitled "Pupilla: That in the Church all the Members, even Sisters as well as Brothers, have a right to all Church-affairs; and may not only implicitly but explicitly vote and offer or object, etc." Rogers also contradicts himself—but rapturously, not anxiously. He certainly does not propose an absolute equality for women, but he does suggest some of the openings within male-dominated sectarian ideology for female self-creation.[9] He concedes that women should maintain a "civil subjection to men in their economical [household] relations," but he also imagines the congregation as a "democratical" space of almost complete gender equality.[10] He recalls the arguments of Reformers, Presbyterians, and Independents from Calvin to Thomas Hooker, who founded anti-Episcopal English Protestantism, then turns them against the male episcopate still ruling the gathered churches: Antichrist's "seminary of discord," which previously enforced absolute differences between clergy and laity, now enforces an unnatural distinction between men and women.[11] Acknowledging the importance of women's continued "subjection," he redefines this subjection as their active participation in church government—that is, as a liberating subjection not *to* men, but *with* men *to* the church.[12]

Rogers's egalitarian faith outruns his interpretive works: "And many others, had I time to search, I should soon find to bear witness with me, of women's (as well as men's) right to vote, offer, object, concur in and

---

but "much of the writing against women was really about women" ("Women on Top in the English Revolution," in Achinstein, "Special Issue: Gender" 143). The author of *A Discoverie* refers to an Elizabeth Bancroft, who attacked the altar-idolatry of the Laudian bishops in Ely, which had a reputation for plebeian religious radicalism (Thomas, *Religion* 168, 200, 204, 260). At her 1638 trial, Ann Hutchinson and Hugh Peter discuss the "Woman of Elis," a radical preacher or prophetess in England (David D. Hall, ed., *The Antinomian Controversy, 1636–1638*, 2nd edn, Durham, NC, 1990, 380). As Dorothy Ludlow suggests, she may be Bancroft ("Arise and Be Doing: English 'Preaching' Women, 1640–1660," Ph.D. diss., Indiana University 1978). Bancroft's prophecy recalls one of Trapnel's most important English precursors: Jane Hawkins, the peddler prophetess of St Ives, only a few miles from Ely. In 1629 she recited thousands of ecstatic verses in ballad meter, and her preacher took them down. But Bishop Williams of Lincoln called her a "crafty baggage" and destroyed them as "full of detraction and injury" to the bishops, the liturgy, and civil government (John Hacket, *Scrina Reserata*, 2 vols, London 1693, 2.47; *PRO* 16/141/63, 16/142/19). Hawkins later emigrated to Massachusetts and associated with Hutchinson and Mary Dyer (Dorothy Ludlow, "Arise" 171–2, 189n.).

9. Rogers's pagination moves from 563, to 464–5, to 566–7, to 468–77; I'll convert to 563–77. Rogers left Ireland for England in 1652, partly because of controversies over the rights of women in his church (Edward Rogers, *Some Account of the Life and Opinions of a Fifth-Monarchy-Man*, 1867, 33). He records the prophesying of a member of his congregation named Elizabeth Avery (402–6), also probably the author of *Scripture-Prophecies Opened* (1647).

10. 572, 564.

11. 565–8.

12. 569.

consent to all things that concern the benefit of the whole body."[13] With "the whole body," he sidesteps Paul's much-invoked patriarchal description of the man as the head of the woman and argues for organic gender equality inside the church.[14] He includes a typical early modern catalogue of vicious women (Delilah, Jezebel, Pharaoh's daughter), then tempers it with one of virtuous women (Mary Magdalene, Jael, Abigail, Deborah). As sur- or ur-Calvinists, women will form the vanguard in the revolution of the saints, "For where they are bad, they are extreme bad, but where they are good, they are exceeding good, and most fondly affected with the things of God." They are "more readily wrought upon" by church discipline—gold to men's iron or steel. Like Paul, Rogers grants that women must be kept "from public preaching, or prophesying, or teaching as officers or as ministers do."[15] But as Margaret Fell pointed out, Paul also implied that women could prophesy when he called it improper for them to prophesy with their heads bare.[16] Similarly, Rogers had already said that women could be public preachers and church officers, prophets, and private teachers.[17] He makes a patriarchal concession, but qualifies it in the next phrase: "To women, I wish ye be not too forward, and yet not too backward, but hold fast your liberty. . . . [Y]e ought not by your silence to betray your liberty." And he concludes by invoking the words of the Anglican wedding service to depict the church itself as one flesh: "And in a word, I say to all, 'Those whom God hath joined together, let no man put asunder.'"[18] This recalls *Ohel*'s title page, which says that "the Theorick and Practick Parts" of church discipline "come forth first into the World as Bride-groom and bride"—a simile which suggests not only a tempering of gender hierarchy, but also the intense affective charge inhabiting gathered church fellowship. A rigorous critical feminism should note that no sect established gender equality inside the church; a rigorous dialectical feminism should add that women found an opportunity to exercise their creative practical consciousness in the congregation, and beyond.

Anna Trapnel, a Baptist and Fifth Monarchist, prophesied against Oliver Cromwell in 1654, after he dismissed Barebone's Parliament and assumed the office of Lord Protector.[19] Like most seventeenth-century women of

---

13. 568.
14. 565.
15. 574–5.
16. *Womens Speaking Justified*, 1666.
17. 568, 570–71, 564, 571, 568.
18. 576, 577.
19. Trapnel calls herself "Anna," but others alternate "Anna" and "Hannah," perhaps because of the competing precedents of prophetical Hannah (1 Sam. 1.2) and Anna (Luke 2.36). Trapnel and her associates published three of her works in 1654: *The Cry of a Stone* (*TCS*, February 20), *A Legacy for Saints* (*TLS*, July 24), and *Anna Trapnel's Report and Plea* (*TRP*, after July; I'll indicate the second group of pages 25–8 as "25a–28a"). *Strange and Wonderful Newes from White-Hall* simply condenses and simplifies *The Cry of a Stone*, published shortly before (see *TCS* 1–14, 16–18, and 51–2). Her late prophecies survive in two volumes: *A Lively Voice for the King of Saints and Nations* (*TVK*, after February

whom we have any record at all, she was not born and did not die, but
flourished (1642–59); like most plebeian millenarians, her alpha and
omega remain murky. With the decline of the Fifth Monarchy movement
in the 1660s, she lost the collective medium that might have given her a
continuing public role and maintained her memory; the contrast is strong
with English Quakerism, which methodically nurtured the myth of Fell
and her husband George Fox. But Anna Trapnel was one of the most
important public political women to emerge from the sectarian ferment
of seventeenth-century England and New England.

Until recently, historians and critics examining seventeenth-century
radicalism have paid much less attention to women radicals than did
terrified seventeenth-century male heresiographers. Feminist literary critics considering early modern women writers have produced an important
body of work during the last twenty years by focusing on royalists, Anglican
and Catholic, like Lanyer, Wroth, Cary, Philips, Cavendish, and Behn,
who wrote in more conventionally literary genres. But until fairly recently,
they have tended to overlook prophetesses and sectarian writers in general, though their writings constitute a substantial proportion of the
whole.[20] Some dangers of continuing exclusion lurk even inside the recent

---

7 1658), and a 990-page printed folio whose sole surviving copy lacks a title page and
some introductory matter (*T*, after November 1659). I'll give page numbers from both
when they overlap. In "Anna Trapnel's Prophecies" (*English Historical Review* 26, 1911,
526–35), Champlin Burrage identifies Trapnel as the composer of the prophecies in the
longer work, earlier described by Bertram Dobell in "A Unique Book," *Notes and Queries*
9.8, 1901. Its latest prophecy, dated 11/30/59 (78–99), follows a silence of more than
fifteen months. The most important critical studies of Trapnel are by Burrage; Kate
Chedgzoy, "Female Prophecy in the Seventeenth Century," in William Zunder and
Suzanne Trill, eds, *Writing and the English Renaissance*, London 1996, 238–54; Alfred
Cohen (*GZ*); Teresa Feroli, "Engendering the Body Politic," diss., Cornell University
1994, 89–123; Antonia Fraser, *Weaker Vessel* 254–63; Katharine M. Gillespie, "Anna
Trapnel's Window on the Word," *Bunyan Studies* 8, 1998; Hilary Hinds, *God's English-
women*, Manchester and New York 1996, 90–103, 122–8, 150–70; Elaine Hobby, *Virtue of
Necessity*, London 1988, 31–6; Dorothy Ludlow, "Arise" 259–70; Diane Purkiss, "Producing
the Voice, Consuming the Body," in Isobel Grundy and Susan Wiseman, eds, *Women,
Writing, History: 1640–1740*, Athens, GA, 1992, 139–58; Carola Lyon Scott-Luckens,
"'Alpha and Omega, the Beginning and the End': Women's Millennialist Prophecy
1630–1670," diss., University of Southampton 1997; and Nigel Smith, *Perfection* 45–53,
86–90.

20. In "The Challenges to Patriarchalism," in John Morrill, ed., *Revolution and Restoration*,
London 1992, 112–28, Patricia Crawford estimates that seventeenth-century publications
identifiably by women accounted for .5 per cent before the war, 1.2 per cent of a greatly
increased output in the 1640s and '50s (124). For historical and critical surveys, see
Crawford's *Women and Religion in England 1500–1720*, London 1993; Fraser, *Weaker Vessel*;
and Hobby, *Virtue*. For two special journal issues, see Achinstein, "Special Issue: Gender,"
and Amy Louise Erickson and Ross Balzaretti, eds, "Special Issue: Presentations of the
Self in Early Modern England," *Gender and History* 7.3, 1995. For two important reference
books, see Maureen Bell, George Parfitt, and Simon Shepherd, eds, *A Biographical
Dictionary of English Women Writers, 1580–1720*, Boston 1990; Hilda L. Smith and Susan
Cardinale, comp., *Women and the Literature of the Seventeenth Century: An Annotated
Bibliography Based on Wing's Short-Title Catalogue*, New York 1990. For two comprehensive
bibliographies of recent critical work on Renaissance and seventeenth-century English
women writers, see Elizabeth Hageman, "Recent Studies in Women Writers of the
English Seventeenth Century," *English Literary Renaissance* 18, 1988; and Sara Jayne Steen,

historical and literary critical turn toward classical republicanism and the public sphere of seventeenth-century England. Since Habermas, public sphere theory has tended toward relatively secular forms of discourse and practice, whereas the vast majority of public women in seventeenth-century England emerged from sectarian culture. If the three main nurseries of specifically classical republicanism in seventeenth-century England were the coteries of European humanism, the schools and universities, and the political life of Parliament and the Army, we should not be surprised to find so few Englishwomen whom we can confidently call classical republicans.[21] While classical republicanism offered men the lordship of their households, it offered women little or nothing by way of domestic emancipation. Neither the republicans' critique of mystifying patriarchalist metaphors nor their emphasis on voluntary, affectionate, and spiritual rather than dynastic marriage challenged the general custom of female subordination. The exploratory powers of Woodhouse's "separation and analogy" model broke down for questions of gender: republicans struggling to remove the Norman Yoke from the necks of freeborn Englishmen seldom went on to propose lifting the conjugal yoke from freeborn Englishwomen.[22] When Milton attacks "domestic tyranny," he compares tyrannical Stuarts not to tyrannical husbands, but to bad marriage laws, or even to ill-chosen and tyrannical wives. In a revealing analogy, he finds "more difference between king and tyrant than male and female." In *Doctrine and Discipline of Divorce*, he proposes to reform civil government by reforming family government:

> And farewell all hope of true Reformation in the state, while such an evil as this lies undiscerned or unregarded in the house. On the redress whereof depends, not only the spiritful and orderly life of our grown men, but the willing, and careful education of our children. Let this therefore be new examined, this tenure and freehold of mankind, this native and domestic Charter given us by a greater Lord than that Saxon King the Confessor.[23]

"Recent Studies in Women Writers of the Seventeenth Century, 1604–1674," *English Literary Renaissance* 24, 1994. On women and the sects, see Keith Thomas's influential essay, "Women and the Civil War Sects," in Trevor Aston, ed., *Crisis in Europe, 1560–1660*, New York 1965, 317–40; Claire Cross, "'He-Goats before the Flocks,'" in G. J. Cuming and Derek Baker, eds, *Popular Belief and Practice*, Cambridge 1972, 195–202; John Briggs, "She-Preachers, Widows, and Other Women," *Baptist Quarterly* 31.7, 1986; Anne Laurence, "A Priesthood of She-believers," in W. J. Sheils and Diana Wood, eds, *Women in the Church*, Oxford 1990, 345–63. On women prophets and preachers, see particularly Gillespie, "Table Talk"; Dorothy Ludlow, "Arise"; Phyllis Mack, *Visionary Women*, Berkeley and Los Angeles, 1992; Hinds, *God's Englishwomen*; and Diane Watt, *Secretaries of God*, Cambridge 1997. See also Bell et al., *Biographical Dictionary* 250–57; Cope, *Handmaid*; Antonia Fraser, *Weaker Vessel* 244–64; Hobby, *Virtue*; Scott-Luckens, "Alpha"; Rachel Trubowitz, "Female Preachers and Male Wives"; Holstun, *Pamphlet Wars* 112–33; Susan Wiseman, "Unsilent Instruments and the Devil's Cushions," in Isobel Armstrong, ed., *New Feminist Discourses*, London 1992, 176–96.

21. For a striking (but still religiously grounded) exception, see David Norbrook, "Lucy Hutchinson's 'Elegies' and the Situation of the Republican Woman Writer," *English Literary Renaissance* 27, 1977.

22. *P&L* [58–60].

23. *M* 4.407, 2.229–30.

The reformed freehold-household of republicans like Milton, Harrington, and Streater sounds remarkably like the gently masculinist "intimate sphere" of the bourgeois household analyzed by Habermas, which simultaneously nurtures male civic virtue and keeps women out of the public eye. Even if we reject as dubious and nostalgic the argument that republican and bourgeois theories of family government put an end to some premodern era of female empowerment, we should still admit the distinctly limited public role that republican theorists envision for women.[24]

Strangely, actual seventeenth-century women can disappear almost as completely from some forms of feminist analysis as from the most masculinist Cambridge School analysis of republican discourse. In *The Imaginary Puritan*, Armstrong and Tennenhouse describe seventeenth-century England as one big masculinist conduct manual, and the only woman before Mary Rowlandson whom they mention by name is Henrietta Maria. Similarly, Carole Pateman conducts a powerful critique of contract theory, which makes women the excluded "natural" ground of fraternal republicanism.[25] But Katharine Gillespie shows that Pateman focuses too exclusively on the tradition of male-authored social contract theory, and pays little or no attention to early modern women's experiments with voluntary religion—including their decisions freely to engage in sororal contracts with this or that congregation.[26] The core of the problem may well lie in a tendency endemic to cultural studies to overestimate the power of formal ideology. Amy Erickson suggests that we supplement our study of patriarchal ideologies with women's actual practice: "A materialist assessment of economic conditions in early modern England is possible, and must be placed alongside the ideological outpouring that seems to accompany female existence anywhere it goes. Only together do theory and practice approximate to anything like lived experience."[27]

Women's political agency also tends to disappear when critics concentrate on the body, fasting, and discourse to the exclusion of female rationality and group practice. In a trailblazing essay, Christine Berg and Philippa Berry drew on French feminist theory to construct a language-based analysis, arguing that female prophets employed a transgressive *écriture féminine*. Their Anna Trapnel inhabits Julia Kristeva's "semiotic" realm, a primal world of unarticulated desires not yet captured by the

24. I discuss Harrington's proposed reform of family government in *Rational Millennium* 192–5. Streater discusses the republican family in *Observations Historical, Political, and Philosophical*, for 3/19–3/26/54, 18 and 20; 4/25–5/2/54, 26; and 5/2–5/9/54, 36–7. Ann Hughes discusses the distinctly limited potential for a Leveller feminism in "Gender and Politics in Leveller Literature," Amussen and Kishlansky, *Political* 162–88.
25. *The Disorder of Women*, Stanford 1989.
26. "Table Talk."
27. *Women and Property in Early Modern England*, London 1993, 236. See also Dagmar Freist, "The King's Crown is the Whore of Babylon," Erickson and Balzaretti, "Special Issue: Presentations of the Self"; and Amanda Vickery, "Golden Age to Separate Spheres?" *The Historical Journal* 36.2, 1993.

"symbolic" of oppressive state rationality.[28] But this argument asks us to ignore the "semiotic" irruptions of male sectarians like Theauraujohn (Thomas Tany), Abiezer Coppe, and Cromwell himself—no stranger to tears and raptures, as his stalwart Anglican, Presbyterian, and republican enemies noted with disgust. And it requires us to overlook or discount the strongly "symbolic" or "rationalist" writings of female prophets, who struggled not so much to destroy male language as to appropriate it. Phyllis Mack argues for the relatively rational quality of writings by female preachers and prophets, and observes that, "far from being a marginalized, hysterical fringe group in seventeenth-century society, women like Grace Cary and Anna Trapnel were the ones whose spiritual sicknesses were healed"—unlike their silent and suffering sisters.[29] We can see this tendency to rational prophecy in the career of Mary Cary, who never claimed divine illumination and practiced methodical, scriptural exegesis, and in Trapnel, who engaged not only in the genres of "semiotic" or ecstatic prophecy in her songs, but also in more ordered and structured prose prayers, spiritual autobiography in a Foxean mode, published epistles, and forensic debate.

Barbara Foley's comments about postmodernist feminists also bear on their analyses of prophetesses: "It seems more than a little suspicious that centered subjectivity has been pronounced passé at the very moment when women—some women, in any case—are able to overcome their marginality and make a bid for centrality."[30] Postmodern critics risk repeating something strangely like the individuating corporal satire of premodern patriarchal conservatives, which aims to control radical prophecy by tracing it to the lustful and pathological body of an errant prophet, so it's not enough to invert the binary and celebrate the recalcitrant irrationality of the body, or the "semiotic" discourse that issues from it. We should also show the rationalities of prophetic discourse, and the way in which it brings male and female bodies together in a radical collective project. The masculinist unconscious of Habermas's communicative rationality needs Nancy Fraser's feminist critique, but postmodernism's celebration of the transgressive body needs Habermas's critique of its normative aporias. Medusa may laugh merrily, but capitalist patriarchy remains unpetrified.[31]

In the 1640s and 1650s, unprecedented numbers of women entered political life via the flourishing world of sectarian voluntary religion. William Prynne accused Independents of admitting women to preach and vote as members—"a mere politic invention to engage that sex to their

28. "Spiritual Whoredom," Barker et al., *1642*, 39–54, 48. They admit that this semiotic/symbolic opposition does not map clearly onto a female/male opposition (40), but without some such connection it loses its explanatory power and becomes simply a linguistic distinction signifying a linguistic distinction.
29. *Visionary* 93.
30. "Marxism in the Poststructuralist Moment," *Cultural Critique* 15, 1990, 36; she is paraphrasing and developing Nancy Hartsock.
31. Hélène Cixous, "The Laugh of the Medusa," *Signs* 1, 1976.

party."[32] Keith Thomas says that women formed a majority of sectarian churches, which isn't surprising given that they offered "spiritual equality, the depreciation of educational advantages, and that opportunity to preach or even to hold priestly office which they were otherwise denied."[33] Others have challenged Thomas's tabulation, but the sects clearly did draw women in substantial numbers. The spirit levels; it authorizes mechanics to speak to clerics, children to parents, girls to ladies, women to men. When a noble woman sat on the bed beside the teenaged prophetess Sarah Wight and "one whispered to her, that this was a great lady," she responded, " 'It's no more to me, then if it were such a one': naming a meaner woman troubled in spirit, that oft came to her."[34] Quoting Peter, Trapnel observed, "The spirit is not a respecter of persons."[35]

"Handmaid," one of the female prophets' favorite names for themselves, is the female scriptural equivalent to "slave" or "servant," as we can see in Joel's seminal prophecy about prophecy:

> And it shall come to pass afterward, that I will pour out my spirit upon all flesh; and your sons and your daughters shall prophesy, your old men shall dream dreams, your young men shall see visions: and also upon the servants and upon the handmaids in those days will I pour out my spirit.[36]

John Bale quoted from this passage on the title page of his *Lattre Examinacyon of Anne Askew.*[37] John Rogers invokes it.[38] In *A Woman Forbidden to Speak in the Church* (acquired by Thomason during Trapnel's Whitehall trance), the Quaker Richard Farnsworth recalls Joel and emphasizes that the spirit of God more readily fills up the weaker vessel.[39] Horrified, Thomas Edwards reported that a preaching lacemaker, perhaps Mrs Attaway, prefaced her sermon by saying, "That now those days were come, and that was fulfilled which was spoken of in the Scriptures, that God would pour out of his spirit upon the handmaidens, and they should prophesy."[40] John Vicars, in *The Schismatic Sifted*, condemns the "New

---

32. *Fresh Discovery*, 1645, 47.
33. "Women" 320–21, 330.
34. Henry Jessey and Sarah Wight, *The Exceeding Riches of Grace*, 1st edn, 1647, 119. That meaner woman could have been Trapnel; see below.
35. Acts 10.34; *T* 441.
36. Joel 1.28–9; Peter quoted this passage in his Pentecostal address, Acts 2.17–21.
37. *The Examinations of Anne Askew*, New York 1996, 73.
38. *Ohel* 564.
39. 3, 4. For other invocations of Joel, see *Prophetic Writings of Lady Eleanor Davies*, New York 1995, *passim*; Anne Hutchinson in Hall, *Antinomian* 268; Mary Cary, *A Word in Season to the Kingdom of England*, 1647, 5; *The Little Horns Doom & Downfall* and *A New and More Exact Mappe or, Description of New Jerusalems Glory* (continuously paginated), 1651, "136" [i.e., 236]–9; *TCS* 63; *TVK* 31, 53–4/*T* 22, 37, 136, 412; and Fell, *Womens* title page. Nat Turner may also have been drawn to it; see Eric Sundquist, *To Wake the Nations*, Cambridge, MA, 1993, 73–4.
40. *Gangraena*, 2nd edn, 1646, 117.

Light" interpretation of Joel, which emboldens "young saucy boys," "bold botching tailors," and "bold impudent huswifes."[41]

In this chapter, I will pay more attention to Trapnel than have most political historians of the period. At the same time, I pay more attention to the Fifth Monarchy movement than have most feminist historians of female prophets. I'll begin with Trapnel's early days, examining some of the conditions for her emergence into a public role. Then I'll turn to the two primary episodes in her prophetic career: her prophecy at Whitehall in January 1654, and her mission to Cornwall and imprisonment in Bridewell during that spring and summer. I'll conclude by looking at the last traces of her public career in 1657–59, and some later accounts of Fifth Monarchy women. My argument is that Trapnel strategically exploits the gaps and contradictions inside the patriarchal theology of the spirit to create a new political project integrating female praxis and Fifth Monarchist resistance to the Protectorate.

Fifth Monarchy Woman

In chapter 6, I examined three conditions for the emergence of the Agitators: the soldiers' religious praxis in congregations and prayer meetings, their martial praxis in the troops and regiments, and their discursive praxis in the Council of Officers. With the trigger of Parliament's attempt to disband the regiments, they elected their Agitators, setting off the events of 1647. In this section, I want to examine three similar conditions for Trapnel's emergence in 1654: her status as the independent and unmarried daughter of a widow; her education in the separating congregations of London, which offered opportunities for female education, expressive spirituality, and associative self-creation; and the collective millenarian expectations nurtured by the Fifth Monarchy movement. With the trigger of Cromwell's dissolution of Barebone's Parliament, these preconditions gave Trapnel the power, the practice, and the occasion for radical prophecy.

Anna Trapnel was born around 1622, in Poplar, Stepney Parish, just outside of London. She was the daughter of a shipwright named William Trapnel and his wife, whose name we do not know.[42] William's death left his wife and daughter in comfortable and relatively independent circumstances, and so, too, Anna when her mother died in 1642. As the unmarried sole survivor to a fairly wealthy widow, Trapnel, too, remained unusually independent of patriarchal authority—a condition she shared

---

41. 1646, 34.
42. *TRP* 50; *TCS* 3. Ellen Quarby and William Trapnell married in St Dunstan's, Stepney, in 1588, Mary Brooke and William Trapnell in 1597, Agnes Gavell and Symon Trapnell in 1603, and Anne Trapnel and Richard Hanley of Poplar, shipwright, in 1629. See Thomas Colyer Fergusson, ed., *The Marriage Registers of St. Dunstan's, Stepney, vol. 1, 1568–1639*, n.p. 1898, 22, 38, 51, 187.

with a number of other seventeenth-century women prophets.[43] Widows or maids of means, then, like relatively independent small producers, provoked a lustful desire to dispossess and exploit; by avoiding marriage and pregnancy, she retained more control over her own inherited property, her body, and her work. With the prideful self-propriety of the small producer, she later based her right to prophesy publicly on her earlier voluntary contributions to the support of the New Model.[44]

Second, Trapnel grew up inside the Protestant culture of voluntary religion that flourished in seventeenth-century London.[45] The combination of shipbuilding and Puritan religion largely defined Trapnel's Stepney. It was the scene of a number of sailors' riots in the twenties and thirties, and the home of many Huguenot refugees.[46] Maurice Thomson, the Puritan new merchant, was elected a parish sideman in April 1647, and had long associations with the parish, as did many officers and common sailors of Cromwell's navy.[47] In 1641, the year of Trapnel's conversion, Stepney became a hotbed of anti-episcopal activity when it produced the first call to allow parishes to appoint their own weekly lecturers. On September 6 1641, it appointed two new lecturers, Jeremiah Burroughs and William Greenhill. By 1637, Bishop Wren suspended and deprived Burroughs, whereupon he became a chaplain to the Earl of Warwick and one of the most ferocious and eloquent preachers of the era, a radical defender of popular sovereignty, and possibly the author of the classic millenarian sermon, *A Glimpse of Sion's Glory*. In 1638, Wren denied Greenhill his living for refusing to read the *Book of Sports*. Their appointment led to the Commons' unilateral anti-Laudian injunction of September 8—a crucial moment in the legislative revolution. Greenhill established a gathered church in 1644, and Trapnel was a member, or at least a regular visitor.[48] She invokes this sectarian culture by referring to her parents' life and death in the Lord, her early religious training, and her literacy: "trained up to my book and writing" from girlhood, she

---

43. Antonia Fraser, *Weaker Vessel* 81–9. It's difficult to overestimate the role of economic dependence in preventing women from entering the public sphere of the revolutionary era. Most of the notable exceptions prove the rule (Mack, *Visionary* 94–6). Two other phenomena bear on Trapnel's relative autonomy: a fifth of seventeenth-century marriages seem to have produced only daughters, and 10 to 20 percent of seventeenth-century women remained unmarried (Erickson, *Women* 224–5).

44. *TRP* 50.

45. On voluntary religion, see Tolmie, *Triumph*; Tai Liu, *Discord in Zion*, The Hague 1973; and above all, the works of Patrick Collinson.

46. Pearl, *London* 40; G. W. Hill and W. H. Frere, *Memorials of Stepney Parish*, Guildford 1890–91, vii–xiii.

47. Hill and Frere, *Memorials* 188–9; *GZ*; *BMR* passim; B. S. Capp, *Cromwell's Navy*, Oxford 1989, 303. Trapnel calls Christ a "great shipwright" who loaded the ships of the English navy (which she compared to the galleys of Isaiah 33.21) with a cargo of combustible naval stores (*TRP* 58). In her final prophecies, she praised God as he who "gave wisdom for to build ships, / That his works might appear" (*TVK* 44–6/*T* 30–32).

48. *GZ*; *BMR* 351–2, 407–8, 413–14, 423–4n., 439, 440–42, 445–6, 508, 521n., 569n. On Burroughs's possible authorship of *A Glimpse*, see Paul Christianson, *Reformers and Babylon*, Toronto 1978, 212–19, 251–2.

began to feel deep religious stirrings at age nine.[49] At fourteen, she "began to be very eager and forward to hear and pray. . . . I had great parts, in prayer great enlargements, and in discoursing and repeating of sermons, I was very forward."[50] This volatile combination of repetition and discoursing recalls Ann Hutchinson, whose "pretence," John Winthrop said, "was to repeat sermons, but when that was done she would comment upon the Doctrines, and interpret all passages at her pleasure, and expound dark places of Scripture."[51] Patrick Collinson notes that the collective "repetition" of sermons often led in time to the formation of separate churches.[52] Dutiful repetition becomes radical creation; indeed, we might almost define radical Protestantism in seventeenth-century England as repetition gone awry.

During the years before her public prophecy, Trapnel circulated among the gathered congregations of London. Hugh Peter shocked her out of an initial phase of "formal" devotion with his sermon on Isaiah 26.20:

"Come my people, enter then into thy chambers, and shut thy doors about thee, hide thy self as it were for a little moment, until the indignation be overpast." From these words he opened the marriage covenant that is between God and his Spouse; from that word "Come" he shewed the sweet compellation of God, to his covenanted people; then I was convinced of the excellency of that condition, to be in covenant, and to know it upon good grounds, which I was very ignorant of.[53]

Here we see two symbolic actions that would become crucial for Trapnel's public career: self-enclosure in a domestic space as a religious, even prophetic act, and church covenant as a metaphorical substitute for marriage.

Trapnel was "filled with horror" after hearing this sermon. "I ran from minister to minister, from sermon to sermon, but I could find no rest." It's easy to overestimate the neurotic or abstractly theological quality of this restlessness, and to underestimate its status as sheer, voluntary sociability.[54] Gadding to sermons was one of the safer ways for women to go public and get talked about. She offers an array of sectarian chaperones or character witnesses: the congregations of Simpson, Greenhill, Ralph Venning, Hanserd Knollys, and Henry Jessey "have knowledge of me, and of my conversation; if any desire to be satisfied of it, they can give testimony of me, and of my walking in times past."[55] In *The Structural Transformation of the Public*

49. *TCS* 3; *T* 367–74.
50. *TLS* 1.
51. Hall, *Antinomian* 263.
52. *The Religion of Protestants*, Oxford 1982, 266–7.
53. *TLS* 2. Trapnel calls both January and March the first month (*TLS* 8; *TCS* 8). She probably heard Peter late in 1641, since he only returned to England from Massachusetts Bay in September, and left as chaplain to the Irish expedition in 1642, and since she says she heard him before hearing John Simpson preach on January 1 1642 (*TLS* 8; *GZ*).
54. *TLS* 2; Collinson, *Religion* 242–81.
55. *TCS* 3. Knollys, formerly a Massachusetts Antinomian, and Hugh Peter provide two possible links to Ann Hutchinson.

Sphere, Habermas coined the term "audience-oriented subjectivity" to characterize the bourgeois impulse to publicize experiences proper to the intimate sphere, as in the salon, the epistolary novel, and literary culture more generally.[56] I think we can see something similar in what Trapnel calls her "public spiritedness"—public testimony to acts of indwelling divine grace, which help to culture a new collective existence.[57]

During a prolonged spiritual depression, Trapnel pondered murder and attempted suicide. Then, on New Year's Day 1642, she heard John Simpson preaching at Allhallows and underwent a conversion experience that left her feeling shamelessly naked before the luminous saints surrounding her:

> I knew not where I was, nor how to get out of the place where I sat, I apprehended nothing but a clothing of glory over my whole man; I never beheld Saints as I did then, I saw their faces like the face of angels; oh what angelical creatures did they appear before me, full of shining brightness!

Two days later, her mother died.[58] She left her daughter an estate, a blessing, and a model for domestic prophesying: " 'Lord! Double thy spirit upon my child.' These words she uttered with eagerness three times, and spoke no more."[59] Like mother, like daughter: her incantation appropriates a male scriptural voice, Elijah's parting blessing on Elisha.[60] Trapnel's aunt told her, "Cousin, the Lord hath taken your mother from you, now labor to be married to Christ, you have nothing to take up your time, but to labor for Christ." She answered, "I hope I am married to Christ." This heavenly marriage distances earthly suitors and reserves a place for her public vocation—not unlike those soft-focus "fresh fields and pastures new" that the aging virgin Milton imagined for himself four years earlier at the end of "Lycidas."[61] A single life leaves the door open to vocational experimentation through marriage to God, the congregation, or the Commonwealth.

Neither Trapnel nor her aunt seems to have considered her marrying a man of flesh and blood, and there's no good reason to insist that Trapnel was not a lesbian.[62] After her mother's death, and throughout her public

---

56. 29.
57. *TRP* 17; see also *TVK* 30/ *T* 21 and Nuttall, *Holy Spirit.*
58. *TLS* 2–3, 9, 10. In the brief autobiography in the opening of *The Cry of a Stone* (1654), Trapnel says her mother died "nine years ago," and that she experienced her first great sickness "seven years ago" (3), but that jars with her other account (*TLS* 3–4), so I assume she simply miscalculated or that the person compiling the tract drew on a spiritual autobiography she wrote in 1650 or 1651.
59. *TCS* 3. Purkiss misreads the exclamation mark as an "I" ("Producing" 143).
60. 2 Kings 2.9.
61. *TLS* 10.
62. On early modern lesbianism, see Judith C. Brown, *Immodest Acts: The Life of a Lesbian Nun in Renaissance Italy*, New York 1986; and my " 'Will you rent our ancient love asunder?' " *ELH* 54.4, 1988. Foucauldian attempts to historicize premodern same-sex orientation as a matter of practices, not identity, sometimes overestimate the clarity and uniformity of modern lesbian and gay identity for the sake of contrast; they forget, in other words, about high school.

career, Trapnel seems to have sought out women to live with. And she enjoyed close friendships with the ten women who prayed with her the night before she left for Cornwall, the "sisters" who visited her in Bride-well, and particularly with her "sister" Ursula Adman—terms that could indicate blood relation, religious affiliation, or erotic affection.[63] She denied that her delight was ever in men's company, but only in the godly.[64] On the other hand, she saturates her late prophecies with male-centered religious eroticism derived from Canticles, describing herself as Solomon's Queen and the Spouse of Christ and longing to "Drink, and eat of love's meat; / O take in Solomon's plenty."[65] Engaging in a sort of serial cohabitation on her way to Bridewell, she exulted at being held in the room that held the Fifth Monarchist preacher Christopher Feake on his way to prison.[66] And in December 1654, an anonymous but not hostile letter writer describes her as "conversant in, and much taken with" what seems to be a conventicle of young Fifth Monarchist men.[67] So Trapnel may have been sexually oriented to women or to men or to both or to neither—or to various of these in succession. That doesn't really narrow things down much—but maybe we should avoid narrowing things down. One task of historicist feminism should be to reconstruct the emotional textures of early modern women's collective life, with a particular eye to those affective bonds available to women outside of marriage, or inside marriage but lying athwart the reigning models of affect; Freud and Lacan would probably need to consult with Fourier to understand the erotics of sectarian church fellowship *c.* 1642. If we resist the impulse to distinguish neatly among consummated sex, desire, affection, and rapture in church fellowship, we might begin to see congregations and marriages shot through with various erotic bonds, with religious and political antipathies and solidarities.[68]

Some analogies: in "Methought I saw my late espoused saint," Milton half-redeems his misogynous divorce tracts by evoking the ideal of spousal conversational solace through his dead wife's achingly disembodied silence, then absence. After the Massachusetts Bay Colony expelled the Antinomians, its nosy emissaries found William Hutchinson in Rhode Island defiantly proclaiming his spousal and religious solidarity with his wife Anne: "And they conceive one church hath not power over the members of another church, and do not think they are tied to us by our covenant and so were we fain to take all their answers by going to their several houses, Mr. Hutchinson told us he was more nearly tied to his wife

63. John Boswell, *Same-Sex Unions in Premodern Europe*, New York 1994, 3–27, 272–9.
64. *TRP* 43.
65. *TVK* 2–3, 12/*T* 8.
66. *TRP* 37.
67. *CP* 2.xxxiv.
68. Amy Erickson notes eighteenth-century literary representations of marriage "in sentimen-tal terms of romantic love and surrender, rather than in the terms of economic partnership and religious companionship which had prevailed in the sixteenth and seventeenth centuries" (*Women* 232).

than to the church, he thought her to be a dear saint and servant of God."[69] Nehemiah Wallington, a Puritan joiner of revolutionary London, twice wrote that his heart was knit together with that of James Cole, a young tradesman, "like David and Jonathan," suggesting, as Paul Seaver says, "not only the closeness of their friendship but also its religious basis, for they were very much covenanted brothers in the faith."[70] And a Quaker captivity narrative of 1662 provides a complex cluster of spiritual and sexual associations. Once, during their years of imprisonment in Malta, Katharine Evans took her comrade Sarah Chevers by the arm, and, invoking the words of the marriage service, said, " 'The Lord hath joined us together, and woe be to them that should part us.' " Writing her husband, Evans called herself "thy dear and precious wife, and spouse, in the marriage of the Lamb, in the bed undefiled," then added a conjugal P.S. from Chevers: "My dearly beloved yoke-mate in the work of God, doth dearly salute you."[71] Returning to Trapnel, two things stand out. First, she chose the independence of unmarried celibacy over subjugated sex and coverture in marriage, scandalous sex outside of it. Second, her membership in a gathered church, and her public role as a prophet, became an intensely felt affective substitute for or equivalent to sex and marriage.

Starting in 1645, Trapnel "kept house with the means my mother left me," and paid taxes for the support of the Army. Eventually, after selling her plate and rings to support the Army further, she "wrought many nights hard to get money"—she doesn't say at what—then moved in with a minister's widow, and then with one of her daughters.[72] In May 1646, she composed her first "short discourse," published eight years later in *A Legacy for Saints*. In June she underwent her first "distemper of body," recovered briefly, then suffered a severe relapse on July 1.[73] In 1647, Henry Jessey compared the prophesying of "H. T. another in London in sickness, July 1, 1646," to the 53-day visionary fast of Sarah Wight, and noted that "Hanna Trapnel" visited her bedside. Given that Sarah Wight fasted and prophesied from April 6 to June 11, and that this same H. T. fasted and received a special inspiration from God between June 9 and 16 1647, Wight and Trapnel may have been engaging in some prophetic solidarity and competition.[74] She had an inexpressible vision of God, and the next day, God gave her a Christifying promise: "[A]fter two days I will revive thee, and the

---

69. Hall, *Antinomian* 392. This is the real "Canonization."
70. *Wallington's World*, Stanford 1985, 95.
71. *This Is a Short Relation*, 1662, 13–14, 55.
72. *TRP* 50.
73. *TLS* 43–7, 25.
74. Jessey and Wight, *Exceeding Riches* A2^r, 43, 139. On Wight's fasting and prophesying, see Nigel Smith, *Perfection* 45–51; Barbara Ritter Dailey, "The Visitation of Sarah Wight," *Church History* 55.4, 1986; Purkiss, "Producing"; Scott-Luckens, "Alpha"; and Catharine Gray, " 'Froward Writers, Critical Readers': Women's Public Roles and Counterpublic Spheres in Seventeenth-Century England," diss., SUNY Buffalo forthcoming. Trapnel may have been one of those unnamed maidens in distress whose conversations with Wight in 1647 Jessey recorded. For some reason, Jessey eliminated Trapnel's name (but not her initials) from later editions of his enormously popular work.

third day I will raise thee up, and thou shalt live in my sight." About 1648, Trapnel moved in with a kinswoman named Wythe, a merchant's wife living in Fanchurch Street, who turned her out in January 1654 because of her opposition to the Protectorate, whereupon she sought out her own lodgings, on which she paid assessments.[75]

During these early years, Trapnel prepared herself for her later public role. The Lord turned her, like Anne Hutchinson and Sarah Wight before her, into a spiritual advisor "for the refreshing of afflicted and tempted ones, inwardly and outwardly." After thus proving her faithfulness in ministering to "particular souls," God would allow her to reveal him to "the universality of Saints." The gadding, female-gendered healing professions open up dangerously into a public role; even if the household was a site of unmitigated oppressive confinement, Puritan women created a sort of inter-private publicness by moving and ministering from one home to another.[76] Before the New Model's march into London in August 1647 to purge the recalcitrant Presbyterian Junto, Trapnel looked up and down the street outside her house, saw an Army flag at one end and Blackheath hill at the other, and had a glorious revelation of the Commonwealth's future: the flag was the flag of the king of Salem, who would make the hill "fall down and become valleys before it." She embarked on a nine-day fast and had one vision of horns and another of the Army marching through the city.[77]

In 1650, she joined in full fellowship with John Simpson's congregation in Allhallows Street—an event of signal importance in her life. Early that year, she had one vision of Cromwell as a Gideon proceeding against the Scots, and in July, another of the Army's victory over the Scots at Dunbar, six weeks before that victory took place. She embarked on a two-week fast, and those who came to watch and attend saw her prophecies came to pass. In November 1652, she saw an English victory at sea over the Dutch—presumably confirmed by the great battles of February to July 1653—with "ships burning, bones and flesh sticking upon the sides of the ships, the sails battered, and the masts broken." During an intense depression, she took knives to bed to stab herself, thought about throwing herself down a well, and felt herself drawn to the sexual and spiritual temptations of "those familistical ranting tenets"—a bold and dangerous admission which suggests that royalist raillery about the erotic core of

---

75. *TLS* 25–6, 27. See also *TCS* 3; *TRP* 51.
76. *TCS* 3. Winthrop thought Hutchinson's bad influence began with her skills as "a woman very helpful in the times of child birth, and other occasions of bodily infirmities." Being "well furnished with means for those purposes, she easily insinuated herself into the affections of many, and the rather, because she was much inquisitive of them about their spiritual estates." She then went on to establish conventicles and a *de facto* counter-congregation (Hall, *Antinomian* 263). Thanks to Katharine Gillespie for conversations on this topic.
77. *TCS* 4–5.

sectarianism wasn't completely off the mark.[78] She prophesied the dissolution of the Rump Parliament four days before it took place, the ineffectiveness of Barebone's Parliament, the hypocrisy of its speaker, Francis Rous, and its dissolution.

The rise and repression of the Fifth Monarchy movement in the early 1650s provides the immediate context for Trapnel's emergence into public life.[79] Protectorate ideologists seem to have dyed the Fifth Monarchists an indelible, fanatical red, for modern historians usually see their chiliasm as the source of an irrational propensity for violence, an elitist will to power, and a spontaneist disregard for the details of revolutionary social organization. Working from Norman Cohn's psychohistorical linkage of medieval millenarians and modern totalitarians, Alfred Cohen says the Fifth Monarchists prefigured Hitler and Stalin.[80] Even Austin Woolrych, in his sober and thoughtful *Commonwealth to Protectorate*, calls them "clamorous millenarians" guilty of "sectarian fanaticism," "firebrands" guilty of "rantings" and "scurrilous aspersions against the Parliament, the army, the Council of State, indeed everyone in power," and "zealots" to be contrasted with Cromwellian "moderates."[81] But such attacks, from Cromwell to the present, have been strategic attempts to obscure not only the rational, democratic, and carefully elaborated quality of the Fifth Monarchist project, but also the Erastian fanaticism of "moderates" struggling to maintain the state's monopoly of violence and its support for such peculiar institutions as forced tithing.

As B. S. Capp has shown, the Fifth Monarchists differed from so many of their contemporaries not by the mere fact of their millenarianism, but by its specifically *popular* quality. They were primarily urban small producers centered in the clothing trades, but with wealthy gentry and capitalist allies (like Vane and Harrison) in Parliament and in the army, and even

---

78. Ibid. 6–7, 7–10, 10–12. T. J.'s *A Brief Representation and Discovery* (1649) tells of a Suffolk prophetess named Anne Wells. She fasted, fell into trances, and conducted a sectarian ménage-à-trois with Nicholas Ware and Matthew Hall, who helped her perform various "bawdy miracles." Before she married Hall, she "counterfeited a pain in the lower part of her belly, which by revelation Ware, and Hall must cure, by touching it, in the name of Jesus" (A3^{r-v}, 8)—probably an easily mustered invocation. Compare *The Alchemist* and Jonson's bunko team of Subtle, Face, and Dol Common, who feigns a fit of enthusiasm when Sir Epicure Mammon mentions "a fifth monarchy I would erect" (*Five Plays*, Oxford 1988, 4.5.28).

79. On the Baptist congregations, which provided the sectarian basis for the Fifth Monarchy movement, see Tolmie, *Triumph*; and J. F. McGregor, "The Baptists," in McGregor and Barry Reay, eds, *Radical Religion in the English Revolution*, London 1984, 24–63. If many seventeenth-century radicals wound up as Quakers, then, as McGregor points out, they tended to start out as Baptists. On the Fifth Monarchists, see B. S. Capp's masterful *The Fifth Monarchy Men* (*CFMM*). On the "Nominated Assembly" or Barebone's Parliament, see *WCP*; and David L. Smith, "The Struggle for New Constitutional and Institutional Forms," in Morrill, *Revolution* 15–34.

80. Cohn, *The Pursuit of the Millennium*, rev. edn, Oxford, 1970; Cohen, "The Fifth Monarchy Mind," *Social Research* 31, 1964.

81. *WCP* 49, 93, 126, 325, 328.

stronger ties to the poor than the Quakers had.[82] Their critics denounced them as hidden communists. For Richard Flecknoe, the Fifth Monarchist speaks to God with less reverence "then any clown does to his landlord, he so hates a gentleman, as he can't endure God should be served like one."[83] Thomas Hall warned that millenaries would "animate men to seditions" by proclaiming "a jubilee and year of liberty from tithes and taxes and imprisonment, after: have at rents, and debts, and a community of all things."[84] Opening the first Protectorate Parliament in September 1654, Cromwell grounded the interest of the nation in the interest of "A nobleman, a gentleman, a yeoman," and accused Fifth Monarchists of claiming "that liberty and property are not the badges of the kingdom of Christ."[85]

This hysterical anticommunism should not lead us to overlook the Fifth Monarchists' genuine small producer radicalism. In *A Standard Set Up*, the manifesto for his 1657 rising, Venner proposes to abolish tithes, the excise, standing armies, arbitrary imprisonment, impressment of soldiers, insecure tenure by copyhold, and legal privileges based on class or status.[86] Others proposed to abolish inherited rights to nominate clergy, imprisonment for debt, and capital punishment for theft, and to institute poor relief, civil marriages, and other legal reforms. Mary Cary described her New Jerusalem as a commonwealth of small producers and tradesmen, with moderate labor and no excise: "Each man shall enjoy the fruit of his own labors: they shall not be unjustly deprived of it, as now many be."[87] In 1653, she proposed a systematic social program driven by a middling-sort ideal of industriousness. She criticized the Rump for its short work-week, and encouraged the members of Barebone's Parliament not to use their governmental positions to enrich themselves. She proposed to end tithes, nurture voluntary religion by throwing open closed meeting halls, new-model the universities to encourage poor scholars, establish work-houses, simplify law codes, favor the poor in lawsuits and support them through public fees on mail delivery and formal contracts, increase local governmental autonomy, limit government salaries, and hold off the excise by ending the sale of government lands. She imagines a system of poor relief at the level not of the parish, but the state, since "there are many godly people that are not in church fellowship, so there may be many godly poor also that are not in church fellowship." She even

82. *CFMM* 22; "The Fifth Monarchists and Popular Millenarianism," McGregor and Reay, *Radical* 165–89, 170; *CFMM* 82, 88. Amid its learned millenarian exegesis and cries for violent revolt, the manifesto for Venner's fatal 1661 Fifth Monarchist rising proposes to limit exports of fuller's earth, used to remove lanolin from raw wool (Venner, *A Door of Hope* 5). On Fifth Monarchist social radicalism, see Capp, "Fifth" and *CFMM* 82–99; and Hill, *Experience* 51–68 and *English* 307–10.

83. *Aenigmaticall Characters*, 1658, 28.

84. *Chiliasto-mastix redivivus*, 1657, 53.

85. William Cortez Abbott, ed., *The Writings and Speeches of Oliver Cromwell*, 4 vols, Cambridge, MA, 1937–47, 3.438.

86. Medley, *Standard* 7, 20.

87. *Little Horns* 309.

proposes toleration for Anglicans and Presbyterians, but this may be righteously disingenuous: what's a prelate or a presbyter without a parish or a tithe?[88] In 1649, the future Fifth Monarchist Peter Chamberlen proposed in *The Poore Mans Advocate* to use confiscated estates to pay the Army, relieve the poor, and develop trades and schools. He maintained his social radicalism through the fifties. An anonymous Fifth Monarchist pronounced the nation "more beholding to the meanest kitchen maid in it, that hath in her a spirit of prayer, than to a thousand of her profane swaggering Gentry."[89] Vavasor Powell said, "there should be no beggar in Israel, and in well-governed Commonwealths there are not."[90] John Spittlehouse and John More said that Thomas Müntzer preserved true Christianity against Luther's thinly veiled popery—an argument whose boldness it would be hard to overestimate.[91] In 1656, another Baptist scoffed at those who call the work of the saints "a monster . . . called Münster." And in 1660, another noted that Continental Anabaptists were in no position to rebut charges of being cutthroats after their own throats were cut.[92]

As Capp has shown, the Fifth Monarchists were "a pressure group rather than a new denomination or party," and drew together civilians and soldiers from General Baptist, Particular Baptist, and Independent congregations.[93] In this, they strongly resembled the Levellers. True, they grew out of separating London congregations that were by no means friendly to the Levellers in 1647, and the Levellers come closer to modern democratic sensibilities than do the more prescriptive Fifth Monarchists.[94] But after 1649, when Commonwealth forces crushed the Levellers, the Fifth Monarchists took on their role of an organizing oppositional vanguard for small producers and the poor. In 1655, Fifth Monarchists published *A Looking-Glasse*, which reprinted Leveller and Army manifestos stretching back to 1647. *A Standard Set Up* invokes the Army's *Declaration* of June 1647 asserting it was no mere mercenary army, and the Levellers' *Large Petition* of September 1648. It proposes a "sanhedrin, or supreme council," to be elected yearly, and its members subject to all laws, with the franchise limited to "the Lord's freemen . . . those that have a right with

---

88. *Twelve* 3, 4, 9. On Cary, see Alfred Cohen's *GZ* essay; "The Fifth Monarchy Mind"; and "Mary Cary's *The Glorious Excellencie* Discovered," *The British Studies Monitor* 10, 1980; Dorothy Ludlow, "Arise" 241–68; Kate Lilley, "Blazing Worlds," in Clare Brant and Diane Purkiss, eds, *Women, Texts and Histories 1575–1760*, London 1992, 102–33.

89. *The Failing and Perishing of Good Men*, 1663, 13.

90. *God the Father Glorified*, 2nd edn, 1650, 138; perhaps Winstanley echoed him in *The Law of Freedom*: "The glory of Israel's commonwealth is this, / They had no beggar among them" (*W* 524).

91. *A Vindication*, 1652, 14–15.

92. *The Banner of Truth Displayed* 48–9. *The Gorgon's Head or the Monster of Munster Choaked with a Lamb's Skinn* 2.

93. "Fifth" 170.

94. See W[illiam] A[spinwall]'s bloody-minded *The Legislative Power Is Christ's Peculiar Prerogative* (1656), perhaps influenced by John Cotton's equally draconian *Moses His Judicials* (1641), which he republished in 1655 in *An Abstract of the Lawes of New England as They are Now Established.*

Christ in and according to the New Covenant."[95] Even if this grouping does imply some measure of oligarchy, we should remember (as England's ruling class never forgot) that an aristocracy of grace is a larger, more open, more permeable thing than an oligarchy of blood or wealth. In any case, *A Standard* allows no particular church or religion to play a direct role in the state, and it allows the state to play no direct role in churches. The Fifth Monarchists were not "secular," of course—neither were the Levellers. But their impulse to democratize religion by making preachers accountable to their congregations alone, not to a state authority or a lay patron, suggests a vision of power-from-below incompatible with any totalitarian state. In effect, they were theocratic republicans who wished, on a scriptural basis, to build in strict safeguards against a tyrannical executive, and maintain a strict division between state and religious life, so that the voluntary associative democracy of the gathered church could continue to nurture democratic culture, and subject state power to a constant check. Their strangely theocratic separation of church and state becomes clearest when we note their outraged and even violent attack on the Erastian state institutions that would threaten it: lay patronage of church office, the state appointment of triers and ejectors, and state-enforced tithing.[96]

The Fifth Monarchy movement emerged in 1651 when a group of radical Independent and Baptist preachers and military men, including Thomas Brooks, Christopher Feake, William Greenhill, Thomas Harrison, Henry Jessey, Hanserd Knollys, and John Simpson, began meeting and discussing a godly reformation of England. They drew up and subscribed a declaration calling for a government that would encourage election of the godly over "all other qualifications, of birth, riches, or parts," while prohibiting rigid sectarian qualifications or disqualifications for rule—communists, polygamists, Ranters, and malignants excepted.[97] Allhallows the Great (associated with Simpson) and St Anne's, Blackfriars (associated with Feake), became the centers of Fifth Monarchist activity in London.[98] In April 1653, Cromwell called the "Nominated Assembly" or "Barebone's Parliament," the decade's "most radical social experiment."[99] With 139 persons nominated by the separating congregations and selected by the Army Council, and with at least twelve Fifth Monarchists in its ranks, it became the focal point for millenarian expectations.[100] But radicals within and without clashed with Cromwell and his speaker, Francis Rous. According-ing to a letter Thurloe received in early December, an ordinance of Barebone's Parliament made it possible for Christopher Feake, that "bold and crafty orator," to give a lecture at Blackfriars calling Cromwell "the

95. Medley, *Standard* 1, 16–19.
96. See *The Banner* B1ʳ, 77, and *passim*.
97. *CFMM* 60–61; *A Declaration of Divers Elders* 5.
98. *WCP* 18.
99. David L. Smith, "Struggle" 19.
100. *WCP* 410–32.

man of sin, the old dragon, and many other scripture ill names."[101] So on December 12, after defeating another attempt to abolish tithes, the more "moderate" members of the Assembly took advantage of the radicals' absence at a Monday prayer meeting to dissolve themselves and return power to Cromwell. Three days later, the Army Council adopted *The Instrument of Government*, England's first written constitution, which established rule by an elected parliament, which in turn had the power to elect a Lord Protector, who alone had the power to modify the constitution. On the 16th, Parliament made Cromwell Lord Protector.

The Fifth Monarchists reacted furiously. On Sunday the 18th, at Christ Church, Newgate, Feake and Powell called Cromwell "the dissemblingest perjured villain in the world."[102] The next day, they lectured at St Anne's, Blackfriars. Marchamont Nedham reported to Cromwell that Feake began with an incendiary sermon on Daniel's description of the last and most perplexing of four allegorical beasts:

> And after this I saw in the night visions, and behold a fourth beast, dreadful and terrible, and strong exceedingly; and it had great iron teeth: it devoured and brake in pieces, and stamped the residue with the feet of it: and it was diverse from all the beasts that were before it; and it had ten horns. I considered the horns, and, behold, there came up among them another little horn, before whom there were three of the first horns plucked up by the roots: and, behold, in this horn were eyes like the eyes of man, and a mouth speaking great things.[103]

Two years before, Feake had identified the little horn with the executed King Charles.[104] Now, he left little doubt that it had taken on Cromwellian contours. He even built in the watchful Nedham: "[I]n this horn were eyes like the eyes of a man ... that is, he had eyes, his emissaries and spies, in every corner." Powell spoke next, denouncing Cromwell, his spies, his army officers bought off with estates, and his persecutions of the godly.[105] Nedham reported the next day to the Council, which promptly arrested Feake and Powell, examined them, and prohibited Monday lectures at Blackfriars. But the Fifth Monarchists found other forums, including Christ Church, and incurred the further wrath of the Council.[106]

When Cromwell destroyed Barebone's Parliament and imprisoned Fifth Monarchist leaders, he set the stage for Trapnel's public debut by simultaneously turning himself into an enemy worth prophesying against, and

---

101. *B* 1.621.
102. Ibid. 3.641. *Strena Vavasoriensis* (1654) records a radical anti-Protectoral hymn sung at this service (24) and attacks Powell's entire career.
103. Dan. 7.7–8.
104. Preface to Mary Cary, *Little Horns* 6.
105. *CSPD* 6.304–8; *PRO* 18/42/114–16.
106. *WCP* 363–4; *CSPD* 6.308–9, 353.

sealing up the usual conduits for God's wrath.[107] In a sense, he unwittingly pushed Trapnel into the "masculine" public sphere by enclosing male Fifth Monarchists.[108] Some have suggested that male Fifth Monarchist leaders manipulated Anna Trapnel for their own ends.[109] One might say with equal justice that she took advantage of their imprisonment, or, better, that Fifth Monarchy men and women engaged in a complex program of collective revolutionary praxis not without its gender-related tensions, or its proper sorts of solidarity.

God's Handmaid vs the Little Horn: The Prophecy at Whitehall

On January 7 1654, as part of its efforts to roll back the radicalism of Barebone's Parliament, the Council of State called the Welsh preacher and Fifth Monarchist Vavasor Powell to Whitehall. Sitting and waiting for him in a Whitehall anteroom, Anna Trapnel was "seized upon by the Lord," and began praying and singing. Her friends took her to a room in a nearby inn where she stayed for twelve days, neither eating nor drinking for the first five, then drinking some small beer and eating a little toast, once a day. Lying rigid in bed, she alternated prose "prayers" and verse "songs" in ballad or common hymn meter in sessions of two to five hours. On January 11, an amanuensis known only as "The Relator" began writing them down.[110]

This was Trapnel's abrupt entry into the revolutionary public sphere, and it was a sensational one—comparable to that of John Felton at Portsmouth or Cornet Joyce at Holmby House. What did it mean for her to prophesy from a room in a Whitehall inn? I propose to begin by considering not her prophetic language, but her symbolic action, which invoked and transformed four other sites of political and symbolic praxis: the household, the Parliament, the congregation, and the theater. First, Trapnel's room in the inn became a politicized household. When the Council of State attempted to domesticate her by shunting her aside into a waiting room while it examined Powell, she did not stride into the streets with an anti-Protectoral prophecy; indeed, she herself attacks such immodest prophets.[111] Rather, she fell into a prophetic trance and

---

107. Cromwell imprisoned Feake or held him under house arrest from January 1654 to December 1656; Simpson from January to July 1654 and from December 1655 to February 1656; Powell in December 1653; Rogers from July 1654 to January 1657 and again in 1658; Harrison from February 1655 to March 1656 and again in 1657; Carew from February 1655 to 1656; and Courtney from February 1655 to October 1656 (*GZ*).

108. Compare Katherine Sutton, who was part of Hanserd Knollys's congregation in Holland. In 1662, when Restoration persecutions made godly preachers scarce, God gave her a special gift of prophecy. See *A Christian Womans Experiences of the Glorious Working of God's Free Grace*, Rotterdam 1663, 16, 30; and I. Mallard, "The Hymns of Katherine Sutton," *Baptist Quarterly* 20.1, 1963.

109. Alfred Cohen, "Prophecy and Madness," *The Journal of Psychohistory* 11.3, 1984; Raymond, *Making* 162.

110. *TCS* 12, 16.

111. Ibid. 22.

proceeded to turn her prophecy chambers into a hybrid public/private space, like the salon or parlor that Habermas analyzes in the later bourgeois household.[112] Through most of her career as a prophet, Trapnel did not so much venture out of the intimate sphere into the public sphere as break down the division between them: moving her earlier bouts of fasting and prophecy into the public eye, she created a sort of fragmented Fifth Monarchist household by allowing the spirit to move her from one domestic space to another. As Susan Wiseman suggests, Trapnel liberated herself from patriarchal authority not by rejecting it, but by submitting herself so completely to the divine patriarch that she could ignore any merely human ones.[113] We might compare the Fifth Monarchists' servile yet anti-tyrannical fealty to King Jesus.

By lying in bed for twelve days and giving spiritual life to others while risking her own mortal life, Trapnel conjured up the authority of protracted childbirth. From within her inspired trance, Trapnel invoked the self-authorizing Christian rhetoric of the suffering body:

> The Lord is building his temple, it is no time now for them to build tabernacles; now thou art upon thy temple-work, shall they be building great palaces for themselves? The soldiers slight thy handmaid, but she matters not, they shall and must consider in time; they say these are convulsion fits, and sickness, and diseases that make thy handmaid to be in weakness; but oh they know not the pouring forth of thy spirit, for that makes the body to crumble, and weakens nature; in these extraordinary workings thou intendest to shew what is coming forth hereafter; something is a coming forth, there is so Lord; and oh how does thy handmaid bless thee![114]

Trapnel repeated the suffering of those travailing women whom she had counseled, her mother's deathbed effusion, and the prophecy of her namesake: as the temple priest Eli mocked Hannah for drunkenness when she moved her lips while praying silently for a child, so "England's rulers and clergy do judge the Lord's handmaid to be mad, and under the administration of evil angels, and a witch." And as the Lord made Hannah fertile and allowed her to bring forth Samuel, "that typical prophet, who held forth Christ that great prophet," so she prays that he will allow her to bring forth Christ to her listeners.[115] She who was contained at Whitehall becomes the container, a virginal Rebekah, with Jacob and Esau—Barebone's Parliament and Cromwell's Council—struggling in her womb: "Oh, this is a day of Jacob's trouble, thine looked for refreshment, and behold greater trouble, they looked for a birth, and behold it is yet

---

112. *Structural* 5.
113. "Unsilent" 188–9. See also Peter Lake's "Feminine Piety and Personal Potency," *The Seventeenth Century* 2.2, 1987; and Vickery on the increasingly controversial concept of gendered separate spheres ("Golden Age").
114. *TCS* 29.
115. *TRP* A2ᵛ–A3ʳ. 1 Sam. 1; the "Song of Hannah" in 1 Sam. 2 praises the Lord's power to overturn, to make the barren fertile and the hungry full.

in travail." As a virgin mother, she was not worlds distant from Mary Adams, the Ranter who proclaimed herself pregnant with the Messiah.[116]

Diane Purkiss finds it anachronistic to see Trapnel's trances as the self-destructive impulses of an enforced feminine weakness, suggesting that fasting women could gain the considerable symbolic authority of the deathbed.[117] Trapnel's fasts inoculated her against attempts such as those we saw in *A Discoverie* to debunk claims to the holy spirit by tracing them to the rebellious flesh: to gluttony or (worse) lust. They also corrected what sectarians saw as the neo-Laudian devotional practices springing up inside the Protectorate. They formed a radical substitute for the "official literature of hunger and abstinence," such as the fast-day sermons initiated by King Charles and reinstituted by the Commonwealth.[118] These sermons continued under the Protectorate, and may even have taken aim at Trapnel herself. On March 20, in *A Declaration of His Highness the Lord Protector*, Cromwell called for a day of public fasting and national purification, attacking those "false prophets" and "filthy dreamers" who "despise government" and "speak evil of dignities."[119] But for sectarians, these fasts came to resemble the Laudian feasts they partly aimed to replace. In January 1637, the Antinomian John Wheelwright boldly seized the occasion of a fast-day sermon in Boston Church to attack civic fasts as a popish elevation of sanctification over justification.[120] In May 1654, a Fifth Monarchist broadside attacked Cromwell's "hypocritical mock-fasts."[121] In October, a Quaker pamphlet attacked fast days as an idol.[122] Trapnel's fasting, like her singing, had to be *ex tempore*, a spontaneous act of immanent Protestant critique. She tried to restore fasts to their earlier ascetic purity and reveal Cromwell, his Council, and his tithe-fed ministers as versions of their erstwhile Laudian enemies.[123]

Purkiss suggests that Trapnel's fasting returns her to a medieval and

---

116. *TCS* 22. On Adams, see *GZ* and Purkiss, "Producing" 153–4. Revelation's pregnant woman, clothed with the sun (12.1–2), who stands for the persecuted early church, provides an millenarian archetype. See *T* 725, 723 [i.e. 732], 751–7, 827, 867, 872, 873, and Avery (*Scripture-Prophecies* 28). Scott-Luckens notes that Sarah Wight also mimed the rituals of childbirth, a female-controlled rite of passage not yet medicalized ("Alpha" ch. 4).

117. "Producing" 143, 145. Dailey discusses Joan Drake's deathbed empowerment ("Visitation" 443). *The Wonderfull Works of God* (1641) tells the story of a young maid who returned briefly from the dead to preach to her family and community.

118. Feroli, "Engendering" 108. On fast sermons, see Hill, *English* 79–108.

119. 2 Pet. 2.1; Jude 1.8, 10.

120. Hall, *Antinomian* 152–72.

121. *An Alarm to the Present Men in Power.*

122. *A Warning from the Lord.* Hyder E. Rollins discusses the symbolic dimensions of seventeenth-century fasting in "Notes on Some English Accounts of Miraculous Fasts," *The Journal of American Folk-Lore* 34, 1921. See also Thomas, *Religion* 148–9; Purkiss, "Producing"; and Dailey, "Visitation." Some Quakers went so far as to challenge other sects to fasting duels: Henry J. Cadbury, ed., *George Fox's "Book of Miracles"*, Cambridge 1948, 34–5.

123. Katherine Sutton attacks public fasting as a "formal outside way of worship" and insists on the unpremeditated quality of her hymns (*Christian* 6, 44); compare Milton on Adam and Eve's spontaneous hymning (*Paradise Lost* 5.149).

Catholic "*contemptus mundi* at odds with post-Reformation teaching."[124] Like their sisters entering arranged marriages, novice nuns tended to enter monastic life under the pressure of families, so their fasts were a sort of repetition compulsion—an effort to repeat, internalize, and master their imposed asceticism. But Trapnel freely chose her status as an ascetic virgin, asserting her own bodily self-propriety in a public and sacramental refusal of the sacrament of marriage—rather like the public/private fast of Gandhi, a suffragette, or an IRA hunger striker. Nor does her fast call up the Puritan "worldly asceticism" to which Weber traces the origins of capitalist primitive accumulation. Rather, she practices a small-producer's asceticism within Protestant voluntary religion, one that aims not to produce material signs of divine election but to spark a saintly revolution against the Antichristian and capitalist Protectorate.

Engels saw such an asceticism among the peasant rebels of sixteenth-century Germany:

> This ascetic austerity of morals, this demand to forsake all joys of life and all entertainments, opposes the ruling classes with the principle of Spartan equality, on the one hand, and is, on the other, a necessary stage of transition without which the lowest stratum of society can never set itself in motion. In order to develop its revolutionary energy, to become conscious of its own hostile attitude towards all other elements of society, to concentrate itself as a class, it must begin by stripping itself of everything that could reconcile it with the existing social system.[125]

Trapnel's asceticism helped her gather those around her together into an oppositional collective. Her fasting body stood for all the English who helped support Parliament with their money and their labor, now suffering under the reign of Cromwell's Council, and for the temperate holy republic of the future. As the relatively egalitarian spirituality of the separated church becomes an analogical base for the revolution of the saints, so the ascetic body of the fasting prophetess becomes an analogical base for an assault on a corrupt and extortionate social order. Like Milton's virginal Lady, who sits rigid on Comus's throne, rending the decorum of the court masque by attacking courtly gluttony, Trapnel lies rigid in her bed, rending the decorum of Whitehall and the bed chamber by denouncing the emergent court culture of the Protectorate: "Let them see what those were who were thy true ministers, were they such as did

---

124. "Producing" 148–9. Carolyn Walker Bynum discusses the asceticism of medieval nuns in *Holy Feast and Holy Fast*, Berkeley 1987. John Rogers reconstructs a seventeenth-century Protestant cult of apocalyptic virginity in "The Enclosure of Virginity," in Richard Burt and John Michael Archer, eds, *Enclosure Acts*, Ithaca, NY, 1994, 229–50.

125. *MECW* 10.428–9. Compare the "Roundheads" of the early forties (*FCA* 231; Hutchinson, *Memoirs* 86–7), the United Irish Croppy Boys (Catholic peasants imitating close-cropped Jacobins), and Bobby Sands, one of whose IRA comrades recalls, "Bobby went and got a haircut and a shave on the first day of his hunger strike. I thought at the time, 'This is it. The body's wasted here. The body's going out.' It was a marker that a phase had gone obsolete and a new phase had begun" (Allen Feldman, *Formations of Violence*, Chicago 1991, 245).

pamper their bellies, and their backs? were not thine willing to feed upon any thing, to go in skins, to be anything for the gospel of Jesus Christ? Has not their fullness brought blindness upon them?"[126] Or as Milton's St Peter says in "Lycidas," when denouncing Arminian prelates, "Blind mouths!"

Second, Trapnel revives Barebone's Parliament, turning her chamber near the very center of state power into a newsworthy site for meeting, discoursing, note taking, and controversy. *Cry of a Stone* lists eight visitors from the disbanded Parliament: Robert Bennet, John Bingham, Henry Birkenhead, John Chetwood, Hugh Courtney, Captain Francis Langdon, Colonel William Sydenham, and William West, along with Captain Bawtrey (Major Bawden?), Mr (Samuel?) Lee, Christopher Feake, and Ladies Darcy and Vermuyden.[127] One newsbook called her "a virgin prophetess come to Whitehall, who has declared great and wonderful ['things'?] touching this present government, and saith that she comes from God."[128] Another described the sensation she created among those "many hundreds" who "do daily come to see and hear":

> Those that look to her, and use to be with her, say she neither eateth nor drinketh, save only sometimes a toast and drink, and that she is in a trance, and some say that what she doth is by a mighty inspiration, others say they suppose her to be of a troubled mind, and people flocking to her so as they do, causeth her to continue this way, and some say worse, so every one gives their opinions as they please.[129]

The author may be pumping up the numbers, but the reciprocal dynamics of performer and audience seem plausible, given that Trapnel frequently addressed her audience and attempted to drown out hecklers.[130] In generating tumultuous conflicting opinions, she resembled Barebone's Parliament itself during its final, factious months. In the demands she makes, the persons gathered around her in her chamber, and their names gathered around her in a pamphlet, she becomes a singing petition.[131]

Third, Trapnel's room in the inn became a new meetinghouse where Fifth Monarchists could gather and hear a new sort of preacher. Her prophecy empowered her in relation not only to the Protectorate, but also to male preachers in general, including Fifth Monarchists. When preachers came to hear her, take notes on her inspired utterances, repeat and discuss her words, she gained an authority denied her inside the walls of Allhallows the Great. When Jessey and Simpson suggested she was under a self-willed temptation to fast, she passed along God's assurances

126. *TCS* 44; see 8, 29, 38, and 42–4 for further references to fasting. In her late prophecies, Trapnel denounced Cromwell's pomp, French and Spanish-style sumptuary excess, courtly table etiquette, and even gravy (*T* 790, 552–3, 705, 440).
127. *TCS* 2.
128. *The Grand Politique Post* 1/10–1/17/54.
129. *Several Proceedings of State Affairs* 1/12–1/19/54.
130. *TCS* 52, 67.
131. See Dailey, "Visitation" 452.

to the contrary. The editor of *A Cry* related a conversation she had with one listener, in which she claimed an inspired authority greater even than that of her ministers:

> "[W]hat moved you to silence at any time when you ceased from speaking? was it with you as with other good men, ministers, etc. who cease at discretion, either having no more to say, or having spent their strength of body, or having wearied the people?" She answered in these words, "It was as if the clouds did open and receive me into them: and I was as swallowed up of the Glory of the Lord, and could speak no more."[132]

Later, her Cornish listeners asked, "Which of all our ministers can hold out thus many hours without a cordial?"[133]

Modern readers may lack her stamina: anyone who has worked through *Cry of a Stone* and *Voice for the King of Saints and Nations* will echo feelingly Dr Johnson's judgment on *Paradise Lost*: none ever wished it longer than it is.[134] But the sheer length and iteration of her prophecies—and the fascination of her listeners—require some explanation, not just summary aesthetic judgment. As a woman's attempt to graft onto the words of male authority figures, Trapnel's scripture-based prophecy resembles so many genres of early modern women's discoursing, including Mary Sidney's translations of the Psalms, Anne Bradstreet's DuBartasean quarternions, and the translations of (sometimes nonexistent) French male writers by Trapnel's royalist contemporaries, Katherine Philips and Aphra Behn. But their couplets, however erotic, were manifestly written, polished, revised, and *on the page*, while her endless millenarian fourteeners were triply *embodied*, with a gasp for breath during the silent eighth beat, a gasp of exhaustion (or an ascent into heaven) at the end of the session, and the struggle of the Relator to take them all down amid the crush of her fascinated audience. If their works smelt of the lamp, hers smelt of faster's breath in a close and crowded room.

For an audience saturated with sermons and scriptural writing, Trapnel's prophecies no doubt produced the pleasure of the familiar, not so much through specific scriptural quotations as through two- or three-word bursts of scriptural language which hover just beneath the level of a concrete allusion. She created a sort of *Iliad* in reverse: a body of imagery and phrases taken from printed Scripture, sermons, and devotions, then re-voiced as oral formulaic poetry in improvisatory performances of Homeric length. Her prophecies were not rational and political in any forensic sense; though they became the object of controversy and debate,

---

132. *TCS* 5, 14–15.
133. *TRP* 18.
134. The impatience of later readers at Trapnel's "doggerel" reflects on their reading practice as well as her performance. Read in small doses with a concentration that emulates sectarian rapture at the spontaneous generation of the spirit, her songs display considerable power, and her prose prayers even more. See, for instance, her long improvisation on "rest," which draws on Peter's connection of the millennium and the Sabbath (*TCS* 45–8; 2 Pet. 3).

they didn't call for or even permit an immediate response. But they did provide the Fifth Monarchist collective under assault with an occasion for collective solidarity, not without risk—like a group of libel readers gathered together to share in the libel's composition.

Finally, Trapnel created a sort of political theater right outside Whitehall, one of the key sites of theatrical display in seventeenth-century England. First, her physical collapse created an almost sculptural collective set piece of prophetess and (literal) supporters.[135] Theatrical language runs through reports about Trapnel—not only those by skeptics like Marchamont Nedham, who referred to her "playing her part" at Whitehall, but also Trapnel's own account of her unwilling command performance: God forced her out of her "closet" and turned her into a "voice, a sound . . . a voice within a voice, another's voice, even thy voice through her," and forced upon "the word's stage of reports and rumors."[136] England's stage, if not the world's, Whitehall's masquing hall was an important symbolic center of court life from 1603 to 1642, and no less important for the iconoclastic drama of regicidal republicanism when Charles I, Marvell's "royal actor," mounted the "tragic scaffold" just outside. Trapnel's prophecy incorporated both cultural moments. It made her room at the inn the site of a millenarian counter-masque of the holy spirit. And her attack on Whitehall's inhabitant and its emergent court culture frequently verged on tyrannicidal iconoclasm. Trapnel played both good cop and bad cop. Sometimes she interceded with God for Cromwell's life, and warned him against being corrupted by a "wicked council"—a menacing echo of those earlier threats against Charles's evil counselors. At other times, she threatened more directly. On her first day of recorded prophecy, she addressed her scribes in the tones of the Son of Man addressing John of Patmos, telling them to

> Write how that Protectors shall go
> And into graves there lie:
> Let pens make known what is said, that
> They shall expire and die.

In a later prayer, she warned about God's impending judgment: "[S]o the transacting of things here below do come suddenly, and poor man, how is he confounded, he is in a smother in his own judgment, he is in the smoke, and cannot find the door! Let not thy children be blinded and blood shed, oh take them out, and let them take heed that they do not return into such smoky houses again."[137]

We might forgive Cromwell for hearing a physical threat beneath the spiritual warning. The Protectorate feared Trapnel not because she

---

135. Compare the Pentecostal/R&B *tableau vivant* created when James Brown collapses into the arms of his band at the end of each sweat-soaked performance. Thanks to Mike Dunn for this point.

136. *TCS* 42; *TRP* 49.

137. *TCS* 22, 19–20, 37.

exposed her ungovernably female body or uttered a semiotically ecstatic discourse, but because she convened a seditious collective and uttered fairly straightforward threats in their presence. On January 19, the last day of Trapnel's prophecy, the Council of State published an ordinance that made it treasonable "to compass or imagine the death of the Lord Protector" or to declare his government tyrannical or illegitimate.[138] The next day, a group of accommodating preachers wrote a circular letter to Baptist churches condemning the Fifth Monarchists at Blackfriars for encouraging even women and children to judge political leaders. Two weeks later, the Council ordered Feake and Simpson arrested and imprisoned in Windsor Castle under the new ordinance.[139] Trapnel avoided immediate arrest, but even before this ordinance, she began rehearsing her eventual imprisonment: her voluntary immobilization in the inn took some of the sting from involuntary immobilization in jail.

I've been trying to argue for the collective political rationality of what would seem to be Trapnel's most anti-rational episode of embodied ecstatic prophecy, which first brought her into the public sphere. This rationality took one step further when her prophecies circulated in manuscript, and a step further still when they went to press and circulated through the nation. Ecstatic prophecy produces gossip and calumny, which demands a self-vindicating published response: Trapnel responded to scandalous rumors by publishing a spiritual autobiography giving an account of "her relations, her acquaintance, her conversation, the dispensations of the Lord to her in clouds and bitter storms of temptations, in manifestations of light and love, in visions and revelations of things to come," in the words of her editor. This self-definition allowed her to bring a number of previously private visions into the oppositional public sphere of 1654. She wove together her own experience and the political history of the nation by presenting her visions of the king's death, the battle of Dunbar, the dissolution of the Rump, the first Dutch War, and the dissolution of Barebone's Parliament.[140] Her outbursts prompted by inspiration from above and out of time allowed her to construct a public life for herself *in* time, reaching back to prophecies that had been fulfilled, reaching forward to a future she would help to create.

This spiritual autobiography recorded what would become the most famous prophecy of her career. It came to her on the night of December 14 1653, just after the dissolution of Barebone's Parliament:

> I saw great darkness in the earth, and a marvelous dust, like a thick smoke ascending upward from the earth; and I beheld at a little distance a great company of cattle, some like bulls, and others like oxen, and so lesser, their faces and heads like men, having each of them a horn on either side their heads; for the foremost, his countenance was perfectly like unto Oliver Cromwell's;

138. *An Ordinance Declaring that the Offences Herein Mentioned,* 1654; *CSPD* 6.357, 363.
139. *WCP* 349–50; *CSPD* 6.371.
140. *TCS* 3–15, 2, 11.

and on a sudden there was a great shout of those that followed him, he being singled out alone, and the foremost; and he looking back, they bowed unto him, and suddenly gave a shout, and leaped up from the earth, with a kind of joy, that he was their supreme; and immediately they prompting him and fawning upon him, he run at me, and as he was near with his horn to my breast, an arm and an hand clasped me round, a voice said, "I will be thy safety"; he run at many precious saints that stood in the way of him, that looked boldly in his face; he gave them many pushes, scratching them with his horn, and driving them into several houses, he ran still along, till at length there was a great silence, and suddenly there broke forth in the earth great fury coming from the clouds, and they presently were scattered, and their horns broken, and they tumbled into graves; with that I broke forth, and sang praise, and the Lord said, mark that Scripture, "Three horns shall arise, a fourth shall come out different from the former, which shall be more terror to the saints than the others that went before; though like a lamb," as is spoken of in the Revelation, "in appearance a Lamb, but pushing like a beast," being not only one, but many and much strength joined together.[141]

How should we interpret this dream? Trapnel's impulse to shape a future by organizing oppositional praxis takes her closer to Ernst Bloch's revolutionary and forward-tending daydreams than to Freud's backward-tending nightdreams.[142] Her dream condenses several functions. No doubt part of the prophetic pleasure here lies in animalizing Cromwell, as Richard Overton had, to more ribald effect, five years before.[143] Trapnel's main sources are Daniel 7 (the prophecy of the four beasts and the horns), Amos 4.1 (where the Bull of Bashan stands for tyrannical oppressors of the poor), and David's Psalm 22:

> Many bulls have compassed me:
> strong bulls of Bashan have beset me round.
> They gaped upon me with their mouths,
> as a ravening and a roaring lion.

As it continues, the psalm suggests Trapnel's characteristic imagery of liquefying exaltation ("I am poured out like water"), and also the physical effect of a fasting prophecy ("My strength is dried up like a potsherd; / and my tongue cleaveth to my jaws"). Her allusion evokes the Passion, when Christ quoted this psalm's first verse: "My God, my God, why hast thou forsaken me?"[144] But for both Christ and Trapnel, the psalm's desperate opening implies its redemptive conclusion; the bull's threat implies the protective arm and voice that save her.

---

141. Ibid. 13–14.
142. *Principle* 1.77–113. Nigel Smith discusses Trapnel's dreams in *Perfection* 94–5. Scott-Luckens points out ("Alpha" ch. 4, n. 224) that Trapnel is reworking an earlier dream by Wight (Jessey and Wight, *Exceeding Riches* 148–9).
143. In *The Baiting of the Great Bull of Bashan* (1649), Overton depicted plucky Leveller bulldogs whose mouths were burned when they bit Oliver's poxy genitals (6; rpt Morton, *Freedom* 279–92).
144. Matt. 27.46; Mk 15.34. Trapnel later called her body Christ's enclosed garden, which the bulls of Bashan could not tear (*TVK* 80; see also *T* 363).

Trapnel's prophecy put her into competition with her fellow Fifth Monarchists. As we've seen, in his sermon in St Anne's Church on December 19, Feake suggested that Daniel's little horn actually signified Cromwell. Here, in Trapnel's concluding quotation from Daniel, she claims to have pre-empted him by five days. In fact, she claims she had a similar vision in the summer of 1647: when the New Model marched into London, she identified the first three horns with the bishops, the king, and Parliament, and the fourth, evidently, with Cromwell.[145] As early as 1646, she had a vision of a vaguely Cromwellian Antichrist-apostate—a beast "that shall appear like a lamb, but with his two horns shall gore as a beast, for so his nature is."[146] Again and again, she greets some new and unexpected event with a claim that she has foreseen it, turning herself into something like the God of the predestinarian Particular Baptists, and Cromwell into the fulfillment of her prophecy, not her victim or victim-izer.[147] We might also see them as a strategic self-fulfilling prophecy of the persecutions she would suffer largely as a result of the prophecy itself. In *Behemoth, or the Long Parliament*, Hobbes warned that prophecy could become "the principal cause of the event foretold," so that a credible prediction of Cromwell's defeat could have prompted the credulous to join in with the struggle against him.[148] J. G. warned that Fifth Monarchist prophecies against the Protectorate obliged the prophets to foment sedition or be found false.[149] Prophecy transforms prophets, committing them to further action in the same way that Lilburne's defiance of the law committed him to a public prosecution and defense.

On February 7, Nedham reported to Cromwell on "how the pulse beats at Allhallows." With Feake and Simpson imprisoned, things were quieter, but one danger remained:

> One thing more I have to impart to your highness; and that is a twofold design now in hand, concerning the prophetess Hannah, who played her part lately in Whitehall at the ordinary. The one is, to print her discourses or hymns; the other, to send her abroad all over England, to proclaim them, in the name of the Lord, *vivâ voce*. To this she is daily persuaded by one Mr. Greenhill a

145. *TCS* 5.
146. *TLS* 44.
147. Ibid. Mary Cary held off publishing *The Little Horns Doom and Downfall* in 1644 because "men would then generally have been uncapable of receiving of such things ... prophecies are then best understood, when they are fulfilled" (A7ʳ). Compare Milton's headnote to "Lycidas" in his 1645 *Poems*, in which he says his 1638 poem "by occasion foretells the ruin of our corrupted clergy then in their height." Shortly after Trapnel's first public prophecy, *Strena Vavasoriensis* claimed that Vavasor Powell achieved pro-phetic authority by predicting events he already knew about. Compare Porphyry's neoplatonic debunking of the Book of Daniel as in large part a backdated Maccabean fabrication.
148. 188. Gramsci calls providentialist "finalism" not a "mechanical determinism," but "nothing other than the clothing worn by the real and active will when in a weak position" (*Selections* 336–7)—an insight that illuminates the Second International as well as the Fifth Monarchy.
149. *Socratismos; or Dissatisfactions Satisfied*, 1653, 17; *The Loyal Intelligencer* for 1/23–1/30/54 identified the author as John Goodwin.

preacher, and by thousands of the Familist crew, but chiefly by people of Mr. Simpson's congregation. She is now continually frequented, and doth a world of mischief in London, and I believe will abroad in the counties. Her prophecies and hymns I have seen, and read most part of them over, being insufferably desperate against your highness' person, family, relations, friends, and the government, and the publication would be very pernicious: for, however such things be frivolous in themselves, yet the vulgar is a superstitious animal, naturally doting upon such vanities. . . . When I saw these prophecies, they were in the hand of a man, who stayed in the woman's chamber when she uttered them day by day in her trance, as they call it, and he would have lent them me to read quite over, but that he was in haste (he told me) going into London, to confer with the woman herself, and with divers of her friends, about the publishing; and he promised me that one day this week he would send them me to peruse. If I can by any means keep him to his promise, your Highness shall have a sight of them. They will make fourteen or fifteen sheets in print.[150]

Nedham's intelligence was good. By February 20, Thomason collected his copy of *Cry of a Stone*. But whereas Cromwell had no compunction about arresting Feake and Powell the day after their lectures at Blackfriars, and banning all future such meetings, he made no attempt to interfere with Trapnel's twelve-day prophetic fast, or to prevent the publication of her prophecies. In the short term, anyway, her symbolic appropriations seem to have worked. But given that such utterances had been defined as capital crimes, that Fifth Monarchist preachers were already being persecuted, and that conditions in prisons such as the Bridewell cell Trapnel eventually inhabited were, to say the least, unhealthy, it is difficult to overestimate the sheer physical courage of Trapnel's decision to publish.

A Gazing Stock: Cornhell and Bridewell

Late in February or early in March, Trapnel left on a mission to Cornwall: home to a number of radical veterans of Barebone's Parliament (John Bawden, Robert Bennet, John Carew, Hugh Courtney, and Francis Langdon), and to Francis Rous, its former speaker, a member of Cromwell's Council of State, and the Fifth Monarchists' nemesis.[151] This trip became a formal sectarian progress comparable to that of Bunyan's Christiana. It began with Trapnel's staging of her departure, which both diminished and magnified her status as a public actor. Like Feake and Simpson (imprisoned in Windsor Castle) and the other Fifth Monarchist preachers, she risked prosecution under the treason act of January 19; as an unmarried public woman, she risked charges of willfulness, disorderliness, vagrancy, and (the trump card) lewdness. Her solution was not to leave quietly, but to make herself the site of a protracted natural and supernatural struggle that emptied her of individual will while underlining her public status as God's handmaid. On the one hand, she herself and her

150. *PRO* for 2/7/54.
151. See Mary Coate, *Cornwall in the Great Civil War and Interregnum*, Oxford 1933.

London church-fellows wanted her to stay, as did Satan, who temporarily took away her prophetic voice and tempted her to throw herself down a flight of stairs, break her leg, and avoid the trip. On the other, her Cornwall friends invited her down, as did God, who sent her a series of private revelations, comparing her to Moses pondering his visit to Pharaoh, to Paul hearing the visionary plea of the Man of Macedonia.[152]

Throughout her deliberations, Trapnel takes pains to specify the particular houses she visited, the invitations that led her from one to the other. By drawing her forth into a public role almost against her will, these invitations acted as a more mundane version of her spiritual impulses. After visiting Feake and Simpson, and praying all night with ten of her spiritual sisters, she traveled to an inn at Whitehall and, accompanied by several unnamed friends, took the coach for Cornwall. She turned it into a mobile version of her prophecy-chambers by singing and praying aloud.[153] After thirteen days, she arrived at the home of Francis Langdon in Tregasow, Cornwall, near Truro.[154] *The Cry of a Stone* assured that her reputation would precede her, and she became a local sensation, with many visitors. In response to requests, she related her biography. Once, as she recounted her vision at Whitehall, recollection became repetition:

> I spake of so many things, and so largely, that it took up the afternoon for the most part; so that before I spake much of my going to Whitehall, and praying and singing there, I broke forth into singing, my heart being so thoroughly heated with discoursing of God's goodness so many hours. And I sang and prayed a great part of that night.[155]

Predictably, this stirred up trouble, for local clerics feared losing the people's loyalty, and so also "their standing quivers, and their fat benefices."[156]

When Trapnel found that a warrant had gone out for her, she suffered a crisis of courage, until "the Lord made his rivers flow, which soon broke down the banks of an ordinary capacity."[157] God began conferring with her about her forthcoming trial, showing her various clergy, a minister's wife, and a jury conspiring against her. She fell into a trance and took to her bed at Langdon's house, thus resisting the warrant that eventually arrived. The justices came to her chamber and attempted to rouse and examine her, but she remained insensate. Some proposed sending for the local witch-trying woman, who would have probed her with a pin. The next day, she rose and walked in the Gethsemane of Langdon's garden, where God told her to "look to the Lord, who will give thee answers

---

152. *TRP* 1–4; Exodus 3; Acts 16.
153. *TRP* 7.
154. Ibid. 10.
155. Ibid. 17–18.
156. Ibid. 50.
157. Ibid. 20.

suitable to what shall be required of thee." As she walked to the Truro sessions house, the populace mocked her: "some ... stared me in the face, making wry-faces at me, and saying, 'How do you now? How is it with you now?'" She became a "gazing stock," but remained unafraid, finding a model in Christ's meekness.[158]

The sessions house, full of spectators, looked like a Laudian temple, with its rail of separation: "the justices leaned over a rail, which railed them in together; only I espied a clergyman at their elbow, who helped to make up their indictment, so that he could not be absent, though his pulpit wanted him, it being a fast day." When Justice Richard Lobb (the "mouth of the court") read the bill of indictment against her, God told her, "Say 'Not guilty,'" according to the form of the bill"—good counsel, given that the court would have taken her silence as a sign she was a witch.[159] The justices bound her over to the next quarter session, and Langdon and Bawden provided a £300 surety for her appearance.

But then the justices violated the decorum of the preliminary hearing by proceeding to examine her. Like Hutchinson in the General Court of Massachusetts in 1637, like Sexby, Allen, and Shepherd before the House of Commons in 1647, Trapnel violated the form of their irregular proceedings by refusing to behave like a defendant. When they asked her if she would "own" *The Cry of a Stone*, she responded "I am not careful to answer you in that matter"—a strategic response, given the Treason Act of January 19, but also a subtle act of defiance, since it echoes the answer Shadrach, Meshach, and Abednego gave to Nebuchadnezzar.[160] When read her prophecy of the cattle and the horns from that book, she repeated this response and denied Cornwall's jurisdiction over her acts in London. What brought her into Cornwall? "I came as others did, that were minded to go into the country." Why Cornwall in particular? "Why might not I come here, as well as into another Country?" Why Cornwall, when she had neither "lands, nor livings, or acquaintance to come to in this country"? "What though I had not, I am a single person, and why may I not be with my friends anywhere?" Lobb added, "I understand you are not married." She challenged his unvoiced presuppositions: "Then having no hindrance, why may not I go where I please, if the Lord so will?" Asked to name those who invited her to Cornwall, she refused.[161]

This led Justice James Launce (soon to be a member of Cromwell's first

---

158. Ibid. 23–4. The phrase derives from Paul's counsel to the afflicted in Heb. 10.33; Trapnel later applied it to Christ (*TVK* 33/*T* 23).

159. *TRP* 24–5. Thus a capital sentence reaches back in time and produces evidence for itself through the dumbfounded terror of the accused. Shortly before Trapnel's trip, twenty-five people were jailed as witches in Launceston, Cornwall (*Mercurius Politicus* 12/5/53–1/12/54 [*sic*]). That same year, Justice Tregagle, who sat at Trapnel's hearing, ordered the arrest of one Anne Jefferies, whose fasting trances, contact with fairies, and royalist prophecies prompted charges of witchcraft (B. C. Spooner, *John Tregagle*, Mount Durand, St Peter Port, Guernsey, 1979, 8).

160. Dan. 3.16.

161. *TRP* 25–8 and *TLS* 53–7. Dan. 3.16. A Cornish clergyman swore she had repeated *Cry*'s vision of the oxen (*TLS* 49).

Protectorate Parliament) to ask, "Pray Mistress tell us, what moved you to come such a journey?" Predictably enough, she answered, "The Lord moved me, and gave me leave." The court then set her up to repeat Ann Hutchinson's disastrous claim of an immediate revelation from God.[162] But Trapnel was both more aggressive and more cagey:

> *Justice Launce.* "But had you not some extraordinary impulses of spirit that brought you down? Pray tell us what these were."
> *A. T.* "When you are capable of extraordinary impulse of spirit, I will tell you; but I suppose you are not in a capacity now." For I saw how deridingly he spoke. . . . [F]or the Lord carried me to speak, that they were in a hurry and confusion, and sometimes would speak all together, that I was going to say, "What are you like women, all speakers, and no hearers?" but I said thus, "What do you speak all at a time? I cannot answer all, when speaking at once."[163]

In her unvoiced response, Trapnel sounds like Paul responding to a church full of disorderly women prophets, in her voiced one, like a chief justice establishing order in the court. After the judges bound her over to appear again, she warned that they would themselves be judged before "the tribunal seat of the most high, and then I think you will hardly be able to give an account for this day's work." When she left the court, she found she had converted those who mocked her on her way in. Leaving local clerics to direct their "table and pulpit talk against her," she yearned to depart "Cornwell, Cornhell in the west," and rejoin the fellowship of saints in London: "[T]he Lord send me to London, for I shall count it a great mercy to see their faces again, I had said a Bridewell among them shall be sweet to me, and so the Lord made it."[164] She later said the trial had fulfilled her earlier vision of the bull's charge and the Lord's rescuing arm.[165]

Meanwhile, someone in Cornwall wrote Nedham a letter complaining that London had failed to prevent Trapnel from prophesying; he printed this letter, perhaps to tweak Cromwell for failing to act on his earlier report: "The design intended to be made use of by means of this woman, is (it seems) to compass England, and pass from one good town to another to vent her prophecies, and thereby disaffect the people to the present authority." He drew a grim analogy to Elizabeth Barton, the Catholic Maid of Kent, who had also prophesied against a state transition (the establishment of an Anglican Church state), until Henry VIII hanged her at Tyburn in 1534.[166] But on April 11, the Council of State had already ordered Captain John Fox, deputy governor of Pendennis Castle, to

---

162. Hall, *Antinomian* 337.
163. *TRP* 26; the original reads "some of extraordinary impulses spirit."
164. Ibid. 26, 28, 25a.
165. *TLS* 57.
166. This letter appeared in four newsbooks: *Mercurius Politicus* 4/13–4/20/54, *Certain Passages* 4/14–4/21/54, *The Weekly Intelligencer* 4/18–4/25/54, and *The Moderate Intelligencer* 4/19–4/26/54. On Barton, see Watt, *Secretaries* 15–80.

apprehend Trapnel and send her to London.[167] Shortly thereafter, she had a pre-emptive vision that soldiers would come to take her into custody, and the next day they did so. They took her by horse through Foy-town (Fowey) and Lew (Looe) to Plymouth Fort. Along the way, she prophesied, attracted the gaze of crowds, and converted sympathetic listeners. Before and after her departure, she was a stumbling block to the military and religious establishment of Cornwall. The court reprimanded a soldier for smiling in solidarity with her. Local clerics mocked one of their brothers, a Mr Frances, as her "disciple" when he refrained from denouncing her. An Ensign Randal, serving under Captain Fox at Pendennis, lost his place because he visited her and invited her to his home. While waiting for a government ship to Portsmouth, she shared Plymouth Fort with "that famous pirate" Captain Beach and two hundred of his men.[168] On May 6, she wrote Feake and Simpson in a letter addressed "From the Prison to the Prison at Windsor Castle."[169] She finally sailed for Portsmouth, then took a coach to London. On June 2, the Council committed her to a cell in Bridewell, where she languished and prophesied until her release on July 26.

Why did Cromwell and the Council bother to arrest Trapnel, only to keep her waiting five weeks in Plymouth, then seven more in Bridewell? Perhaps they wanted to take her out of circulation during a period of intensified royalist and Fifth Monarchist agitation against the Protectorate. They could simultaneously deny her the opportunity for a prophetic trance in the Council of State (practically a certainty if they had forced her to testify), and turn her radical public spiritedness into a humiliating private corporeality by isolating, individuating, and possibly destroying her body. Her imprisonment and association with the accused prostitutes in Bridewell constitutes a prerogative punchline to the joke, "What happens to spirited young ladies who allow too many visitors to their bedchambers?" The prison matron accused Trapnel of being one of a crew of "ranting sluts," some of whom had passed through before. Trapnel herself began to fear that she would become "a byword and a laughing-stock while I lived, and that everyone would point at me as I went up and down the streets, when I came out, they would say, 'There goes a Bridewell bird,' and then many will gather about thee, to mock and deride thee." Second, by leaving her in a cell infested with sewage and rats, Whitehall may have intended a judicial murder by negligence. Indeed, Trapnel fell gravely ill and feared she would die.[170]

If this was Cromwell's plan, it backfired. In a sermon of May 28 at St Thomas Apostles, John Rogers asked the Lord to "Remember thy handmaid, who is brought to town, and threatened by the worldly powers."[171]

167. *CSPD* 7.86, 89.
168. *TRP* 27–35; *TLS* 50; on Captain Beach, see *The Weekly Intelligencer* 3/14–3/21/54.
169. *TLS* 57–60.
170. *TRP* 38, 39–40.
171. *B* 3.483.

Later, he called for the liberation of Feake, Simpson, and Trapnel.[172] When the prison matron accused her in Bridewell Court of eagerly desiring the company of men in her cell, she responded, "That word went to my heart, I knowing my bashful nature, and my civil life was known to many; and I said to them truly, Gentlemen, my delight is not nor never was in men's company, but in all people as they are godly, I delight in their company."[173] The feeling was mutual: as crowds flocked to see Felton in the Tower in 1628, Feake and Simpson at Windsor, and Rogers at Lambeth Palace, so Feake's and Simpson's congregations continued to visit Trapnel in Bridewell. The porous early modern prison easily became part of the public sphere.[174]

In her cell, Trapnel staged prophecies and conducted nightlong prayer sessions with her "holy sisters."[175] She singles out her "Sister" Ursula Adman, who kept her company through almost all her time in prison.[176] The crowds were so great that Trapnel herself, in a sick and weakened state, asked to have them limited.[177] While she was still in Bridewell, sometime between July 6 and 9, Allhallows published *A Legacy for Saints*: a collection stretching from her devotional writings of 1646 to her letters from Plymouth of a few months before. Trapnel's pamphlet verges on deathbed testimony—a "legacy of experience ... when I am gone hence."[178] By referring to Trapnel as "the testatrix," Allhallows turned her imprisonment into a Foxean drama of potential martyrdom with public political importance. She experienced rapturous divine visions related to her full baptism.[179]

Trapnel did her best to short out the circuits of penal power. When some people (she doesn't say who) advised her to petition for release, she responded, "I had not offended man, whereby to seek to him." She refused release under base terms, demanding that the Council acknowledge "the reproach and odium they have brought upon me, through this their prison." She would not promise not to prophesy against the state, for "I will never engage to that which lies not in me to perform, for what

172. *Mene, Tekel, Perez*, 1654, 12.

173. *TRP* 43.

174. In late May, the Council directed the Governor of Windsor Castle to keep Feake and Simpson in close custody. They had been receiving constant visits and letters from the "disaffected ... who take the opportunity of such assembling to vent their own discontents, leavening others thereby" (*CSPD* 7.188–9). John Rogers preached through the windows of Lambeth Palace each Sunday to a "great concourse of people" until transferred to Windsor in March 1655 (*CFMM* 106).

175. *TLS* 59. *Perfect Account* 6/7–6/14/54.

176. *TLS* 44.

177. Court Minute Book of Bridewell Hospital, October 1642–July 1658, vol. 9: 661 (Guild-hall Library, Microfilm 515). Thanks to Ariel Hessayon for this reference.

178. 12. Thomas Brewster printed *TLS* and *TRP*. *TCS* reveals no printer, but its ornaments (A1ʳ) resemble those in *TLS* (A2ʳ). Brewster served as an official printer to the Council of State until the dismissal of Barebone's Parliament, when he became an oppositional printer issuing works by Thomas Collier, John Spittlehouse, Marchamont Nedham, James Harrington, and Henry Vane (Plomer).

179. On her baptism, see *T* 130–31; she doesn't say just when this baptism occurred.

the Lord utters in me, I must speak."[180] Finally, under the prompting of the Cromwellian Baptist Henry Lawrence, Lord President of the Council (she called him her "Bridewell Lord"), the prison authorities asked her, "if the order come, and give you liberty freely, will you accept of it?" She was silent, "only my sister said, 'if we can have liberty, we will choose it rather than bonds.'" The next week, she frequently lay in trances, and "often desired that they in high places had some of the dainties with me at Bridewell."[181] On July 26, the Council of State issued a warrant for her release.[182] When it finally arrived, she claimed to have foreseen it weeks before, waited a bit, then left with a threat: "Go tell your masters, though they will not see me they shall be sure to hear from me."[183]

She made good by sending self-vindicating letters to the Council, and by publishing her final pamphlet of 1654, *Anna Trapnel's Report and Plea.* Her name appears twice on the title page, with a subscription reading "Commended for the justification of the Truth, and satisfaction of all men, from her own hand," and it contains no prefatory epistles by male "gatekeepers."[184] The very titles of Trapnel's 1654 tracts reveal a striking movement into a public identity and voice, as we move from *The Cry of a Stone*, with its suggestion of an inanimate object forced into a voice against its nature; to *A Legacy for Saints*, whose prematurely posthumous title protects Trapnel from accusations of self-will and forwardness; to *Anna Trapnel's Report and Plea*, with its public, forensic, and combative assertion of her own (and the Fifth Monarchist) case. As such, it marked her movement from orality to literacy—from memory to performed speech to reinforced memory to avowedly public writing:

> [A]nd though I fail in an orderly penning down these things, yet not in a true relation, of as much as I remember, and what is expedient to be written; I could not have related so much from the shallow memory I have naturally, but through often relating these things, they become as a written book, spread open before me, and after which I write.[185]

In this tract, she omits "The Visions and opening of the Scriptures, that the Lord brought to my soul, while I was in Bridewell"—in other words, precisely the sort of ecstatic prophesying that first brought her into the public eye.[186]

Her tract begins with a defiant letter "To the Reader," which employs the misogynous idioms of English antipopery: she rails against the "Scarlet Whore" and calls for "Babylon's Brats" to be executed. After a long narrative of her Cornwall trip and imprisonment, she concludes with an

---

180. *TRP* 45–6.
181. Ibid. 46–7.
182. *CSPD* 7.438.
183. *TRP* 48.
184. See Bell et al., *Biographical Dictionary* 278–87.
185. *TRP* 34. Wiseman considers female prophets' movement between oral and written discourse ("Unsilent").
186. *TRP* 45; thanks to Christopher Nalls for this point.

address entitled "A Defiance to all reproachfull, scandalous, base, horrid, defaming speeches, which have been vented by Rulers, Clergy, and their Auditors, and published in scurrilous pamphlets up and down in cities and countries, against Anna Trapnel, late Prisoner in Bridewell for the Testimony of Jesus Christ."[187] She claims, once again, that God forced her into the public eye, and alludes to the antisectarian rhetoric of corporal signs:

> I am forced out of my close retired spirit, by rulers and clergy, who have brought me upon the world's stage of reports, and rumors, making me the world's wonder, and gazing stock: and as some have said they thought I had been a monster or some ill-shaped creature, before they came and saw, who then said, they must change their thoughts for I was a woman like others that were modest and civil. . . . I am compelled, as I told you, to bring my private spirit forth to the world.

She rebuffed accusations that she was a witch and an imposter.[188] Accused of vagrancy, she recited yet again her places of habitation and her status as a rate payer who impoverished herself supporting the Parliament's army: "I Anna Trapnel am no vagabond, nor runagate person, though I have and may sometimes live in the city, and sometimes in the country, as yourselves do, and why should I be accounted a vagabond more than you?"[189] She denounces the Cornwall jurors, Captain Fox, Bridewell, university-trained clerics, the wealth of the Protectorate, and the false Lord Protector who has usurped the true one:

> Therefore get you to your strongholds, O Israel, and prisoners, for you are prisoners of hope, you seek not great things for your selves, but for the Lord's anointed ones; you cry to the Lord, and not for earthly palaces, nor Whitehall garden walks, nor kitchen-belly-cheer, nor lardery-dainties, nor banquet-sweet-meats, nor Council-robes, nor Parliament tithes, nor Emperor advancement, nor great attendance, nor for colonels and captains' silken buff, and garnished spangled coats, and gilded cloaks, and brave London and country houses.[190]

In response to charges that she is a whore, "which language hath proceeded from court, I hear so," she laments the inadequacy of libel laws, invokes Solomon ("The name of the righteous is as a precious ointment"), and rejects the Ranter justification for orgiastic antinomianism: "I will not sin that grace may abound." She confesses or boasts that "my iniquity is passion, apt to be hasty," not lustfulness of the flesh or eye. Nowhere in her writings does her passionate nature appear more strongly than in "A

187. *TRP* A4ʳ, 49–59. I haven't turned up any of the implied anti-Trapnel pamphlets.
188. At Whitehall, she prophesied that God would cause witches to be discovered and suppressed (*Severall Proceedings* 1/12–1/19/54). While I have emphasized the emancipatory force of Fifth Monarchist radicalism, it's worth noting that Trapnel calls for Protestant imperialism, and for evangelizing Indians and Africans (*TVK* 90, 19–20, 29/*T* 13–14, 20.
189. *TRP* 49, 50, 50–51.
190. Ibid. 58.

Defiance," where she describes herself as one of "the Lord's chosen Baruchs . . . and truly he now makes use of them, to meditate terror."[191]

Britomart II

Trapnel left few traces after her release. In London, she seems to have moved away from moderates like Simpson and Jessey toward intransigent opponents of the Protectorate like Pendarves, Tillinghast, Rogers, Feake, and Carew.[192] In October 1654, she sent a message of solidarity to John Rogers, imprisoned in Lambeth House.[193] In December, an anonymous witness pondered the millennial meaning of her ascetic body: "I think God in this dispensation doth teach his people that when our communion with him is enlarged a very little of the creature will satisfy us."[194] She resumed her travels about England, for she repeatedly spoke of the country saints.[195] In December 1655, she visited Cornwall in the company of three young men, hoping to visit the regicide and Fifth Monarchist John Carew, imprisoned in St Maurs. When a trooper asked them their business, they responded, "Thy Lord Protector we own not; thou art of the Army of the Beast." When examined by her old acquaintance Richard Lobb and the governor of Pendennis Castle, she fell into a protective trance.[196] In May 1656, she visited Cornwall again, contemplating cooperation with Quakers and emigration.[197]

Meanwhile, rifts developed within the Fifth Monarchy movement. On January 5 1657, Christopher Feake, recently released from a year's imprisonment, addressed a meeting at Allhallows in incendiary tones that alienated him from the moderate ministers present. After alluding to the intelligence report by Nedham that led to his arrest, he declared that "This power and the old monarchy are one and the same," and defended radical millenarianism. Thurloe's spy (Nedham?) reported in disgust, "I am almost weary of repeating this kind of stuff. This is all I could collect, being far from candlelight, and my shoulders laden with a crowd of women riding over my head, upon the tops of the seats; so this is hardly the fortieth part of what he rambled over."[198] Was Trapnel among the holy sisters riding Nedham's shoulders, struggling for a better view of thundering Feake, while Kiffin, Jessey, and Simpson, neither hot nor cold,

---

191. Ibid. 51–2, 54.
192. On Pendarves and Tillinghast, see *TVK* 52–3/*T* 36, 249–51.
193. Rogers, *Jegar-Sahadvtha*, 1657, 28–9.
194. *CP* 2.xxxiv–xxv.
195. *T* 131, 245, 358, 443, 485, 592, 885.
196. *The Public Intelligencer* 12/24–12/31/55.
197. *Mercurius Politicus* 5/29–6/5/56. On New England connections, see James F. Maclear, "New England and the Fifth Monarchy," *William and Mary Quarterly* 3.32.2, 1975. Cornish authorities imprisoned George Fox and other Quakers in Launceston from January to September 1656. Robert Bennet, alumnus of Barebone's Parliament and Trapnel's associate, finally released them (*The Journal of George Fox*, New York 1963, 204–46).
198. *B* 5.755–9; 756, 759. On this sermon, see *CP* 3.85–6, and the epigraph to my chapter 3 for an excerpt.

looked anxiously on? Thomas Venner's Coleman Street congregation rose in April, but Cromwell's troops easily crushed them. No prominent Fifth Monarchists joined them, but this may have been more a matter of millenarian timing than moderation. In June, Thurloe heard that Feake, Rogers, Harrison, and Canne had been meeting regularly to plan an armed insurrection, since "the three years and a half is at an end, in which the witnesses have lyen dead," thus linking the "time and times and half a time" of Revelation 11.3 with the three and a half years since the Protector dismissed Barebone's Parliament.[199]

On September 1 1657, a radical faction split off from Simpson and the rest of Allhallows, and it would appear that Trapnel went with them.[200] This crisis prompted Trapnel's final episode of public political activity, when she reverted to extended bouts of ecstatic prophecy. Two overlapping sources preserve these prophecies, which extended from October 11 1657 to November 30 1659: a 95-page quarto entitled *A Voice for the King of Saints and Nations* containing six prophecies, and a 990-page folio containing five of these and forty-five more. The sheer effort, expense, and danger of producing this seditious Leviathan suggest that Trapnel continued a significant public career, though no independent references to it seem to have survived, and the "remnant" whom she addresses did not reconstitute itself as a church.[201] In the absence of a regular preacher, she became a lecturer: in one session, seemingly not spoken out of a trance, she delivers an *ex tempore* sermon on 1 Peter 3.14–15.[202] But the bulk of the work consists of songs in hymn meter, which had grown more polished with practice. She alternates between prophetic critique based in the apocalyptic idiom of John's Revelation, and utopian rhapsodies based in the erotic idiom of Canticles. Speaking as "the Voice," "the Instrument," and "the little stone," she repeatedly denounces Cromwell by name.[203] Given that she thought spies present, she must have been trying to provoke state persecution, but Cromwell seems to have learned the wisdom of repressive toleration.[204] Speaking as "the Spouse," she exhorts her "companions" to maintain solidarity, presenting herself as an enclosed garden, a handmaid lubricated with the holy spirit, and Christ's Rose of

199. *B* 6.349.
200. Simpson, released from Windsor by July 24 1654 (*The Faithful Scout* 7/21–7/28/54), became one who "owns and prays for the present powers" (*Several Proceedings* 8/10–8/17/54)—a far cry from Trapnel in the roughly contemporary *Report and Plea*. On Simpson's "apostasy," see *TVK* 53/*T* 37; *CP* 2.xxiv–xxvi; Richard Greaves, *Saints and Rebels*, Macon, GA, 1985, 122; *CFMM* 276–8; and *Old Leaven*, the schismatics' account of the break, signed (63) by John Proud and Caleb Ingold. As Deacon and Elder of Allhallows, they had introduced *TLS* (A4r).
201. On the "remnant," see *T* 721, 757–62.
202. Ibid. 427–38.
203. As the "little stone" falling on Cromwell (ibid. 574–5); on Cromwell (*T* 59, 146, 247, 248, 250, 272–3, 314, 395, 408, 413, 458, 461, 486, 533, 539, 563, 564, 574–6, 598, 618, 637, 641–2, 647, 680, 684, 736, 740, 774, 787, 790, 796–7, 806, 814, 824, 840, 889).
204. Ibid. 606–9, 702.

Sharon, with no need for other men.[205] She fuses the two idioms when she sings herself into the role of the laboring woman clothed with the sun/Son of Revelation 12.[206] She emphasizes particular points for her amanuenses, but cautions them not to pick and choose, and warns listeners not to come in to hear her by "fits and starts."[207]

In these late prophecies, Trapnel turns more directly to female predecessors. She diminishes Adam's role by saying he was fast asleep during Eve's creation, and stresses the Serpent's delusion of "poor Eve," not her temptation of Adam. The Serpent's assault on the Tree of (Fore)knowledge resembles that of Arminians on free grace—a strong indication of her Particular Baptist faith.[208] In misogynous attacks focused, rather boldly, on female loquacity, she recommends the "bridling of the tongue," and warns "handmaids" to shun the bad example of Eve, who was "so forward at first / To talk with the Serpent's cheat."[209] But she also praises female prophecy. Like Milton in *Paradise Lost* 11–12, Trapnel invokes Paul's list of lone just men in Hebrews 11: Abel, Enoch, Noah, Abraham, Lot, Isaac, Jacob, Joseph, Moses. Unlike Milton, she retains Sarah and adds Hannah, Deborah, Abigail, and Jael, that nurturing, tyrannicidal provider of dairy products and tent pegs, whom she imagines, perhaps, on Charles's scaffold: "For brave Jael hath severed so / His body and his head."[210]

But these late prophecies also reveal the serial dispersal of the anti-Protectoral pledged group of 1654. On her radical plebeian left, she rejects Venner and his "rash brains" through an allusion to Venner's *A Standard Set Up*:

> The Voice and Spirit hath made a league
> Against those rash brains too,
> That have not the standard set up
> That is the Ensign new.[211]

On her accommodationist right, she attacked Simpson as Cromwell's fellow "apostate."[212] She endeavors to drive out heretical "mixtures," stresses water baptism and her own orthodox Calvinist theory of election, and rejects the idea (at the center of New England controversies over "the Halfway Covenant") that believers' children could have faith imputed to them automatically.[213] She attacks the beliefs of "spiritual notionists,"

---

205. *TVK* 1/*T* 1, 353, 762, and *passim*.
206. *T* 725, "723" [i.e. 732], 751–7, 827, 867, 872, 873.
207. *T* 76, 640, 231, 341, 703.
208. *TVK* 47, 48–9/*T* 33.
209. *T* 211, 235.
210. Ibid. 57, 69, 706–7, 928–31. Gillespie discusses the use of Jael by Katherine Chidley ("Table Talk"), whom Trapnel may have seen preach in William Greenhill's church in 1645.
211. *T* 273–4; see also 312.
212. *TVK* 53/*T* 37, 273.
213. *T* 73–4, 668, 434, 78, 402, 421, "941" [i.e. 931], 131.

paedobaptists, Ranters, Antinomians, and particularly Quakers.[214] One prophecy records her clash with a group of Quakers, who cried foul when she descended from her rapture long enough to respond to their questions, until "the Lord sent down a louder voice" that allowed her to drown them out—a hollow victory at best.[215] Her very reversion to ecstatic prophecy may have been an effort to distinguish herself from the upright, scandalous, and non-ecstatic public speech of Quaker women. Heroic as these late prophecies are, in substance and in magnitude, they never move into anything like a structural analysis of the late Protectorate or a strategic revolutionary program of sectarian alliance or a utopian vision of a new polity. No radical can perform every task, but it's hard to avoid seeing Trapnel's final prophecies to her remnant as, in part, a failure or defeat, as we begin leaving the pledged group of revolutionary Puritanism for the ossified, serializing sects of Restoration Dissent.

Most Restoration references to the Fifth Monarchists occur in the shadow of Venner's second London rising, in January 1661, which grew out of his congregation in Swan Alley, Coleman Street.[216] In *A Door of Hope*, their remarkable manifesto of 1661, they combine detailed and learned millenarian theory based in Mead and Tillinghast with a platform for a saintly republic and a ferocious call to arms. The pamphlet's title suggests tyrannicide: Israel slays Achan in the valley of Achor (Josh. 7) and lays waste its courtly finery dedicated to Baal, before making it a "door of hope" (Hos. 2.15). At least fifty mounted saints threw London into a panic, but the trained bands finally defeated them. Venner and his comrade Roger Hodgkin were hanged, drawn, quartered in Swan Alley, and hung in pieces on the city gates and London Bridge. Samuel Butler's "Character of a Fifth-Monarchy Man" commemorated their passing with typical corporal wit, saying that "their whole outward Men were set on the gates of the city; where a head and four quarters stand as types and figures of the fifth monarchy."[217] Other hangings followed, as did other Fifth Monarchist risings, but we have no reason to think that Trapnel participated in them.[218] Our last public view of her may date from July 1661, when an Anne Trapnel married one Thomas Semicraft in Woodbridge, Suffolk, where Frederick Woodall, a Fifth Monarchist before the Restoration, led a gathered church between 1652 and 1681.[219]

Five afterwords on Fifth Monarchy women. In *Behemoth* (1668), Hobbes discusses the political force of prophecy and mentions three particular prophets: the Quaker James Naylor, the "mere cozener" William Lilly, and

---

214. Ibid. 76, 266, 919.
215. *TVK* 70–76/ *T* 47–51.
216. See David A. Kirby, "The Radicals of St. Stephen's, Coleman Street, London, 1624–1642," *Guildhall Miscellany* 3, 1978.
217. *Characters* 79–81.
218. *CFMM* 200–28.
219. Ibid. 266, 269, 274, and personal correspondence. Thanks to Professor Capp for sharing his research.

an unnamed prophetess who appeared in Cornwall in 1654, "much famed for her dreams and visions, and hearkened to by many, whereof some were eminent officers. But she and some of her accomplices being imprisoned, we heard no more of her." Naylor and Lilly still have names, but not Trapnel, though she was "much famed."[220] If the modern canon of seventeenth-century writing has tended to exclude female prophets on more mediated, formal grounds, then the seventeenth-century exclusion was cruder: a woman, and a sectary, so heard no more.

Second: in 1661 appeared a coarse closet drama entitled *The Holy Sisters Conspiracy against their Husbands, and the City of London, Designed at Their Last Farewell of Their Meeting-houses in Coleman Street*. The locale suggests Feake and Venner, but its body-focused humor suggests the drunken, pork-eating prophetesses of *A Discoverie*, and the Council's attempt to turn Trapnel into a Bridewell bird. The sisters lament Charles's proclamation against the Fifth Monarchists and mourn their imprisoned leaders (Feake, Canne, Kiffin, Henry Hills the printer, Knollys, and Jeremy Ives, among others), who filled them with "holy seed" and encouraged them to slit their husbands' throats. They seek solace in burned claret, wine, rolls, potato pies, jellies, and broths. One holy sister is named "Hannah," and Sister Faith rails against "the great Bulls of Bashan, our husbands!"—thus returning Trapnel's public and political prophecy against Cromwell to a safer domestic context. Before they set out to "fire the city," they break into a "psalm of mercy . . . composed by our father Feake." But their husbands return with the rape cure for wifely intransigence: "Let's lay'um, says Nat, and splay'um, says Wat, / And then we shall make'um safe." Like so much anti-sectarian and anti-republican rhetoric, this pamphlet attempts to deny popular collective political praxis by tracing it to a libidinal core of oversexed women and the husbands who fail to satisfy them.[221]

Third: Abraham Cowley's *Cutter of Coleman Street*, a play of 1661 set in 1658, integrates two Restoration projects by restoring sequestered estates to their royalist owners, and gadding sectarian women to conforming patriarchal households. The soap-boiler Mr Barebottle became wealthy buying up sequestered estates, including that of Colonel Jolly. When he dies, Jolly regains his property by marrying Barebottle's Baptist widow. Her Fifth Monarchist daughter Tabitha "was wont to go every Sunday afoot over the Bridge to hear Mr. Feake, when he was Prisoner in Lambeth House; she has had a Vision too herself of Horns, and strange things." Cutter, a "merry sharking fellow" in disguise as the sectarian "Abednego," woos and weds her with the help of a bottle of sack, which transforms a ranting Protectorate prophetess into a randy Restoration wench. If

220. 187. Keith Thomas first noted this reference in "Women."
221. 11, 6, 8, 15. Thus Wiseman explains the recurrent turn to sexual raillery in so much political polemic of the period ("'Adam, the Father of all Flesh,'" Holstun, *Pamphlet Wars* 134–57). *Rump* (1662), a Restoration compendium of body-oriented antisectarian poetic satire, reprints the songs concluding this drama (2.192–200).

wartime enables women to create public identities for themselves, postwar patriarchs struggle to redomesticate them.[222]

Fourth: John Reynolds's *A Discourse upon Prodigious Abstinence* of 1669—a medical study presented to the Royal Society—begins with a learned scientific argument for the possibility of fasts, then considers the thirteen-month fast of one Martha Taylor. Reynolds concludes that "Her non-pretensions to Revelations, and the constant visits she receives from persons of all forms, may serve to occlude not only the mouths that are so unevangelical as to cry her up for a miracle, but those also who are so unphilosophical as to cry her down for the cheat of a faction." Here we see science separating itself off from the spheres of radical religion and conservative politics—a gain in knowledge, but not without its costs. As a political agent becomes a clinical patient, a prophetess an anorexic, the independent activity that Trapnel embodied begins to disappear. Here, we approach the disenchanted but murderous world of Victorian neurasthenia and Soviet psychiatry.[223]

But this is all a little too absolute. So fifth: women participated actively in both of Venner's risings. In 1657, "the sisters that meet together" were to distribute copies of the the group's manifesto, *A Standard Set Up*. Some of these were found with Trapnel's friend Captain Langdon in Tregas, Cornwall, and some with a Mrs Abigaile Marshall in Lincoln. A Sister Kerwit hid pistols.[224] One intelligence report from 1661 mentions a Cheapside widow named Hardy or Harding—"a very violent woman," who may also have been involved in the '57 rising.[225] And after denouncing the rebels of the '61 rising as the scum of the earth, the anonymous author of *Londons Glory* lists three women among those imprisoned at the Poultry Counter in its aftermath: Elizabeth Gittens, Mary Farnby, and Mary Whitlock. His account of the government's mopping-up operation leaves us with the rumor of a final Fifth Monarchy woman:

> But by six a clock in the morning all the whole city was all quiet, and not one to be seen, except in Newgate Bridewell, and other prisons, in which there were

---

222. *The Complete Works in Verse and Prose*, Vol. 1, 1881; rpt Hildesheim 1969, 191. It played to packed houses with doubled admission (*CFMM* 14).

223. 36. Alfred Cohen diagnoses seventeenth-century prophets, including Trapnel, as genuinely mad ("Prophecy"); Christopher Hill traces this sort of psychohistory to Cold War rhetoric in "Under the Tudor Bed," review of Lacey Baldwin Smith, *Treason in Tudor England* (London 1986), in *New York Review of Books* 34.8, May 7 1987, 36. Cohen's argument jars with his anti-Stalinism, as we can see in the study of Soviet political psychiatry by Zhores A. and Roy A. Medvedev, *A Question of Madness*, New York 1971. See also Hawes, *Mania*; Jonathan Sawday, "'Mysteriously divided,'" *HS* 127–43; and Scott-Luckens ("Alpha" ch. 4), who notes the conflict of medicine and religion even in the earlier seventeenth century, and Trapnel's refusing the offices of a physician (*TLS* 30).

224. Champlin Burrage, "The Fifth Monarchy Insurrections," *English Historical Review* 25, 1910, 735–6, 746.

225. *B* 6.186–7.

about the number of forty: it was certainly reported that one woman was taken all in armor, which if it be true it deserves to be chronicled.[226]

No other crossdresser could so terrify a seventeenth-century patriarch. Spenser's Britomart dons her armor in order to find her destined husband, and gains a prophetic vision of the dynasty they will produce, culminating distantly in Elizabeth. This spectral Britomart dons her armor to fight alongside her fellow saints, and bring King Jesus to life before her very eyes.

Was Trapnel an early feminist? That's a good, cut-to-the-chase question, but it's also a question badly posed: a version of that binary blackmail ("early, or modern?") to which revisionists hold so many early modern radicals, with starkly predictable results—typically, a weary reminder that Citizen X (Lilburne, Milton, Winstanley, Fox, Bunyan, etc.) was, after all, a devout seventeenth-century Protestant, not a secular twentieth-century radical. In this argument, "religion" typically guards the early modern world against intrusions by slapdash modernizers. It stands as a marker for the traditionalism, authoritarianism, and instrumental consciousness that pervades the writings even of ostensible radicals. Even Keith Thomas, in his great essay on women and the Civil War sects, stresses the division between female sectarians of the seventeenth century and feminists of the eighteenth, who grounded their practice not in the holy spirit, but in claims to natural right.[227] But this approach, I think, is the truly reductive vision of early modern religion, for it denies religion's tremendous power as creative practical consciousness. The question of "feminist or nonfeminist?" cuts off the discussion too early, and hinders us from reconstructing those early, religiously grounded experiments in collective praxis that form the feminist long revolution in Britain: from Baptist conventicles to Quaker meetings to the culture of Rational Dissent to abolition and women's suffrage to socialist feminism. Anyone more interested in the actual history of feminism than in patrolling the Great Wall of Modernity will want to look for those religious sites for women's collective activity that help to make the eighteenth-century emergence of feminism intelligible, and which continue to fuel feminism in the present.

In *The Making of the English Working Class*, E. P. Thompson examines the complex heritage of Dissent, and argues that Methodism, as a creature of capitalist work discipline, contained, controlled, and deformed workers' energies within the walls of the chapel. Yet he also argues that Methodist discipline and church fellowship provided a training ground for early

226. 14. Thus she rigorously cancelled Deuteronomy's sumptuary Old Law, as retranslated by John Selden: "A man's armor shall not be upon a woman" (22.5). See Jason P. Rosenblatt and Winfried Schleiner, "John Selden's Letter to Ben Jonson on Cross-Dressing and Bisexual Gods [with text]," *English Literary Renaissance* 29.1, 1999.
227. See, for instance, B. J. Gibbons, "Richard Overton and the Secularism of the Interregnum Radicals," *The Seventeenth Century* 10.1, 1995; Davis, "Religion"; and Mulligan and Richards, "Winstanley." Thomas, "Women" 338.

labor radicals. Putting a more hopeful face on melancholy Max Weber, we might subtitle Thompson's book *The Methodist Ethic and the Spirit of Socialism*. Similarly, we can trace important currents of bourgeois patriarchy to seventeenth-century sectarianism; we could call to witness Anne Hutchinson, Elizabeth Poole, and Anne Wentworth, among many others. Yet that same sectarianism authorized and was substantially composed of women's experiments in public political activity, writing, and collective praxis. Without these experiments, it is impossible to imagine, for instance, Mary Wollstonecraft. We might subtitle Trapnel's writings of 1654 *The Baptist Ethic and the Spirit of Feminism*.

8

Forlorn Hope:

Edward Sexby and the Republic

And this informant saith, that both the said bundles of books had
paper about them, and were tied up with pack-thread; but the paper
being loose and ruffled up, the titles of the said book were very visible,
they being severally entitled *Killing no murther*: and said, that one of
the said bundles he did tell over, which contained 154 in number;
one of which said books this informant hath in his custody, and
believes, that the other bundle did contain as many; but that in taking
them from the said Sturgeon, divers of them were scattered and lost.
And this informant further saith, that the said Sturgeon, upon his
apprehension, had a pistol about him, which had four barrels, and
was charged ready for execution.

—Thomas Banks, *The Thurloe Papers*

Hope is not confidence. If it could not be disappointed, it would not
be hope. That is part of it. Otherwise, it would be cast in a picture. It
would let itself be bargained down. It would capitulate and say, that is
what I had hoped for. Thus, hope is critical and can be disappointed.
However, hope still nails a flag on the mast, even in decline, in that
the decline is not accepted, even when this decline is still very strong.
Hope is not confidence. Hope is surrounded by dangers, and it is the
consciousness of danger and at the same time the determined
negation of that which continually makes the opposite of the hoped-
for object possible.

—Ernst Bloch, "Something's Missing"

My sect thou seest.

—Abdiel to Satan, *Paradise Lost*, Book 6

Centrifugal Charisma

Clifford Geertz has exercised an influence on new historicist literary
critics second only to Foucault's, and for much the same reason.[1] He, too,

---

1. See, for instance, Goldberg, *James I* 32–3; Greenblatt, *Renaissance* 3–4, and *Shakespearean*
55; see also Underdown, *Revel* 4; and Sharpe, *Politics* 279. The summer 1997 issue of
Representations celebrates Geertz's work.

arrives trailing clouds of extra-disciplinary authority, but bearing comforting news about the fundamentally *interpreted* quality of social reality. He, too, criticizes certain totalizing methods in the name of an alternative model of totality that claims an empirical, pre-methodological fidelity to local symbolic practice: "There is a certain value, if you are going to run on and on about the exploitation of the masses, in having seen a Javanese sharecropper turning earth in a tropical downpour."[2] Wet spectatorship confers intimate authority. And if Geertz's Wordsworthian encounter with this solitary shoveler is any clue, a bourgeois anthropologist of a culturalist bent can towel off and forget about the steaming earth turners pretty quickly. But that's all right, for the non-reductionist social sciences have begun to abandon any concern with labor. Their defining analogies come "more and more from the contrivances of cultural performance than from those of physical manipulation—from theater, painting, grammar, literature, law, play. What the lever did for physics, the chess move promises to do for sociology. . . . Life is just a bowl of strategies."[3]

Geertz's essay titled "Centers, Kings, and Charisma," which turns sharply from sharecroppers to potentates, has strongly influenced the new historicism. Focusing on political progresses and pageants in fourteenth-century Java, sixteenth-century England, nineteenth-century Morocco, and the modern United States, Geertz considers the "paradox of charisma": though it inhabits the political center, "its most flamboyant expressions tend to appear among people at some distance from the center, indeed often enough at a rather enormous distance, who want very much to be closer. Heresy is as much a child of orthodoxy in politics as it is in religion."[4] To understand the apparent subversive or revolutionary, "we must begin with the center and with the symbols and conceptions that prevail there," and remember that "the charisma of the dominant figures of society and that of those who hurl themselves against that dominance stem from a common source: the inherent sacredness of central authority."[5] In this filial world of parents, children, and inheritance, of the "glowing center" and those moth-like outsiders who blindly hurl themselves against it, charisma and "anti-charisma" form a closed loop—a sort of determining "spiritual electricity," much like Foucault's *power* and Greenblatt's *social energy*.[6]

Geertz's model of charisma has at least some local value, particularly for those inclined to overestimate the provenance of rationality in the modern world. But it doesn't work so well as a new principle of social totality. There's something to be said for resisting the impulse to let charisma take over the whole social field and lose its analytical specificity. By contrast, Max Weber distinguished charismatic from traditional and

2. *The Interpretation of Cultures*, New York 1973, 22.
3. *Local Knowledge*, New York 1983, 22, 25.
4. Ibid. 121–46.
5. 143–4, 146.
6. 123, 136. See Greenblatt, *Shakespearean* 65.

from *rational-legal* authority, associating it with the periphery, not the center—with movements and prophetic leaders who arise in opposition to established power.[7] Like many literary critics and cultural anthropologists, Geertz overestimates the power of these charismatic displays, whose very reiteration suggests that they didn't altogether succeed in reducing the extra-courtly world to order. He simply ignores non-charismatic activities like plowing, pregnancy, carpentry, and teaching children how to talk—practices still primary in any society that has not yet solved that pesky problem of material reproduction. And he underestimates the human capacity to reflect critically on centripetal charisma from some vantage-point not utterly saturated with it.

Renaissance England reveals a systematic and extraordinarily complex attack on courtly charisma. This does not mean charisma disappeared. Charismatic modes of social power persisted in Interregnum England, and even (as Geertz indicates) drew new life from opposition to them. Charles I, that clumsy, tongue-tied prince, was perhaps never more charismatically eloquent than in his (at least partially his) *Eikon Basilike*. But the century does show us a qualitative change from the self-mystifying patriarchalist and centralized courtly fictions of Jacobean England to the world of the revolutionary public sphere, which lacked a sovereign center. Revived medieval theories of ascending power and new utopian theories of collective association (the godly people, the republic, democracy, communism) emerged from the periphery at a rate that horrified conservative social theorists. Along with them came new critical theories of charisma—notably, theories of tyrannicide. *Eikon Basilike* found its *Eikonoklastes*. Which won? *Eikon Basilike*, probably, in the short term. But when Dr Johnson demanded what lasting mark Oliver Cromwell had ever made on history, Boswell's father responded, "God, Doctor! he gart kings ken that they had a *lith* in their neck!"[8] Awestruck and bedazzled, Geertz compares rulers marking the landscape with their symbolic presence to "some wolf or tiger spreading his scent through his territory, as almost physically part of them."[9] But from time to time, lesser magistrates and even sharecroppers turning the earth get tired of being pissed on, and start planning a tiger hunt.

This chapter focuses on an unsuccessful but glorious hunt conducted by Edward Sexby, whom we last saw at Putney, annoying Oliver Cromwell, his future quarry. Sexby willfully fled the center for the periphery, and vigilantly opposed the re-emergence of a new sort of monarchical charisma under the Protectorate. At the same time, his conspiratorial swashbuckling, republican eloquence, and oppositional self-fashioning in the court of the future made him one of the most charismatic figures of the

---

7. *From Max Weber*, London 1958, 52. For some of Weber's writings on charisma, see *On Charisma and Institution Building*, Chicago 1968. Weber was sometimes disquietingly eager for the resurgence of charismatic rule in central Europe.
8. *Boswell's Life of Johnson*, 6 vols, Oxford 1964, 5.383n.; "lith" is Scots for "joint."
9. *Local* 125.

revolutionary years: "There is no more remarkable career in the annals of the New Model army."[10] If his charisma was radically individualistic, that individualism lay precisely in its ability to attract a wide variety of allies to his revolutionary project—including some whose social status that project aimed to abolish. In "Strange Engines: Serial Conspiracy," I will narrate Sexby's conspiratorial efforts in England and on the Continent. In "Sardonic Ethics in *Killing Noe Murder*," I'll analyze his remarkable republican pamphlet, focusing on his use of a radical theory of natural law to legitimize the tyrannicide he proposes. And in "Aftermath: Tyrannicide as Critique," I will consider his capture and death, the historical reception of his pamphlet, and the nature of tyrannicide as a stunted but still significant form of revolutionary political practice.

Strange Engines: Serial Conspiracy

Sexby's early life is largely a blank to us. He seems to have been born into the decayed gentry, for the coroner's jury pronouncing on his death referred to him as "Esquire."[11] G. E. Aylmer suggests he may be "Edward, son of Marcus Sexby *alias* Saxbie of London, Gentleman, who was apprenticed to Edward Price of the Grocers' Company, in 1632."[12] David Wootton suggests that, in 1645, he wrote the remarkable Leveller and republican tract *England's Miserie and Remedie*.[13] He entered public life in the spring of 1647 when he helped organize the New Model soldiery and petition its generals. After examining him in April, the House of Commons described him as a "Suffolk man, trooper in the General's own troop, served four years, before he served the General he served the Lieutenant General in that troop which is now the General's."[14] Though only a private, Sexby

10. *FD* 1.66.
11. *Mercurius Politicus* 1/14–1/21/58. On the meaning of "esquire," see G. E. Aylmer, *The State's Servants*, London 1973, 394–5.
12. "Communication: Gentlemen Levellers?" *WIR* 101–8, 102. In 1638, a Widow Saxeby was a ratepayer of All Saints, Stayning, and a John Saxby of St Botolph's, Aldgate (Dale, *Inhabitants* 17, 217). Olivier Lutaud studies Sexby, his pamphlet, and its tradition in *Des Révolutions d'Angleterre à la Révolution Française* (The Hague 1973), which includes a full bibliography on Sexby (109–16, 367–70), and reprints the 1659 edition of *Killing Noe Murder* (371–404). Wootton reprints the 1657 edition but omits its learned notes to humanist authorities (*DRD* 360–88). See also Eduard Bernstein, *Cromwell and Communism*, New York 1963, 172–84; and Perez Zagorin, *A History of Political Thought in the English Revolution*, London 1954. Firth discusses Sexby's plots in larger historical context in *The Last Years of the Protectorate, 1656–1658*, 2 vols, London 1909. Underdown gives a wide-ranging account of Leveller–royalist plots against Cromwell in *Royalist Conspiracy in England, 1649–1660*, New Haven, CT, 1960.
13. *DRD* 53–4; Wootton may be right. *England's Miserie* says "princes, or what estate soever, when they arrogate to themselves an unlimited jurisdiction do degenerate into tyrants" (*DRD* 277), while an Agitator pamphlet of 1647 co-written by Sexby denounces "some who have lately tasted of sovereignty; and being lifted beyond their ordinary sphere of servants, seek to become masters, and degenerate into tyrants" (*The Apologie of the Common Soldiers* 4).
14. *CP* 2.431. That same month, he was also called a private soldier in Captain Arthur Evelyn's troop, Colonel Thomas Sheffield's regiment (*CM* 41.13ᵛ, 90.8ᵛ).

played a prominent role in forming the Agitators and linking them with the London Levellers. In July 1647, he took part in the General Council's debates in Reading and was one of only two soldiers joining eleven officers in presenting *The Heads of the Great Charge*, the Army's petition of impeachment against the Eleven Members.[15] In September, the imprisoned Lilburne called Sexby the conduit to his printers and the distributor of his books.[16] And as we have seen, he was one of the leading Agitators representing the New Model soldiery in their debates with Cromwell and Ireton at Putney. As much as anyone, he would show that the collective will and identity born in the New Model soviets would not go without remainder into a dictatorial Protectorate.

The abiding mystery of Sexby's public career lies in his seven years of apparent intimacy with Cromwell between their rancorous engagement at Putney and their deadly split in September 1654. In 1647, after the mutiny at Ware, Sexby left the Army, but continued to serve as a go-between for the grandees and the Levellers. In August 1648, at the battle of Preston, he delivered to Cromwell a characteristically defiant letter from Lilburne and perhaps led the Parliament's "forlorn hope," the avant garde designated to take the brunt of an attack, against Sir Marmaduke Langdale— or so he claimed, years later, to Langdale himself.[17] The House awarded him £100 when he returned to London with news of Cromwell's victory, and, according to a royalist newspaper, he was part of Cromwell's camp in the autumn of 1648.[18] In February 1649, the Council of State sent him to Gravesend to arrest the Scottish Commissioners, whom it suspected of departing for Holland to invite King Charles to Scotland.[19]

Throughout the turbulent Leveller spring of 1649, Sexby continued to work diligently for the Commonwealth. In early May, he examined mail packets in Dover, and the Council appointed him captain of foot and Governor of Portland, directing him to monitor the foreign post.[20] John Milton, then Secretary for Foreign Languages, reported that "One Sexby or Saxby offers how packets and letters may be opened and sealed again, if he or his associates may be entrusted with letter-office"—a suspiciously obliging offer.[21] By this time, he met the parliamentary radical and Council member Thomas Scot, who became the head of the new republic's intelligence service in July. Sexby traveled on intelligence missions to Rye, Hastings, Canterbury, and Ware.[22] In June 1650, the Council

15. *CP* 1.183, 151.
16. *Juglers Discovered*, 1647, 1–2.
17. *CP* 2.254; *CCSP* 42; Sexby also promoted himself to "Adjutant General" (Agitator General?). A Major Smithson may actually have led the forlorn hope of horse (*FD* 1.266–7).
18. *GZ.*
19. *CSPD* 1.21–2, 26. On the Scottish Commissioners, see *GHCP* 1.20–22.
20. *CSPD* 1.135, 140, 533.
21. Sheffield University Library, Hartlib Papers (H50 28/1/138; *Ephemerides*, 1649). Thanks to Tim Raylor for the reference. Did they discuss Milton's *Tenure*, to which Sexby alludes in *Killing Noe Murder?*
22. *PRO* 18/71/118ʳ.

promoted him to colonel and ordered him to lead a regiment of foot to Ireland, appointing George Joyce to replace him as Governor of Portland.[23] After a series of shifting orders and delays, Sexby's regiment joined the Scottish campaign, where it helped besiege Tantallon ("Timptallon") Castle in February 1651.[24] In June, Sexby was court-martialled in Edinburgh for executing a soldier without due process and for misappropriating funds by mustering absent soldiers. On Arthur Haselrig's testimony, the court acquitted him on the first count, and, after a long debate on the second, concluded that he had only withheld some soldiers' pay to encourage them to go with him to Ireland as ordered.[25]

He was cashiered but not disgraced, for later in 1651, a secret committee of the Council of State (Cromwell, Scot, Whitelocke, and perhaps also Neville and Marten) sent him to Huguenot France as an emissary and intelligencer, with a yearly salary of £1000. Given the hopes that Commonwealth England might lead an upsurge of Protestant republican internationalism, this was a vital appointment.[26] Nedham and Harrington theorized this republican project in the 1650s, but Sexby had already been actively engaged in it.[27] He left with a party of four, including his servant Samuel Dyer, John Tubbing, Thomas Arrundel, and perhaps Richard Overton, the Leveller.[28] He established headquarters in Bordeaux and, for the two years of his mission, reported twice a week to Scot and the Council. In September 1652, as "Stephen Edwards," he wrote a passionate letter to Henry Marten, "truth's solicitor" and "liberty's champion." He reveals his mistrust of Cromwell and arranges to continue communication with Marten by interlinear writing with invisible ink. Turning Paul's pleading Man of Macedonia into a Frondeur, Sexby encourages Marten to view the French tumults as a chance to make good the opportunities missed by the Commonwealth:

> 'Tis to be lamented his many prizes have been put into your hands, [and] what hath not been weakly managed hath been covetously monopolized: not becoming the worthies of a commonwealth: now you have another ball thrown you. . . .

23. *CSPD* 2.206, 223.
24. *Mercurius Politicus* 2/20–2/27/51.
25. *FD* 2.562–3; see also *CM* 19.26–7. Frances Henderson's forthcoming Oxford dissertation will transcribe Clarke's shorthand record of Sexby's court martial. Later, perhaps trying to save face, Sexby claimed he had left the Army after the battle of Dunbar and a quarrel with Cromwell (*NP* 2.342).
26. On the mission to France, see *GHCP* 2.156–8; Charles H. Firth, "Thomas Scot's Account of His Activities as Intelligencer During the Commonwealth," *English Historical Review* 12, 1897, and *The Journal of Joachim Hane*, Oxford 1896, xvi–xvii; Brailsford, *Levellers* 671–92; Philip A. Knachel, *England and the Fronde*, Ithaca, NY, 1967, 161, 198–202; and Sexby's account of his mission and its expenses in *CP* 3.197–202; *CSPD* 7.160–61; and *PRO* 18/71/115ᵛ–123ʳ.
27. Worden discusses republican internationalism in "Milton and Marchamont Nedham," in Armitage et al., *Milton* 156–80, 173.
28. *B* 6.829, 832. Tubbing was captured and tortured to death; his widow Susan petitioned the Protector and Council for relief on September 9 1657, which suggests that Sexby helped support her until his own imprisonment in August (*CSPD* 7.160, 11.90). Overton's possible participation (*NP* 3.51) would fill a gap in his history.

[T]he people's score is the best and safest interest to come in upon and this when you are fit to hear shall be spoken loud enough—"Oh England come and help your laws shall be ours."

But the popular republicanism of the Ormée, based among the artisans and apprentices, had already begun to clash with the aristocratic republicanism of Condé, creating a situation not unfamiliar to agitator Sexby.[29] Characteristically, Sexby proceeded to exceed his commission: the papers of Mazarin and Condé contain a document from early 1653 entitled *L'Accord du Peuple*, a poorly translated version of the Third (May 1649) *Agreement of the People*, which was endorsed by "les sieurs Saxebri et Arrondel" and intended as a revolutionary manifesto for the Huguenots of Bordeaux and Guienne. Its program of religious toleration and radical political and social reform included a republican "Manifeste" advocating an alliance between Guienne and Huguenot republicans in the Ormée, a proposal to abolish servile legal status for peasants, and a memorable declaration:

> We find that no man is born a slave. . . . The Governor of the universe, maker of everything in it, and of man as the glorious head of all, made us a rational people, and for a guide he gave us his word, which tells us that all men were equal in their first state, and will be the same at the end. The peasant is as free as the prince, for he comes into the world with neither sabots on his feet nor a saddle on his back—no more than the child of a king is born with a golden crown on his head.[30]

Aristocratic Frondeurs were not amused: Pierre Lenet wrote "I do not approve" on the copy he forwarded to Condé. Recalling Buckingham's bungling at La Rochelle, they declined to give England a second chance.[31]

The Bourbons defeated the Fronde in August 1653, leaving Condé the primary noble holdout. Sexby returned to England in August.[32] In a long undated report to Cromwell, he proposed that England lend ships, men, and horses to help Huguenots secure La Rochelle, St Martin, and the Isle of Casow in the River Garonne.[33] Cromwell sent Joachim Hane to examine La Rochelle and other fortified sites in France, and he agreed to send some ships and six thousand men under Sexby's command to aid Guienne, if Spain would foot the bill. But by November, the Spanish navy left the coast of Gironde and Sexby went to work monitoring mail packets

---

29. Thanks to Sarah Barber for this transcript from the Marten Papers (ML 72/519) and for this comparison. On the Ormée, see Sol Alexander Westrich, *The Ormée of Bordeaux*, Baltimore 1972.

30. Olivier Lutaud, *Cromwell, les Niveleurs et la République*, 2nd edn, Paris 1978, 260, 263. Lutaud provides a fully annotated edition of the French texts (249–74, 263). Others, including Richard Rumbold (*GZ*), John Harris (*GZ*), Defoe, Jefferson, and Taine (Hill, *Experience* 37), employed the saying.

31. Knachel, *England* 201–2.

32. *B* 6.829; *GHCP* 4.53n.

33. *CP* 3.197–202.

for John Thurloe.[34] He pressed for reimbursement of his expenses stretching back to his intelligence work in 1649, and worked with Condé's agents to secure an English alliance with Spain on the Fronde's behalf.[35] But Cromwell demurred, and nothing came of Sexby's mission. Instead, in April 1654, when the Council of State ratified the Treaty of Westminster and settled the first Anglo-Dutch War, Cromwell steered the Protectorate into war with Spain and an attempt to seize its colonies in the Caribbean—the "Western Design."[36]

Sexby had hoped to turn Bordeaux into a Leveller republic; instead, he saw Whitehall turning into a Bourbon palace. After Cromwell dismissed Barebone's Parliament, English radicals (including ex-Levellers, republicans, Fifth Monarchists, and Quakers) began to form an opposition, one which sometimes ventured into tyrannicidal arguments. In May, an Englishman in Amsterdam preached that one might kill Cromwell with a clear conscience, and that he was of a mind to do so.[37] John Streater issued a number of menacing anti-Cromwellian works in 1654.[38] In *A Politick Commentary*, he compared Cromwell to Julius Caesar, who rebelled in his youth against Sylla the dictator: "I have much wondered oftentimes to read of flatterers, that have to those in power said, 'Sir, you are like Caesar,' when it would better have become them to be like Timoleon of Corinth: to be like Caesar is in effect to say they deserve to be killed by a Brutus, as he was."[39] A royalist pamphlet of October 1654 presents an argument remarkably like the one Sexby would develop in *Killing Noe Murder*, asking why an Army that fought against Charles as a tyrant should hesitate to slay a Protector who gives laws "like a conqueror." The author warns Cromwell against trying to make his rule hereditary, for all his authority would vanish with his death, and his family would be "destroyed (like that of the great Alexander's) by your own friends and followers, if you yourself should scape such a cup of poison as he met with or such a dagger as finished the ambition of Julius Caesar."[40]

Sexby began meeting with this opposition, perhaps as early as December 1653, shortly after Cromwell had himself declared Lord Protector.[41] In August 1654, he may have spoken at the trial of Humphrey Marston, who was hanged for counterfeiting, coin clipping, and killing two messengers

34. Ibid. 3.xvi; *GHCP* 3.54–5, 112, 199–200n.; Abbott, *Writings* 3.271–2.

35. *CSPD* 6.266; 7.160, 325, 347; *PRO* 18/71/117ʳ, 18/75/3ʳ; Abbott, *Writings* 3.111–12.

36. On the Western Design, see *GHCP* 4.120–76; and Timothy Venning, *Cromwellian Foreign Policy*, New York 1995, 71–112.

37. *B* 2.319. On the culture of republican resistance to the Protectorate, see Norbrook, *Writing* 299–325.

38. On Streater, see Nigel Smith's "Popular Republicanism in the 1650s," in Armitage et al., *Milton* 137–55; and Adrian Johns, *The Nature of the Book*, Chicago 1998, 266–323.

39. This short piece appeared as a preface to *Perfect and Impartial Intelligence* (5/16–5/23/54). In *A Rational Millennium*, I discuss Marvell's subtly menacing comparison of Cromwell to Caesar the young general and Charles to Caesar the old tyrant (220–23).

40. J. H., *An Admonition to My Lord Protector and His Council*, 1654, 4, 10.

41. *B* 6.829.

of the Council of State.[42] In August, the Council of State reimbursed him £1000.[43] Thereafter, he burned his bridges and moved into implacable opposition. This shift appears even more dramatic if we take seriously his story to the royalist court in exile:

> He had been, in the beginning, a common soldier of Cromwell's troop, and afterwards was one of those Agitators who were made use of to control the Parliament; and had so great an interest in Cromwell that he was frequently his bedfellow, a familiarity he frequently admitted those to whom he employed in any great trust, and with whom he could not so freely converse as in those hours. He was very perfect in the history of Cromwell's dissimulations, and would describe his artifices to the life.[44]

Politics makes strange bedfellows.[45] Even if we primly distinguish modern and early modern sleeping practices, it's intriguing to picture Edward and Oliver in bed together, swapping political intimacies. Sexby's claim to insider status might be no more than an attempt to puff himself up in the eyes of the exiled court, but it does jibe with the privileged trajectory of his career in the preceding years.[46] His capacity for republican solidarity and deep personal loyalty explains both his early commitment to a fraying ideal of Cromwell the Commonwealthsman, and his later ferocious hatred of him as a tyrant. His abrupt shift was not unlike that of Fifth Monarchists in December 1653, when Oliver the godly prince dismissed Barebone's Parliament and became the Little Horn.

Sexby worked with his Putney ally, John Wildman, and a coalition of radical soldiers, sailors, parliamentarians, Baptists, and Fifth Monarchists in "the Overton Plot" of late 1654—the first of a series of "poniarding conspiracies, / Drawn from the sheath of lying prophecies."[47] In the previous chapter, we saw the growth of Fifth Monarchist agitation against the Protectorate in 1654. As Cromwell's semi-monarchical regime under the Instrument of Government alienated his former allies, this opposition spread further. In the summer of 1654, when they were elected to the first

42. Since Sexby had been the main intermediary between Lilburne and the Agitators, he may have been that advocate, "one of Lilburne's old friends," who spoke for Marston, and *Several Proceedings* may have intended Sexby when it called Marston "formerly one of the Agitators at Putney, and one very intimate with John Lilburne." The large size of Marston's funeral train suggests that, like Robert Lockyer's in 1649, it may also have been a Leveller/Agitator rally (8/17–8/24/54). Marston had signed *The Levellers (Falsly so called) Vindicated* of August 1649; he left behind *The Confession of Mr. Humphrey Marston*, and *Marston's Declaration*, a manuscript among the Thomason Tracts.

43. *CSPD* 7.325.

44. Hyde, *History* 15.133.

45. "To be someone's 'bedfellow' suggested that one had influence and could be the making of a fortune" (Bray, "Homosexuality" 42).

46. He later boasted to Peter Talbot that almost all of Cromwell's soldiers at Preston deserted him and joined Sexby, leading him to promise Sexby his daughter's hand in marriage if he would join in battle (*GHCP* 4.224–5).

47. Marvell, "The First Anniversary," *Andrew Marvell* 171–2. For the Overton Plot—named after Colonel Robert, not Leveller Richard, who participated—I draw on the *DNB* and *GZ* entries on Robert Overton; Ashley, *Wildman* 82–94; and Barbara Taft, "*The Humble Petition of Several Colonels of the Army*," *Huntington Library Quarterly* 42, 1978–79.

Protectorate Parliament, John Wildman, colonels Thomas Saunders and
John Okey, and (Ludlow reported) Lord Grey of Groby refused to pledge
loyalty to the government as constituted, and the Council of State
excluded them.[48] Cromwell opened the Parliament on September 3 with
a speech conflating Levellers, Diggers, and Ranters, saying that the
Levellers were out to "make the tenant as liberal a fortune as the
landlord," and that their motto was Ezekiel's "Overturn, overturn, overturn"—a favorite phrase of Abiezer Coppe's. Cromwell gained a pliant
Parliament, but only by driving the opposition into extra-parliamentary
action.[49] Excluded parliamentarians with republican sympathies, such as
Grey and Marten, began to meet with the Levellers.[50] Discontents also
emerged in the Navy, where Vice-Admiral Lawson began to organize
political meetings which drew up grievances.[51]

An intelligence report to Thurloe tells of meetings in September 1654
at the house of a Mr Allen, a merchant in Birchen Lane, London,
including the three colonels (Okey, Saunders, and Matthew Alured),
Lawson, Wildman, Marten, Captain Bishop, Lord Grey, and Sexby.[52] In
the Army, officers with Fifth Monarchist sympathies (including Major
General Harrison) began to meet, and, with Wildman's assistance, the
three colonels drew up *The Humble Petition of Several Colonels of the Army*.[53]
Barbara Taft calls this "the last of the Army–Leveller manifestos," and
indeed, the emergent opposition of 1654–55 frequently recalls the Army
in 1647.[54] It pronounced the Instrument of Government an attempt to
reinstate monarchy and denounced the reduction of the Army to a
mercenary "standing army under a single person," who had assumed
Charles's old "negative voice" over all civil matters. It recalled "the
expense of all the blood and treasure in these three nations" that had
brought Cromwell where he was, and demanded the restoration of free
parliaments and the "birthrights" of the Englishmen who had fought.
Wildman (probably) had it published as a broadside, after the arrest of
the three colonels.[55] On October 18, Thomason acquired his copy, and
the next day, *Some Memento's for the Officers and Souldiers of the Army*, which
echoes phrases in the petition. But its direct address to the Army, its
character of a tyrant, and its particular antityrannical arguments also
suggest *Killing Noe Murder*. Nedham attacked both works, calling the
colonels' petition an attempt to "infect the soldiery, and bring the little
Agitators to town again, and make the wheels of time and the world run a

48. Ashley, *Wildman* 84; Taft, "*Humble*" 20; Ludlow, *The Memoirs of Edmund Ludlow*, 2 vols,
    Oxford 1894, 1.390.
49. Ashley, *Wildman* 84–9.
50. Taft, "*Humble*" 32–3.
51. See Capp, *Cromwell's Navy* 136–7. See also *GHCP* 3.195–225.
52. *B* 3.147–8.
53. Also in *CSPD* 6.302–4, misfiled in papers for December 1653.
54. Taft, "*Humble*" 15.
55. [Wildman,] *A Declaration of the Free-born People of England*, 1655.

madding back to the year 1647."[56] Sexby continued meeting with Wildman, Lord Grey, and Lawson, and helped distribute copies of the petition
and pamphlet to Scotland, Bristol, Warwickshire, and Leicester.[57]

In December 1653, Robert Overton, formerly a major general in the
Scots campaigns, told Wildman of his discontent with Cromwell.[58] Overton
returned to Scotland, where he met with Army radicals, mainly Baptist,
who began to plan action against the Protectorate.[59] He did not join
them, but did not warn his superiors, either. Samuel Dyer, Sexby's former
servant, later said that Sexby told him Overton planned to seize General
Monck and his headquarters in Scotland, that he and Wildman had
plotted against Cromwell's life, and that Sir Arthur Haselrig promised
Sexby his support once the rebellion was in progress.[60] Anthony Salter,
formerly a sergeant in Sexby's regiment in Scotland, reported that Sexby
kept two horses to speed his getaway after the royalist Penruddock's Rising
in Salisbury, which did not occur until March.[61] Cromwell's intelligence
network acted with its usual efficiency. In December 1654, he dismissed
Saunders, forced Okey out of the Army, and court-martialled Alured,
imprisoning him until the end of 1655. In January, Monck arrested
Overton, and he remained in custody until March 1659.[62] On February
10, Cromwell's forces arrested Wildman while he was putting the finishing
touches to a manifesto—a piece of stagecraft, it seems, since at least one
other copy survived, to be published in March as a broadside with the title
of *A Declaration of the Free-born People of England, Now in Armes Against
the Tyrannie and Oppression of Oliver Cromwell, Esq.*[63] They imprisoned
Harrison until March 1656, Wildman and Lord Grey until July. In January,
they arrested William Allen in Devonshire.[64] Captain Unton Croke was
seeking Sexby in the west of England on February 3. On the 19th,
G. Forsington wrote Cromwell about an unsuccessful search in Salisbury.
On the 21st, Croke assured Cromwell of his diligent search in Devonshire
and Dorsetshire. In March, Croke visited Weymouth and the house of
Sexby's "mistress," Mrs Ford, "to whom for many years he had professed

---

56. *The Observator* 10/24–10/31/54 and 10/31/54–11/7/54.
57. Ludlow, *Memoirs* 1.406–7, 414–15; see also *B* 6.829. John H. F. Hughes suggests that, in
    late 1654, someone connected with the colonels' plot attempted to meet with Ludlow in
    Ireland ("The Commonwealthsmen Divided," *The Seventeenth Century* 5.1, 1990, 66–7n.15,
    referring to *TM* A41, 560). This may have been Sexby, or Wildman's servant, William
    Parker (*B* 6.830).
58. On Overton, see *FD* 2.546–61; *GZ*; Firth's *DNB* entry; and Barbara Taft, "'They that
    pursew perfection on earth . . .': The Political Progress of Robert Overton," Gentles et
    al., *Soldiers* 286–303. In his *Second Defense* (May 1654), Milton referred to Overton as his
    dear friend (*M* 4.676).
59. Ashley, *Wildman* 88.
60. *B* 6.829, 832.
61. Ibid. 3.271, 6.693–4.
62. Ashley, *Wildman* 82–96; *GZ*.
63. For a transcript and admiring commentary, see Whitelocke, *Memorials* 606–"601" [i.e.
    607]. See also Ashley, *Wildman* 90–92.
64. *GZ* on Harrison and Wildman. On Grey, *DNB*; *CP* 1.433. Hardacre, "William Allen"
    301–2.

friendship." She promised to help him contact Sexby, but not to bring them together physically. Croke speculatively linked Sexby with "Joyce" (presumably George Joyce) and with Hugh Courtney (Cornish Fifth Monarchist, former MP, and visitor to Trapnel's bedside). By March 10, a party of horse at Hartley Rowe seized Sexby's portmanteau "with some writings of concernment therein, and likewise a suit of extraordinary arms."[65] But Sexby had already fled to the Continent with Richard Overton and William Parker, Wildman's manservant, after the Mayor and the Governor of the Castle at Portland detained the soldiers sent to arrest him.[66]

Ludlow says Cromwell kept tabs on Sexby by feigning friendship and funding his trip as an unofficial emissary to the Huguenots of Bordeaux, where he was betrayed and barely escaped; this account either fills in the missing months of Sexby's life from February to May 1655, or confuses them with 1651–53.[67] A pamphlet of October 1655 suggests the former, if its account of the Protectorate's low credit among Continental Protestants derives from Sexby.[68] In any case, Sexby arrived in Antwerp by May. His wife followed, settling in Ghent; she gave birth to a son in late 1656.[69] By late May, Sexby began conspiring with exiled royalists—first, perhaps, Colonel Robert Phelipps.[70] He eventually contacted a remarkable range of persons, including Father Peter Talbot (Irish Jesuit and Professor of Theology in the Jesuit College of Antwerp), Charles II and his court (Phelipps, the Earl of Norwich, Edward Hyde, Silius Titus, Sir Marmaduke Langdale, the Duke of Buckingham), and Spanish officials (Count Fuensaldaña, governor of the Spanish Netherlands; Don Juan of Austria, his

65. On the hunt for Sexby, see *B* 3.140, 143, 162–3, 165, 194–5; *CP* 3.25; *CM* 25.140, 143, 194–5; and *GHCP* 3.269–70.
66. *B* 6.830; *CCSP* 55.
67. *Memoirs* 1.415.
68. *The Protector, So called, In Part Unvailed*, 64.
69. *CCSP* 183. Sexby's aliases (including "Thomas Hungerford," "Thomas Brookes," and perhaps "Hester Broadbent," "H. C.," and "J. C.") complicate efforts to track his comings and goings. He may be the "Colonel Ogle" who wrote "Mrs. Ogle" (*B* 5.338–9, *TM* A50, 273), and Thurloe identified him as the "Jo. Smith" who wrote a letter "for his best friend E. C." Its gently patriarchal tones recall Donne's "Valediction Forbidding Mourning": "My Dearest Love:. . . . There is nothing in this world, that I more wish and pray for, than our happy and speedy meeting; neither have I the least reason to doubt of it; but yet if it shall please God otherwise to determine, it would argue us guilty of a great deal of impatience and imprudence to impair our healths by a voluntary afflicting ourselves for what lieth not in our power to prevent or remedy. Let not my love therefore harbor the least thought that way, but refer all to God's blessed will, from whom we daily receive better things than either we can deserve or know how to ask, who in his good time will bring us together to his own glory and our comfort. My best love, forget not to send me the sympathy powder by Mr. H. All things go as well as we can desire. I pray God send your new landlady to be kind to you. My best respect to our best friend. If thou lovest me, be merry. He desires it, who loves thee dearlier than himself, and shall ever remain, Thy truly loving husband. J. C." (*B* 5.307). If Mrs Ford of Weymouth (see below) was Sexby's common-law wife, she may have been the same person as Elizabeth "Sexby." But one Elizabeth Cole (NB—"E. C."), servant to Samuel Rogers in St Catherine's dock, received seven parcels of *Killing Noe Murder* (ibid. 6.315).
70. *NP* 2.299.

successor, and the king's illegitimate son; Don Alonso Cardeñas, former Spanish ambassador to England, whom Cromwell had expelled in October). He even sent out feelers to the Pope.[71] Two years earlier, Sexby encouraged Cromwell to ally with Spain and French Huguenots against King Louis of France; now he encouraged English radicals to ally with Spanish and English royalists against the person who he was convinced would soon become King Oliver I of England. More than anyone else, Sexby worked to create a conspiracy between the Leveller left and the royalist right, a Protectoral nightmare memorably captured in Thurloe's letter to Henry Cromwell: "The Spaniard, cavalier, papists, and Levellers are all come into a confederacy. What monstrous birth this womb will bring forth, I cannot tell."[72] But Sexby's conspiracies suggest a marked shift in his political practice. In 1647, he worked as an organic intellectual on behalf of a fused group; as a democratically elected Agitator, he attempted through petitions, manifestos, and communication networks to fabricate a new egalitarian party that would democratize the English state. In 1655–57, he worked as a conspiratorial *bricoleur* on behalf of a merely serial collective; as a self-authorized conspirator, he attempted to cobble together a makeshift alliance among preconstituted political parties united only by a shared opposition to Cromwell, and constantly threatening to fragment. This precarious ensemble helps to explain Sexby's frantic but finally inconclusive activities during the following two years.

While on the Continent, Sexby maintained contact with English radicals, as we can see in his passionate and reassuring letter of March 18 1656, to Wildman in the Tower:

> Oh what would I give for an hour's discourse; but know that cannot be; let us converse this way, I desire, if possible. I understand thou art much dejected. I cannot but exceedingly blame you for it; you have as little cause so to be as ever had prisoner in thy condition; for though your unrighteous judge and his janissaries think they sit so sure that there is no condition of falling, yet I tell thee he will not be himself of that opinion long. . . . That apostate thinks he knows me, but if as he pretends he would not be jealous of me, being in any petty design, I hate foolish businesses; those undertakings and only such can render him in this falling condition. He is inconsiderable, mark what I say to you; his way within few months will be hedged up by that necessity his own designs will bring upon himself; being frustrated therein his soul (as proud as Lucifer's) will fail within him. . . . Thine to command till death.[73]

Pondering the republic's religious composition, Sexby proposed toleration for all Christians and Jews – the latter because they were "necessary for a kingdom."[74] If, as many believed, the Flood took place 1656 years

71. *CCSP* 40, 42, 52, 76, 137.
72. *B* 5.45.
73. Ashley, *Wildman* 99–100.
74. *NP* 3.43–5, 51.

after creation, a timely conversion of the Jews might set off a resonant apocalypse.[75]

Sexby's attention turned to Spain, whose colonial war with the Protectorate opened the possibility of an alliance. Many English radicals militantly opposed the war, particularly after England's humiliating defeat in Hispaniola in April and May 1655. Despite their ostensible godly fanaticism, Fifth Monarchists hesitated to embark on a fight to the death with the Spanish Antichrist, perhaps because the London cloth trades depended so heavily on Spanish markets.[76] They also feared that, by seeking an empire before completing the revolution at home, Cromwell's England would degenerate into a Roman tyranny, growing "so low and cowardly" as to turn its back on those whom it pretended to liberate, "as it's generally reported the Protector's army did upon a few inconsiderable cowkeepers in Hispaniola."[77] In 1656, I. S. predicted, "Sir, first, his Highness will cleanse the commonwealth of her money, the love of which is the root of all evil: secondly, he will cleanse her of superfluous members, and send them to Hispaniola, either to be killed by the Spaniards, or else to starve there for want of bread."[78]

By May 1655, Sexby contacted Don Luis de Haro, warned him of the Western Design, and offered to help subvert the English fleet.[79] By June 3, he had established contact with Marmaduke Langdale and Count Fuensaldaña.[80] By late June, George Goring, Earl of Norwich, sent Sexby to Spain with Samuel Dyer, Don Francisco de la Hoste, and another Spanish noble. They arrived by August 16.[81] In Madrid, Sexby lobbied the Council of Spain to help him overthrow the Protectorate. Offering himself as hostage until the proposed conquest was complete, Sexby proposed that Spain and the Pope provide £100,000 for a force of Irish mercenaries who would invade England, with the assistance of that part of the fleet friendly to his ally, Admiral Lawson. Charles would then regain the crown, so long as he agreed it was a gift from the people, not a possession by right of conquest. He could then introduce liberty of religion for Catholics in a new Leveller constitutional monarchy. During his trip, using the aliases of "Thomas Brookes" and "Thomas Hungerford," Sexby kept up a correspondence with many of his allies, but Richard Overton heard nothing from him between the end of July and the end of October.[82] By

75. On philosemitism in the 1650s, see the letter of an Overton conspirator in Scotland in *CP* 3.12–14; *CCSP* 42–3; David S. Katz, *Philo-Semitism and the Readmission of the Jews to England 1603–1655*, Oxford 1982.

76. *GHCP* 4.171.

77. *The Protector* 67. See also David Armitage, "The Cromwellian Protectorate and the Languages of Empire," *Historical Journal* 35.3, 1992.

78. *The Picture of a New Courtier*, 1656, 12.

79. *CCSP* 40.

80. Ibid. 38.

81. *B* 6.831; *CCSP* 54. Norwich knew Sexby well, from his days in prison after the second civil war (*NP* 2.347–8).

82. *NP* 3.102.

October, Sexby was back in Calais.[83] And in early November, he had returned to Antwerp with some money and promises of additional support.[84] In December 1655 or January 1656, he sent Overton to England with weapons and Spanish gold; they corresponded for some months.[85] On April 12 Sexby's lobbying produced a treaty signed by Ormond and Rochester for King Charles, by Cardeñas and another for King Philip: Spain would provide four thousand foot and two thousand horse if he could secure an English port for their debarkation, and England promised to aid Spain against Portugal, restore Caribbean conquests made since 1630, and forgo any further conquests. Peter Talbot's brother Gilbert began assembling Irish troops at Ghent.[86] In August 1656, William Lockhart, English ambassador to France, told Thurloe of Sexby's meeting with Cardeñas and his invasion plan: a port near London, Spanish troops, mutiny in the fleet and Ireland, Charles declaring open war.[87] But Cromwell's agents intercepted Sexby's payment of £800 aimed at suborning an officer in charge of a port, and the invasion never came to be.[88]

Three key points emerge about Sexby's conspiracy. First, Cromwell and spymaster Thurloe took it seriously, monitoring it through counterspies, mail interception, and interrogation of suspected English allies. In January 1656, Cromwell examined Captain Richard Talbot, later the Duke of Tyrconnel, on the probably well-founded suspicion that he was involved in an assassination plot. After escaping to Antwerp, Talbot reported that Sexby "is the greatest enemy Cromwell has, and is looked upon here as a person of great interest in England."[89] In July, his brother Father Peter Talbot reported to Charles a conversation with Sexby's wife, who had told him the Duke of Buckingham was planning to meet with Sexby in France, and might thus "bring to him the man whose daughter he desires to marry"—thus raising the arresting prospect of a conspiracy among Sexby, Buckingham, and Sir Thomas Fairfax.[90] Lockhart wrote Thurloe in August, with tremulous hesitation, about Fairfax's possible connection with Sexby's plans for an invasion.[91] In an August letter to Henry Cromwell, Thurloe seems to be taking Sexby's threat quite seriously.[92] In September, Major Ralph Knight wrote General Monck that Cromwell had informed his officers at Whitehall that Charles Stuart had ready an invasion force of eight thousand, which Sexby would admit to England

83. *B* 4.84.
84. *NP* 3.114, 128.
85. *B* 2.590, 6.829–33.
86. Philip Aubrey, *Mr. Secretary Thurloe*, London and Rutherford, NJ, 1990, 108; *CCSP* 91, 109–10; *CCSP* 116.
87. *B* 5.319–20.
88. *CP* 3.71; *B* 5.407.
89. *CCSP* 84–5.
90. Ibid. 147; see also 103, 108, 121, 201. Royalists contacted Fairfax or his circle as early as September 1654, and Buckingham may have been interested in Mary Fairfax as early as 1653; they married in September 1657 (Underdown, *Royalist* 118–23, 224).
91. *B* 5.319–20.
92. Ibid. 5.349.

through a betrayed port garrison, and that they would be joined by English Fifth Monarchist allies.[93] On November 27, the Protectorate issued *An Act for the Security of His Highness the Lord Protector* aimed at the recent conspiracies against him. It set up a body of approved commissioners who would have the power to conduct inquiries and try cases of treason.

Second, Sexby's conspiracy impressed royalists in exile, who held back only because they feared Sexby would attempt to institute a monarch-free republic. A royalist–Leveller alliance is likelier than it might seem. Even before the execution of Charles, Levellers such as John Lilburne and Francis White began to resist the pressure toward regicide on the republican grounds that Charles was a citizen suffering under tyrannical authority.[94] Royalists in exile contemplated a treacherous alliance as early as September 1649, when Hyde sent Charles II a long report on how to deal with Levellers and Presbyterians: noting the considerable Leveller strength in the Army and Navy, Hyde advocated some "specious concessions" to liberty of conscience, law reform, poor relief, chastening of privy advisors, protection of common fields, and frequent calling of parliaments.[95] On January 27 1655 an anonymous broadside entitled *A Declaration of the Members of Parliament Lately Dissolved by Oliver Cromwell, Esquire* called Cromwell a tyrant, yearned nostalgically for a republican government by replaceable king, Lords, and Commons, and pointed toward the possibility of a Leveller–royalist alliance. In July 1655, Peter Talbot wrote the king that Sexby was "a man of more than ordinary judgment and sagacity; after many discourses, professes not to be opposed to the king's prerogative so far as it agrees with the liberty of the people, to whom he would give the legislative power." He also tied Sexby to an important oppositional group in England: "Lord Grey of Groby, Wildman, Allen and some Anabaptists are sure to him, above fifteen colonels, a great part of the navy, and some sea ports." In October, Talbot asked the king to write a friendly letter to Sexby, saying that "If the King gains him, he gains his kingdom without much bloodshed."[96] More than any other Leveller, Sexby came to embody the royalists' hopes for an alliance; indeed, royalists began calling him "*The* Leveller."[97]

But they had misgivings. In June 1655, Phelipps wrote Nicholas that Sexby and other Levellers shared with their new Presbyterian contacts that "pernicious state doctrine" that "the king is the people's creature"— quoting John Cooke's notorious phrase from Charles's trial.[98] In July 1655, Norwich wrote Nicholas that Sexby might well be "a knave," but he was "no fool."[99] In June 1655, Langdale wrote Charles that Sexby was

93. *CP* 3.71–2; see Baines's concurring report in *B* 5.407.
94. Gregg, *Free-Born John* 259–60; White, *Copies of Severall Letters*, 1649, 4–5.
95. *NP* 1.138–47.
96. *CCSP* 51, 183.
97. *NP* 3.10.
98. Ibid. 2.352.
99. Ibid. 3.15.

soliciting £150,000 from Count Fuensaldaña, hoping "to pull down Cromwell and set up a Parliament."[100] He remained skeptical in October, when he commented that "killing Cromwell will little avail, if in his stead they set up a Commonwealth, which is the greatest fear I have." In November, he described Sexby as one not "inclinable to the king's interest." Nicholas concurred.[101] In January 1656, *The King's Answer to the Proposals of "Mr. S"* observed that if Sexby's plan for an invasion with one thousand Irish horse were successful, "the king might only find that he had changed his enemy, while failure would deject his whole party and give credit to Cromwell."[102] In November, Talbot wrote Charles about Sexby's plans; a little later, Hyde responded that Charles would meet with Sexby, but "As for the overture of 1000 foot and 400 horse, the king cannot conceive the ground of such an undertaking."[103] In December, Charles contrasted his own party, a unified group combining "all the considerable fortunes and families in the kingdom," with Sexby's—men of "very different humors," united only by their opposition to Cromwell. Their radical proposals would lessen the Crown's power, "devolving an absurd power to the people."[104] The king's party began to demand that Sexby demonstrate his monarchist good faith by assassinating Cromwell.

Third, Sexby's conspiracy was indeed an attempt to use his Presbyterian, Anglican, and Catholic allies against Cromwell in an effort to re-establish a republic. Some of Sexby's most appealing moments in these letters suggest his difficulty in professing a royalism he did not feel. In a letter of March 1656, Hyde counseled Ormond on strategy in dealing with Sexby, saying that "the privileges of Magna Charta and the power of free parliaments must be magnified as much as possible, and if it is necessary to consent to any unreasonable propositions, let it be with the clause, 'If a free Parliament think fit to ask the same of his Majesty.'" Furthermore, Sexby "complains that the cavaliers are his mortal enemies; it is necessary that they take no notice of him, or else seem to be his friends."[105] Talbot noted Sexby's abhorrence of the Cavaliers, whom he called "a generation God cannot prosper, for their swearing, drinking, whoring, and little secrecy, and that Cromwell had been down before but for their folly." In a letter of November, attempting to negotiate an audience with Charles, Talbot warned that Sexby "desires to be excused from kneeling, for he thinks that to be a kind of idolatry, and says the king's father dispensed with him in that matter; he does not despair of Cromwell's being cut off."[106] In December 1656, Sexby wrote Don Juan of Austria with a request

100. *CCSP* 38.
101. *NP* 3.76–7, 118, 145.
102. *CCSP* 91.
103. Ibid. 202–3, 206.
104. Ibid. 213–15; J. R. Jones, *Charles II, Royal Politician*, London 1987, 31.
105. *CCSP* 101–2.
106. Ibid. 51–2, 202–3, 206. When was Sexby in contact with Charles I? During the summer of 1647, after Joyce took him into custody? In October, when Lilburne was scheming to

for a thousand Irish foot and four hundred horse. He detailed plans for an invasion, asking that no mention be made of the king before Cromwell was killed, and that royalists speak only of the liberty of the country until that time.[107] Still, Sexby's claim that monarchy might have a role in this republic may have been more than a stratagem. He may have begun to prefer a *de jure* mixed monarchy in something like the 1689 settlement to what he saw as the merely *de facto* tyranny of the Protectorate. He told the Earl of Norwich that if there were proper safeguards for the people's rights, he could agree to the restoration of Charles II.[108]

In June 1656, Sexby may have returned to England briefly.[109] A brilliantly written work entitled *The Picture of a New Courtier* had been "cast about in the streets" in April. In it, "I. S." laments the imprisonment of Fifth Monarchists and godly participants in the Overton Plot, including Sexby's associates Ludlow, Courtney, Lilburne, and Sturgeon, but he also attacks Cromwell's hypocritical piety and his Blasphemy Ordinance from the perspective of something like a rational religion.[110] He menacingly compares Cromwell to Strafford, invokes the "good old cause" (the first printed use of the phrase), recalls the New Model's expense of blood, and concludes with the language of apocalyptic tyrannicidal prophecy that concludes *Killing Noe Murder*.[111] Sexby may have carried back to the Continent a remarkable petition from the Levellers to Charles, which arrived the following month. It proposed to restore the Long Parliament, elevate Charles to the throne on the terms of the treaty of the Isle of Wight, establish liberty of conscience, end tithing, and declare amnesty to all those save inveterate supporters of Cromwell. It was signed by, among others, John Wildman, John Sturgeon, and William Howard, the Leveller Baron.[112] By August 10, Sexby was back in Amsterdam when he wrote Wildman that

> [T]hey are madmen, if not worse, if worse can be, that think either paper polities, or great words, can free us from our oppressors; no it's that must free us from it, [that] hath brought it upon us; the sword is that now enslaves us, and it's that must deliver us. . . . [B]e not afraid, or doubt I have jackals in the

---

bring the king together with radicals in a coalition against Cromwell (Dyve, "Tower" 91–2)? In 1648, as an emissary between Charles and the Levellers?

107. *CCSP* 213–14.
108. *NP* 2.351.
109. *B* 5.100, 319, 362.
110. I. S., 4, 9.
111. 6, 7, 5, 11. Johns (*Nature* 287) and Abbott (*Writings* 4.143) tie "I. S." to John Streater, and Abbott also suggests the Fifth Monarchist John Spittlehouse, whom the tract mentions (4). We might add John Sturgeon, Sexby's agent "John Speedwell" (perhaps Richard Overton—see below), and Sexby himself writing under the alias of "Jo. Smith" (*B* 5.307). *The Picture* bears a number of resemblances to R. G.'s proto-Harringtonian *A Copy of a Letter*, ostensibly written in 1654 but published in June 1656, two months after *The Picture*, and frequently attributed, on slim evidence, to Streater.
112. Hyde, *History* 15.103–31; *CCSP* 145–6. An officer of the king delivered this petition (Hyde, *History* 15.104), but this wouldn't rule out a hand-off from Sexby, perhaps to Titus.

forest among the lions, and some cubs too who hath seasoned claws and teeth. . . .[113]

Sexby may have been thinking of the summer's explosion of oppositional republican theory, contrasting it with the anti-Cromwell network he had helped set up in England during his trip, a network that numbered thirty or forty committed assassins, at least in the official account, *The Whole Business of Sindercome*.[114] Later speculation included Lawson, Harrison, Colonel Rich, and Major Danvers.[115]

All these plans hung on the assassination of Cromwell, the special task assigned to Miles Sindercombe—formerly "one of the levelling party."[116] Sindercombe had been a quartermaster in Colonel John Reynolds's regiment and a leader in the Leveller mutiny at Burford in 1649. After the Overton Plot, Monck dismissed him from the Army in Scotland as a suspicious character, only to find that he was a chief conspirator, perhaps assigned the task of assassinating Monck himself.[117] To aid him in his plots against Cromwell, Sindercombe engaged John Cecil, with whom he had served under Monck, and a man named "Boyes," who may have been Richard Overton.[118] They hoped to assassinate Cromwell on September

---

113. I've modified Ashley's transcription (*Wildman* 106) of *TM* A40, 661–2.

114. 1657, 6.

115. *CSPV* 31.46.

116. *Mercurius Politicus* 1/29–2/5/57; see also the accounts for 1/15–22, 1/22–29. On Sindercombe, see Giavarina (*CSPV* 31.7–12, 18, 20, 45–6); Burton, *Diary*, 1.354–8, 4.483–6); *Whole Business*; Firth (*DNB*); William Cobbett and Thomas Bayly Howell, eds, *Cobbett's Complete Collection of State Trials*, 34 vols, London 1810, 5.842–71; Philip Aubrey, *Thurloe* 110–14; Ruth Spalding, *Contemporaries of Bulstrode Whitelocke, 1605–1675*, Oxford 1990, 328–30.

117. *FD* 133–4; *CSPV* 31.18; *Whole Business* 6; *DNB* on Sindercombe.

118. After Sindercombe's plot failed, Cecil described Boyes as a frequent traveler between Flanders and England, "a man of somewhat a low stature, and small boned, brownish hair curling to flaxen, sanguine complexion, and wore his beard long," and with "great skill in fireworks" (*B* 5.776). What little we know of him conjures up Overton. Overton may have spent the early thirties as an actor (Margot Heinemann, *Puritanism and Theatre*, Cambridge 1980, 243). Cecil observed "That Boyes goes by several names, and in several habits; sometimes as a poor priest in ragged clothes; sometimes well clad as a gentleman" (*Whole Business* 6–7). After January 1656, Overton left the public eye, disappearing completely from *The Nicholas Papers* and *The Clarendon State Papers*. Samuel Dyer, Sexby's former servant, testified that Overton took most of Sexby's Spanish money over to England in December or January, and in a letter of January 29, Sexby (as "Hungerford") wrote "John White" (Sindercombe?) that he would send "a small parcel by John Speedwell, master"—perhaps a Bunyanesque pseudonym for Overton/Boyes (*B* 6.831, 4.436). "Boyes" spent much of his time between January 1656 and February 1657 shuttling incognito between Flanders and England. Dyer testified about Sexby's conspiracy that "Overton knows all"; Cecil testified that the Sindercombe conspirators were organized in cells, so "that not one above two should know each other," but "Boyes knew the whole number" (*B* 6.833; *Whole Business* 6). In late 1655, waiting for Sexby to return from Spain, Overton revised his mortalist classic, *Mans Mortalitie* (1644), into *Man Wholly Mortal*; Sindercombe, who associated frequently with Boyes during 1656–57, was a mortalist, "owning the universal point of redemption," claiming "that the soul died with the body or slept with the body till the resurrection, and then it may be it should rise," and "that by the grave Hell was meant" (*Whole Business* 11). See Firth on "Boyes" (*Last* 1.37n.) and Marie Gimelfarb-Brack on Overton and Sexby in *Liberté, Egalité, Fraternité, Justice!*, Berne 1979, 381–4. Sturgeon was in custody when Dyer and

17 1656, while he was on his way from hearing a sermon at Westminster Abbey to open his second Parliament. Sexby sent over a large trunk of weapons from Flanders, including "strange engines"—rifles that fired twelve bullets and a slug.[119] In Westminster, the conspirators rented a room fronting Cromwell's projected route, and smuggled in a cache of weapons—Chicago-style, in a viol case. This attempt failed, for Cromwell was protected by a crowd and proceeded to Parliament, where he delivered a long speech that recalled the Overton Plot, named Spain the inveterate and natural enemy of England, and immodestly compared its design against him to that against Elizabeth, the conspiracy of Fifth Monarchists and Commonwealthsmen to that of Herod and Pilate. He also spoke of Sexby's trip to Antichristian Madrid, calling him "a fellow, a wretched creature, an apostate from religion and all honesty."[120]

The conspirators monitored Cromwell's comings and goings through John Toope, a member of his lifeguard.[121] Several opportunities arose to attack Cromwell while he was out riding, but they failed to press the attack. On January 8 1657, they planted an incendiary device that would have burned Whitehall down around Cromwell's ears if Toope had not betrayed the plan. The Protector's troops captured Cecil and Sindercombe—the latter only for want of a weapon, as he boasted to Cromwell when interrogated, and after his nose was almost severed.[122] On January 23, *A True Narrative of the Late Trayterous Plot* gave a brief account of Cromwell's escape. On February 2, Cromwell revealed his deliverance in a work entitled *A Declaration of His Highness*, calling for a day of public thanksgiving on the 20th.[123]

In February, Sexby wrote Talbot that Cecil had confessed, but that Sindercombe would "die ten thousand deaths before he will impeach any one, but he will take it all on himself."[124] In March, Giavarina reported that Sindercombe's captors tried and failed to scare him into naming his confederates.[125] Asked to name his accomplices, he replied that, "if he were minded to destroy innocent blood," he would name Fleetwood, Lambert, Barkstead, and Thomas Pride. On February 9, the Bar of the Upper Bench, with a jury consisting of "a very substantial company of men, most of them being justices of the peace," heard the testimony of

---

Cecil testified, so if he were "Boyes," the Protectorate would likely have identified him and punished him severely.

119. *CCSP* 202.

120. Abbott, *Writings* 4.260–79, 261–2, 267–9.

121. The lifeguard was dangerously disaffected. Sexby's associate Sturgeon was a lifeguard until 1655, and Baron William Howard until February 1656, when the whole troop seems to have been purged of Baptists (*GZ*; *CCSP* 415). In January 1657, a Mr Carpenter testified that five lifeguards told him that they, along with three-fourths of their fellows, were in on Sindercombe's plot (*B* 5.790).

122. Burton, *Diary* 1.333; see also Abbott, *Writings* 4.380–82. Thurloe made payments to Toope in 1657 and as late as 1659 (Philip Aubrey, *Thurloe* 113).

123. Burton, *Diary* 1.371–2.

124. *CCSP* 244.

125. *CSPV* 31.20.

Toope and Cecil. After turning up a statute from the reign of Edward III that covered plots against a Protector, they found Sindercombe guilty of high treason. They sentenced him to be drawn on a hurdle to Tyburn and hanged until half dead, then to have his entrails removed and burned before him, then to be quartered, with the pieces distributed at the Protector's pleasure.[126]

However, while in the Tower awaiting execution, Sindercombe confessed his guilt, proclaimed his mortalism and belief in universal redemption, and on Friday the 13th, took poison and died—or so Nedham reported.[127] On Saturday the 14th, the coroner's jury met and deferred their judgment until the sixteenth. The same day, two doctors found his brain engorged with blood in a fashion not consistent with apoplexy or other known diseases of the brain, "except when caused by contusion, and other the like extraordinary violences," and a Mr Laurence Loe, along with two wardens from the Company of Surgeons, found none of the usual signs of poisoning. On Sunday the 15th, his warders claimed to have discovered a suicide note proclaiming his desire to avoid a spectacular public death—a little out of character for this mortalist desperado, though it's easy enough to imagine wanting to avoid the smell of one's own cooking bowels. Two days later, the coroner's jury rendered a unanimous verdict of death by suicide, and Sindercombe was buried beneath a scaffold on Tower Hill, with an iron-clad stake through his heart, its butt-end visible above ground.[128]

The official account, *The Whole Business of Sindercome*, contained a narrative of the trial, the autopsy report, the burial, and corroborating testimony by wardens, physicians, coroners, and surgeons, and interviews with Sindercombe's mother Elizabeth, his sister Elizabeth Herring, and others. Like the official manuscript report on the suspicious death of King James in 1625, it tries to make public an irreducibly private and hidden act, but it leaves room for doubt by recording the qualms and delays described above and by failing to suggest who could have brought poison to Sindercombe. Many have been quick to name his sister, but even the official account stresses her horror at the idea of his suicide and his wardens' care in keeping her from giving him anything. Later, speaking to a group of her son's friends, Sindercombe's mother blamed Cromwell for his death and prophesied his imminent execution.[129] Lucy Hutchinson believed he had been poisoned by others, while Hyde said Cromwell feared a rescue attempt by his allies and accusations that he was afraid to bring him to public justice.[130] Giavarina was initially suspicious at the

---

126. *Whole Business* 19–20; *B* 6.53.
127. *Mercurius Politicus* 2/12–2/19/57. *Whole Business* 9; see also *B* 5.774–7; and Whitelocke, *Memorials* 645.
128. *Whole Business* 12–15.
129. *B* 6.531–2.
130. *Memoirs* 335; *History* 15.144.

delay of his official execution on the 12th.[131] Among modern historians, only Ruth Spalding has seriously questioned the suicide verdict of the coroner's jury.[132] But conflicting dates in *The Whole Business* raise further doubts: Thomason obtained this pamphlet on February 16 (the catalogue misreads this as "February 10"), the day of Sindercombe's burial, according to the title page, but the body of the pamphlet, like the later account in *Mercurius Politicus* (also published by Thomas Newcomb), dates the verdict and the burial on February 17.[133]

Cromwell intended Sindercombe's iconic burial as "an example of terror to all traitors for the time to come," but to no avail: "There was, in effect, scarcely a moment from this time to his death that he was not in danger of assassination, and that became a definite factor in the politics of the ensuing months."[134] Sexby did not slacken his efforts, and he continued to hold the qualified confidence of his royalist associates. On January 27, Titus wrote Hyde that Sexby was resolved to go to England with one Major Wood, a Presbyterian, to assassinate Cromwell himself, and that he planned to alienate Cromwell from Lambert by arranging for Thurloe's agents to intercept compromising letters from the king to Lambert.[135] In March, Titus wrote Hyde about allies in the Navy, including Lawson, who was "well beloved" and "totally governed by Sexby and Wildman."[136] Adding to the turmoil, Thomas Venner led his first abortive Fifth Monarchist rising in early April. In late April, before he returned to England for the last time, Sexby bragged to Talbot that "So long as Sexby lives there is no danger but Cromwell shall have his hands full, and I hope his heart ere long. . . . either I or Cromwell must perish."[137] In May, Sir Henry Bennet wrote the Earl of Bristol that Don Alonso de Cardeñas "expects to see Cromwell destroyed by Sexby and his party, and succeeded by them in the government rather than by the king."[138]

The conspirators hoped that Cromwell would solidify resistance to his

131. *CSPV* 31.18, 20.

132. *Contemporaries* 330.

133. On January 24, the Stationers registered a commemorative ballad, *Matchlesse treason plott discovered, &c.* (*A Transcript of the Registers of the Worshipful Company of the Stationers, from 1640–1708 A.D.*, 3 vols, London 1914, 2.108).

134. *Whole Business* 16; Abbott, *Writings* 4.292. On conspiracies against Cromwell, see *CSPV* 31.103 and *B* 6.441–2, 447. In February, Charles Perrot wrote of "gunpowder treasons, the like of which never heard of since King James . . . that at one blow would have sent the Protector to heaven in a fiery chariot. A strange motion for that grand a body." He added that five lifeguards had been imprisoned and that Lambert barely escaped execution as the plot's prime mover (*PRO* 18/153/97ʳ⁻ᵛ).

135. *CCSP* 237; on Wood, see *CSPD* 8.246. In June, Sir Allan Broderick reported that Lambert had been in touch with the king (*CCSP* 317), and certainly he had grown estranged from the intolerant and courtly aspects of the Protectorate, particularly after the *Humble Petition* (*CSPV* 31.22, 27, 28, 35, 96, 103).

136. *CCSP* 257.

137. Ibid. 278.

138. Ibid. 288.

continued rule by allowing himself to be declared king.[139] On May 18, Titus wrote Hyde that "The republical party pray for nothing so much as that Cromwell would take the title of a king, which they have no great reason to distrust."[140] But in a speech to the House ten days before, Cromwell had declined the crown. *The Humble Petition and Advice*, which may refer to Sindercombe in its denunciation of "turbulent and unquiet spirits in our own bowels," named him only "Lord Protector."[141] Later that month, Titus found Sexby morose at the news. On June 26, Titus wrote Hyde that Sexby and Major Wood were about to depart when news came that John Sturgeon had been apprehended with a bundle of pamphlets against Cromwell—*Killing Noe Murder*, as we will see—prompting them to delay their mission.[142] But Sexby soon left for England, taking time to write his wife an optimistic letter: "Sweet Love: I am blessed to be got safely at Dunkirk: by the next thou shall hear from me, of my success." She never read it, but John Thurloe did.[143]

Sardonic Ethics in *Killing Noe Murder*

J. G. A. Pocock's body of work gains much of its force—and much of its importance for literary historians—by turning from the history of political *thought* to the history of political *languages*. This linguistic turn need not be at odds with social history; indeed, Pocock has insisted that any charge that "we do not relate thought to social structure should be utterly untenable."[144] But more recently, Pocock has said that the "historian of discourse" should pay no attention to the practical, extra-discursive results of political writing:

> This is to say, of course, that we are historians of discourse, not of behavior, but it is also to read Machiavelli and Hobbes as they were read by everyone whose response to them we possess in written form; these responses are, without exception, concerned not with their practical political consequences, but with the challenges they present to the normal structures of discourse. . . . Language is self-reflective and talks largely about itself; the response to new experience takes the form of discovering and discussing new difficulties in language.

For Pocock, this discourse/praxis divide is also a class divide, and the proper historian of discourse turns to readers whose "responses were verbalized, recorded, and represented," not to the "*mentalité* of the silent and inarticulate majority." Moreover, the historian of discourse "is characteristically interested in the performances of agents other than himself and does not desire to be the author of his own past so much as to

139. On the controversies surrounding Cromwell's title, see Firth, *Last* 1.128–200.
140. *CCSP* 292.
141. Abbott, *Writings* 4.512–14; Gardiner, *Constitutional* 448.
142. *CCSP* 294, 310.
143. *TM* A50, 273; I think Sexby wrote this letter—so does the indexer of the Rawlinson Manuscripts—but I can't be sure.
144. *Politics* 36.

uncover the doings of other authors in and of it. This is probably a reason why his politics are inherently liberal rather than aimed at *praxis*." Such historians have abandoned "a modernist history of consciousness organized around such poles as repression and liberation, solitude and community, false consciousness and species being." They attend with philological rigor to the recorded utterances of a literate elite, while marxist historians of society or praxis or *mentalités* attend loosely and tendentiously to the consciousness of inarticulate or silent plebeians.[145]

Pocock thus eliminates in a flash the methods of sociologists and social historians, who are neither struck dumb nor reduced to wanton speculation when writing about plebeians who are illiterate, unrecorded, or silent (not quite the same thing as "inarticulate," incidentally). Like the postmodernists whom he has begun to invoke, Pocock reduces practice to discourse, discourse to elite discourse, and plebeian oppositional writing and speaking to silence.[146] But what happens when Pocock's republicanism becomes elite *discourse* only, disconnected from material interests? Pocock's majestic republican narrative in *The Machiavellian Moment* stretches from Aristotle to Davy Crockett, but its synchronic social resonances are a little thin: "The upshot of the monumental chain of ideas . . . appears moderate to minimal. It is as if discourse, once emancipated from undue social reference, is also delivered of explanatory power."[147] Indeed, Pocock's own examples desert him here by venturing out beyond the hermetic confines of a discursive universe: Machiavelli read Livy to create a Florentine republic, while Hobbes read republican theorists to protect his new-modeled absolutism against them, and James Harrington, to whom Pocock has devoted so much work, read Livy, Machiavelli, and Hobbes in hopes of fabricating an immortal British commonwealth. Since *Politics, Language and Time* (1971), Pocock's methodological work has stagnated. One can only wonder what might have been the result had he seriously engaged the important marxist work (by Bakhtin, Vološinov, Sartre, Williams, Habermas, and many others) that begins precisely with a critique of the language/society split that he takes for marxist gospel.[148] Thus, while his work has sparked among post-revisionist historians and literary critics a salutary resurgence of interest in the republic, this work risks coming to a dead end so far as it shares in his resistance to history from below, and his effort to separate discourse from interest and from non-discursive practice.[149] Academic anticommunism stunts intellectual

---

145. *Virtue* 14, 29, 18, 9, 34.
146. In *Virtue, Commerce, and History*, Pocock invokes *langue* and *parole*, game theory, and the postmodernist criticism of Jonathan Goldberg, Stanley Fish, and Dominick La Capra (1, 14, 19n.20, 20n.21, 27n.30).
147. Anderson, *English* 293n.
148. "Texts as Events," Sharpe and Zwicker, *Politics* 21–34, 25–6.
149. For some of this work on republicanism, see Norbrook, *Writing*; David Wootton, ed., *Republicanism, Liberty, and Commercial Society, 1649–1776*, Stanford 1994; Armitage et al., *Milton*; and Gisela Bock, Quentin Skinner, and Maurizio Viroli, eds, *Machiavelli and Republicanism*, Cambridge 1990. Blair Worden's much-invoked essays on early modern

inquiry not only by repressing marxist scholars in more and less subtle ways, but also by encouraging anticommunist scholars to dismiss relevant marxist work with a quick, blocking sneer, untainted by knowledge of the field.

The republican theory of divided sovereignty becomes most menacing and pregnant with dangerous praxis when it raises the question of tyranny—those moments when the "one" threatens to extinguish the powers of the "few" and the "many," or when the sovereign representative begins to override the *salus populi*. Pocock has shown that, after Cromwell purged the republican Rump in April and the godly Barebone's Parliament in December 1653, the political languages of republic and millennium came together in an oppositional dialogue. This dialogue culminated in 1656 with three important works: Henry Vane's *A Healing Question* (May), Marchamont Nedham's *The Excellencie of a Free State* (June), and James Harrington's *Oceana* (September–November). All three responded to "a crisis in the relations between Army and nation, Protectorate and Army, which was apparent enough to idealists of the good old cause in the summer when Cromwell was abandoning the major-generals, summoning a Parliament, and moving towards the conservative experiment of the *Humble Petition and Advice*."[150] Vane's *A Healing Question* insists that a good old cause of saints and soldiers has claims by right of nature and conquest against any part of the body politic claiming sovereignty over them; he compares any such usurper to Achan.[151] In early July, Vane's pamphlet became the center of a discussion group aimed at bringing together Commonwealthsmen and Fifth Monarchists in opposition to the Protectorate.[152] When Vane suggested that he intended to stand for Parliament, Cromwell, ever a reader concerned with practice and behavior, summoned him before the Council to make him submit to the Instrument of Government. When Vane refused to appear, Cromwell imprisoned him in Carisbrooke Castle.[153]

Pocock argues that Nedham's decision to republish his 1651–52 *Mercurius Politicus* editorials in 1656 as *The Excellencie of a Free State* was a subtle act of political critique, for in their new context, they turn from the tyrannous potential of the Rump to the tyrannous practice of the Lord Protector.[154] Nedham's earlier railing attack against the Levellers as zealous anarchists and communists in *The Case of the Commonwealth Stated* becomes an attack on monarchy as the true leveler of private property

republicanism (for instance, his essays on Harrington and Nedham in Wootton, *Republicanism* 45–110) overlap too much with Pocock's work and with each other.

150. "Historical Introduction" to Harrington, *The Political Works* 1–152, 38.

151. 14–15.

152. *B* 5.185; Firth, *Last* 2.209. See Barbara Taft, "That Lusty Puss, the Good Old Cause," *History of Political Thought* 5.3, 1984; and Blair Worden, "Oliver Cromwell and the Sin of Achan," in Derek Beales and Geoffrey Best, eds, *History, Society and the Churches*, Cambridge 1985, 125–45.

153. *GHCP* 4.266–7.

154. "Historical Introduction" 13.

and the virtue proper to a republic. Following Machiavelli, he insists that the people form an independent, armed militia, guarding their liberty by maintaining their grasp on the sword. He concludes by discussing the tradition of capital punishment for those "grandees" (his recurrent, indiscreet word) who betray "the interest and majesty of the people."[155] And Harrington's fictional utopia concludes with a "Corollary" in which Olphaus Megaletor tyrannically transforms Oceana into a classical republic, then tyrannicidally deposes himself—a heroic action, with its ultimate precedent in Plutarch's Lycurgus, but an awkward suggestion for a work dedicated to Cromwell. While the client prophesies his patron's dynastic immortality, the republican theorist warns the Lycurgan legislator to cut himself off from a self-perpetuating dynasty.[156]

These questions bear directly on Edward Sexby and his place in English republicanism. But so far, the Pocock-inspired rebirth of interest in English republicanism has not yet shown much interest in Sexby— certainly nothing like that devoted to Milton, Vane, Nedham, Harrington, and Sidney, perhaps because Sexby emphasizes republicanism's Reformation dimensions as popular praxis over its Renaissance dimensions as elite discourse.[157] More than any antityrannical predecessor or contemporary, Sexby made plain his desire to translate his reading into practice, and he can enrich our appreciation for the practical impulses in those antityrannical works Pocock sees as discursive structures only. In *Killing Noe Murder,* Sexby answers Vane's healing question by asserting that Cromwell *is* Achan, and that he should be dealt with accordingly. He revises Nedham's *Excellencie* by encouraging England's army to remember its former virtue and turn its sword against Cromwell, who has betrayed its expense of blood and the interest and majesty of the people. And he revises the "Corollary" of *Oceana* by separating Harrington's unlikely Lycurgan Olphaus into his constituent parts. Some Junius Brutus must slay the Tarquin of Whitehall; the legislating founder of Sexby's republic—perhaps Sexby himself—will be neither an abdicating tyrant like Olphaus, nor a republican theorist like Harrington, but a tyrannicide.

Sexby finished his pamphlet between mid-April and mid-May.[158] He had it printed—in the Low Countries, Firth suggests—in small type on thin

155. *The Case of the Commonwealth of England, Stated,* Charlottesville, VA, 1969, 96–110; *Excellencie,* 83–93, 199.
156. Harrington, *Works* 341–59. Sexby calls Lycurgus one of those good princes who "abridge their own powers, it may be distrusting themselves, they would not hazard the welfare of their people" (*S* 13). On the conclusion of *Oceana* and the self-consuming sovereignty of the utopian *rex absconditus,* see my *Rational Millennium* 91–101, 220–32.
157. For related critiques, see Mark Gould, *Revolution in the Development of Capitalism,* Berkeley and Los Angeles 1987, 404n.17; Daly, "Saith the Spirit" 68n.3; and Neal Wood, *The Foundations of Political Economy,* Berkeley and Los Angeles 1994, 254n.1. Gramsci contrasts the circumscribed vision of Renaissance and Crocean idealism with the expansive and revolutionary vision of the Reformation and marxism (*Selections* 132n.).
158. He refers to Cromwell's *A Proclamation Prohibiting Horse-Races* of April 8 (*S* 5), and assumes throughout that Cromwell would accept the crown that he declined on May 9.

paper for ease in mass distribution.[159] It arrived in London by May 18, when "divers abominable desperate pamphlets" which were "written to infect men's minds with that inhumane and damnable doctrine of privy murder and assassination" were dispersed "by some Jesuited villain." State agents in St Catherine's Dock seized 1700 copies and arrested John Sturgeon carrying a bale of 1500. They imprisoned him in the Tower, and announced his suspected ties to Sindercombe.[160] The circumstances of the pamphlet's arrival suggest a republican–Fifth Monarchist alliance—a practical correlate to the intersection of millennialist and republican discourses that Pocock examines. Sturgeon was a General Baptist, a Fifth Monarchist, and one of Cromwell's lifeguard, until he was dismissed in August 1655 on suspicion of having written *A Short Discovery of His Highness the Lord Protector's Intentions Touching the Anabaptists in the Army*. In May 1656, William Goffe accused him of dangerous preaching in Reading, and Thurloe later said he was involved in the Sindercombe plot and fled into Holland when it failed.[161] Sturgeon signed the Levellers' appeal to Charles II.[162] It seems likely that he traveled to Holland, picked up several bales of pamphlets, and returned with them to England. When arrested, Sturgeon was with Edward Wroughton, a London haberdasher and member of Venner's congregation.[163] Cromwell himself examined Sturgeon, but he refused to answer any question asked of him, "though it be whether two and two make four." He remained committed to the Tower until the Restoration.[164]

Thurloe tried to suppress the pamphlet, but that seems only to have increased its notoriety, and people paid up to five shillings for the copies that got loose.[165] In June, his assistant Samuel Morland wrote John Pell that

> there has been the most dangerous pamphlet lately thrown about the streets that ever has been printed in these times. I have sent you the preface, which is more light, but, believe me, the body of it is more solid; I mean as to showing the author's learning, though the greatest rancor, malice, and wickedness that

159. *Last*, 1.229n.3.
160. *The Public Intelligencer* 5/18–5/25/57, 5/25–6/1/57.
161. *B* 3.738–40, 4.752, 6.311.
162. Hyde, *History* 15.119; *CCSP* 145.
163. Thurloe and Barkstead examined Wroughton in August 1656 regarding his distribution at a Venner prayer meeting of *Englands Remembrancers* (*B* 5.272–3; Jeaffreson, *Middlesex* 3.253; *CP* 3.68; *GHCP* 4.261–2). This pamphlet called Cromwell an Absalom and a Mordecai, attacked the Western Design, and urged voters to support godly members in the crucial parliamentary elections of the summer and frustrate the "fruitless designs of one man" (4, 8).
164. *B* 6.315–20; *GZ*; *The Public Intelligencer* 5/25–6/1/57. Sturgeon's name, ideology, and temperament connect him with the Fifth Monarchist Rebecca Sturgeon or Spurgeon: after the Overton Plot, she told Thurloe's agents "that she must be one of them, that must pluck down Cromwell; and she would tell him so to his face" (*B* 3.160). In 1674, a John Sturgeon was arrested for attending conventicles (Jeaffreson, *Middlesex* 3.324, 334).
165. *B* 6.291.

ever man could show—nay, I think the devil himself could not have shown more.[166]

Thurloe sent Henry Cromwell a copy in Ireland.[167] Giavarina wrote the Doge of the pamphlet's circulation in London and Cromwell's nervous attempts to destroy all copies.[168] Michael Hawke said it was "covertly dispersed among discontented and seditious persons, which they embrace as their Apostles' Creed, and communicate and extol it to others, as an indubitable, and sacred truth, whereby many well disposed people may be debauched, corrupted, and withdrawn from their due obedience to their prince."[169] Someone threw a copy into Cromwell's coach.[170] Hyde remarked, "The whole piece is so full of wit that I cannot imagine who could write it," and the king's party found it vastly amusing, despite its republican principles.[171]

The question of authorship is vexed, but interesting for the light it casts on historians' reluctance to acknowledge the possibility of systematic plebeian learning. In what seems to have been a rough practical joke, the title page credits one William Allen, a Baptist and Army radical, who as an Agitator had appeared with Sexby before the House. When Cromwell called Allen in, he "desired to see the book, which Oliver lent him to read; and then Allen told him, that he knew well enough that he had not the capacity enough to be the author; but that if he had been able to have writ it, he would with all his heart have done it."[172] According to later reports of his captors, Sexby admitted or claimed authorship. So did Silius Titus, his Presbyterian liaison with the royalists in exile, but not until 1669. At first, Firth assigned primary authorship to Sexby. Later, in "*Killing Noe Murder*," he assigned him the general conception and the fervent epistle to the Army, and Titus the witty dedication to Cromwell and the erudite body of the pamphlet, on the grounds that "Sexby was not a learned man, but when the question what constitutes a tyrant comes to be discussed the pages are full of quotations from Aristotle, Plato, Cicero, Machiavelli, Grotius, and other writers on politics." This argument recalls the sublime upper-class twittery of Edward Hyde, who said that, for "an illiterate person," Sexby "spake very well and properly, and used those words very well the true meaning and signification whereof he could not understand."[173] But Sexby was an uncommon commoner—the intimate of nobles and monarchs of several nations—so some humanist learning would not seem to be out of the question. Moreover, if Anthony Wood rightly attributes to Titus the wooden, aristocratic, and bloodline-obsessed

166. C. H. Firth, "*Killing No Murder*," *The English Historical Review* 17, 1902, 308.
167. *B* 6.311.
168. *CSPV* 31.60.
169. *Killing Is Murder, and No Murder*, 1658, Preface.
170. Abbott, *Writings* 4.522.
171. *CCSP* 297.
172. Hardacre, "William Allen" 303; see also *B* 5.670.
173. Firth, *DNB*; "*Killing*" 310. Hyde, *History* 15.133.

A Brief Character of the Protector Oliver Cromwell, he was neither a fluent stylist nor a radical republican.[174]

Who stood to gain? When the pamphlet had already created a sensation among exiled royalists and Titus had nothing to risk by claiming authorship, he continued referring to it as the work of another person.[175] In late 1657, when Sexby was in Cromwell's custody and could have eased his captivity or ended his torture by naming a few hateful cavalier names, he persisted in claiming full authorship. In 1665, when Titus finally claimed authorship, he had no living rivals to contradict him and something quite specific to gain: an addition to his coat-of-arms earned "by his pen and practices against the then usurper, Oliver," when "he vigorously endeavored the destruction of that tyrant and his government."[176] Lutaud suggests that Peter Talbot and John Wildman aided Sexby and Titus in the pamphlet's composition.[177] Barber suggests Henry Marten had a hand in it.[178] We might also nominate Sturgeon, Streater (see below on the second edition), and Richard Overton.[179] Finally, I am inclined to assign full credit to Sexby, but we need not rule out collective authorship: tyrannicidal discourse slips and slides around, and in 1657, the Presbyterian Titus might well have co-authored the pamphlet with Sexby, that inveterate hammer of parliamentary Presbyterians ten years earlier. Further, Sexby and Titus were together in Breda from March 15 until at least April 10 1657.[180] Lutaud observes, "The reader will form his own opinion. But there's no doubt that we find ourselves here before a work in which the faith of d'A. d'Aubigné combines with that of Suárez, where Puritans and Jesuits become temporary allies. And the continuing odyssey of the pamphlet confirms this original heterogeneity."[181] In any case, we should avoid jumping from the work's stylistic diversity to a hypothesis of joint authorship, as if a single (plebeian) consciousness could not move from an ironic courtly dedication, through a learned humanist republican argument, to a thundering jeremiad.

Killing Noe Murder, "the most brilliant republican polemic of the 1650s," ranks with Milton's great antityrannical pamphlets, and it deserves to be better known.[182] It begins with two epigraphs from 2 Chronicles describing the serial tyrannicide of Athaliah and Amaziah.[183] Just as Amaziah

---

174. *DNB*. William Godwin credits Sexby, on the grounds that the author must have been a Leveller, and provides the first full account of Sexby's post-Putney career, in *History of the Commonwealth of England*, 4 vols, London 1828, 4.278–83, 331–3, 388–90.
175. *CCSP* 397–8.
176. *DNB*.
177. *Des Révolutions* 56, 70–74.
178. *Regicide* 213.
179. Overton had invoked Othniel and Ehud in tones of exhortation much like those that conclude *Killing Noe Murder* (*LM* 172–3).
180. *CCSP* 269.
181. *Des Révolutions* 74.
182. Norbrook, *Writing* 324.
183. Both Buchanan and Knox turned to Athaliah when they wrote against Mary Queen of Scots; so did Languet and Mornay in *Vindiciae, Contra Tyrannos*, when they wrote against

succeeded one slain tyrant, and was himself slain after he turned away
from the Lord, so Oliver Cromwell succeeded the tyrant Charles, and
must now be slain because he has degenerated; and so Edward Sexby may
adapt to Cromwell's case arguments originally directed against Charles.
Sexby's first introductory epistle, "To His Highness, Oliver Cromwell," is
by far the best-known part of the pamphlet, no doubt because of its finely
controlled irony, and because it was short enough to have been circulated
as a manuscript separate, even by those, like Samuel Morland, who copied
it out for friends while claiming to be appalled by it.[184] Like most parody,
it has a double audience: it addresses Cromwell directly, speaking in the
voice of an obsequious client, and England indirectly, exhorting all
readers to create a republic by assassinating him at the first opportunity.
Sexby, formerly a Commonwealth functionary and now a fugitive, begins
by gratefully acknowledging a previous "gift" from Cromwell (his years of
employment? his Continental exile? both?): "How I have spent some
hours of the leisure your Highness hath been pleased to give me, this
following paper will give your Highness an accompt."

He yearns "to procure your Highness that justice nobody yet does you,
and to let the people see, the longer they defer it, the greater injury they
do both themselves and you: to your Highness justly belongs the honor of
dying for the people." Sexby sardonically parodies the symbolic economy
of patronage: like all clients, he tries to dissimulate his actual relation to
his patron, but to ironic effect, for that relation is homicidal, not economic.[185] In the filial world of patronage, clients piously attempt to graft
themselves onto powerful political patrons and matrons. Sexby turns it
into the comedic world of generational conflict: "All this we hope from
your Highness' happy expiration, who are the true Father of your Country:
for while you live, we can call nothing ours, and it is from your death that
we hope for our inheritances." The act of killing remains comically
obscene: offstage, unspeakable, but powerfully present. The Lord Protector does not exactly die, but restores "justice" to his people, becomes the
"true reformer," "true father of your country," who will free his country
"from a bondage little inferior to that from which Moses delivered his."
Thus Sexby steps outside the language of clientage, for this pamphlet is
not a *plea* for recognition, but a self-contained *message* whose force, unlike
the client's plea, does not depend on the patron's recognition. While the
client and the patron aim at mutual advancement within a fixed and

---

Catherine de Medici. See Lutaud on Racine's *Athalie* (*Des Révolutions* 151–97). Christopher Feake compared Cromwell to Athaliah in *The Oppressed Close Prisoner in Windsor
Castle*, 1655, 118.

184. *S* 1. Firth, "*Killing*" 308.

185. "Sardonic" derives from "sardonian," meaning "bitter or scornful laughter," with
"reference to the effects of eating a 'Sardinian plant' . . . which was said to produce
facial convulsions resembling horrible laughter, usually followed by death." A "sardonian" is also "one who flatters with deadly intent" (*OED*). No doubt, the pleasure so
many took in the pamphlet derived from its assault on patronage rhetoric as well as
Cromwell.

hierarchical social order, the tyrannicide wagers his life against the tyrant's in hopes of transforming that order, either by killing the tyrant, or by losing his life gloriously and providing a heroic example to others.

In the second epistle, to the "Officers and Soldiers of the Army," Sexby takes an altogether different tone—not obsequious malice in a parody, but prophetic solidarity in a lay sermon calling for civic virtue.[186] He recollects the Army's founding covenant with English liberty, laments its present-day lapses, and exhorts it to kill Cromwell and leave behind a heroic memory: "This if you defer too long to do, you will find too late to attempt, and your repentance will neither vindicate you, nor help us." He speaks as a peripheral prophet—as "one that was once one amongst you, and will be so again when you dare be as you were," reassuring himself that he will either excite them to acts of courage, or "exprobrate your cowardice and baseness"; the aggressive tone resembles that of Felton's suicide note. The rest of *Killing Noe Murder* alternates between the ideology critique of the first epistle, with its savage iconoclasm directed against the mystifying fictions of *de facto* monarchical rule, and the utopian association of the second, with its passionate effort to recall, construct, and prophesy the righteous collectives of the godly republic.

This latter, associative impulse is immanent and textual as well as extrinsic and political. In the course of a sixteen-page pamphlet, Sexby invokes Plato, Aristotle, Plutarch, Tacitus, Augustine, Machiavelli, Appian, Seneca, Cicero, Suetonius, Ames, Hooker, Bacon, Grotius, and Milton, in addition to extensive scriptural sources.[187] Sexby engages in the philological conversation defining Renaissance humanism. In a letter to Francesco Vettori, Machiavelli describes donning his special robes to commence his scholarly conversation with the ancients.[188] But for both Sexby and Machiavelli, this leisurely humanist conversation, which associates scholars in a historical genealogy, moves out of the study into the forum: "The conversation with the ancients which results in knowledge is affiliated with the conversation among citizens which results in decision and law." The republican genealogy of writer to writer is a *made* thing, quite conscious of its associative quality, and, in this, like the republican association of citizen with citizen, republic with republic. Unlike the traditional vision of monarchy as a timeless and hierarchical reflection of the heavenly order, the republic is a civic entity existing in time:

---

186. *S* 2.
187. Hughes's review of Milton's antityrannical sources also bears on Sexby's (*M* 3.110–25). For reviews of resistance and tyrannicidal theory, see Bushnell, *Tragedies*; Oscar Jászi and John D. Lewis, *Against the Tyrant*, Glencoe, IL, 1957; Donald Kelley, "Ideas of Resistance before Elizabeth," in Heather Dubrow and Richard Strier, eds, *The Historical Renaissance*, Chicago, IL, 1988, 48–78; vol. 2 of Quentin Skinner's *The Foundations of Modern Political Thought*, Cambridge 1978, 189–359; and Robert Zaller, "The Figure of the Tyrant in English Revolutionary Thought," *Journal of the History of Ideas* 54, 1993.
188. *The Letters of Machiavelli*, New York 1961, 142.

The republic of Florence, stated as a high ideal but existing in the present and in its own past, was affiliated only with other republics and with those moments in the past time at which republics had existed. The republic was not timeless, because it did not reflect by simple correspondence the eternal order of nature; it was differently organized, and a mind which accepted the republic and citizenship as prime realities might be committed to implicitly separating the political from the natural order.[189]

Republican citizens associate themselves through rational and voluntary discursive forms, not through the client's mystifying assertion of a filial relation to his patron. If any force of nature binds them together, it is the associative human nature of the *salus populi*, not the hierarchical transmission of dynastic authority.

This humanist concept of human nature derives from the philological comparison of different nations. In the "Prolegomena" to *The Law of War and Peace*, Grotius announces that he will avail himself "of the testimony of philosophers, historians, poets, finally also of orators," and those of many nations, for "when many at different times, and in different places, affirm the same thing as certain, that ought to be referred to a universal cause."[190] The contrast with Hobbes couldn't be stronger. Hobbes reduces communicative rationality and intersubjectivity to a sort of biomechanical reflex: he avoids "the ornament of quoting ancient poets, orators, and philosophers," for opinions taken from antiquity "are not intrinsically the judgment of those that cite them, but words that pass (like gaping) from mouth to mouth." The exemplary history produced by humanist republican scholarship could have a disastrous outcome. The proper political philosopher, Hobbes says, speaks not from "examples, or authority of books," but on the basis of a long involvement with the affairs of government. The English Revolution itself was the product of an ill-advised attempt to imitate the republics of the Low Countries, and the ungoverned reading of Greek and Roman history:

> From the reading, I say, of such books, men have undertaken to kill their kings, because Greek and Latin writers, in their books, and discourses of policy, make it lawful, and laudable, for any man so to do; provided, before he do it, he call him tyrant. For they say not *regicide*, that is, killing of a king, but *tyrannicide*, that is, killing of a tyrant is lawful.

This imitation infected them with a kind of "*tyrannophobia*, or fear of being strongly governed," and just as hydrophobic dogs fear the water that would relieve them, so these tyrannophobes fear the monarchical government that would cure them of their inward turmoil.[191]

Hobbes could have found no madder dog in Protectorate England than Sexby, and no tract further in genre and form from *Leviathan* than *Killing*

---

189. Pocock, *Machiavellian* 62, 53.
190. Indianapolis 1925, 23; see also Ernst Bloch, *Natural Law and Human Dignity,* Cambridge, MA, 1987, 48–9.
191. *Leviathan*, Oxford 1960, 490, 180, 233–4, 226.

Noe Murder. Whereas the abstractive marginal heads of the former lead Hobbes's readers inward to the closure of his philosophical text and its advice to sovereigns, Sexby's marginal invocations of republican textual authorities lead his readers outward to a destabilizing civil conversation and to tyrannicide. In 1647, Sexby deflected attacks by the House and then by Cromwell and Ireton on his individual willfulness by saying he was no more than the representative of a regiment. Here, he says that, if he errs, he was "drawn into that error, by the examples that are left us by the greatest and most virtuous, and the opinions of the wisest and gravest men, that have left their memories to posterity."[192] He resembles Milton's Samson, who prompts the feckless Danite chorus to remember the heroic Israelite exempla of Gideon and Jephtha, then adds, "Of such examples add me to the roll."[193] Anticipating prosecution for his extra-legal action, Sexby assembles an array of precedents, creating *Killing Noe Murder* as a sort of prevenient court brief.

From Aristotle to the Renaissance, antityrannical writing turns so frequently to certain topoi that they serve not only to clarify and develop arguments, but also to beat out a sort of rhythmic solidarity. We might chart these out as a series of casuistical binaries:

1. St Paul says in Romans 13.1, "Let every soul be subject unto the higher powers. For there is no power but of God: the powers that be are ordained of God." So, other things being equal, obedience is more just than resistance.
2. Lesser magistrates resist tyrants more justly than do private persons.
3. Private persons inspired by God resist tyrants more justly than do private persons acting on their own authority.
4. One may resist a tyrant without title (*sine titulo*) more justly than a tyrant by practice (*exercitio*).
5. One may slay new tyrants more justly than tyrants who have ruled for some time.
6. One may slay tyrants who break God's law more justly than tyrants who break only man's law.

So if obedience becomes impossible, it's better for a divinely inspired lesser magistrate to slay an impious and newly established tyrant without title than for an uninspired private person to slay an established tyrant by practice who breaks only men's laws.

Or so it would seem. In practice, the exceptions overwhelm the rule. Romans 13.1, that favorite of sitting rulers and their house philosophers, may be the most aggressively interpreted political text in the Western canon.[194] For Languet and Mornay, the "higher powers" include God

192. *S* 8.
193. *Samson Agonistes*, line 290.
194. *M* 3.58–64.

himself, and "every soul" includes kings, so obedience to the higher powers might require resistance to a disobedient king.[195] Ever the humanist philologist, Buchanan argued that Paul's epistles, interpreted in their particular historical context, show him to be prohibiting not all resistance to wicked magistrates, but just the antinomian claim to complete freedom from all secular magistrates, even good ones. Moreover, rulers must submit to "the higher powers" of lesser magistrates, as well as the other way around. Submission to a ruler's powers might entail resistance to that ruler's person.[196] Christopher Goodman agrees that Paul is to be understood only as resisting absolute antinomianism among new Christians, which would make them "Anabaptists and Libertines"; but obedience to God must take precedence over obedience to rulers and magistrates, or one would have to obey the Prince of Hell.[197] Francisco Suárez concedes Paul's phrase but, glancing at James I of England, adds that "nowhere did he add: Let all be subject even to powers that have been excommunicated or deprived by the Pope."[198] In 1647, a resistant New Model, including Fairfax and Cromwell, reminded Parliament that it had pronounced it "no resisting of Magistracy, to side with the just principles and law of nature and Nations."[199] In 1654, a group of Baptist ministers recalled this declaration and turned it against the new Lord Protector.[200] In *The Tenure of Kings and Magistrates*, Milton called superior powers only those that are good, and he devoted much of the third chapter of *A Defence* to the same argument.[201]

Resistance theorists practice strong interpretation so as to collapse or invert the binaries. Buchanan prefers tyrants without title if they govern justly.[202] Ponet forthrightly defends the rights of private persons to slay tyrants.[203] Languet and Mornay admit that tyrants by practice frequently degenerate further and further, while tyrants without title frequently become worthy rulers, and one who "performs his function badly seems more worthy of the name tyrant than he who has not received his function in the proper fashion. . . . I obviously prefer for a thief to succor me, than for a pastor to devour me." If the lesser magistrates grow corrupt, they become as bad as tyrants themselves, for their sluggishness allows tyrants

---

195. *Vindiciae* 32.
196. *Powers* 113–14, 119.
197. *How Superior Powers Oght to be Obeyd*, Geneva 1568, 108, 116–17, 110.
198. *Selections from Three Works*, 2 vols, Oxford and London 1944, 2.723.
199. *D* 40. Compare the Army's arguments in *A Cleere and Full Vindication*, 1647, 6–7; those in the Leveller newspaper *The Moderate*, for 10/10–10/17/48; and Thomas Collier's *A Discovery* 33–4.
200. *A Declaration of Several of the Churches of Christ* 11.
201. *M* 3.196, 209–10; 4.373–9.
202. *Powers* 146–7.
203. [John Ponet], *A Shorte Treatise of Politike Power*, [Strasburg] 1556, H5ᵛ–H6ʳ. Ellen Meiksins Wood and Neal Wood suggest that England's rapid transformation into a capitalist state, without the constitutionally sanctioned corporate sovereignties surviving inside feudal and absolutist France, made it hard for Ponet to find any sanctioned lesser magistrates (*Trumpet* 53).

to gain some color of legitimacy. Because the Hebrew magistrates did not resist the titled but tyrannical kings of Canaan, God stirred up special private persons like Ehud, Deborah, and Jehu.[204] These days, God tends not to work so much by miracles, so we should be cautious in claiming divine inspiration, lest we fall into Anabaptist outrages. But just as God sends modern-day Pharaohs and Ahabs to scourge us, so he may sometimes raise up "extraordinary liberators" to rescue us, designating them by miraculous signs, or by interior effects—"a mind empty of all ambition, authentic and earnest zeal, and finally conscience and knowledge, so as to prevent him being led on by error to foreign gods, or becoming overexcited by the frenzy of ambition to serve himself rather than the true God."[205] Despite the moderate and measured tone, this effort to ground the uninspired private person's tyrannicidal project in his practice of Protestant discipline and meditation would provide small comfort to the Catholic or Lutheran powers that be. As we saw in chapter 5, John Felton put himself through a similar spiritual exercise in August 1628, before setting out to kill the Duke of Buckingham.

An early regicidal pamphlet of 1642 reveals an even subtler shift. The author first observes that David, being a "private man," lawfully defended himself against the tyrant Saul, who sought his life; but the author demurs, and then demurs again:

> Again, 'tis a different case for a private man to lay violent hands upon the person of a tyrannical king, to take away his life, (which I utterly disallow) and for a whole state to stand up to defend themselves against tyrannical usurpation. David would not, nor durst do the former: but he and his men did the latter, so far as it concerned them and theirs, for their safety.

An ethical opposition (private man, public authority) begins to look prudential: David's six hundred armed accomplices both stand for the whole state, and assure his success. At first, the focus on "usurpation" would seem to spare Charles, but the author proceeds to suggest that Charles has unkinged himself by setting up a standard and marching on his loyal subjects.[206]

Resistance theorists may negate a "horizontal" imperative within one binary by subordinating it to a "vertical" hierarchy between two binaries. "Breaking God's law"—a flexible category, to say the least—frequently becomes the trump card. In his influential discussion of resistance, Calvin begins by affirming Romans 13, saying that men must obey all monarchs, even unworthy ones, or risk sanctioning the rebellion of wives and children against an unworthy patriarch. But obedience to God sometimes requires disobedience to kings and magistrates, and God will sometimes appoint an Othniel if lesser magistrates shirk their duties. When earthly princes rebel against God, "We ought, rather, utterly to defy

---

204. *Vindiciae* 140–41, 61–2, 160–61.
205. Ibid. 61–3.
206. *King James His Judgement* A3ʳ, A4ᵛ.

them [*conspuere in ipsorum capita*, "to spit on their heads"] than to obey them."[207] Writing from the opposite side of the Continental wars of religion, Suárez constructs a similarly flexible argument: of course, one ought never to resist legitimate kings, only usurpers, except when one acts in self-defense, "For the right to preserve one's own life is the greatest right," and *a fortiori* a state may resist a legitimate king who attempts to slaughter its citizens, or one like the heretical King James of England, who has been deposed by the people or the Pope.[208] Tyrannicidal writing sets up analytical distinctions as a bulwark against disorder, then dissolves them in the contingencies of particular cases—perhaps with Cicero's *salus populi* as a natural-law limit. Quentin Skinner sees "the essence" of Huguenot resistance theory in the action of lesser magistrates alone.[209] But resistance theory has only a mixed, republican essence, in which the power of one argument tends to be limited and checked by the power of another, or a casuist essence that opens itself up into particular cases and into practice.

Sexby's arguments are extraordinary not only for sanctioning the more radical side of these binaries, but for straightforwardly aiming at a particular named tyrant.[210] Sexby begins with a conventional modesty topos, protesting that he published not out of ambition, but because he had been goaded into writing by *A Declaration of His Highness the Lord Protector*, which called on the public to give thanks for Cromwell's deliverance from Sindercombe: if Pharaoh had asked the Hebrews to pray for his long life and for "daily increase of the number of their bricks," it could have been no more galling.[211] Sexby turns with contempt to "a late pamphlet" that "tells us of a great design discovered against the person of his Highness"—presumably either *A True Narrative of the Late Trayterous Plot* or *The Whole Business*. Sindercombe's death not only forced him into writing and direct action, but traumatized him, leading him to write *Killing Noe Murder* as a fierce elegy for his fallen comrade, whom he commemorates with passionate classical republicanism: "The brave Sindercombe hath shewed as great a mind, as any old Rome could boast of, and had he lived there, his name had been registered with Brutus, and Cato; and he had had his statues as well as they." He proposes an ironic monument on Tower Hill that would replace the stake through Sindercombe's heart with the pillow and mattress used to smother him, and he threatens Cecil and Toope for their "treachery and perjury."[212]

The first section in the body of the pamphlet addresses the question, "Whether my Lord Protector be a tyrant or not?" Invoking the classic distinction between the tyrant without title and the tyrant by practice,

207. *Institutes of the Christian Religion*, 2 vols, Philadelphia 1960, 2.1519n.
208. *Selections* 2.706–9, 709, 709–10, 705–25.
209. *Foundations* 2.336–7, 338–9.
210. Compare Buchanan, who delivers one of the most unqualified defenses of the right of private persons to slay all tyrants, yet says repeatedly that he describes only what may lawfully be done, not what should or must be (*Powers* 134).
211. *S* 3.
212. Ibid. 3, 15, 16.

Sexby concludes that Cromwell is both. First, he shows that Cromwell has no title—neither by compact, nor by divine appointment, nor by natural right. He distinguishes the consensual or elective rule of all political rulers from the natural authority of the father: in a state, only divine pronouncement or "consent of the society itself" can determine authority among several families.[213] Absolutist discourse frequently responds to republican resistance theory by comparing it to an indefensible assault on paternal rule itself. For James VI/I, any subject questioning the king's power is an unnatural child, and the worst of these, the tyrannicide, is a "parricide."[214] Much of Filmer's political theory meditates on this filial analogy, and Sexby admits that even some good Puritans like William Ames compare tyrants to bad parents, whose mischiefs one must simply endure.[215] But finally Sexby denies the analogy and joins the mainstream of fraternal republicanism. Languet and Mornay say that subjects are brothers to the king, not his slaves. Indeed, tyrants, not tyrannicides, are political parricides, for they attack the subjects who made them kings.[216] Johannes Althusius rejects the patriarchal analogy, and, indeed, analogical argument in general.[217] Buchanan concedes that assaults on patriarchy and familial piety are unnatural, but less so than tyranny, and he notes the republican praise accorded Thebe for killing her husband, Timoleon his brother, and Cassius, Fulvius, and Junius Brutus their sons.[218] For Sexby, the state will become a tyrannical Roman *familia* if anything like a Stuart-style patriarchy returns and breaks down this separation of family and state: "to be under a tyrant, is not to be a commonwealth; but a great family, consisting of masters and slaves." Even if Cromwell claims divine nomination, he has usurped over his brethren: "And it is plain in that place that God gives the people the choice of their king, for he there instructs them whom they shall choose, 'Emedio fratrum tuorum,' one out of the midst of thy brethren."[219]

Next, Sexby shows Cromwell's tyrannous practice by drawing up a fourteen-point "character" of a tyrant—the one "character" generally absent from the conservative character book. While shattering any remaining customary or casuist bonds to the Protectorate, Sexby also inserts himself into a long-standing anti-tyrannical tradition: "I shall not give you any [character traits] of my own stamping but such as I find in Plato, Aristotle, Tacitus, and his Highness own evangelist, Machiavell." Sexby's pages are thick with allusions to earlier political writers, to Hebrew, Greek, and Roman tyrannicides, and to the honors accorded them by their

---

213. Ibid. 3, 4.
214. *The Political Works of James I*, Cambridge, MA, 1918, 177.
215. *S* 6.
216. *Vindiciae* 108–10.
217. *Politica*, Indianapolis 1995, 198–9.
218. *Powers* 143–4. Compare Philip Sidney's ascetic republican prince Euarchus, who refuses to rescind the death sentence pronounced on his son and nephew when he learns their true identities (*The Countess of Pembroke's Arcadia*, Harmondsworth 1984, 841–2).
219. *S* 12, 4.

states.[220] When searching for tyrannicidal exempla, Sexby favors scriptural sources, "which we may much more safely imitate," but this does not mean that we are headed for a theocratic or sacred critique of secular tyranny. Rather, like the Fifth Monarchist republicanism I examined in the previous chapter, *Killing Noe Murder* reveals a ferociously religious assault on those Erastian state institutions that would replace the voluntary democratic culture of the gathered congregations with a mystifying cult of Cromwell the godly prince. Appropriating conservative rhetoric, he accuses tyrants of claims to "inspirations from Gods, and responses from oracles to authorize what they do, and his Highness hath ever been an enthusiast." He poses to Cromwell the quarrelsome Hebrews' unanswered challenge to Moses in Exodus 2.14: "Who made thee a prince and a judge over us? If God made thee, make it manifest to us." And he attacks the Erastian aspects of Cromwell's polity: "his Highness his Chaplains, and Triers who are to admit none into the ministry that will preach liberty with the gospels" should be hanged before their pulpits, as was Baal's priest Mattan, after the execution of Athaliah.[221]

Sexby transforms the religious discussion by locating political action and right in an order of nature authored by God, but not directly manipulated by him. He treats the Hebrew Scriptures as Harrington did when he combined them with the records of classical civilization as a chronicle of the struggles between the republican "ancient prudence" and the monarchical "modern prudence." What connects the apparently private act of tyrannicide to a public purpose is not a special divine dispensation, but the equitable first principles of natural law—a law ultimately of divine origin, but accessible to human study and understanding. Sexby does, in fact, associate himself with Old Testament tyrannicides—not by asserting his special inspiration, but by denying theirs. When Moses killed the Egyptian for striking a Hebrew, when Samuel slew Agag for making women childless, when Samson smote the Philistines for burning his first wife and father-in-law, they acted on the basis of retaliation and natural law, not divine inspiration. No doubt, divine inspiration guarantees the success of tyrannicide, but, in a sort of casuist hermeneutical loop, its success also indicates its inspiration: Jehoiada had no pretence to authorize killing Athaliah but "the equity and justice of the act itself. He pretended no immediate command from God for what he did, nor any authority from the Sanhedrin, and therefore any man might have done what Jehoiada did as lawfully, that could have done it as effectually as he."[222]

220. Ibid. 5, 6, 5, 9.
221. Ibid. 9, 6, 4, 11.
222. Ibid. 10, 11. A remarkable unpublished paper from the summer of 1647, copied by an amanuensis not Clarke, makes a similar argument for the public value of private acts: "And therefore the Army hath reason as Samson did to take advantage rather of the particular injury done to them to rescue the whole nation from bondage than by their particular sufferings to involve also the whole kingdom in unrecoverable slavery" (*CM* 41.56ʳ–60ᵛ; 57ʳ). The author compares the Army acting apart from Parliament to

Sexby particularly fancies Ehud, who also speaks with grim irony and conceals the identity of a tyrannicide beneath the appearance of a client. He forges a special dagger one cubit long and straps it to his thigh, under his clothing. He then goes to an audience with Eglon, the Moabite who had ruled over the Hebrews for eighteen years. After presenting him with a gift in his private chamber, Ehud tells him,

> I have a message from God unto thee.... And Ehud put forth his left hand, and took the dagger from his right thigh, and thrust it into his belly: And the haft also went in after the blade; and the fat closed upon the blade, so that he could not draw the dagger out of his belly; and the dirt came out.

The smell reinforces the hypothesis of Eglon's retainers that he is relieving himself, allowing Ehud to make his getaway—perhaps through a sewer hole in the floor—and organize Israelite resistance. After slaying ten thousand Moabites, Israel lives free for eighty peaceful years.[223]

Ehud fascinates early modern political theorists because he seems to come from nowhere, writing Israelite history from below with his dagger. Peter Martyr emphasizes Ehud's lowliness and superficial lack of qualification for such a heroic act, his prudent superiority to Brutus and Cassius in instantly rousing up allies, and the divine inspiration of his guile and lying.[224] Mariana agrees, for while it is, "indeed, more manly and spirited to show your hate openly, to rush upon the enemy of the state in public ... it is not less prudent to seize the opportunity for guileful stratagems."[225] Invoking Aquinas, Suárez defends Ehud on the grounds that Eglon was an enemy and a tyrant.[226] John Ponet says that "witty messenger" acted privately on God's special inspiration, not publicly as a lesser magistrate appointed by his people, "for by that means, one Judas or other would have betrayed him."[227] Richard Rogers emphasizes Ehud's

---

Esther, who had no "formal call" from God but still made use of a providential opportunity to destroy Haman and save her people: "In such a case the divine Providence hath not so ill provided for the preservation of human societies as that they cannot be saved without a miracle, but where God hath placed power to help he hath given a power to put in execution that supreme law of all states the safety of the people, and if this hold in the case of a private man, much more so when the safety of a whole kingdom is concerned." The speaker appeals to "the practice of all nations" and "the law and light of nature that when all politic constitutions fail either through disability or corruption, those that have power and means in their hands to save the commonwealth ought not to doubt their care and warrant to undertake it" (58^{r-v}). If this was Sexby, then *Killing Noe Murder* adapted to Cromwell these arguments against Charles.

223. Judges 3.20–22, 30. In an unpublished paper, "The Oracle is a Sword: Irony as Sociology in the Story of Ehud's Deliverance of Israel from the Moabites," Lewis Daly highlights Ehud's status as a subaltern bearer of tribute, and the material force of prophetic peasant religion (Ehud's "message") against Canaanite overlords. Baruch Halpern considers the episode as a textual/architectural murder mystery in *The First Historians*, San Francisco 1988, 39–75.

224. *Most Fruitful and Learned Commentaries of Doctor Peter Martir Vermil Florentine*, 1564, 81^v–91^v.

225. *The King and the Education of the King*, Chevy Chase, MD, 1948, 153.

226. *Selections* 711.

227. *Short Treatise* H5^v–H6^r.

status as a "private person" with a lame right hand, and God's decision to work through "weak means."[228] Responding to aristocratic raillery against his popular commonwealth, Harrington's Lord Archon classifies Ehud—who, after all, seems to know his way around a smithy—among such lowly republican heroes as Othniel, Gideon, Jephtha, Samson, Miltiades, Aristides, Themistocles, Cimon, Pericles, Papirus, Cincinnatus, Camillus, Fabius, and Scipio—"smiths of the fortune of the commonwealth, not such as forged hobnails but thunderbolts."[229] Gilbert Burnet recalled a talk with an intimate of Cromwell, who claimed that his circle appealed to "the practices of Ehud and Jael, Samson and David" to excuse them from "the common rules of morality."[230]

Ehud shows Sexby that revolutionary piety requires a practical supplement:

> In a tyrant's case process and citation have no place, and if we will only have formal remedies against him, we are sure to have none. There's small hopes of justice where the malefactor hath a power to condemn the judge. All remedy therefore against a tyrant is Ehud's dagger, without which all our laws were fruitless, and we helpless. This is that high court of justice where Moses brought the Egyptian, whether Ehud brought Eglon: Samson the Philistines: Samuel Agag: and Jehoiada the she tyrant Athaliah.

To those who insist that the Hebrew tyrannicides acted as special instruments of God, not as private persons, Sexby responds,

> The example of Ehud shews us the natural and almost the only remedy against a tyrant, and the way to free an oppressed people from the slavery of an insulting Moabite, 'tis done by prayers and tears, with the help of a dagger, by crying to the Lord, and the left hand of an Ehud. Devotion and action go well together; for believe it, a tyrant is not of that kind of devil that is to be cast out only by fasting and prayer: and here the Scripture shows us what the Lord thought a fit message to send a tyrant from himself: a dagger of a cubit in his belly, and every worthy man that desires to be an Ehud, a deliverer of his country, will strive to be the messenger.[231]

Rather than limiting "religion" to a safely enclosed sphere, Sexby allows its collective energies to infuse active political life. He aspires to be a Machiavellian "armed prophet" like Moses, Cyrus, Theseus, and Romulus, who can enforce piety with the republican sword.[232] Speaking of these

228. *A Commentary Upon the Whole Booke of Judges*, 1615, 161–2, 173, 176, 179.
229. *Political Works* 291.
230. Burnet, *History* 1.78.
231. *S* 9–10. In January 1655, while Sexby was still in England, someone visited John Rogers, imprisoned at Lambeth Palace, and claimed that "we did not live in an age to expect miracles; that Babylon cannot be destroyed, nor the saint at Windsor [Christopher Feake] be released by only faith and prayer; but you must be of courage, and make use of material instruments, and proceed by force" (*B* 3.136). In 1653, shortly after Sexby returned from Bordeaux, Rogers faulted Cromwell for abandoning the Huguenots and issued a rousing call to arms based in Scripture, classical sources, and English precedent (*Sagrir*, 1653, 14–19).
232. *Prince* 16–18.

armed prophets, who are also inspired republican legislators, Pocock observes, "We must not say that divine inspiration is being lowered to the level of *Realpolitik* without adding that *Realpolitik* is being raised to the level of divine inspiration."[233]

Sexby sacralizes his call for apparently secular tyrannicidal action by invoking the writing of a former acquaintance: "I answer with learned Milton, that if God commanded these things, 'tis a sign they were lawful and are commendable."[234] Sexby probably recalls Milton's claim in *The First Defence* that "It was not however permissible and good to put a tyrant to death because God commanded it, but rather God commanded it because it was permissible and good," or his response in *The Tenure of Kings and Magistrates* to the idea that God gave Ehud a "special warrant" to kill Eglon: "It cannot be granted, because not expressed; 'tis plain that he was raised by God to be a Deliverer, and went on just principles, such as were then and ever held to be allowable, to deal so by a tyrant that could no otherwise be dealt with."[235] For Sexby as for Milton, something we might misrecognize as "secular thought" emerges from the divinization of history and human activity; no longer the special province of a lesser magistrate or an inspired divine agent, tyrannicide becomes a revolutionary career open to godly talent.[236] The tyrannicide operates according to his own reason, but in a divinely authored order of nature and natural law.

In the second section of *Killing Noe Murder*, Sexby asks, "Whether it be lawful to kill a tyrant?" and responds with his radical theory of political violence sanctioned by natural law.[237] Almost all early modern political theorists have some conception of natural law, and Merritt Hughes suggests that its "mounting prestige" and "declining clarity" show it was "fast becoming a transcendent principle of essentially emotional appeal."[238] But at least one distinction remained: theorists continued to differ sharply over whether natural law enjoined obedience to positive law and the powers that be, or authorized resistance to both. In the 1650s, this conflict took shape as the Engagement Controversy between theorists of *de facto* political rule, who downplayed the oppositional force of

233. *Machiavellian* 171.
234. *S* 11.
235. *M* 4.407, 3.215. See also 1.454.
236. *S* 10. In "Milton's Radical 'Admirer' Edward Sexby," *Milton Quarterly* 15.2, 1981, Richard F. Hardin suggests Milton responded to this embarrassing tribute by having Samson say, "I was no private but a person raised / With strength sufficient and command from heaven / To free my country" (1211–13). But in his prose, Milton left it an open question whether Samson "acted in pursuance of a command from Heaven, or was prompted by his valor only"—God could "raise" a tyrannicide through second causes with no immediate "special warrant" (*M* 4.402, 3.215). Even in his play, the source of Samson's final inspiration (from within? from above?) is notoriously ambiguous. Milton's Samson, like Sexby's, puts a notion into practice to see if it has divine warrant.
237. *S* 4.
238. *M* 3.68. On early modern natural law theory, see ibid. 3.65–80; Tuck, *Natural Rights*; and *P&L* [87–91].

natural law, and opponents to the Protectorate (Anglicans, Presbyterians, sectarians, and republicans) who used it to legitimize resistance.[239]

Referring to the former group, Quentin Skinner has argued that the regicide generated a complex body of casuist philosophy that considered the extent to which non-Cromwellians might accommodate themselves to the new regime. The Presbyterian-turned-Independent Francis Rous, arguing from Romans 13, read Cromwell's very ability to rule as a sign of his divine appointment. The Cromwellian Independent Anthony Ascham agreed, in his *Of the Confusions and Revolutions of Government*. Hobbes, on the other hand, derived the legitimacy of a *de facto* ruler from the necessity for social order.[240] Skinner emphasizes this movement from the relatively theocratic first position to the relatively secular second, but the two come together in their attempt to reduce or remove the distance between power and right, sovereign act and political norm, undoing the subversive normative potential of natural law in the process. Royalists and Presbyterians might have disagreed with Hobbes on many counts, including his effort to legitimize Cromwell's rule, but as Merritt Hughes says, they "could welcome his theory of nature's first laws as precluding any social contract *between* kings and their subjects, which limited royal 'power to put to death, imprison, banish, whip, or fine any of them.'"[241] *De facto* theory tended to avoid or ignore the question of tyranny without title, and reduce the question of tyranny by practice to a question of order. In a neo-feudal or proto-fascist formulation of 1650, "protection and allegiance are relatives."[242] The next year, Hobbes provided the more canonical formulation: the purpose of *Leviathan* was to convince humankind of "the mutual relation between Protection and Obedience."[243]

Pocock makes the Engagement Controversy the center of his case for a paradigm shift in the historical study of the English Revolution. The earlier approach of liberals like William Haller and marxists like Christopher Hill focused on the struggle for spiritual and social liberation and the Putney Debates. The new approach of John M. Wallace, Quentin Skinner, and Pocock himself focuses on the languages of political authority and legitimation and the Engagement Controversy. To claim such a shift is not simply "an ideological reaction by conservative scholars to the events of 1968 or 1970," but an attempt to describe a number of "singularly tough-minded responses" by Hobbes, Harrington, Ascham, and others "to the question how men left with nothing but the sword could restore the rule of reason and authority."[244] Despite Pocock's protest, we may indeed hear an echo of Thatcher's *de factoist* "There is no

239. John M. Wallace, *Destiny His Choice*, London 1968, and "The Engagement Controversy, 1649–1652: An Annotated List of Pamphlets," *Bulletin of the New York Public Library* 68, 1964.
240. Quentin Skinner, "Conquest and Consent," Aylmer, *The Interregnum* 79–98.
241. *M* 3.72.
242. Skinner, "Conquest" 92.
243. 491.
244. *Virtue* 55–6.

alternative" in "tough-minded." But finally, the question is not whether there is some connection between one's political situation and one's historical arguments, but the extent to which one allows a particular class-bound idiom to swell into an episteme, whether in 1656 or 1985. For Pocock, I think that extent is considerable, and, as a result, the specifically *controversial* elements tend to disappear from his account of the Engagement Controversy. Though he acknowledges the earlier liberal and marxist argument, and suggests that he is simply making a modest historical claim about the transition from the 1640s to the 1650s, he is actually making a more global argument about historical writing and political authority itself, and opening a new front in the war he has waged in Restoration and eighteenth-century historiography to elevate a neo-Harringtonian republican discourse of virtue, corruption, and authority over a Lockian liberal discourse of property, class, and right, much emphasized by both liberals and marxists.[245]

But try as they may, historians of the Engagement can't remove the taint of class, since the Engagement aimed primarily to ensure the orderly establishment of a new landed ruling class that would include both compounding royalists and the parliamentary new men who had bought up portions of their estates, along with king's and church lands. Indeed, I think we should see the Negative Oath of 1645, whereby compounders regained some of their property in exchange for swearing never again to bear arms against Parliament, as a dress rehearsal for the Engagement, which denied process of law, and so also full property rights in the event of a suit at law, to any nonscriber.[246] Ten years later, in yet another engagement controversy, ex-parliamentarians set about reconciling themselves to the *de facto* rule of monarchy, forswearing previous allegiances, negotiating land transfers, and forming the strategic marriages that engendered a new English ruling class.

---

245. Michael Oakeshott is a likely influence. Attacking Locke's conception of political authority rising from the consent of the people, he concludes that "the authority of the state can reside nowhere save in the state itself as such"—its Hobbesian power to provide satisfaction to "the needs of concrete persons" (*Religion, Politics and the Moral Life*, New Haven, CT, 1993, 86–7). Power and norm, act and authority, collapse in a fashion that might appeal to Carl Schmitt or a Nietzschean postmodernist. Oakeshott defines civil life as a sort of conversation among political speakers, who make statements of greater or lesser aesthetic value, which suggests Pocock's focus on (ruling-class) political speech acts, and the postmodern attempt to substitute an aesthetics of existence for an ethics. See Perry Anderson, "The Intransigent Right at the End of the Century," review of Oakeshott's *Rationalism in Politics and Other Essays* (London 1991), *London Review of Books*, September 24 1992, 10. Oakeshott claims that German fascism did not negate liberalism, but perfectly embodied the "characteristic liberal project of a science of politics"; its true enemy, parliamentary government, is "not liberal at all, but of a far more ancient lineage in European politics" (*Religion* 102). Though Young Conservatives like Lyotard and Foucault might resist Oakeshott's primeval parliamentarianism, they could happily join him in collapsing liberalism and fascism under the heading of an oppressive modern "science."

246. *GHCW* 3.198; *DRD* 357–8; Mary Anne Everett Wood Green, ed., *Calendar of the Proceedings of the Committee for Compounding, 1643–1660*, 1889–92; rpt Nendeln, Liechtenstein 1967.

Moreover, even if we remain strictly inside the domain of political theory, Protectorate republicans were by no means bereft of arguments for resistance. With their militant insistence on the government of laws not men, they are closer to Commonwealth Levellers than to Protectorate *de factoists*. The movement from 1647 to 1657 suggests a complex continuity, not a paradigm shift. Just as 1640s radicals like Parker, Milton, Rainsborough, Wildman, and Private Edward Sexby faced *de factoists* like Henry Ireton, who stressed the binding force of prior engagements to a sitting parliament and a political nation grounded in freehold tenure (the continuing, unvoiced ground of *de facto* theory), so *de factoists* of the 1650s like Hobbes, Hawke, and Cromwell himself faced theorists of social liberation like the Fifth Monarchists, republicans, Winstanley, and Colonel Edward Sexby—theorists armed not just with the sword, but also with radical theories of natural law and the *salus populi* that would not fit neatly into the genres of casuist discourse, whether or not they supported the Engagement. Pocock and his followers have underestimated the extent to which *de factoist* arguments responded not just to general civic instability, but to attacks by Levellers, Baptists, Fifth Monarchists, and republicans on the legitimacy of the Cromwellian regimes.

In fact, tyrannicidal theory proposes what we might call a counter-casuistry defining cases in which one may, not obey, but slay an illegitimate or even a legitimate monarch, or an anti-casuistry that doesn't try to reconcile the subject's individual conscience to the power of *de facto* rule, but emboldens him to slay the tyrant and reconcile the state itself to his own individual conscience, which temporarily embodies the authority of natural law. Where *de factoists* fear the prospect of social disorder and a breakdown of authority, Sexby fears a slavish tendency to honor oaths and compacts grown unnatural and corrupt, because tending to the harm of the compactors. Where *de factoists* argue that long obedience to a ruler implies "tacit consent," Sexby (like Milton) praises the tyrannicidal resistance of Ehud and Jehoiada, despite the Israelites' years of obedience to Eglon and Athaliah.[247] He rails against clerical *de factoists*: as Samson heard the admonitions of the Judahites, "so we have the men of Levi, crying to us out of the Pulpit, as from the top of the rock Etam, know you not that the Philistine is a ruler over you?"[248]

Turning to two favorite examples of the antityrannical tradition, Sexby attempts to delegitimize *de factoist* ethical critiques of resistance: if slaves may resist their masters' depredations, why can't free subjects resist their appointed rulers? If a householder can slay a thief in the night without bringing him to civil justice, why can't he slay a tyrant, "that is the common robber of mankind . . . whom no law can take hold on? . . . As if

---

247. *S* 9, 11; *M* 4.401, 402. Hobbes says anyone living openly under a government "is understood to submit himself to the government" (*Leviathan* 485). The doctrine of "tacit consent" tried to defang radical contract theory (Ellen Meiksins Wood and Neal Wood, *Trumpet* 120–21).
248. *S* 10.

to rove with two or three ships were to be a pirate, but with fifty an admiral."[249] Sexby alludes to Augustine's account of Alexander's encounter with Diomedes the pirate: when Alexander asked "what he was thinking of, that he should molest the sea," Diomedes responded, "the same as you when you molest the world! Since I do this with a little ship I am called a pirate. You do it with a great fleet and are called an admiral."[250] Diomedes criticizes the quantitative hypocrisies of ruling-class ethics, using the fundamentally ethical conception of "molestation" to do so. A similar tension inhabits the very title of Sexby's pamphlet, which maintains a conception of justice even as it attacks a particular regime of civil law.

For Hobbes, the only natural right is the right to self-preservation, adjudicated by each individual: "The notions of right and wrong, justice and injustice have there no place. Where there is no common power, there is no law: where no law, no injustice."[251] No one can act *unjustly* in the state of nature, for "injustice against men presupposes human laws, such as in the state of nature there are none," and the laws of nature, though they may exist abstractly, are "silent":

> Theft, murder, adultery, and all injuries are forbid by the laws of nature; but what is to be called *theft*, what *murder*, what *adultery*, what *injury* in a citizen, this is not to be determined by the natural, but by the civil law. For not every taking away of the things which another possesses, but only another man's goods, is theft; but what is ours, and what another's, is a question belonging to the civil law. In like manner, not every killing of a man is murder, but only that which the civil law forbids. . . .

Hobbes's state of nature is not an actual place or time. For instance, no son can inhabit a state of nature, for he is under the authority of his parents from the moment he is born.[252] Still, he manages to separate and periodize rigorously: where there is a state of nature, there civil society and sociability cannot be.

But for the radical republican tradition, natural law is the product of divine law, the foundation of positive law, and a figure for human sociability itself; the state of nature inhabits the present like a dormant virus, or a touchstone, or a whetstone. This tradition derives ultimately from Aristotle's theory of man as the political animal, and, closer to hand, from Grotius, whom Sexby invokes four times.[253] Bloch helpfully contrasts Grotius and Hobbes: "It was not the *drive for self-preservation* motivated by the *fear* of one's neighbor, but the social drive, *appetitus socialis*, that led to

---

249. Ibid. 8.
250. *The City of God Against the Pagans*, 7 vols, London and Cambridge, MA, 1957–72, 2.17. Languet and Mornay used the anecdote to defend tyrannicide (*Vindiciae* 149), John Rogers to attack Protectorate tithing (*B* 3.484).
251. *Leviathan* 90.
252. *DRD* 459, 471, 458.
253. *S* 7–8.

the social contract."[254] Similarly, Buchanan sees an impulse to association, not mere expedience, underlying the civil bond.[255] We have seen the same tradition in the Levellers and Agitators. It reappears in the writing of a later republican, Algernon Sidney, whose "ultimate political appeal was not to immemorialism or to any particular code of positive law, but to the general law of nature, reason, truth, and justice written by God in the heart of every man."[256] And it reappears in the natural law theory that would have world-transforming implications in the bourgeois revolutions of the eighteenth through the nineteenth centuries, and in their proletarian revolutionary subplots.

In Sexby's moral philosophy, Calvin bumps into Aristotle: the "depravity of man's will" makes people somewhat unfit for society, but a human impulse to sociability mitigates it. Where Hobbes sees natural law as the drive to individual self-preservation, Sexby sees it as the quest for collective *happiness*:

> We are therefore to consider that the end, for which men enter into society, is not barely to live, which they might do dispersed, as other animals: but to live happily; and a life answerable to the dignity and excellency of their kind. Out of society, this happiness is not to be had, for singly we are impotent, and defective, unable to procure those things that are either of necessity, or ornament for our lives; and as unable to defend and keep them when they are acquired. To remedy these defects, we associate together that what we can neither enjoy nor keep, singly, by mutual benefits and assistances, one of another, we may be able to do both.[257]

Reasoning not the need, Sexby refuses to separate necessity and ornament. In beginning with this credo about human sociability, he moves even beyond Milton, who says that "No man who knows ought, can be so stupid to deny that all men naturally were born free," and need society only after they fall.[258] But Sexby sees humans born lonely, yearning for social happiness—like Milton's Adam—and tyranny violates "the law of nature, that is, the law of human society, in which human nature is preserved."[259]

Perhaps chastened by Grotius, Sexby holds back at first from the radical implications of *salus populi* and retreats to the safer pole of the resistance theory binary: tyrants without title are Ishmaels or Cains who should be "destroyed by him that found him first," but tyrants by practice are a different matter, for "none, of sober sense, makes private persons judges of their actions; which were, indeed, to subvert all government." But he quickly shakes off this fit of sober sense and places the tyrant by practice among the Ishmaels: "Justice dispenses with her forms" for anyone who

254. *Natural* 48.
255. *Powers* 46–7.
256. Jonathan Scott, *Sidney* 38.
257. *S* 7.
258. *M* 3.198–9.
259. *S* 7.

gains control of the laws and "secures himself against all ordinary course of justice." Under a tyranny, the power that more conservative resistance theorists reserved to lesser magistrates devolves to each individual man. This leads not to a Hobbesian war of all against all, but to a Grotian war of all against one:

> A tyrant, as we have said, being no part of a commonwealth, nor submitting to the laws of it, but making himself above all law: there is no reason he should have the protection that is due to a member of a commonwealth, nor any defense from laws, that does acknowledge none. . . . He that flies justice in the court, must expect to find it in the street. . . . And certainly by the law of nature, *ubi cessat judicium,* when no justice can be had, every man may be his own magistrate, and do justice for himself, for the law (says Grotius) that forbids me to pursue my right but by a course of law: certainly supposes, *ubi copia est judicii,* where law and justice is to be had; otherwise that law were a defense for injuries, not one against them: and quite contrary to the nature of all laws, that would become the protection of the guilty against the innocent, not of the innocent against the guilty.

The "laws of God and nature" insist that sovereignty must be social—that men should not be judges of themselves, that each individual man denied justice may justly repel force with force.[260]

This emulative killing prefigures the hoped-for future collective solidarity of the republic. But when Sexby turns from the abstractly heroic English People to the actual people of England, he sounds considerably less sanguine, for he senses their substantial accommodation to a dictatorial regime. In a moment of identification that suggests Milton's in *Samson Agonistes,* he justifies Samson's war on the Philistines, though "not only not assisted, but opposed by his servile countrymen." He calls the English "a people of great faith, but little wit," easily taken in by Cromwell's pious pretenses and "spongy eyes." At the end of his pamphlet, recalling and balancing his initial antityrannical character of Cromwell, he conducts a desperate anatomy of England's civic virtue in the form of a republican jeremiad.[261] The nobility have "not so much as the generous vices that attend greatness, they have lost all ambition and indignation." The ministers are simply tithe-seeking time servers, who "rake Scriptures for flatteries. . . . and impudently apply them to his monstrous Highness." London is "but a great tame beast, that eats and carries and cares not who rides it." Parliament are the "pimps of tyranny, who are only employed to draw in the people to prostitute their liberty." The Army are "but janissaries, slaves themselves; and making all others so." And the people in general are "knaves, fools, and cowards, principled for ease, vice and slavery." During a stagnant tyranny, the republican conviction that civic form produces civic virtue leads to despair: "Nor must we think we can continue long in the condition of slaves, and not degenerate into the

260. Ibid. 6–8; Grotius, *Law* 138–63.
261. *S* 10, 5, 14–15.

habits and temper that is natural to that condition: our minds will grow low with our fortune; and by being accustomed to live like slaves, we shall become unfit to be anything else." The people are on the verge of losing all their virtue, "and then his Highness hath completed his work to Reformation."[262] Using the idioms of 1647, Sexby tries to refabricate the intimate solidarity of soldiers and agitators:

> Hitherto I have spoken in general to all Englishmen, now I address my discourse particularly to those that certainly deserve that name, ourselves, that have fought, however unfortunately, for our liberties under this tyrant; and in the end cozened by his oaths, and tears, have purchased nothing but our slavery with the price of our blood.[263]

Still, like a good Jeremiah, Sexby meets his pious but small-witted country-men halfway. He concludes with a millenarian exhortation based in Zophar's description of the portion of the wicked in Job 20, combining a last attack on Cromwell with a prophecy of England's conversion into a heroic collective of emulous tyrannicides:

> There's a great roll behind, even of those that are in his own muster-rolls, that are ambitious of the name of the deliverers of their country: and they know what the action is that will purchase it. His bed, his table is not secure; and he stands in need of other guards to defend him against his own. Death and destruction pursues him wherever he goes: they follow him everywhere, like his fellow-travelers, and at last they will come upon him like armed men. Darkness is hid in his secret places, a fire not blown shall consume him; it shall go ill with him that is left in his tabernacle. He shall flee from the iron weapon, and a bow of steel shall strike him through. Because he hath oppressed, and forsaken the poor; because he hath violently taken away a house which he builded not: we may be confident, and so may he, that ere long, all this will be accomplished: for the triumphing of the wicked is but short, and the joy of the hypocrite but for a moment. Though his Excellency mount up to the heavens, and his head reacheth unto the clouds, yet he shall perish forever like his own dung. They that have seen him, shall say, where is he?[264]

In this striking utopian prophecy, the tyrannicide contrasts starkly with the client: if the latter seeks filial recognition from a pre-existent authority by promising to memorialize him, Sexby attempts to expunge his enemy's name from the Book of Life while writing for a patron who does not yet exist—a virtuous English republic that the stab of his pen will shock into being.

Aftermath: Tyrannicide as Critique

Of course, Sexby did no such thing. After Cromwell declined the crown on May 8 1657, Sexby remained, as Titus said, "still sanguine, which is

262. Ibid. 12.
263. Ibid. 14.
264. Ibid. 16.

either his artifice or his disease."[265] He followed his pamphlet to England in June. But he was captured on July 24, as he attempted to board the ship *Hope* for a return to the Low Countries, dressed "in a mean habit, disguised like a country man, and his visage altered by an overgrown beard; who being brought before his Highness, was after examination sent prisoner to the Tower of London."[266] The examination seems to have been clandestine and rather thorough: the warrant ordering Barkstead to receive and keep Sexby close prisoner in the Tower is dated August 4, eleven days after his capture and at least five days after Nedham and seven days after Thurloe reported him in the Tower.[267] Talbot wrote Hyde of Sexby's betrayal in both England and Holland.[268] Someone wrote "Wyld-man" on an anonymous intelligence letter to Thurloe of February 25 1657 about royalist invasion plans.[269] In October, Nicholas wrote Sir Henry Bennet about the splintering of Leveller opposition: "Col. Courten saith Major Wildman is a juggler and Sexby saith Wildman hath brought him into the condition he is, being a prisoner in the Tower; and Wildman saith Sexby is a knave." Nonetheless, Wildman became the center of continuing efforts to cement a Leveller–royalist alliance against the Protectorate.[270]

No official word of Sexby appeared for six months. His wife returned to England in early September and attended him constantly save around the time she gave birth.[271] He seems to have been sick, but not too sick. In October, the Middlesex Sessions called one "Katherine Whitehead *alias* Linsey widow" to answer for "her uncivil carriage in going to bed to Colonel Sexby when she kept him in his sickness."[272] In September appeared an anonymous response with the thudding title of *Killing Is Murder: Or, an Answer to a Treasonous Pamphlet Entituled, Killing Is No Murder*. The second edition identified the author as one "Mich. Hawke, of the Middle-Temple, Gentl."[273] Hawke displayed the dogged alliterative energy of a determined placeman in dedicating his work to "The Most Puissant and Prudent Prince, Oliver Cromwell."[274] With generic but

---

265. *CCSP* 294, 316.
266. *Mercurius Politicus* 7/23–7/30/57. Philip Aubrey discusses Thurloe's intelligence about Sexby's plot (*Thurloe* 111–15).
267. *CSPD* 11.48, 549; *Mercurius Politicus* 1/14–1/21/58; *B* 6.425.
268. *CCSP* 349.
269. *TM* A47, 281.
270. *NP* 4.16; on Wildman's possible betrayal, see *GHCP* (4.258–9), Firth (*Last* 1.35n.), and Ashley (*Wildman* 112). Because Overton offered Thurloe his services in 1654 (*B* 2.590), Gardiner suggests he betrayed Sexby in 1657 (*GHCP* 4.233n.)—a stretch, I think.
271. *CCSP* 357; *Mercurius Politicus* 1/14–1/21/58.
272. Jeaffreson, *Middlesex* 3.266.
273. I'll quote from the second edition, *Killing Is Murder, and No Murder* (1658).
274. In *The Right of Dominion, and Property of Liberty* (1656), a treatise dedicated to Cromwell, Hawke compares "our late ambitious Levellers" to the first tribunes of republican Rome, saying that they were "the cause of many turbulent commotions, which like Hydras' heads, one being lopped, others instantly sprouted up" (77–8). Hawke's courtly petition of May 28 1656 begs Cromwell for something, please, anything, by way of state office (*CSPD* 9.338–9); *Killing Is Murder* looks like another such petition.

strangely accurate paranoia, he ties the pamphlet's author with the Jesuits (including "his Ghostly Father Mariana"), the Levellers, and the Fifth Monarchy men, and threatens him repeatedly with the halter.[275] He defends Cromwell's legitimacy on the grounds of popular consent, scriptural warrant, and a *de factoist* argument combining Genesis and Hobbes:

> After the fall of our first parents, the natural state of men, before they were settled in a society, as Master Hobbes truly saith, was a mere war.... The foundation of government ... is not election or consent of the people, as this Imposter would have it, but force and arms which first raised and established it.... No law hath more power than arms; for as every one is more potent, so doth he seem to say and do all things more justly.

Following Hobbes, Hawke suggests that there is no such thing as a tyrant, for *tyrannus* is simply another name for *king*. He even puts in a *de factoist* good word for Nimrod: Genesis calls him a "mighty hunter before the Lord" because he received his power from the Lord.[276] Commenting, perhaps, on Hawke's pamphlet, Titus said "'tis wonder Cromwell, as impudent as he is, would give allowance to come forth, for it is to make him as absolute as the Grand Turk."[277]

The January 7–14 issue of *Mercurius Politicus* announced the second edition of Hawke's work, and Sexby's death in the Tower on January 13. The next issue narrated his final months.[278] Nedham's Sexby confesses that he wrote *Killing Noe Murder*, worked for Spain, conspired with Charles II, and organized the Sindercombe Plot. He admits that Cromwell's refusal of the crown put a completely different complexion on things, and ruefully apologizes for accusing Cromwell and Barkstead of smothering Sindercombe. Thus Nedham asks us to accept the testimony of one person who died in custody as to the mode of death of another. Though most historians have complied, Olivier Lutaud remarks laconically, "Bref, une belle confession."[279] Three points are worth remembering. First, wardens, torturers, executioners, and editors of government newspapers tell lies—and Marchamont Nedham was not exactly known for stiff-necked resistance to helpful hints from upstairs. Second, tortured

275. A1ᵛ, 3, 20, 41, 42.
276. 7, 10, 28, 9. On Nimrod and the Puritans, see Hill, *English* 217–22.
277. As Macray suggests, Titus may be attacking Hawkes's pamphlet, but in referring to "The Answeare to *Killing No Murder*" (*CCSP* 397), he may intend another pamphlet, now apparently lost, which Hawkes refers to as "the Answer to *Killing Noe Murder*" in his second edition (A3ʳ). On August 5 1657, Henry Rumbould reported the arrival in Spain of "the book of which *Killing no Murder* was the preface" (*CCSP* 3.344); perhaps this is simply a complete pamphlet, with a manuscript separate of the preface misidentified as the whole thing.
278. See also *The Public Intelligencer* 1/18–1/25/58.
279. *Des Révolutions* 59. Sometime between Cromwell's death and the Restoration, perhaps responding to the second edition of Sexby's pamphlet, much of this account, along with most of *The Whole Business* and a plate of Sindercombe's naked body being dragged to burial, appeared in *A Further Narrative of the Passages of These Times in the Common-Wealth of England.*

prisoners tell lies in hopes of ending their torture. And third, the voice of resistance sometimes miraculously survives inside the official story. Thurloe noted Sexby's tendency to fall into "his former distraction and wild speeches" when pressured to confess his assassination plot, but even in this state, Sexby, like Sindercombe before him, refused to name his confederates.[280] The republic of the future survives only as the solidarity of conspirators, but that's not nothing. Nedham hears madness in Sexby's tendency to respond "that it was a lie" to anything said to him, and in his repeatedly waking the Lieutenant of the Tower to hear his late-night confession, only to complain that "The Devil would not let him speak out the truth." But surely Sexby was prudent to give the lie to capital charges, and his toying with the screws suggests his sardonic wit become gallows humor. Nedham sounds a little nervous when he describes Sexby's final illness in lurid detail, lists multiple witnesses to his death by natural causes, then notes that the coroner's jury found "blackness and seding [settling] of blood about his shoulders, which they judged to come from the violence of the fever."[281] Might not a calculating warder, eager to stifle the cult of a tyrannicidal martyr, choose to smother him at a time when he was sick anyway—a time never long in coming, it seems, for guests in Julius Caesar's ill-erected tower?[282] We can at least leave the possibility open. The Tower reported Sexby's death to his wife, then staying in Whitefriars with her mother. She sent forty shillings and, on January 15, Sexby's body was interred on the Tower grounds.

But one could plausibly argue that his effort failed long before—that it was flawed in its very conception. Sexby, like Sindercombe, seems to have thought that, after Cromwell's assassination, "the great ones of the King would never agree, who should succeed, but would fall together by the ears about it, and then in that disorder the people would rise, and so things might be brought to a commonwealth again."[283] Here we see the secular millennialism of the assassin: the obsessive dream ("fanatical" doesn't seem too strong a word) that a single, carefully planned act of violence would automatically inaugurate a new age—a negative equivalent to the fanatical belief of republicans like Harrington that a new Lycurgus could instill political order through a miraculous act of utopian legislation. This mystified individualism marks the spot where republicans fail to work out an adequate theory of revolutionary class agency. Without a revolutionary transformation of society, without transitional institutions of popular democracy, tyrannical power could easily outlive any particular tyrant, or even government by a single person. *Killing Noe Murder* doesn't even hint at any transformation of productive relations in the republic of

---

280. *B* 6.560.
281. *Mercurius Politicus* 1/14–1/21/58.
282. Thus Richard's unhappy queen calls it in *Richard II*, alluding to the tradition tracing its original construction to that archetypal tyrant (*William Shakespeare*, Baltimore 1969, 5.1.2).
283. *B* 5.775.

the future, and it maintains a strategic silence even on the question of the franchise.

When we move from Sexby's rhetoric to his practice, further problems emerge. His ability to concoct a conspiracy ranging from John Sturgeon to Pope Alexander VII testified to his considerable charisma and political ability. But finally, he created only a series united by its opposition to Cromwell. When he says that Cromwell's death is "the only thing wherein all sects, and factions do agree in their devotions," the irony is two-edged.[284] He opens himself not simply to a demonizing critique of his apostasy, but also to an immanent critique setting Sexby against Sexby. In 1647, he was an organic intellectual reliant on the union dues of a unified rank and file, but in 1657 he was, no less than Nedham, a traditional intellectual working for a succession of governmental bodies and factions, and lacking any clear popular mandate. His later career reveals a disturbing readiness to trim his Agitator principles to fit a republican end. In 1651, when he withheld his soldiers' pay to encourage them into the Irish campaign, and executed one of them to restore their discipline, he repeated Parliament's actions in the spring of 1647 and the grandees' at Corkbush Field. In 1653, when he proposed to Cromwell that English troops be told of their commitment to a Spanish-led campaign against the King of France only after they had set sail, he grossly violated *The Solemne Engagement.*[285] And in 1655–57, his willingness to conspire with the blood enemies of the Commonwealth suggests at best the narrowed possibilities for radical opposition, at worst a real betrayal. In February 1658, after Sexby's death, his former servant Samuel Dyer testified that, when he objected to collaborating with "the malignant party," Sexby had him imprisoned in Ghent Castle.[286] Even if Dyer concocted this story for John Thurloe, it carries some real force.

Still, Sexby didn't create the straitened political possibilities of the late 1650s, when even Winstanley had made his peace with the powers that were. Any republican assault on the Protectorate with a prayer of success would have had to integrate the threat or the reality of royalist and foreign support, and nothing in Sexby's writing to his republican and sectarian colleagues is incompatible with the idea that he planned a strategic alliance with royalists against the Protectorate, then a final conflict with them that would establish a republic or a constitutionally fettered monarchy. His silence on the question of social revolution doesn't altogether remove his pamphlet from the history of anticapitalist struggle. His address to the Army and recollection of Agitator idioms and arguments suggest that he may have wanted to repeat and perfect the 1647 rise of popular democracy in the New Model. Moreover, an assassination plot is not necessarily an individualist delusion, for in a moral economy like early

284. *S* 1.
285. *CP* 3.201.
286. *B* 6.829–32.

modern England, assassination, like bread rioting, was far from an irrational and impulsive bodily reflex.[287] The transition from feudalism to capitalism changed the state from a coercive mechanism for extracting surplus labor into a formally neutral mechanism protecting the property rights of capitalists extracting surplus value by strictly economic means. Henceforth, the state would back capitalist rule from behind the scenes, through its monopoly on the legitimate exercise of coercion and violence. But just as capital punishment, the exercise of ultimate state violence against human bodies, underwrites capitalism and its imperatives to accumulate, so tyrannicide, as a seized and inverted capital punishment, can underwrite anticapitalist populism. The compressed, cynical joke of the title has a distinctly modern feel: I can't imagine it connecting properly in precapitalist England, or failing to do so in the three-and-a-half capitalist centuries since Sexby's death.[288]

Antityrannical writing itself tends to lead a distinctly anticapitalist existence. Despite the considerable dangers of writing, publishing, and circulation, it keeps reappearing at moments of political crisis, moving handily from one side of a conflict to another via strategic reappropriation, from one nation to another through translation. Ponet's *Short Treatise* (1556), one of the most radical works of Marian resistance theory, was reprinted in 1639 and 1642.[289] Buchanan wrote *De Iure Regni Apud Scotos* in the late 1560s, and it was published in 1579 with a dedication to his pupil, James VI. Dutch translations appeared in 1598 and 1610 during the Low Countries' struggles with Spain. In 1683, Oxford burned the English edition of 1680, but it was reissued in 1689. German editions followed in 1796 and 1821. As John D. Lewis observes, it had a "habit of turning up whenever trouble was in the air."[290] Buchanan's antityrannical drama *Baptistes* was translated in early 1643 as *Tyrannicall-Government Anatomized.* *Vindiciae, Contra Tyrannos* appeared in 1579 with a double homage to Buchanan and the Scots monarchomachs: its title page lists its place of publication as "Edimburg" and its author as "Stephanus Junius Brutus, Celta." It was frequently reprinted in Latin, and in French, German, and Dutch translation.[291] The first English translation appeared in 1622, and it was reprinted in 1631 as *Vindiciae Religionis.*[292] In March 1643, William

---

287. Indeed, even inside modern bureaucracies, assassinations have had important collective implications. Lincoln's death cut Reconstruction short, redeeming the Southern plantocracy and damning generations of sharecroppers to near-feudal exploitation, while John Kennedy's may have saved Cuba from a more savage American assault and a generation of Latin Americans from uncontested capitalist exploitation. Thanks to Ed White for this point.

288. On capital accumulation, capital punishment, and proletarian resistance to both, see Peter Linebaugh's *The London Hanged*, Cambridge 1992. On coercion and the capitalist state, see Wood, *Democracy* 19–48.

289. Ellen Meiksins Wood and Neal Wood, *Trumpet* 50.

290. Jászi and Lewis, *Against* 55.

291. Languet and Mornay, *Vindiciae* lxxxiv–lxxxviii.

292. *A Defence of Liberty Against Tyrants. A Translation of the Vindiciae Contra Tyrannos*, 1924; rpt New York 1972, 60.

Prynne translated sizeable extracts as an appendix to his *Treachery and Disloyalty of Papists to their Soveraigns*.[293] Two editions of a full translation appeared in 1648, attributed to William Walker, Charles's executioner! It was reissued in 1660 and again in 1689.[294] Milton's *Tenure of Kings and Magistrates*, first published in two 1649 editions, in 1689 appeared in excerpted form as a Williamite tract with the title *Pro Populo Adversus Tyranno*. In 1784, a slightly modified version appeared in Dublin in support of emergent Irish republicanism.[295] Even before his death, Harrington's writings embarked on a sustained career in the Atlantic republican tradition, joining the works of Milton, Neville, and Algernon Sidney.[296]

And as Olivier Lutaud has shown in *Des Révolutions d'Angleterre à la Révolution Française*, Sexby's pamphlet had the most remarkable history of all. In the last words of the 1657 edition, he promised "another sheet or two of paper of this subject, if I escape the tyrant's hands." He didn't, but others eagerly provided the sheets, and his pamphlet became a practical and applied supplement to the high republican theory of Milton, Nedham, Harrington, and Sidney. In June 1659, someone brought out a second edition entitled *Killing, No Murder: With Some Additions, Briefly Discourst in Three Questions, Fit for Publick View; To deter and prevent Single Persons, and Councils, from Usurping Supream Power*. Its appendix refers to Cromwell's death, eight months after Sexby's. Most readers have attributed this edition to Silius Titus, and in fact, he was in England in May, helping to prepare for Booth's Rising in August.[297] But it's difficult to see Titus taking time off from royalist conspiracy to pen the new appendix, with its nostalgia for the Rump and its proposed death sentence for anyone attempting to gain the supremacy, or even to circulate the original pamphlet's ferocious republicanism, with its backhanded compliment to the late king: "If there be no remedy to be found, we have great reason to exclaim ... We wish we had rather endured thee (O Charles) than have been condemned to this mean tyrant, not that we desire any kind of slavery, but that the quality of the master something graces the condition of the slave."[298] Such a sentiment accords with Sexby's professed willingness to see England become a constitutional monarchy, but not with Titus's vengeful and reactionary royalism. The more likely parentage is the springtime flurry of republican pamphleteering aimed at bringing back the good old cause, with John Streater, the radical republican and

293. David Wootton, "From Rebellion to Revolution," *English Historical Review* 45, 1990.
294. G. K. Fortescue, comp., *Catalogue of the Pamphlets, Books, Newspapers, and Manuscripts*, 2 vols, London 1908, 1.597.
295. Lieb and Shawcross, *Achievements* 313.
296. Harrington, *Political Works* 128–52; Caroline A. Robbins, *The Eighteenth-Century Commonwealthsmen*, Cambridge, MA, 1959.
297. Underdown, *Royalist* 258.
298. *S* 14; 2nd edn 13.

printer, as midwife.[299] Streater's other publications of the period suggest this edition aimed to assist the republican machinations of Sexby's former allies, Ludlow, Vane, and Haselrig, the Rump Parliament that they helped recall, and the new Council of State that the Rump had constituted. Its tyrannical target would seem to be the late Lord Protector's truculent allies and Charles himself—the most likely "single person" on the horizon, after the gentle purge of Richard Cromwell.[300]

For the next two centuries, many editions of the pamphlet appeared in English and French, under the names of Sexby, Allen, and Titus. The opening epistle appeared in a 1707 work entitled *Hypocrisy unveil'd*.[301] Four editions appeared in 1689, and others in 1695 (possibly), 1708, 1715 (possibly), 1734, 1741, 1743, 1745, 1749, 1762, 1775, 1777, 1784, 1792, 1804, 1809/10, 1819, 1864, and 1900. The 1784 edition came out of Dublin; the 1741, 1745, and 1749 editions out of Jacobite Edinburgh, the last with an appended discourse linking corrupt governmental counselors to the corrupt courtiers of Charles I and Charles II. The 1775 edition claims to have been "reprinted for the great grandson of Algernon Sidney"—who never married. The 1792 edition celebrated the assassination of Gustavus III and the death of Emperor Leopold II, and prayed for the deaths of Catherine the Great and of any others "puffed up by the pride of rank."[302] Godwin and Shelley both read Sexby's pamphlet. In a caricature directed against the Cato Street Conspiracy, Robert Cruikshank (George's brother) linked Sexby and Shelley by depicting a murderous anarchist with a placard reading "Queen Mab or Killing No Murder."[303] The Chartist George Holyoake republished the 1792 edition in his *Collected Writings* (1845, 1853, 1864, 1888), with a new Preface attacking Louis Napoleon and the Tories. The (anarchist?) London edition of around

---

299. Taft discusses the ideological climate ("That Lusty Puss"). Streater's authorship looks likely if we compare four pamphlets sometimes attributed to him:

1. I. S., *The Picture of a New Courtier*, collected by Thomason on April 18 1656. Abbott (*Writings* 4.143) and Johns (*Nature* 287n.48) suggest the author may be Streater.
2. J. S., *The Continuation of This Session of Parliament, Justified*, collected May 16 1659—a strongly antityrannical, pro-Rump piece. Johns (*Nature* 292n.67), Donald Goddard Wing (*Short-Title Catalogue*, 3 vols, New York 1982–94) and Zaller (*GZ*) credit Streater. Its type ornaments and republican sentiments resemble those of *The Picture*.
3. J. S., *Government Described*, collected June 1. Johns (*Nature* 293) and Wing (*Short-Title*) credit Streater.
4. "William Allen," *Killing No Murder*, collected June 9. Zaller (*GZ*, "Sexby," "Streater") names Streater the printer, though without explanation. It refers (3) to *The Continuation*, printed three weeks before, while its newly written Appendix (16, lines 6–9) echoes *Continuation* 13, lines 22–6. Its imprint ("London, Printed MDCLIX") derives from the same distinctively battered block of type used to print that of *Government Described* a week before.

300. See Edmund Ludlow, *Memoirs* 2.65–9.
301. 23–4.
302. In addition to Lutaud's list of English and French editions (*Des Révolutions* 367–70), there are at least six more English editions, attributed variously to Allen, Sexby, and Titus, and dated 1741 (Edinburgh), 1784 (Dublin), and 1762, 1775, 1777, 1819 (London).
303. Lutaud, *Des Révolutions* 239, 348–9.

1900 claims to have been "Re-printed for the heirs of J. Brutus." Sexby's
pamphlet was quickly translated into French and published in 1658, 1793,
1798 (possibly), and 1800. A new translation of 1804, published in
London, addressed Napoleon I; an 1856 version of the 1658 translation,
probably published in Brussels, addressed Louis Napoleon.

The work's title circulated, sometimes with no evident knowledge of its
contents. In 1800, Maria Edgeworth concluded her novel *Castle Rackrent*
by glossing the Irish idiom of "kilt" for "much hurt": "In Ireland, not only
cowards, but the brave, 'die many times before their death.'—There *killing
is no murder.*"[304] In 1809, Theodore Edward Hook published *Killing No
Murder: A Farce in Two Acts*, with no discernible connection to Sexby.[305] In
Killing No Murder; or, A Plain Proof (1811), an anonymous writer advocated
parliamentary reform in a response to a letter by Lord Selkirk. In 1823,
an anonymous "Yorkshireman" attacked the feudal despotism built into
British game laws in *Legalized Murder: Or, Killing no Crime*. In 1846, Sir
Peter Laurie wrote *"Killing no murder"; or The Effects of Separate Confinement
on the Bodily and Mental Condition of Prisoners in the Government Prisons and
other Gaols in Great Britain and America*. In 1870, "One of the Million"
attacked the oppression of the poor by railways, bubble companies, and
the Bank Act of 1844 in *Stealing No Theft and Killing No Murder*. In 1871, it
provided the title for a temperance poem.[306] In Volume 3 of *Capital*, Marx
said that capitalists had formed a "union" to combat legislation against
industrial accidents and prove "that KILLING WAS NO MURDER when
it occurred for the sake of profit"; Engels glossed this as a reference to
Sexby's pamphlet.[307] James Keir Hardie used the phrase for the title of his
1911 defense of railway strikers against the government. And in 1834,
writing as "Agrarius" in the journal *Man*, George Petrie adapted not just
Sexby's title but his arguments, calling imperial capitalism a

> combination of murderous villains denominated kings, lords, and priests,
> together with their myrmidons, the masters, merchants, capitalists, and their
> hired assassins. This combination of miscreants has caused millions upon
> millions of men to be murdered in what has been termed "honorable war,"
> which establishes the maxim that "one murder makes a villain, millions the
> hero." . . . I reiterate the sentiment I formerly expressed, that KILLING, under
> the present circumstances, IS NOT MURDER!

Petrie echoes Sexby, but his linkage of kings, priests, and capitalists sounds
more like Winstanley.[308] *Killing No Murder* rivals *Antigone* in its power to
attract Creon-hating adapters, and its practical and discursive legacy
presents us with something more than the irruption of irrational violence

304. London 1965, 85; thanks to Deidre Lynch.
305. 3rd edn, New York 1809.
306. Lutaud, *Des Révolutions* 368.
307. *MECW* 37.93, 904n.19; thanks to Ed White.
308. Louis James, ed., *English Popular Literature 1819–1851*, New York 1976, 263–4; thanks to
     Simon Joyce.

or the containment of tyrannicidal subversion. In its reception, at least, Sexby's pamphlet succeeded beyond his dreams, for it outlived him and continued to function as part of antityrannical republican practice.

I'll conclude by comparing Sexby's natural rights-based struggle against *de facto* political theory to the contemporary struggle of liberal and marxist proponents of "essentialist" natural right against conservative theorists of decisionism. Then I'll compare his tyrannicidal project with contemporary acts of political violence.

Between the world wars, the decisionism of German conservative revolutionaries like Oswald Spengler, Ernst Jünger, Martin Heidegger, and Carl Schmitt promoted an antidemocratic political ethic promising that radical will would abrogate the rule of constitutional law, forming a new Nietzschean authenticity through what Schmitt called "a pure decision not based on reason and discussion and not justifying itself . . . an absolute decision created out of nothingness. . . . This decisionism is essentially dictatorship, not legitimacy."[309] In *The Concept of the Political*, which he published in 1932, the year before he joined the Nazi Party, Schmitt reveals an unflagging hostility to any ideology that attempts to advance the interests of a particular group in the name of universalist principles such as natural law, justice, freedom, and the interests of humanity. Political legitimacy resides in the ability to conduct practical politics, which is nothing more than the act of distinguishing *friends* clearly from *enemies*, and making that distinction stick by initiating a condition of actual or potential warfare.[310] Schmitt idolizes Hobbes, "by far the greatest and perhaps the sole truly systematic political thinker," and praises his attempt "to instill in man once again 'the mutual relation between protection and obedience.' . . . Hobbes himself had experienced this truth in the terrible times of civil war, because then all legitimate and normative illusions with which men like to deceive themselves regarding political realities in periods of untroubled security vanish." Schmitt sees Hobbes's social contract as the militant association of "friends" in a nation, who exist in a state of war with "enemy" nations, so that the "high points of politics are simultaneously the moments in which the enemy is, in concrete clarity, recognized as the enemy."[311]

As a virtuoso use of this friend/enemy paradigm, Schmitt turns to Cromwell's speech opening his second Protectorate Parliament on September 17 1656, which I considered earlier in this chapter.[312] Firth calls this speech the turning point of the Protectorate, presumably because

309. *Political Theology*, Cambridge 1985, 66.
310. Chicago 1996, 54, 66, 72. On Schmitt and decisionism, see Strong's introduction (ix–xxxi) and Habermas, *The New Conservatism*, Cambridge, MA, 1989, 128–39. Anderson groups Schmitt with Strauss, Hayek, and Oakeshott as conservative thinkers who found a common agenda in "holding popular sovereignty at bay" ("Intransigent" 11).
311. *Concept* 92n., 52, 67.
312. Ibid. 67–8; Abbott, *Writings* 4.260–79.

Cromwell used it to turn decisively toward something like a dictatorship
or monarchy with only a *de facto* legitimacy.[313] Cromwell begins his speech
in classic Hobbesian fashion, arguing that "the first lesson of nature . . . is
being and preservation," then moves on with reiterative decisionist clarity
of purpose to specify the satanic Spanish threat to England's being:

> Why, truly, your great enemy is the Spaniard. He is. He is a natural enemy, he
> is naturally so. He is naturally so, throughout, as I said before, throughout all
> your enemies, through that enmity that is in him against all that is of God that
> is in you. . . . And truly when I say that he is naturally throughout an enemy, an
> enmity is put into him by God. *I will put an enmity between thy seed and her seed,*
> which goes but for little among statesmen, but it is more considerable than all
> things.[314]

Cromwell effectively reduces the political landscape to a binary field of
"friends" and "enemies" by invoking the defensive Armada as a precedent
for his own distinctly offensive imperial ventures in the Spanish Caribbean. Despite his own Catholic background, Schmitt admires Cromwell's
theological view of the world, which leads, "just as does the distinction of
friend and enemy, to a categorization of men and makes impossible the
undifferentiated optimism of a universal conception of man." For both,
the designation of friend and enemy occurs not only between nations, but
within them: "As long as the state is a political entity this requirement for
internal peace compels it in critical situations to decide also upon the
domestic enemy. Every state provides, therefore, some kind of formula for
the declaration of an internal enemy."[315] Cromwell and his friends har-
rowed the 1656 Parliament thoroughly, excluding one hundred members
and prompting fifty or sixty more to refuse their seats out of solidarity.[316]
As we have seen, Cromwell's speech excoriates Edward Sexby as a
"wretched creature" whose trip to Madrid revealed him as "an apostate
from religion and all honesty."[317] The hateful apostate roving the borders
sharpens up the contours of the dictatorial nation state. In his character
of a tyrant, Sexby responded to this decisionist art of rule: tyrants "make
war to divert and busy the people: and besides to have a pretence to raise
moneys and to make new levies, if they either distrust their old forces or
think them not sufficient. The war with Spain serveth his Highness to this
purpose, and upon no other justice was it begun at first, or is still
continued."[318] Similarly, Protectorate republicans such as Harrington,
Vane, and Milton opposed premature imperial conflicts with the European powers.[319]

313. *Last* 1.1.
314. Abbott, *Writings* 4.260, 261–2.
315. *Concept* 65, 46.
316. Firth, *Last* 1.1, 16.
317. Abbott, *Writings* 4.261–2, 264, 267–9.
318. *S* 5.
319. David Armitage, "Cromwellian"; and "John Milton: Poet Against Empire," Armitage et
    al., *Milton* 206–25.

I don't want to press so hard on this analogy as to collapse Cromwell and Hitler, English antipopery and German antibolshevism, Sexby and the Jews. But I do think Schmitt's fascist admiration for Cromwell's speech can help us feel anew the loathing it inspired among many observers. Titus found the speech "insolent beyond all show of prudence."[320] William Howard, like many of Cromwell's opponents, fastened on what Milton would call the satanic "tyrant's plea" of necessity, observing that Cromwell made it the "great standing law of the world to which all other municipal laws ought to give place."[321] Giavarina wrote the Doge that Cromwell's speech attempted to cover up his irregular declaration of war against Spain without parliamentary consent.[322] In responding to this "decisionist" Cromwell, Sexby approaches (but does not quite reach) something like a counter-decisionism. As we have seen, he argues that the success or failure of tyrannicide indicates its legitimacy: Jehoiada had no special warrant to kill Athaliah, and "any man might have done what Jehoiada did as lawfully, that could have done it as effectually as he." In his suggestion that the tyrannicide will become his own precedent, Sexby verges on a decisionist collapse of act and norm, but only with regard to God and the Sanhedrin. He stops short of a Hobbist or *de facto* decisionism, for any action must remain responsible to "the equity and justice of the act itself"—the collective and democratic imperatives of the *salus populi*.[323] Sexby's decisionism is to Cromwell's as Sartre's is to Schmitt's.

Schmitt's decisionism has enjoyed a revival among his anti-humanist, anti-liberal, and post-marxist admirers. Writing on California's Proposition 187, designed to deny social services to illegal immigrants, Paul Piccone and Gary Ulmen recall Schmitt's friend/enemy distinction and even Cromwell's Hispanophobia:

> If there is not a common cultural horizon, if it is all open to the world and it becomes impossible to distinguish between inside and outside, the US as a distinct cultural and political entity will sooner or later cease to exist. There have to be shared traditions, customs, values, etc. . . . And if there are particular ethnic groups who are unassimilable or unwilling to assimilate to American society, does it make sense to have them join communities already on the verge of dysfunctionality?[324]

And there are strong formal analogies to certain currents of anti-humanist French thought—with a link to Schmitt, perhaps, through Nietzsche and Heidegger. In chapter 3, we saw Noam Chomsky's natural law anarchism in debate with Michel Foucault's Nietzschean decisionism. The debate continues today, in the conflict between "essentialist" arguments (by

---

320. *CCSP* 309.
321. Firth, *Last* 9–10. *Paradise Lost* 4.394. See Armitage, "Cromwellian" 551.
322. *CSPV* 31.266; Abbott, *Writings* 4.279.
323. *S* 11.
324. Quoted in Elias José Palti, "Is There a *Telos* Right?" *Telos* 107, 1996, 121. See also *Telos* 72, 1987, a special issue devoted to Schmitt.

liberals and some marxists) about human nature and the *salus populi*, and "anti-essentialist" social constructionist arguments for decisionism and the will to power. The latter haven't worn particularly well outside the university, or even inside, and we have yet to see any notably successful anti-humanist liberation movements; the jury is still out, and it won't return so long as anti-humanist theorists continue to practice critique without specifying its normative grounds.[325] Too frequently, left anti-humanists forget the lesson—embodied nowhere better than in the chilling career of Carl Schmitt and his followers—that bourgeois humanism may be negated in a fascist direction as well as a socialist, feminist, and democratic one. A consideration of the normative grounding of resistance theory in relatively democratic conceptions of natural law could have an important role in revising a conception of early modern political culture still dominated by an *a priori* hypothesis of universal authoritarianism.[326]

Second, I think we can usefully compare Sexby's project to contemporary acts of political violence. I'm not inclined to claim any abstract truth or beauty for assassination and terrorism—I'll leave that to Marinetti, Baudrillard, and other gleeful exploders of Enlightenment rationality. To my eye, there's a world of difference between ruling-class assassinations of popular political leaders (Pearse, Connolly, Sandino, Evers, King, Allende, Aquino, Romero, Biko, Hani, Mendes) and popular and insurrectionary assassinations of ruling-class leaders (the Romanovs, McKinley, Ceaucescu, Somoza).[327] But both sorts of assassination suggest the impossibility of a totally administered world, revealing the ruling class's inability to maintain such a world through administration alone, or the people's refusal to be administered. Jürgen Habermas—that notable non-incendiary—gives a surprisingly sympathetic account of terrorism's structural position in the contemporary neo-feudal world of bureaucratic administration:

> Terrorism should be seen together with neo-populism as a reaction against the contraction of politics to administration on the one hand, and pure acclamation on the other.... Terrorism does not fall from the sky. It is a structural phenomenon.... Although this may be a very unpopular view, I think we must say that terrorism is not an irrational phenomenon but should be categorized

325. Nancy Fraser, *Unruly* 17–34.
326. Bloch, who attacks Schmitt's fascist decisionism, also says that "The natural law of a real enlightenment could put tyrannicide as well as the social contract to good use," instancing Calvin, Mariana, and other early modern resistance theorists (*Natural* 149–52, 35).
327. See Claribel Alegría and Darwin Flakoll, *Death of Somoza*, Willimantic, CT, 1996. Of course, some political assassinations (Huey Long, Malcolm X) resist easy classification under either heading, and most political murderers aren't exactly "assassins" since they kill unknown civilian workers and their children—in Korea, Southeast Asia, Belfast, El Salvador, Beirut, Baghdad, Chechnya, Kabul, Chiapas, Waco, Oklahoma City, Rwanda, Sarajevo, *et bloody cetera*. Americans tend not to think of themselves as political murderers, since they and their allies drop their righteous retributive bombs from above, while their enemies without air forces explode their wretched apostate bombs from the side.

with other attempts to react against the same structural processes: in its own way, it is an attempt to reaffirm politics in the face of pure administration.[328]

Habermas does not celebrate terrorist violence, but tries to reflect critically on what we might call Cromwell's ethical vantage point: the Whitehall or White House view that denies the terrorism of friends, demonizes the terrorism of enemies, and purges terrorist violence of its ideological substance.

For instance, British efforts to depict Irish republican violence as wanton Gaelic savagery fail to blot out the venerable history of colonial violence in Ireland, including invasion, colonization, impressment, massacres, enclosure and eviction, free market genocide through starvation, deportation, illegal trials and detention, and century after century of extracted surplus labor. Similarly, American historians have worked long and hard to obscure the ideological commitments of our seemingly endless queue of crazed lone gunmen, but their diverse motives remain visible. After shooting Abraham Lincoln, John Wilkes Booth voiced his racist Confederate republicanism by sending a cry of "Sic semper tyrannis!" through Ford's Theater. Booth's given names, along with those of his father and brother (Junius Brutus Sr and Jr), also resonate with a certain republican tradition. In 1901, the revolutionary anarchist Leon F. Czolgosz momentarily dimmed Buffalo's Pan American Exposition—that festive, electric-lit masque celebrating the dawn of the American Century—by shooting President William McKinley in the stomach and pronouncing him "an enemy of good working people." Horrified at the state murder of the Rosenbergs and the Kennedy brothers' attempts to assassinate Castro, Lee Harvey Oswald became a committed Communist and, in 1963, shot John Kennedy. Posthumous hagiographies have tried to forget the American ruling class's virulent hatred of Martin Luther King Jr in the late 1960s, when he moved from liberal civil rights reformism toward anti-imperialist socialist internationalism; his death in April 1968 remains mysterious. Two months later, the fervent anti-Zionist Sirhan Sirhan, a Christian Arab displaced from his native Jerusalem, shot Bobby Kennedy, the fervent sponsor of fighter planes for Israel.

The modern ethics of murder in the contemporary US recalls Diomedes the pirate's thesis about quantitative changes becoming qualitative. Murderers of one or two, if caught, get jail or the needle or the chair. Two-figure serial murderers become the demonic centers of a journalistic, literary, and cinematic cult. Political assassins or three-figure political murderers like the Oklahoma bombers provoke a sense of national trauma, with accompanying threats of summary justice, martial law, and the nationwide erosion of civil liberties. But four-, five-, six-, or seven-figure political murderers become sages and celebrities, write their memoirs, and walk the streets in safety. After scrubbing off a few million

---

328. *Autonomy and Solidarity*, rev. edn, London 1992, 76.

damned Indochinese spots, Henry Kissinger gave interviews, taught seminars, and starred in sympathetic revisionist accounts of the Nixon era. He
continues to enjoy quite a few nice meals out.[329]

Killing Noe Murder has not found its way into the Hobbes-and-Locke-
dominated history of political philosophy, or the Pocock-inspired history
of republican discourse. Its remarkable publication history, and the
radical pamphlet literature of the English Revolution more generally,
have no place inside the new historicist and revisionist models of literary
culture as textual production, subjectification, and the quest for personal
advancement within a unified system. The client's ode to the patron
appears as a commodity, consumed once and for all, and falls silent when
either the client or the patron dies. If it should be reborn in the author's
collected works, it remains a commodity, consumed and assimilated in the
literary marketplace. But resistance literature resists consumption. Its
proper rhythm of existence is not the circuit of commodity exchange but
the serial immortality of the phoenix, for it can actually feed on the death
of its author or its victim. If the literature of patronage enables envious
people to negotiate for themselves an increase in status and wealth within
a relatively fixed hierarchy, then antityrannical writing enables discontented people to associate in a project aimed at unfixing that hierarchy
and replacing it with something better.

If we hold *Killing Noe Murder* to a rigorously practical standard, it comes
up short—as the shards of a bad utopia, or, at best, a premature one that
failed to realize itself. But such a whiggish perspective would slight its
manifest appeal for a succession of radical, plebeian, and proletarian
translators, publishers, and readers. They kept its forlorn negativity alive
for two centuries after Sexby's death, using it to help imagine an alternative to the hopeless present. Neither the Protectorate nor any succeeding
regime could consume and assimilate this indigestible pamphlet, which
was, like St John's apocalyptic little book, sweet in the mouth but bitter in
the belly. There is still something tonic in Sexby's reminder that a servile
client can become a republican tyrannicide—that Ehud arrives at Eglon's
court with a gift in his hand and a dagger strapped to his thigh.

---

329. In *Pirates and Emperors: International Terrorism in the Real World*, New York 1986, Noam
  Chomsky maintains Diomedes' outrage at America's Alexandrian ethics.

9

The Diggers' *Hortus Inconclusus*

For "mine" and "thine"—those chilly words which introduce innumerable wars into the world—should be eliminated from that holy Church. . . . The poor would not envy the rich, because there would be no rich. Neither would the poor be despised by the rich, for there would be no poor. All things would be in common.

—St John Chrysostom, on Acts 4.32

A certain kind of capitalism, nourished at the expense of the peasants through the agency of the State, has risen up in opposition to the commune; it is in its interest to crush the commune. It is also in the interest of the landed proprietors to set up the more or less well-off peasants as an intermediate agrarian class, and to turn the poor peasants—that is to say the majority—into simple wage-earners. This will mean cheap labour! And how would a commune be able to resist, crushed by the extortions of the State, robbed by business, exploited by the landowners, undermined from within by usury?

—Karl Marx, draft letter to Vera Zasulich

> Then Clubs and Diamonds cast away,
> For Hearts and Spades must win the day.

—Anonymous, *The Diggers Mirth*

Rational Hunger

The canon of early modern English literature has opened up to women and the writers of many marginal or non-literary texts, but it seems less interested in the voices of the hungry. Desire and deprivation may produce language itself, but some sorts of deprivation still seem to be more audible than others. Erotic deprivation produces the love lament, deprivation of political power the poem of patronage, both sorts of deprivation the Petrarchan political sonnet. Deprivation of bodily freedom produces the wife's diary or the prison journal or the Foxean captivity narrative, of political liberty the philippic or manifesto. Even deprivation of life produces, through the melodious tear of a bereft swain, the pastoral elegy. But no parallel genre responds to the deprivation of food. Early modern writers typically invoke hunger as the vehicle for metaphor, speaking of the communicant's spiritual hunger for the Eucharist, or the Petrarchan *devoto*'s hunger for love. But they usually treat hunger itself as the condition of *the other*, as in that cruel Renaissance epithet *starveling*, which almost suggests an elective character type or profession. Frequently, they depict the poor as mouths without brains—perhaps a vision of their actual hunger, perhaps a guilty displacement of ruling-class voraciousness: Sidney's hungry (and therefore hangable) rebellious peasants in *The Countess of Pembroke's Arcadia*, Shakespeare's famished (and therefore stabbable) Jack Cade in *Henry VI, Part II*, Spenser's starving (and therefore crushable) Irish kerns in his *View of the Present State of Ireland*, which serves the imperial project by turning an effect of English barbarism into its cause, as if to say, "See how savage the Irish are when deprived of food? Let us starve such savagery back into the bog from which it came."[1] This objectivizing point of view reappears in the modern study of "the vagrancy problem" in early modern England, which scholars might (but seldom do) describe as "the next meal problem."[2]

Anorexia is the exception that proves the rule. In both its modern and premodern forms, it has commanded a good deal of recent critical attention, but if anorexia isn't exactly voluntary, neither is it altogether imposed from without. Indeed, it may lie at the border of volition, thus inviting a meditation on will itself: its social construction, its capacity for self-reflection and self-destruction. But sheer, brutal, involuntary hunger is another matter. It provokes an analytical embarrassment not unlike that prompted by the sight of the hungry through a restaurant window. Hunger's object of desire, if not exactly a brute fact free of symbolic systems, remains somehow impoverished, semiotically meager, too thin to bear up under sustained analysis. For one thing, the hungry and the literate tend to be mutually exclusive groups. Even when they aren't, the hungry tend to be less interested in writing about their hunger than in eating. And when literate people record their voices, they usually want to hear their legal testimony, their religious confessions, and their deferential greetings—not stark, embarrassing cries like "We want to eat!" Because hunger suggests a primal existential *need* instead of *desire*, anyone who discusses it risks that indelible epithet "essentialist humanism," and perhaps even a damning link with Sartre, who left the ontological category of "lack" for the social and natural category of "need."[3]

Because *need* and *hunger* resist a talking or writing cure, psychoanalysts feel more comfortable with *absence* and *lack*, whether the Freudian lack of the mother or the Lacanian gap in being and language. Mistrusting the idea of any "beyond" and reluctant to discuss material nature, anti-Sartrean postmodernists follow suit, and even go so far as to make lack the positive product, not the negative cause, of desire. Jean Baudrillard admits that the "'functional need'" for food is "not symbolic." But he

1. Sidney, 753–4; Spenser, Oxford 1970.
2. A. L. Beier, *Masterless Men: The Vagrancy Problem in England*, London 1985.
3. Though Sartre rejected Engels's dialectics of nature, his concepts of "scarcity" and "need" imply an untranscendable level of nature (*SSM* 91; *SCDR* 29–32, 79–82, 122–52).

quarantines this need in scare quotes, ignores its structural relation to desire, calls "need" the mythological byproduct of the subject's ideological separation from the object, rejects the idea of use value, and asks, "Is loss of status—or social non-existence—less upsetting than hunger?"[4] Well, yes, it is. But the question is badly posed: those who lose food unwillingly have always lost status, too, so they face social as well as natural non-existence. A prudent postmodernist, hesitant to call hunger an effect of discourse or the traumatic symptom of a cleft in being, might simply say that it always exists within discursive and conceptual systems, so that no one can point to hunger-as-such. But this statement, while formally true, rings a little hollow, and is of interest, perhaps, only to those still digesting a recent meal. The easiest way around these problems is simply to ignore them, and so also the majority of humankind throughout history whose lives have been shaped by hunger and (just as important) the fear of hunger.

I want to approach this problem through a portion of Ernst Bloch's 1400-page Expressionist prose poem, *The Principle of Hope*, which criticizes several psychoanalytical visions of the unconscious:

> The unconscious of psychoanalysis is . . . *never a Not-Yet-Conscious*, an element of progressions; it consists rather of regressions. Accordingly, even the process of making this unconscious conscious only clarifies What Has Been; i.e., *there is nothing new in the Freudian unconscious.* This became even clearer when C. G. Jung, the psychoanalytic fascist, reduced the libido and its unconscious contents entirely to the primeval. . . . On a bi-sexual foundation, Adler posits, in supreme capitalist fashion, the will to power as the basic human drive: primarily man wants to rule and overpower. He wants to get from the bottom to the top, wants to lie on top, to pass from the female line in him to the male, feel himself individually confirmed as the victor. . . . Sexuality is itself only a means to the final goal, the attainment of power.

The drives animating these various models of the unconscious—Freud's oedipal/sexual drives, Jung's frenzy-drive, Adler's power-drive—all face backward, and Bloch links them with what he calls the "filled emotions (like envy, greed, admiration) . . . whose drive object lies ready, if not in respective individual attainability, then in the already available world."[5]

The contemporary study of Renaissance culture shows us versions of these familiar psychological drives. After the brief and contained heyday of Frye, polite literary critical society banished Jungian myth criticism as improperly ahistorical and universalist, but another sort of archetypalism survives among the more thematic sorts of deconstructive criticism and in the carnival of happy orifices celebrated by Bakhtin, with its festive gorging, vomiting, and excretion. Whereas *not eating* and *starving* slink down the hall to the gray departments of economic or social history, *feasting* as self-fashioning can belly up to the copious table of cultural

---

4. *For a Critique of the Political Economy of the Sign*, St Louis, MO, 1981, 69n., 70, 81. See also Ebert's critique of Deleuze and Guattari on need and desire (*Ludic* 55–7).
5. 1.56, 57, 74.

history and Geertzian thick description. Freud's analysis of the sexual/ oedipal drive flourishes, particularly as criticized and adapted by structuralist and feminist psychoanalysis.[6] Adler's theory has barely touched literary studies, but if its father is Nietzsche, its Foucauldian half-sibling thrives among new historicist genealogists of power/knowledge. And the accompanying "filled emotions" of envy, greed, and admiration have received sustained critical attention in studies of patronage, the literary marketplace, and theatricality inside the theater and out. Indeed, historical revisionists employ an implicitly Freudian paradigm, though Jonathan Clark and Kevin Sharpe might blanch at the thought. Just as Freud demotes conscious rationality as a principle of explanation, so revisionists demote ideological struggle. Just as Freudians see successful patients as those who adjust their id-driven quest for power to an immutable reality principle, and neurotics as sons and daughters who misrecognize their continuing quest for the love of the mother or father, so revisionists see loyal subjects as those who adjust their quest for advancement to a fixed and patriarchal patronage system, and sullen rebels as those who misrecognize their personal failure as political oppression. More than one Cambridge history seminar room might be fetchingly adorned with that ever-vigilant warning sign in the psychological advice bureau of Freud's Vienna: "Economic and social questions cannot be treated here."[7]

In criticizing these psychoanalytical drive theories, Bloch yokes historicism and humanism. On the one hand, he sees ostensibly universal drives as historically determinate products: Freud's "libido man lives—together with his dreamed wish-fulfillments—in the bourgeois world a few decades before and a few decades after 1900 (the key year of the secessionist 'liberation of the flesh from the spirit')." At the same time, he draws

---

6. Janet Adelman says "the unsatisfied ravenous attack of the infant on the breast provides the motive force for warfare" ("'Anger's My Meat': Feeding, Dependency, and Aggression in *Coriolanus*," in David Bevington and Jay L. Halio, eds, *Shakespeare: Pattern of Excelling Nature*, Newark, DE, 1978, 108–24, 111). The provident tit of the capitalist academy seldom sends such whimsies to bed unfed. But compare Winstanley's dialectical psychoanalysis (*W* 519–20) and Sartre's: "No one has the right to regard the fear of famine which is so striking in underdeveloped societies, or the Great Fears of peasants under feudalism confronting the spectre of starvation, as mere subjective feelings. On the contrary, they represent the interiorisation of objective conditions and are in themselves an *origin of praxis*" (*SCDR* 149; see also *SSM* 117–18).

7. Bloch, *Principle* 1.66. This sign—since translated into French, Slovenian, and English—is the *Real* Freudo-Lacanian *nom/non-du-père*. In *Civilization and Its Discontents*, Freud attacks the communists' idea of a class struggle for justice: "To be sure, if an attempt is made to base this fight upon an abstract demand, in the name of justice, for equality for all men, there is a very obvious objection to be made—that nature, by endowing individuals with extremely unequal physical attributes and mental capacities, has introduced injustices against which there is no remedy" (New York 1961, 60n.1). Similarly, Slavoj Žižek says that proletarians attacking capitalism and feminists attacking patriarchy merely externalize and misrecognize the ineradicable trauma, the "autonegativity," that founds and constitutes their very identity ("Beyond Discourse Analysis," in Ernesto Laclau, *New Reflections on the Revolution of Our Time*, London 1990, 249–60, 251, 253). No historical revisionist or Presbyterian landlord could ask for more: tricked out as nature or being, capitalist productive relations blot out all thought of the *novum*.

attention to "the drive that is always left out of psychoanalytical theory"—
the drive to self-preservation, with hunger as its primary expression:

> Very little, all too little has been said so far about hunger. Although this goal
> also looks very primal or primeval. Because a man dies without nourishment,
> whereas we can live a little while longer without the pleasures of love-making. It
> is all the more possible to live without satisfying our power-drive, all the more
> possible without returning into the unconscious of our five-hundred-thousand-
> year-old forefathers. But the unemployed person on the verge of collapse, who
> has not eaten for days, has really been led to the oldest needy place of our
> existence and makes it visible. . . . In the late bourgeoisie, to which Freud's
> psychoanalysis also belongs, hunger was deleted. Or it became a subspecies of
> the libido, its "oral phase," as it were; subsequently, self-preservation does not
> occur as an original drive at all.[8]

Hunger seems almost purely subjective, focused on the subject's own
stomach, not the erotic or political object of desire. But it always has a
political potential as well as an existential reality, and it can help produce
class consciousness and revolutionary action:

> Hunger cannot help continually renewing itself. But if it increases uninter-
> rupted, satisfied by no certain bread, then it suddenly changes. The body-ego
> then becomes rebellious, does not go out in search of food merely within the
> old framework. It seeks to change the situation which has caused its empty
> stomach, its hanging head. The No to the bad situation which exists, the Yes to
> the better life that hovers ahead, is incorporated by the deprived into *revolution-
> ary interest*. This interest always begins with hunger, hunger transforms itself,
> having been taught, into an explosive force against the prison of deprivation.

Hunger has not only an unconscious, but a not-yet-conscious; it can
produce not only the emptily "filled" emotions, but also the utopian or
"expectant" emotions of anxiety, fear, and hope, emotions "whose drive-
intention is long-term, whose drive-object does not yet lie ready, not just
in respective individual attainability, but also in the already available
world, and therefore still occurs in the doubt about exit or entrance."[9]

"Venter non habet aures," said Cato the Elder, but sometimes, the
empty stomach does have ears, and pauses for a moment to ponder its
own growling. And sometimes, early modern literature presents hunger
sympathetically as the condition not just of starveling *others* but of the
hungry *self*. We hear this sort of hunger in the folktales of peasants, which
turn not to the church-sanctioned ritual feast, but to the luminous utopia
of the next meal.[10] We hear it in Milton, that compulsive humanizer of
God and angels, with his laboring, sweating, hungering, and eating cosmos
in *Paradise Lost*, his hungry Christ in *Paradise Regained*. We hear it in Mary
Rowlandson's captivity narrative, which changes her from an English

---

8. *Principle* 1.68, 64, 65, 67.
9. Ibid. 1.75, 74.
10. Robert Darnton, *The Great Cat Massacre*, New York 1984, 9–74.

housewife to a fugitive gleaner of corn and chewer of horse hooves.[11] And we hear it in the food riot that begins Shakespeare's *Coriolanus*:

> *First Citizen.* You are all resolved rather to die than to famish?
> *All.* Resolved, resolved.[12]

This desperate resolve sounds at first like a hunger-crazed non-choice, but it also suggests a significant distinction between a passive death inside the customary order of the Roman polis, and an active death that attempts to transform the polis and the sorts of hunger it produces. At such a revolutionary moment, individuals "are directly threatened, in practico-inert necessity, by the impossibility of life," and "thus the group constitutes itself as the radical impossibility of living, which threatens serial multiplicity."[13] And indeed, this very rebellion pushes Rome into granting the plebeians formal representation through the *tribuni plebis*, thus creating the triune Roman republic. Necessity gives birth to a grim freedom: the desperate resolve of Shakespeare's plebeians announces the economically motivated movement of previously voiceless persons out of the crisis-wracked private sphere of customary labor into the public sphere of political debate and revolutionary struggle.

The non-choice faced by Shakespeare's plebeians crops up repeatedly in the context of early modern food riots, which tended to appear not as the spontaneous eruption of bodily needs, but as customary and orderly communal actions.[14] The food riot is a rebellion of the belly, which Bacon calls the worst kind, but it's also a rebellion of wounded reason.[15] In 1607, the author of *The Diggers of Warwickshire to all other Diggers*, a manifesto for the Midlands Rising, denounces depopulation through enclosure, and calls it better to "manfully die, then hereafter to be pined to death for want of that which those devouring encroachers do serve their fat hogs and sheep withal."[16] In January 1642, a crowd of artificers and the poor marched on the House of Commons with a petition warning that "many of us had not, nor can tell where to get bread to sustain ourselves and families," so that without food, they would be "enforced to lay hold on the next remedy which is at hand . . . and rather than your petitioners will suffer themselves and their families to perish through hunger and misery, though hitherto patiently groaned under, they cannot leave any means unassayed for their relief."[17] A short time later, fifteen thousand impoverished porters warned that they would soon be forced "to extremities, not

11. *The Captive*, Tucson 1990.
12. *William Shakespeare* 1.1.4–6.
13. *SCDR* 342.
14. Thompson, *Customs in Common*, New York 1991, 185–351.
15. *Works* 12.126.
16. J. Halliwell-Phillipps, *The Marriage of Wit and Wisdom*, London 1846, 141. This may be the first reference to agrarian rebels as "Diggers."
17. *To the Honourable the House of Commons Assembled in Parliament.*

fit to be named, and to make good that saying, 'That necessity hath no law'; it is true, that we have nothing to lose but our lives."[18]

In March 1650, nine Northamptonshire starvelings issued a broadside with a typically verbose but eloquent seventeenth-century title: *A Declaration of the Grounds and Reasons Why We the Poor Inhabitants of the Town of Wellinborrow, in the County of Northampton, Have Begun and Give Consent to Dig up, Manure and Sow Corn upon the Common, and Waste Ground, Called Bareshanke, Belonging to the Inhabitants of Wellinborrow, by Those that Have Subscribed, and Hundreds More that Give Consent.* Poor relief has broken down, and though the justices at the recent quarter sessions ordered that a charity stock be established for 1169 receivers of alms, charity does not yet reign in Wellinborough:

> We have spent all we have, our trading is decayed, our wives and children cry for bread, our lives are a burden to us, divers of us having 5, 6, 7, 8, 9 in family, and we cannot get bread for one of them by our labor; rich men's hearts are hardened, they will not give us if we beg at their doors; if we steal, the law will end our lives, divers of the poor are starved to death already, and it were better for us that are living to die by the sword then by the famine:[19] and now we consider that the earth is our mother, and that God hath given it to the children of men, and that the common and waste grounds belong to the poor, and that we have a right to the common ground both from the law of the land, reason and scriptures; and therefore we have begun to bestow our righteous labor upon it, and we shall trust the spirit for a blessing upon our labor.[20]

The rhythmic opening indictment leads these tenants and wage laborers to the familiar painful choice of passive death by famine or active death by struggle, when they take up the patrician sword. But a third option appears immediately, when they begin beating it into a plowshare. The Northamptonshire Diggers reflect on their own experience in the light of popular religion and, with filial piety, speak of "bestowing" their labor on Bareshanke's Mother Earth—a bit grandiose, but then, what else does anyone have to bestow? "No man can be rich, but he must be rich, either by his own labors, or by the labors of other men helping him."[21] The hungry poor articulate themselves with utopian force, trying to end not

18. *To the Honourable the Knights, Citizens and Burgesses in the Commons House of Parliament Now Assembled.*

19. "They that be slain with the sword are better than they that be slain with hunger" (Lam. 4.9)—later the motto of the Anti-Corn Law League (*MECW* 4.658). "If we fight we die and if we do not fight we die. So we will fight" (the Taiping leader Shih Ta-kai, quoted in Smedley, *Great* 199).

20. *W* 650. Fellow-travelling sentimental anachronists may hear a remarkable choral response in an 1860 manifesto by English hand-mule spinners and self-actor minders: "Plainly speaking, our lives are to us a burthen; and, while we are confined to the mills *nearly two days a week more* than the other operatives of the country, we feel like helots in the land, and that we are perpetuating a system injurious to ourselves and future generations. . . . This, therefore, is to give you most respectful notice that when we commence work again after the Christmas and New Year's holidays, we shall work 60 hours per week, and no more, or from six to six, with one hour and a half out" (*MECW* 35.299).

21. *W* 511. Winstanley also speaks of "bestowing" labor on the commons (ibid. 384, 387).

only their hunger but also the social structure that allows it to exist in the first place. Their hunger has ears, a voice, and a rational revolutionary potential.

Gerrard Winstanley, the Diggers' chief spokesman and theorist, sees hunger as the fundamental drive. Humankind fell not through pride, but through fear of hunger and want, which

> begets hypocrisy, subtlety, envy, and hardness of heart, which makes a man to break all promises and engagements, and to seek to save himself in others' ruin, and to suppress and oppress every one that does not say as he says, and do as he does. . . . For imagination begins to tell the soul; if thou enjoyest not fullness of all objects, thou wilt want and starve for food, and so presently fear of poverty takes the throne and reigns; and fear bids thee go, get what thou canst, by hook or by crook, lest thou want, and perish, and die miserably.[22]

The Digger commonwealth will punish those who maintain private property or steal by leaving them to labor and eat without the benefits and pleasures of community, thus repeating the isolation implied by their actions.[23] Winstanley's very writing proceeds from hunger, for he customarily forsook his companions, his ordinary labor, and his food for days at a time in order to write.[24] In this isolated, voluntary hunger, he adopts the traditional ascetic technic of the impoverished prophet seeking individual and spiritual transcendence, but his visions seek the collective and political extirpation of involuntary hunger.

Gerrard Winstanley was born in Wigan, Lancashire, probably in 1609.[25]

---

22. Ibid. 379, 460.
23. Ibid. 265, 196–7.
24. Christopher Hill, *Winstanley: The Law of Freedom and Other Writings*, Harmondsworth 1973, 156.
25. Sabine's excellent edition of Winstanley (*W*) omits his first three tracts (*The Mysterie of God*, *The Breaking of the Day of God*, and *The Saints Paradise*, all probably 1648), which I'll quote from the collected 1649 edition, entitled *Several Pieces*, and his Preface to that collection, which I'll quote from Hill's edition of Winstanley. In "A Newly Discovered Pamphlet by Gerrard Winstanley," G. E. Aylmer presents *Englands Spirit Unfoulded*, and Keith Thomas does the same for the Digger *Declaration* from Iver in "Another Digger Broadside" (*WIR* 109–23, 124–37). Paul Hardacre found a letter Winstanley wrote his landlady, the prophetess Lady Eleanor Davies/Douglas; see "Gerrard Winstanley in 1650," *Huntington Library Quarterly* 22, 1958–59. Sabine's Introduction remains the best short guide to Winstanley's life and work (*W* 1–70). For others, see Hill's Penguin edition, his discussions of Winstanley in *The World Turned Upside Down*, and his "Religion of Gerrard Winstanley" (*Collected* 2.185–252). Andrew Bradstock usefully narrates Winstanley's career in *Faith in the Revolution*, London 1997, 69–81; Manning narrates the story of the Diggers as a group in *1649*, 109–34. In *The Alchemy of Revolution*, New York 1990, David Mulder combines a standard critique of "anachronism" in Winstanley studies, a strained argument that his dialectical thought cloaks an alchemical core, an important survey of agrarian history in Winstanley's Surrey, and a thorough biographical survey of the known Diggers (249–86, 215–48, 299–331). In "Gerrard Winstanley and the Digger Movement in Walton and Cobham," *The Historical Journal* 37.4, 1994, John Gurney definitively establishes the local roots of the Diggers' second settlement, at Cobham. J. C. Davis's study of Winstanley in *Utopia and the Ideal Society*, Cambridge 1981, 170–203, has strongly influenced revisionists. Timothy Kenyon compares More and Winstanley in *Utopian Communism and Political Thought in Early Modern England*, London 1989. For other book-length studies of Winstanley, see Lewis H. Berens, *The Digger Movement in the Days of*

He was apprenticed to a London cloth merchant in 1630, and in 1637, became a freeman of the city. In 1640, he married Susan King, daughter of a London barber surgeon. In 1643, after being cheated by Matthew Backhouse, a London merchant and future slave trader, he went bankrupt.[26] He moved to Cobham, Surrey, the home of his father-in-law, and found work as a cowherd. In 1648, he published four extraordinary religious pamphlets which seem traditional only by comparison with his own later work.[27] In these works, he attempted to reconcile scriptural accounts of a final judgment with his belief in general redemption (illegal under the 1648 Blasphemy Act, as Bradstock points out) by reintroducing a sort of Purgatory: God will redeem the elect immediately, while the rest will linger until the last hour.[28] Winstanley conflates humankind with the earth, presents the angels as regenerate saints, characterizes God and Satan as spirits within humankind rather than outside forces at a distance, and describes tilling the ground as a sort of prayer.[29] He denounces any form of established church and reveals a deep sympathy with the English poor.[30] But he also advises against revolutionary action: the persecuted saints should "wait patiently on the Lord," not fight, and "If thou lie under temptations of men, of losses, of poverty, of reproaches, it is God's dispensation to thee, wait with an humble quiet spirit upon him, till he give deliverance."[31] He acknowledges the temporal sufferings of those who have "no riches, no certain dwelling place, no way to get a subsistence," then counsels trust in God, who sees hungry and naked people and advocates charity, not revolutionary action.[32] Invoking Foxe's *Book of Martyrs* and the mainstream tradition of English antipopery, he limits his

---

the *Commonwealth*, 1901, rpt London 1961; David W. Petegorsky, *Left-Wing Democracy in the English Civil War*, London 1940; T. Wilson Hayes, *Winstanley the Digger*, Cambridge, MA, 1979; George Shulman, *Radicalism and Reverence*, Berkeley and Los Angeles 1989; the collection of essays in *Prose Studies* 22.2, 1999, rpt as Andrew Bradstock, ed., *Winstanley and the Diggers 1649–1999*, London 2000; and particularly Olivier Lutaud's *Winstanley: Socialisme et christianisme sous Cromwell*, Paris 1976. Typically, Anglophone scholars exalt or snub Winstanley in the national context of English political history and radical religion, but the comparative study of peasant revolt and radical religion are at least as important. Berens begins with a chapter on the Reformation in Germany and includes "The Twelve Articles of the German Peasantry" of 1525 as an appendix (*Digger* 1–11, 235–40). Bradstock examines the liberation theology of Winstanley and Thomas Müntzer. In " 'Saith the spirit,' " Lewis Daly contextualizes Winstanley's project amid popular struggles for the land from ancient Canaan to contemporary Latin America.

26. See R. J. Dalton, "Gerrard Winstanley: The Experience of Fraud 1641," *The Historical Journal* 34.4, 1991. Since new merchants like Backhouse, enriched by the slave trade and colonial plantations, played a crucial role in the English Revolution, this episode reveals the interrelation of black and white proletarian labor and struggle in the seventeenth-century Atlantic world.

27. On Winstanley's early writings, see Nicola Baxter, "Gerrard Winstanley's Experimental Knowledge of God," *Journal of Ecclesiastical History* 39.2, 1988; and J. Sanderson, "The Digger's Apprenticeship: Winstanley's Early Writings," *Political Studies* 22.4, 1974.

28. *Mysterie* A3ʳ, 15, 51; *Saints* 133; Bradstock, *Faith* 89.

29. *Breaking* 18; *Saints* A3ʳ, 51, 68, 85, 89; *W* 136–7.

30. *Breaking* 64, 79, 115; *Mysterie* 33; *Saints* 2.

31. *Breaking* 133; *Mysterie* 59.

32. *Saints* 33, 123.

criticism to the hireling clergy, declining to blame the "magistrates" (king or Parliament) misled by them. Social evils have an internal, moral origin: "All outward abominations in men's practices came from the indwelling of the beast in every man's heart."[33]

Was Winstanley "caught inside" a theological form of thought in these early works? For him, as for so many seventeenth-century writers, the sacred/secular opposition falls flat.[34] But an opposition between an "idealist" and a "materialist" religion—between a serial collective of expectant saints waiting on Jesus, and a pledged group of agrarian saints recreating him in their very praxis—is a different matter. The great change seems to have arrived in January 1649. On the day before King Charles was sentenced to death, Winstanley completed *The New Law of Righteousness*, one of the most remarkable works of the seventeenth-century sectarian imagination. It formulated a communist program for peacefully revolutionizing English society. Winstanley heard a divine command to the poor laborers and copyholders of England to begin communal cultivation of the waste lands and commons: "Work together. Eat bread together; declare this all abroad."[35] This Genesis-based exordium, which fuses production, consumption, and prophecy, generated the Digger movement. In the Preface to *Several Pieces*, Winstanley insists on both the spiritual origin of his Digger revelation, and its distance from his early works:

> And therefore though some have said I had done well if I had left writing when I had finished *The Saints Paradise*: surely such men know little of the spirit's inward workings; and truly what I have writ since or before that time, I was carried forth in the work by the same power, delivering it to others as I received it, and I received it not from books nor study.[36]

During the next eighteen months, the Diggers established at least ten communes in Surrey, Northamptonshire, Kent, Buckinghamshire, Gloucestershire, and Nottinghamshire.[37] Winstanley's own commune, under the leadership of William Everard, took shape near Walton, Surrey, at St George's Hill, which the Diggers desanctified (and resanctified) as "George Hill," thus unhorsing George and changing him from a saint and a knight to a farmer tilling the earth—a *georgos* tilling *gea*. On April 1 1649, a small group of Diggers broke ground, sowing parsnips, carrots, and beans. Winstanley published fourteen new works during the next year. Nine Digger pamphlets by other hands appeared between December

---

33. *Breaking* 128–31, 124.
34. Bradstock (*Faith* 82–107, 117–19) astutely criticizes Hill's occasional attempts to move past Winstanley's religious language and George Juretic's effort to distinguish an early "millenarian" and late "secular" Winstanley in "Digger No Millenarian," *Journal of the History of Ideas* 36, 1975.
35. *W* 190.
36. Hill, *Winstanley* 156–7.
37. Thomas, "Another" 58–9.

1648 and April 1650.[38] In the summer of 1649, after sustained resistance, the George Hill colony moved to nearby Cobham Heath, where it enjoyed substantial local support.[39] We know little about the fate of the other communes, but this one folded in April 1650, after a series of gentry-led legal actions, boycotts, and physical attacks. Late in 1652, Winstanley published his communist utopia, *The Law of Freedom in a Platform*. In later life he probably became a Quaker. He died in 1676.[40]

The capitalist transformation of English agriculture has hovered over each chapter of this book. In this chapter, I will argue that the Diggers produced the most important seventeenth-century critique of this trans-formation from the point of view of its victims. With their vision of a true commonwealth's freedom rooted in the land, the Diggers take us beyond the desperate republican negativity of the tyrannicides and even the associative martial praxis of the Agitators. In "Paternalists, Improvers, and Fellow Creatures," I contrast the Diggers' attitude toward agrarian improvement with those of paternalists who criticized it, and the capitalists who advocated it. "Natural Law *in Loco Parentis*" examines the Diggers' efforts to replace the nostalgic ethic of paternalism with an anti-nostalgic social ethic and theory of natural law. "Green Millennialism" examines the Diggers' efforts to replace the instrumental ethic of capitalist improve-ment with an ethic of self-creation through agrarian communism. "Geor-gic Prophets and Pastoral Poets" examines the conflicting views of seventeenth-century agrarian life offered by aristocratic country house poems and Digger pamphlets. "Common Futures" examines two historical dialogues: the first between the Diggers and those historians who would attempt to cut them off from a communist tradition, the second between the Diggers and contemporary agrarian communist resistance to enclo-sure—particularly that of the Amazonian Forest People.

Paternalists, Improvers, and Fellow Creatures

The moment of the Diggers in 1648–50 occurred at the critical juncture of three cycles or "times": one long-term, one medium, one short. The first, long-term cycle was economic, a product of class struggle: the fundamental transformation of early modern English agriculture from feudal to capitalist that has come to be known as "primitive accumulation," "the enclosure movement," or "improvement." Like the Diggers, I will

38. See Lutaud's very helpful tabulation in *Winstanley* 520–23.
39. Gurney, "Gerrard Winstanley."
40. Winstanley said farewell in a spiritual materialist poem at the end of *The Law of Freedom*: "Come take this body, and scatter it in the Four, / That I may dwell in One, and rest in peace once more" (*W* 600). The "Diggers 350" commemoration briefly conjured him up again in April 1999, when associated members of The Land is Ours set up a camp on the George Hill common (now surrounded by luxury estates) and tried to install a stone memorial to the Diggers. Local authorities delivered a notice of their intent to evict them, along with their accomplice, one "Gerald Winstanley." At last report, the stone was scheduled for installation.

favor "enclosure," but the term requires some comment, since not all enclosure was oppressive, and not all oppression was enclosure. As Thirsk points out, though the poor usually resisted attempts to divide and enclose the traditional commons, they sometimes supported certain other sorts of enclosure. Furthermore, agrarian improvement entailed not only enclosure but improving wastes, draining fens, engrossing scattered smallholdings, converting arable land to pasture, developing new agricultural technologies, and developing new schemes of social welfare and poor relief to respond to the resulting social turbulence. It might be more accurate to describe the conflict over enclosure as a struggle between rival models of the human relationship to the land: between a rights-based model that gave the direct producers some measure of immediate access to the agrarian means of production, and a model of absolute property that gave them such access only through the mediation of the capitalist wage form. Early modern England saw the large-scale transformation of commons into absolute property, and of copyhold from a customary tenure (which implied heritable land and fixed low rents) into tenancy-at-will (which implied something like modern forms of rental—subject to rackrenting at the landlord's pleasure, with no guaranteed heritability).[41]

The second, medium-term, cycle was primarily natural: an accumulating series of bad harvests. Peter Bowden comments that the twenties, thirties, and forties "were probably among the most terrible years through which the country has ever passed." But like most natural contingencies, this one worked itself out in a socialized nature, and brought disproportionate suffering to agrarian workers. Agricultural produce in 1647–49 brought the highest prices of the revolutionary era, and the disastrous harvest of 1648, immediately preceding Winstanley's move to communism, doubled the price of bread and led to widespread hunger and scattered incidents of starvation.[42]

The third, short-term, cycle or time was political and ideological. The regicide of January 1649 created a classic revolutionary situation by capping off a period of rising hopes following a period of oppression with a fear of betrayal. Charles's Personal Rule and the early forties raised the suffering and ideological conflict produced by enclosure to a higher pitch, through a complex dialectic of politics and economics, city and country. Charles dismissed a parliament that demanded consultation in response for provision, and attempted to "improve" his extra-parliamentary sources of revenue, including the royally owned forests, wastes, and fenlands.[43] These attempts aggravated the agrarian crisis and helped generate the provincial crowds that came to the aid of the London

---

41. On enclosure and forms of tenancy, see Joan Thirsk, ed., *The Agrarian History of England and Wales*, 8 vols, Cambridge 1967, 4.200–55, 5.2.198–230; and her "Agrarian Problems" for an overview.

42. Thirsk, *Agrarian* 4.621, 5.2.847. See also Hill, *Winstanley* 22.

43. On antebellum agrarian conflict, see Manning, *English* 15–18, 181–211, 266–81; and Thirsk, "Agrarian Problems" 170–71.

crowds, which had come, in turn, to the aid of the Long Parliament. In the 1640s, some of the English poor began to hope for a fundamental social revolution that would remove not only the great tyrant in the palace but the lesser tyrants in the manor, the law court, and the parish church. These libertarian expectations appear in the increasing number of attacks on enclosures, with twenty-six counties experiencing rioting in the early forties.[44] In the late forties the victorious parliamentarians had confiscated and sold the bishops' lands, but they still held other liberated property, and it was not yet clear that it would pass from an absolutist to a capitalist ruling class. In *A New-Yeers Gift*, Winstanley stakes the commoners' claim to the "crown lands, deans, bishops, forests lands and commons"—a considerable fraction of the English countryside, forming, quite literally, the English common wealth.[45]

The paternalist critique of enclosure from the point of view of a half-imagined, half-remembered ideal economy of the past draws strongly on the rights-based model of land tenure. One cannot identify it too readily with any particular class or time, for a paternalist rhetoric fires an important body of resistance to enclosure among tenants, some landlords, clergy, and nobles from the fifteenth to the nineteenth century. "Nowe A Dayes," a sixteenth-century ballad, laments the violation of proper social spaces and relations:

> Envy waxith wonders strong,
> The Riche doth the poore wrong:
> God of his mercy sufferith long
> 　　The devill his workes to worke.
> The townes go down, the land decayes;
> Off cornefeyldes, playne layes:
> Gret men makithe now a dayes
> 　　A shepecott in the churche.

Frequently, paternalist writers appeal to an idealized monarch who will set all to rights when informed of abuses. Recalling an eroded feudalism, an anonymous petitioner of the 1550s warns the King's Council and the Lords of Parliament that enclosure and the conversion of arable to pasture would weaken the nation, since "shepherds be but ill archers."[46]

This paternalism could turn a conservative religious rhetoric against private enclosures. In his 1550 epigram "Of Rent Raysers," Thomas Crowley constructs a religious critique of improvement:

> A Manne that had landes of tenne pounde by yere,
> Surueyed the same, and lette it out deare;
> So that of tenne pounde he made well a score
> Moe poundes by the yere than other dyd before.

44. Morrill, *Revolt* 34.
45. *W* 363.
46. R. H. Tawney and Eileen Power, eds, *Tudor Economic Documents*, 3 vols, London 1924, 3.18–19, 55.

But when he was tolde whan daunger it was
To oppresse his tenauntes, he sayed he did not passe.
For thys thynge, he sayde, full certayne he wyste,
That with hys owne he myghte alwayes do as he lyste.
But immediatlye, I trowe, thys oppressoure fyl sicke
Of a voyce that he harde, "geue accountes of thy baliwicke."

Rewriting Christ's Parable of the Talents—that favorite of Christian capitalists—Crowley turns the absolute property owner into a bailiff held accountable for his stewardship to the godlike voice of the violated paternal economy.[47]

The paternalist critique continued strong through the seventeenth century. John Moore described articles of enclosure as a Faustian devil's pact: "At least one snatched the pen, subscribed his name, and bid them follow him all in the Devil's name." Later, he told improvers, "Surely they may make men as soon believe there is no sun in the firmament as that usually depopulation and decay of tillage will not follow enclosure in our inland counties. We see it with our eyes. It is so."[48] In *Depopulation Arraigned*, Robert Powell sanctioned certain sorts of enclosure, but, using the generative language that pervades these debates, he condemned depopulation as "the strangling or choking of the womb" of the commonwealth. After presenting his opponents' argument that they may buy as much land as they can and do with it what they will, he offers a conservative communitarianism: "Where every man is for himself, *non deus, sed diabolus*, the Devil is for all.... where hospitable farms, and plentiful fields of corn have been, nothing remains but a champant wilderness for sheep, with a cote, a pastoral boy, his dog, and crook and a pipe."[49] Such enclosure would also inevitably lead to idleness and a decay of rents and tithes. Depopulating enclosers are tyrannical Nimrods, the opposite of benevolent King Charles. Powell concludes with a paternalist plea that the king heed earlier examples of anti-depopulating legislation: "The King shall cover us under the wings of his royal and religious protection, and we shall render to him the dues of our faith and obedience."[50]

We can readily detach this critique of rural decay from its social referent and expose it as a deluded yearning for metaphysical presence or an idealized childhood. In his introduction to *The Country and the City*, Raymond Williams traces agrarian nostalgia for a golden age ever further backward, showing that the impulse to contrast a glorious past with the mundane and oppressive reality of the present inhabits not only the shattered rural landscape of industrial Britain, but also ancient Britain, with its memory of "an Iberian world, before the Celts came, with their

---

47. Ibid. 3.62.
48. *The Crying Sin of England*, 1653, 23; *A Scripture Word Against Enclosure*, 1656, in Thirsk and Cooper, *Seventeenth-Century* 149.
49. 1636, 4, 43, 46, 54–5.
50. 32, 76, 118.

gilded barbarism." But he adds that such demystifying critiques do less than justice to the paternalist critics: as their nostalgic fictions recalled an archaic, regulated economy that never really existed, they helped rural people conceptualize and resist real social transformations and real economic and physical violence.[51] A wry smile at nostalgic fictions may divert us from that more sordid idealism which universalizes the histori-cally determinate assumptions of capitalism, including the improver's unshakeable faith (epidemic from the sixteenth century to the present) that a net increase in production will benefit all classes. E. P. Thompson remarks,

> It is not easy for us to conceive that there may have been a time, within a smaller and more integrated community, when it appeared to be "unnatural" that any man should profit from the necessities of others, and when it was assumed that, in time of dearth, prices of "necessities" should remain at a customary level, even though there might be less all round.[52]

Furthermore, these paternalist complaints prompted royal commissions investigating anti-enclosure riots (in 1517 and 1607) and royal proclama-tions from the time of Henry VII onward designed to limit the decay of habitations and the sufferings of rural populations: the Act against Pulling Down of Towns (1489), the Act for the Maintenance of Husbandry and Tillage (1597–98), the Statute of Artificers (1563), the Statute on Cottages (1589), and the Book of Orders (1630–31).[53]

Still, because pater's helping hand readily clenches into a fist, we should distinguish carefully between laboring-class and ruling-class paternalism. Whereas rural laborers and artisans struggled first to protect their tra-ditional rights to commons and forests, rural gentry and their city cousins sought primarily to preserve social order. When the latter attempted to maintain a traditional economy, they easily resorted to violence when disobeyed or frustrated, as in the Tudor statutes against vagrancy that accompanied the statutes against depopulations and the decay of houses. If radical paternalists attacked those rackrenting, grainhoarding, and leasemongering interlopers between rulers and subjects, then conservative paternalists warned against those evil messengers named "Discontentation or murmur" and "Arrogancy, nigh cousin to pride" who will "promise to set you on high and to be lords and governors, and no longer to be churls as you were before." Indeed, these two paternalisms could coexist: Protec-tor Somerset authored both a powerful body of anti-enclosure legislation and an act that would have enslaved "vagrants"; Robert Crowley's *The Way to Wealth* of 1550 begins with conventional warnings against rebellion, and concludes with an attack on the oppressions of the poor

---

51. New York 1973, 11, 12.
52. *Customs* 252–3.
53. Tawney and Power, *Tudor* 1.84–6, 325–83.

by enclosure.[54] In a sermon responding to the Midlands Corn Insurrections, Robert Wilkinson reverses this emphasis. Examining Christ's saying, "Man shall not live by bread alone," he remarks that "two things may be distinctly considered: first, that man liveth by bread, and then secondly that he liveth not by bread alone." He notes Satan's temptation to Christ to turn stones into bread, then accuses depopulating enclosers of turning bread into stones. Echoing More's Hythloday, he asks, "What sheep were these that throw down houses, towns, and churches?" then observes, "For the belly saith bread must be had, and the soul subscribeth that bread must be had too; and though reason may persuade and authority command, and preachers may exhort with obedience and patience to sustain the want of bread, yet for all that, *venter non habet aures*, in case of extreme hunger men will not be persuaded, but they will have bread."[55]

Yet he then argues, like the precommunist Winstanley, that the corn rioters should have waited for God to work a miracle. Preaching to the belly's absent ears, he warns, "Therefore, consider and see I beseech you, whence arise conspiracies, riots, and damnable rebellions; not from want of bread, but through want of faith, yea want of bread doth come by want of faith." Sometimes, God actually wills the hungry to starve, and they should accept this quietly. Rioters impiously attempt to turn thrown stones into bread, and fail to "look up to heaven from whence you shall have bread." They come forth "like Adam's sons ... with shovels and spades," then turn into "Tubal-Kain's sons, armed with swords and weapons of iron." Most damning of all, they rudely threaten Great Britain with coitus interruptus: "Was this a time of all times to disturb the peace of the land; now that king and state were so earnest in hand to unite two kingdoms into one, now to attempt the rending of one kingdom into two?" Political order takes priority over hungry poverty, and Wilkinson draws potential rioters' attention to the pendant lesson of their predecessors on the gallows. The radical and seemingly unselfconscious contradiction between the two tones of this sermon dramatizes a fundamental weakness in the conservative paternalist case: since it can only explain economic crisis as moral turpitude, it can respond to the disorder it produces only with horror and state violence.[56]

The second attitude toward enclosure, capitalist improvement, introduces absolute property relations by turning the early modern land and the populations inhabiting it into raw materials subject to pure instrumental reason. This ideology of economic rationalization certainly appears among sixteenth-century improvers—for instance, in Alderman Box's 1576 letter to Lord Burghley, proposing a compulsory division and sowing of the wastes.[57] But it comes into its own in the seventeenth century, when

54. Ibid. 2.296–369, 3.14–15. C. S. L. Davies, "Slavery and Protector Somerset," *Economic History Review* 2.19.3, 1966. Crowley in Tawney and Power, *Tudor* 3.57–60.
55. *A Sermon Preached at North-hampton*, 1607, C2ʳ, C4ʳ, D3ʳ.
56. E3ʳ⁻ᵛ, E4ᵛ, F3ᵛ, F4ᵛ, F4ʳ.
57. Tawney and Power, *Tudor* 1.72–7.

improvers accelerated their efforts to enclose waste lands and commons, end their customary use by the poor, and set up charity plots in nominal compensation. Poor commoners thus exchanged the relative independence of an income supplemented by access to the commons and wastes for the relative dependence of parish charity. Supporters of enclosure began to depict the commons as an unmarked *prima materia* sure to breed up a population of idle rogues, rather than a space rich in traditions and marked by multiple uses and rights. In *Wast Land's Improvement* (1653), E. G. distinguishes the orderly enclosures from the "wild howling wildernesses" and "deformed chaos" of the wastes. Parliament can survey and divide the wastes, providing work for the poor, or it can risk creeping gaelifaction, for neglect "may in time make England's wastes a receptacle and harbor for troops of assassinating rogues like the tories in Ireland, and the moss-troopers in Scotland."[58] The commons are "nurseries of thieves and horse-stealers."[59] They are one of the "great nurseries of idleness and beggary, etc. in the nation," and "the nurseries of beggars."[60] In 1656, "Pseudonimous" preached that "God is the God of order, and order is the soul of things, the life of a commonwealth; but common fields are the seat of disorder, the seed plot of contention, the nursery of beggary." With a radical humanist attack on irrational custom, he says he can find no precedent for common fields in Scripture, or "in any skillful author writing of husbandry, as Virgil, Tully, etc." If enclosure chances to produce depopulation and human suffering, then the fault lies "in the men, not the ground; and if it be evil in the beginning thereof, then it is likewise evil in the continuance of the same. Yet a man may drink strong beer without drunkenness, and eat fat meat without gluttony, and enclose land without depopulation."[61] Whereas sixteenth-century paternalist critics tended to see enclosure as the cause of vagrancy, seventeenth-century improvers saw it as the cure: they would limit vagrancy by enclosing common land and supporting the deserving poor with the rents derived from charity plots.[62] Richard Halpern notes that capitalism makes vagrancy and unemployment functional as the "industrial reserve army" of the unemployed, as Marx calls it, which helps to depress wages.[63] Andrew McRae shows that the language of improvement developed not just against but within the genre of the conservative husbandry manual: what had been a relatively small-scale and communally oriented rhetoric became a new rhetoric of political economy integrating individual gain and specifically national enrichment.[64]

The improvers' view of the land led to a similar view of the persons

58. Thirsk and Cooper, *Seventeenth-Century* 135, 136–7.
59. Adam Moore, *Bread for the Poor*, 1653, 21.
60. Silvanus Taylor, quoted in Buchanan Sharp, "Common Rights," Eley and Hunt, *Reviving* 107–38, 115; *A Consideration*, 1607, quoted in Thirsk and Cooper, *Seventeenth-Century* 107.
61. Thirsk and Cooper, *Seventeenth-Century* 144, 146–7.
62. Sharp, "Common Rights."
63. *Poetics* 75.
64. *God Speed the Plow*, Cambridge 1996, 135–68.

living off it. Gervase Markham refers to "some boys and girls, or other waste persons," as likely candidates for cheap, unskilled labor. McRae notes that he "transforms the poor from a problem of charity into an unexploited 'productive resource' within an expanding commonwealth."[65] At their cruelest, the enclosers compared displaced tenants to livestock. Writing in 1607 on the Midlands Corn Rising, the anonymous author of *A Consideration* says that "as there is now a labor to suit our dwellings for as much stock of people as the commonwealth will bear, it must likewise be fit, as good husbands do with their grounds, to provide that you do not overburthen it." In *A Good Speed to Virginia* (1609), Robert Gray compares a canny prince burdened with an excessive population to a good husbandman, who finds his grounds "overcharged with cattle," then "removes them from one ground to another, and so he provideth well both for his cattle and for his grounds."[66] In this tortuous figure of speech, the bovine vehicle crowds the human tenor right out of the metaphor. Wealthy landlords and tenants frequently caused agrarian distress by overstocking commons and producing a "surplus" of commoners. As Winstanley notes, "In Parishes where Commons lie, the rich Norman freeholders, or the new (more covetous) gentry, overstock the commons with sheep and cattle; so that inferior tenants and poor laborers can hardly keep a cow."[67] These cattle thus turned the impoverished tenants into human stock, who were driven to pasture elsewhere— frequently, to the New World, where they in turn displaced Native American commoners. So runs the carcinogenic logic of primitive accumulation.

As these tracts suggest, improvement had a crucial national and even colonial role to play. Adam Moore underscored the Old/New World dialectic of enclosure, saying that "We have now ... discovered a new plantation on our own continent. ... how much more able might we be to accomplish those happy plantations by the increase of people, wealth and provisions, which the improvement of the lands would yield us?"[68] If improvement once threatened national security by turning hardy yeoman-archers into febrile shepherds, it now becomes the very motor of capitalist imperialism. In his *General Considerations for the Plantation in New England*, John Winthrop calls the Algonquians "savage and brutish men" who "range up and down" like "wild beasts." He anticipates Locke when he asks why Europeans should

> suffer whole countries, as profitable for the use of man, to lie waste without any improvement? ... That which is common to all is proper to none. This savage

---

65. Ibid. 135–68, 168.
66. Thirsk and Cooper, *Seventeenth-Century* 109, 758.
67. *W* 506.
68. *Bread* 38, 30–31. As Dick Gaughan remarks of the Diggers, "Sometimes we (Scots and Irish) forget that the first colony of the British Empire was in fact England." Liner notes for *Handful of Earth*, Advent Records, 1981, on which Gaughan performs "The World Turned Upside Down," Leon Rosselson's great song about the Diggers.

people ruleth over many lands without title or property; for they enclose no ground, neither have they cattle to maintain it, but remove their dwellings as they have occasion, or as they can prevail against their neighbors.

John Eliot, the "Apostle to the Indians" of the Massachusetts Bay Colony, remarks that "Men of new plantations are subject to much distress and unquietness until all commons lands be divided, an humor which after nations have no occasion to see unto."[69]

The improving projector turns the paternalist's nightmare of social disorder into an investment opportunity—a moment of capitalist serendipity that suggests we should group him with early modern utopists such as Eliot, More's fictional Raphael Hythloday, Vasco de Quiroga (who tried out More's principles in New Spain), Francis Bacon, William Petty (the "political anatomist" of Ireland), Gabriel Plattes (agrarian reformer and author of the utopia *Macaria*), and James Harrington (author of *Oceana*). All searched for the geographic *tabula rasa* of a waste land, a common, or a conquered territory that could be surveyed, divided, improved, and turned into a productive new polity. Similarly, they searched for the human raw material of a displaced population (vagrants, the people of Interregnum England, conquered Indians or Irish) which could be settled on the land and made productive according to a rational and anti-customary scheme of discipline. Again and again, these prophets see improvement as a sort of inscription: the one-way writing of utopian reason on a human or geographical *tabula rasa*, which masks the fact that human populations are already creating and re-creating themselves through the rational use of the lands they inscribe through their praxis.[70]

In *Novum Organum*, Bacon reveals a classically utopian vision of knowledge as will-to-power when he observes that the difference between native inhabitants of the New Indies and European explorers equipped with print, gunpowder, and the compass was "great enough to justify the saying that 'man is a god to man.'" In *The New Atlantis*, the workers in Salomon's House research ways to make animals "greater or taller than their kind is; and contrariwise dwarf them, and stay their growth; we make them more fruitful and bearing than their kind is; and contrariwise barren and not generative." They also invent horrific new weapons.[71] Most of Bacon's seventeenth-century followers pursued a similar program of utopian improvement, in which the project of class domination finds an authorizing analogy and alibi in God's domination of humankind, and a technological supplement in the progressive human mastery of nature. In *Dialectic of Enlightenment*, Max Horkheimer and Theodor W. Adorno see a similar impulse at the heart of all Western enlightenment: "What men

69. My *Rational Millennium* 107. E. P. Thompson discusses the role of English theories of absolute property, enclosure, and improvement in the theft of Indian, Maori, and South Asian common lands in *Customs* 164–75.

70. My *Rational Millennium* 34–48. On Petty, see Patricia Coughlan, "'Cheap and Common Animals,'" *HS* 205–23.

71. *Works* 8.162; 5.402, 408.

want to learn from nature is how to use it in order wholly to dominate it and other men."[72] This near-postmodernist critique casts its net too wide and not wide enough, for it denounces all science, all rationality (including, presumably, itself), while letting slip the historically specific capitalist form of rationality. But it can help us understand the utopian vision of seventeenth-century improvers, who characteristically present their schemes as the encounter of an eschatologically tinged absolute reason with a neutral or recalcitrant subject matter—waste land, commons, fens, forests, the New World, and the displaced or displaceable peoples inhabiting them.

The utopian encounter between "culture" and "nature" that we see in the literature of improvement is always an encounter between a dominant and a subordinate culture, for the nature that preceded human history "is not by any means the nature in which Feuerbach lives, it is nature which today no longer exists anywhere (except perhaps on a few Australian coral-islands of recent origin) and which, therefore, does not exist for Feuerbach either."[73] This may seem almost self-evident, but the opposition between ordering culture and disordered nature, or some version of it, continues to organize a good deal of historical work. British historians follow their seventeenth-century anticommunist forebears in juxtaposing "order" and "disorder," as if a conflict between two social groups could be explained as the conflict of form and matter.[74] American historians of ideas still fancy concepts like "discovery," "frontier," "wilderness," and "expansion," all of which dissimulate the genocidal origins of their nation. An indigenous human population always already works over "Nature" to some degree. Whenever anyone designates some area as "wilderness," we are hearing either a prologue or an epilogue to the eviction and murder of its inhabitants.

Capitalist improvement came with irrationalities of its own, but it did prevail over paternalism. Its expansive vision of unification and profit adapted better to imperial conquests and the subjugation of Celtic Britain, Ireland, and the Western hemisphere.[75] Moreover, its techniques—engrossment, enclosure, decay of dwellings, depopulation, starvation, etc.—tended to be one-way processes. Despite legislative attempts to restore arable land and dwellings, such regressions were infrequent and

72. New York 1972, 4.
73. *MECW* 5.40.
74. See Fletcher and Stevenson, *Order and Disorder*, particularly the Introduction and Morrill and Walter's "Order and Disorder in the English Revolution" (1–40; 137–65). In their study of "Dearth and the Social Order in Early Modern England," John Walter and Keith Wrightson draw an interesting distinction between "the populace" and "society": "That popular disorder was limited should not blind us to the very real, albeit localized, threat it might pose to the social order. . . . Seventeenth-century English society was not capable of eliminating the spectre of dearth, but it was capable of interpreting and resisting this phenomenon in such a way as to preserve itself" (27, 42). Hungry grain rioters might be forgiven for seeing the true social order in themselves, not in those starving them into specters.
75. On England's relation to the "dark corners of the land," see Hill, *Change* 3–47.

short-lived. A depopulated village tended to become a childhood remembered in a London tenement, a poem by Goldsmith, a picturesque vista of crumbling crofts, and a faint irregularity in an aerial survey. Moreover, capitalist improvers adopted an authoritative religious rhetoric of their own by embracing the millennial advancement of learning.[76] The title page of Bacon's *Instauratio Magna* features an engraving of imperial ships venturing westward through the Pillars of Hercules, with a millennial motto from Daniel 12.4: "Many shall run to and fro, and knowledge shall be increased."

Finally, capitalist improvers effectively assimilated the powerful social rhetoric of the conservative paternalists, with whom they shared an overriding concern for social order. Indeed, this assimilation began as early as 1516. The first part of More's *Utopia* does indeed suggest the medieval moral economy much beloved by his anticommunist interpreters, for it presents a paternalist critique of contemporary England, with its starving displaced populations created by feudal decay, enclosure, and the conversion of arable to pasture. But the second part proposes a surprisingly modern solution: complete enclosure and transformation of the landscape according to an instrumental scheme of urban and agrarian improvement. In the rationalized Utopian countryside, there will be "no hiding places; no spots for secret meetings"—a hygienic ideal attractive not only to sixteenth-century paternalists but also to seventeenth-century improvers.[77] In *A Discovery of Infinite Treasure Hidden Since the World's Beginning* (1639), Gabriel Plattes presents a utopian program for improvement with a title that suggests the revelations of Matthew 13.35: "I will open my mouth in parables; I will utter things which have been kept secret from the foundation of the world." He reveals a sympathy with the poor which we should not dismiss out of hand. But he sees both the origin of and the cure for agrarian distress in essentially non-political processes: the suffering born of natural population increase would be eliminated by an innovative, class-neutral technology.

In *The English Improver Improved* (1652), Walter Blith offers a capitalist utopianism free of More's anti-hierarchical vision. On the one hand, he laments the suffering wrought by enclosure and depopulation, but finds its cure in a technologically improved version of his own hierarchical England, based in a "clear understanding of the Mystery of Improvement," including the new implements, planting techniques, procedures for flooding, draining, and enriching soils, for transforming waste lands into arable, that he presents in the body of his book. On the other hand, his introductory matter presents the received English class structure as an

76. See Charles Webster, *The Great Instauration*, London 1975.

77. 49. Here as in my *Rational Millennium*, I've slighted the genuinely emancipatory aspects of More's Utopia—the six-hour workday and relatively egalitarian government, the prohibition of dynasty and accumulated wealth. Bloch highlights these aspects by contrasting More's "utopia of social freedom" with Campanella's "utopia of social order" (*Principle* 2.515–34).

immutable given. In the tones of a benevolent patriarch on his deathbed, Blith addresses separate epistles to each class, "to each a portion as I conceived most suitable to work their spirits into a flexibleness of practice and acceptance": one for Cromwell and the Council of State, one for the industrious reader, and others for the nobles and gentry, the houses of court and the universities, the Army, the husbandman or farmer or tenant, the cottager or laborer or "meanest commoner." But this isn't to say that class struggle has disappeared. Blith sees a new binary structure emerging in the relation between the new class of capitalist improvers and the new class of agrarian proletarian wage laborers, and warns the latter that they must rest "content" with their "portion," even if it's no more than expropriation softened with the promise of wage labor.[78]

Blith's primary antagonists in this work are not the paternalists, whose cause seems by mid-century to be fading, but the Diggers:

> Although I endeavor so mainly to work my improvements out of the belly of the earth, yet I am neither of the Diggers' mind, nor shall I imitate their practice, for though the poor are or ought to have advantage upon the commons, yet I question whether they as a society gathered together from all parts of the nation could claim a right to any particular common: and for their practice, if there be not thousands of places more capable of improvement than theirs, and that by many easier ways, and to far greater advantages, I will lay down the bucklers.

Blith then mocks Digger "parity" with a perennial anti-eschatological joke: the Diggers will ultimately fail, he says, "unless they bring us to the New Jerusalem, or bring it down to us."[79] But for Winstanley, the Diggers' New Jerusalem is no place "above the skies, in a local place . . . like the seeing of a show or masque before a man." It will arise within the individual conscience, or among the saints gathered together in agrarian praxis. Like Milton's newly created tawny lion pawing to get free of the earth, "commonwealth government" will "arise from under the clods, under which as yet it is buried, and covered with deformity."[80] It derives from a mundane vision of commoners as a national class joining together in non-hierarchical communal praxis, creating themselves anew. Blith's anticommunist calumny diverts critical attention from his own fantastic and perpetually deferred vision of a world improved for all persons and classes by technical means alone, which will "make the poor rich, and the rich richer."[81] This is the perennial, ever-receding, capitalist New Jerusalem, which always glimmers just past that transitional pile of groaning rags. Its prophets still walk the earth.

---

78. C3^r, C2^v, B2^r–E3^v, E3$^{r–v}$; compare the political marxist effort to replace or supplement the "bourgeois revolution" model with an account of the internal transformation of the ruling class. On Blith, see *GZ*; Manning, *1649* 77–8; and McRae, *God* 226–8.

79. C2^v–C3^r.

80. *W* 226, 533.

81. C3^r.

Natural Law *in Loco Parentis*

Responding to the misery and dislocation born of enclosure, the Diggers turn not to the paternalists' mythical past, not to the improvers' enriched version of an oppressive present, but to the revolutionary praxis of an egalitarian future. In this section, I contrast the Diggers with neo-feudal paternalists, dealing first with space (the Diggers' critique of deferential localism), then with time (their critique of nostalgic history). In the next, "Green Millennialism," I consider the Diggers' engagement with capitalist improvers, arguing that they propose an alternative, communist vision of improvement, and a monist integration of subject and object.

Joan Thirsk comments, "After enclosure, when every man could fence his own piece of territory"—except, of course, those who couldn't—"and warn his neighbours off, the discipline of sharing things fairly with one's neighbours was relaxed, and every household became an island unto itself." She wonders why the opponents of enclosure never availed themselves of their most forceful argument: that enclosure and strict property rights would destroy the vigorous, communal, and cooperative spirit preserved in the practice of traditional agriculture in smallholdings and common fields. Only an "observer from a later age" could appreciate such an argument, but by that time, this way of life was lost.[82] But a wage laborer gazing at a common field is precisely an observer from a later age. Winstanley derived his utopian program from precisely this experience of communal agricultural praxis. But the Digger project required Winstanley to detach this experience from the localist paternalism that could turn it into a form of hierarchical oppression.

The last three decades have witnessed an interdisciplinary renaissance of local studies. Revisionists have underlined the continuing importance of local paternalism in an epoch of political conflict. Peter Laslett begat this argument in *The World We Have Lost*, which portrays early modern England as a one-class, traditional society.[83] Local historians such as Alan Everitt have followed up by setting the local against the national, saying that the English Revolution did not really trouble the stolid hierarchy of the gentry-dominated county communities.[84] Kevin Sharpe observes that "the key to English political thought was not theory but circumstance, practical politics rather than philosophy." Larger principles of explanation such as economics may be "less important than family and upbringing, than the influence of manorial lord, vicar, or schoolmaster, than personal relations and even individuality in determining attitudes."[85] The localities form the rooty rural site of proto-Burkean customary resistance to the deracinated proto-Jacobin ideologies of minuscule radical groups. Waxing almost Heideggerean, John Morrill says that "a rhythm of worship, piety,

82. *Agrarian* 4.255.
83. See chapter 4 n.53 and the critique of Laslett in Thompson, *Customs* 16–96.
84. *The Community of Kent and the Great Rebellion*, Leicester 1966.
85. *Politics* 287.

practice ... had earthed itself into the Englishman's consciousness and had sunk deep roots in popular culture."[86] Fletcher and Stevenson define rural plebeians by their plucky resilience, "rooted in the sense of belonging to a local environment." Their culture was an unreflective and pre-ideological amalgam of local rituals, traditions, festivities, rural sports, even music, which "lifted men's spirits at work and play." We may hear an echo, with banjo obbligato, in paternalist reveries about the happy slaves of antebellum Dixie.[87]

Even non-revisionist historians incline toward localist explanation. David Underdown sees the English Revolution foundering on "the stubborn resilience of traditional culture" in the localities.[88] Roger B. Manning defines early modern village revolts as "sub-political" localism.[89] And Buchanan Sharpe distinguishes the "essentially nonideological" disturbances of oppressed rural laborers and artisans from the relatively unimportant "irrational excesses" of that tiny minority of antinomians analyzed by Hill in *The World Turned Upside Down*.[90] As Fletcher and Stevenson's analysis of "the popular mentality" indicates, revisionist localism can find allies in the French *histoire des mentalités*, with its emphasis on the *longue durée* of unchanging and unconscious custom.[91] It could also look to recent literary criticism influenced by Bakhtin, Foucault, and Geertz, which turns from society, state, revolution, ideology, and dialectics, toward carnival, village festivity, the body, and local knowledge.

Like so many postmodernist celebrations of micropolitics, this turn to the local can begin to sound reductively global. Despite its air of particularity, it threatens to reduce a host of overlapping and potentially conflicting determinants of identity: the geographic region, the county, the town, the family, the parish, religious affiliation, relations of production, etc. Ideological and other sorts of divisions could so rend the locality that, as Clive Holmes notes, "in many counties the court–country dichotomy is more analytically useful than a romantic evocation of an organic gentry community."[92] Ann Hughes suggests that the tacit revisionist decision to focus on the county derives less from its existential priority than from its

---

86. *Nature* 174.
87. *Order* 9, 10; Frederick Douglass saw drunken slave holidays as "safety-valves, to carry off the rebellious spirit of enslaved humanity." As an alternative, he created a Sunday club to encourage literacy and religious study among slaves; *Narrative of the Life of Frederick Douglass, an American Slave, Written by Himself*, New York 1997, 51, 55.
88. *Revel* 286.
89. *Village Revolts*, Oxford 1988, 3.
90. *In Contempt of All Authority*, Berkeley and Los Angeles 1980, 8.
91. *Order* 6. To the monographic imagination of localist French historical writing, Darnton observes "The peasants of the Old Regime did not think monographically. They tried to make sense of the world, in all its booming, buzzing confusion, with the materials they had at hand" (*Great Cat Massacre* 64); in other words, they *totalized*. One of the main theses of this book is that early modern working people had not just a *mentality* coterminous with the parish or with official ideology, but reflective *consciousness* that could take both for its object.
92. "The Country Community in Stuart Historiography," *Journal of British Studies* 19, 1980, 69.

status as a locus of record-keeping, and that the English Revolution was remarkable for the extent to which two nationwide ideological affiliations overcame local loyalties.[93] Leah Marcus shows that such micropolitical matters as carnival and festivity tended to work themselves out in the macropolitical context of a conflict between royalists and parliamentarians.[94] *The Puritan Moment*, William Hunt's study of godly and revolutionary Essex, shows that revisionist localists have tended to concentrate on royalist localities as if they represented a traditionalist whole. Buchanan Sharpe shows how semi-independent rural artisans complicate our picture of a deferential rural arcadia.[95] Cynthia Herrup shows that "participatory situations" such as the assizes bound together the localities and the nation as a whole.[96] So did correspondence, petitioning, newsbook writing and reading, publishing, and the national peregrinations of the New Model Army. Traditional and unifying institutions such as the two Erastian universities could work to bring national conflicts to the localities, as Underdown shows in his study of the Reverend John White's effect on Dorchester.[97] In his study of John Lilburne's work in the 1650s for the fenmen, Clive Holmes shows that local and national movements could discover strong formal and substantive ties.[98] And the Diggers made their local experience the ground for a totalizing critique of the incomplete national revolution: the hedge kings—the lords of manors—could easily survive the execution of the national king, and even grow more kingly by accumulating sequestered lands.[99]

Theories of neo-paternalist localism rely heavily on the concept of deference—that hoary but hardy civil offshoot of the Great Chain of Being: "The traditional concept of order was suited to a localized society in which hierarchy, together with obligation to those below and deference to those above, made sense of people's lives."[100] But even if we agree that deference was an important aspect of seventeenth-century social life, we should resist inflating it to the status of a historically specific *mentalité*— thus overestimating its premodern provenance (witness the Lollards, the Anabaptists, and the Marian martyrs), and underestimating its modern one (witness the annilingual pursuit of symbolic and material patronage in a modern university or corporation). Too often, looking at the early modern world, we simply assume deferential plebeian consciousness or derive it automatically from deferential actions. We might reasonably

93. "Local History and the Origins of the Civil War," *CH* 224–53, 228–9.
94. *Politics of Mirth*, Chicago 1986.
95. *Contempt* 6.
96. "The Counties and the Country," Eley and Hunt, *Reviving* 289–304.
97. *Fire from Heaven*, London 1993.
98. "Drainers and Fenmen," in Fletcher and Stevenson, *Order* 166–95. Leo F. Solt discusses Winstanley's "local" involvement in a 1649 court case and his contact with John Lilburne in "Winstanley, Lilburne, and the Case of John Fielder," *Huntington Library Quarterly* 45.2, 1982.
99. *W* 353. See also his critique of the capitalist revolutionaries who overthrew the court of wards without overthrowing feudal copyhold (*W* 387).
100. Fletcher and Stevenson, *Order* 2–3.

apply to illiterate plebeian culture the same skepticism we apply to elite literate patronage culture, in which deferential public statements coexist with resentful and satiric statements made in the relative privacy of a diary or newsletter, the retrospective insulation of a memoir, or the protective alias afforded by poetry and drama.

And the Digger pamphlets reveal a literate, public, and plebeian critique of deference. In *A New-Yeers Gift*, Winstanley looks at a group of poor men paid to pull down Digger houses, sees the powerful but imperfect social construction of deference, and concludes with a measure of hope: they "smiled one upon another; being fearful, like a dog that is kept in awe, when his master gives him a bone, and stands over him with a whip; he will eat, and look up, and twinch his tail; for they durst not laugh out, lest their lords should hear they jeered them openly; for in their hearts they are Diggers." In *A Mite Cast into the Common Treasury*, the Digger Robert Coster inverts the idyllic but ideologically partial view of manorial life with a laborers'-eye-view of patriarchal ritual:

> If the Lords of Manors, and other gentlemen who covet after so much land, could not let it out by parcels, but must be constrained to keep it in their own hands, then would they want those great bags of money (which do maintain pride, idleness, and fullness of bread), which are carried unto them by their tenants, who go in as slavish a posture as may be; namely, with cap in hand and bended knee, crouching and creeping from corner to corner, while his Lord (rather tyrant) walks up and down the room with his proud looks, and with great swelling words questions him about his holding. If the lords of manors, and other gentlemen, had not those great bags of money brought before them, then down would fall the lordliness of their spirits, and then poor men might speak to them; then there might be an acknowledging of one another to be fellow creatures.[101]

In April 1649, Winstanley and William Everard came to Whitehall to give Fairfax an account of their digging. When asked why they kept their hats on, they responded, "he was but their fellow creature."[102] A revolutionary program of labor withdrawal would abolish the deferential hierarchy of landlord, tenant, and wage laborer, and replace a verbal economy of one-sided domineering questioning with reciprocal speech. If courtly lyric shows us the client's deferential address to a patron, then the Digger pamphlet shows us one behatted fellow creature addressing another, face to face.

The author of *Light Shining in Buckinghamshire*, a near-Digger pamphlet published by December 1648, insists on bringing an anti-deferential attitude home from court: he attacks kings as such, but also "petty kings" (earls, dukes, marquesses, viscounts), "vice kings" (deputies and mayors),

---

101. W 368, 657.
102. *A Perfect Weekly Account* 4/18–4/25/49. Everard led the Digger colony in April, but left it in May. A William Everard signed the Leveller/Agitator works of 1647, *The Humble Petition* and *Englands Freedom, Soldier's Rights*.

"kings of patents," and, most hated of all, "hedge kings, viz. those called lords of the manors, those fellows that can keep a court-leet, and enslave all within their territory." He calls tenantry another name for slavery, and attacks "the chief encloser, called the Lord of the Manor, or some wretch as cruel as he," for enclosing the land and forbidding rights to timber, commons, game, and fish. He distances himself from the rituals of public order through a railing satire of a civic processional, which begins with a "Major" followed by "a Just-ass of Peace and Coram" and

> twelve Aldermen following after in their coney-skin gowns, as so many fools in a midsummer ale, and those petty-tyrants shall domineer over the inhabitants by virtue of their patent, and enclose all, letting and setting of the poor's lands too, and moneys, stocks of moneys to their own use. . . . so that you see all tyranny shelters itself under the king's wings: is it not time then to throw down the king, and bring his person to his answer: these patents and charters is the main wheel and prop that upholds the king's tyranny.

The king shelters his subtyrants, who uphold him and tyrannize in turn, like "the subtle nasty fox with his dirty tail":

> And because the Lord Keeper, Privy Seal, and Treasurer's long tails should not daggle in the dirt, they must have each another sycophant slave apiece to carry up for them with their hats off doing homage to their breech. Oh height of all baseness! Why, oh, his majesty's breath of honor it may be blows out there, and therefore he holds up his gown that it might blow him that holds it up, and makes him be called Sir.

This satire offers neither a carnivalesque celebration of the body's lower functions nor a trace of psychoanalytic spore in a seventeenth-century context, but an exercise in excremental levelling.[103]

The Diggers threatened the landed ruling class precisely because they inserted local knowledge into a national revolutionary project: preaching and publishing epistles to other disaffected tenants and wage laborers, to the Army, to Parliament, to London, to the universities; forming links among the scattered Digger communes; and developing a program for revolution based in a transformation of productive relations at the local level. In *Englands Spirit Unfoulded*, Winstanley entered into the national debate over engagement to the Commonwealth by linking it to his local utopian project. He pledges loyalty to the new republic, which will, of course, be true to itself by establishing the egalitarian commonwealth of

---

103. *W* 636, 620, 618. The author transfers a favorite Reformation image to a political and economic context. Compare Spenser's Duessa, with her bedunged fox's tail (*Faerie Queene* 1.8.48). Like Hill (*English* 132n.), I think George Shulman (*Radicalism* 26–30) and Stephen Greenblatt (*Learning* 74–6) make too much of Winstanley's few references to the "dunghill" pride of the rich (*W* 145, 216, 447, 448). Seventeenth-century Surrey cowherds, for whom (cow)dung was an unpleasant but familiar aspect of daily life, may have been more inclined than twentieth-century Viennese psychoanalysts to imagine flinging it at the rich, less inclined to correlate psychological maturation and the development of bowel control.

the soil.[104] In his preface to *Several Pieces*, he says that "the matter of Digging" had sprung up among others, unknown to him, whereupon his commune began trying to establish links of communication and mutual aid among the various Digger communes. As we have seen, the specter of this communist collectivity emerging from the localities troubled Walter Blith's parallel proposal for a national reformation through local capitalist improvement. And it may explain the seemingly disproportionate anxiety of the Council of State, which at least twice ordered Fairfax to disperse the Diggers. Christopher Kendrick observes that the persecutions of the Diggers accelerated soon after they began this expansion and unification.[105] John Bradshaw, regicide and President of the Council, wrote Fairfax in April 1649, directing him to take a troop of horse and disperse that

> tumultuous sort of people assembling themselves together not far from Oatlands, at a place called St. George's Hill; and although the pretence of their being there by them avowed may seem very ridiculous, yet that conflux of people may be a beginning whence things of a greater and more dangerous consequence may grow, to the disturbance of the peace and quiet of the Commonwealth.[106]

The real fear is not so much that Diggers arrive from outside the locality as that they threaten the very definition of the locality as a site of traditional exploitation.

Compared to most of his Protestant contemporaries, Winstanley is resolutely anti-nostalgic. He conjures up no ideal virtuous reign of a godly prince, no ancient constitution preserving Saxon liberties, no era of idyllic medieval housekeeping before the arrival of the flocks. And despite some predictable sympathy for the apostolic communism in the Book of Acts, he seems not to be terribly interested in denouncing popish deviations from the doctrinal purity of the early church.[107] True, he does seem at times to subscribe to the populist nostalgia for Saxon liberty.[108] He sees villainous "Norman" freeholders, gentry, and even toll-takers, and alludes to the Conquest: "This difference between Lords of Manors and the poor, about the common land, is the great controversy that hath risen up in this 600 years past." But his anti-Normanism remains highly metaphorical, as when he depicts a gentry-led attack on the cattle in his charge as a full-tilt

---

104. *WIR* 109–23.
105. "Preaching Common Grounds: Winstanley and the Diggers as Concrete Utopians," Zunder and Trill, *Writing* 213–37, 234n.2. Kendrick also notes the traditionalist and localist dimensions of the attack on the Diggers by cross-dressed gentry flunkies. See also Hill (*Collected* 3.268), the itinerary of the Digger emissaries Heaydon and Knight (*W* 440), and the map of their likely fund-raising circuit drawn up by Lutaud (*Winstanley* 454).
106. *CP* 2.209–10. In late May, after crushing the Levellers at Burford, Fairfax himself came to visit the Diggers (*The Speeches of the Lord Generall Fairfax, and the Officers of the Armie,* 1649).
107. *W* 184, 204, 582, 616.
108. Christopher Hill, *Puritanism and Revolution,* London 1958, 58–125.

Norman assault on freedom and liberty.[109] And with a refreshing historical skepticism, his anti-Normanism seldom becomes philo-Saxonism. He undercuts any image of a pre-Conquest paradise when he says that William the Conqueror "took the land from the English, both the enclosures from the gentry, and the commons and waste lands from the common people, and gave our land to his Norman Soldiers." The Norman conqueror

> took freedom from every one, and became the disposer of both enclosures and commons. . . . When the enemy conquered England, he took the land for his own, and called that his freedom; even so, seeing all sorts of people have given assistance to recover England from under the Norman Yoke, surely all sorts, both gentry in their enclosures, commonality in their commons, ought to have their freedom, not compelling one to work for wages for another.

In this strategically confused account, Winstanley shifts the definition of freedom from a national and political to an economic basis. Saxon England included both commons and enclosures, and the Normans established their "freedom" or political power by redistributing these lands. His proposal to give all classes the freedom to do what they will with their rightful property seems at first quite accommodating to the gentry. But in the last phrase, we find that freedom must be economic as well as political: since enclosures cannot exist without wage labor, Winstanley's limits on those social forces that compel wage labor will level them, and, by extension, the gentry. Winstanley attacks the Saxon and grandee as well as the Norman Yoke; he proposes to "restore" a gentry-free egalitarian state that never existed before.[110]

In other words, Winstanley uses a historical rhetoric to fashion a natural rights argument, following a path taken by many mid-century radicals. Winstanley's "state of nature," like Sexby's, calls up not Hobbes's vision of human depravity and absolute magistracy, but Aristotle's vision of human sociability calling for association and resistance to tyrannical power. In *Fire in the Bush*, he says that some call the state of nature that "power in man, that causes divisions and war . . . which every man brings into the world with him. But this law of darkness in the members is not the state of nature; for nature, or the living soul is in bondage to it, and groans under it, waiting to be delivered from it, and is glad to hear of a savior." Like the most radical of the debaters at Putney, he abandons any common law or constitutionalist argument for rebellion: the "*salus populi*, the safety, peace, and preservation of the whole body of the people, excepting none

---

109. *W* 506, 420, 330. With its mixture of political/historical high and bovine low, this passage may sound farcical, until we remember the economic and imaginative importance of cattle as concentrated wealth for rural society and its bards; cf. the Ulster epic of cattle raiding, the *Táin-Bó-Cúailnge*, and the cattle raids underlying *The Iliad* (M. I. Finley, *The World of Odysseus*, New York 1978, 46, 60).

110. *W* 304, 287; see also 292. At Putney, Henry Lilburne said "The Norman laws are not slavery introduced upon us, but an augmentation of our slavery before" (*CP* 1.368). Winstanley finds an aspiring "spirit of self-love" even in Eden (*Mysterie* 2), where *Fire in the Bush* also finds "stinking weeds" of self-love, envy, pride, and covetousness (*W* 446).

... gave life and strength to the Parliament and army to take up arms against the king; for they had not the least letter of any written law for their warrant at that time, all the laws being from the king, and none against him."[111] In this relative indifference to the claims of a historically based authority, Winstanley approaches Henry Marten, who said in 1649 that England would be "restored to its ancient government of a commonwealth." John Lenthall recalled the reaction:

> Sir Henry Vane stood up and reprimanded and wondered at his impudence to affirm such a notorious lie. H. M., standing up, meekly replied that there was a text had much troubled his spirit for several days and nights of the man that was blind from his mother's womb whose sight was restored at last, i.e., was restored to the sight which he should have had.[112]

The "mother's womb" here suggests Winstanley's only true utopia, the unalienated communal life which he locates variously in Eden (where "the whole creation lived in man, and man lived in his maker, the spirit of righteousness and peace, for every creature walked evenly with man, and delighted in man") or during the reign of Christ (when "there was a sweet community of love between all members of that humane body"), but perhaps most powerfully in the prophetic future.[113]

Winstanley spends relatively little time locating this state in history, for a linear history, with its enclosures of time, can be as tyrannical as enclosures of space: as the latter can deny the human praxis integrating mother earth and the earth of humankind, so the former can justify present-day inequality by asserting an all-determining fall from Eden into the hierarchy of the present, a distant millennium that shines no light on today's poverty, or a punishing and rewarding afterlife invented by a clergy to justify their expropriated tithes in this life. In *The New Law*, Winstanley constructs a half-attack on the historicity of Adam, and reinforces it by pointing to Cain's paradoxical fear of (nonexistent) enemies: "Therefore, certainly this Adam, or first man that is spoken of, is he that is within, as I have spoke of, which kills or suppresses Abel, who is the anointing; I am sure I have found him the cause of my misery, and I can lay the blame on no man, but my self."[114] Later, he extends this argument to Christ, attacking the "Fleshly wisdom and learning" that "teaches you to look altogether upon a history without you, of things that were done

---

111. *W* 493, 430. On Winstanley and Hobbes, see Hill, *World* 387–94; and Shulman, *Radicalism* 245–57.
112. John Aubrey, *Brief* 267. Struggles for gender liberation also recoded natural rights arguments as historical arguments. Aemila Lanyer pleads for women, "Let us have our liberty again" (*The Poems of Aemilia Lanyer*, New York 1993, 87). Captain Edward Rigby turns a similar argument to a different end: "Then Rigby sitting on Minton's Lap, kissed him several times, putting his tongue into his mouth, asked him, if he should f——— him, "How can that be?" asked Minton, "I'll show you," answered Rigby, "for it's no more than was done in our forefathers' time" (*An Account of the Proceedings against Capt. Edward Rigby*, 1698; elision original).
113. *W* 155, 204.
114. Ibid. 176, 210.

6000 years ago, and of things that were done 1649 years ago." With georgic fundamentalism, he quotes God's prelapsarian exordium in Genesis 1 to subdue the earth and insists that labor itself, "That bare and simple working in the earth, according to the freedom of the Creation, though it be the sweat of men's brows, is not the curse."

Similarly, enclosure and class oppression are not the punitive consequence of the Fall, but the Fall itself: "But when mankind began to quarrel about the earth; and some would have all, and shut out others, forcing them to be servants; this was man's fall, it is the ruling of the curse, and it is the cause of all divisions, wars, and pluckings up."[115] Enclosure continues throughout history. The traditional law of kings repeats the act of "the soldier, who cut Christ's garment into pieces, which was to have remained uncut and without seam; this law moves the people to fight one against another for those pieces, *viz.*, for the several enclosures of the earth, who shall possess the earth, and who shall be ruler over others."[116] The Calvinist gathered church "hedges in some to be heirs of life, and hedges out others."[117] The kingdom of heaven itself will consist of communal agriculture without enclosure. Adapting Christ's vision of heaven as a place where the saints "neither marry, nor are given in marriage, but are as the angels of God in heaven," Winstanley describes New Israel's commonwealth as a place where "the king of righteousness himself shall be governor in every man; none then shall work for hire, neither shall any give hire, but every one shall work in love: one with, and for another; and eat bread together, as being members of one household; the Creation in whom Reason rules king in perfect glory."[118] In place of the ascetic heaven of Scripture and the enclosed gardens of aristocratic *otium*, Winstanley envisions an open field of paradisal love and labor.

Green Millennialism

In *The Great Instauration*, Charles Webster links Winstanley and the Diggers to the seventeenth-century Puritan Enlightenment of the Hartlib Circle, which combined the Baconian advancement of learning with millenarian theories of progress.[119] McRae shows that Winstanley adopted some of the rhetoric of improvement.[120] Like many of the utopian improvers, Winstanley is an agrarian millennialist; following Everard, as early as *The New Law*, he suggested that the communal cultivation of the soil would

---

115. Ibid. 423–4.
116. Ibid. 589. The author of *Light Shining* says that Nimrod and his successors strove to see who could be "the greatest encloser and tyrant" (ibid. 628–9).
117. Ibid. 445–6. Hugh Latimer called non-preaching prelates "spiritual enclosers" in his *Sermon on the Plowers* (*Selected Sermons*, Charlottesville, VA, 1968, xxiv, 28–49).
118. Matt. 22.30; *W* 190–91. Hill discusses the metaphors of wilderness, garden, and hedge (*English* 126–53).
119. 367–8.
120. 129–31.

lift the Adamic curse and make the earth more fruitful.[121] As in so much agrarian capitalist literature, Digger visions of improvement could even acquire an imperial and expansive tinge: in a manifesto of March 1650, the Diggers prophesied that this improvement would increase England's wealth, so that it would "rule over the nations of the world." Just as Israel became "a terror to all oppressing kings," so will a communist England, whose knowledge will "spread to cover the earth, even as the waters cover the seas," and *The Law of Freedom* shows us Winstanley proposing lectures in natural science.[122] Nigel Smith says that, in *The Law of Freedom*, Winstanley is "nothing more than a neo-Hartlibian projector."[123] But if he is that, he's something more, too. He turns the imperial, capitalist, and technocratic millennialism of the Hartlib Circle into the green millennialism of an agrarian communist. He envisions a monist unity that removes any radical distinction between spirit and matter, God and humans, humans and nature, human and human. And he proposes a dialectics of social deracination that will replace localist paternalism with communist, not capitalist, improvement.

The Digger utopia is not by any means a pastoral assault on urbanism, or a reactionary proposal for a return to traditional peasant smallholding, with its structural resistance to any sort of genuinely labor-saving improvement. Indeed, Winstanley leaves the practice of agriculture strangely underelaborated in his formal utopia, while he conspicuously integrates his London experience with his revolutionary rural localism: "the government of the halls and companies in London is a very rational and well ordered government." He uses guildhall fraternal communalism as a model for the rural commune, reminding London that "I am one of thy sons by freedom, and I do truly love thy peace; while I had an estate in thee, I was free to offer my mite into thy public treasury guildhall, for a preservation to thee, and the whole land."[124] Particularly in *The Law of Freedom*, he surveys the rhetoric of capitalist improvement not with abhorrence but with an eye to communist appropriation. Sounding quite like Bacon, Winstanley claims that "To know the secrets of nature, is to know the works of God." But he moves on directly to level spirit and matter, god and man, by saying that "to know the works of God within the creation, is to know God himself, for God dwells in every visible work or body."[125] He discusses the "five fountains" of the arts and sciences, including agriculture, horticulture, animal husbandry, mining and chemistry, and wood science:

---

121. *W* 153, 187, 199.
122. Ibid. 414, 516, 517, 563.
123. *Literature* 334.
124. *W* 549, 315. Corns notes that Winstanley's conception of the rural stock and the storehouse derives in part from the London livery companies (*Uncloistered* 173). On radicalism among the London guilds, see Carlin, "Liberty."
125. *W* 565.

The fourth fountain is the right ordering of woods and timber trees, for planting, dressing, felling, framing of timber for all uses, for building houses or ships. And here all carpenters, joiners, throsters, plow-makers, instrument makers for music, and all who work in wood and timber, may find out the secret of nature, to make trees more plentiful and thriving in their growth, and profitable for use.[126]

At first, with the orthodoxly Baconian "profitable for use," these activities sound like they would be right at home in Salomon's House. But Winstanley integrates research and artisanry: no separate sphere of scientific inquiry stands apart from the people, and no special caste of researchers raises the specter of a technocratic priesthood.

Like Bacon, Winstanley proposes "deserved honor" for "every one who finds out a new invention"; but he also sees communism, not kingly subsidies, calling forth a host of mute inglorious Bacons through a Fourierist liberation of the (vocational) passions:

And certainly when men are sure of food and raiment, their reason will be ripe, and ready to dive into the secrets of the Creation, that they may learn to see and know God (the spirit of the whole creation) in all his works; for fear of want, and care to pay rent to task-masters, hath hindered many rare inventions.[127]

Winstanley new-models the Sabbath itself, changing it from a disciplinary Puritan enclosure of time to an egalitarian holiday combining rest, fellowship, and rational inquiry.[128] A Sabbath is "rational and good" for three reasons: it allows people to have "some bodily rest for themselves and cattle"; it enables them to "meet together to see one another's faces, and beget or preserve fellowship in friendly love"; and it brings them together to hear news of the commonwealth and improving discourses on the law, history, and "all arts and sciences, some one day, some another; as in physic, chirurgery, astrology, astronomy, navigation, husbandry, and such like."[129] Winstanley was a Hartlibian improver improved, who proposed a communist utopia in which the immediate producers would maintain control of the means of production and the processes of improvement. Could such a thing have been possible? Perhaps we too readily identify improvement itself with a particular regime of class exploitation. Both Marx and N. G. Chernyshevsky, the Narodnik writer and activist, believed that the Russian peasant commune

---

126. Ibid. 578.
127. Ibid. 580; cf. Bacon, *Works* 5.411–12. Gabriel Plattes, for instance, died for want of food in December 1644 (Charles Webster, "The Authorship and Significance of *Macaria*," *WIR* 369–85, 375).
128. On the Puritan Sabbath, see Christopher Hill, *Society and Puritanism in Pre-Revolutionary England*, 2nd edn, New York 1967, 145–218; my *Rational Millennium* 124–6, 302.
129. *W* 562–3.

could incorporate mechanized agriculture and other technologies of improvement.[130]

This vision of improvement has its roots in Winstanley's levelling monist theology (and vice versa). He pushes the Protestant critique of idolatry to its breaking point when he renames God "Reason" to avoid presenting him as a being separated from man and nature. Reason is the very spirit of community, which tells man, "Is thy neighbor hungry, and naked today, do thou feed him, and clothe him, it may be thy case tomorrow, and then he will be ready to help thee."[131] Reason aims "not to preserve a part, but the whole creation." In *The New Law*, Winstanley's syntax fuses God and humans:

> As it is said, that the king of righteousness takes delight in nothing, but what is within himself, and what proceeds out of himself: so the heaven of an enlivened heart is not a local place of glory at a distance from him, but the seeing and feeling the Father within, dwelling and ruling there; and to behold the glory of that power proceeding forth of himself, to which he is made subject, through which he walks righteously in the Creation, and in which he rests in peace.[132]

Winstanley's first sentence presents God as both the container of creation and its emanating source; his second likewise presents the enlivened human heart both as the container of God, and as subject to him. A strategic confusion runs through the long concluding infinitive phrase. Presumably, the "beholder" is a human "made subject" to a power. But like God in the first sentence, he or she sees that power "proceeding forth of himself" and "walks righteously in the Creation" as God walked in the Garden of Eden. Winstanley's allusions, half-parallelisms, and confusions lie halfway between mere syntactic awkwardness and an effort to break down the relations of domination and hierarchy in received theology.

A little later in *The New Law*, when Winstanley moves toward an orthodox division between infinite God and finite humans, things go interestingly awry:

> If you were possible to have so many buckets as would contain the whole Ocean, and every one is filled with the ocean, and perfect water is in all; and being put all together, make up the perfect Ocean, which filled them all.

130. Chernyshevsky, "Selected Writings," and Marx, "Drafts of a Reply" and "The Reply to Zasulich," Shanin, *Late Marx* 181–203, 99–126, 187, 106. "Whether small-scale agricultural production was incapable of innovation is a matter for debate not only among historians but also among those concerned with surviving modern (especially Third World) peasantries. One might suggest that the question is not necessarily blocked by the fact that England, pioneer of industrial capitalism, did happen to develop, to begin with, an agrarian capitalism based on the destruction of the peasantry" (Rodney Hilton in *BD* 8). The inverted "green" version of "forces first" technologism, which sees something demonic in technology as such, finds some strange opponents (poor, tired farmers—including Winstanley) and allies ("Agriculture is today a motorized food industry, in essence the same as the manufacture of corpses in gas chambers and extermination camps"—Martin Heidegger, former Rektor-Führer of Freiberg University, quoted in Richard Wolin, *The Politics of Being*, New York 1990, 168).
131. *W* 40; *Saints* 123.
132. *W* 105, 217.

Even so, Christ, who is the spreading power, is now beginning to fill every man and woman with himself; he will dwell and rule in every one, and the law of reason and equity shall be Christ in them; every single body is a star shining forth of him, or rather a body in and out of whom he shines; and he is the Ocean of power that fills all.[133]

As he moves into the second paragraph, Winstanley delivers not the expected contrast between the finite multitude of buckets and the infinite, sublime magnitude of Christ, but a discussion of the historical process of *spreading*—a favorite Digger word, rooted in agrarian praxis—that emphasizes the great ocean of humanity, and the "in and out" reciprocity of human and divine being. Creator and creature merge easily, not just in the Incarnation, or moments of special grace, or the New Jerusalem, but in everyday life: "For if the creation in all its dimensions be the fullness of him, that fills all with himself, and if you yourself be part of this creation, where can you find God but in that line or station wherein you stand?"[134]

Just as orthodox religious hierarchy allowed King James to imagine himself as a petty god in relation to his subjects, so it allowed landlords to conceive of themselves as petty gods to their tenants and laborers—a common conceit of country house poems. Because the Diggers no longer lay claim to a God beyond the creation, they give up Bacon's analogical rationale for exercising sheer instrumental domination. The attempt "to reach God beyond the Creation, or to know what he will be to a man, after the man is dead, if any otherwise, then to scatter him into his essences of fire, water, earth and air, of which he is compounded, is a knowledge beyond the line, or capacity of man to attain to while he lives in his compounded body." Anyone attempting such an inquiry "doth as the proverb saith, build castles in the air, or tells us of a world beyond the Moon, and beyond the Sun, merely to blind the reason of man," and risks falling into religious obsession.[135] Machiavelli and More took one step toward a critical sociology of religion by arguing that threats of divine retribution in the next world could help enforce social discipline in this one.[136] Winstanley took a step further by denying any other reality to hell, and by arguing for its economic motive: "The former hell of prisons, whips, and gallows they preached to keep the people in subjection to the King: but by this divined hell after death, they preach to keep both king and people in awe to them, to uphold their trade of tithes and new raised maintenance."[137]

---

133. Ibid. 225.
134. Ibid. 565.
135. W 565, 567.
136. Machiavelli, *Discourses* 139–52; More, *Utopia* 75.
137. W 523. Menocchio, the heretical miller of sixteenth-century Montereale, attacked the exploitation of the rural poor, rejected the idea of an immortal soul and a punishing and rewarding afterlife, and generated a cosmology strongly resembling Winstanley's spiritist materialism. He told his inquisitors, "I believe that the earthly paradise is where there are gentlemen who have many possessions and live without working" (Ginzburg, *Cheese* 16, 47, 77).

Like the ideologists of capitalist improvement, Winstanley compares the people and the land, but without instrumentalizing either. The Diggers' earth never lies down flat as the neutral substrate of instrumental reason; it stands up straight as a living substance marked by and interwoven with the divinity of human praxis. The "whole creation of fire, water, earth and air; and all the varieties of bodies made up thereof" are "the clothing of God," while the English countryside and the displaced and resettled English people who will cultivate it communally are "the two earths."[138] The utopian improvers call for a new law to enclose wastes and the common, that bad mother or "nursery of beggars"; Winstanley calls the law itself a "nursery of idleness" and the art of buying and selling a "nursery of cheaters." He agrarianizes the fifth commandment, calling the father the spirit of community, and the mother "the earth, that brought us all forth: that as a true mother, loves all her children. Therefore do not thou hinder the mother earth, from giving all her children suck, by thy enclosing it into particular hands."[139]

In *Truth Lifting Up Its Head*, Winstanley presents an evocative and metaphoric version of his agrarian monism in a dialogue between a speaker like himself and an orthodox questioner, who attempts to hold him to Nicene fundamentals and a rigorous distinction between earth and heaven, body and spirit. The questioner asks whether Christ's body was "killed, laid in the earth, and raised again from the dead, and ascended up to the Father into heaven?" Winstanley responds with an even-tempered radicalism that substitutes human patience for the miraculous resurrection:

> He was killed by the curse that ruleth in the Jews, and was laid in the earth; here was the wisdom and the power of the Father seen, that though all the powers of hell, or covetous proud flesh, did combine together to oppress, and then to kill a body wherein he himself dwelt bodily; yet they could not distemper him, for he was still patient, and he was not heard to complain.

Christ descended into the earth and stayed there—as a chthonic deity, a divine manure: "Now the body of Christ is where the Father is, in the earth, purifying the earth; and his spirit is entered into the whole creation, which is the heavenly glory, where the Father dwells; which is a glory above the flesh." Christ's death was like pouring a bucket of water back into the sea; his body merely dispersed itself into its four constituent elements.[140] *The Law of Freedom* describes a symbiosis of the creatures: "as man is compounded of the four materials of the creation . . . so is he preserved by the compounded bodies of these four, which are the fruits of the earth." Winstanley concludes that work with a poem asking Death to scatter his body among the four elements. Like the feudal remnant of the common field, this medieval metaphysics acquires a utopian function

138. *W* 451, 375.
139. Ibid. 361, 580, 265.
140. *W* 112–13, 115, 116–17.

in an era of Baconian improvement and instrumental reason; materialist monism is a true leveller.[141]

Winstanley's monistic metaphysics turns into a rational physiocratic sociology when he discusses the origins of social conflict. In *A New-Yeers Gift* he says that "All this falling out or quarrelling among mankind, is about the earth who shall, and who shall not enjoy it." In *The Law of Freedom*, he places rival definitions of freedom inside a materialist hierarchy of determinations. Freedom of trade is only "freedom under the will of a conqueror." Freedom of religion is "an unsettled freedom." The Ranters' sexual freedom is "the freedom of wanton unreasonable beasts." And the freedom of the elder brother to be a landlord of all the earth is "but a half freedom, and begets murmurings, wars, and quarrels." True freedom, he says,

> lies where a man receives his nourishment and preservation, and that is in the use of the earth. . . . Do not the ministers preach for maintenance in the Earth? the lawyers plead causes to get the possessions of the earth? Doth not the Soldier fight for the Earth? And doth not the landlord require rent, that he may live in the fullness of the earth by the labor of his tenants? And so, from the thief upon the highway to the king who sits upon the throne, do not every one strive, either by force of arms, or secret cheats, to get the possessions of the earth from one another, because they see their freedom lies in plenty, and their bondage lies in poverty?

Reversing the priority of his earlier works, Winstanley argues, "the inward bondages of the mind, as covetousness, pride, hypocrisy, envy, sorrow, fears, desperation, and madness, are all occasioned by the outward bondage, that one sort of people lay on another." Winstanley's "is occasioned by," like Marx's "conditions" and Williams's "determines," emphasizes the quantitative and logical priority of social and collective life over individual ethics, while stopping short of mechanical causality.[142] Later in *The Law of Freedom*, an imagined "zealous, but ignorant professor" objects that Winstanley proposes a "low and carnal ministry indeed," which "leads men to know nothing, but the knowledge of the earth, and the secrets of nature, but we are to look after spiritual and heavenly things." Winstanley responds with a materialist catechism, asking again if all zealous professors, as well as ministers, soldiers, and lawyers, do not struggle to enjoy the earth: "Why do you heap up riches, why do you eat and drink, and wear clothes? why do you take a woman, and lie with her to beget children? Are not all these carnal and low things of the Earth? and do you not live in them, and covet them as much as any? nay more than many which you call men of the world?" Winstanley's mixed tone suggests not only a traditional Christian condemnation of hypocrisy, but also a Ranterish attempt to seduce his readers into acknowledging and

---

141. Ibid. 519, 600. John Rogers discusses the monist and vitalist materialism of Winstanley, Milton, Cavendish, and others in *The Matter of Revolution*, Ithaca, NY, 1996.

142. *W* 380, 519–20; *MECW* 29.263; Williams, *Problems* 31–49.

embracing the carnal and material desires underlying their spiritual pretensions.[143]

Winstanley's corporate ideal differs from the order-based ideals of dominant culture in its egalitarianism, its constant focus on common-preservation rather than oppressive order, and its basis in an agrarian praxis simultaneously sensuous and rational. Even in his precommunist pamphlet *Truth Lifting Up Its Head*, he depicts God and his creation coming together as a monist gathering of spinsters: "The spirit of the father is pure reason: which as he made, so he knits the whole creation together into a oneness of life and moderation; every creature sweetly in love lending their hands to preserve each other, and so upholds the whole fabric."[144] In *The New Law*, he extends this into a theory of subjectivity, whereby "all the glory and content that man takes in other creatures of the earth, it is but a rejoicing in himself." The new heaven and new earth will appear when "a man shall be made to see Christ in other creatures, as well as in himself, every one rejoicing each in other, and all rejoicing in their king."[145] For Marx, the "realm of necessity" always undergirds the "realm of freedom"; for Winstanley, "the law of necessity, that the earth should be planted for the common-preservation and peace of his house-hold," undergirds *The Law of Freedom*. He contrasts the original impulse to "common-preservation," which is "a principle in every one to seek the good of others, as himself, without respecting persons," with "self-preser-vation," which has regard for itself and for members of its own class, but none for "the peace, freedom, and preservation of the weak and foolish among brethren." This ethical opposition has deep roots in the residual traces of a precapitalist mode of production.[146] Winstanley's communal emphasis extends even to his theory of sexuality. He criticizes the Ranters not for antinomian disorder, but because their predatory love creates bondage, whereas "universal love . . . seeks the preservation of others as of one self." Consistently enough, he warns, "Let none go about to suppress that ranting power by their punishing hand."[147]

In criticizing "self-preservation," Winstanley leveled the order-based models of dominant culture. Taking up the absolutist body politic metaphor,

---

143. *W* 565–66. Compare the "Postscript" to the Ranter pamphlet *Justification of the Mad Crew* 26–7.
144. *W* 108.
145. Ibid. 169–70.
146. Ibid. 536–7. Winstanley alludes to Peter in Acts 10.34 ("I perceive that God is no respecter of persons")—a passage invoked by laboring-class radical Christians as often as ruling-class *de factoists* invoked Romans 13.1.
147. Ibid. 401, 402. As early as 1648, Winstanley attacked practical antinomianism not as anarchy but as "the serpent's law of works" (*The Saints Paradise* "11" [i.e. 5]–6). For other references to the Ranters, see *Englands Spirit* (*WIR* 122–3), *A New-Yeers Gift* (*W* 364), and *Fire in the Bush*, where Winstanley refers to anti-dualists who claim to "see every thing and power with a single eye" (ibid. 477). He refers to Luke 11.34, but also, perhaps, to the Ranter Laurence Clarkson, who visited the Diggers. Clarkson's *A Single Eye* appeared seven months later, in October 1650, and he later condemned Winstanley as a hypocrite (Nigel Smith, *Collection* 161–75, 182).

he emphasizes the connectedness rather than the hierarchical differentiation of the parts, and omits the traditional head. The "mystical body" of Christ—St Paul's recurrent metaphor, much beloved of Christian hierarchs—remains a headless body, which spreads throughout the "sons and daughters which are members," creating "a sweet community of love between all the members of that humane body." It "made every member a servant to the other, and so preserved the whole body in peace." He tells the city of London that "whole mankind was made equal, and knit into one body by one spirit of love, which is Christ in you, the hope of glory, even as all members of man's body, called the little world, are united into equality of love, to preserve the whole body."[148] This corporate ideal resembles the republican theory of the *vivere civile*, which we might trace back to Aristotle's discussion of humans as political animals. It resembles even more the spirit of the New Model agitators in 1647, with their attempt to base political authority in their own martial praxis. But Winstanley bases his corporate ideal in the agrarian labor that formed the actual foundation of the English economy. Thus, he moves away from those various repressive corporate ideals that instrumentalize human labor and degrade those who practice it. Labor creates not just rents and commodities, but humanity itself: "it is for the health of their bodies, it is a pleasure to the mind, to be free in labors one with another."[149]

In politics as well as material science, Winstanley comes surprisingly close to the capitalist vision of improvement, for he takes a dialectically optimistic view of contemporary social disorder as destroying customary irrationalities, and creating the human and geographic raw materials for a new, rational polity. In *Fire in the Bush*, the tumults and displacements of the revolutionary era become the signs not of a Babel-like confusion, but of an imminent emancipation: "Before you live you must die, and before you be bound up into one universal body, all your particular bodies and societies must be torn to pieces."[150] For Winstanley, as for the radicals at Putney, the powerless and landless English people are the subjects, not the objects, of the Revolution, as he reminds Cromwell and his grandees. The English people demand freedom of the commons

> to be quietly given us, out of the hands of tyrant-government, as our bargain and contract with them; for the Parliament promised, if we would pay taxes, and give free quarter, and adventure our lives against Charles and his party, whom they called the common enemy, they would make us a free people.[151]

Rather than following the instrumental utopists in proposing schemes for forcibly resettling the poor on the land, he proposed to accelerate the process of depopulation through a program of voluntary labor withdrawal. In *The New Law*, directly after the voice in his trance tells him to "Work

148. *W* 204, 323.
149. Ibid. 593.
150. Ibid. 445.
151. Ibid. 276.

together. Eat bread together; declare this all abroad," it gives him some practical advice for attaining this goal: " 'Whosoever it is that labors in the earth, for any person or persons, that lifts up themselves as lord and rulers over others, and that doth not look upon themselves equal to others in the creation, the hand of the Lord shall be upon that laborer: I the Lord have spoke it and I will do it'; Declare this all abroad."[152]

This program is modest in the short-term, but revolutionary in the long. It differs markedly from the deferential patience recommended by the "tithing priest," who enjoins silence "while the kingly power swims in fullness, and laughs at the others' misery." But neither is it, like the war against the king, an exercise of physical force that perpetuates economic tyranny: "For this is the fruit of war from the beginning, for it removes property out of a weaker into a stronger hand, but still upholds the curse of bondage."[153] Rather, in this proposal for labor withdrawal, Winstanley tries to envision a new, pacific use of power. Previously, tenants and wage laborers enjoyed a merely formal freedom to withdraw their labor—the freedom to starve. Now, joined to the Diggers' revolutionary project, this formal freedom becomes actual and leads to a new form of collective life. Unlike earlier anti-enclosure rioters, who attacked hedges and other creatures of enclosure, the Diggers attack the agrarian capitalist system that created them. They propose a quantitative increase in anti-paternalist depopulation that would lead dialectically to a qualitative change in land tenure. When enough tenants leave their landlords behind, the landlords will have to work their own fields, and the distinctions between landlord and tenant, enclosure and common field, will disappear: anyone who lays sole claim to any piece of land, "let such an one labor that parcel of land by his own hands, none helping him."[154]

This elective displacement suggests Woodhouse's Puritan dialectic of separation and analogy, or, more concretely, the emigration to New England. Sacvan Bercovitch has characterized New Englanders as separatists on a mission for God—dialectical Protestants whose religious withdrawal from the persecuting City of Man would in time help to transform it into the City of God.[155] The Diggers practice a similar withdrawal on an economic level—and they claimed the English commons and wastes more

152. Ibid. 431–2, 190.
153. Ibid. 388–9, 355.
154. Ibid. 195. Underestimating Winstanley's non-violent radicalism, John Morrill says that he proposed simply to persuade the rich to surrender their superfluous property (Morrill, "The Impact on Society," Morrill, *Revolution* 91–111, 97)—a position closer to the eloquent radical idealism of *Tyranipocrit Discovered* (1649). Winstanley's idealism lay not in thinking the English ruling class would disempower itself, but in hoping it would refrain from crushing him as soon as he attempted to show English workers how to reclaim the means of production. When critics and historians refer to the Diggers' "failure," implying some sort of interesting internal or tragic flaw, they avert their eyes from a simpler explanation: agrarian capitalists rightly saw them as a threat and wiped them out. Nigel Smith says it was "the laws of supply and demand, and of pure survival" that laid the Diggers low (*Literature* 175); Winstanley says it was "club-law" (*W* 373).
155. *The American Jeremiad*, Madison 1978, 38.

legitimately than the Puritans claimed Algonquian Massachusetts. More-over, this economic withdrawal has a religious component: just as Winstan-ley's communism encourages copyhold tenants and wage laborers to break with manorial and capitalist discipline, so, too, his anticlericalism encour-ages them to break with parish discipline. If paternalism longs to put displaced people back into their old place, and if utopian improvement aims to displace them from this old place and fix them fast in a new one, then Digger communism encourages them to withdraw from an old place and create a new place by electing it as their own.

Still, despite his considerable skills as a dialectical theorist of society, Winstanley fell short as an economic theorist and historian. His account of enclosure might lead one to view it as a uniform and simple phenom-enon: from Eden to the Norman Conquest to George Hill, he derives all social conflict from the same struggle between landlords and laborers. Regional variations in enclosure and systemic causes of long- and short-term economic crises remain quite invisible to him. And the economic status of a metropolis like London simply does not figure in his utopia, except, perhaps, as something to be dispersed and transcended, like the pastoralized London of Morris's *News from Nowhere*. Neither does industry, finance, colonialism, or international trade. For a concrete seventeenth-century theory of economic history and its relations to political history, we should turn to the work of James Harrington, the other great materi-alist social theorist of the English Revolution. Harrington formulates a complex theory of history as a series of conflicts between the "superstruc-tures" and the "foundation"—between governmental forms and the capacity to make war based on the distribution of property. This is a remarkable achievement in the history not only of republicanism, but of materialist thought.[156]

However, some problems remain. For Harrington, land is important primarily for "its" ability to generate rent income, and so to support an independent legislature and militia; whatever the weaknesses in Macpher-son's view of Harrington as a possessive individualist, wage labor does indeed form the true lifeblood of his two-chambered cardiac republic.[157] Harrington's signal contribution to seventeenth-century republican the-ory—his "agrarian" regulating inheritance—would have limited primogen-iture, but it would have left untouched seventeenth-century relations of agrarian production. He has a soft spot for landless younger sons of the gentry, but not for rural wage laborers and copyholders, for his republic would have perpetuated the institutionalized theft Winstanley criticizes in *The Law of Freedom*: "If the land belong to three persons, and two of them buy and sell the earth, and the third give no consent, his right is taken

---

156. On Harrington, see Pocock's "Historical Introduction," my *Rational Millennium* (166–245), and Norbrook's *Writing* (357–78).
157. Macpherson, *Political* ch. 6.

from him, and his posterity is engaged in a war."[158] His theory of the transition to the utopian republic of *Oceana* underlines this vision. On the one hand, the new distribution of English landholding works almost automatically to generate new political orders; Harrington was "an economic determinist: he conceived of economic change as a blind impersonal force which somehow produced political change of its own accord, without the lever of mass political action."[159] On the other hand, this process required an anti-monarchical but authoritarian imposition of will from above—the legislative fiat of the Lord Archon Olphaus Megaletor, his fanciful amalgam of the Lord Protector and Lycurgus, will instill civic form into the "herd" and "rout" of an ungoverned people.[160] But Winstanley writes not primarily to convince a dictator prince, but to win over a rural proletariat (and other sympathetic groups) to the mass political action of labor withdrawal. He dedicates *The Law of Freedom* to Cromwell and calls on him to institute the communist state, but he also reminds him that "the kingly conqueror was not beaten by you only as you are a single man, nor by the officers of the army joined to you, but by the hand and assistance of the commoners, whereof some came in person, and adventured their lives with you; others stayed at home, and planted the earth, and paid taxes and freequarter to maintain you that went to war."[161]

Insofar as he is able to describe historically distinct ensembles of landholding, Harrington is the better economic historian. But Winstanley is the better psychologist and sociologist, for he stays focused on the process of exploitation and the way in which individual and collective human identity intertwines with agrarian praxis. Winstanley was painfully and eloquently conscious of the material constraints forming and deforming the consciousness of tenants compelled to participate in the assaults on the Cobham commune, even though "in their hearts they are Diggers."[162] In *Fire in the Bush*, he moves beyond mere moral denunciation of the "imaginary power" of acquisition by tracing a universal, three-stage phenomenology of class consciousness. First comes the "plain-hearted state," which is peaceful but malleable and unstable, identified with human infancy rather than a historical period: "you need not look back

---

158. W 511; see the similar passage in Winstanley's *Appeale to the House of Commons* of July (*W* 309). In late 1649, just before Cavalier assassins killed him, Anthony Ascham alluded to the latter in *Of the Confusions and Revolutions of Governments* (1649). He defends private property by speaking of Adam's sin in Eden against God's property in the tree, but he also speaks at length of the Diggers and summarizes their argument fairly: "They plead, that he who buys, and he who sells the earth to a fellow creature, removes the landmark from a third person, to whom the same land belongs as well as to the other two. . . . I wonder not so much at this sort of arguing, as to find that they who have such sort of arguments in their mouths, should have spades in their hands: for they contain the most intricate points of the constitution of societies, of the laws of nature and nations" (18, 19).

159. Hill, *Puritanism* 312.

160. Harrington, *Political* 838; the improvers' bestial metaphor returns.

161. W 501; see also 574–5.

162. Ibid. 368.

six thousand years to find it; for every single man and woman passes through it."[163] This time is "the image of God, but not the strength and life of God; it is wise, but not wisdom itself," and he associates it with the strength of Peter, which "proved weakness," and calls it "the first time of the Beast, or self, which is full of peace, while a man is in it; but it is a state like wax, flexible and easy to take any impression."[164]

Next comes the "time of the curse" implied by the immoderate use of "the creatures" (material objects)—a time which forms the "second estate of mankind."[165] Here, the acquisitive Adam

> fears where no fear is: he rises up to destroy others, for fear, lest others destroy him: he will oppress others, lest others oppress him; and he fears he shall be in want hereafter; therefore he takes by violence, that which others have labored for. . . . For Imagination begins to tell the soul; if thou enjoyest not fullness of all objects, thou wilt want and starve for food, and so presently fear of poverty takes the throne and reigns; and fear bids thee go, get what thou canst, by hook or by crook, lest thou want, and perish, and die miserably.[166]

This sympathetic account, which suggests Sartre's analysis of seriality, is all the more remarkable given its publication in March 1650, when sustained attacks from without threatened the Cobham commune, and when Winstanley's words may have described defecting Diggers.[167] Finally comes the "third estate of mankind . . . the day of Christ, or the rising up," and restoration from this state of bondage. This is more than the restoration of the first stage: "Now no man hath, or can have true peace, till he be able to see this clear distinction within himself; he that sees nothing but one power, nor never saw any other but one power in him, that man as yet is a slave to the Devil." Winstanley's vision suggests the traditional *felix culpa* model, but it comes closer to a phenomenology of consciousness in the mode of Hegel or Wordsworth.[168]

Winstanley also remained superior to Harrington as an economic *sociologist*, charting a fundamental structural relationship that we may mistake for a merely ethical one. Without losing a sense of differences among city and town, king, nobles, gentry, yeomen, and wage laborers, Winstanley saw the determining early modern movement toward a binary capitalist system of surplus appropriators and surplus producers, with the rural "middling sort" splitting between freeholding yeomen joining with the lords of manors, and proletarianized copyholders forced into joining with landless wage laborers. At the same time, he developed a theory of the complex English social structure, with all its cultural and ideological determinants, and the subjective internalization of that structure. In the

163. Ibid. 482.
164. Ibid. 482, 479–80.
165. Ibid. 482–3.
166. Ibid. 456–7, 460–61.
167. See Keith Thomas, "The Date of Gerrard Winstanley's *Fire in the Bush*," *WIR* 138–42.
168. *W* 483–4. See also T. Wilson Hayes on the dialectical psychology of Marx and Winstanley (*Winstanley* 199–206).

third chapter of *Fire in the Bush*, he engages in an extended piece of allegorical exegesis that resembles Gramsci's theory of hegemony. He calls the antagonist of Christ rising "a fourfold power, much idolized," comparing it to the four beasts of Daniel 7: "the imaginary teaching power" (a beast, indeterminate in species, but with iron teeth), "the imaginary kingly power" (like a lion with eagle's wings), "the imaginary judicature" (like a bear), and the "imaginary art" of "buying and selling the earth" (like a leopard). In other words, religion, civil politics, law, and economy. But matters get more complicated, and Winstanley's allegory grows clotted, for the imaginary teaching power of the clergy, "though he come last, yet indeed he is the father, that begot the other." Moreover, the leopard of buying and selling has four heads: "the power of the sword," "the power of the law," "the power of the covetous imaginary clergy," and "the power of a blind deceived heart, over-awed with fear of men." The economic level, then, is inseparable from the levels of politics, the law, and religion—and from the subjective internalization of all these oppressive powers. These beasts "differ in shape, and yet they agree all in one oppressing power, supporting one another; one cannot live without another; and yet they seem to persecute one another; and if one truly die, all dies."[169]

Winstanley's green millennialism seeks an alternative to seeing social spheres as utterly determined or utterly independent, shifting focus from questions of priority (religion first or politics first?) to questions of concrete social interrelation (how do church and civil rulers differ from each other and reinforce each other?). Whereas the university-trained gentry humanist James Harrington and the utopian improvers turn the people and the lands they inhabit into simple objects of domination, the plebeian autodidact Winstanley produces a sophisticated theory of class hegemony, which preserves a sense of the interconnectedness and inter-dependence of religious, political, legal, and economic power, while insisting that material production forms the foundation of social life. His allegories blend levels of meaning, classes, and social spheres which a rigorous Augustinian or a social scientist might want to distinguish, but which a liberation theologian or a political marxist must strive to connect. To James Stuart's anxious "No bishop, no king," Gerrard Winstanley responds hopefully and more complexly, "No priest, no king; no king, no judge; no judge, no landlord; no landlord, no priest."

But we should hesitate slightly when speaking of Winstanley's "allegorical" reading of the Hebrew Scriptures, and examine the metaphoric ground beneath our feet. As I said in chapter 2, radical sociologists of religion have argued that pre-Davidic Palestine presents us with a series of struggles for the land between an exploited multiethnic peasantry and

---

169. *W* 463–6. "Every pre-condition of the social production process is at the same time its result, and every one of its results appears simultaneously as its pre-condition" (Karl Marx, *Theories of Surplus-Value*, 3 vols, Moscow 1971, 3.507).

their Canaanite lords—a history redacted in a monarchist direction by the whiggish Davidic scribes when they read back their own ethnic/nationalist concerns into earlier accounts. So when Winstanley says that "the land of England shall be a common treasury to all English men without respect of persons: even as the several portions of Canaan were the proper birthright and livelihood of such and such a tribe: neither hedging in the elder, nor hedging out the younger brother," and that "The glory of Israel's Commonwealth is this, / They had no beggar among them," and we say he is reading a fundamentally theological (i.e., "non-economic") text allegorically, we may be repeating that redaction, and obscuring the liberation theology of Joshua's Canaan and Winstanley's Surrey.[170] Sitting and shivering and writing in a cold room, Winstanley theorized his society's reliance on the agrarian labor of working people, its hegemonic system of class domination, and the way in which it might move toward a worldly, non-hierarchical alternative. He was the least allegorical reader of Scripture and the foremost social theorist of seventeenth-century England.

Georgic Prophets and Pastoral Poets

As the Jonsonian city comedy dominates our literary vision of seventeenth-century city life, so the Jonsonian country house poem dominates our vision of the countryside.[171] For this remarkably coherent group of poems we might begin with Aemilia Lanyer's long-neglected "To Cooke-Ham," move on to the generic touchstone of Jonson's "To Penshurst," and follow it up with his own "To Sir Robert Wroth," Carew's "To Saxham" and "To My Friend G. N., from Wrest," and Herrick's "The Country Life," "A Panegyrick," and "The Hock Cart, or Harvest Home." Marvell expands and mutates the genre in "Upon Appleton House," which celebrates the Yorkshire estate of Sir Thomas Fairfax, the recently retired general of the parliamentary armies. Country house conventions also appear in adjacent aristocratic genres: pastoral romance such as Sidney's *Arcadia* (with its idealizing portrait of Kalander's House), fairy poems and celebrations of rural sports and festivals such as we see prominently in Herrick, topographical poetry such as Denham's "Cooper's Hill," and epithalamiums from Spenser to Jonson to Donne to Marvell.

In the opening sections of *The Country and the City*, Raymond Williams wrote the watershed critical analysis of the country house poem, and it

---

170. *Englands Spirit* (*WIR* 117); *W* 524.
171. Alastair Fowler collects seventy-seven poems in *The Country House Poem*, Edinburgh 1994. For critical studies, see Fowler's "Country House Poems," *The Seventeenth Century* 1.1, 1986; William Alexander McClung, *The Country House in English Renaissance Poetry*, Berkeley and Los Angeles 1977; and Charles Molesworth, "Property and Virtue," *Genre* 1, 1968.

takes us at least halfway to the Diggers.[172] Like aristocratic pastoral more generally, the country house poem creates a myth of the pastoral golden age by magically erasing the lapsarian curse of agrarian labor:

> What is really happening, in Jonson and Carew's celebrations of a rural order, is an extraction of just this curse, by the power of art: a magical recreation of what can be seen as a natural bounty and then a willing charity: both serving to ratify and bless the country landowner, or, by a characteristic reification, his house. Yet this magical extraction of the curse of labour is in fact achieved by a simple extraction of the existence of labourers.

For Williams, the poets' presentation of deferential tenants dissimulates the existence of rural exploitation, transforming a productive terrain into an object of aesthetic contemplation.[173] They build this transformation on a strategic reversal: with courtly *sprezzatura*, they turn consuming lords into providers and the tenants whom they exploit into consumers. This is a perennial task for capitalist ideologists, even German economists, whose "gibberish" Engels helpfully glosses: "one who for cash has others give him their labour is called a labour-*giver* [Arbeit*geber*] and one whose labour is taken away from him for wages is called a labour-*taker* [Arbeit*nehmer*]."[174]

The country house poem effaces the practical reality of agrarian labor by viewing it as an endless, effortless feast:

> A charity of production—of loving relations between men actually working and producing what is ultimately, in whatever proportions, to be shared—was neglected, not seen, and at times suppressed, by this habitual reference to a charity of consumption, an eating and drinking communion, which when applied to ordinary working societies was inevitably a mystification. All uncharity at work, it was readily assumed, could be redeemed by the charity of the consequent feast.[175]

For instance, in "To Saxham," Carew argues that, rather than Sir John Croft's tenants preserving him, the charity of his table preserves them, and they in turn bless his table with their prayers. Mildmay Fane calls a personified "Retiredness" the "Great patron of my liberty." Thanks to this

---

172. New York 1973. Williams's book, a remarkable intellectual achievement, provides the best historical survey of the country house poem and allied topographical genres in Britain, from the seventeenth century to the present. James Grantham Turner's *The Politics of Landscape* (Cambridge 1979) studies both seventeenth-century aristocratic topographic poetry and opposing plebeian voices, including Winstanley's. Chris Fitter's *Poetry, Space, Landscape* (Cambridge 1995) studies classical, medieval, and Renaissance English topographic poetry; particularly strong are his discussions of Marvell's "Upon Appleton House" and the ruling-class structure of feeling implicit in seventeenth-century enclosure, landscape painting and poetry, and wonder cabinets.

173. 32.

174. *MECW* 35.28. Thirsk says that improvers struggled to invent "work they would give to the poor" (*Agrarian* 5.2.321), while Mulder observes that "Far from enslaving the poor, as Winstanley claimed, the great landowners of Cobham provided the poor their livelihood" (*Alchemy* 259).

175. Williams, *Country* 31.

tautology, he can become his own client, and at the same time turn the true patrons of his liberty—his "hinds" and their labor—into mere objects for pastoral contemplation:

> Then turning over nature's leaf,
> I mark the glory of the sheaf,
> For every field's a several page
> Deciphering the Golden Age.
> So that without a miner's pains,
> Or Indies' reach, here plenty reigns.[176]

Turner notes that "The harvest of 1647 gave Fane about 5,750 pounds in rent and over 1000 pounds worth of grain; each laborer that year received five pounds and a dinner."[177] *The World Is Turned Upside Down*, a broadside poem of 1646, opines that the country houses' hospitable Yuletide welcome of the poor is now counted "a sin": "Christmas was killed at Naseby fight: / Charity was slain at that same time."

Williams resists the impulse to reduce agrarian unrest to a timeless struggle between tenants and landlords, the poor and the rich, for classes are dynamic and malleable relationships, not fixed objects. But he also insists that any morally responsible criticism should work to maintain an imaginative sympathy with exploited laborers:

> There is only one real question: where do we stand, with whom do we identify, as we read the complaints of disturbance, as this order in its turn broke up? Is it with the serfs, the boardars and cotters, the villeins; or with the abstracted order to which, through successive generations, many hundreds of thousands of men were never more than instrumental?[178]

In a later interview, referring to a critique of this passage and to Jonson's "Penshurst," Williams comments,

> Jonson had to find a patron, and in order to find a patron he had to pay that kind of compliment in that kind of house: such was the nature of the convention. But if I cannot be seriously offended that in the poem he wrote out the labourer, what affiliation can I now make to labourers? . . . I found it necessary to say in the crudest way that these houses were primarily sites of exploitation and robbery and fraud.[179]

Williams's critics have said that the country house poets either could not have felt his sort of sympathy with agrarian laborers, or that they actually did.[180] Fowler responds that "In manorial society, communal eating—joint

---

176. "To Retiredness," in Hugh Maclean, ed., *Ben Jonson and the Cavalier Poets*, New York 1974, 206.
177. *Politics* 151.
178. *Country* 38.
179. *Politics and Letters* 307, 312.
180. McClung, *Country House* 21–2; George Parfitt, *Ben Jonson*, London 1976, 161; William E. Cain, "The Place of the Poet in Jonson's 'To Penshurst' and 'To My Muse,'" *Criticism* 21, 1979, 39.

consumption of what all joined to produce—had symbolic as well as real value."[181] Kevin Sharpe notes that the ideal order of Carew's country house poems offers "unlimited hospitality to the poor and strangers as well as those of 'finer thread.' "[182] The difficulty that Williams's critics have had in addressing his rather clear distinction between a nonexistent charity of production and a sporadic and symbolic charity of consumption suggests not a failure but an active refusal to comprehend. Williams has faced similar criticisms from those who share his assumptions about the worldliness of literature and literary criticism. Jonathan Goldberg says "To Penshurst" "embraces the reality of workers, encroached-upon landowners, mean-spirited lords, unchaste wives, servants, and begging suitors" and "presents an image of an absolute totality, an inclusive fantasy of containment. And the poem in its royal largesse manages to contain rebellion as well."[183] Don Wayne agrees substantially with Williams, but objects that he labors under a "weight of moral indignation that is not really adequately supported by a thorough, close analysis of the texts," and warns that "Anachronism is one of the dangers of any criticism that is fundamentally a moral polemic (whether of the right or of the left)."[184]

I'm less bothered by the close and hot-breathed sort of anachronism that sees recognizable conflicts in the past than by the detached and genteel anachronism that turns a historical epoch into a closed system by purging it of those internal social contradictions that create its proper temporality and (through their dialectical working-out) its connection to us. But Williams's treatment of the seventeenth-century country house poem does invite charges of anachronism, even from a marxist perspective. First, how can these poems represent something like the "fetishism of commodities" two centuries before that form dominates the economy and Marx describes its logic, and in the countryside, not the urban world of consumer capitalism?[185] The indubitable anachronism here lies not so much in Williams's reading as in the English economy itself. For Marx, the capitalist mode of production appeared first not in the modern English factory, but in the early modern English field. Robert Brenner has followed up forcefully, arguing that England moved away from use rights still prevalent in Continental Europe to a new system based in absolute property held by landlords, rented by large capitalist farmers, and worked by agrarian proletarians: "By the middle decades of the

181. *Country* 8.
182. *Criticism* 130.
183. *James I* 26.
184. *Penshurst* 17, 20. Leftist opponents of left moralism forget the ferocious moral polemic that Marx mixes with his analysis, as when he describes Edmund Burke as a "sycophant . . . who always sold himself in the best market. . . . In face of the infamous cowardice of character that reigns today . . . it is our bounden duty again and again to brand the Burkes, who only differ from their successors in one thing—talent" (*MECW* 35.748n.). It's not clear that the unspeakability of such sentences inside modern academic discourse derives from an advance in scientific rigor.
185. *MECW* 35.81–94.

seventeenth century, after a long evolution, a strong majority of English landlords, titled and untitled, great and small, were maintaining themselves in the same way, deriving the bulk of their income from taking competitive rents from commercial farmers for the lease of their absolute landed property."[186] Like anything new, this historical change felt and perhaps still feels like a traumatic anachronism. The birth trauma of capitalism in agrarian England called forth the country house poem's compensatory fantasy of an organic society and unproduced wealth. Ellen Meiksins Wood distinguishes early modern England's multifaceted capitalist culture of improvement with France's absolutist and bourgeois Enlightenment.[187] We can extend this to the country house poem: the generalized and meditative French topographic poetry and landscape poetry of the period, such as Saint-Amant's "La Solitude" and Théophile's "La Maison de Silvie," offers no corollary to the literary vision of improvement in a particular site that defines contemporary English poems. If the English countryside, with its classic triad of large landholder, capitalist tenant, and proletarian wage laborer, gives birth to capitalism, then the English country house poem, with its characteristic mystified triad of munificent patron (capitalist landlord), adoring client-poet (capitalist ideologist), and deferential hind (agrarian wage laborer), gives birth to commodity fetishism. McRae finds a vision of improvement throughout seventeenth-century literature, even in Herrick's ostentatiously traditionalist pastoral.[188] The country house myth continues its symbiotic relation with capitalism in *Country Life* magazine, the cult of the Anglo-Irish country houses (favorite objects of rebel arsonists during the War of Independence), and the American obsession with *Gone With the Wind*—that perniciously resonant, Klan-happy country house novel and movie.

The second potential anachronism: if the seventeenth-century country house poem forms a determinate class project, not a culturally immanent *mentalité*, why can't we hear the contemporary oppositional voices that reveal its particular class perspective? Williams's earlier seventeenth century lacks those plebeian voices protesting agrarian expropriation that he hears in later eras—voices like those of Duck, Goldsmith, Crabbe, and Cobbett. Beginning with Williams, left critics of the country house poem have typically constructed an immanent critique, focusing on the gaps, fissures, and moments of ideological bad conscience revealed in the poems themselves. In "To Robert Wroth," for instance, Jonson praises the country life as one in which Wroth can feast on "unbought provision"—a cunning expression that condenses paradisal plenty and sweaty-browed

---

186. *BD* 10–63; *BMR* 641.

187. *Pristine* 81–94. See Marx on England as "the most revolutionary country in the world. . . . '*Clearing of estates*,' a technical term [well known] in the United Kingdom, will not be found in any continental country" (*Theories* 2.237).

188. *God* 262–99. Kendrick examines "Upon Appleton House" in the context of English agrarian capitalism, the Diggers, and the improving agrarian utopia of Cressy Dymock in "Agons of the Manor," David Lee Miller, Sharon O'Dair, and Harold Weber, eds, *The Production of English Renaissance Culture*, Ithaca, NY, 1994, 13–55.

payment in kind, or wage-paid house gardens. Herrick's "The Hock-Cart," written about Mildmay Fane's estate at Apthorpe, reminds the jolly rural celebrants, "Feed him ye must, whose food fills you"—a line that moves with indecent haste from economic realism to patriarchal idealization.[189] Despite its origin and circulation in a dominant landholding subculture, the country house poem does not simply express that subculture's desires and will to power. Working from Jameson's conclusion to *The Political Unconscious*, which proposes to uncover the dialectic of ideology and utopia within canonical and high cultural literary works, Wayne argues that even so manifestly aristocratic a poem as "To Penshurst" reveals a Bloch-style utopian surplus.[190]

This yields excellent results, but a new formalism looms if we assume too quickly that ruling-class cultural artifacts contain their own utopian critique and supplement, and if we avoid looking (as Bloch habitually did) to out-of-the-way and non-canonical sources. If we admit that the laboring classes can imagine a utopia not mechanically passed down from the ruling classes, one can also find this dialectic in the gap between the texts of the ruling classes and those of the laboring classes. Here, the Diggers provide a crucial seventeenth-century supplement to Williams's study: the period's most powerful country-born critique of agrarian capitalism. At the end of the era of transition from feudalism to capitalism, the Digger pamphlets offer a communist utopian critique of the capitalist ideological fetishism at work in the country house poem. This critique remains implicit, for Winstanley shows no familiarity with the Sons of Ben. But of course, the Diggers had country houses of their own. They are less familiar to us than those of the hereditary aristocracy—partly because poets took little notice of them, partly because they tend not to exist any longer. But had they never existed, neither would have the great houses. We can see one such house in a letter of 1649 written by seven Diggers, who place themselves quite consciously in opposition to the values of their intended readers, General Thomas Fairfax and the Council of State:

> But now sirs, this last week upon the 28th of November, there came a party of soldiers commanded by a cornet, and some of them of your own regiment, and by their threatening words forced three laboring men to help them pull down our two houses, and carried away the wood in a cart to a gentleman's house who hath been a cavalier all our time of wars, and cast two or three old people out who lived in those houses to lie in the open field this cold weather (an action more becoming the Turks to deal with Christians than for one Christian to deal with another); but if you inquire into the business you will find that the gentleman that set the soldiers on are enemies to you, for some of the chief had hands in the Kentish rising against the Parliament, and we know, and you will find it true if you trust them so far, that they love you but from the teeth outward.[191]

189. Maclean, *Ben Jonson* 125.
190. Jameson, *Political* 281–99; Wayne, *Penshurst* 130, 208n.
191. *W* 344.

This account of eviction, demolition, and property transfer suggests "Upon Appleton House," which tells how one of Thomas Fairfax's ancestors (William Fairfax) abducted another (Isabel Thwaites) from a nunnery and married her, and how their sons made that nunnery a quarry for renovations to the family estate after the dissolution of the religious houses by Henry VIII. Fairfax himself profited enormously from estates acquired during the war, but also looked after the estates of George Villiers, Duke of Buckingham, while he was in exile. Marvell's poem concludes by prophesying the marriage of Thomas Fairfax's daughter Maria—as it turned out, to Buckingham. Both country house poems reveal the logic of property in dividing former revolutionary allies and reconciling former revolutionary enemies on class lines. But finally, the substantive contrasts predominate over these formal parallels. For the easy, edible cosmos of Penshurst, we have a world of commands, threats, and force. For the eternal present of the country house poem's commemorative verse, we have the juridical specificity of November 28 1649, rendered in plain, reportorial prose, and the grinding quotidian familiarity of these rural brute facts: force conquers need, the rich evict the poor, and poor people's houses are fragile things, easily pulled down. For the pious perpetuity of a dynasty, celebrated by happy fireside feasters, we have soldiers and laboring men ordered to destroy two houses and ordered to cast two old people impiously out into the cold.

The country house poem operates according to a fundamentally spatial vision, which consistently attempts to reduce lived human processes to iconic or topographical artifacts. In a poem prefacing William Cartwright's posthumous *Comedies, Tragi-Comedies, with other Poems* (1651), Edward Sherburne asserts a class conflict between two topoi, attacking the "Levellers of Wit" and "Delvers in poetry . . . that only skill / To make Parnassus a St. George's Hill"—referring, perhaps, to *The Diggers Song* and *The Diggers Mirth*.[192] Country house poems invite examination inside the tradition of contemporary landscape painting, for they present the houses, the surrounding landscape, and the local tenants through an iconic imagination that effaces the reality of rural production, and, indeed, of time itself.[193] Country house topography figures a fantasy of uncreated wealth and dynasty. The houses themselves are "piles" of native stone that have emerged, as if by themselves, from the soil. The trees surrounding them are dynastic emblems, whose persistence in time naturalizes the ruling-class transmission of real property: the oak representing Margaret Clifford in Lanyer's "To Cooke-Ham," the oaks of Sir Philip Sidney and Lady Leicester and the copse of Gamage in "To Penshurst," the allegorical Caroline oak ruling over the troubled lesser trees of James Howell's

---

192. Thanks to Chris Kendrick for this thought.
193. See Fitter's discussion of "landskip" as "the particular complex of values by which a highly advanced commercial civilization, of secular and materialist tendencies, engages and construes the natural world"—beginning with the ancient world and medieval world, but flourishing in the capitalist English seventeenth century (*Poetry* 10).

Dodona's Grove. In "Upon Appleton House," things are, as usual, more complex, but finally not much different. Marvell flees the postlapsarian georgic labor of "the Bloody Thestylis" and her levelling cohort to the emblematic "ark" of the wood, where he sees a Caroline oak infected by a Villiersesque traitor worm and felled by a Cromwellian hewell. And at the end of the poem, Marvell focuses on the dynastic "Fairfacian Oak."[194]

The country house poem tends to present tenants iconically. In "To Penshurst," they bashfully bear gifts, "emblems of themselves," to the Sidney family. In "The Hock Cart," Herrick's striking partial demystification of the genre, we see tenants most thoroughly instrumentalized:

> Come, sons of summer, by whose toil
> We are the lords of wine and oil;
> By whose tough labors and rough hands
> We rip up first, then reap our lands.[195]

"Appleton House" opens with a "stately frontispiece of poor," and concludes with a "vitrified" nature that utterly effaces the labor of the poem's middle sections.[196] As country house poets efface agrarian praxis, they retreat from the chaotic military praxis of Civil War England. Mildmay Fane, who had supported the king in the early phases of the Civil War, suffered as a result two sorts of non-pastoral enclosure (in the Tower, and then restriction to an area near London). He retreated to Apthorpe in 1644, where he rested "out of fears or noise of war," and heard no other contest than his tenants' whimsically presented attempts to "make the tenth [their tithes] go less."[197] The year after receiving the Diggers' petition, Fairfax resigned his command of the parliamentary armies because of his reluctance to invade Scotland, and retreated to Appleton House, where Marvell says he enjoyed an enclosed floral simulacrum of the battlefield—there, bees "fire fragrant volleys" and "the gardener has the soldier's place."[198]

But the Digger poor are no longer topoi in a landscape. They are literate authors or articulate subscribers—speakers in their own voices about themselves and their practical activity. Their charity of production reassembles the laborer's arm, the landlord's stomach, and the poet's tongue in a human whole: "Work together. Eat bread together; declare this all abroad."[199] In their plebeian georgic, the earth is never a contemplative landscape but a site of communal praxis: seeded, manured, bled into, fought over in the continuing struggle between Norman landlord and freeborn Briton. Trees are not emblems, but obstructions to plows,

---

194. Stanzas 51, 57, 61, 93.
195. Maclean, *Ben Jonson* 123–4.
196. Stanzas 9, 86.
197. Maclean, *Ben Jonson* 207.
198. Stanzas 38, 43.
199. *W* 190; "He is a monster who is all tongue and no hand" (ibid. 567).

or the source of fuel and timber, and so an object of class struggle.[200] In *A Declaration from the Poor Oppressed People of England*, the Diggers promise to "lay hold upon, and as we stand in need, to cut and fell, and make the best advantage we can of the woods and trees, that grow upon the commons," hoping to sell wood to tide them over until their crops come up.[201] This concrete struggle adds material resonance to the arboreal tyrannicide presented in *A New-Yeers Gift*:

> For kingly power is like a great spread tree, if you lop the head or top-bow, and let the other branches and root stand, it will grow again and recover fresher strength. . . . But alas oppression is a great tree still, and keeps off the sun of freedom from the poor commons still, he hath many branches and great roots which must be grubbed up, before every one can sing Sion's songs, in peace.[202]

First the grubbing-up, then the song of the Lamb: a georgic millennialism breaks out of the paternalist cycle of extorted labor and carnival, the capitalist dialectic of enclosure, displacement, and improvement.

For the Diggers, the idea of an aristocratic retreat from the battlefield to the cornfield is an absurdity, for they see a fundamental continuity between military praxis, which has overthrown the king, and communal agrarian praxis, which will overthrow the hedge kings and the tithe-supported tyrants of a state church.[203] In *The Law of Freedom*, Winstanley submits the alpine imagination of courtly and monarchical pastoral to the levelling georgic imagination of Digger prophecy:

> A Monarchical army lifts up mountains, makes valleys, viz., advances tyrants, and treads the oppressed in the barren lanes of poverty. But a commonwealth's army is like John Baptist, who levels the mountains to the valleys, pulls down the tyrant, and lifts up the oppressed: and so makes way for the spirit of peace and freedom to come into rule and inherit the earth.[204]

200. In *The Blazing World*, Cavendish expresses pastoral distress at the levelling of her husband's Colchester forests to construct warships (*The Blazing World and Other Writings*, Harmondsworth 1994, 193); the poor of Colchester also poached timber to help them feed their starving families (Manning, *1649* 95). Trees function in aristocratic pastoral as tokens of dynastic hierarchy, in utopian improvement as objects of intense programs of research, and in popular struggle as the source of "crops and tops" claimed by commoners, who also sought out forests as a space of liberty. On arboriculture and improvement, see Keith Thomas, *Man and the Natural World*, Harmondsworth 1984, 192–223.
201. *W* 272.
202. Ibid. 353, 357. Anthony Low discusses Winstanley as a georgic poet/prophet and the affinities of georgic and millennialism in *The Georgic Revolution*, Princeton 1985, 215–20, 351.
203. See Winstanley's discussion of Israel's collective warfare and distribution of land and his elegant argument about the collective right born of the Revolution (*W* 524, 509).
204. Ibid. 575. John (Luke 3.4–6) echoes Isaiah (40.3–5). Compare Spenser's mighty Gyant: "Therefore I will throw downe these mountaines hie, / And make them levell with the lowly plaine / . . . . Tyrants that make men subiect to their law, / I will supresse, that they no more may raine" (*Faerie Queene* 5.2.2). *The Faerie Leveller* (1648) quotes this passage and provides a key identifying Charles with Artegall, and Cromwell, improbably enough, with the levelling giant.

The enclosed gardens and fields of Thomas Fairfax and Mildmay Fane try to return to Eden through pastoral nostalgia and utopian improvement; the disenclosed fields of the Digger pamphlets open up into a communal future through revolutionary agrarian praxis and prophecy.

Bloch distinguishes enclosed or filled emotions from expectant emotions, which open out entirely into the horizon of time.[205] Perhaps we should also distinguish filled or sated genres like the country house poem from expectant or hungry ones like the Digger pamphlet. The country house poem lives contentedly in a landscape enclosed in time and space. The future appears as a dynastic fantasy of pure replication through primogeniture, improvement, entailment, and the genial infusion of legitimate paternal virtue, which will help find "a Fairfax for our Thwaites," in the strangely incestuous phrase of "Upon Appleton House."[206] The closed couplets favored by most country house poets, and Marvell's foursquare stanzas, readily enclose the landlord's world of fields, gardens, and private prospects. The Digger pamphlet, on the other hand, is ill at ease in its own present. With its repetitions, structurelessness, ungrammaticality, serial being, and dialogical plea for a response, it suggests a not-yet-existent novum, not a timeless plenum. Anyone disappointed at its descriptive poverty is employing an aesthetic foreign to its class experience, for the worked earth is not a landscape. Rather, it arrives in a "torn country garment," but with a glowing Blakean body beneath: "take off the clownish language, for under that you may see beauty."[207] Its lament over two worlds clashes with the ideological country house ode to one world. Despite the seemingly epochal execution of a king, the hedge kings still rule England:

> Monarchy is twofold; either for one king to rule, or for many to rule by kingly principles; for the king's power lies in his laws, not in the name: and if either one king rule, or many rule by king's principles, much murmuring, grudges, troubles and quarrels may and will arise among the oppressed people upon every gained opportunity.[208]

Just as Egyptians persecuted the Jews, and Jews the early Christians, so Christians now persecute those who prophesy the Joachitish third age, when the spirit will rise in every son and daughter.[209] The country house's *now* defined by a simulacrum of the Golden Age jars with the Digger *now* defined by the chafing of the Norman Yoke; the cryptic "time and times and half a time" of Old and New Testament apocalyptic appears as a social conflict: "Time shall dash against times, and times shall dash against the dividing of time; and the divisions in the dividing of time shall destroy him [kingly power]; till the Creation be cleansed of all these plagues. . . .

205. *Principle* 1.74.
206. Stanza 94.
207. W 510.
208. Ibid. 527.
209. Ibid. 160–63.

And this makes way for Christ, the universal love, to take the kingdom, and the dominion of the whole earth." The "dividing of time" in England may be seen in "the variety of Churches, and differences in religion, that is amongst men; every one pleading his privilege, or else it is called the dividing of time, in regard the Government of the land is taken out of the hands of one man, and put into the hands of many."[210] These clashing times suggest Bloch's "nonsynchronism," that present-sense defined by the felt experience of contradictory temporalities, of distinct modes of production, in a single historical moment.[211]

Country house poems have attracted considerably more critical attention than the Digger pamphlets, for they lend themselves much more readily to regnant spatially oriented forms of interpretation. A conventional account, frequently associated with Lukács, argues that, in a literary analog to commodity fetishism, modernism privileges space over time, reifying temporality by turning it into a purely interior or subjective experience.[212] I think this conventional account retains a good deal of explanatory force—not only for modernism, but for its semi-detached postmodernist offspring. The very category of temporality has tended to evaporate from recent Renaissance studies, along with the allied concepts of intention, utopia, consciousness, and revolution. Neither antimodernist revisionism (with its contempt for "whig" history and its model of a deferential social system), nor modernist New Criticism (with its refutation of the intentional fallacy and its emphasis on the verbal icon), nor postmodernist deconstruction (with its critique of phenomenology and its vision of temporality as spacing and endlessly deferred presence), nor new historicism (with its focus on homological emblems and the system of power/knowledge) has shown much interest in the temporality of Renaissance literature. But questions of method are inextricably tied to questions of canon, and no attempt to argue for spatial form and the literary system can prove convincing which simply overlooks oppositional prophetic writing like Winstanley's. When the ruling class of early modern England listens to the violent clashing of times and peoples in the English Revolution, it hears an irrational chaotic Babel, and retreats into the filled *hortus conclusus* of a country house or some analogous meditative site. But the Diggers hear this clash pregnant with utopia. Their expectant *hortus inconclusus* opens up into the socialist future.

Common Futures: The Diggers and the Forest People

But this connection I'm suggesting has not gone unchallenged. Five techniques have emerged for disconnecting the Diggers from their properly

---

210. Ibid. 467, 485. See also *Breaking* 109; *Mysterie* 34, 39; *W* 208, 261, 383; and Bradstock, *Faith* 114–25.
211. "Nonsynchronism and the Obligation to Its Dialectics," *New German Critique* 11, 1977.
212. See particularly "Narrate or Describe?" in *Writer & Critic and Other Essays*, New York 1970, 110–48.

improper future: *snubbing, periodizing, sneering, stalinizing,* and *patriarchaliz-ing.*[213] The first and most effective technique simply ignores plebeian history. The positive evidence here is, understandably, somewhat lacking, but the snubbing occasionally becomes audible. To mention Winstanley is to elicit a sigh at one's—not *error,* exactly, but—*soixante-huitish* gaucherie. Joan Thirsk's massive *Agrarian History of Britain and Wales* spares the Diggers barely a page. She agrees with their gentry opponents that their project constituted a gross affront, and that the land they cultivated was poorly chosen anyway—as if the gentry would have been more reluctant to trample a better-situated commune. Of their theory of the land, she says nothing.[214] Kevin Sharpe observes that Winstanley and his partisans have overlooked the benefits of enclosure, "which were not merely the invention of Tory apologists." He laments the "tired old marxist preoccu-pation with nascent popular movements" such as the Diggers, particularly since "Land and liberty never became the slogan of the English Revolu-tion; radical millenarianism never infected the poor; the radical groups, especially the most important, never appealed to the poor."[215] Never, never, and especially never; except, of course, when they did.

The second technique, periodization, casts the Diggers as premodern religious thinkers, not modern social revolutionaries—a strange argu-ment, which implies that religion existed outside of early modern society, and that it has fled the modern world. In "Economic and Social Thought of Gerrard Winstanley: Was He a Seventeenth-Century Marxist?" Winthrop Hudson answers, unsurprisingly, "no," then adds, dumbfoundingly, that the Diggers "did not conceive of their venture as a means of effecting social change or as a way of gaining desired ends."[216] Richard Schlatter says Winstanley was "not a proto-Marxist or a creator of humanistic utopias" but a "religious mystic."[217] Paul Elmen dismisses marxist readings of Winstanley, then observes that, "far from being a secular program, Winstanley's vision of a new heaven and a new earth was not unlike John's on Patmos"—an observation presumably meant to etherealize Winstanley, not to make us recall John's apocalyptic curses at the merchants of Babylon.[218] David Mulder finds even Elmen too much of a modernizer: his argument that, for Winstanley, an elimination of hunger would

---

213. These techniques have some corollaries in scholarship on More. R. W. Chambers attempted to enclose *Utopia* in the past by arguing for its fundamentally medieval vision (*Thomas More,* London 1953), while C. S. Lewis and many others wish to insert it in an eternal ludic present as an exercise in playful gaming or bloodless satire (*English Literature in the Sixteenth Century,* Oxford 1954, 167–71), and J. C. Davis allows its connection to the anticapitalist present only by emphasizing its totalitarian tendencies (*Utopia* 41–62).

214. *Agrarian* 5.2.321–2; see also 4.465. The barrenness of George Hill and Cobham Heath was no news to the Diggers (*W* 260). In a later assessment, Thirsk says that the landlords' defense of their property defeated the Diggers ("Agrarian" 182–3).

215. "Religion" 279; "Battles"; *Politics* 306.

216. *Journal of Modern History* 18.1, 1946.

217. *GZ.*

218. "The Theological Basis of Digger Communism," *Church History* 23, 1954, 213.

reconcile men to each other and to God "is a reasonably good expression of the religious ethic behind the Salvation Army and is, therefore, a nineteenth-century mode of thought."[219] John Knott argues that "digging itself is best understood not as a revolutionary act but as a sign, a symbolic witness to the impending age of the Spirit when the earth would again be a 'common treasury.' . . . What may look like striking progressive social theory, anticipating some of the central concerns of marxism, can better be understood as a profound nostalgia for an idealized life of perfect simplicity and 'plain-heartedness.' "[220] Lotte Mulligan, John K. Graham, and Judith Richards criticize Hill and others for scanting Winstanley's religious language, for "minimizing the part theology played in his theories of social and moral change," for failing to see that Winstanley's God is transcendent as well as immanent, and for ignoring his belief that the world would be transformed not by the action of people but by a literal second coming.[221]

False binaries thicken the air. To begin with, "theology" is a troublesome ally, particularly if one intends the formal university discipline of that name, for Winstanley refers to the "City Divinity" as "that great City Babylon" and proposes to execute professional ministers.[222] But even if we mean an internally coherent religious idea system existing prior to social change, significant problems remain: only a desiccated version of the history of ideas can set an absolute opposition between "religion" and "society"; any sociologist of religion, whether theist, agnostic, or atheist, would find that nonsensical—analogous to a rigorous opposition between apples and fruit (or fruit and apples). Of course, the sociology of religion talks about a structurally demarcated sphere of religious experience and institutional life within a social totality. But why attribute faith in a distinct religious sphere to the Diggers, who spent so much time attacking the social institutions (tithing, universities, a caste of professional clerics) and the conceptual oppositions (between spirit and matter, clergy and laity, heaven and earth, labor and prayer, Eden and England and the New Jerusalem) that helped to produce and reproduce that sphere? Winstanley sees no opposition between secular life and the millennium, for "community of ownership in the earth and the resurrection of Christ are interchangeable concepts," while "True religion, and undefiled, is to let every one quietly have earth to manure, that they may live in freedom by their labors."[223] These historians have been unable to assimilate Sabine's fifty-year-old insight: "By what may seem at first sight a paradox, the very universality of religious experience in the life of the saint gives to Winstanley's personal philosophy a tone of secularism. . . . In short,

219. *Alchemy* 16n.
220. *The Sword of the Spirit*, Chicago 1980, 86, 114.
221. "Winstanley: A Case for the Man as He Said He Was," *Journal of Ecclesiastical History* 28.1, 1977, 58, 71, 65.
222. *W* 570, 590.
223. Pocock, "Historical Introduction" 96; *W* 428.

religion was for him a way of life, not a ceremonial, a profession, or a metaphysic."[224] We might compare the surreligious secularism of *Tyranipocrit Discovered*, which trumps the godly by arguing that one ought to add six days to the Sabbath.[225] Winstanley does, in fact, distinguish a transcendent and an immanent God—not absolutely but structurally, as "The Father," a "universal power, that hath spread himself in the whole globe," and "The Son," who is "the same power drawn into, and appearing in one single person."[226] The immanent, indwelling spirit of God achieves transcendence through rational reflection, preaching, writing, and communal praxis.

Third, *sneering*: where these historians of ideas have tried to enclose Winstanley in a sealed theological past, others try to enclose him in an eternal capitalist present, where his prophetic socialism becomes no more than the petulant, non-ideological pursuit of personal gain inside a fixed social system. Richard T. Vann led the way by examining Winstanley's whole career and constructing a psychological explanation for the Digger movement. He suggests (with no evidence) that Winstanley was a destitute gentleman's son, and that "The experiment in Digger communism would seem to have come between the ruin of a career as a Merchant Tailor and the scarcely propitious beginning of one as a steward and corntrader. These few facts about his life seem to invite the interpretation of the radical as one who turns on a system in which he personally has failed."[227] In a series of essays, James D. Alsop has taken a sterner tone, pursuing Winstanley with the dogged ferocity of a delinquent accounts collector. Winstanley's inability to cut it in the business world led to his resentful radicalism with a sort of fumy necessity, while his later small success in that world confirms with stunning force the insincerity of his Digger days—an unusually coarse example of the genetic or "whig" history that revisionists claim to find offensive in liberal and socialist historians.[228] It may seem ungenerous to fault a poor man for seeking some measure of financial security for himself, his wife, his children, and his blind father-in-law. Winstanley's alternative, of course, was not continued Digging (gentry violence made that impossible), but starvation. Even if someone discovers decayed aristocratic origins for Winstanley—the Holy Grail of anti-Winstanley studies—his five years as a farm worker in Surrey before he began publishing would seem to insulate him adequately against attempts to present him as a gentry wastrel gone slumming. A structural

---

224. *W* 48.
225. 38–9.
226. *W* 168.
227. "The Later Life of Gerrard Winstanley," *Journal of the History of Ideas* 26.1, 1965, 136. For related arguments, see Davis, *Utopia* 176; and Kishlansky, *Monarchy* 196.
228. "Gerrard Winstanley's Later Life," *Past and Present* 82, 1979; "Gerrard Winstanley: Religion and Respectability," *Historical Journal* 28, 1985; "Ethics in the Marketplace: Gerrard Winstanley's London Bankruptcy, 1643," *Journal of British Studies* 28, 1989; "A High Road to Radicalism? Gerrard Winstanley's Youth," *The Seventeenth Century* 9.1, 1994; "Gerrard Winstanley: A Reply," *The Historical Journal* 38.4, 1995.

explanation for the "inorganic" relation between Winstanley's early life
and his agrarian communism might note the frequent birth of peasant
rebellions in the union of an oppressed peasantry and a leader with some
experience of a distinct culture: this paradigm extends from the Hebrews
liberated from Egyptian bondage leading the ancient Canaanite peasant
revolts, to Winstanley of Wigan and London leading the Surrey Diggers,
to Ho Chi Minh (that former merchant marine and pastry sous-chef to
L'Escoffier) leading the Vietnamese almost to independence, to Subcomandante Marcos (a former professor from Mexico City) "leading" the
Zapatistas.

The fourth technique, Stalinizing, has strong ties to the third. In his
account of Winstanley, J. C. Davis partly echoes Vann and Alsop, but he
also insists on Winstanley's connection to contemporary socialism: particularly in *The Law of Freedom*, Winstanley reveals an authoritarianism endemic
to all socialism—scratch a socialist and find a Stalinist. Winstanley's utopia
certainly does show an increasing concern with social discipline, but Davis
exaggerates the severity of the Digger disciplinary mechanism when he
says Winstanley proposes "slavery" for lawbreakers.[229] On the very page
Davis references, he forbids "imprisoning, punishing and killing," and
specifies only that malefactors who attempt to reinstitute property should
be made to work and eat by themselves until they see the reason of
communal cultivation.[230] Davis also accuses Winstanley of proposing "judicial slavery"—a nasty name for a nasty thing, but, of course, every nation
on earth still turns some of its citizens into judicial slaves. Mine boasts the
highest proportion of all, and puts down its judicial slave rebellions with
ruthless efficiency. Still, next to Albion's fatal tree, judicial slavery looks
blazingly progressive. Unless Davis proposes a universal practical antinomianism in the mode of the Ranters, or a Digger/socialist attack on the
roots of crime in earth-mongering, his alternative remains unclear.[231]
Winstanley does indeed call for "laws for every occasion, and almost for
every action that men can do," which may conjure up fears of totalitarianism. But perhaps we need to resensitize ourselves to the sheer material
power of the early modern prerogative rule which such law codes aimed
to counteract: the monstrous delight it brought to its proponents, the
rebellious loathing it inspired in its victims. Winstanley's continuing
horror at prisons, his emphasis on mediation between those with grievances, and his desire for amendment rather than exemplary punishment
seem mild by comparison with the Levitical rigor of such Puritan codes as
John Cotton's *Moses His Judicials*.[232]

---

229. *Utopia* 169–203, 180. The superficially oxymoronic title derives from "the law of liberty"
   in James 1.25, 2.12.
230. *W* 192.
231. *Utopia* 196. On the Winstanley-as-totalitarian argument, see Michael Rogers, "Gerrard
   Winstanley on Crime and Punishment," *Sixteenth Century Journal* 27.3, 1993; and Kenyon,
   Utopian 203–5.
232. *W* 597–8, 528, 545, 553.

Davis also underestimates the extent to which Winstanley was responding to the systematic attacks on the Digger colony from its inception to its
demise. He suggests that the influence of these attacks has "perhaps been
exaggerated"—that the Diggers' embarrassing association with the Ranters
and Winstanley's own proclivities pushed him into authoritarian fantasies.[233] But at the hands of gentry and freeholders and their servants,
the Diggers suffered economic boycotts, threats, lawsuits, pullings-down
of houses, trampling of crops, and vicious beatings—as a result of which
one Digger miscarried, while another almost died.[234] G. E. Aylmer reminds
Davis that "it was largely through the apparatus of the coercive state—
troops, lawyers, the rights of private landowners, and the consequent
employment of both legal action and physical force—that the Diggers
were defeated."[235] But such arguments won't wash with Davis, for whom
any socialist attempt to envision political authority conjures up the Gulag,
while the customary or capitalist coercion practiced by English property
owners remains silent, natural, part of a picturesque landscape. When
Davis listens to what Winstanley calls the "pitched battle between the lamb
and the dragon," he hears only the bleating of the lamb.[236] We might
compare the bicentennial paroxysms of French historical revisionists like
François Furet: "Today, the Gulag leads to a rethinking of the Terror, in
virtue of an identity of project."[237] Such leaps help drown out the
customary economic and political violence of the *ancien régime* and
counterrevolutionary Europe: "There were two 'Reigns of Terror,' if we
would but remember it and consider it; the one wrought murder in hot
passion, the other in heartless cold blood; the one lasted mere months,
the other had lasted a thousand years."[238]

Davis points the way to the final critique when he finds a "strong
element of patriarchalism" in Winstanley.[239] In *Visionary Women*, Phyllis
Mack follows up, finding him "conservative to the core" on questions of
gender, despite his political radicalism. She sees his warnings against
orgiastic Ranters as a masculinist effort to maintain authority over the
bodies of women.[240] *The Law of Freedom* clearly shows Winstanley moving
toward traditional patriarchal forms. He speaks of fathers as natural
magistrates, mentions mothering not at all, and never even hints that
pregnancy and childrearing might be forms of work.[241] He never explains
how the patriarchal household can remain as a locus of private property
administered by the father without corrupting the ruler or oppressing the

233. Davis, *Utopia* 183.
234. *W* 284–5, 295–6, 433.
235. "The Religion of Gerrard Winstanley," McGregor and Reay, *Radical* 91–119, 111.
236. *W* 281.
237. Quoted in Callinicos, "Bourgeois" 120.
238. Mark Twain, *A Connecticut Yankee*, Harmondsworth 1979, 127.
239. *Utopia* 197.
240. 72. Achinstein agrees in "Women" 162n.75.
241. *W* 544–5.

ruled.[242] In Winstanley's ideal England, as in Milton's Paradise, a gentle but distinctly possessive patriarchy becomes "sole propriety ... of all things common else."[243]

But the moderating of this patriarchy should also be of some interest. In *The New Law*, Winstanley does gender "the powers of the curse in flesh" as a feminine moon, but within a page he condemns the fleshly power of the first Adam infecting (among others) husbands, who "do carry themselves like oppressing lords over such as are under them; not knowing that their wives, children, servants, subjects are their fellow creatures, and hath an equal privilege to share with them in the blessing of liberty."[244] In *The Saints Paradise*, he says that the "evil masculine powers" of pride, covetousness, hypocrisy, self-love, and imagination, rule over "the created flesh, which is the feminine part, and leads it captive in unrighteousness."[245] Particularly in his earlier writings, he emphasizes Christ rising in his sons *and* his daughters, quoting the prophetesses' touchstone in the Book of Joel.[246] In a letter of 1650, he protested to the prophetess Lady Eleanor Davies that she had shortchanged him and the workers he represented for helping her remove the sequestration from her estate and for threshing her grain. He addressed her in distinctly misogynous terms, but he also acknowledged the existence of true prophetesses in the Scriptures, adding that they did not hesitate to work with others.[247] In *The Law of Freedom*, he establishes strict laws against rape based on the rights of women, not men, calling rape "robbery of a woman's bodily freedom"— a remarkable definition all by itself, even more so by contrast with contemporary alternatives.[248] As Norah Carlin has argued, peasant families being pauperized and broken apart by proletarianization might have been drawn to Winstanley's finding "every man's wife and every woman's husband proper to themselves," and "their children at their dispose till they come of age."[249] But this bears little resemblance to the Filmeresque patriarchy that Mulligan and Richards hear.[250] Where Filmer uses a "natural" rule of fathers to naturalize monarchy, Winstanley tries to present the rule of fathers as almost elective, the product of a sort of vote by the mute political necessity of the children. Moreover, the Digger

242. Kenyon emphasizes Winstanley's increasingly traditional attitude toward fathers' rule over sons (*Utopian* 196–7, 210–16).

243. *Paradise Lost* 4.751–2.

244. *W* 157, 158.

245. 75.

246. *Mysterie* 32.

247. Lutaud, *Winstanley* 329–31.

248. *W* 599. Compare W[illiam] A[spinwall]'s *Legislative Power*, which proposes to punish rape with whipping and a fine—"not unto the Court, but unto the Father, who suffers wrong" (31). Aphra Behn celebrates a Restoration ethic of aestheticized rape when she excitedly encourages her noble Prince Oroonoko "to seize his own, and take the rites of love" from Imoinda (*Oroonoko, The Rover and Other Works*, Janet Todd, ed., London 1992, 94).

249. "Marxism" 123; *W* 527.

250. "A 'Radical' Problem" 136.

storehouse will put an end to patriarchal wedding portions, "for we are all of one blood, mankind; and for portion, the common storehouses are every man and maid's portion, as free to one as to another."[251]

Anticommunist polemicists habitually denounce economic communism as a lecherous alibi for sexual community. This attitude was alive and well in 1653, when Adam Moore warns traditionalists who see the commons as an "inseparable spouse" that they are "so cuckolded by foreigners and strangers, and your common used before your face, even as commonly as by yourselves. . . . Were it not better therefore and more secure to take her home to your chamber, and keep her with a guard where she cannot be abused? which you may do by distinguishing each one's part properly to himself."[252] But Winstanley refused to protect himself by policing female sexuality. He never mentioned adultery and denounced "witches" only in the form of professional preachers.[253] His warnings against Ranter paramours simply do not mention husbandly or fatherly authority, only the hardships Digger women might suffer when infected, made pregnant, and abandoned.[254] In "A Watch-Word," a poem appended to a pamphlet on the Engagement Controversy, he offers some motherly advice:

> For if a child you get, by ranting deeds
> The man is gone and leaves the child your gain,
> Then you and yours are left by such free-men,
> For other women are as free for them.[255]

Unlike the absolutist, gentry, or bourgeois writers of early modern England, Winstanley seems to be uninterested in reproducing aristocratic patriarchalism or creating bourgeois/republican domesticity. This shouldn't be altogether surprising: since a new seventeenth-century ethic of bourgeois domesticity produced a new mode of anxious misogyny, we probably shouldn't expect to find that sort of misogyny in the writings of a plebeian prophet.

The Diggers' *hortus inconclusus* opens up more readily into the traditions of Quakerism and communist sectarianism, British and American prophetic literature (Milton, Bunyan, Blake, Whitman, Ginsberg, King), and social utopia (Covell, Bellers, Plockhoy, Spence, Wedderburn, Fourier,

---

251. *W* 538, 599.
252. *Bread for the Poor* A1ᵛ–A2ʳ. As Marx and Engels note in *The Communist Manifesto*, this sort of raillery suggests that ruling-class men view their wives as property (*MECW* 6.502). Early modern conservatives associated sexual community with economic community because of polygamous Münster, and with mortalism. If, as Christ says, the resurrected "neither marry, nor are given in marriage" (Luke 20.35), then mortalists (like Winstanley) who believe in the annihilation of the soul at death might believe in some sort of resurrection and so also, perhaps, some sort of sexual community in this life—a charge lustily embraced by the anonymous Ranter author of *A Justification* (13–16), and flung at Anne Hutchinson during her second trial (Hall, *Antinomian* 358; and James F. Maclear, "Anne Hutchinson and the Mortalist Heresy," *New England Quarterly* 54, 1981).
253. *W* 242, 343, 597.
254. Ibid. 538, 599, 399–403.
255. Winstanley, *Englands Spirit* (*WIR* 122).

Owen, Morris).[256] Here, I'd like to concentrate on the context of continuing agrarian resistance to capitalist accumulation. Resistance to primitive accumulation in England continued into the eighteenth and even nineteenth centuries. In *Whigs and Hunters*, E. P. Thompson studies the conflict between sylvan rebels and capitalist improvers in the forests of Robert Walpole's England.[257] In *Commoners*, J. M. Neeson shows the persistence of common right in plebeian practice into the nineteenth century. In Scotland, the disruption of traditional agriculture by improving enclosure did not reach its height until the Highland Clearances of the eighteenth and nineteenth centuries. They disrupted the patriarchal economies of the clans, as scientific improvers from England or the Lowlands worked with Highland nobility and landowners to evict crofters and convert their communal smallholdings into pasture and deer parks. Harriet Beecher Stowe characterized the Clearances as "an almost sublime instance of the benevolent employment of superior wealth and power in shortening the struggles of advancing civilization."[258] Marx reported with disgust a reception for Stowe held by the Duchess of Sutherland, the scourge of the crofters: "The enemy of British Wages-Slavery has a right to condemn Negro-Slavery; a Duchess of Sutherland, a Duke of Atholl, a Manchester Cotton Lord—never!"[259] This conflict continued to the Crofters' War and the Battle of the Braes on the Isle of Skye in 1882, and to March 1999, when the community of Knoydart successfully concluded a fifty-year campaign to buy its land for itself. In the cult of Scots picturesque built on bleak landscapes and ruined crofts, we see that elegiac aesthetics concludes the attempted destruction of a culture.[260] The seventeenth-, eighteenth-, and nineteenth-century Anglo-American invaders of North America presented their genocidal clearing and enclosure of the indigenous commons as a program of providentially sanctioned rational improvement. Something like a country house ethic reappears among North American environmentalists for whom national parks tended to be nature reserves rather than monuments to exterminated social ecologies.

256. See William Covell's *A Declaration unto the Parliament* (1659), and J. Max Patrick, "William Covell and the Troubles at Enfield in 1659," *University of Toronto Quarterly* 14, 1944–45. Compare the Diggers' critique of the Levellers and Thomas Spence's critique of Paine. Like Ireton, Spence insists that the vote be grounded in property right; like Rainsborough, he insists on a democratic franchise; like Winstanley, he reconciles the two positions by insisting on communal property ownership in the agrarian soviet of the reformed parish (Thomas Spence, *The Meridian Son of Liberty*; Marilyn Butler, *Burke* 189–94, 191).

257. Harmondsworth 1990.

258. John Prebble, *The Highland Clearances*, Harmondsworth 1963, 292.

259. *MECW* 11.486–94. See also Marx's discussion of the Clearances in *Capital I* (*MECW* 35.718–23).

260. Thanks to Justin Dyer for the information about Knoydart. See www. scotland.gov.uk/news/release99_3/pr0766.htm or, earlier, www.smo.uhi.ac.uk/ leabharlann/1-luibh/clippings/november97/nov19scot/html. On depopulation and aesthetics, see David Worrall, "Agrarians against the Picturesque," in Stephen Coplay and Peter Garside, eds, *The Politics of the Picturesque*, Cambridge 1994, 240–60. Thanks to Alan Gilbert for this reference.

For instance, Yosemite National Park began with the decimation of the Miwok nation of "Digger" Indians.[261]

The controversy over the commons continues to this day in Central and South America. The North American Free Trade Agreement was to have been the keystone for at least the western wing of the capitalist New Jerusalem, bringing Canada, the United States, and Mexico together, unifying labor and commodity markets, and inaugurating a new era of hemispheric prosperity. But on January 1 1994, the day it took effect, the Zapatista Army of National Liberation launched a peasant rebellion in rural Chiapas, Mexico, aimed primarily at President Salinas de Gortari's efforts to expropriate peasant smallholdings. In a series of military and non-military actions, and a string of communiqués by "Subcomandante Marcos" and others, the Zapatistas attacked the expropriations and NAFTA, articulated a multilevel program for social and cultural revolution, and attempted to reclaim the commons, resisting efforts to create capitalist absolute property of the *ejidos*, systems of inalienable communal land tenure instituted by the Mexican Revolution of 1915.[262]

Amazonia has recently witnessed a similar struggle. An aestheticized environmentalism leads most North Americans and Europeans to see the struggle over the rainforest as a battle between tree and bulldozer, but it is more fundamentally a struggle between two economies: the destructive economy practiced by ranchers and log-harvesters, and the renewable economy of small production (rubber tapping, small farming, nut gathering) practiced by two million Forest People—Indians, river-bank peoples, and rubber tappers. "The extinction," Hecht and Cockburn point out, "is not only of nature but of socialized nature: what is also being exterminated in the Amazon is civilization." The last thirty years have proved particularly devastating:

> From the sixties until today the entire Amazon has been convulsed by an enormous enclosure movement easily rivaling the conversion of public land to private property in early modern Europe.... Indeed, the Amazon is the site of one of the most rapid and large-scale enclosure movements in history as more than 100 million acres pass from public to private ownership.[263]

This process has provoked responses analogous to those of the Diggers: new political collectives such as unions of rural workers, new organic intellectuals like Chico Mendes (murdered by a landowner in 1988), and new techniques of resistance to enclosure such as the *empate*, or sit-down strike of Forest People resisting loggers.[264]

The Digger declaration from Iver in Buckinghamshire, which sets the

261. Susanna Hecht and Alexander Cockburn, *The Fate of the Forest*, New York 1990, 271.
262. George A. Collier and Elizabeth Lowery Quiaratiello discuss the Zapatistas and Mexican land tenure in *Basta! Land and the Zapatista Rebellion in Chiapas*, Oakland 1994. See also *Shadows of Tender Fury: The Letters and Communiqués of Subcomandante Marcos and the Zapatista Army of National Liberation*, New York 1995.
263. Hecht and Cockburn, *Fate* 62, 142, 107.
264. Chico Mendes and Tony Gross, *Fight for the Forest*, London 1992, 72.

mark of Cain on what it calls "Earthmongers," says that "we affirm that they have no righteous power to sell or give away the earth, unless they could make the earth likewise, which none can do but God the eternal spirit."[265] The green millennialism of the Diggers echoes in the *Forest Peoples' Manifesto* of 1985 and 1989, which calls for extractive reserves, an end to the division of the forest into lots for colonists, a new technology that will benefit the people of the forest, and the maintenance of "Administration and control of reserves directly by the extractive workers and their organizations."[266] The extractive reserves of rubber and brazil nut trees envision a new/old variety of collective life on the land and resonate strongly with the Digger utopia. Ailton Krenak, a Krenak Indian, describes the extractive reserves of rubber and brazil nut trees in terms that the Diggers would recognize:

> Extractive reserves bring into play part of the population which came to the Amazon to "civilize" it along with the Indians, but who instead learn from them a new way of living with nature. Rubber tappers learn how to humanize nature and themselves. Thus the reserve brings a new form of social culture, and economic character. Migrants to this region came in search of land, but the property of the people cannot be commercialized. An extractive reserve is not an exchange item, and it isn't property. It is a good that belongs to the Brazilian nation, and people will live in these reserves with the expectation of preserving them for future generations. This is tremendously innovative.[267]

Of course, Mendes's Brazil clearly differs from Winstanley's England in many ways. In place of a national revolution with strong but stifled egalitarian elements, we have a fascist military government moving toward an ostensibly democratic one. In place of a long-term religious conflict, we have long-term ethnic conflict, in which developers have tried to depopulate the forests by sending diseased settlers to infect and extermi-nate Indians with no resistance—a primitive but effective mode of germ warfare.[268] The process of enclosure has proceeded much more rapidly in the Amazon, and the conversion of Brazilian rainforest to pasture (and, rapidly thereafter, to waste land) is even less reversible and more devastat-ing than the conversion of English arable, commons, and wastes to pasture and private holdings.

But these differences should not blind us to the process tying the two times and places together: the primitive accumulation or "original theft" by which capitalists divorce direct producers from the means of produc-tion and force them to become mere sellers of their labor power. To link early modern England and contemporary Brazil in this fashion is not to venture into anachronism, since capitalism is not a system, not even a mechanical sequence of stages (early, middle, late), but a complex,

265. Thomas, "Another" 129.
266. Hecht and Cockburn, *Fate* 261–5.
267. Ibid. 244.
268. Ibid. 154.

non-synchronous human history. A single "phase" like capitalist primitive accumulation may recur as agrarian accumulation again and again in different places. Conversely, any given historical moment incorporates more than one "time," more than one mode of production, as Marx came to see while contemplating the possibility of a direct movement from the Russian peasant communes of his day to a decentralized, non-statist communism.[269] Winstanley's England contained the remnants of feudal serfdom, small-holding communism in the commons and common fields, an agrarian capitalism driven by a dynamic of improvement, and revolutionary communism among the Diggers. Our own historical moment includes the primitive communism of a few uncolonized aboriginal peoples, small production of some persons not yet completely proletarianized, capitalist accumulation in the industrializing Third World nations, early capitalism to rival Engels's Manchester in the industrialized Third World (and in the ununionized and environmentally degraded First and former Second), and even the holographic specter of a post-industrial "information order." Socialists should resist the impulse to equate history itself with a rigorous, enclosing periodization, which carries us along from "sacred" to "secular," or from one homogeneous mode of production to another. They must remain sensitive to these different times within a single historical moment, since critical consciousness lives inside the nonsynchronous clashing of time, and times, and half a time that pervades the everyday life of commoners. As they try to create communist democracy, they might well want to consider the radicals inhabiting an earlier moment of rational hunger, when precapitalist economies did not yet seem doomed, when capitalist ones did not yet seem foreordained.

In a 1986 essay on economic development, Robert Brenner drew two "speculative conclusions. . . . The first is that pre-capitalist economies have an internal logic and solidity which should not be underestimated. The second is that capitalist economic development is perhaps an historically more limited, surprising and peculiar phenomenon than is often appreciated."[270] During the last decade, these conclusions have become even more utopian—more shaded with doubt, more fired with hope. For we have witnessed an epochal event whose full importance we are only beginning to grasp: the global maturity of the capitalist mode of production. Nobody who views this event as a happy ending will feel any need to examine its history, which is "written in the annals of mankind in letters of blood and fire."[271] But others of us, who see the blood still flowing and the fire still burning, may feel compelled to sneak a backward glance at early modern England. There, we will see not just blood and fire, but hopeful eyes looking back at us, necks craning to see around and past us—working men and women engaged in small production, self-organized

---

269. Marx, "Drafts" and "The Reply."
270. "Social" 53.
271. *MECW* 35.706.

communal labor, religious fellowship, martial solidarity, free debate, antityrannical conspiracy, and other struggles to imagine and create a better future. Their experience of non-capitalist collective life gave them a practical model for radical, oppositional projects embodying their hope that they would not inevitably be dragged into the slough from which we are still struggling to extricate ourselves.

This praxis of hope makes their lives and their words shine out and shout over a gulf of 350 years. When the Diggers cultivate George Hill, the broken enclosures open up into the rainforest and reveal the common desire of Diggers and Forest People to create themselves freely through collective labor on the land. The Diggers' pursuit of common-preservation and love withdraws from the capitalist vision of self-preservation and exploitation, and joins with Ailton Krenak's pursuit of a once-and-future Amazon: "It is for this that the region is so beautiful, because it is a piece of the planet that maintains the inheritance of the creation of the world. Christians have a myth of the garden of Eden. Our people have a reality where the first man created by god continues to be free. We want to impregnate humanity with the memory of the creation of the world."[272] In Ernst Bloch's phrase, this pregnant memory of a communist future is the Diggers' not-yet-conscious. It might still be ours, too. *Ça ira.*

272. Hecht and Cockburn, *Fate* 1.

Index

I have indexed both text and notes, indicating the page number of the first, full reference for cited works by boldfacing the appropriate page number after the author's name or, for anonymous works, the title. Except for monarchs, I have generally listed persons by their proper names, omitting military, ecclesiastical, and hereditary titles.